A Changing of the Guard: Anglo-American Relations, 1941–1946

Randall Bennett Woods

The University of North Carolina Press
Chapel Hill and London

The paper in this book meets the guidelines for permanence and
durability of the Committee on Production Guidelines for Book
Longevity of the Council on Library Resources.

94 93 92 91 90   5 4 3 2 1

Library of Congress Cataloging-in-Publication Data

Woods, Randall Bennett, 1944–
    A changing of the guard : Anglo-American relations, 1941–1946 / by
Randall Bennett Woods.
      p.   cm.
    Includes bibliographical references.
    ISBN 0-8078-1877-1 (alk. paper)
    1. United States—Foreign relations—Great Britain.   2. Great
Britain—Foreign relations—United States.   3. United States—
Foreign economic relations—Great Britain.   4. Great Britain—
Foreign economic relations—United States.   5. International
finance—History—20th century.   6. World War, 1939–1945—Diplomatic
history.   7. United States—Foreign relations—1933–1945.   8. Great
Britain—Foreign relations—1936–1945.   I. Title.
E183.8.G7W93   1990
337.73041'09'044—dc20   89-22615
                                                                        CIP

To my mother,
Mary Dorothy Stokes Woods

Contents

Preface

THE DOMINANT SCHOOL of thought in American diplomatic history during my formative years was the New Left. William Appleman Williams, Lloyd Gardner, Walter LaFeber, Gabriel Kolko, and their disciples argued in various ways and to varying degrees that the foreign policy of the United States at any given time is a response to the needs and demands of American capitalism. Through political and economic clout, and manipulation of the myth of free enterprise, the economic elite in this country had bent a sometimes willing and sometimes unwilling foreign policy establishment to its will. Like George F. Kennan, who has spent much of the past twenty-five years trying to explain that he really did not mean what he said in the containment article, the pioneers of the New Left have devoted a great deal of time and energy arguing that they were not and are not simple economic determinists, that their explanations then as now are multicausal, and that their books and articles accurately reflect the complexities of America's foreign policy.

Be that as it may, I, like most students of foreign affairs, find the question of the relative influence of economic interests and capitalist ideology on the foreign policy of the United States fascinating. Thus, when some ten years ago Professor Robert Divine suggested that I investigate the British loan of 1946, I eagerly agreed. I anticipated producing a couple of articles and perhaps a monograph. But what I quickly discovered, of course, was that the loan was only a patch in a large and complex quilt, and that it was the culmination of a process the last stage of which began in 1941. To understand the loan, I would have to delve into the mysteries of lend-lease, reconversion, the sterling area, the issue of Britain's gold/dollar balances, commercial policy, Bretton Woods, and multilateralism in general. I soon learned, too, that practice could not be separated from theory, and that, if my study were to be thorough, financial and commercial policies would have to be traced to their intellectual as well as their political roots. Nor could I ignore the role of bureaucratic politics in an era when the British and American foreign policy establishments, stimulated by World War II, were mushrooming. And I quickly learned that the economic foreign policies of the United States and the United Kingdom at any given time were reflections of or reactions to domestic social and economic policies. Finally, Anglo-American diplomacy unfolded in the context of the rise and fall of the Grand Alliance. International politics restrained and at times defined national policies during the Anglo-American alogue of the 1940s, just as it had during the 1780s, 1890s, and 1920s. What I have attempted, then, is a history and analysis of Anglo-American financial and commercial relations during World War II and the early stages of the Cold War.

It is with some trepidation in this, the heyday of the new social history, that I admit that *A Changing of the Guard* is about power and elites. It is about the efficacy of money and markets, of ideas, personalities, and bureaucracies. It is about diplomatic machinations and political imperatives. And, quite simply, it is a chapter—a crucial one, I believe—in the story of America's arrival as a super-power and Britain's departure. The United Kingdom wanted desperately to maintain the empire and sterling area intact and, failing that, to resurrect the old multilateral trading apparatus and balance-of-power political system that it had managed in the late nineteenth century. Forced to acknowledge that their nation had not the resources and influence to be the arbiter of such a system, British officials looked to the United States to seize the helm. America agreed, but on its own terms. The United States, a traditionally self-sufficient and isolationist nation, was ill-suited to play the role of world banker and power broker. Congress and economic nationalists in the Roosevelt-Truman administrations modified multilateral mechanisms and institutions into devices to promote United States exports and acted to ensure that Washington controlled any and all mechanisms for currency stabilization and trade regulation that emerged from World War II. In so doing, the United States denied Britain and the other trading nations the commercial and financial wherewithal to participate in a multilateral system. At the same time the Roosevelt and Truman regimes not only backed away from a commitment to the military security of Western Europe but also refused to condone a spheres-of-interest arrangement between Britain and Russia while the war was still undecided. Eventually, the United States, with British prompting, decided that, in menacing Western Europe and the eastern Mediterranean, the Soviet Union simultaneously posed a threat to American security. But while isolationism metamorphosed into Cold War interventionism in the political sphere, nationalism did not give way to multilateralism in the economic. The Anglo-American Financial Agreement of 1946 provided the United Kingdom with enough capital to enable it to survive in the short run, but the loan actually retarded Britain's long-term rehabilitation and thus its ability to act as an effective counter to Soviet expansionism in Europe.

This book was eight years in the making and would not have been possible without grants from numerous foundations and agencies. I am indebted to the National Endowment for the Humanities for awarding me a senior fellowship and to the American Philosophical Society, the American Council of Learned Societies, the Roosevelt and Truman libraries, and the Fulbright Institute of the University of Arkansas for research and travel grants. The reference staffs of the National Archives, the new Public Record Office in Kew, London, and the presidential libraries were instrumental in guiding my research. But perhaps most helpful in this regard was Professor David Reynolds of Cambridge University who steered me through the labyrinth of John Maynard Keynes's papers. Theodore Wilson, Howard Jones, John Milton Cooper, Timothy Donovan, Robert Hathaway, Johnathan Utley, and William Rock read all or part of the manuscript and made invaluable suggestions for revision. Jeanie Wyant, Suzanne Stoner, Kathryn Cantrell, Betty Skinner, and Terry Garrity typed tirelessly and accurately. My thanks finally to my wife Rhoda and my children, Nicole and Jeff, for their tolerance and support, and to Lewis Bateman for his faith in this project. All errors in style, content, and judgment are, of course, mine.

Fayetteville, Arkansas
June 1989

A Changing of the Guard

Introduction

WORLD WAR II accelerated the decline of British power in every realm except perhaps the moral. Forced to bear the brunt of fighting against the Axis powers from 1939 to 1941, the United Kingdom liquidated overseas assets, abandoned traditional markets, and borrowed billions of pounds from the sterling area. The war, moreover, burst apart the old European nation-state system, momentarily destroying British power in the Far East and stimulating anticolonial sentiment throughout the Third World. Each of these factors contributed to the disintegration of the financial and colonial empire. In its weakened condition Great Britain turned for aid to the United States, first for the material and munitions with which to defeat the Axis and then for the resources that would guarantee Britain's economic and military security in the immediate postwar period.

In its efforts to use American power to shore up its postwar position, London pursued two primary objectives—a United States commitment to the military security of Western Europe, and a massive program of economic aid that would (1) forestall the necessity of imposing an unprecedented austerity program on the British people, (2) enable Britain to maintain its strategic outposts around the world, and (3) make it possible for the United Kingdom to participate in a system of multilateral trade.

The Roosevelt and Truman administrations recognized the importance to America of a stable, democratic, noncommunist, and nonfascist Europe. Moreover, both governments embraced multilateralism as a mechanism that would promote full employment in the United States, raise living standards in underdeveloped areas, and strengthen the British economy. The White House and the State Department were, moreover, willing to furnish the foreign aid necessary to maintain a balance of power in Europe and make multilateralism work. The creation of an integrated world economy through the reduction of trade barriers and economic specialization was, they believed, a prerequisite to lasting peace. Both presidents, however, were circumscribed in their policy and decision making by the forces of nationalism, fiscal conservatism, and isolationism within Congress and the federal bureaucracy, and among the American people as a whole. Despite the untiring efforts of the Churchill and Attlee governments and the cooperative attitude of the White House, the United States proved unwilling through 1945 to make a commitment to the military security of Western Europe or to an authentic system of multilateral trade.

No matter how compelling the drama of World War II, Anglo-American leaders during the period from 1941 to 1946 could not escape elections nor could they avoid the socioeconomic issues that usually dominate domestic politics. Ever sensitive to the mood of the American people, a mood that grew increasingly conservative during the course of the war, FDR searched for a mechanism, an ideology that would prevent unemployment in the United States and at the same time deflect charges from conservatives that he was taking America farther down the road toward state socialism. Meanwhile, on the eastern shore of the Atlantic, Winston Churchill was increasingly distracted from his duties as minister of defense by worries about his own political future and that of the Conservative party. Britons no less than Americans, he perceived, were concerned about their economic and social security in the postwar period. And he was right. "Food, Homes, and Work" became the domestic battle cry of the average person by late 1943. When Churchill stopped to look at the state of British opinion, he, unlike FDR, saw a rising collectivist tide that, unless halted, foreshadowed a Labour victory at the first general election after the war and, ultimately, socialization of the British economy. If Churchill were to preserve a modicum of free enterprise in Britain and at the same time perpetuate his own political leadership, he would have to find an alternative to planning, countercyclical deficit spending, and massive state intervention into Britain's industrial life.

In their search for a noncollectivist weapon for dealing with unemployment, a device that would also hopefully guarantee their political future, both men turned in 1944 to foreign economic policy. Roosevelt embraced multilateralism, a concept that called for a mutual, simultaneous reduction of trade barriers among the principal trading nations of the world. Because V-E Day would find America in possession of a large portion of the world's industrial capacity and because the rest of the world, ravaged by war, would be in desperate need of finished and semifinished products, multilateralism promised to banish unemployment from America in a generation while leaving the free enterprise system relatively intact.

Churchill saw Britain's salvation as well as his own and that of the Conservative party in a massive program of American aid. A continuation of lend-lease or an interest-free credit during Stage II, the period between V-E Day and Japan's surrender, would allow Britain to reconvert part of its economy to civilian production and then to compete with the United States for foreign markets as the war wound to a close. Subsequently, a large postwar credit would enable Britain to retain its empire in the eastern Mediterranean and Middle East, and make it possible for Churchill and the Conservatives to provide the British electorate with food, homes, and work. But the prime minister wanted United States aid without multilateral strings attached. To protect Britain's vulnerable export industries and shelter British markets from aggressive American exporters, Churchill intended to retain the system of empire preferences that had been in place since the Ottawa Conference in 1932. The reality for Britain was, however, that America possessed the gold, dollars, and goods upon which the fate of Britain and the Conservative party hinged, and Washington was not going to part with those resources unless and until London abandoned preferences and exchange controls.

For multilateralism to work—that is, for members of the trading community to lower their barriers and end their controls, and still achieve a balance of payments and an ever-rising volume of trade—the United States would have to meet two conditions. Washington would have to provide adequate liquidity to its trading partners, and it would have to agree to a horizontal tariff reduction tied to simultaneous reductions made by other countries. Without adequate reserves or credit, nations with less developed or war-distorted economies could not compete for any length of time in a multilateral world.

During World War II a battle raged within the Roosevelt administration between those who wanted to provide adequate liquidity to Britain in the form of lend-lease or credits, and those who did not. Harry Hopkins and his circle of advisers, a group of professional economists in the federal bureaucracy, and liberal internationalists such as Henry Wallace advocated a generous foreign aid program for Great Britain on political, strategic, economic, and ideological grounds. In opposition were a coalition of isolationist-nationalists in Congress, bureaucratic imperialists in the United States Treasury, and, of course, special interests who feared foreign competition. Congressional opponents of liberal aid to Great Britain consisted of those who believed the object of foreign trade was to enrich America at the expense of the rest of the world, those who saw foreign aid as a first step to United States entanglement in European affairs, and, after July 1945, those opposed to subsidizing a collectivist state. They were joined by Henry Morgenthau and his underlings, who were determined that the United States and specifically the United States Treasury monopolize the circulating medium in any new international financial set-up.

The isolationist-nationalist alliance proved too much for the economic internationalists in the State Department and on the White House staff. The Bretton Woods Agreements hammered out between Anglo-American representatives in 1944 guaranteed that a United States monopoly of the world's gold/dollar supply would continue. A year later Congress ratified a revised Reciprocal Trade Agreements Act (RTAA) that reserved to Congress and the special interests it represented the right to maintain high duties on goods threatened by foreign competition. Harry Truman was even more sensitive to conservative, nationalist, and isolationist opinion in Congress than his predecessor, and as a result the United States failed to provide Britain with a postwar aid program substantial enough to restore its economic health. The president stood idly by in 1946 as the United States saddled Great Britain with a loan agreement that forced a premature end to exchange controls and drained the Exchequer of its gold/dollar reserves.

Winston Churchill fought a losing, rearguard action against multilateralism. Though it was clear that the Bretton Woods Agreements and the Financial Agreement of 1946 were not in Britain's interest, the honorable member from Woodford capitulated and agreed to support them. He did so for a variety of reasons. Rejection of multilateralism would leave Britain alone in a devastated world to face Soviet imperialism or a totalitarian threat from some other quarter. If Britain refused to ratify the Bretton Woods Agreements and the British loan, neither long-term nor short-term aid would be forthcoming from America. Balance of trade considerations aside, without United States dollars, Churchill would have to impose an austerity program on Britain at once. Popular revulsion in turn might very well destroy conservatism and the Conservative party in Britain.

In addition, the United Kingdom eventually embraced multilateralism because those officials responsible for British foreign policy—including a broad coalition of reform Tories in the Foreign Office and professional economists in the Treasury and War Cabinet Secretariat—believed that multilateralism would, in fact, achieve peace and prosperity. Moreover, their vision of postwar Britain—a mixed economy in which the government intervened to maintain aggregate demand and a framework of social services—was no less dependent on short-term American aid than Churchill's view of the good society. These officials, especially James Meade and John Maynard Keynes, took the lead in convincing the War Cabinet that multilateralism, even as modified by Congress and the United States Treasury, would not damage vital British interests.

As in so many other areas, there was little loss of continuity in foreign economic policy when Clement Attlee and the Labour party swept to victory in July 1945. Attlee, Ernest Bevin, Hugh Dalton, and other Labour leaders, frequently dubious before 1945 about the benefits of an unfettered multilateralism, became ardent converts once they came to power. Members of the new Labour government no less than Churchill and Anthony Eden perceived that their political survival and their dreams for Britain, which were not so different from those of the reform Tories and the professional economists, depended on a continuation of American aid into the postwar period. Though the Labour government knew that neither the International Monetary Fund (IMF), the International Bank for Reconstruction and Development (IBRD), nor the Anglo-American Financial Agreement of 1946 provided the Exchequer with the liquidity necessary to permit elimination of exchange controls, it successfully urged parliamentary ratification of all three. In sum, Britain's need—its strategic need, its financial need, but particularly its political need—for American resources put it at the mercy of economic nationalists in Congress and the federal bureaucracy, and led to acceptance of mechanisms and agreements that were not in the national interest.

An American commitment to the military security of Western Europe proved almost as difficult to obtain as a liberal foreign aid program and for many of the same reasons. During World War II, those in Whitehall and at No. 10 Downing Street concerned with boundaries, armies, and alliances attempted to hammer out a spheres-of-interest arrangement with Russia while searching for allies that would help defend the status quo thus achieved. Jealous of burgeoning American power and apprehensive over the ambivalence and uncertainty that traditionally characterized American foreign policy, groups within the British foreign policy establishment advanced a number of alternatives to an Anglo-American alliance and a permanent United States military presence in Europe. Men around Churchill and Eden fashioned several variations on the federation–of–Western Europe theme while empire isolationists clung to their dreams of a commonwealth/ sterling area bloc capable of guaranteeing independence and continued great-power status for the United Kingdom. But in the strategic as in the financial arena, there seemed to be no substitute for a dominant American role.

In its quest to commit the United States to the military security of Western Europe in the postwar era, Whitehall was forced to contend with the same elements in America that subverted multilateralism. In addition, however, unlike the economic realm, there were no true internationalists—advocates of an authentic collective security system in which nations willingly relinquished a portion of their national sovereignty and submitted to majority rule—in positions of power. This was true in both London and Washington.

The Roosevelt foreign policy establishment thought not in terms of world community or even binding collective security. For Roosevelt, Hopkins, Acheson, and subsequently Truman, diplomacy was the art of reconciling contending national interests strategically and economically defined. These policymakers longed to be free of congressional and popular opinion so they might identify threats to America's national interest and respond to them in a pragmatic, case-by-case fashion.

But the efforts of the executive branch during and immediately after the war to practice hard-headed pragmatism in the international sphere were blocked by a nascent isolationism. United States participation in World War II was a specific response to a particular perceived threat—Nazi Germany. Most Americans considered Hitler an aberration and the nation's struggle against him did not mark an end to isolationism—that deep-seated desire in the United States to remain aloof from Europe's rivalries, ideologies, and wars. Despite its all-out effort to defeat the Axis powers, America demonstrated repeatedly from 1941 to 1945 that it was unwilling to become an active and permanent participant in the European balance of power after V-E Day.

Responding to the need to counter Axis propaganda and to demands from the American electorate for a plan that would guarantee peace and security in the postwar world, FDR came up with the Four Policemen concept. Each of the four principal allies—the United States, Russia, Great Britain, and China—would police their respective areas of the world, nurturing democracy and preventing aggression. The Four Policemen idea, subsequently ensconced in the charter of the United Nations, seemed to be harmonious with the tenets of American isolationism. In dividing the world into quadrants and relegating the United States to the Western Hemisphere, Roosevelt's stratagem conformed to the two-spheres clause of the Monroe Doctrine.

By 1943 Roosevelt and his advisers were discovering, however, that partitioning the world into four static spheres each policed by a great power was not as simple a task as the president had imagined. Little agreement existed among the four as to the boundaries of their respective spheres (or even as to whom the four should be). United States domination of the Western Hemisphere was relatively certain, but Britain, Russia, and China seemed determined to take advantage of the chaos caused by the war to regain lost colonies or carve out new areas of influence in Europe, the Middle East, and Asia. The White House recognized that it was in the nation's interest to have these spheres delineated as quickly as possible in order to check Russian imperialism in Europe, prevent the reemergence of British colonialism in the Far East, and render unnecessary the permanent stationing of American troops in Europe following World War II. But Congress and the American people were in no mood for "power politics."

Though the Four Policemen stratagem was consistent with the Monroe Doctrine, isolationists worked to thwart administration efforts to delineate spheres of interest during World War II. These men and women, primarily Republicans, were motivated—just as they had been in the commercial and financial fields—by a simple desire to limit the power of the executive in foreign affairs and augment that of Congress. In addition, World War II left them unconvinced that British and American interests were identical. Distracted by visions of a strong, democratic China nurtured by the United States and by nightmares in which the United States continually pulled British chestnuts out of the fire in Europe, isolationist-nationalist leaders objected not only to a United States commitment to the postwar collective security of Europe and a substantive aid program to Great Britain, but also to efforts by Washington to help mark out respective spheres of interest. They were, ironically, aided and abetted for a time by American internationalists who saw spheres-of-interest deals and power politics as inimical to the principles of the United Nations. As a result, attached though he was to the Four Policemen concept, FDR twice refused to endorse specific spheres-of-interest arrangements worked out by the British and the Russians.

Hemmed in by congressional chauvinism, isolationist opinion, and popular, romantic notions of internationalism, Roosevelt fell back on a policy of personal diplomacy and appeasement of the Soviet Union. He catered to public and congressional opinion by attempting to build bridges to Russia through unrestricted lend-lease, promises of a postwar credit, and attacks on British colonialism. That policy culminated at Yalta, where the president agreed to occupation zones that left Russia in control of Eastern and part of Central Europe, and recognized Soviet claims to large tracts of previously Chinese real estate in return for a promise by Stalin to participate in the Japanese war.

Gradually the British War Cabinet and Foreign Office began to realize that the United States was not going to become a makeweight in the European balance of power in response to abstract notions of collective security or loyalty to the ideal of Anglo-American solidarity. As in the past, Washington would be willing to identify and subsidize European proxies and, if necessary, commit troops to their defense, only in reaction to a specific perceived threat. If Whitehall were to ride the American horse, it would have to convince its headstrong steed that Stalin was as evil as Hitler, and Russia as great a threat to Western civilization as Nazi Germany. There were those in the British foreign policy establishment who accepted this analogy and those who did not, but, if the interventionist impulse in

America were to be appealed to, there was no room for gray areas. London was aided in its task by a series of events in the international, bureaucratic, and political milieus from fall 1944 through spring 1946. A provocative Soviet foreign policy beginning with the Warsaw uprising in 1944 and culminating with the Iranian intrigue in 1946, coupled with the advent of a clique of hard-liners in the State Department and the continuing proddings of Churchill and Bevin, pushed the United States toward a policy of Anglo-American solidarity and confrontation with the Soviet Union. A key element in this shift was the conversion of isolationist-nationalists in the United States to Cold War interventionism.

Eager to shed the onus of appeasement and anxious to wrest control of the presidency from the Democrats, prominent Republican members of Congress became ardent Cold War warriors in spring 1946. In an effort to turn the tables on their domestic foes, Republican leaders charged the Roosevelt-Truman administration with appeasing the forces of international communism and exposing the United States to grave danger. This new bellicosity brought the GOP into line with the southern wing of the Democratic party, which up to this point had voted with the Republicans only on domestic issues. The Dixie component of the conservative coalition in Congress proved to be as aggressive in defending the nation's honor in 1946 as it had in 1941. At the same time, the new Labour government in Great Britain, no less eager to halt Soviet expansion and protect British interests than the Churchill regime, adroitly disarmed internationalist sentiment in the United States by confronting the Soviets within the context of the United Nations and portraying Stalin as the chief postwar threat to the world organization.

Harry Truman was if anything more of a prisoner of the political and diplomatic forces that swirled about him than FDR. After initially attempting to appease the Soviet Union and hold Great Britain at arm's length as his predecessor had done, Truman responded to Soviet truculence, British machinations, and congressional bellicosity by adopting a get-tough stance with the Soviet Union in spring 1946 and accepting the necessity of a tacit Anglo-American alliance.

Throughout World War II and the early stages of the Cold War, then, the United States pursued economic policies toward Great Britain that were counterproductive of its strategic and political objectives in Europe. Confronted with a coalition of fascist powers from 1941 to 1945 that threatened its very survival and with the menace of Soviet imperialism in 1945–46, Washington nonetheless labored to hold British gold/dollar reserves to a minimum and to commit the United Kingdom to a multilateral trading system in which it could not compete. Great Britain received enough aid to enable it to survive and to play a role in the war against the Axis, but not enough to preserve its overseas investments and markets, to maintain its military outposts, or to participate in a system of multilateral commerce. This occurred despite the fact that informed observers on both sides of the Atlantic recognized that financial and commercial weakness inevitably translates into military weakness. Lend-lease aside, then, British efforts to "manage" the United States during this crucial period in world history were only minimally successful. Why America refused to identify its interests with those of Great Britain and how the British failed to educate their "cousins" in the ways of realpolitik are the subjects of this book. The Anglo-American dialogue is a complex mixture of bureaucratic conflict, conventional politics, transatlantic alliances, national characteristics, mutual images, and circumstance. It is the story of the birth pangs of one superpower and the death agonies of another, a story made all the more poignant by the fact that the two were blood relations.

1. An American Ideology: Modified Free Trade and Lend-Lease, 1941–1942

AFTER THE OUTBREAK of war in Europe in September 1939, the administration of Franklin D. Roosevelt struggled to provide the United Kingdom with moral and material aid while still preserving America's neutral status. As 1940 drew to a close, however, it was apparent that Britain would soon run out of the gold and dollars with which to purchase supplies in the United States. In December President Roosevelt decided to heed Winston Churchill's call for all-out aid to the Allies short of military intervention. What followed was the introduction of a massive aid bill, intense public and congressional debate between isolationists and interventionists, and then in spring 1941 passage of the Lend-Lease Act. This measure, involving as it did a huge congressional appropriation, the risk of war with the Axis, and a tacit alliance with Great Britain, forced the United States to think simultaneously about its national security, the state of its domestic economy, and, tentatively, the postwar order it hoped to see emerge from World War II.

Gaddis Smith, A. J. P. Taylor, Warren Kimball, and more recently David Reynolds have speculated at length on Roosevelt's motives in the lend-lease matter. Taylor implies that the United States intended from the first to use Britain's predicament to drain it of gold and dollars, weaken its overseas financial position, and undermine its capacity to compete with the United States in the markets of the world. Others argue that, while Britain's replacement by the United States as the dominant economic power in the world was a result of lend-lease, it was not a cause. The president concluded that the European members of the Axis alliance were bent on world domination and that, after the fall of France, Hitler posed a direct threat to the Western Hemisphere. Quite aside from a natural sympathy for Britain and a desire to see it survive, Roosevelt, Cordell Hull, Henry Morgenthau, Henry Stimson, and company viewed that country by early 1941 as America's first line of defense.[1] These historians admit that Secretary of the Treasury Morgenthau forced the sale of American Viscose Corporation, a subsidiary of the British textile combine, Courtalds, at approximately half its market value,[2] but point out that this was a pittance compared to the reduction of British holdings the Roosevelt administration could have required. According to this view, Morgenthau believed that Congress would never agree to the unprecedented subsidy that lend-lease called for unless the administration could dissipate widely held notions concerning British opulence by demonstrating that the Exchequer was out of dollars and gold. These latter scholars tend to neglect an important point, however.

United States policymakers, assuming that Britain was, like America, capable of economic self-sufficiency, would seek in return for wartime and postwar aid the break-up of the sterling bloc and the elimination of imperial preferences, not the destruction of British interests narrowly defined. That this double-barreled campaign was due more to ideological, political, and bureaucratic factors than domination of the administration by special interests made it no less potent. Thus, while the average person on the street in London and New York saw lend-lease simply as a mechanism to achieve speedy and complete destruction of the Axis, shrewder heads on both sides of the Atlantic viewed it as a device that could be used to alter the structure of international trade and finance, and determine the global balance of power in the postwar world.

Throughout 1941 and early 1942 various bureaucratic entities and interest groups in the United States fought for control of foreign economic policy at the intranational and international levels. A variety of American politicians, exporters, bankers, and bureaucrats coalesced in support of multilateralism, a concept that promised to achieve social justice at home and abroad without sacrificing American prosperity or offending American conservatives. The chief stumbling block to the creation of a multilateral trading world, which required the simultaneous reduction of trade barriers and abolition of exchange controls, was Great Britain. The sterling area was a closed system which discriminated against the goods of nonsterling countries. But the American foreign policy establishment perceived that it could take advantage of Britain's wartime dependency on the United States to force London to abandon the sterling bloc and accept multilateralism.

Roosevelt perceived immediately how important the task of administering lend-lease would be. If Washington so desired, it could use its aid program to determine the course of wartime strategy and the shape of the postwar settlement. Lend-lease would, in addition, have a drastic impact on the American economy and could become a political football in the struggle between liberals and conservatives for control of domestic and foreign policy. The aid program was much too important to turn over to Henry Morgenthau, who often acted impetuously and independently, or to Secretary of State Cordell Hull, who often did not act at all. FDR turned instead to his trusted lieutenant and alter ego, Harry Hopkins. Hopkins was a social worker from Chicago who had come to the New Deal early as head of the Federal Emergency Relief Administration. In the years that followed he carved out an empire for himself, gaining control in 1935 of the Works Progress Administration (WPA), the gigantic apparatus that was the heart of the government's relief program. After serving a stint as secretary of commerce during Roosevelt's second administration, Hopkins resigned at the president's request and moved into the White House. He was until Roosevelt's death the president's chief bureaucratic watchdog at home and his principal envoy abroad. Like Colonel Edward House, Woodrow Wilson's adviser and confidant, Hopkins could anticipate his chief's wishes and even his moods, a crucial attribute since the two were often closely related. A man who once dreamed of occupying the highest office in the land, Hopkins, after becoming assistant to the president, satisfied his immense ego by identifying totally with FDR. Throughout the war Hopkins served as unofficial personnel officer for the administration. He placed at the second and third echelons of various agencies people who were loyal to him and hence to the president and who reported directly to him. Not surprisingly Hopkins, who was equally intolerant of New Deal ideologues and selfish private interests, was one of the most hated and feared men in wartime Washington.[3] This gaunt, chain-smoking, acid-tongued man could cut short a career with the scribble of his pen. He and his secret clique of advisers would play a central role in the evolution of American foreign policy during World War II.

In 1941 Roosevelt agreed to the formation of the Lend-Lease Administration and named Hopkins to head an interdepartmental committee to oversee it. Hopkins in turn chose Edward Stettinius, Jr., a former General Motors executive and ex-Republican, to serve as the first lend-lease administrator. Stettinius had no constituency and no power base within the Democratic party or the Roosevelt bureaucracy. He was dependent on and hence loyal to the White House.

Lend-lease was not a treaty or an executive agreement with a foreign nation. It was a request for $7 million for the production of munitions and the authority to allocate some of those items to countries whose survival benefited the United States. In the Lend-Lease Act Franklin Roosevelt had eliminated the "dollar sign" from aid to Great Britain, but that nation soon learned that the president, Congress, the Treasury, the State Department, and various American interest groups expected something in return for their largess. To be eligible for lend-lease aid, each recipient nation was required by law to negotiate a master agreement with the United States. Anglo-American discussions began almost before the final Senate vote had been tabulated, but a master agreement was not finally approved by London and Washington until February 1942, nearly a year after passage of the Lend-Lease Act. The issue that more than any other prevented early ratification was that of compensation.

The United States Treasury made a concerted effort to control negotiation of the master agreement just as it had the formulation of the Lend-Lease Act, but in the end it was forced to defer to the White House and the State Department. Although Morgenthau viewed Hopkins as arrogant and flamboyant, he also perceived him to be devoid of personal ambition. More importantly, his ties to the president made him a man not to be trifled with.[4] Hence, two days after the Senate approved lend-lease, Morgenthau wrote Hopkins urging him to negotiate the quid pro quo with the British. FDR's former neighbor from Dutchess County was not ready to bow out completely, however. From mid-March through April

1941, the treasury secretary met several times with Hopkins and FDR and pushed adoption of a draft master agreement prepared by Treasury. In that document Morgenthau presented a compensation plan that reflected the president's thinking as of December. At the close of the war Britain would return unused and undamaged goods, and compensate the United States for expended and damaged goods by payment in kind—similar defense articles or raw materials.

The State Department, which had no intention of abdicating its role as chief negotiator of the compensation agreement, got wind of the draft and pointed out to the White House that payment in kind could lead to a war debt that would dwarf that created during World War I. The United States should instead write off expendable munitions, require the return of ships and planes that survived the war, and insist on British acquiescence in United States plans for a postwar economic order.[5] In fact, Cordell Hull and his subordinates saw in the lend-lease master agreement an opportunity to commit Great Britain, sure to be the second most powerful capitalist society to survive World War II, to the principle of multilateralism.

The secretary of state, seventy years old in 1941, was the embodiment of old-fashioned southern liberalism. The son of a petty merchant trader, Hull was born in a log cabin in Overton County, Tennessee, in the foothills of the Cumberland Mountains. After his graduation from Cumberland University law school and a stint in the army during the Spanish-American War, he entered politics. In 1906, the young lawyer was elected to Congress where he served first in the House and then, beginning in 1930, in the Senate. His adopted political mentors were Thomas Jefferson and a Tennessee politician named Benton MacMillan, who had waged a prolonged struggle in Congress for tariff reduction and an income tax. Hull was, moreover, indelibly affected by the agrarian radicalism that had swept rural America in the 1890s. Northern business interests, in his view, were plundering farmers, workers, and small business people through a system of special privilege. Wall Street bankers and industrial magnates such as John D. Rockefeller, W. H. Harriman, and Cornelius Vanderbilt controlled the Republican party and through it national and state governments. With the blessing of the state, these malefactors had established monopolies, restricted the size of the money supply, and erected tariff barriers, all in an attempt to maximize profits at the expense of the living standards of the average American. The solution to the problem was not to control or regulate this conspiracy, Hull believed, but to destroy it. Anticipating Woodrow Wilson, who was to become the third in his pantheon of heroes, Hull in his maiden speech in Congress demanded the "suppression of lawless combinations and the proper curbing of corporate wealth."

Hull and Roosevelt had met during the Wilson years, and FDR cultivated the Tennessean throughout the 1920s. Because Hull supported him at Chicago in 1932, and because he represented two great constituencies—Congress and the South—FDR asked him in 1933 to be his secretary of state, a post Hull would retain until his retirement in 1944.[6]

Hull's stock-in-trade as America's chief diplomat was, of course, commercial liberalism. Trade barriers—particularly the tariff—retarded production, raised prices, created inefficiency, held down living standards, and thus bred hostility among nations. "Economic wars," he told the House of Representatives in September 1918, "are but the germs of real wars."[7] He would certainly have agreed with Richard Cobden, the spiritual leader of the nineteenth-century British free traders, who claimed to see "in the Free Trade principle that which shall act on the moral world as the principle of gravitation in the universe—drawing men together, thrusting aside the antagonisms of race and creed, and language, and uniting us in the eternal bonds of peace."[8]

Intellectually, if not politically, Cordell Hull was a lightweight. As Arthur Schlesinger puts it, this "serious, meditative, gentle, frail" epitome of the "southern gentleman" appeared to believe that the articulation of a lofty principle was tantamount to its realization.[9] Alexander Cadogan, permanent undersecretary in the British Foreign Office, was less kind. On their first meeting, he described Hull as "a dreadful old man—vaguer and wordier than Norman Davis, and rather pig-headed."[10] Dean Acheson later recalled: "Hull gave the same speech over and over, a dissertation on the benefits of unhampered international trade and the road to it through reducing tariffs."[11] The complexities of international economics eluded Hull. To his mind they were irrelevant anyway. Like his Populist forebears, Hull chose to believe rather than understand, to put his faith in a few simple truths rather than to clutter his mind with price structures, demand curves, and demographic trends.[12]

It remained to Hull's subordinates to translate the secretary's simple obsession into reality. The authentic architects of multilateralism were Francis B. Sayre, an economics professor and assistant secretary for economic affairs who was also Woodrow Wilson's son-in-law; Henry Grady, who later succeeded Sayre; Harry Hawkins, a career foreign service officer who headed the Division of Commercial Policy Agreements in the late 1930s and early 1940s; Clair Wilcox, director of the Office of International Trade Policy; and Herbert Feis, an economist and historian whom Hull made his economic adviser in 1933.

The program advocated by economic internationalists in the State Department rested on two cornerstones: nondiscrimination and a simultaneous lowering of all trade barriers. In their trade, tariff, and currency exchange policies, nations should not favor one member of the international community over another. Moreover, no exporter or importer, no matter what the person's nationality, should have to contend with "artificial impediments." That is, trade should be conducted purely on economic and not political grounds.

The multilateralists were reacting in part to contemporary developments in international economics. Bilateralism, the signing of exclusive trade agreements between two nations, was the norm in international commerce in the 1930s. As the Versailles peace structure disintegrated, a number of nations moved to put their economies on a war footing. This involved imposing state control over raw materials, import quotas to conserve foreign exchange, and long-term commodity agreements designed to enable the purchaser to monopolize overseas sources of strategic materials. The competition to build arsenals and control strategic materials precluded any chance of a simultaneous reduction of trade barriers. All of the great European powers signed bilateral pacts with their smaller neighbors and with developing nations in Latin America and the Far East in which the trading partner was granted increased import quotas and a special low tariff rate in return for allowing the larger power to monopolize the imported product. Germany was particularly blatant in using the threat of military power and/or economic leverage in the form of German markets and finished products, particularly steel, to force its neighbors to sign long-term trade pacts very favorable to Berlin. Although the United States may have followed a more liberal trade policy than other nations, the Roosevelt administration's cherished Reciprocal Trade Agreements Act of 1934 with its most-favored-nation clause was largely nullified by the method of its administration, by the hedges imposed by special interests, and by the subsequent imposition of import quotas.

Each country, then, by raising tariffs, imposing quota restrictions, negotiating preferential arrangements, utilizing restrictive and discriminatory exchange controls, and subsidizing its exports, tried to take care of its own exporters and producers at the expense of those in other countries. In consequence, the multilateralists asserted, international trade was in large part destroyed. The foreign economic policy of nations became a struggle for a shrinking world trade. To Hawkins, Wilcox, Feis, and other multilateralists in the State Department, bilateralism was a form of mercantilism. The negotiation of trade pacts that discriminated against the other members of the international community stemmed from the atavistic notion that nations, like biological organisms, were involved in a constant struggle for limited food supplies, energy sources, and raw materials, and that in order to survive a country had to reduce the wealth of its competitors.[13]

Multilateralists maintained that competition among countries for the wealth of the world restricted trade, wasted resources, and bred war; competition between individuals and corporations based on price, product quality, and market demand bred efficiency and economic expansion, and raised living standards. The world had not begun to realize its productive potential, they insisted. As long as nations tried to protect infant industries and inefficient agricultural operations with artificial, "uneconomic" trade barriers, the world would continue to be made up of relatively inefficient national economies or clusters of national economies.[14] The multilateralists looked forward to the creation of a world market in which the citizens of each region concentrated on producing the commodity that they could produce most cheaply and efficiently. This specialization, coupled with the elimination of trade barriers, would mean production and distribution of the greatest number of goods at the cheapest possible price. There would be temporary dislocation and unemployment as inefficient industries and high-cost farming operations went under, but the end result would be ever-rising living standards and maximum employment throughout the world. They looked forward, in other words, to a process at the international level similar to that which had taken place at the national level in the United States in the late nineteenth century.[15]

The multilateralists were both heirs to and dissenters from America's open-door tradition.[16] The concept includes strains of both economic nationalism and economic internationalism. Many of those urging adoption of an aggressive foreign economic policy believed that the object of that policy should be the unlimited expansion of American exports. They were not interested in lowering the American tariff and worked to exclude third parties from markets the United States already dominated—certain parts of Latin America, for example. Others, most notably Woodrow Wilson, saw foreign trade in terms of balance and equilibrium, and believed that a concert of interest among the principal trading nations was possible. America could acquire new markets overseas only by opening its domestic market to foreign competition. Wilson and the internationalists looked forward to a multilateral expansion of international trade, not national aggrandizement. The multilateralists of the 1940s belonged to the internationalist rather than the nationalist branch of the open-door movement.

In many ways multilateralism was a throwback to progressivism. Like Wilson, the men who shaped American trade and financial policy during World War II were generally committed to social justice at home and abroad. "A Liberal trading system," wrote one foreign service officer, "is the means by which the world's productive resources can yield the maximum of material well-being." It seemed to be the only approach, moreover, that could do so without undermining economic democracy and destroying individual liberty.[17] "Because we desire to preserve our democratic system of individual enterprise, a policy of bilateralism under strict government control would be contrary to our national interest," insisted Harry Hawkins in a report prepared for the Executive Committee on Commercial Policy. America's "democratic institutions" required that "the promotion of our foreign trade should be accomplished with a minimum of government interference with or participation in trading operations."[18] There could be no justice without freedom and freedom was indivisible.

In the late 1930s a number of State Department technicians and economists viewed multilateralism as merely a specific device with which to combat German bilateralism and help finance United States–Latin American trade, but after the outbreak of World War II they began to see the concept as the economic phase of internationalism.[19] Indeed, as time passed, multilateralism seemed to be the only ideological alternative to communism on the one hand and fascism on the other. It was a uniquely American stratagem that combined humanitarian ideals with free enterprise and the profit motive. For Hawkins and Clair Wilcox, social justice—whether in Mississippi or Kenya, Tallahassee or Beirut—meant primarily equality of opportunity. State control of and particularly state competition with the private sector undermined freedom and was in fact totalitarianism. Multilateralism was a device, then, that could forestall collectivism in the domestic sphere by preventing unemployment and raising living standards, and in the global arena by keeping the role of national governments in international economics to a minimum.

Unfortunately for the American heirs of Adam Smith, John Bright, and Richard Cobden, a consensus had developed within the international community early in World War II that multilateralism was an anachronistic throwback. Due to a combination of history and circumstance, the major trading nations of the world, developed and underdeveloped, were by 1941 committed to the concept of a closely regulated and tightly controlled economy, both domestic and foreign. Europeans believed that the United States had still not resolved the problems that developed in the late nineteenth century when capitalism became wedded to democracy. They noted that the majority of Americans, who regarded the depression as a monumental aberration, believed that individuals ought to be left relatively free to do with their property as they wished. Laws and regulations that diminished individual liberty in the economic sphere also somehow diminished democracy. A number of European nations, most notably Great Britain, were convinced that in a postindustrial environment state intervention into the economic sphere strengthened rather than weakened democracy.

Cobdenite liberals who argued that laissez-faire at home and free trade abroad perpetuated democracy and promoted internationalism were extremely influential in Britain until 1914. World War I, however, shattered the liberal dream for most Britons. After the Great War the Labour party, an increasingly important element in the Conservative party, and the average citizen fully accepted planning and a mixed economy as requisites to prosperity and social justice. Their own experience as well as that of their neighbors across the channel taught Britons that the key to preventing revolution—which often produced totalitarianism—was economic security. Because economic security in modern industrial societies required planning and economic controls, the latter promoted rather than eroded democracy and individual liberty. Circumscription of property rights was a small but necessary price to pay.

Preindustrial no less than postindustrial nations were committed to state regulation of their economies. Many developing nations in Latin America, Africa, and the Far East acted on the assumption that the key to raising living standards was economic diversification. Most had experienced a colonial relationship with an economically more advanced nation in which the weaker sent raw materials to the stronger in exchange for finished goods. Leaders of these countries believed that agricultural diversification coupled with stimulation of domestic industries would give them greater leverage in the marketplaces of the world. New enterprises require protection, however; few could survive free competition, even in their own home markets, with the products of the American colossus. World War II accelerated existing trends toward planning and control in both Europe and the Third World countries. The environment with which the multilateralists would be dealing during and after the war, then, would be hostile to laissez-faire economics and notions of free enterprise.

In 1941 multilateralists in the State Department, ignoring these broader trends, identified two obstacles to the realization of their dreams—economic nationalism in the United States and empire isolationism in Great Britain. In the domestic sphere, multilateralism promised to offend economic nationalists by requiring a general reduction of tariffs and exposing inefficient industries to extinction. Just as had been the case in 1919, America would emerge from World War II as the principal creditor nation in the world. As a result of its massive economic and military supply program, it would have accumulated most of the world's gold supply. Because the United States would be the arbiter of any multilateral system, the dollar would be the strongest currency in the world and would dominate foreign trade. Or, conversely, control of the world's gold/dollar supply would guarantee that America would be the arbiter of any multilateral system created. Yet without dollars America's trading partners could not participate in a dollar-dominated system. Anticipating this situation, a number of State Department officials argued that after World War II the United States would have to import more than it exported in order for America's trading partners to earn gold and dollars.[20] Only after general currency equilibrium emerged could multilateralism work. But how could this truth be reconciled with the political reality of vested interests and their clout in Congress, and with the lingering strength of economic nationalism in general?[21] Moreover, the architects of multilateralism admitted that there would be some "temporary dislocation" in national economies as nations abandoned marginal industrial and agricultural enterprises to concentrate on activities they did best. While temporary dislocation did not constitute a major obstacle to economic theorists, it caused a very real problem for political realists, especially in a democracy such as the United States where the national legislature was set up to represent local and regional economic interests. Franklin Roosevelt and Cordell Hull were above all else political realists, and the economists and civil servants who worked for them had to respond to their priorities.

Refracted through the prism of American politics, the multilateralism advocated by the State Department differed from the absolute economic liberalism propounded by Adam Smith. Smith, a true free trader, had argued against all restraints on imports, either through tariffs or quotas. But his free market ideas were spawned during a period when Britain, vitally dependent on a large volume of imports, had possessed a great colonial empire and was the world's leading trading nation. Twentieth-century America, by contrast, did not possess a great colonial empire and did not depend on a high level of imports for economic survival. Acutely aware that there would be circumstances under which American industries would have to be protected against foreign imports and sensitive to Congress's historic opposition to any drastic reduction of American tariffs, the majority of State Department officials concerned with foreign economic policy were forced to concede the need to retain modest rates. As a result, liberals in the State Department pushed not free trade but modified multilateralism, a scheme under which low import duties were permitted as long as they were uniformly applied and did not discriminate against the goods of any other nation.[22]

Finally, there was an ideological inconsistency associated with multilateralism that would bring heat from economic nationalists inside and outside Congress.

Because existing trade patterns were bilateral and protectionist, the realization of multilateralism would require massive planning, an active foreign policy, and far-reaching interference with established economic relationships and mechanisms either by the United States or by an international authority committed to multilateralism. In their efforts to build an interdependent world economy, the multilateralists would run into opposition not only from vested interests but also from American conservatives who were simultaneously attracted by the scheme's emphasis on private enterprise and a free marketplace, and repelled by the need for national and international agencies to implement it.

In 1941 economic liberals within the State Department perceived the primary external factor in the continuing battle between neo-mercantilism and multilateralism to be Great Britain. In 1932 in the Ottawa Agreements, the United Kingdom and other members of the Commonwealth had formed themselves into a trading bloc within which member nations awarded each others' exports preferential treatment, that is, lower rates. The exigencies of World War II compelled Britain to strengthen this bloc and generally to expand governmental control of international finance and trade. London entered into long-term purchasing agreements with exporters of primary products, strictly limited imports from nonsterling nations, and blocked sterling payments to members of the sterling area. The British Treasury also refused to make the sterling it did release to its trading partners freely convertible into other currencies—dollars, for example—in order that sterling bloc members might buy from third parties such as the United States. American policymakers perceived that if Britain used the leverage of its blocked sterling balances and the dollar pool to maintain and strengthen its trading and monetary union into the postwar period, multilateralism would never come to pass.[23] As one American official put it: "What England does about her currency and trade controls determines whether the world will be one large and prosperous international trading group or whether it will be broken up into conflicting economic blocs."[24]

The particular bête noire of State Department multilateralists was imperial preference. To their minds it combined the twin evils of discrimination and politicization of foreign trade. As Hawkins, Wilcox, and Feis saw it, Britain under the Ottawa Agreements granted special low tariff duties and signed long-term bulk-purchasing agreements with its empire trading partners in order to monopolize their raw materials and make sure that they took only British-manufactured products. In other words, Britain used special incentives and the leverage of its market to force its trading partners not to sell to or buy from third nations. London might, for example, withhold railroad equipment from a former colonial area whose rails had been built to British specification in order to secure a monopoly on a vital raw material produced by that nation. Imperial preference could be used, then, not only to monopolize the trade of a particular nation or region; it also could be used to isolate and punish political and military rivals. In a political as well as an economic sense, the structure established by the Ottawa Agreements seemed the antithesis of multilateralism.[25]

State Department multilateralists, however, were generally undaunted by the winds of economic nationalism and collectivism that seemed to be sweeping the world. They were certain that their moment in history had arrived; the United States possessed unparalleled leverage which could be used to eliminate discrimination and reduce tariff barriers. "The economic strength of the United States," wrote Hawkins in a memo prepared for the State Department leadership, "is greater than that of any other country. Its production and consumption is a large part of the production and consumption of the entire world. It is the greatest creditor nation. Policies that it pursues and advocates will be decisive in determining whether mutual impoverishment or mutual prosperity will characterize economic policies in the post-war world." The economic dislocation and disorganization that would follow close on the heels of World War II presented the multilateralists with a golden opportunity. Old patterns of trade characterized by bilateralism and discrimination would be destroyed, opening the way for the introduction of a new order. "But it is an opportunity which we will have only for a relatively brief time," Hawkins continued; "production and trade will tend to revert to what they were and will solidify into the pre-war patterns that Secretary Hull and the present Administration sought so persistently but found so difficult to change because of the resistance of vested interests."[26]

Another group of policymakers in the State Department led by Undersecretary Sumner Welles, Assistant Secretary Dean Acheson, and Special Assistant to the Secretary Leo Pasvolsky defined multilateralism in primarily political and strategic terms, and, while not responsible for its formulation or even aware of all of its implications, supported the stratagem as a necessary corollary to collective security. Welles, a Groton classmate of FDR, was an experienced foreign service officer who specialized in Latin American affairs. A principal architect of the Good Neighbor policy, Welles was devoted to the concept of an Inter-American System based on the juridical equality of all states. Attributing the rise of fascism and the outbreak of World War II to the failure of collective security during the 1930s, he looked forward to the creation of a collective security organization in the postwar era, a kind of Inter-American System writ large. Pasvolsky was brought into the department to design just such an organization.[27] Although Welles and Cordell Hull were bitter rivals—Welles enjoyed independent access to the White House until his abrupt departure from the State Department in 1943—the undersecretary fully supported multilateralism. At the Argentia Conference in 1941 he told his counterpart in the British Foreign Office, Sir Alexander Cadogan, that he looked forward to Anglo-American cooperation in the reconstruction of the world economy and to the establishment of a system "without manifold economic barriers which had . . . been so clearly responsible for the present world collapse."[28] Welles was one of the main authors of Roosevelt's Four Freedoms speech in January 1941. To him and others concerned primarily with politics and war, equal access to the raw materials and markets of the world was a prerequisite for security and thus for peace.

Dean Acheson, "the tall man with the bristling mustache and cold eyes," as Charles Bohlen would describe him,[29] was also a multilateralist and in fact one of the principal authors of the lend-lease master agreement with Great Britain. Acheson, also a graduate of Groton and Harvard, took essentially a balance-of-power view of international affairs. He looked forward to a postwar world in which peace would be maintained in Europe through an Anglo-American concert of power. If Britain continued imperial preference into the postwar period and embarked on an aggressive policy of bilateralism, the United States, prodded by Congress and the special interests it represented, would respond in kind. The resulting trade war would threaten Anglo-American cooperation in the political and military spheres and give American isolationism in general a huge shot in the arm.

Had it been the property merely of a handful of economic theorists and professional diplomats in the State Department, multilateralism might well have been a relatively insignificant phenomenon. In fact, by war's end a number of influential Americans had come to see in the concept an answer to the human dilemma of security versus freedom. Its appeal to conservatives was strong. At their initial meeting in 1912, Louis Brandeis convinced Woodrow Wilson that the most important public issue of the day was preservation of economic freedom in the United States. Monster monopolies, a privately controlled banking system, and corrupt government were threatening the liberties of the people. He persuaded Wilson to use the federal power to sweep away special privileges and artificial barriers to the development of individual energies, and to preserve and restore competition in business. The Wilson-Brandeis tradition survived the Republican twenties and became one of the two principal themes in the New Deal. Through Brandeis himself, through his distinguished protégé, Felix Frankfurter, and through Frankfurter's chief representatives in Washington, Thomas G. Corcoran and Benjamin V. Cohen, the New Freedom philosophy was injected directly into the New Deal organism.[30]

Multilateralism was an ideological branch of the Jeffersonian, Wilsonian, Brandesian tree. That social justice be placed in a free enterprise setting was no less important to multilateralists than it had been to progressives. Early in 1944 Clair Wilcox wrote an article for the *New York Times* entitled "No Private Collectivism: A Challenge." In this piece, one of the prime architects of multilateralism warned America that business people and financiers who attacked the Office of Price Administration (OPA), War Production Board (WPB), Combined Shipping Board, and other wartime agencies set up to control the economy and maximize production were not really as interested in competition and free enterprise as they claimed. Rather, these giants of industry and finance wanted to be free to set up monopolies and cartels, to conclude enterprise-stifling agreements, to restrict output in order to artificially raise prices, and to control the growth of the money supply. "Freedom of enterprise means that new firms are free to enter an industry and that old firms are free to leave it; that there are no artificial barriers either to investment or bankruptcy," Wilcox proclaimed. "Privacy of enterprise means that business stands on its own two feet, that it does not lean for support on a governmental crutch."[31] Wilcox and the other theorists of multilateralism believed that nondiscrimination, elimination of exchange controls, and reduction of trade barriers would restore competition and private control to international trade. Their paeans to free enterprise and rugged individualism would strike a responsive chord in the average American.

Liberal reformers found multilateralism no less congenial than progressives. Indeed, one of the concept's foremost supporters in the Washington hierarchy was a man with impeccable liberal credentials: Vice-President Henry Wallace. This planner, centralizer, and author of the Agricultural Adjustment Act had survived the conservative resurgence within the New Deal bureaucracy and, sitting atop his labor and liberal constituencies, continued to be a powerful figure in wartime Washington. Wallace, editor of *Wallace's Farmer*, agricultural geneticist, and son of Warren Harding's secretary of agriculture, was in many ways a typical agrarian radical. The sensitive and idealistic Wallace had been raised in rural Iowa and had internalized farm grievances at an early age.[32] Like Wilson and Brandeis, Wallace believed that it was the duty of the federal government to break up monopolies and regulate business and financial houses clothed with the public interest; but unlike them (at least from 1913 to 1915), he was convinced that Washington should help unorganized elements in the marketplace—such as farmers and laborers—organize in order to bargain more effectively with business for a larger share of the economic pie.

Wallace was attracted to multilateralism for a number of reasons. As the person most responsible for developing New Deal farm policy, Wallace was determined to respond to the truth that overproduction was the root cause of low living standards among farmers. Wallace viewed the Agricultural Adjustment Act, which paid farmers not to plant, as only a temporary solution to agrarian problems, however. A champion of scientific farming, he looked forward to ever-expanding agricultural production. As secretary of agriculture, Wallace could see no long-range solution for American farming except through an increase in exports and could see no increase in exports except through an increase in imports. "Frankly," Wallace wrote Roosevelt in September 1933, "I am convinced that sooner or later we must be prepared to lower our tariffs very radically."[33]

During World War II the Iowan's broadening political and intellectual horizons caused him to see unemployment as the number one problem of the postwar era and multilateralism as a possible solution to that problem. In 1940 FDR chose Wallace as his running mate; and by the time he became vice-president, the Iowan had expanded his constituency to include organized labor. His support of the sit-down strikes of the late 1930s at a time when antiunion sentiment was mounting in many quarters won him the undying gratitude of the CIO and to a lesser extent the AFL. Wallace, who now saw himself as sound presidential timber, expanded his area of concern to include not only farm surpluses and other agricultural concerns but labor problems and the condition of small business as well. The issue that seemed to skewer all of these groups was unemployment.[34]

In fact, unemployment, or rather full employment, became the great liberal preoccupation on both sides of the Atlantic during World War II. Signs pointing to an overproduction-produced depression in America following the defeat of the Axis were numerous. The war proved to be a tremendous stimulus to United States industry. Eighteen million Americans were employed in war-related industries by 1944; including members of the armed services, 28 million people or 24 percent of the nation's work force produced goods used directly in the Allied war effort. From December 1941 through August 1945, the nation's industrial output increased by 75 percent and total plant capacity by 50 percent. In 1944, the last full year of the war, the United States exported goods valued at almost $15 billion—five times the 1938 level. In August 1945 the director of the Office of War Mobilization and Reconversion declared that as soon as hostilities ended 18 million Americans would be released from war-related jobs. By spring 1946 some 8 million Americans would be jobless, he predicted. Theodore A. Sumberg wrote that it would be possible theoretically for the United States to achieve full employment without any exports at all, but to do so, he believed, the nation would have to move away from a free enterprise economy.[35]

Henry Wallace espoused multilateralism because it simultaneously promised to alleviate unemployment and preclude the domination of the federal government by special interests.[36] World War II had so augmented the power of big business, Wallace argued, that economic democracy and political democracy were threatened with extinction. "These corporations say—give us old-fashioned Americanism; give us free enterprise," he proclaimed in 1943. "By old-fashioned Americanism they really mean corporation-controlled government—not the free Americanism of the United States in the pre-corporation days."[37] The corporations that posed the greatest threat to the economic well-being of average citizens as well as to their political liberty were the ones engaged in international trade, he alleged. Ever interested in gaining subsidies from their governments, these firms moved to control state departments, foreign offices, and the whole apparatus of diplomacy. In pursuit of profits, they formed international monopolies—cartels—and pursued restrictive and exploitive policies on the international as well as the national level.[38] In calling for the elimination of monopolistic practices in international trade, and particularly the breakup of cartels, multilateralism would not only promote general prosperity in the United States but serve the cause of democracy as well.

Finally, Wallace championed multilateralism because he was an internationalist. The "century of the common man," a phrase he later used as the title of a best-selling book, was not for Americans alone but for all the citizens of the world. By 1941 he had rejected the notion of inevitable stagnationism; he believed that the world economy had only begun to grow. Decrying colonial relationships that featured exploitation of underdeveloped, raw material–producing areas by economically advanced, industrialized nations, Wallace advocated a program that combined large-scale capital investment in underdeveloped areas with a reduction of trade barriers throughout the world. "Foreign trade is ready for vast expansion," he wrote in 1944. "War torn Europe will need our foreign products, consumer and capital goods in vast quantities. But more important, Latin America, Asia, Africa, and most of Europe are ripe for a speedy and long-term industrialization which will raise their buying power . . . to unthought of heights."[39] Wallace supported multilateralism, a system based theoretically on free enterprise and competition, because he believed it would be preceded by a United States–financed, international New Deal. He recognized that much of the world's trade took place between industrialized nations exchanging a variety of finished goods, services, and technologies, and not between industrial and preindustrial areas. The export of American capital to Peru, India, Malaysia, and Nigeria, together with the sharing of technology and the sale of capital goods on credit, would allow these countries to diversify their economies. At this point these formerly underdeveloped nations would be able to compete. They would join in a multilateral system of international trade in the context of an expanding world economy. "It begins more and more to look as if the backward areas of the world have to be led to a high standard of living either by way of American organization, British organization, or Russian organization," he observed. "Neither the British or the Russians care much for raising the standard of living of the people. The British raised the standard merely as a by-product of exploitation. The Russians raised the standard of living as part of their effort to enlarge the field of influence of the communist doctrine."[40]

By 1944 multilateralism, though it was vaguely understood by the general public, came to enjoy widespread support outside the administration among those who took an interest in foreign affairs. Republicans, Democrats, and independents claimed to have learned a lesson from the events of 1938 and 1939, namely, that isolationism did not pay. A consensus developed early in the war that America's ostrichlike posture had contributed to the rise of Hitler and Mussolini. The American people would become self-consciously "internationalist" during the war, resurrecting and adulating the memory of Woodrow Wilson and pledging full support for a postwar international collective security organization.[41] Multilateralism seemed to constitute the economic phase of internationalism, emphasizing, as it claimed, cooperative action to achieve nondiscrimination, general prosperity, and peace. A man who frequently exhibited this generalized support for multilateralism was John Foster Dulles. A member of a prominent New York law firm, a leading Presbyterian layman, and a member of the liberal wing of the Republican party, Dulles was asked to testify before Congress in behalf of renewal of the Reciprocal Trade Agreements Act in 1943. Unable to attend, he sent a letter of support instead. "Two propositions seem to me to be indisputable," he wrote the chairman of the House Ways and Means Committee. "The first is that no nation of any importance can any longer consider its fiscal and trade policies to be matters of purely domestic concern. The world has become so interdependent that the trade and monetary policies of one country may have serious repercussions on others . . . in the second place, the trade conditions which ought to prevail in the world need to be given some stability by international agreement."[42] In the view of Dulles and many Americans, the lack of long-range plans and agreements to reduce trade barriers and to provide for equal access to raw materials and markets prompted the strong to prey on the weak and provoked a general sense of economic and social insecurity.

A final but very significant interest group in the United States that supported multilateralism consisted of exporters and bankers specializing in overseas investments. By the turn of the century a number of American manufacturers had become convinced that their products were the cheapest and best that the world had ever seen, and that in situations of nondiscrimination they could compete successfully with the merchants of any other nation. As numerous historians have pointed out, investment bankers, exporters, and manufacturers played a prominent role in progressive-era administrations. Capitalists pressed the federal government to open new fields for investment, to acquire new markets, and to preserve existing ones. Statesmen in turn strove to use money and material to protect areas of strategic interest. Both were successful. The coming of the depression, accompanied as it was by the massive liquidation of United States holdings in Europe and the disruption of an already distorted foreign trade, forced the export/investment branch of the business community into temporary eclipse. The political isolationism of the 1930s acted as an added fillip to economic nationalism.[43] But with the coming of World War II and the resurgence of internationalism, and with memories of the depression still fresh in the public's mind, business people who lived off of international trade and investment were in a position once again to prowl the corridors of power. Manufacturers of every kind—those that produced primarily for the home market as well as those preoccupied with exports—supported multilateralism, Franklin Johnston, publisher of *The American Exporter*, wrote Robert Taft, "because it aims to correct a worldwide condition instead of merely treating its symptoms."[44] American investors and exporters argued that multilateralism would promote private enterprise and healthy competition at home and abroad, and they clearly expected the federal government to do everything in its power to establish conditions under which the system could take hold and flourish.[45]

The officials in charge of drafting a lend-lease understanding with Great Britain in 1941, then, were convinced by their reading of history and politics that multilateralism was an idea whose time had come. The individual selected to oversee negotiation of a master agreement was Dean Acheson. A lawyer and former assistant secretary of the Treasury, Acheson seemed to Cordell Hull and the White House to have the right combination of technical expertise, bureaucratic clout, and diplomatic skill to settle the matter of compensation with the British.[46] Acheson's counterpart was John Maynard Keynes, the famed economist and in 1941 an adviser to the British Treasury. More than any other person, Keynes would bestride Anglo-American economic and financial talks during the war and immediate postwar period like a colossus, a temperamental, abrasive, inconsistent, and self-centered colossus, but a colossus nonetheless.

Born in 1883, the son of a Cambridge don, young Keynes led a sheltered if stimulating childhood. He absorbed the ancient university's traditionalism, its aura of security, its purposefulness. The predominant mood in late nineteenth-century Cambridge was one of conservative reform, rational change directed toward preserving the best elements of Western civilization. The institution's mission became the man's mission. Keynes studied political economy with the best minds in England and, following graduation with highest honors, settled down to a long and distinguished academic career with his alma mater. At Cambridge Keynes was inducted into a highly select discussion group known as the Society of Apostles, a coterie dedicated simply and solely to "the pursuit of truth." In later years he would become a leading light in a much less sophomoric association, the Bloomsbury Group, a glittering assemblage of British literati, artists, historians, and economists.[47]

As Charles Hession has noted in his controversial biography of Keynes, the English economist adopted a holistic approach to life and learning. Humankind could advance only if its educated elite combined intuition and reason to solve the world's problems. The passionate perception that he brought to life and that he urged others to practice focused initially on self rather than community. Keynes's early life through the Bloomsbury period was devoted to the pleasures of homosexuality, intellectual stimulation, and self-development. World War I worked a profound change on the brilliant young hedonist. Turning his attention to public life and public problems, he spent the rest of his years in an intense quest for theories and mechanisms that would ease the world's pain. As Keynes turned outward, his homosexuality, which many psychologists regard as a form of immaturity, receded into the background. His most productive period unfolded within the context of his marriage to the Russian ballerina, Lydia Lopokova.[48]

Keynes believed that civilization had been entrusted to its intellectual elite, and that no problem was beyond solution, or at least amelioration, through rational discussion. Ideas were paramount, and economics always controlled politics. "Practical men," he wrote in the *General Theory*, "who believe themselves to be quite exempt from any intellectual influences, are usually the slaves of some defunct economist. Mad men in authority who hear voices in the air are distilling their frenzy from some academic scribbler from a few years back." Though he started out firmly rooted within traditional, classical economics, Keynes moved away from it because of what he perceived to be its often erroneous economic assumptions and policies, and its antisocial consequences. Quite simply, he found traditional laissez-faire theory unable to predict or explain reality. Classical assumptions were applicable, he believed, only under conditions of full employment, and England experienced massive unemployment throughout much of Keynes's adult life. He devoted a good part of his time to proving that governmental acceptance of more responsibility for the smooth working of the economy could increase human freedom and choice. Although he valued tradition and social stability, upheld the virtues of the middle class, and was something of an elitist, Keynes was no admirer of the Conservative party. The Conservatives' historic attachment to laissez-faire, undergirded by the presumption of the working of natural economic law, offended him. Man made economics and not economics man. Keynes was keenly alive to great social evils and sensitive to human suffering; he believed statesmen, guided by their intellectual mentors, could render the human condition much improved.

But neither was Keynes a socialist; he had no egalitarian sentiment. Keynes never questioned the fundamental principles of private property, competition, self-interest, the market mechanism, or profit making. They should be harnessed and regulated but not destroyed. Individualism was a theme in all of Keynes's major works, from the *Economic Consequences of the Peace* through the *General Theory*. Increased governmental intervention in the economy was necessary to protect individuals in pursuit of their interests.[49]

In heart, brain, and spirit Keynes was a pragmatic reformer. It is ironic that he came to be perceived, especially in America, as an economic doctrinaire, a rigid ideologist. Capitalism in and of itself could not achieve social justice, he argued; it must be modified and adapted to changing circumstances. If capitalism did not evolve, it would die and with it much of what was good about Western civilization. Keynes viewed money as a means to an end, not an end in itself. That was the difference, he insisted, between himself and those counting-house barbarians who advocated laissez-faire and fiscal conservatism for their own sake and who dominated the Bank of England.[50]

Not surprisingly, Keynes was interested above all else in the factors that created employment and unemployment. Involuntary unemployment existed, despite what the classicists said. He successfully debunked the theory that supply creates its own demand, with the economy moving toward equilibrium at full employment. Rejecting the frictionless marketplace, Keynes insisted that economists shift their attention from prices, wages, and interest rates and focus on aggregate demand as the key determinant of employment. Aggregate demand was composed of two factors—investment and consumption—and together they determined output and employment. Consumption, Keynes stated, was a function of income, income equaling the wages and salaries of those employed in the production of goods and services. With few exceptions, the *General Theory* insisted, the amount consumed was not equal to that earned and the difference represented what society wished to save. According to Keynes's theory, each rise in the national income would produce a corresponding rise in consumption, but it would be less than the increase in income. The overall effect would be to widen the gap between national income and consumption. Investment thus became the crucial determinant of employment; no automatic process existed, however, to ensure that the savings of one group would be utilized by another for investment purposes. It was clearly demonstrable that investment did not equal savings, and, therefore, unemployment existed. In light of these truths, only the government could maintain aggregate demand at full employment levels. Through its expenditure and taxation policies the government could compensate for deficiencies in investment, add to the nation's purchasing power, and stimulate prior investment.[51]

Keynes began his public life as a modified free trader and a member of the Liberal party. But with the advent of widespread unemployment in the 1930s, the "undismal scientist" embraced tariffs, exchange controls, commodity agreements, and the whole structure established by the Ottawa Conference. Britain must protect itself from the disturbances of the outer world while it pursued planned stability at the national level. By refusing to enter into currency stabilization agreements and to promise a sweeping reduction of trade barriers, the London Economic Conference had acted correctly. Deflation could easily spread from one nation to another and Britain, given its dependence on foreign trade, was especially vulnerable. But Keynes was a living example of the aphorism that a foolish consistency is the hobgoblin of small minds. He was nothing if not flexible, and he had no vested interest in his own theories. There was a saying among British economists: "Where five economists are gathered together there will be six conflicting opinions and two of them will be held by Keynes."[52] Although 1941 saw Keynes committed to protection and national policies to secure full employment, events late that year and early the next led him to abandon his previous position and embrace multilateralism—with certain conditions attached.

Keynes was no stranger to the United States or the Roosevelt administration when as special Treasury representative he arrived in May 1941 to explain Britain's perilous financial situation and its need for an immediate cash advance. As Roy Harrod, Keynes's first biographer, notes, the acerbic economist was not predisposed to admire the American way of life. American civilization, he believed, was characterized by materialism, superficiality, political turmoil, and parochialism; it was a sort of distorted offshoot of European civilization.[53] In spring 1934 Keynes had visited the United States to receive an honorary degree from Columbia. His friend Felix Frankfurter arranged a meeting with the president, and on May 28, 1934, Keynes went to the White House. The Englishman was urbane, suave, articulate, and intellectually aggressive. He could be condescending and even cruel to his intellectual inferiors. "Insulting arguments darted out of him with the swiftness of an adder's tongue," Bertrand Russell once wrote.[54] He had already delivered several articles and speeches on the New Deal. He refrained from lecturing the president, but FDR was cool nonetheless. Roosevelt did not like to be upstaged. Keynes was not particularly impressed with Roosevelt either. He admired the president for his willingness to experiment but found no rationale behind the New Deal. The president was disappointingly shallow; "I don't think your President Roosevelt knows anything about economics," he told Alvin Hansen after their meeting.[55]

Conservatives in the United States, of course, viewed Keynes as the great ogre.

Everywhere he was portrayed as the champion of centralized planning, big government, and deficit spending; the British economist seemed to Liberty Leaguers the number one enemy of private enterprise. Some even insisted on viewing him as the evil genius behind the New Deal. The prevailing consensus among historians and economists is that, while Keynesian theory served as a point of departure for a number of New Deal planners, particularly Alvin Hansen and Marriner Eccles, his direct influence on the New Deal and Franklin Roosevelt was minimal. They point to FDR's reaction to the economic upturn of 1936–37 and argue, correctly, that he never felt comfortable with countercyclical deficit spending and was committed to the concept of a balanced budget. But, as shall be seen, so was Keynes in the long run.

In many ways Franklin Roosevelt and John Maynard Keynes were similar in philosophy and approach. Both were committed to saving capitalism and to the idea that it could survive only through constant modification. Both were committed to achieving social justice within the context of a political and economic system that provided for a maximum of individual freedom. Neither believed in the absolute working of economic laws and both were willing to experiment. Indeed, Roosevelt and Keynes were two of the twentieth century's great pragmatists, one intellectual and the other political.

In his role as ombudsman for the British Treasury, Keynes opened talks with Henry Morgenthau on the implementation of the lend-lease program in early May. Machinery had to be set up, orders placed and processed, and production in the United States adjusted to new demands. Although just over $4 billion worth of goods had been delivered to England by the end of 1941, lend-lease did not halt the drain on the Exchequer's hoard of gold and dollars. Britain had to continue paying for orders placed in 1940 and delivered in 1941. Payment under these old commitments had reduced the total gold reserves of the Bank of England to less than $50 million by June and the cash reserves of the British Treasury to less than $100 million. This was hardly enough to maintain the "backing" for British currency and operate the sterling area, Keynes complained.[56] The matter of Britain's immediate cash-flow situation was overshadowed, however, by negotiations over compensation for lend-lease.

Keynes and Churchill differed strongly over the position Britain should take in regard to compensation. In the negotiations over a master agreement, the prime minister was determined first to prevent a reoccurrence of the World War I war debts imbroglio and second to protect Britain's freedom of economic action in the immediate post–World War II period. In mid-June Churchill wrote Keynes and "strongly argued" that the agreement should not provide for repayment or installment payments in either cash or commercial goods. Moreover, Britain's financial and economic condition during the first five years following World War II would be so precarious that the Bank of England and the Treasury would have to be free to impose whatever controls were necessary to maintain the prewar standard of living. Britain should under no circumstance bind itself to give up those controls. Churchill, who was also minister of defense, declared that, anyway, discussions concerning the economic shape of the postwar world were premature.

As he pointed out repeatedly to Keynes, the cabinet then presiding over Britain's fortunes was a patchwork affair that included socialists, imperialists, traditional liberals, and everything in between; cooperation among these disparate elements had been made possible only by the greatest external threat Britain had faced since Napoleon. Debates over the social and economic policies that Britain should pursue at home and abroad could fracture that fragile consensus. Consequently, Churchill advised Keynes that he and Acheson should look for compensation "in the field of military and political considerations and the field of economic collaboration."[57]

Keynes was disappointed by Churchill's negative attitude. Though he was but a temporary in the Treasury, Keynes's fertile mind was already toying with the idea of an international agreement on postwar finance that would safeguard Britain's interests and simultaneously promote international economic expansion. Churchill was adamant, however, and Keynes turned his energies to avoiding any commitment whatsoever.

Shrewdly, Keynes recognized that in Washington the first person to reach the president usually got what he or she wanted. "It is vitally important that the President should give the right kind of instructions," he told Lord Halifax. "If we draft the phrases we can give them the turn we prefer." Consequently, the first week in July, through Harry Hopkins, Keynes arranged for a personal meeting with FDR.[58]

According to Keynes, Roosevelt declared that he felt under no pressure from Congress for early publication of a lend-lease agreement with Britain but, nevertheless, it would be helpful to have a preliminary agreement by January 1942. Any document agreed to, he asserted, ought to be vague. Keynes, together with Lord Halifax, explained Churchill's position. They emphasized the importance of not creating a money debt and "suggested phrases that indicate that considerations should not be such as to interfere with the economic and commercial relations between the countries or between either of them and other countries."[59] Without realizing that the overriding goal of his British visitors was to preserve their country's absolute freedom of action, Roosevelt concurred.

Immediately after his interview with Roosevelt, Keynes called on Dean Acheson. The president, he declared, had given them the green light to frame a preliminary agreement, and he repeated FDR's instructions. Understandably, Acheson, Hull, and their colleagues in the State Department were furious at Keynes's arrogance. Already chaffed raw by Roosevelt's penchant for bypassing State and relying on Hopkins, Acheson and company were particularly incensed that the representative of a foreign nation felt free to execute an end run. But their anger was quickly allayed by the realization that the British had outwitted themselves. Churchill had ordered Keynes to insert phrases in the master agreement stipulating that consideration should not in any way interfere with economic and commercial relations between countries. The prime minister meant that the agreement should include nothing that would distort trade, as the war debts–reparations payments had, or interfere with the operation of the sterling area. Acheson and his cohorts believed, however, that the proposal to include in the master agreement a pledge by both countries not to impede commerce between them, and between them and other nations, could be turned into an Anglo-American ban on trade discrimination and a commitment to reduce barriers. Quite simply, the State Department intended to use the Lend-Lease Master Agreement to commit Great Britain to participate in a postwar system of multilateral trade, and it was not about to be undone by either Churchill's stonewalling or Keynes's bureaucratic arcing and forking.

Throughout July Acheson and his subordinates in the Division of Trade Agreements and other related areas worked independently on a draft, which the assistant secretary presented to Roosevelt the last week of July 1941. The eight-point document was short and direct. The United States promised to continue to supply defense-related articles to the United Kingdom as needed, and the United Kingdom would reciprocate. Britain was prohibited from transferring to a third party any article furnished under lend-lease. It also was obligated to return all lend-lease items not "destroyed, lost or consumed" minus reverse lend-lease provided to the United States by Britain after March 1941. The key clause in the agreement as far as the multilateralists were concerned and, although they did not realize it at the time, as far as the British were concerned, was Article VII: "The terms and conditions upon which the United Kingdom receives defense aid . . . and the benefits to be received by the United States of America in return therefore . . . shall be such as to not burden commerce between them and the betterment of world-wide economic relations: they shall provide against discrimination in either the United States of America or the United Kingdom against the importation of any product originating in the other country; and they shall provide for the formulation of measures for the achievement of these ends."[60]

At this point Franklin Roosevelt's commitment to or even grasp of multilateralism was uncertain. Characteristically he had avoided making his position clear, thus keeping his options open. Yet he approved Acheson's draft; more than likely the State Department, using the British suggestion for a clause prohibiting compensation arrangements that would in any way burden commerce between the two countries, had convinced the president that Article VII would be acceptable to all parties. Nonetheless, when it subsequently became apparent that the United Kingdom had grave objections to multilateralism, FDR stuck by the State Department and Article VII. Hull, Wallace, and other multilateralists had had a number of conversations with him concerning international trade, and there was no doubt he was committed to lowering trade barriers. Thus, although he was not yet aware of either the immense political and diplomatic possibilities of multilateralism or its specific strategic and economic implications, Roosevelt was favorably disposed toward the idea. Keynes later would make much of the fact that the president had approved the State Department's draft over the phone, which, he argued, indicated a lack of understanding and commitment.[61] But for a man like FDR, for whom conversation was the primary mode of communication, phone approval was common and certainly significant.

Acheson presented the document to Keynes on July 28 and told him that the president had approved the draft as a basis for discussion. On reading the document, Keynes was at first apprehensive and then irate. The prohibition against discrimination in trade between the United States and the United Kingdom "raised serious questions." Would Article VII be applied to imperial preference and to exchange and other trade controls in the postwar period? Acheson said it would, but there were no binding obligations.[62] Keynes was not mollified. He "burst into a speech such as only he could make," Acheson recalled.[63] Economically, Article VII was archaic, an "ironclad formula from the nineteenth century." It attempted "the impossible and hopeless task" of returning to a gold standard under which international trade was controlled by rigid monetary devices.[64] The only hope for the future was to maintain national economies in balance without great surpluses of either exports or imports, and this could be achieved only through the very exchange controls that Article VII promised to ban.[65]

What did the British expect? Acheson retorted. The compensation that Keynes had suggested—that in response to the extension of lend-lease, Britain should return what was "practicable" for it to return, and that London would be glad to talk about other matters—was wholly impossible. He wanted something for nothing. The United States had disposed of the war debts issue; it was reasonable to expect Britain to refrain from discriminating against American products in the postwar period and to work toward the elimination of barriers to international trade generally. "Then, as coldly as I could," Acheson recalled, "I added that the British should realize that an effort of the magnitude of the Lend-Lease program on our part imposed upon them at least an obligation to work in good faith for the establishment of a multilateral trading system sometime in the future."[66] Keynes ended the stormy interview by declaring that he would take the proposal back to London and discuss it with the War Cabinet.[67]

The July 29 draft and the ensuing clash between Keynes and Acheson actually marked the culmination of a month-long breach between the British economist and the multilateralists in the State Department in which the two sides had grown progressively farther apart. In discussions with Harry Hawkins, Dean Acheson, and others, Keynes had taken an extreme procontrol, proimperial preference position.

Hawkins and the other multilateralists believed that Keynes's advocacy of bilateralism was a natural outgrowth of the views he had propounded in *Collected Works* (1925) and the *General Theory*. They assumed that Keynesian theory translated into the international sphere spelled economic nationalism. Such was not the case. In view of his later efforts to cooperate with multilateralists in Britain and the United States, the extreme position that Keynes espoused in June–July 1941 probably constituted an attempt to bluff the United States into allowing

Britain some freedom of action in the immediate postwar period. It also was in part an effort to convince chauvinist elements in Britain that the Treasury had done its best to safeguard British and imperial interests. He confided to Acheson, as they prepared to part company on the twenty-eighth, that the British government was deeply divided over foreign economic issues; there were in Britain essentially three points of view on international trade: the free traders, the imperialists, and a middle group, to which he belonged, that "believed in the use of control mechanisms."[68]

2. To Pay the Piper: Multilateralism and the British Dilemma, 1942

EVEN WHILE confronting the Battle of Britain and the threat of invasion by Nazi Germany, the Churchill government was distracted by fear of having to compete with the United States for the markets of the world without benefit of the sterling area and protective financial controls, and by fear of having to defeat the Axis and reconstruct Europe without adequate support from the United States. The War Cabinet and the British foreign policy establishment quickly divided between those who supported multilateralism on strategic and economic grounds and those who insisted that Britain could have its financial empire and its American ally as well. Fortunately for Churchill and his ability to rule, the issue split the Conservative and Labour parties rather than pitting the two principal components of the national government against each other.

Among Conservatives, those who opposed multilateralism came to be known during the war as empire isolationists. Some were simple reactionaries while others were more enlightened, but all agreed that the continuation of British power depended on the preservation of the sterling area and that the cornerstones of the financial empire were empire preference and exchange controls. Opposing them was a group of reform Tories who advocated a mixed economy at home and a modified multilateralism abroad. Motivated by a sense of social justice and an instinct for political preservation, they regarded empire isolationism as both outmoded and politically suicidal. Most officials in the Conservative-dominated Foreign Office supported multilateralism because they believed that American participation in a postwar collective security system, and hence Britain's physical security, depended on its realization. A small but influential clique of Conservatives equated multilateralism with free enterprise and thus advocated it as a barrier to socialism.

Labour was as divided as the Conservatives over the stratagem. The left-wing of the party opposed multilateralism for the same reason some right-wing Conservatives favored it—they equated it with laissez-faire and free enterprise. Moderates and Conservatives were ambiguous. Trade union leaders and the party's pragmatic politicians coveted American aid but were afraid that elimination of preferences and relaxation of controls would make possible the transfer of unemployment and depression from America to Britain. They were willing to tolerate multilateralism only until and unless the United States embraced domestic policies designed to guarantee full employment.

Thus splintered, the Churchill government proved unable, indeed unwilling, to devise a coherent foreign economic policy of its own during the early stages of the war. Despite pressure from Washington, No. 10 Downing Street and Whitehall succeeded in dodging a binding commitment regarding multilateralism in 1942. Their victory would be temporary and ephemeral, however.

As Winston Churchill had pointed out so emphatically to John Maynard Keynes in his instructions, Great Britain was ruled by a multiparty, national government during World War II, a most unusual situation in that country's political history. A virtue of the parliamentary system was that it featured parties that took fairly clear-cut stances on the major issues of the day and offered the voters a choice. The monumental crisis spawned by World War II placed a premium on unity and efficiency, however. Churchill's selection as prime minister in May 1940, following the development of widespread public discontent with the Chamberlain government after the German invasion of Norway, occurred in large part because he was perceived to be the one person who could unify the nation and lead it to victory. To do this Churchill believed he had to construct a truly national government, a coalition of the three major parties. The cabinet he built in 1940 and rebuilt in 1942 was, according to Maxwell Schoenfeld, a monument to his skill as a political leader and administrator.[1] That may have been so, but, as Churchill recognized, establishing and maintaining a multiparty government are two different things. His ability to hold together the seventy-odd socialists, parliamentary Labour leaders, high Tories, reform Conservatives, and Liberals that came and went in his government between 1940 and 1945 depended on his being able to provide the government with an organizing and defining principle. "What holds us together is the conduct of the war, the prosecution of the war," he declared to his colleagues. "No Socialist, or Liberal, or Labour man has been in any way asked to give up his convictions. That would be indecent and improper. We are held together by something outside, which rivets all our attention. The principle we work on is: 'Everything for the war, whether controversial or not, and nothing controversial that is not *bonafide* needed for the war.' "[2] The prime minister repeatedly expressed hope that his government could postpone making decisions and taking positions on postwar social and economic matters. Unfortunately, in areas such as commercial policy and international finance, where foreign affairs and matters of domestic, social, and economic concern intervened, that proved impossible. Churchill quickly recognized that this was so and moved to steer events and policy to conform to his philosophy and the interests of his party.

Reacting to Dean Acheson's specific efforts to secure Britain's approval of a Lend-Lease Master Agreement, the Churchill government began in late 1941 to splinter along three axes, each one delineated by a different approach to commercial and financial policies. These were the three lines Keynes mentioned in his parting shot to Acheson.

The first group, the empire isolationists, advocated exactly the course of action that Keynes had propounded in Washington in June and July. That is, they believed that Britain's survival—and they used no less a word than that—depended on the preservation and expansion of the sterling area and the extension of imperial preference through the conclusion of additional bilateral agreements. The chief spokesmen for this point of view within the Churchill government were Leopold Amery, secretary of state for India; Robert S. Hudson, minister of agriculture; and Max Aitken, Lord Beaverbrook, who was consecutively minister of aircraft production, minister of production, and Lord Privy Seal. Probably the most conspicuous but, ironically, the least influential member of this group was Beaverbrook. He was the only one of the three who was even a member of the War Cabinet, that inner group of five or six ministers established in November 1940 and reconstructed in February 1942 that Churchill relied so heavily upon, and he was a frequent, personal adviser to the prime minister. Yet his extremism, his abrasiveness, and his intermittent irrationality kept him from being as effective an advocate for empire isolationism as he otherwise might have been.

William Maxwell Aitken was a Canadian millionaire who emigrated to Britain in 1910, having assembled a press empire that included the *Daily Express*, the *Sunday Express*, and the *Evening Standard*. He dabbled in politics as a Conservative unionist M.P. from Austin-under-Lyne. For his journalistic contributions, that is, his political clout, he was knighted in 1911 and, after a stint as minister of information during World War I, was created Baron Beaverbrook in 1917.[3]

Beaverbrook was a sharp, intense, unpredictable man. He was something of a firebrand, tending to overstatement and even irresponsibility in his editorials and public utterances. Though a lifelong Conservative, Beaverbrook felt free to support a specific political figure and then criticize his policies. This was not disloyalty but "independence." His ideal, as A. J. P. Taylor has said, was for there always to be a Conservative government in power with Beaverbrook tending to every detail of policy. Conspiracy was second nature to him. While a member of the War Cabinet in 1942, he plotted briefly to supplant Churchill, supposedly his best friend, as prime minister. In conversation Beaverbrook was constantly exaggerating and embellishing. An inveterate name-dropper, he appears to have suffered from an intense inferiority complex stemming from either his provincial origins, his self-doubt, his inability to build a true political constituency, or all three. The truth is that while many people found "the Beaver," as Hugh Dalton and others referred to him, colorful and entertaining, no one, not even Churchill, trusted him.[4]

According to his principal biographer, Beaverbrook had one conviction that he put above party—a desire to promote the economic unity of the British Empire. He was, somewhat paradoxically, a disciple of Cobden and Bright and even thought that a closed imperial system could be reconciled with liberal tradition by calling it "Empire Free Trade," the name he gave to an official movement he started in 1929. The idea of Empire Free Trade assumed that Great Britain was industrially powerful enough to supply the entire empire with finished goods and that the Dominions would be content to be solely producers of foodstuffs and raw materials. Britain should use the leverage of its huge market, especially for food, to obtain duty-free entry for British-manufactured products into the other nations of the imperial association. An empire free of internal trade barriers would, through quotas, tariffs, and other external shields, shut out the rest of the trading world. "At bottom this was pure sentiment," writes A. J. P. Taylor—"a desire to be British as well as Canadian and a desire, also characteristic of a Canadian, that the British Empire should maintain its independence of the United States."[5]

Beaverbrook's friendship with Winston Churchill is well known. When he assumed control of the government on May 10, Churchill turned first to Beaverbrook for advice. On May 14 the prime minister named his confidant minister of aircraft production, and three months later the Canadian became a member of the War Cabinet. After a brief and stormy stint in that post and an equally tumultuous tenure as head of all war production, he resigned in February 1942. Eventually Churchill was able to appoint him Lord Privy Seal and, though alienated from the cabinet after 1942, he retained Churchill's ear.[6] "He's [Churchill] like a man who's married a whore," observed Ernest Bevin of the relationship; "he knows she's a whore, but he loves her just the same."[7] This may or may not have been true. Churchill was an inspirational and charismatic wartime leader, but he could not long have retained his post without being a calculating politician. The prime minister knew who and what Beaverbrook was and used him mercilessly.

Robert Spear Hudson was a man with less flamboyance but more power than Beaverbrook. His constituency was an ancient and powerful one in Britain and in the Conservative party—agriculture. Following his graduation from Oxford, Hudson entered the diplomatic service and served with distinction from 1911 to 1923. Elected Conservative M.P. from Whitehaven, he served in a variety of cabinet posts in the Conservative governments of the 1930s. From 1940 to 1945 he was minister of agriculture and fisheries.[8]

Great Britain was during the nineteenth and twentieth centuries the world's largest importer of agricultural products, especially wheat. As one of the world's great exporters of farm produce, particularly cereals, the United States became a major agricultural trading partner of the United Kingdom after repeal of the Corn Laws in 1846. During the interwar years, however, the idea, encouraged by British farmers, took hold that for strategic reasons Britain should try to decrease its dependence on foreign food by encouraging home production. Under the Imperial Preference System, Britain was allowed to pay large subsidies to its farmers. This, together with the fact that the Ottawa Agreements of 1932 shifted British agricultural imports to members of the sterling area, sharply reduced purchases of American farm surpluses.[9]

During Anglo-American wheat talks held in 1941 and 1942, the Roosevelt administration attempted to use the leverage of lend-lease to force Britain to sign a long-term commodity agreement in which London made a commitment to take a fixed amount of American wheat each year at a fixed price.[10] Given the position U.S. negotiators took during these conversations, Hudson regarded Washington's advocacy of multilateralism as the height of hypocrisy. Throughout the war the minister of agriculture maintained that, because his constituents were highly vulnerable to competition from cheaply produced milk, cheese, butter, wheat, beef, and other foreign foodstuffs, laissez-faire and free trade would bankrupt them. Hudson advocated massive subsidies for British agriculture and long-term commodity agreements but only with those nations with whom Britain had the upper hand, either economically or politically.

But the true spokesman for the empire isolationists and their most influential advocate was Leo Amery, secretary of state for India. Amery came to public life without important family or political connections and with only modest means, but he had an imposing intellect and wide experience as a journalist. In South Africa, where he served as a correspondent during the Boer War, Amery came under the powerful influence of Alfred Milner, the British governor, and Cecil Rhodes. Milner, described by one scholar as the leading theoretician of British imperialism, had designed a mechanism for the efficient development of the resources of the British Empire both to advance national goals and to improve conditions of life. Rhodes added to Milner's views his romantic vision of the civilizing mission of the English-speaking peoples and the practical contribution capitalism could make to this mission. Amery returned from South Africa determined to devote his life to welding the self-governing colonies and colonial dependents that made up the loose-knit Victorian empire into a more perfect union, united for defense, for foreign affairs, for trade, for investment, and for migration. This concept of empire was for him a coherent system of thought to which every issue—political, social, or economic—could be related.[11]

Gradually, Amery's views won him support in the Conservative party, and in 1911 Joseph Chamberlain found him a safe constituency in Birmingham, a seat he would retain for thirty-four years. During the 1920s in the House of Commons and as First Lord of the Admiralty, he convinced Stanley Baldwin that tariff reform and imperial preference offered the best and perhaps the only conservative solution to Britain's economic problems. In the domestic sphere Amery advocated the kind of private collectivism that Clair Wilcox seemed to be warning America against. Large firms already dominated British industry, and if Britain were to compete, he insisted, there would have to be still more bigness. The government should encourage the corporate world to organize, consolidate, and nationalize.[12] As secretary of state for dominions and colonies from 1924 to 1929, he espoused a far-reaching scheme of imperial development with Britain the source of labor and capital, and with the Dominions and Britain as mutually interdependent markets. In some ways the Ottawa Agreements and the creation of the sterling area were the culmination of a dream for Amery, but in his opinion they did not go far enough.

During the late 1930s Amery became more and more immersed in foreign affairs. An outspoken critic of Adolf Hitler and appeasement, he is generally credited with bringing down the Chamberlain government in 1940. Despite this and despite his support of Churchill for prime minister, Amery was rewarded with the relatively insignificant post of secretary of state for India. It was from this position that he led the fight against multilateralism. Physically unimposing at five feet four inches, Amery was vigorous, forceful, brilliant, and at times pugnacious.[13] Harold Macmillan, no mean evaluator of his fellow man, has left a lasting portrait:

> Hard working, well informed, a ripe scholar, imaginative and passionately sincere, he had a far better grasp of world affairs than all the Hoares and Simons put together. He knew the empire intimately and was on terms of close friendship with the leading imperial statesmen . . . he had a grasp of the fundamentals of great problems which few of his colleagues could boast. He was small in stature but could be persistent, like a well-trained terrier. He was at this time [1940] well-liked in all parts of the House; his advanced views on social welfare and progressive ideas had especially attracted many Labour members. In his own party both the Right and Left wings admired him.[14]

Amery gained a degree of notoriety by being the last member of the House of Commons to punch and knock down a colleague. In Amery's view the knave had impugned his honor—an ominous sign for the multilateralists.

In memos, in cabinet white papers, in speeches, and in private conversation, Amery labored to refute the arguments of the multilateralists and to warn his fellow Britons that, if they heeded the siren's song being sung by the Americans, disaster would follow. The multilateralists, Amery pointed out, based their case on the assumption that low trade barriers, nondiscrimination, and the refusal by national governments to manipulate the terms of trade to benefit their nations would automatically increase aggregate world demand, stimulate production, and raise living standards. History simply did not bear out this contention. The economic expansion of any particular nation depended on its natural resources, on the skill and energy of its people, and, not least, on the policy of its government. This last must be so because nations vary in resources, skilled labor, and technology. What was economically beneficial for one nation was not necessarily so for another.[15] "The unregulated and unbalanced flow of international trade on *laissez-faire* principles may, like the unregulated flow of water, prove disastrous to all concerned," Amery wrote in 1943. "Deluge and draught, boom and slump, over-production side by side with under-consumption, are in each case natural concomitants of leaving water or trade and investment to find their own level."[16]

Intellectually, Amery was a historian, and it was on history that he depended primarily to make his case against the multilateralists. Britain had not risen to the top rank of world power through free trade. London wrested control of merchant shipping from the Dutch through the Navigation Acts. Acting on the knowledge that an industry with a large and stable home market had a competitive advantage in the export trade, various British governments had carefully cultivated the woolen and cotton industries through import quotas for raw wool and finished cotton products, and massive export subsidies for both. Britain's great economic rival in the twentieth century became so not through a policy of free trade. Importation of capital and capital goods coupled with high tariffs to protect "infant industries" moved America from fourth to first among the manufacturing nations of the world between 1865 and 1914. Alexander Hamilton, not Thomas Jefferson, was the architect of the American economy, Amery asserted. Whatever the defects of its political system and social policies, the Soviet Union, a land with immense but undeveloped national resources and a massive but untrained population, had achieved an economic miracle—through comprehensive planning and state trading. Free trade is beneficial, Amery argued, only to a particular nation in a particular situation. Those nations and those situations were rare in the history of Western civilization.[17]

The multilateralist erred, the secretary of state for India insisted, in blaming the depression on tariffs, quotas, preferences, and other trade barriers. The primary cause of the global economic crisis was American financial and economic irresponsibility in the 1920s and the determination of the major trading nations to cling to a gold standard that sacrificed domestic wage and price stability on the altar of international currency stabilization. The tariffs and quotas erected in the 1930s, halfhearted and unsystematic though they were, had contributed significantly to recovery. It was no accident that Britain, having abandoned the gold standard and entered into the Ottawa Agreements, recovered faster than any other Western power and in the process pulled much of the empire up with it.[18]

In Amery's opinion, the United States was now advocating multilateralism because its economy closely resembled that of Great Britain during the last half of the nineteenth century. Washington's goal was "self-sufficient expansionism." The United States was an interdependent economic entity with a huge and prosperous home market and surplus capital to invest. Its manufacturers were certain that they could dominate any market in the world given an equal chance. "The new blend of Puritan quasi-religious Free Trade fervor with an aggressive Imperialism presents us with a problem of no little difficulty," Amery wrote. "Nothing could be more disastrous for this country than the literal fulfillment of Article 7," a provision that stemmed from an impulse that was at once "utopian and reactionary."[19] In the postwar period Britain would be extremely vulnerable. Most of the other great trading nations of the world would be in the same boat and would have to pursue an economic policy of planning and control for many years. Government policy and international trade, by definition, involved selection and discrimination. Moreover, the developing nations of the world, whose numbers would increase because of the impetus given to anticolonialism by World War II, would seek to emulate the present Russian or past American models. Multilateralism would be disastrous for both war-damaged and underdeveloped economies.[20]

Multilateralism, Amery claimed, called for a kind of internationalism for which the world was not ready. Given the imperatives of modern war, governments would not relinquish their sovereignty in areas that affected the nation's ability to defend itself, areas such as the acquisition and preservation of oil, iron ore, chromium, copper, and other strategic materials. Nor would military planners be anxious to see their nation become economically and financially vulnerable to the vagaries of an unregulated international economy. It was inconceivable that national politicians would be willing to entrust the prosperity of their people and their own careers to the whims of a multilateral economy and the decisions of a group of international bureaucrats.[21]

Amery, Hudson, Beaverbrook, and the empire isolationists spoke, of course, for a number of important special interest groups in Britain. Hudson's position and his connection with British agriculture are obvious. Scottish politicians representing, as they did, an agricultural area, vehemently opposed multilateralism. "It will be impossible to deal with the [agricultural] situation in this country," wrote an official in the Scottish Office to Minister of State Richard Law, "unless imports are quantitatively controlled either by regulation or state purchase. The use of one of these is essential for economic agricultural stabilization in Great Britain."[22] A number of industries in Great Britain, many of which had failed to modernize equipment and management techniques in the interwar period, opposed multilateralism and favored protection. Textile leaders were particularly adamant about the maintenance of economic controls and trade barriers. They may have been, as Keynes sneered, "old joiners who want to live out the rest of their lives in peace," but they still wielded some political clout.[23] Defeatist with regard to the future, they did not want to be bothered with either new ideas or machinery, and they dug in during World War II for a last-ditch fight.

Empire isolationism was a curious blend of reality and illusion. Amery and company's analysis of multilateralist arguments was quite cogent. Nations did differ dramatically in the areas of natural resources, skilled labor, and living standards. Members of the international community develop at different rates, and different stages call for different policies. They were also realistic in perceiving that in the absence of a world government political and strategic imperatives would make true multilateralism, in which an international marketplace was policed by supranational agencies, unworkable.[24] The empire isolationists were, however, unrealistic in two vital areas—the degree to which Britain would become economically and strategically dependent on the United States and the willingness of the Dominions to participate in a commercial and financial apparatus dominated by the United Kingdom.

There were multilateralists in England, free traders who called for a return to the halcyon days of Queen Victoria when the Royal Navy ruled the waves and the pound sterling the world's countinghouses. The interest of the United Kingdom in a multilateral system that promised a continual expansion of international trade was obvious, they argued. Britain, a densely populated island, could not be self-sufficient. Its dependence on overseas supplies of foodstuffs and raw materials, its reliance on foreign markets for its finished goods, and its traditional role as financier, carrier, and insurer gave Britain a huge stake in expanding the volume of world commerce.[25] Japan had faced a similar situation in its modern history and had chosen to safeguard its future by conquering and securing an economic empire through military force—the Greater East Asian Co-Prosperity Sphere—

rather than through the peaceful expansion of trade. For most Britons the Japanese alternative was unthinkable. Given the impending breakup of the empire—Canada had already been drawn into the American sphere, Australia and New Zealand wanted to establish their own trading systems, and India was determined for political and emotional reasons to reduce its economic ties to the United Kingdom—the only alternative seemed to be multilateralism. A number of senior civil servants, Richard N. V. Hopkins in Treasury and Sir Percival Leishing in the Board of Trade, held these views as did several distinguished "temporaries," academic economists who had entered government service at the beginning of the war. Lionel Robbins and James Meade, who in turn headed the Economic Section of the War Cabinet Secretariat, a staff body created for the purpose of advising, informing, and coordinating the work of the War Cabinet, had written powerful defenses of liberal trade.[26] The Liberal party, though in eclipse, was still alive, and living, breathing disciples of William Gladstone still strolled the halls of power. Winston Churchill, it will be remembered, had been one of Britain's staunchest free traders, once having defended the gold standard as "reality" and all else as economic illusion.

But no one with any influence was advocating pure, unadulterated multilateralism in 1941. The truths that Amery had penned were too glaring to ignore. Britain's economy, not to mention the war-devastated economies of Western Europe and the developing systems of the African, Asian, and Latin nations, would be much too vulnerable for a competitive free-for-all with the United States. Rather, a variety of individuals representing different viewpoints and interest groups struggled to present alternatives to empire isolationism, alternatives that held out a chance of accommodation with American multilateralism.

Two groups within the Conservative party advocated a modified multilateralism, one for primarily socioeconomic reasons and the other strategic. The first centered on Harold Macmillan and the Next Five Years movement. Macmillan—Oxford graduate, publishing giant, Conservative M.P.—had argued in *The Middle Way* that prosperity and social security were always to be the highest, if not the exclusive aims of statesmen. Macmillan insisted that a stable and well-ordered internal economy and a prosperous and expanding international commerce were inseparable. Like the American multilateralists, he accepted the maxim that the roots of war were basically economic and social, that hunger, deprivation, and inequality of opportunity had bred autarky and international rivalry. In phrases Keynes and Roosevelt no doubt would have approved, Macmillan wrote: "The preservation of freedom is intimately related to social and economic progress. The cultural gains of the past can only be carried over into the future if the essential changes in the structure of society can be accomplished by peaceful means. When social evolution slows down, the tide of revolution rises."[27] He rejected classical economic theory and hailed the depression for shaking politicians and economists out of their thralldom to Cobden and Bright. Tariffs, compulsory reorganization of inefficient industries, and the exchange equalization fund were all steps in the right direction, Macmillan argued, but government intervention into economic affairs had been piecemeal and unco-ordinated.

What Macmillan called for was comprehensive planning and regulation of the national economy by the central government. He envisioned neither the emer-gence of a socialist state with means of production owned entirely by the govern-ment nor the maintenance of a totally free enterprise economy. The former could not exist without the destruction of individual liberty and political totalitarianism and the latter without exploitation, cyclical depression, and inequality of opportu-nity. The answer was a state-planned and regulated economy with certain ineffi-cient, noncompetitive industries owned and operated by the government, and others—stronger, healthier—controlled by private interests and run in accordance with free market, competitive principles. The yardstick should be always employ-ment, national income, and production.[28]

In foreign trade, international specialization and cooperation in the context of a multilateral payments system was the ideal, Macmillan believed. But like Amery he admitted that because politicians were responsive to special interests at the national level, because nations made war, and because various countries were at different stages of economic development, the possibility of such an interdepen-dent world economy becoming a reality was "still remote."[29] Macmillan's views on foreign trade were consistent with his ideas on domestic economics in that he rejected both free trade and state trading. What was needed was a central foreign trade authority able to make decisions in the national interest in the area of total volume of imports to be received, and to devise means by which they could be received without disturbing internal prices. Through the maintenance of empire preference and negotiation of trade agreements with other nations and blocs, Britain should move gradually toward reduction of tariffs, quotas, and other impediments to the free flow of international trade.[30]

The Middle Way and the Next Five Years movement paved the way for the formation of the Tory Reform Committee in the House of Commons early in World War II. Led by Quentin Hogg, David Eccles, and Macmillan, and with ties to both Anthony Eden and Winston Churchill, the committee became a major force in British politics by early 1944.[31] In foreign trade as in domestic affairs, the key was pragmatism, a mixed economy involving measures "primarily inter-nal" to protect British industry and labor from fluctuations of the world economy, and trade agreements leading to the gradual, selective reduction of trade barriers. Doctrinaire multilateralists in America viewed the Tory Reform Committee much as the abolitionists viewed Free-Soilers in the 1850s—dangerous and unprinci-pled compromisers who posed a greater danger to the true faith than its outright opponents.

Conservative politicians, namely Anthony Eden and Richard Law, comprised the political leadership of the Foreign Office throughout World War II, and from that vantage point gave strong support to the establishment of an Anglo-American multilateral system after the war. Like Macmillan and Hogg, they accepted the need for a modified welfare state and a mixed economy in postwar Britain; they too saw the need for expanded exports and balanced international accounts to achieve a prosperous and progressive society. But Law as minister of state and Eden as foreign secretary voiced a different but potentially decisive reason for acquiescing in American multilateralism. The alternative was the division of the capitalist world into a sterling bloc and a dollar bloc, with accompanying trade barriers and perhaps all-out trade warfare between the two rival systems. Economic nationalism would provoke a revival of political isolationism in the United States. As had been the case following World War I, a disillusioned America would withdraw from Europe, leaving Britain alone to restore a shattered continent and maintain the balance of power. Such a situation was unthinkable. At the time of Hitler and Mussolini's demise France and the Netherlands, Britain's traditional allies, were sure to be devastated. Hunger and unemployment would rage through Europe unchecked, opening the way for political extremism in the guise of either Russian communism or a revived German fascism. If democracy, capitalism, and Western civilization were to survive, and, perhaps more importantly, if Britain was to face the postwar era with a modicum of economic and strategic security, the United States would have to finance the economic reconstruction of Europe and participate in a collective security system capable of maintaining the balance of power. Washington would be willing to do neither, Law, Eden, and a number of their subordinates in the Foreign Office believed, unless and until Britain acquiesced in multilateralism.

There were in the Conservative party those who were repelled by both the empire isolationists and the half-breed Tory Reform Committee who, they alleged, had "sold out" to the planners and centralizers. Harcourt Johnstone, a right-wing Conservative, a Churchill intimate, and a senior official in the Department of Overseas Trade, was typical. The Board of Trade, charged as it was with accelerating Britain's life-giving flow of exports in the postwar world, generally favored multilateralism. Its bureaucracy shuddered at the prospect of an all-out trade war with America's already muscular industrialists, who had been further strengthened by the steroids of wartime contracts. Johnstone's motives in supporting multilateralism were ideological as well as economic. "The very foundations of Socialism and the Socialist Party are threatened by successful Anglo-American cooperation developed on a wide international front," Johnstone wrote Churchill. "For what does such cooperation mean but, broadly speaking, an attempt to make the Capitalist system work?" Echoing such American missionaries of free enterprise as Bernard Baruch and Thomas Lamont, Johnstone asserted that capitalism would be the hope of the world after the Axis had finally succumbed. "If, as I believe, Capitalism, purged of its elements of poison and decay and rebuilt upon strong and wholesome foundations, can beat collectivism hollow at supplying the material needs of mankind, then the enterprise should be undertaken without regard for prejudices and without delay."[32] The true enemies of multilateralism thus were bound to be not the empire isolationists, but the leaders of the "Socialist" Labour party who saw in multilateralism the eventual triumph of capitalism and their own eclipse at the British polls.

And there was indeed opposition within the British Labour party to the American plan for a better world through multilateralism. Left-wing socialists and miscellaneous radicals advocated in 1941–42 a thorough reordering of society in which the free market system would be replaced by a centralized, planned economy with severe restrictions on the ownership of private property. At the party's Forty-first Annual Convention in May 1942, the left's leading ideologue, Harold Laski, submitted a resolution entitled "For a Planned Economic Democracy," which declared that measures of government control needed for mobilizing the nation's resources to win the war "are no less necessary for securing their best use in peace and must, therefore, be maintained after the final victory." In introducing the resolution, Laski said: "This is not one of those dynastic wars of the 18th century, with Mr. Churchill playing the role of Marlborough and Hitler that of Louis the XIV. This is a revolutionary war of the 20th century. It is blasting the foundations of all society."[33] Emmanuel Shinwell, abrasive socialist leader and M.P., had declared a month earlier his total opposition to any compromise with capitalism after the war. Influenced as it was by the writings of Marx and Lenin, this group feared the effects of capitalism in the international no less than in the domestic sphere. Laski, G. D. H. Cole, E. H. Carr, and other intellectuals attacked liberalized trade policy as a recipe for social injustice, depression, and even war. Kingsley Martin, editor of the radical and semipacifist *New Statesman*, and Konni Zilliacus, chief commentator for the *Tribune*, argued that the competitive struggle for markets, raw materials, and investment outlets constituted one of the major causes of international conflict.[34] Moreover, they, like the economic multilateralists in the State Department, believed that nations could not follow socialist policies at home while adhering to free enterprise, competitive doctrines abroad. Unlike the American group, however, they decried multilateralism because it would reinforce capitalism and the free market system within Britain's domestic economy.

The center and right wings of the British Labour party were much more ambivalent about multilateralism. The chief spokesmen for the rank and file were Clement Attlee, Lord Privy Seal; Hugh Dalton, president of the Board of Trade; Herbert Morrison, home secretary; and Ernest Bevin, minister of labor and national service. It was these men, rather than Laski and Shinwell, who would be most directly concerned with matters of international finance and economics. And it was these men who controlled the party in 1941. The outbreak of World War II saw the Labour party cohesive and unified as never before. During the previous decade virtually every organized group within the party that had dissented from the official leadership had been eliminated or discredited. The Independent Labour party had reduced itself to isolation and impotence in 1931. The events of September 1939 had sealed the doom of the pacifists. Whatever communist or fellow-traveling influence there was within the party collapsed overnight with the publication of the Nazi-Soviet Non-aggression Pact.[35]

Attlee, the quiet, circumspect, but decisive leader of the parliamentary Labour party, and Dalton, a flamboyant economist and Labour politician who would become chancellor of the Exchequer in 1945, were influential in the cabinet's foreign economic decisions, but it was Ernest Bevin perhaps who was most typical and most outspoken. The son of an agricultural laborer, Bevin was orphaned when he was eight. His formal education ended two years later. Bevin began his career in organized labor as a minor official in the Dockworker's Union. His rise was meteoric; as head of the Transport and General Workers' Union (TGWU) which he founded in 1922, he controlled the Trades Union Congress which in turn decided the policies, generally, of the entire Labour party. In many ways his views paralleled those of Samuel Gompers and William Green. As a successful trade unionist, interested almost exclusively in raising the wages and improving the working conditions of his membership, Bevin early in his career developed a disdain for both professional politicians and socialist intellectuals. He battled Winston Churchill during the General Strike of 1926 and subsequently the communists and the *Daily Worker* when they tried to seize control of his union. Personally, the founder of the TGWU was something of a paradox. He was short and stocky, packing more than two hundred pounds on his five-foot, four-inch frame, pugnacious, and abrasive. He hated Beaverbrook and Laski with equal intensity.[36] He had, according to Hugh Dalton, "mountainous defects of egoism, garrulity and peasant-minded suspicion." His speeches were rough and too long; so were his memos. Nevertheless, Dalton considered him "by far the best of all my colleagues."[37] Attlee respected and deferred to Bevin. So did Churchill.[38]

Bevin, like Dalton, Attlee, and Morrison, claimed to be a socialist, but, also like his fellow leaders, he was flexible and pragmatic. Nationalization of basic industries and financial institutions was essential. Yet private enterprise would have its place in postwar Britain. Social justice could be achieved through centralized planning in a mixed economy. Thus, the stance taken by Bevin and by Labour's center and right wings was not much different than the position adopted by Macmillan and the Tory Reform Committee. The difference was that Bevin believed that planning must be done by the workers and their representatives and not by the capitalists and theirs.[39]

Bevin distrusted multilateralism in general and the United States in particular. During the depression he and his colleagues had hammered away at the workings of the free trade, gold standard system. Here was a mechanism, Bevin argued, tailored by financiers and bankers to maintain international equilibrium through domestic deflation. It was a given in the gold system that external stability could be achieved only at the cost of instability in the national economy. In the event of an American depression, a development that moderate as well as left-wing Labour leaders considered a certainty, prices in the United States would fall. This would in turn stimulate the flow of British imports from and retard British exports to America; Britain would experience a drain on its gold supplies until a similar deflation in its domestic price structure occurred. At the same time, American interest rates would rise and capital would be drawn across the Atlantic until British interest rates increased to the same level. Finally, the decline in employment and income would reduce the demand for British goods in America, thus ravishing the export industries of Great Britain. Bevin trusted neither the Republican nor the Democratic party in this regard. The New Deal had not proven to his satisfaction that Roosevelt was committed ideologically or politically to antidepression measures to the extent that would warrant Britain tying its economy to America's. How much less so would be a Thomas Dewey or a Wendell Willkie?

Yet Bevin, like most socialists, was an internationalist. Empire isolationism and its economic corollaries were an anathema to him. Trade barriers and the formation of economic blocs seemed to breed nationalism and militarism. A foreign economic policy dictated by political and military considerations—Germany's prewar economic policy under Dr. Schacht was a prime example—inevitably pitted the workers of one nation against those of another to the detriment of all.[40]

Bevin, of course, was wrestling with the dilemma that faced socialist politicians everywhere: how to reconcile internationalism with the perceived need for planning and regulation in the domestic sphere to achieve prosperity and social justice. In the absence of a world government and in the face of the political and economic diversity of the world's social systems, the two could not be reconciled. When push came to shove Ernest Bevin, like Attlee, Dalton, and Morrison, was a hard-headed representative of the working classes of England. The blue-collar living standard was the bottom line for these Labour politicians. Britain had to export to live, and it stood a better chance of acquiring a bigger slice of the international trade pie if there was a bigger pie. Britain could and should participate in a multilateral system—but on two conditions: first, the United States would have to adopt comprehensive measures guaranteeing full employment, thus reducing the chance of another depression; and second, America would have to lower its tariff barriers, which, even with the trade agreements program, stood at approximately the 1931 Hawley-Smoot level. Labour leaders, in other words, would not agree to participate in a multilateral trading system supervised by an international agency until all members of the community accepted centralized planning and control of their economies.[41]

But where did Churchill stand? At times he feigned disinterest in social and economic matters and frequently tried to put them out of his mind. But periodically he could not, and he was interested—vitally interested. Personal and political considerations aside, how could anyone dedicated to the perpetuation of British power not be? Churchill held, as historian David Reynolds recounts, a number of deep convictions of his own regarding international economics. His long-standing support for free trade was real. His commitment in this area had led him to join the Liberals in 1904; and even after he returned to the Conservative party in 1924, he retained his orthodox views on commercial policy. Moreover, it was Churchill as chancellor of the Exchequer who, over Keynes's protests, had returned England to the gold standard. He totally rejected Beaverbrook's urgings that he join the Empire Free Trade movement. "It will hand over South America to the Yanks, split the Empire forever, and shatter the Conservative Party to smitherines [*sic*]," he told Harold Nicolson.[42] Yet Churchill realized fully that multilateralism was fraught with both political and economic danger. The Amery group was still a powerful force in the Conservative party. Labour's attitude, still nebulous in 1941, would be crucial to the Conservatives' chances for retaining power after the defeat of the Axis. A too clear identification with multilateralism, which left-wing Labour figures equated with laissez-faire and free enterprise, could be used against the Conservatives in a future general election. Churchill was aware, moreover, that in the short run England would be vulnerable and unable to compete. Finally, there was some question as to America's sincerity. Was Washington planning to use multilateralism as a cloak for a program of economic nationalism? Despite these fears and reservations, however, Churchill allowed himself to be sucked into the multilateralist vortex.[43]

The prime minister's chief adviser on foreign economic matters was Frederick Alexander Lindemann, Lord Cherwell, son of an American mother and Alsatian father who had immigrated to Great Britain in the 1870s. A physicist and Oxford don, Lindemann worked during and after World War I for the Royal Air Force investigating and describing the aerodynamics of aircraft spin. At the same time, he acquired, much to the distress of his Oxford colleagues, a taste for politics.[44] His views were ultraconservative. "Lindemann, I quickly discovered, regarded all miners, if not all the working classes, as species of sub-humans," recalled Thomas Jones after meeting him in 1926.[45] According to John Colville, Jews and nonwhites fit into an only slightly higher category. Elected a member of the Other Club in 1927, Lindemann met Churchill and the two quickly developed an intimate relationship. Tall, trim, and balding, Lindemann was a teetotaler, a vegetarian, and a bachelor. Churchill, as his daughter Sarah recalled, deplored these habits but found the contentious professor not only entertaining but also a veritable encyclopedia of information. He was arrogant and vindictive, yet good company when in the mood, and never boastful of his own achievements.[46] From the mid-1920s until his death, "the Prof," as Churchill called him, was a regular guest at Chartwell. "He swore by Lindemann," Sarah Churchill recalled. "Anything that was a query, which Winston did not know, he would say 'What do you think about that Prof,' 'What is that about.' If Prof said it was all nonsense, Winston believed it was nonsense."[47] From 1940 to 1941 Cherwell served as Churchill's personal assistant and from 1942 to 1945 he held the title of paymaster general. Among other duties he oversaw the work of the War Cabinet Secretariat.[48]

Cherwell was obsessed with Anglo-American cooperation in the postwar period. He fully concurred with Harcourt Johnstone in believing that, if capitalism was to be saved from communism and Western Europe protected from Russian aggression, America and Britain would have to act almost as one in the economic and strategic spheres. Article VII he saw as a means of tying the knot. Anglo-American cooperation in the construction of a multilateral system could lead to a mutual understanding to defend Europe and Western civilization. In 1942 he would write to Churchill in connection with the forthcoming talks on the implementation of Article VII: "The conversations in our view concern the best way of building up Anglo-American economic cooperation within a capitalistic framework after the war. To bring in Russia now could not possibly be helpful and would raise the Communist Problem in its most acute form . . . it is surely essential first of all to hammer out an Anglo-American plan, and at a time agreed between us to put it jointly before Russia and the other nations."[49]

These, then, were the various perspectives from which Britons viewed international economics in 1941. Creating a viable response to the onslaught by American multilateralists and molding a political consensus in Britain around that response would be formidable tasks. But one Englishman thought he was equal to the job.

After his negotiations with Dean Acheson, John Maynard Keynes found his first opportunity to relax and reflect as he flew back to England aboard one of Pan American World Airways' giant clippers. Gradually, it began to dawn upon him that Britain, and perhaps Western civilization itself, stood at a crossroad. Neither capitalism nor democracy could stand another cycle of depression and world war. Rival ideologies—both political and economic—stood ready to bid for the allegiance of Latin America's peasants, the teeming masses of India, and the tattered and battered European survivors of Axis aggression and Allied liberation. Britain, home of the world's freest and most cultured people, would face bankruptcy at war's end. His beloved nation would hardly be able to defend itself and the empire, much less deal with the massive economic and social problems in Europe and elsewhere that would follow V-E Day. The only option available seemed to be Anglo-American cooperation. If Britain rejected multilateralism out of hand, the United States well might resurrect the Fortress America concept and settle for an economic closed door in Latin America, leaving Britain and Europe to face the future on their own. "If we adopt bilateral arrangements," he wrote Sir Hubert Henderson, "they will be adopted to our detriment by other countries such as Germany and the United States. The American continent is the natural area for United States bilateralism and Central and Southwestern Europe for German bilateralism."[50] And if America decided to pursue multilateralism without British participation—that is, create an aggressive "dollar area" and a United States–dominated customs union—and Britain retreated into empire isolationism, the prospect was no better. As the world's primary supplier of capital, capital goods, and even food, the United States could lure members of the Commonwealth away from the sterling area until it was reduced eventually to England, Jamaica, and the Seychelle Islands.[51] This was not a cheering prospect. "I do not believe," he told Henderson, "that we shall ever successfully persuade the Americans that discriminatory bilateral arrangements are fair and desirable, and I think we shall fail in our major aim of successful cooperation with the Americans if you try to do so. I think that cooperation with the Americans is worthwhile, even if it involves a considerable reduction in our standard of living as compared with what would be possible if we pursue a policy of which the Americans are bound to disapprove."[52]

The broader question of Anglo-American cooperation aside, Keynes had grave doubts about the economic and financial efficacy of bilateralism. The great desideratum in the postwar period as far as Britain was concerned would be "equilibrium," that is, the creation of a situation in which Britain's exports and earnings from overseas investments and insurance were sufficient to pay for "necessary" imports. Necessary imports meant imports sufficient to provide a middle-class living standard to all Britons. The bilateralists—Amery, Beaverbrook, Hudson—assumed that under a bilateral system a state of equilibrium would automatically exist. "You exaggerate the extent to which payments agreements are, as such, self-righting or productive of automatic equilibrium," he told a proponent of bilateralism. "In the absence of government trading, both ways, it is far from being the case that they are self-righting. For one thing the initiative to make them lies with the creditor rather than with the debtor country; yet the potential importers and creditor country have no particular motive to discriminate in favor of the goods of the debtor country."[53] British-Argentine trade offered a good example. The fact that British imports of Argentine grain created a surplus of sterling in favor of Argentina did nothing to make British cotton more attractive to private Argentine importers. As individual business people they had no economic motive to redress the imbalance of trade and payments. Keynes noted that the phenomenon of bilateralism frequently arose out of the struggle among states for economic and financial security, and he readily admitted that collective security and individual security were legitimate objects of international policy. He acknowledged, in addition, that unrestricted, multilateral trade tended to destroy security, particularly for small states engaged in very specialized trades. Keynes asserted, however, that, although bilateralism might advance the welfare and security of individual states, "it did not necessarily contribute to the sum total of world economic security." A bilateral arrangement might secure a guaranteed market for one country while completely denying access to another. "It is very much like a crowd of people in the water all trying to secure themselves from drowning by standing on the others; the stronger or the luckier ones will survive, but a good many may drown."[54]

Moreover, in Keynes's view the bilateralists were stagnationists. They assumed that the volume of world trade was fixed and that Britain could only increase its share by reducing that of the other trading nations. Keynes was an expansionist. "If there is sufficient expansion," he told Henderson, "we may obtain a sufficient market for our exports without the United States having to contract any part of hers. This is why expansionism is the most hopeful line of solution." Just as was the case with domestic economies, the key to equilibrium and prosperity at the international level was aggregate demand. Projecting the theories he had outlined in *General Theory* and *Collected Works* into the international sphere, he declared: "If effective demand throughout the world is adequate, the demand for exports will always be equal to the supply of them, and gluts will not occur." Every increase in effective demand reduces the severity of the problem, he argued. Increase in effective demand in the United States would reduce surpluses available for exports and intensify demand for imports. Unlike Bevin and many of the empire isolationists, Keynes in 1941–42 believed that there was a distinct possibility the United States would adopt aggressive measures to ensure full employment.

"Adversity may well drive us to barter agreements," he confided to his colleagues. "But to start off on so pessimistic a hypothesis will lose us that support from general outside opinion without which nothing can be done." If Britain should be forced on a bilateral course, it would most likely take the form of state-negotiated barter agreements "much more on Russian lines." He wrote: "There is the American bias and the Russian bias. I doubt if there is much between which is likely to be practical politics. And whether or not we end up with a Russian bias, is there not much to be said for having a try with the American bias first of all?"[55]

But John Maynard Keynes was perhaps first and foremost a British patriot, and he was no less willing to endanger the financial independence of the United Kingdom and members of the empire than Churchill or Bevin. Keynes and others within Whitehall who favored cooperation with the United States and the establishment of a system of multilateral trade placed several distinct conditions on British participation. First, the government could not support any system that seemed to be aimed indiscriminately at weakening Commonwealth ties. In addition, there would have to be safeguards to protect full employment and social welfare programs in the domestic sphere from fluctuations in an unregulated international economy. And, of course, Britain could not be part of a multilateral system as long as it suffered a negative balance of payments.

During the immediate postwar period, referred to as the transitional period because it would allegedly bridge the gap between wartime measures of control and restriction and the multilateral trading system envisioned by the expansionists, Britain would have to have available to it some means of making payments for imports while repairing war-damaged areas and rebuilding its export trade. Even beyond the transitional period, which Treasury officials estimated as five years minimum, there might be a balance-of-payments problem. Nor would multilateralism work unless and until creditor nations took steps to correct their positive balance of trade. At the very least America would have to agree to a drastic reduction in tariff rates and embark on an aggressive overseas lending program. In other words, the extent to which Britain participated in trade liberalization depended, in Keynes's view, on how nearly equilibrium in the world's balance of payments was achieved.[56]

Keynes believed that no one was better suited to tailor American dreams to Britain reality than himself. "For your private information," he wrote Ben Cohen, a Frankfurter protégé he had met during his 1934 trip,

> I myself am working along two lines: one of them a protective plan for arrangements after the war, which can remain dormant, but necessary against possible contingencies. And separately from this a Utopian Plan which would solve all our problems on international lines. I call it Utopian because it is the sort of thing

that never seems to happen. But it is entirely practical and requires nothing more for its success than a mental attitude on the part of the powers that be. I hope I shall be allowed to put forward something along these lines for American consideration. But it has not run the full course of criticism here and so must be kept confidential.[57]

Meanwhile, there was the matter of Article VII. Keynes had promised to consult with his superiors in London and get back to Acheson in due course. The multilateralists in the State Department had no intention of allowing the British to put them off, however, and when Churchill and Roosevelt met at Argentia Bay, Newfoundland, the first week in August 1941, the Americans pressed the attack.

The president and the prime minister had been awaiting an opportunity to meet in the flesh and cement the relationship, diplomatic and personal, that had begun with the former naval person's first letter in May 1940. Roosevelt, with a sense of the dramatic that rivaled even Churchill's, had insisted on the utmost secrecy for their first meeting. Abandoning the presidential yacht *Potomac* in Long Island Sound where he was reputedly on a fishing trip, Roosevelt and his entourage boarded the heavy cruiser *Augusta* and set sail for Canada. Early on August 9 the president, Undersecretary of State Sumner Welles, and the American military chiefs rendezvoused with Churchill. He and his advisers had crossed the Atlantic aboard the massive *Prince of Wales*, still scarred from its encounter with the *Bismarck*. Harry Hopkins, on special assignment in Britain, accompanied Churchill. Roosevelt's only other nonmilitary adviser was Welles, while the prime minister's diplomatic second was Sir Alexander Cadogan, permanent undersecretary for foreign affairs. Despite the cordiality, even sentimentality, of the encounter, the Argentia Conference involved hard-nosed bargaining between the two heads of state. Interspersed between broiled chicken, cigars, brandy, and Churchill's enthralling accounts of battles won and lost, the two leaders discussed Hitler, the situation in the Pacific, American public opinion, and lend-lease.[58]

On the morning of August 9, Welles and Cadogan met and took up where Acheson and Keynes had left off. Unlike Keynes, however, Cadogan forthrightly articulated the views of British multilateralists. The permanent undersecretary was poised, efficient, bright, and thoroughly conservative in domestic social and economic matters.[59] On reading Harold Laski's *Reflections on the Revolution of Our Time*, he penned a scathing indictment of British socialists: "I'd like to put them in power and give them responsibility—not for more than ten minutes, but that might be sufficient to prove, even to their stunted intelligence, their futility, prejudice, and chicanery."[60] He wrote on another occasion of Aneurin Bevan, left-wing Labour M.P.: "He and his kidney are mere barnacles on the bottom of the ship of state. In any decent country, they'd be bumped off. To that extent am I 'Fascist'—and proud of it."[61] In foreign affairs Cadogan was both advocate and practitioner of realpolitik. For strategic, ideological, economic, and political reasons, cooperation with the Americans in constructing a multilateral system seemed to him not only unavoidable but desirable. In other words, he and Cherwell saw eye to eye.

Welles opened the conversation by insisting on "the need, when the time came.

for reconstruction to be undertaken with the freest possible economic interchange without discrimination, without exchange controls, without economic preference utilized for political purposes, and without all of the manifold economic barriers which had in my judgment been so clearly responsible for the present world collapse."[62] Cadogan, if he is to be believed, needed no persuading. Off the record, he confided to Welles, the Ottawa Agreements had been a disaster and he had "bitterly" opposed them. If Britain and America could not agree to press for the resumption of liberal trade practices and the abolition of discrimination, there was no hope for the future.[63] He found Article VII "exactly what was required." According to Welles's account, however, "he [Cadogan] did not yet know what the Prime Minister's considered judgment on this issue might be."[64]

It had not yet dawned on the British that what the American multilateralists were gunning for was nothing less than the inclusion of the generalized portion of Article VII in the joint communiqué scheduled to come out of the Argentia Conference. That became obvious the next morning when Cadogan handed Welles the first draft of the Atlantic Charter. Point Four read: "They will strive to bring about a fair and equitable distribution of essential produce not only within their territorial jurisdiction but between the nations of the world." This was not exactly what Welles, who was in continual contact with Cordell Hull and Harry Hawkins, had in mind. The British draft conjured up visions of supernational agencies working through cartels, international commodity agreements, and state trading agencies at the national level to ensure equality not of opportunity but of condition. There was, most unfortunately of all, no mention in the British proposal of that magic word "discrimination." The undersecretary informed his opposite member that his draft was totally unacceptable.

On August 11, Roosevelt, Churchill, Hopkins, Cadogan, and Welles all met in the admiral's quarters on the *Augusta* to resolve the issue. Welles presented a redraft of Cadogan's document. Churchill read aloud: "Fourth, they will endeavor to further the enjoyment by all peoples of access without discrimination and on equal terms, to the markets and raw materials of the world which are needed for their economic prosperity."[65] The American draft emphasized *access* not distribution and provided for *markets* as well as produce. Moreover, there was to be no *discrimination*. Did this apply to imperial preference? Churchill inquired. Indeed it did, said Welles. Roosevelt, whose informality and cordiality stood in stark contrast to Welles's notorious coldness and self-righteousness, pled with Churchill to consider the public relations angle. The Germans and the Japanese were making bales of propaganda hay by attacking British imperialism. Here was a chance to counter their anticolonial appeal. The nonwhite, underprivileged peoples of the Pacific basin, Asia, and the Middle East must be able to look forward to a postwar world in which they had a chance to grow and prosper, in which they were not confronted with giant colonial mechanisms that denied them any chance at upward economic and social mobility.

Welles's proposal went much farther than Churchill wanted to go. A British commitment to end "discrimination" would prevent the use of exchange and trade controls in the immediate postwar period. Equal access to markets and raw materials was a potential hammer blow that could shatter imperial preference. Roosevelt's goodwill notwithstanding, it appeared to many Britons that Americans were simply trying to horn in on empire and sterling area trade.[66]

Churchill found himself in a diplomatic and political box at Argentia Bay. Between those in Great Britain who advocated continuation of economic controls into the postwar period and those who wanted to cling to imperial preference there was little political room. The American proposal, it seemed to the British leader, would alienate both and possibly break up the coalition government. Moreover, in 1940 His Majesty's Government and the British trade associations had entered into arrangements whereby the nation's largest industries were to be protected against competition from any new industries or corporations in their fields of action for a sufficient time after the war to enable wartime losses to be recouped. The "arrangements" could be interpreted as official guarantees of closed monopolies without a definite time limit.[67] Yet Churchill had worked long and hard to draw the United States closer to Britain and to intervene in the struggle against the Axis. The Argentia Conference and the joint communiqué that would come out of it promised to be a major step in that direction. In the final analysis, however, the prime minister chose to jeopardize Anglo-American solidarity against the Axis over Point Four.

Personally, Churchill told the Americans, he was an economic liberal and had always opposed the Ottawa Agreements. But there were the Dominions to think about; yes, there were the Dominions. They would have to be consulted and that would take at least a week.[68] (This would be the first of numerous appearances during World War II by the Dominions as a stalking horse for those interests in Britain that were opposed to American multilateralism.) "It was inconceivable that the issuance of the joint declaration should be held up by a matter of this kind," interjected Harry Hopkins, who was almost more avid in promoting Anglo-American cooperation against the Axis than Churchill. Could not Welles and Cadogan get together and draft "new phraseology"? It was not a matter of phraseology, snorted the prickly Welles; it was a matter of "high principle." If Britain and the United States did not cooperate in restoring liberal trade policies in the postwar world, they might as well "throw in the sponge"; and if they did that, it meant that one of the principal causes of the present war would continue into the future.[69]

Suddenly Churchill suggested a way out of the impasse. The British could live with Point Four if it contained the phrase "with due regard to our present obligations." Apparently Hopkins went to work on Welles over lunch, for that afternoon the undersecretary informed Cadogan that "inasmuch as Point Four was broader and more satisfactory than the minimum" that FDR had instructed him to obtain, the United States would accept the British redraft. Point Four of the Atlantic Charter read: "Fourth, they will endeavor, with due respect for their existing obligations, to further the enjoyment by all States, great or small, victor or vanquished, of access, on equal terms, to the trade and to the raw materials of the world which are needed for their economic prosperity."[70]

Churchill had successfully fought off a binding commitment on multilateralism without alienating the Americans. Indeed, the joint statement of war aims seemed a prelude to full United States participation in the war against the Axis. But the multilateralists could afford to wait. Power is the ultimate arbiter of international relations and America was the repository of Britain's strength. Just as the British would never be satisfied until the United States became a full-fledged belligerent, neither would the Americans be content until Britain accepted a fully implemented Article VII. The State Department's overriding objective, Harry Hawkins wrote Dean Acheson shortly after the Argentia meeting, must be to compel Britain to implement Article VII. This meant, in his opinion, "the virtual abolition of Empire preferences and renunciation of bilateralism."[71]

During the dark days of August and September 1941, as Japanese diplomats came and went in Washington and the situation in the Pacific deteriorated alarmingly, the State Department had Ambassador Gilbert Winant press the British for a reply to the July 28 draft of the master agreement. Acheson pointed out that during an appearance before the House Appropriations Committee he had had to obfuscate—"lie"—when asked what had been done toward defining compensation under lend-lease. Anthony Eden promised that Lord Halifax, then in Britain for consultation, would return with the War Cabinet's response.[72]

The ambassador returned with an answer—but not one that was satisfactory to the multilateralists. The cabinet that Keynes, Churchill, and Halifax found on their return to London was deeply divided over and generally opposed to Article VII. The version approved by FDR and put forward by Acheson, it will be remembered, stipulated that as part of the compensation the United States was to receive for lend-lease, both nations would agree not to "discriminate" against the imports of the other. The empire isolationists, with a strong anchor in the Treasury in the person of Sir Hubert Henderson, insisted that acceptance of Article VII meant an end to empire preference. Clement Attlee, Hugh Dalton, Herbert Morrison, and other Labour leaders were still responsive to left-wing warnings that multilateralism abroad meant the triumph of free enterprise at home and to doubts that America would be willing to adopt measures of full employment. There was also the matter of controls. The chancellor of the Exchequer in 1941 was Sir Kingsley Wood, an orthodox Tory who had risen from humble origins. This son of a Wesleyan minister had been one of capitalism's greatest defenders before the war. Ironically, Wood implemented a policy that "liquidated the millionaire." Churchill made him head of an Exchequer that would levy a 57 to 90 percent income tax on Britons. Nonetheless, the chancellor wanted to save as much of capitalism as he could, and he believed that import quotas, subsidies, and exchange controls in the transitional period would be necessary if Britain were to reconvert quickly and successfully to civilian production and to resurrect its export trade.[73]

More specifically, Wood and his underlings in the Treasury were extremely concerned about the massive indebtedness Britain was incurring in the Dominions and sterling area countries. From September 1939 to September 1941 Britain had purchased billions of pounds worth of oil, cotton, iron ore, and finished products from India, Malaysia, Egypt, and its other raw material suppliers, and paid for these items in sterling placed in blocked accounts in London. "The present position is that our overseas obligations are increasing at the rate of 400 million pounds sterling to 500 million pounds sterling a year," Wood wrote Eden in 1942.[74] The sterling debts would be monumental by war's end. Britain would need time to scale them down and pay them off. Article VII seemed to deny Britain that time. Consequently, Wood, a paradigm of pragmatism, joined in ironic union with his Labour colleagues in 1941 to oppose an American initiative that would, he believed, turn Britain over to socialism at war's end.

The third week in October Halifax called on Acheson and presented a British redraft of Article VII that reserved complete freedom of action to all parties. The proposed agreement would bind the two nations "each working within the limits of their governing economic conditions . . . to securing as part of a general plan the progressive attainment of a balanced international economy, the avoidance of harmful discrimination and generally the economic objectives" of the Atlantic Charter. Acheson recorded his reaction in *Present at the Creation*: "A glance was enough to show that the insertion of some slippery words and phrases had robbed of all meaning our prohibition of discrimination against the importation of American goods into Britain."[75]

Actually, British multilateralists, who were as concerned about British living standards and security as Wood, Leo Amery, Robert S. Hudson, and the Labour leaders, were uneasy with the United States version of Article VII. It smacked of unilateralism—that is, requirements unilaterally imposed on Great Britain.[76] The multilateralists did not want to venture out upon the seas of free market competition unless the United States and other trading nations did also. "We do not want to get into the position in which control or discrimination is applied against our interests by Russia, Germany, and other countries while we are not at liberty to employ them when it safeguards our interests," Sir David Waley, a Treasury multilateralist, wrote Henderson. "If, therefore, we advocated a general non-discriminatory attitude, I think it should be on the basis that this be adopted universally and not by us alone." Keynes agreed. "The U.S. Administration has been quite clear that they want us to get rid of preferences," he wrote. But why should preferences be in a different category from tariffs and other restrictive devices? If Britain unilaterally gave the advantage to its competitors, it would be destroyed.[77]

Underlying the British draft was the general mistrust of the Roosevelt administration's ability and even its willingness to control the forces of economic nationalism. "One can take nothing whatever for settled in the U.S.A., for the sufficient reason that the Administration, not being in control of Congress, is not in a position to enter into commitments on anything," Keynes observed in 1941. "We shall have to bear this in mind in all the negotiations for Anglo-American economic cooperation. What our representatives say bind the British Government. What the State Department or the Treasury or the departments of Commerce or Agriculture may intimate in the course of our conversations with them can and does bind no one. Thus, every bargain can, and very likely will, be overthrown by Congress . . . we shall, therefore, have to be very careful in tying up our side of the bargain with theirs."[78] The British expressed doubt that FDR and his colleagues were willing to work for an across-the-board reduction of tariff rates. No such comprehensive cut had been made since the Underwood Tariff, and the Reciprocal Trade Agreements program dealt with the tariff on an item-by-item basis. It seemed to many British officials that the Roosevelt administration was asking the Churchill government to affront its special interests without any guarantee that it was willing to do the same.

What followed was a two-month charade. The State Department asked Winant to appeal directly to Churchill to accept Article VII without qualifying phrases—"each working within the limits of their governing economic conditions," for example. The prime minister, claiming to be grief-stricken over the loss of the HMS *Prince of Wales* and HMS *Repulse* off the coast of Malaya, and preoccupied with strategic matters, referred Winant to Wood.

Meanwhile, the Japanese attack on Pearl Harbor had drawn America at last into the war against both Germany and Japan. Churchill was exultant; he moved at once to fulfill his promise that a British declaration of war would follow within the hour if and when Japan attacked the United States. On December 8, after a dramatic address by the prime minister, both houses of Parliament voted for war with Japan. When, the following day, some of his advisers continued to advocate a velvet-gloves approach to the United States, Churchill stopped them: "Oh, that is the way we talked to her while we were wooing her; now that she is in the harem, we talk to her quite differently."[79] Churchill immediately asked Roosevelt if he could come over for military talks, and the president readily agreed. The prime minister set sail on his new battleship, the *Duke of York*, and then flew to Washington after disembarking at New York. FDR met with Churchill at National Airport. After a semiformal dinner for seventeen, Churchill was installed at the White House in the large bedroom near Hopkins's quarters. Suddenly the White House metamorphosed into an imperial command post. During the hectic days that followed, the two leaders and their staffs discussed in detail plans for turning the strategic tide in Europe and the Pacific. Interspersed among the whiskey, martinis, cigars, cigarettes, and anecdotes were discussions of lend-lease and Article VII.

The man who presided over British affairs during World War II has earned a reputation as an Anglo-American romantic of the first order. During his stint in the service in India Churchill began to read widely in history, particularly the works of Gibbon and Macaulay. He was fascinated by power, war, and empire, and tended to think of world affairs in terms of the broad-brush historian that he himself later became. "Mr. Churchill sees history—and life," Isaiah Berlin observed, "as a great Renaissance pageant . . . he sees vivid historical images—

something between Victorian illustrations in a child's book of history and the great procession painted by Bonozzo Gozzol in the Riccardi Palace."[80] Churchill seemed driven by an almost mystical belief in the solidarity of the Anglo-American peoples. A shared political tradition—democracy, free enterprise, individual liberty—formed the cornerstone of Western civilization. God, in his wisdom, had singled out Britain and America to rule the world. True, Americans could be provincial, introverted, rude, and most difficult to deal with, but they were basically innocent and well intentioned, "a great lusty youth who treads on all your sensibilities . . . but who moves about his affairs with a good-hearted freshness which may well be the envy of the other nations of the earth."[81] In one sense America was superior to Britain. Socialism, which Churchill detested only slightly less than communism, was well established in the latter, whereas it had made almost no headway in the former. Churchill stood in awe of the material achievements of American capitalism. After experiencing public transportation in New York, he wrote a relative: "And when one reflects that such benefits have been secured to the people—not by confiscation of the property of the rich, or by arbitrary taxation, but simply by business enterprise—out of which the promoters themselves have made colossal fortunes—one cannot fail to be impressed with the excellence of the entire system."[82]

Churchill's emphasis on Anglo-Saxon cooperation grew in part out of his family background and educational experience, and in part out of his experience as politician and diplomat. His American-born mother, whom he worshipped, had been a devout believer in Anglo-Saxonism and had founded the *Anglo-Saxon Review*. The special relationship was also for Churchill a matter of the common language shared by the two peoples. At Sandhurst and later during his process of self-education, he came to revere the English language, a love affair that culminated with the publication of his *History of the English Speaking Peoples* in the early 1930s. Also, by the late 1930s Churchill had become obsessed with the threat of Nazi world domination and the belief that only Anglo-American solidarity could stop it. As early as 1935, he had written:

> The first and surest of all methods for maintaining the peace of the world would be an understanding between Great Britain and the United States whereby they would together maintain very powerful air forces and navies decisively stronger than those of other countries put together; and secondly that they would use these forces, as well as the whole of their influence and money power in support of any state which was the victim of unprovoked aggression.[83]

The events of World War II only increased his belief in the efficacy of a Pax Anglo-America. At a luncheon in Washington in May 1943, Henry Wallace recalled that Churchill "made it clear that he expected England and the United States to run the world" and he expected staff organizations that had been set up for winning the war to continue when the peace came."[84] Not surprisingly, then, he was far more unequivocal than Neville Chamberlain in 1939–40 about bringing America into the war. Initially, he saw no threat to British interests or prestige in an Anglo-American alliance that would first rid the world of Hitler and Mussolini and then establish a lasting peace structure. Churchill even went so far as to propose common Anglo-American citizenship. According to Henry Butter-field Ryan, however, that proposition was not to be taken literally, but rather was designed to create an atmosphere in which specific military and diplomatic linkages could occur.[85]

Indeed, Winston Churchill was more than a simple romantic, and his paens to Anglo-American solidarity should not obscure the fact that he was a hard-headed patriot who knew where his and his country's interests lay. He was a pragmatic politician who would subsume ideology and party to the goal of gaining and holding office. And he was a resourceful diplomat who would join hands with the devil himself in order to preserve Britain's great-power status. Eventually Churchill would have to choose between his diplomatic and political goals—that is, between retaining office and preserving Britain's independence in world affairs—but that dilemma was not yet apparent in 1941. Until 1944 Churchill was confident that he could control American power, using it first to help defeat the Nazis and then to guarantee Britain's economic and military security in the postwar period. Despite his rhetoric, Anglo-American solidarity was a means to an end, not a goal in itself. That he also believed a strong Britain was in America's interest was incidental. Under his leadership the United Kingdom would once again call upon the New World to redress the balance of power in the Old.

Despite his anti-imperialism and his distrust of British diplomacy, Franklin Roosevelt had already begun to think of America and Britain as allies well before Pearl Harbor and Churchill's subsequent visit. The Western democracies were America's first line of defense against Hitler and Mussolini.[86] Despite strong isolationist opinion in the United States, FDR looked forward to increasingly close Anglo-American cooperation, but he was determined that it would be a cooperation on American terms.

Both Roosevelt and Halifax commented later that during his post–Pearl Harbor trip to America Churchill seemed totally disinterested in lend-lease, Article VII, trade barriers, and exchange controls. The president told Acheson that he brought up Article VII several times, but Churchill wanted to postpone economic and financial questions or delegate them to someone else.[87] Halifax recalled Churchill as being inattentive: "I don't suppose he will read any of the telegrams [from various multilateralists in Whitehall] and I don't think he will apply his mind to it . . . he is, of course, as you know, pretty bored with anything except the actual war."[88]

Churchill may have been more interested in battle strategy than the politics of economic aid, but he had his eye on the postwar balance of power and America's role in it. Cherwell saw to that. In conversation before and telegrams after the prime minister's departure from Washington, Cherwell advocated the multilateralist case, justifying it on strategic grounds. "To annoy her [the United States] and sacrifice her cooperation, merely in order to retain a free hand to extend these undesirable [bilateral] practices would surely be disastrous pusillanimity . . . it seems that the time for us has come to abandon our suspicions and decide to play in with the Americans."[89] Churchill agreed, but he told "the Prof" that he must avoid a political donnybrook at home. Churchill insisted, moreover, that there was no hurry. Hull and the State Department were the only bureaucratic constituency in Washington clamoring for Article VII. "Morgenthau assured me he is not troubling about it," he told Halifax. Churchill recalled that when he suggested postponing international economic questions until the close of the war, Roosevelt agreed: "I told the President Imperial Preference would raise great difficulties in England if raised as a separate issue now, but that if raised at the end of the war as part of a large economic settlement, in which the United States would become a low tariff country, it would probably be easy to handle." More importantly, Churchill believed, America's entry into the war had changed everything. The whole notion of compensation was formed before America had become an active belligerent. Now that the United States was in the war "lend-lease was practically superseded," he asserted.[90] Rather naively the prime minister assumed that the Roosevelt administration and Congress would agree to a complete merger of the British and American war machines. Each partner would contribute oil, cotton, food, tanks, and planes according to its ability to contribute, and each would take from this pool according to its needs.

In deference to Churchill and to the calamitous military situation, Roosevelt did not press the matter of compensation and Article VII during the prime minister's visit to Washington. According to the British leader, FDR agreed that postponement was "very sensible." He felt "as I do, that we had better address our minds to the struggle upon which the lives of our people depend." After his post–Pearl Harbor visit to Washington, Churchill advised Halifax: "I recommend you stall any demand from the State Department with the usual diplomatic arts."[91]

Halifax and his staff thought Churchill dangerously obtuse regarding foreign economic policy; delay had in it the seeds of disaster. It is not at all unusual for an ambassador, and an embassy, swayed by the immediacy of their contact with the host government, to act as an advocate for the policies of that government. Halifax and his staff were not immune to those forces; but the ambassador, in addition, reflected the prejudices of the Foreign Office and the strategic multilateralists. "Unless my judgment and that of all my principal advisors here is at fault," he wrote Eden on December 29, "there is not the smallest chance of the U.S.G. revising their main position on this contentious clause."[92] Eden agreed and notified Halifax that he would take up the cudgels with the cabinet.[93]

What Halifax and Eden needed to overwhelm opponents and doubters, including those among the economic multilateralists, was proof that Roosevelt was foursquare behind multilateralism. They communicated that to Dean Acheson, and on January 29 the assistant secretary called at the White House. There was some question as to where he stood, Acheson told the president. Could he tell the British that Article VII had the full support of the White House? It did and he could, FDR replied.[94]

In fact, despite what he had told Churchill, the president's patience was wearing thin. Britain must know that cooperation was even more in its interests that in America's. Hearings on fiscal 1942 appropriations would begin the first week in February. When Acheson inquired how he should respond when Congress asked why no agreement had been reached with the British, FDR told him to make it clear that Britain and Britain alone was responsible for the delay.[95] Roosevelt concluded the interview by telling Acheson to make another effort to gain British acceptance of the United States draft and if that failed to eliminate Article VII entirely, leaving the matter of compensation to future negotiation. "I strongly hope the British will accept (1)," he told Acheson, "because (2) leaves them in a much more difficult future economic situation."[96]

Just what the president meant became clear during a meeting at the British Embassy the following day. After fending off a half-hearted effort by Halifax to sell the Churchill delay strategy, Acheson and Herbert Feis declared that failure to reach agreement now would throw the whole question of compensation open to Congress. Congressional committees were, as everyone knew, capable of an infinite amount of ignorance and mischief. It was probable that Anglophobes would attach a dollar sign to the compensation clause and the whole war debts imbroglio would repeat itself. According to Halifax, his two visitors asserted that the "United States Government hold the view strongly that both countries would lose by allowing these other ideas to creep in but that Britain would lose most."[97] The message was clear: if Britain wanted to head off a resurgence of economic and political isolationism in the postwar world, it had best accept Article VII. Put another way, in the absence of an early compensation agreement, the law of the jungle would prevail, with America playing the role of a very rich lion and Britain that of a very poor and aging buffalo.

Halifax had received no concession statement from London, however, and he once again rejected the American draft. On February 4 Roosevelt sent a personal appeal to Churchill: "I understand your need of maintaining unity at home in the great task of winning the war. I know you also understand how essential it is that we maintain unity of purpose between two Governments and peoples in this and equally important in the unfinished tasks that will follow it. I am convinced that further delay in concluding this agreement will be harmful to your interests and ours."[98]

Churchill convened a special cabinet meeting on the sixth and summarized its results for Roosevelt in a telegram the next day. "I found the cabinet at its second meeting on this subject," he wrote, "even more resolved against trading the principle of imperial preference as consideration for lend-lease." A majority of the cabinet felt that acceptance of Article VII was tantamount to accepting "intervention in the domestic affairs of the British Empire."[99] Churchill, who would soon remark that he had not become first minister to preside over liquidation of the empire, fully concurred with the empire isolationists in this case. British acceptance of Article VII, the former naval person concluded, "would lead to dangerous debates in Parliament as well as to a further outbreak of the German propaganda of the kind you read to me on the second night of my visit about the United States breaking up the British Empire and reducing us to the level of a territory of the Union."[100]

In the wake of this apparent British stonewall, the multilateralists in Washington conferred. It was agreed that imperial preference could not be excluded from the talks provided for in Article VII, but that the British could be reassured on two points. First, acceptance of Article VII did not involve any commitments on imperial preference per se, and, second, preference reductions would always be linked to tariff reductions. Moreover, the United States could recognize the right of the Dominions to approve or disapprove any arrangement regarding their trade agreements with Great Britain. On the eleventh Roosevelt telegraphed these concessions to Churchill. "What seems to be bothering the Cabinet is the thought that we want a commitment in advance that empire preference will be abolished. We are asking for no such commitment; and I can say that Article VII does not contain any such commitment. I realize that that would be a commitment which your government could not give now if it wanted to; and I am very sure that I could not, on my part, make any commitment relative to a vital revision of our tariff policy."[101]

Linking imperial preference with United States tariff rates and assurances about the nonbinding nature of Article VII served to tip the scales in favor of Eden, Cherwell, and the other British multilateralists. On the thirteenth London cabled the Dominion governments for permission to sign the Mutual Aid Agreement with Article VII as it stood. That permission was forthcoming and on February 23, 1942, Halifax and Hull exchanged signed documents.[102]

The battle was over but the struggle had just begun. American multilateralists were bound and determined to use World War II and Britain's vulnerability to end "Schachtian" practices once and for all. They continued to believe that unilaterally imposed tariffs at the national level were not in the same category as exclusive regional blocs, no matter what rhetorical concessions had been made to the British. If the United States could not persuade its closest ally to part with imperial preference, what chance did it have of persuading other nations to abjure bilateralism? Britain for its part hoped to educate American opinion, public and private. How long could State, Commerce, and Treasury officials continue to attack Great Britain for pursuing bilateralist policies when the sterling bloc represented the most advanced form of regional multilateralism then in existence? British officials repeatedly pointed out that, most-favored-nation clause notwithstanding, the Reciprocal Trade Agreements program came closer to bilateralism than imperial preference. But, of course, the balance of power would continue to tip heavily in favor of the United States. Britain's military struggle against overwhelming odds would be paralleled by a struggle against similar odds with the American multilateralists to preserve a modicum of British economic independence and to create a postwar world that was safe not only for capitalism but for social democracy as well.

3. Good as Gold: Liquidity, Bureaucracy, and the Keynes-White Plans for International Currency Stabilization, 1942–1943

RECOGNIZING THAT Britain's economic and strategic interests required intimate and continuous cooperation with the United States during and after World War II, John Maynard Keynes designed in spring 1942 an apparatus for international currency stabilization. His mechanism was intended to provide Britain and other debtor nations with the liquidity necessary for participation in a multilateral system. Continuing its furious struggle with the State Department for control of foreign economic policy, the United States Treasury advanced its own plans for a stabilization fund and an International Bank for Reconstruction and Development. The principal difference between the Keynes Plan and the American structure designed by Harry Dexter White was that the former was intended to secure British financial independence while the latter was designed to ensure United States domination of international finance.

Meanwhile, some members of the War Cabinet and certain officials in the British Foreign Office came to the conclusion that the postwar prosperity and security of Western Europe depended primarily on the willingness of the United States to commit its resources to the reconstruction of the Continent. In addition, most were convinced that such a commitment hinged on British acceptance of multilateralism. As a result, the coalition government decided to propose the negotiation of a multilateral commercial convention that mandated an across-the-board cut in tariffs, quotas, and preferences for nations experiencing a positive balance of trade. Realizing that Britain could never participate in such a system without adequate liquidity, the cabinet at the same time instructed its economic experts to persuade the United States to accept the Clearing Union. Indeed, Washington's endorsement of Keynes's proposal would be a precondition to the conclusion of a commercial convention. Though Anglo-American negotiators agreed to a joint statement of principles in fall 1943, neither side, in fact, compromised on their respective stabilization schemes. Britain's determination to erect a structure that redistributed the world's supply of gold and dollars and gave the United Kingdom an equal say with the United States remained as strong as ever, while Henry Morgenthau and Harry White refused to abandon their plans for an American-dominated financial system.

The United States Treasury's position was buttressed by burgeoning isolationism and economic nationalism within Congress. Opponents of European intervention, guardians of the national sovereignty, and fiscal conservatives banded together in 1943 to ensure that Congress retained control of foreign economic policy and that the Roosevelt administration did not launch any "international New Deals" that would once again entangle America in European affairs. So intimidated was the White House by this nationalist resurgence that it not only supported Treasury in its uncompromising stand over a stabilization plan, but also rejected the common pooling theory of lend-lease and backed Morgenthau and his bureaucratic allies as they labored to hold British gold-dollar balances to the barest minimum. Roosevelt held firm to this course despite warnings from Whitehall and its allies in the State Department that British participation in a multilateral trading system without guarantee of adequate reserves would ultimately destroy America's staunchest European ally.

Keynes longed to get back to England, to his wife, to his friends, and to his suffering fellow Britons. Yet like General George S. Patton, the economist sensed that World War II constituted an immense opportunity for him. It was his destiny, he believed, to reconstruct a chaotic world economy in a manner that would eradicate the roots of economic and social insecurity, and check the advance of revolution, fascism, and communism in the years to come. Men of affairs and the philosophers who stood behind them could not win the war—that was up to Montgomery, Dill, Marshall, and Mountbatten—but they could win the peace. Though Keynes was an economist he never lost sight of strategic and political factors. In the political sphere, he believed, Britain must organize Western Europe in the postwar era. If it did not, Russia would. Communism spelled totalitarianism, and totalitarianism seemed inevitably to produce armed aggression. Fascism must be stamped out and communism contained. In this Churchill and Keynes were in full agreement. In the economic and financial spheres, Britain must be protected from an adverse balance of trade and a negative balance of payments. Either or both would produce bankruptcy, disarmament, and the removal of Britain as a significant element in the international balance of power. Equilibrium, Keynes recognized, was the key. And that was the key not just for Britain but for every nation. When exports equaled imports, when capital outflow equaled capital inflow, not only would multilateralism be possible, but also it would have arrived. Equilibrium opened the door for the unlimited expansion of the world economy, a process which Cordell Hull and company had been dreaming about but which seemed beyond their mental capacities to set in motion.

From May 1941 through February 1942, British and American officials in charge of framing an economic policy for the postwar world had been preoccupied with commercial policy—with tariffs, imperial preferences, quotas, cartels, commodity agreements, and the most-favored-nation principle. But to Keynes it seemed that London and Washington were putting the cart before the horse. "It is extraordinarily difficult to frame any proposals about tariffs if countries are free to alter the value of their currencies without agreement and at short notice," he observed. "Tariffs and currency depreciations are in many cases alternatives. Without currency agreements you have no firm ground upon which to discuss tariffs."[1] Trade was substance and finance was form, to be sure, but form often determined substance.

In finance as well as trade, radical imbalance rather than equilibrium would characterize the international economy at war's end. The United States would hold nearly two-thirds of the world's gold supply and it would be the West's chief source of finished products, capital goods, capital, and even some food and fiber. Continuing high tariffs would mean that America's positive balance of trade and payments would accelerate dramatically after V-E Day, especially if, as the multilateralists wanted, commercial and exchange controls were removed. Britain, without gold, deeply in debt to its sterling area partners, and unable to reach prewar export levels for at least five years, would be a decided debtor. This would be more or less true of Belgium, France, and the other Western European countries. For multilateralism to work, all of the major trading nations needed substantial resources of gold and currency to accommodate the natural fluctuations in trade that occurred in an unregulated system. Unless some means for redistributing the monetary resources of the world's greatest creditor nation were found, Britain, France, and the other members of the trading community would become commercial and financial colonies of the United States.[2]

Keynes perceived, correctly, that this was not the end goal of the American multilateralists. Harry Hawkins, Clair Wilcox, Henry Wallace, and Dean Acheson all realized that, given the advanced state of America's economy, most of its overseas trade was and would continue to be with the industrialized nations of Europe and Asia. Reduction of living standards was in the interest, then, of no one. There were the ideological and strategic dimensions to be considered as well. The Germans and the Japanese had done, and the Russians would do, everything in their power to exploit anticolonial sentiment in Eastern Europe and in the underdeveloped areas of the world. A multilateral system that failed to take into account existing inequities and the desire by developing countries to build balanced economies and achieve a degree of economic sovereignty would play into the hands of the totalitarian powers whoever they might be.[3] But there was no guarantee that the multilateralists would be able to talk special interests in the United States out of their traditional tariff shelters. There was, moreover, nothing per se in the multilateral program that would achieve a basic redistribution of wealth at war's end.

Finally, despite his statements to the contrary, Keynes was as concerned as Ernest Bevin and Leo Amery about the possibility of postwar depression and deflation in the United States. During the 1930s the Cambridge don had not only defined and emphasized the role played by aggregate demand in preventing unemployment and ensuring prosperity, but he also had outlined a mechanism for stimulating and maintaining aggregate demand in a capitalist society—countercyclical deficit spending. Keynes had coupled this theory with protectionism, creating, in effect, a blueprint for full employment in one country. Keynes together with reform Tories and Labour moderates recognized that in conditions of nondiscrimination, low trade barriers, and free convertibility of currencies, Britain would be able to pursue Keynesian policies in the domestic sphere only if the other major trading nations of the world followed suit.[4]

The task ahead, as Keynes saw it, was to devise an international structure that would give to the have-not trading nations the financial reserves they needed to survive in a multilateral environment and compete successfully with the United States. Moreover, if possible, that system should include a compelling incentive for the United States to pursue full employment policies in the domestic sphere. Keynes was not at first sanguine about the possibility of bringing such a system into being.

From the day he took office in the Treasury in mid-1940 through his return to England in August of the following year, Keynes preached the necessity of exchange control. When asked to write a laissez-faire response to Germany's New Order and Japan's Co-Prosperity Sphere, he refused. What the people of Europe, including Britain, would want after the war was security, not the vagaries and the turbulence of the international gold standard. But just as had been the case with his thinking on commercial policy, by spring 1941 Keynes's fertile mind began to spot weaknesses in his own defense of exchange control and bilateral payments agreements. The Payments Agreements Plan, which Britain had been able to negotiate with some of its trading partners in the 1930s, was the simplest way to protect Britain from an adverse balance of payments. Under such a system, for example, if the United Kingdom bought maize from Argentina and paid in sterling, Argentina could make no use of that sterling except to buy goods from Britain. The first great disadvantage with such a proposition, Keynes recognized, was that "it would involve a discrimination against the United States if she persisted in maintaining an unbalanced creditor position."[5] Second, there would be little pressure the United Kingdom could bring to bear on sterling area partners to force them to sign such agreements after the war. America could supply their needs and Britain could not. Even bilateralism required a partner. Finally, Keynes began to have grave doubts about the ability of unilateral currency manipulation to maintain high wages, high profits, and full employment in England. British exchange depreciation would merely touch off competitive depreciation elsewhere and everyone would be back where they started. Exchange depreciation could not be used against other members of the sterling area without destroying the entire system.

What, then, was the alternative? What Keynes had in mind when he informed Ben Cohen that he had been working on a utopian alternative to bilateralism and protectionism was a plan that would provide for flexible currency stabilization, furnish the have-not trading nations with the currency reserves they needed to operate in a multilateral system, and provide the United States with incentive to lower tariffs and allow its capital to be used for reconstruction and development abroad. Over the years, Keynes's ideas on an international monetary system had begun to crystallize, but he had never put forward a comprehensive plan. Full employment in one country had been his obsession. In *A Tract on Monetary Reform* he had, however, discussed the "evil consequences" of the unstable international currency system; later, in *A Treatise on Money*, he had explored the possibility of tying the national currencies of the world together in a managed international system, taking the gold standard as a starting point.[6] Back in London after his disappointing trip to Washington in summer 1941, Keynes discussed the implications of Article VII with several of his colleagues in the Treasury, the Board of Trade, and the Foreign Office. Gathering their comments and arguments, he retired to the country for a few weeks. When he returned, he brought with him "Proposals for an International Currency Union."[7]

"To suppose that there exists some smoothly functioning automatic mechanism of adjustment which preserves equilibrium if only we trust to methods of *laissez-faire* is a doctrinaire illusion which disregards the lessons of historical experience without having behind it the support of sound theory," he insisted.[8] The inability of laissez-faire to achieve social justice and equality of opportunity had been responsible for the maze of restrictive and protective devices erected by the trading nations of the world in the 1930s, not vice versa. But the Schachtian device had its drawbacks too; state trading in vital foodstuffs and raw materials and bilateral payment agreements might suit Britain in the short run, but its value to a nation so dependent on foreign trade was questionable in the long run. More importantly, it would be totally unacceptable to the Americans. The Clearing Union, Keynes wrote, would provide Britain with a modicum of protection while at the same time satisfying the United States. Admitting that it was "complicated and novel and perhaps Utopian," he argued that it was well worth presenting to the Americans. "If not this, we can ask, what then? Now that you are fully seized of the Essential elements of the problem, what alternative solution do you offer us?" he asked the cabinet.[9]

The Clearing Union project proposed realistically not to bypass national governments but to make them the foundation of the system. It assumed that all foreign exchange would be held by a central bank, which would act as an intermediary between the international community and its public. Central banks would trade their currencies not directly but through an international clearing bank. A central bank would have control over the purchase of foreign exchange by its own citizens, but would be prepared to sell its own currency to another central bank on demand. There would, then, be free convertibility of currency. Currencies would have a fixed value, expressed in terms of the currency of the clearing bank, which would itself be expressed in and theoretically convertible to gold. Although in Britain the "Gold Standard" had become something of a bogeyman—Keynes had played no small part in squashing the gold bug—the Americans, having stored some $21 billion worth of the precious stuff in the vaults at Fort Knox, would insist that it retain its value. Thus, any plan for international currency stabilization that was not based on gold would obviously be unacceptable to the Americans. Keynes had no intention of playing William

Jennings Bryan to Henry Morgenthau's William McKinley. Keynes suggested the name "bancor" for his new gold-based currency.

The world's central banks would set up accounts with the clearing bank. Nations whose currencies were bought would have their accounts debited and those who sold their currency, credited. A central bank whose account was in debt by a certain amount, and for a given time, would be allowed to depreciate its currency at a rate not to exceed 5 percent in a year. It could also borrow. If, however, its debit exceeded half its quota—an amount of credit would be assigned each participating country at the outset—the governors of the clearing bank could require a depreciation, compel the offender to hand over the gold in its possession, force the nation in question to prohibit the export of capital, or even kick it out of the Clearing Union. Debtor nations—Great Britain, for example—could not continue to be debtors forever.[10]

Conversely, a central bank whose account ran too much in the black could be required to appreciate its currency; it could also grant loans to deficit banks. At the close of each year, the credit balance of any member in excess of its quota would be transferred to a reserve fund. Creditors, then, could not continue to be creditors forever. The system was set up so that the surplus capital accumulated by creditor countries—the United States in the postwar period—would be used to aid debtor countries. Debtors could borrow directly from creditors; moreover, an account could be set up with the clearing bank in the name of an international organization charged with postwar relief and reconstruction.[11] Keynes claimed that this mechanism was designed to prevent any one country from having to bear alone the burden of postwar reconstruction but, in fact, it was designed to ensure that the one country—the United States—that could bear it, did.

The overriding object of the Clearing Union was, of course, equilibrium. Like domestic banking systems, it would aim at "equality of credits and debits, of assets and liabilities."[12] In fact, members would have to pay charges on their outstanding balances with the Clearing Union, credit or debit, and these charges would be progressively higher. Obviously it would be to the advantage of members to keep their accounts as close to equilibrium as possible.

The stabilization plan was, in addition, designed to maintain aggregate demand. An international bank would create credits sufficient to allow national governments to pursue full employment policies at home. It would, moreover, ensure that capital did not lie idle but would be invested in those areas where unemployment was high and demand low. Since balances were resources that a country voluntarily chose to leave idle and represented a potential purchasing power it was entitled to use any time, it would suffer no harm if these balances were put at the disposal of other countries, Keynes rationalized. Indeed, it would be helped, as that capital could be used to develop a debtor's economy, increase aggregate demand, and swell the volume of international trade.[13]

The United States and the United Kingdom, as founder states, would be given a special position under the Keynes Plan. The two would agree between themselves on the value of dollars and sterling in terms of bancor, which in turn would be expressed in terms of gold. When other states had established a central banking system they could apply and be admitted. At that point their currencies would be pegged to bancor. No state could change the value of its currency without the permission of the board of governors. Member countries could add bancor credit to their accounts by paying in gold but could not demand gold for bancor. Between gold and bancor, and only between these two mediums, would there be one-way convertibility.[14]

Before submitting the Clearing Union plan to the cabinet, Keynes first asked his colleagues in Whitehall for their comments. The two relevant bureaucracies were Treasury and the Economic Section of the War Cabinet Secretariat. The Exchequer was divided into four sections: Overseas Finance, Home Finance, Supply, and Establishment. Heading Overseas Finance was Sir Wilfrid Eady, a man whose forte, as Sir Richard Clarke recalled, was mediation and conciliation, not original thought, a veteran Treasury man with "razor sharp intelligence, likableness, and the cynicism and waspishness born of thirty years of British and European Finance." Assisting him was a gregarious Irishman named Ernest Row-Dutton, who headed eight territorial divisions.[15] Keynes was one of two principal economic advisers to the department; the other was Sir Hubert Henderson, who served from 1939 to 1944. Eady and Henderson were anti-expansionists who labored to develop an alternative to countercyclical deficit spending and warned continually about the dangers of inflation. A group of younger officials—P. D. Procter and Frank Lee, for example—defined themselves as "Keynesians," and they together with civil servants in the Economic Section of the War Cabinet Secretariat accepted the role Keynes set out for government in the *General Theory*.[16]

This group, not surprisingly, was enthusiastic about Keynes's scheme for international economic stabilization. Lionel Robbins, a Liberal, was typical; "I sat up late last night reading your revised proposals with great excitement and a growing hope that the spirit of Burke and Adam Smith are on earth again."[17] Professor Dennis Robertson and the all-important Sir Richard Hopkins were positive, as were James Meade and Sir Edward Bridges of the Economic Section. Meade, who later succeeded Hopkins, would become the leading apologist for commercial multilateralism in Great Britain—Whitehall's Harry Hawkins. In fact, with the exception of Henderson, the Treasury and the Economic Section lined up solidly behind the Clearing Union plan, at least as a basis for negotiation.

Nonetheless, Henderson was the government economist who, next to Keynes, had the most influence outside departmental circles. He rejected the prescriptions for domestic recovery contained in the *General Theory* and was an avid bilateralist and protectionist in foreign policy. Britain would have to resort to every conceivable device to protect its balance of trade in the postwar period and should be free to do so. To Henderson, the Clearing Union tied Great Britain too closely to the gold standard and exposed it to the dangerous vagaries of a free market system. Commercial policy was his obsession, however, and he did not choose to make a last-ditch stand over the Clearing Union.

On February 11, 1942, the Clearing Union plan was submitted to the cabinet as a basis for discussion with the Americans; Whitehall suggested that it constitute Britain's response to the discussions that had been called for under Article VII. Two foci of opposition to the Clearing Union concept soon emerged. One centered on Leo Amery, Lord Beaverbrook, and the Bank of England. During the war, the latter two were virtually indistinguishable. The Bank was jealous of its role as historic center of the financial world. Despite the fact that its preeminent position had eroded steadily since World War I and would continue to do so during the current conflict, hope sprang eternal in the hearts of Lord Catto and the other directors.[18] The key to the Bank's power was the strength of sterling, its acceptability as an international currency. The Clearing Union would, the Bank insisted, undermine sterling and create a new international currency and a new worldwide central bank. The empire isolationists joined the Board of Governors of the Bank of England and launched a bitter, emotional attack on the Clearing Union idea. "This is the Gold Standard all over again," cried Beaverbrook, running up the Union Jack. "And at a moment when the U.S. has all the gold and G.B. has none of it." An unholy alliance between the United States and "the professors" was in the offing and "we should not allow the United States to lasso us this time."[19]

Ernest Bevin and the Labour center took a position on the Clearing Union not radically different from the empire isolationists. After studying the Treasury draft, Bevin protested that the proposals called for an automatic return to the gold standard "with just a little more rope before the unfortunate debtor is hanged." The minister of labor reminded his colleagues that he had already been forced to take part in one bloody and divisive general strike by a return to the gold standard, and he had no intention of seeing Britain involved in a second. An interview with Keynes in which the architect of the Clearing Union insisted to Bevin that no nation should be required to adopt deflationary policies under the scheme somewhat mollified the former dockworker, but he remained intensely suspicious.[20]

Ever the pragmatist, Keynes answered each of these criticisms in turn, sometimes patiently, sometimes not. After much gnashing of teeth and tearing of hair, the cabinet gave the Treasury permission to approach the Americans and use the Keynes proposal as a basis for discussion.

To the Churchill government's consternation, however, the Americans were not ready to be approached, even though the United States government had pressed Article VII on Britain with great urgency. Keynes had intended that, before developing his ideas into an integrated proposal, he should submit his views to a group of American experts and listen to what they had to say. Such a procedure would prevent the crystallization of ideas that were unacceptable to both. To the Foreign Office and Treasury's irritation, repeated British initiatives through both Gilbert Winant and Lord Halifax were at first ignored and then turned aside on the grounds that the United States was not ready to discuss currency stabilization.[21] Nigel Ronald speculated that Keynes's authorship of the Treasury plan had "touched up some old wounds," but that was not the primary reason for American procrastination.[22]

Washington's policy of delay stemmed from a bitter bureaucratic rivalry between the departments of State and Treasury, one of a dozen major interagency conflicts that punctuated the history of the Roosevelt administration during World War II. In fact, Anglo-American negotiations concerning the commercial and financial makeup of the postwar world were frequently affected and at times dominated by Washington's bureaucratic politics.

The modern federal bureaucracy was a direct outgrowth of the New Deal and World War II. Relief, reconstruction, and then wartime agencies multiplied, and the number of bureaucrats increased geometrically from 1933 to 1945. In the Roosevelt administration, individuals were chosen for cabinet- and department-level posts and for the super-grade positions for a variety of reasons—they represented a powerful constituency, they were loyal to the president, they had proven experience in a given field.[23] The least important factor was ideological consistency and the most important, loyalty. In Franklin Roosevelt's Washington all bureaucratic roads led to the White House.

In his search for new ideas with which to combat the depression, Roosevelt stimulated rather than eliminated bureaucratic conflict and personal rivalries within his administration. Thinking that out of conflict and compromise would come the best possible solution, he deliberately assigned advisers or groups of advisers with diametrically opposed views to work on the same problem. In practice, however, the president's techniques often blurred lines of authority and responsibility and led to bitter rivalries that distorted the decision-making process.[24] The burgeoning of Washington during the New Deal and World War II coupled with FDR's willingness to grant personal access to dozens of bureaucrats up and down the hierarchy meant that bureaucratic and personal goals frequently eclipsed definitions of national interest rationally arrived at as policy determinants.[25]

There were, in addition, a couple of war-related traits that came to distinguish the Roosevelt bureaucracy from its predecessors. Not surprisingly, a deep split developed between military and civilian agencies. Treasury, State, and the War Production Board, for example, were all extremely suspicious of the War and Navy departments, convinced that they were determined to use the war to encroach upon economic, political, and diplomatic policy-making. Civilian agencies worked feverishly to keep the soldiers' attention on the battlefield and limit their influence to strategic issues. Henry Stimson, Frank Knox, and the Joint Chiefs of Staff were often persuaded, on the other hand, that the civilians were putting political and ideological concerns ahead of winning the war. As a result, the military and civilian branches of government often negotiated with each other as if they were foreign governments—to use William Roger Louis's analogy— rather than colleagues.[26]

Moreover, during World War II there developed a troublesome gap between those who were planning for the postwar world and those who were in control of day-to-day policy. That chasm was especially apparent in the State Department. The planners tended to work in a vacuum, drawing up blueprints frequently unsuited for practical application. Decision makers, by contrast, often implemented short-range policies totally unconnected to the long-range plan being formulated by their fellows. Not surprisingly, consistency and, at times, rationality were scarce commodities in the Roosevelt foreign policy establishment.[27]

Finally, after Sumner Welles's departure in 1943, Roosevelt did not trust the State Department to make foreign policy and conduct day-to-day diplomacy. Cordell Hull was too slow-witted and cautious. Yet, due to the Tennessean's clout in Congress and his stature within the Democratic party, particularly with Southerners, FDR could not replace his secretary of state. As with all obstacles he could not remove, Roosevelt simply bypassed Hull and the State Department. He did so with special assistants and envoys to whom he assigned specific tasks. Harry Hopkins, who was openly contemptuous of the State Department and professional diplomats in general, was the best example. Averell Harriman, wealthy New York Democrat and long-time Roosevelt supporter, was another.

British-American relations were strongly affected by Roosevelt's sashays around State. From 1941 to 1943 Harriman was the president's special envoy to Churchill. During this period he, rather than Gilbert Winant, met with the prime minister, Anthony Eden, and Lord Beaverbrook, and he traveled both to Moscow and Washington with Churchill. "The work of the Embassy is seriously interfered with by the increasing number of people who negotiate with the British Government often without definite assignment to the Embassy as well as by efforts to reach agreements on both sides of the water at the same time," Winant complained to Hopkins in 1941. "Your help is greatly needed." Winant, of course, was appealing to the wrong man.[28]

In their dealings with the United States the British were well aware of the importance of presidential and congressional politics and the interplay of special interests, but the internecine strife that characterized the Roosevelt bureaucracy was a new and baffling phenomenon to them. Due in part to the nature of the parliamentary system, there was no parallel in Britain, though the patchwork nature of the Churchill government gave rise to more infighting than normal. British diplomats spent much of the war studying the Roosevelt administration in an effort to learn the principal players and the rules of the game. The chaos that seemed to prevail in Washington amazed and frequently appalled the British. As Keynes once advised the cabinet:

> Remember that, in negotiations lasting weeks, the situation is entirely fluid up to the last minute. Everything you are told, even with the greatest appearance of authority and decision is provisional, without commitment. . . . I liken them [American officials] to bees who for weeks will fly around in all directions with no ascertainable destination, providing both the menace of stings and the promise of honey; and at last, perhaps because the queen in the White House has admitted some faint, indistinguishable odor suddenly swarm to a single spot in a compact, impenetrable bunch.[29]

Frequently the Churchill government's ability to protect Britain's interests and to reach agreement with America depended on its insight into the power struggle in Washington.

No one was a more enthusiastic, skilled, or energetic bureaucratic warrior than Henry Morgenthau, Jr., Roosevelt's secretary of the Treasury and the person the British would have to deal with in all matters pertaining to currency stabilization. In 1941 Morgenthau was fifty years old, a tall, balding, dour man who had headed the Treasury since 1933. The Morgenthaus and the Roosevelts became Dutchess County neighbors in 1913, and the two young couples virtually grew up together. FDR took Morgenthau with him to Albany in 1929 and subsequently to Washington. Roosevelt prized him for his loyalty and administrative ability. Privately gentle and considerate, the public Morgenthau was most unattractive— "Henry the Morgue," Roosevelt called him. Inarticulate, stubborn, and suspicious, Morgenthau displayed at times an inferiority complex that bordered on paranoia. He was a Jew who hated the banking establishment—Wall Street and the City of London—placing much of the blame for the depression on its shoulders.[30] Capable of excruciating self-doubt one moment and overweening self-confidence the next, Morgenthau wielded great power in Washington through a combination of determination and frequent access to the president—the two lunched together every Monday through 1944.[31] He had ideas of his own— Morgenthau believed in a free, regulated economy and active American participation in a collective security organization abroad. In the 1930s he struggled to make the Treasury, rather than the private banking establishment, arbiter of domestic financial and economic matters.

Morgenthau shared American ambivalence in regard to Great Britain. One moment he admired Britons for their freedom and gallantry; the next he reviled them for their imperialism and elitism. Morgenthau basically did not trust the English and was magnanimous toward them only when he felt them in his power. The Treasury chief had been an internationalist prior to Pearl Harbor; but just as he had been determined to shift control over the domestic economy from Wall Street to the Treasury, so too was he determined to see Washington supplant London as the financial and commercial center of the world. Morgenthau was a multilateralist, not so much for ideological or strategic reasons, but because he saw in it a mechanism that would facilitate the transfer of power. Once the White House and the Treasury gained control of the economic levers of the world, poverty and war were sure to be eliminated and democracy would be perpetuated. The important thing was to affect the transfer.[32]

Morgenthau's commitment to multilateralism becomes all the more meaningful in view of his well-known hatred of Cordell Hull and his general contempt for the State Department. He believed the secretary of state to be a dull-witted, southern conservative who was soft on fascism and dictatorships. In 1940 he criticized the State Department for appeasing fascism by maintaining relations with Vichy France and then for exposing the United States to grave danger by freezing Japanese assets in July 1941. The department was dominated by a pro-British clique, he believed, with a penchant for anti-Semitism, that conviction becoming stronger as revelations concerning State's insensitivity to the Jewish refugee problem came to light after 1943. In short, Morgenthau believed Hull and the State Department were not fit to preside over American foreign policy at this crucial juncture in world history. Treasury would just have to expand its horizons.[33]

It was with these goals and prejudices in mind that Morgenthau called his chief assistant, Harry Dexter White, on Sunday morning, December 14, 1941, exactly one week after Pearl Harbor, and ordered him to begin work on an "Inter-Allied Stabilization Fund." What the secretary envisioned was "a Fund to be used during the war to give monetary aid to actual and potential allies and to hamper the enemy; to provide a postwar 'international currency.' "[34] By his own admission Morgenthau lacked theoretical expertise in international finance. If his dream of an American-run international financial system were to become reality, White would have to be the conjurer. A week before making this assignment Morgenthau had announced to his staff that he was going to grant Harry White the status of assistant secretary, although he could not give him the title. White would be, as Morgenthau later told Hull, the Treasury official in charge of foreign affairs and relations with the State Department.

While Harry White's qualifications as a sorcerer were open to question, his credentials as a theoretical economist were not. Born to Russian immigrant parents in Boston in 1892, White in turn graduated from high school, worked in the family hardware stores, entered the military (serving in France), farmed, and ran a public institution for war orphans. Having experienced the worlds of business and social work, White married and, nearly thirty years old, decided on an academic career. After earning a Ph.D. at Harvard for his dissertation on French international finance, he taught for a period and then in 1934 went to Washington where he found a minor position in the Treasury Department. His hard work, determination, and intelligence paved the way for his steady advance and culminated with his promotion to Morgenthau's right-hand man for international finance.[35]

Harry White was convinced of two things: that political and social problems—revolution, tyranny, racism, war—were economic in nature, and that people were rational beings who could shape their environment to produce a better world. "Without a clear grasp of the principles, a moderate mastery of analysis of the economics of international relationships, it is utterly impossible to distinguish between the real causes and the alleged causes of international conflict," he wrote in 1939.[36] International and domestic economics, moreover, were inseparable. The policies a nation followed in the international sphere inevitably affected living standards, wages, production, and profits at home. Real economic isolationism, similar to the strategic isolation the United States enjoyed in the nineteenth century, was impossible. But how was it possible to insulate domestic economies, particularly underdeveloped and unbalanced ones, from the fluctuations of unregulated international trade and at the same time provide these economies with the fruits of a vigorous and expanding foreign commerce? That was the central question of the twentieth century.[37]

Like his boss, White's chief drawback was his public personality. Humorless, abrasive, arrogant, and impassioned, he drove his arguments home like battering rams. He shared Morgenthau's distrust of Wall Street bankers, the British, and rival bureaucracies—especially the State Department.[38] That distrust, turning at times to dislike, was returned in spades. "I have been so outraged by Harry White's capacity for rudeness in discussion," Dean Acheson declared, "that the charges made against him [he was accused in 1948 by Elizabeth Bentley of being a communist] would have seemed mild compared to the expressions I have used."[39] But Morgenthau was in search of a theorist not a diplomat (although Treasury was in desperate need of one), and White was certainly a theorist.

As Japanese troops followed up their victory at Pearl Harbor with air attacks and amphibious landings in the Philippines and Shanghai, White worked on his assignment. By the first week in January 1942 he was ready. In his "Suggested Program for Inter-Allied Monetary and Banking Action," White identified two objectives: (1) the stabilization of foreign exchange rates, and (2) the creation of an international agency capable of providing capital to reconstruct war-ravished economies and to finance the expansion of foreign trade. Where Keynes would combine both functions in a single entity, White proposed the creation of two autonomous mechanisms: an Inter-Allied Stabilization Fund and an Inter-Allied Bank. Like the Clearing Union, the stabilization fund would deal only with the central banks of the participating nations. Instead of each nation being assigned a quota or credit line, as was the case in the Keynes Plan, the members would contribute, or invest, a total of $5 billion in gold, currency, and government securities in the fund, a nation's share being determined by its wealth, volume of foreign trade, and other factors. The fund would be run by a board of directors elected by the members. Each member's vote would be determined by its share of investment. "The U.S.," White advised Morgenthau, "should have enough votes to block any decision, i.e., more than 20 percent."[40]

The principal currency of the Inter-Allied Stabilization Fund would be the dollar. The central authority could sell dollars to members for their local currency but only to help them settle their international accounts, that is, to achieve equilibrium in their balance of payments. The fund could not sell dollars to a country whose gold/dollar holdings rose above a certain level. The fund would peg currencies to gold, act as a clearinghouse, and in general facilitate a multilateral system of payments. To become a member, a nation would have to agree to a long list of conditions. Among other things, participants could not alter exchange rates without permission of the board, could not impose foreign exchange controls, could not negotiate bilateral clearing agreements, could not deflate or inflate its currency without permission, and would have to agree to embark on a program of tariff reduction.

The Inter-Allied Bank, also capitalized at $10 billion, would act as an international bank of reconstruction and development. A board elected by the members on the basis of their contribution to the total capitalization would provide low-interest loans to governments and private concerns for specified purchases. The bank, White wrote, was designed to eliminate worldwide economic fluctuations, reduce the likelihood and intensity of depression, stabilize prices of essential raw materials, and raise living standards.[41]

There was no need, White asserted, for an international currency. The dollar would fulfill that function. "For many decades the British pound sterling was regarded virtually as an international currency unit," he wrote. "But when sterling lost its stability in terms of gold, its use as a unit of account rapidly diminished. Only the United States dollar has any chance of serving that capacity now."[42]

By fall 1942 the objectives of the Treasury Department were clear. As the White Plan revealed, Treasury looked forward to a postwar financial order in which an American-controlled international agency implemented and supervised a currency stabilization agreement that linked the major trading currencies of the world firmly to each other and to gold. This agency would ensure that enough credit existed for a system of multilateral payments to work. Dollars and gold would be to international finance in the post-1945 period what sterling had been to nineteenth-century multilateralism. United States preponderance on the governing board would ensure that dollars and gold would be sold only to finance current transactions and not to build up the gold/dollar reserves of other nations. If other nations could build up their reserves through normal trade, so be it, but Morgenthau and White were determined that the United States would not voluntarily turn over its gold and dollars to its competitors. There would be no international "Share Our Wealth" plan under their aegis.

Morgenthau received the plan enthusiastically; it seemed to fit his preconception as precisely as any theoretical plan could. He initially favored an international currency but quickly relented in the face of White's arguments against one. On May 15 Morgenthau sent a copy of the White Plan to the White House with his endorsement. The project had tremendous strategic as well as economic significance, he told FDR. It would serve as a perfect propaganda counterpiece to Germany and Japan's New Order. This "New Deal in international economics" would give hope to the downtrodden. The United States should call a general conference of the Allied finance ministers to discuss implementation of the plan as quickly as possible, he advised.[43]

"A Suggested Program" may have been "bold and idealistic" and "a notable departure from powerful traditions of political isolation and financial orthodoxy," as Richard Gardner has claimed, but it was at the same time a mechanism designed to give the United States a substantial amount of control over international finance and commerce.[44] There was no question as to who would determine the policy of the bank and the fund—the United States, and more specifically the United States Treasury. Certainly White and his associates believed that American hegemony would expand trade, raise living standards, and provide economic stability for all members, but political considerations and bureaucratic imperialism were strong motives as well.

In the wake of White House approval of the fund and bank concepts, the next logical step would seem to have been an amalgamation of the White and Keynes plans. There were obvious differences between the two approaches. The Clearing Union, for example, did not provide for the elevation of the dollar to the status of a universal currency nor did it arrogate to the United States control of a stabilization and reconstruction mechanism. The British and American treasuries also differed on procedure. London favored the negotiation of an Anglo-American agreement to which the other Allied nations could subsequently adhere, while Morgenthau envisioned a general inter-Allied conference and multilateral negotiations. Yet there were broad similarities between the Keynes and White plans in both means and ends, certainly enough similarity to allow negotiations to begin. The British were anxious to get started, and Morgenthau believed that the sooner the fund and bank were fleshed out in an inter-Allied agreement the better. The State Department, however, had no intention of allowing Treasury to preempt the field of international economics.

When Morgenthau discussed the White Plan with the president in May, Roosevelt had given his blessing but advised his old friend to consult with Cordell Hull before making it public. Morgenthau, who conceived of the State Department under Hull as a mist-enshrouded swamp, swallowing every new idea that dared enter it, was apprehensive. But he had no choice. In late May Treasury submitted the White Plan to the State Department for its comments and the bureaucratic waters closed over it.[45]

By 1941 the Department of State was more fragmented, compartmentalized, and divided against itself than ever. Its organizational problems were a product of the existing structure, of Hull's leadership, and of Roosevelt's administrative style. The department had failed to keep pace with America's burgeoning role in world affairs. Prior to 1947 and the reorganization pushed through by George Marshall, there was no central policy-planning staff in State. Departmental divisions— defined both geographically and functionally—expanded as the department's responsibilities grew in a certain region (Latin America, for example), or in a certain field (petroleum, for instance). Departmental divisions with topical or geographic jurisdiction became the primary instrument for formulation and execution of policy. Bureaucratic power came to reside with the division chiefs and their advisers—political, economic, and legal. Aside from the "recipwocal twade agweements pwogwam"—Cordell Hull was famous for his lisp—postwar collective security, and Argentina, the secretary exerted little policy leadership.

The decision-making waters were further muddied by the notorious rivalry between Hull and his undersecretary, Sumner Welles. Welles made enemies easily. Aristocratic, acid-tongued, and a man who did not suffer fools lightly, he swept away or bypassed everything and everyone who stood in his path. Decisive where Hull was cautious, and energetic where the secretary was deliberate, well educated where his superior was limited, Welles would have threatened Hull under normal conditions. But, in addition, Welles, a Groton classmate of FDR, enjoyed privileged and direct access to the White House. In many situations the president consulted and relied on Welles rather than Hull—to the latter's enragement. Because of his work on the Good Neighbor Policy, Welles's reputation outside of the United States was much greater than Hull's.[46] The secretary, as Dean Acheson put it, spoke softly but carried a long knife. The Hull-Welles rivalry produced administrative chaos and made the State Department a kind of microcosm of the Roosevelt administration as a whole. According to Acheson, "The heads of these divisions, like barons in a feudal system weakened at the top by mutual suspicion and jealousy between king and prince, were constantly at odds, if not at war."[47]

Aside from Hull and Welles, two other frequent combatants were Acheson and Adolf Berle. Berle, a former brain truster and general counsel to the Reconstruction Finance Corporation (RFC) from 1933 to 1938, had joined the State Department as assistant secretary of state for Latin American affairs in 1938. By 1941 he had been shifted from Latin American to financial matters. Where Acheson was to coordinate commercial and economic questions with major policy concerns, Berle was to do the same in the area of finance. The two men disliked each other personally and differed philosophically. Acheson was a disciple of Louis Brandeis and a protégé of Felix Frankfurter. Bigness in business was bad; the overriding objective of government policy should be decentralization—regulation without control. Berle was a planner, a centralizer. Bigness in business was not only inevitable, it could be a positive good. But government, the federal government, must oversee, regulate, plan. Berle believed, moreover, that the business community should be told not only what it could do but also what it should do.[48]

There were old scars that carried over into the Acheson-Berle relationship in the State Department. Berle had been a major part of the first New Deal, but by 1935 he, Raymond Moley, and Rexford Tugwell were in eclipse. The second New Deal was dominated by Brandeis and Frankfurter—Acheson's mentors and cohorts. In addition, Berle along with Welles tended to be extremely suspicious of the British. They looked forward to the formation of a vigorous Inter-American System that would serve as a power base for the United States in world affairs and as a model for a postwar international cooperation. The United States should avoid being sucked into the British vortex and giving Soviet Russia the idea that Anglo-America was ganging up on it. Despite his stormy encounter with Keynes over Article VII, Acheson was an Anglophile who believed strongly in the cultural solidarity of the two countries and in the identity of their interests in international affairs. He pushed multilateralism on Britain in large part to save it from itself. Finally, Acheson regarded Berle as an intruder. He and his chief adviser on economic matters, Herbert Feis, did not believe commercial and financial matters should be separated; they ought to be unified under Acheson.

Acheson recalled: "For four years, until he [Berle] became Ambassador to Brazil, we maintained a wary coexistence on the second floor of Old State, separated by the offices of the Secretary and Undersecretary, who side by side, managed to do the same thing."[49]

Harry Hawkins, Clair Wilcox, and other commercial policy experts in the department clearly recognized and acknowledged that, in order for multilateralism to work, "national exchange controls would probably have to be abolished" and "vast international controls" erected.[50] But the White Plan alarmed Cordell Hull. He saw it as a plot hatched by his ambitious colleague to horn in on a diplomatic bailiwick. Currency stabilization and reconstruction were State not Treasury concerns. Berle, who had resented the prominence Acheson had gained in the course of the lend-lease–Article VII negotiations, agreed. The department would have to assert itself. From May through August, as a result, Hull and Berle sat on the plan while the Tennessean lobbied the White House to turn over Anglo-American financial negotiations to State. Berle, who still enjoyed independent access to the White House, worked on Roosevelt separately. Their labors bore fruit when, during the first week in August, the president approved Hull's recommendation that Berle be put in charge of all negotiations dealing with international postwar finance.

Without a plan of their own, Hull and Berle's bureaucratic victory over Treasury would be meaningless, however. The problem, therefore, was to hold off both the British and the Treasury until Berle could come up with an alternative to the Keynes and White programs. To White's barrage of memos insisting that a general conference of finance ministers of all friendly nations be scheduled at once, the State Department replied that such a conference would be premature. The department had been in contact with the British and the Russians, and both agreed that a general conference must be preceded by bilateral talks. At the same time, State put off British requests for Anglo-American discussions.[51]

By the end of September Berle had come up with a stabilization mechanism that the State Department could call its own. Given the press of time and his unfamiliarity with international finance, the former brain truster chose to adopt something close at hand. On September 28, 1942, he proposed the creation of an international version of the Federal Reserve System. Participants in his International Reserve Bank would subscribe to its stock in gold according to a mutually acceptable ratio. Like the Federal Reserve Board, it would have the power to issue notes redeemable in gold and to buy commercial paper with these notes. The bank would not have its own currency but would issue notes in the form of national currencies—francs, dollars, pounds—that the holder of gold or seller of paper wished to purchase. Because such issuance could significantly expand the money supply of the country in question, the central bank of the nation whose currency was being issued would have the right to approve or disapprove each issuance. Only central banks or national treasuries could do business with the International Reserve Bank.[52]

Berle admitted that the Treasury would object to any plan not of its own creation. Their amour propre would be wounded, as he put it. Hull should therefore get the president to call a series of cabinet meetings and in the course of these persuade Morgenthau to make the International Reserve Bank plan his own. Berle was engaging in wishful thinking. It quickly became apparent that the State Department, divided against itself, was no match for Treasury in the area of finance, and the International Reserve Bank was never heard of again.

While turf wars raged in Washington, a tenuous consensus emerged within the Churchill government in favor of commercial multilateralism. What converted a number of waverers was Keynes's stabilization plan and its promise of permanent liquidity for debtors.

Following a period of intense study and discussion, the Special Cabinet Sub-committee on Commercial Policy in April 1943 put forward three alternatives for presentation to the United States. Alternative A called for an Anglo-American convention open to all states providing for restriction of tariffs to a "moderate" level, reduction of preferences, elimination of export subsidies, regulation of state trading so as to avoid discrimination, and implementation of quantitative import restrictions only within clearly defined limits. Members of the international community could retain trade restrictions during a postwar transitional period on a diminished basis. Alternative B, a variation of A, went farther toward preserving national prerogatives. Trading nations would sign a single, multilateral convention. Each, however, would retain the right to impose quantitative import restrictions whenever warranted by balance-of-payments problems, and those restrictions would not be subject to approval by an international organization. Alternative C was essentially empire isolationism. This approach insisted that quantitative import restrictions, quite apart from balance-of-payments problems, were a positive good, and Britain would need them in the postwar period, especially to protect agriculture.[53]

Despite Amery and Hudson's arguments, which were half-heartedly supported by such left-wing Labour figures as Aneurin Bevan and Emmanuel Shinwell, the multilateralists prevailed. As Lord Cherwell put it, "The U.K. is too small an economic unit to act alone in the post-war world. We must throw in our lot either with the U.S.A. or with Europe. An economic union of the English-speaking peoples would provide a nucleus around which many other countries would tend to crystallize."[54] The cabinet voted to take the initiative with the Americans at once and propose alternative A—with one major modification: participating nations would retain the freedom to maintain quantitative restrictions without obtaining permission from the regulatory body if the country in question could show that it was experiencing an adverse balance of payments. The problem, acknowledged by nearly everyone, was liquidity. Multilateralism was feasible for Britain only if adequate credit and/or monetary reserves were available. British representatives ought, therefore, to seek the establishment of a Clearing Union or similar structure at the same time they negotiated on commercial policy proposals.[55]

Throughout late 1942 and early 1943, frustration had built within the British Treasury over Washington's refusal to negotiate a compromise between the Clearing Union and stabilization fund concepts. "It [Clearing Union] has been discussed with the Americans, but in only a preliminary, rather perfunctory, and altogether dissatisfying way," Keynes wrote James Meade. "They have put up an alternative scheme of their own. This goes a good way and is a great deal better than nothing. But it is half-baked and a poor second-best. Moreover, as usual, it is *not* a firm offer, and they make it very plain that they are not committed to their own plan. If we were to accept it, they would probably repudiate it."[56]

Although Keynes and White had been working on their respective plans for more than a year, as of 1943 neither had been made public. White was the first to break silence, outlining his plan before the annual meeting of the American Economic Association in early March 1943. At the same time Morgenthau included a copy of the plan with his call to the finance ministers of thirty-seven countries to send technical experts to a meeting in Washington. But the British wanted full publication and distribution of both plans. The great danger in Keynes's mind was that the Americans would do nothing. Once the Anglo-American plans were a matter of public record, the Roosevelt administration would have to act or lose face, he reasoned. Even publication of the British plan alone would be a plus in that it would leave Washington the choice either of acquiescing or publicizing its own plan.[57]

By spring 1943, however, the chief obstacle to Anglo-American consultation and publication was no longer the State Department but rather Franklin D. Roosevelt. On March 15 Hull told Eden that Congress and the American people were at long last prepared to move ahead in the area of postwar international cooperation. To guard against "fickle and sudden lapses or changes in public sentiment," the people must be kept "educated and up to date with respect to each of the important methods, plans or proposals calling for international cooperation."[58] Encouraged, the British pressed Morgenthau to approve joint, simultaneous publication. On the seventeenth the secretary approached Roosevelt. After mulling over the matter for two weeks, FDR said no. The tide had not yet fully turned on the battlefield, and publication would be premature. The president was still concerned about Russian sensibilities, rubbed raw by the continuing failure of Britain and America to establish a second front in Europe. Joint publication could further arouse Soviet suspicions that Britain and the United States intended to fashion a Pax Anglo-Americana and then present the USSR with a fait accompli. Moreover, while multilateralism was beginning to appear more and more attractive to the president, he was not yet ready to sell the program to Congress and the American people; indeed, he did not even have a clear picture, especially in the financial area, of how the system would operate.

Treasury officials, fearful of losing the initiative in international financial policy to Britain and/or to some bureaucratic rival, grew frustrated. Morgenthau had now to agree that the British plan be published alone. He did announce to a press conference that a United Nations Monetary Conference would be held in Washington and that tentative proposals for the stabilization of currencies had already been presented to a number of countries. In London arrangements were made to publish the Clearing Union plan on April 8. Then, on April 5, 1943, the London *Financial News* printed full details of the American scheme on its front page. Verbatim reports of the article were immediately cabled back to the American press by its correspondents in England. According to Armand Van Dormael, one of the ten governments-in-exile based in London was responsible for the leak. Morgenthau, he writes, did not blame the British.[59] He may not have blamed them, but he certainly believed them responsible. London had everything to gain—the appearance of an Anglo-American tie and hopefully bilateral negotiations leading to a permanent solution to Britain's postwar liquidity problem. Nonetheless, because it introduced the issue of postwar currency stabilization into the public forum and presented the White House with a fait accompli, the leak served Treasury's purposes as well as those of the Exchequer.

On the day of the leak, the secretary had to respond to questions on monetary policy at a press conference, and that afternoon he outlined for the Senate Banking Committee the White Plan for postwar currency stabilization. On April 7, the American plan was released in Washington and the British plan in London. Neither made reference to the other.[60]

Keynes, meanwhile, had persuaded all of the European governments-in-exile to endorse his scheme. The financial ministers, in anticipation of their forthcoming trip to Washington, asked how best to convert the Americans. Question, do not object, advised a self-satisfied Keynes, and the Americans were bound to see reason and come around.[61] Strangely, Keynes seemed to have momentarily lost sight of the fact that, between haves and have-nots, money and not logic drives arguments.

On May 12 Kingsley Wood explained the main features of both plans to the House of Commons. A week later Keynes, lately ennobled as Baron Keynes of Tilton, made his maiden speech in the House of Lords. In vivid, lucid prose he described the Clearing Union and stabilization fund plans and predicted a successful synthesis. Privately, too, Keynes expressed the belief that compromise was possible, but the British must establish priorities. The most fundamental question and the one London should be slowest to give way on was that of subscribed capital versus the banking principle. "If we can hold firm on the banking principle, we might compromise freely on everything else."[62]

Meanwhile, throughout April 1943 financial experts from the invited governments, including governments-in-exile and members of the British Commonwealth, arrived in Washington for talks on postwar finance. Treasury did not invite British experts and made it clear that embassy officials would not be welcome to sit in on the talks. To Keynes's dismay, each and every country that had expressed avid support in London for the Clearing Union succumbed to

American pressure in Washington and expressed strong preference for the White Plan.[63]

By late July 1943, the British Treasury had decided that bilateral talks on monetary policy must be held at once lest the United States produce additional proposals "not in the general interest." Keynes, the Foreign Office, and the Board of Trade persuaded the cabinet to ask Washington for comprehensive talks on the whole field of subjects included in Article VII. Washington, assured that other members of the trading community would support the White over the Keynes Plan, subsequently informed Lord Halifax that it would be ready to receive a delegation to discuss financial questions as well as commercial policy.[64]

At this point three major differences distinguished the two nations' monetary plans. First, the American scheme called for actual capital subscription while the Clearing Union relied on the banking principle, credit to be based on an overdraft capacity. Second, White's approach limited the liability of creditors to provide credit to debtor members while Britain wanted to expand the size of the fund from $5 billion, the American figure, to $10 billion. And third, the Keynes Plan called for each member to retain sovereignty over the exchange rate of its currency while the United States wanted a fixed ratio of $4 to £1, any future changes to be approved by the international authority.[65] The differences were formidable, particularly Britain's insistence on maintaining control over its exchange rate, but Keynes was, à la Franklin Roosevelt, supremely confident that his logic and force of personality could forge a compromise satisfactory to all. More tangibly, he believed he had an important bargaining chip. The British Treasury would never support United Kingdom participation in a multilateral trading network without a monetary system that guaranteed adequate liquidity to creditors and that accorded Britain parity with the United States within the governing body, and multilateralism could not work without British participation.

The British War Cabinet met on August 27 and September 2 to frame instructions for their delegation to the Washington talks. Ernest Bevin, Hugh Dalton, and other Labour leaders, supported by the empire isolationists, were adamant—Keynes and his colleagues must not give way on the principle of national control of exchange rates. The issue bore directly on the whole concept of convertibility of currencies. The British were afraid of free convertibility, and maintenance of the right of unilateral depreciation was one way to undermine the concept. The Labourites in the cabinet took a dim view of convertibility because they believed it would drain away British reserves, thus making it impossible for the national government to expand social services and guarantee full employment. The empire isolationists feared it because many believed that it would lead to nothing less than a dissolution of the empire. Britain's debt to India and the Dominions was so great by 1943 that, if at war's end the sterling balances were funded at even half their value, and Britain was at the same time forced to make sterling freely convertible, the United Kingdom would be placed in an untenable position.[66]Not only would convertibility and funding drain away Britain's entire reserve of gold and dollars, but it also would abolish a tie—the sterling debt—that would bind the empire together.

Nonetheless, after much pounding of palms and gnashing of teeth, Dalton, Leo Amery, and company finally conceded to the multilateralists that exchange rates and the ability of national governments to manipulate them could be subjected to some "objective" international standard if the United States insisted. Under no circumstances, however, should the right of a country to alter its exchange rate be the subject of debate and vote within the governing body.

The compartmentalization within the American foreign policy establishment, in which the State Department was responsible for commercial policy and the Treasury Department for financial policy, was paralleled in Whitehall. The Economic Section of the War Cabinet Secretariat dealt primarily with commercial matters and the Treasury with monetary affairs. The British delegation that arrived in Washington in fall 1943 included representatives of both these agencies as well as officials from the Board of Trade and the Bank of England. Richard Law, the able and diplomatic minister of state in the Foreign Office, headed the contingent. The voyage over was punctuated by seasickness and periodic strategy sessions on how to deal with the Americans. During these meetings James Meade and his colleagues labored to ensure that commercial policy discussions were not trampled in the dust by the Treasury in its drive to secure approval of the monetary union. After some prodding Keynes and Sir David Waley agreed to emphasize in Washington the interconnectedness of trade and finance, and Law was persuaded to address all plenary sessions in lieu of Keynes lest the Americans get the idea that the proposed commercial union was of secondary importance. But Meade and company remained suspicious of Treasury and uncertain of Keynes. They could not forget his periodic flirtation with bilateralism and feared that under pressure he would trade commercial multilateralism for an exchange stabilization scheme.[67]

The British delegation stopped off in New York long enough to do some sightseeing. Meade was dazzled by the view from the Empire State Building at dusk. "The brightly colored taxis and buses moving about the streets like colored insects, or locked in traffic jams; the vast sky scrappers; the huge liners in their berths and the shipping going up and down the Hudson; the cars disappearing in underground roads; and over all 'brilliant light' " seemed to him to comprise a picture that was positively "Wellesian."[68] The "brave new world" aura both attracted and repelled him, his ambivalence no doubt heightened by an awareness of the carnage then taking place in Asia and Europe. The British delegation entrained for Washington, where talks on commercial and financial policy were scheduled to open simultaneously.

Sir Percival Leishing, James Meade, and Lionel Robbins, the chief British negotiators on commercial policy, quickly found themselves in agreement with Dean Acheson, Harry Hawkins, and other interested American officials on the need for a multilateral convention on commercial policy to be implemented by an international trade organization that could interpret the convention, investigate complaints, and settle disputes between members. Both sides agreed on the need to eliminate quantitative restrictions, and on the desirability of finding an automatic tariff-reducing formula that would make possible elimination of imperial preference. The whole affair was remarkably harmonious. These conversations marked the beginning of a deep and abiding friendship between Meade and Hawkins. Their personal security, equanimity, and commitment to Anglo-American multilateralism would stand in sharp contrast to Keynes and White's attitudes. Meade committed his impressions of Hawkins to his diary:

> Hawkins personally seems to be almost the ideally happy man. He has a most interesting and responsible job which he thoroughly enjoys and does extremely well; he has the most beautiful home in the country with horses and other country occupations; he is a happily married man with affectionate children; and he himself is intelligent, well balanced, good tempered and contented. . . . In our commercial policy talks he has been consistently acute and on the spot, but at the same time very sensitive to any difficulties or embarrassments which we may have been in; and instead of trying to score off any such embarrassments, he has always tried to help us out of our difficulties.[69]

Yet the talks were informal and inconclusive; Washington and London were no closer at the end of 1943 to signing a convention or even agreeing on the principles governing the writing of such a convention than they had been in 1942.[70] In part, the inconclusiveness of these talks stemmed from the fact that financial negotiations had simultaneously ground to a halt. As Meade was forced to admit, everything commercial or political hinged on the conclusion of a satisfactory currency agreement.[71]

The British delegation included financial experts from the War Cabinet Secretariat, the Bank of England, the Foreign Office, the Board of Trade, and other agencies as well as a bevy of Treasury officials. White led a coalition of "experts" from Treasury, State, the Office of War Mobilization, the Federal Reserve System, and the Foreign Economic Administration. Each nation's standard was carried and the brunt of the conversations was borne, however, by the authors of the monetary plans under discussion—Keynes and White. The two had met and talked only briefly during White's visit to London the previous October. There was not, as it turned out, a good mix of personalities. Keynes's condescension, glibness, imperiousness, and cutting wit found no better reception with the Americans than White's irascibility, bluntness, and general irritability did with Keynes.

Keynes was in fighting trim when he arrived in Washington. He had entertained his colleagues on the trip down from New York with set pieces on Hitler and the sterility of the American countryside. After reading reams of United States periodicals in record time, he and Nigel Ronald engaged in heated debate over modern painting while Lydia Lopokova sang the *Casse-Noisette* at the top of her voice and danced it with her hands. Meade recalled that "we had been instructed to slip into Washington unnoticed," but that "as far as the Keynes party was concerned, I do not think we attained our objective."[72]

The first meeting on finance was held in Washington on September 15. Keynes and White proceeded to bump heads over the relative freedom of member nations to depreciate their currencies, the powers of the governing body, the amount of liability each state would assume, and whether the proposed international financial system should rely on an artificial currency of gold-backed dollars.

The currency talks were characterized throughout by discord and ill-temper, especially when compared to the commercial policy conversations. "What absolute bedlam these discussions are," remembered Meade. "Keynes and White sit next to each other, each flanked by a long row of his own supporters. Without any agenda or any prepared idea of what is going to be discussed they go for each other in a strident duet of discord which after a crescendo of abuse on either side leads up to a chaotic adjournment of the meeting."[73] Out of these confrontations came just one significant compromise. On September 28 White confirmed that he was in favor of increasing aggregate quotas from $5 billion to $10 billion. Keynes thereupon agreed to accept a limitation on United States commitments to the stabilization fund of $3 billion.

On 9 October 1943, White gave Keynes a draft statement of what was supposed to be the record of their conversations and the principles agreed upon by the two groups. Keynes read the document and threw it on the floor. It was useless to continue the negotiations, he said. White was furious, but he restrained himself. He had the upper hand in the Anglo-American dialogue over postwar financial policy; America and America alone could guarantee the future economic and military security of Europe. Yet no system of postwar monetary stabilization could hope to succeed without British participation. Even if it wanted to, the Roosevelt administration could never persuade Congress and the American people to undertake relief and reconstruction without some promise of benefits. Only if other countries shared or appeared to share through participation in an international organization the responsibility for curing the world's economic ills would the people and their representatives go along. White could not afford to let the talks collapse. "We will try to produce," he shot back at Keynes, "a document Your Highness can understand."[74] Later in the day, the Americans submitted a statement outlining the areas of agreement and disagreement.

Keynes's fit of temper was the result as much of constraints placed on him by the War Cabinet as American intransigence. The British delegation in Washington had, after much discussion, recommended to London that Britain compromise and accept agreement on the variation of exchange rates that did not include an "objective test," a precise arithmetical formula (percentage of imports in excess of percentage of exports; payments deficits, etc.) under which a member could depreciate its currency without the approval of the fund. Instead, British representatives recommended a formula that allowed members to devalue 10 percent unconditionally, a further 10 percent subject to subsequent approval, and even perhaps another 10 percent contingent on prior approval. The cabinet had resisted. "Certain circles in the Treasury and the Bank of England have always been afraid of the council of the international body lining up against us and voting us out of the possibility of manipulating our exchanges," Cherwell wrote Churchill.[75] These forces, led by Sir Hubert Henderson had, with Keynes, Sir David Waley, and other multilateralists away in Washington, gained temporary ascendancy over Sir John Anderson, the new chancellor of the Exchequer. An ardent empire protectionist in commercial policy, Anderson believed that 10 percent or even 20 percent would not meet the difficulties of a country that found its monetary resources being drained away.

Cherwell intervened in behalf of Keynes and the 10/10/10 proposal. Britain must go along with the concept of currency stabilization, he told Churchill. "After all, we must assume that the Council of the Fund will behave reasonably." If it did, there would be no problem; if it did not, the whole international monetary scheme would fail. Cherwell still envisioned a governing body dominated by Anglo-America anyway: "The Americans seem to be coming round to the view of a small executive committee, which it may be hoped the Empire and the United States would control; if this is done, the [British] Treasury's anxiety should be superfluous."[76]

Despite Attlee's protests, the paymaster general secured a partial victory for Keynes and the British delegation over the forces of nationalism, but it was partial indeed. Under the terms of the Joint Statement that ended the financial phase of Anglo-American discussions on October 9, Keynes agreed that parity changes past an initial 10 percent could not be made without the approval of the fund. The governing body would have to grant permission if the change was essential to the correction of a fundamental disequilibrium; and it could not reject on the grounds that the disequilibrium was being caused by the domestic social or economic policy of the requesting country. Who was to decide if a fundamental disequilibrium existed was not clear, and no attempt was made to define the concept.[77]

Thus, the Joint Statement that emerged from the Washington conversations did not include British acceptance of the principle of convertibility. There was wide agreement on the purpose of the stabilization fund and on the method of operation, but on the crucial issue of free exchange of currencies at stable rates—nothing. Britain reserved the right of unilateral depreciation and even the imposition of exchange controls during periods of "disequilibrium." The essence of internationalism in the economic as well as the political sphere is the renunciation of unilateral action and a willingness to trust the community to look after the interests of its individual members. In 1943 even between Britain and America, two nations that were "fighting as one," that trust was missing. Indeed, at the cabinet's insistence the British experts inserted into the Joint Statement an absolute disclaimer; the conversations had committed Britain to nothing.[78]

4. No Entangling Alliances: Isolationism, Anti-imperialism, Appeasement, and the Politics of the Grand Alliance, 1942–1943

MULTILATERALISM was a drama played out within the wider political and strategic context of the Grand Alliance, and the Roosevelt administration's policy toward its two principal partners was determined largely by its perception of public and congressional opinion. Actually, Franklin Roosevelt and his advisers were devotees of realpolitik, and they longed for the freedom to deal in a pragmatic fashion with the international crises that threatened American interests. But the White House dreamed an impossible dream.

Passage of the Lend-Lease Act in March 1941 marked the culmination of an effort by the federal executive to reassert itself in foreign affairs. Isolationism, defined both as nonintervention into European affairs and the preservation of congressional prerogatives in foreign policy-making, was driven into temporary eclipse. But the isolationists had no intention of allowing the Roosevelt administration and internationalism, which they equated with interventionism and executive control of foreign policy, to go unchallenged. Isolationist Republican leaders such as Arthur Vandenberg, Robert Taft, and Gerald Nye had opposed lend-lease in 1941 because they believe that passage would lead directly to United States involvement in the war. For many, the Japanese attack on December 7 simply confirmed their suspicions. As the war progressed, the isolationists, often in uneasy and ironic alliance with Wilsonian internationalists, acted to see that Britain gained no political or economic "advantage" as a result of American aid and to ensure that the Roosevelt administration refrained from making meaningful commitments to the physical security of postwar Europe. The residual strength of the isolationists and their ability to make limited common cause with American internationalists had profound implications for Anglo-American relations.

In the economic sphere, the Roosevelt administration, led by the Treasury Department, and, after 1943, by the Foreign Economic Administration (FEA), reflected isolationist-internationalist sentiments by laboring assiduously to hold British gold/dollar balances to a minimum. Responding in part to Congress's fiscal conservatism and in part to Treasury's determination to dominate any postwar financial system that came into being, Washington manipulated lend-lease in such a way as to prevent London from building up its cash reserves. In the process, the United States government rejected the pooling concept of lend-lease in which all nations contributed according to their ability and shared according to their need, and insisted instead that America was making up "deficits" in its allies' war production. Under the latter approach, the United States was entitled to compensation at war's end and to control distribution of lend-lease during the war. In strategic matters Washington responded to isolationist-internationalist pressure by thwarting an early attempt by the United Kingdom and the Soviet Union to work out a spheres-of-interest deal for postwar Europe. At the same time, Roosevelt and his lieutenants launched both rhetorical and substantive attacks on British imperialism. Denied access to "sphere of interest, power politics" and forced to distance itself from its principal wartime ally, the administration sought the stabilization of postwar Europe by attempting to conciliate the Kremlin. In pursuit of this policy the United States from 1942 to 1943 held Britain at arm's length while allowing Soviet gold/dollar balances to rise, and assured Stalin of America's determination to look after Russia's security needs following V-E Day.

As Richard Darilek has pointed out, the lingering tendency of isolationist leaders in Congress to blame Pearl Harbor on lend-lease indicates that they still clung to the isolationist position, basically refusing to recognize the worldwide aims of the Axis or admit that the United States had a responsibility to confront aggression abroad. Taking their cue from Robert Taft, congressional Republicans in 1942 were soon able to depart from a purely defensive posture and began to hold the administration, in Arthur Vandenberg's words, "strictly accountable" for effective and efficient prosecution of the war. GOP congressional members, sensing strong public support for criticism in this area, cast themselves as watchdogs over the administration's conduct of the war and acted out the role by stepping up attacks on executive personnel and organizations.[1] By autumn 1942 the national unity generated by Pearl Harbor seemed to be disintegrating. The war was not going well. The successful North African landings and the Battle of Midway were two dim stars in the strategic void. The home front seemed to be faring no better. Despite rationing and price controls, shortages abounded. The Office of Price Administration (OPA) was already a lightning rod for public discontent.[2]

The conduct-of-the-war issue not only diverted attention from the GOP's prewar isolationism, it also freed it to renew its assault on the New Deal. Republicans and some southern Democrats began supporting Taft's call for cuts in nondefense spending and for elimination of such New Deal agencies as the Civilian Conservation Corps, the Farm Security Administration, the National Youth Administration, and the WPA. By April Taft had drafted a resolution to be presented to the Republican National Committee, scheduled to meet that month in Chicago, which called on the party to oppose all administration efforts to use the war as an excuse for launching unsound domestic programs. The resolutions, which also pledged the party to preserve free and private enterprise as well as equal opportunity for all, was accepted unconditionally at the meeting. This aggressive posture, coupled with dissatisfaction with the course of the war and low voter turnout, produced an astounding Republican rebound in the 1942 midterm congressional elections.

On November 3, five days before the first Allied landings in North Africa, voters went to the polls and gave Republicans forty-four additional seats in the House and nine in the Senate, the party's best showing in a national election since the 1920s. Roosevelt's margin of support was cut to the lowest level of his presidential career.[3] Both of the president's forays into the campaign—to defeat arch-isolationist Hamilton Fish in New York and reelect George Norris in Nebraska—were failures.

Despite these successes, Republican isolationists could hardly oppose lend-lease when the measure came up for renewal; public opinion was overwhelmingly in favor of passage in 1943, and Vandenberg made it clear that he and his colleagues would vote "yes." It soon became apparent, however, that Republicans in Congress, in line with Vandenberg's objective of holding the administration to "strict accountability," intended to scrutinize and seek justification for every provision. Their hope, of course, was to weaken the executive's power over administration of the program while strengthening Congress's. Led by Hugh A. Butler (R-Nebr.), the Republicans began their drive in the Senate in January when they demanded a complete congressional investigation of the aid program. Butler criticized it for being based on "the dole" and compared the program to a global WPA. He argued that it would eventually wreck the American Treasury and contribute to the spread of communism.

If congressional rhetoric is any guide, Republican isolationists were worried lest FDR use lend-lease to involve the nation in postwar commitments in the areas of foreign aid, tariffs, finance, and military bases without congressional approval. Various statements by administration officials during renewal hearings in spring 1943 heightened those suspicions. In response to a question from J. William Fulbright (D-Ark.), Edward Stettinius expressed the view that lend-lease would be an appropriate and constitutional means of helping to restore order and economic health in war-devastated countries. Vandenberg responded in behalf of the conservative majority by asserting that lend-lease was a mechanism for wartime use only. In the House, John M. Vorys (R-Ohio) introduced an amendment to the lend-lease extension bill. It reserved to Congress ultimate control of any "final determination of benefits" under the program. Vorys's proposal stated, in essence, that Congress refused to be bound by Article VII and in so doing seemed to bear out John Maynard Keynes's gloomiest predictions about the American executive's inability to make commitments in diplomatic negotiations.

In their effort to weaken the executive's control over foreign aid, congressional isolationists charged that Great Britain and the Soviet Union were concealing and misusing American supplies. Representative Hamilton Fish (R-N.Y.), buoyed by his recent personal victory over the White House, alleged that the British were selling lend-lease materials to their own people, depositing the proceeds in the British Treasury, "and not returning one cent to us for the goods."[4]

Congressional demands for legislative oversight of lend-lease were part of a general deterioration of relations between Congress and the executive that occurred in mid-1943. The White House ruffled legislative feathers when it announced that no members of Congress or reporters were to be permitted to attend the United Nations Food Conference scheduled for May 1943 in Hot Springs, Virginia. But the flap over the food conference was mild compared to the outburst of congressional jealousy that occurred in June, when Roosevelt informed House and Senate leaders that he intended to secure United States participation in the proposed United National Relief and Rehabilitation Administration (UNRRA) by means of executive agreement rather than by treaty.[5] Arthur Vandenberg declared the procedure to be "clearly a preview of the method by which the President and State Department intend to bypass Congress in general, and the Senate in particular, in settling every war and post-war issue by the use of more 'Executive Agreements.' "[6] To Charles McNary he later remarked privately that, as it was written, "this 'draft agreement' pledged our total resources to whatever unlimited scheme for relief and rehabilitation all around the world which our New Deal crystal gazers might desire to pursue."[7]

Congress chose to strike back by launching two official inquiries into lend-lease. In fall 1943 five members of the Senate Military Affairs Committee returned from a tour of the war's battlefronts and made their report to Congress. They confirmed charges of widespread waste and mismanagement of lend-lease funds among the Allies, particularly the British. The senators accused Britain of using lend-lease supplies to win friends and influence people at the expense of the United States in areas of interest to both, particularly the oil-producing regions of the Middle and Far East. One of the five senators, Owen Brewster (R-Maine), called for a Senate investigation of all lend-lease operations abroad. Immediately, the Senate Committee to Investigate the National Defense Program (the Truman committee), set to work, and on November 5 its chairman, Harry S. Truman, issued a report on lend-lease. Asserting that the aid program was never intended as a device to shift Allied war costs to the United States, the committee proposed that, if the beneficiaries could not repay in dollars after the war, they might transfer some of their international assets to America.[8] The report further insisted that America's allies be compelled to utilize their resources to the maximum before requesting additional aid from the United States.

There were Anglophiles and "internationalists" in the House and Senate who fought against what they considered the pettiness and parsimony of Congress. "It discourages me that we have fallen to a status in our thinking that leads us to give prominent, and almost first, consideration to the question of who is furnishing the most money in this war," Congressman John Folger (D-N.C.) wrote FDR. Congressional investigations of lend-lease with accompanying debates and controversies would "furnish to our enemies the greatest measure of satisfaction and jubilation."[9] But those who argued for liberal implementation were in a minority.

The State Department, the White House, and indeed most of the foreign policy establishment, with the exception, perhaps, of Jesse Jones, viewed Congress's efforts to assert itself over lend-lease with extreme alarm. Harry Hawkins, Dean Acheson, Cordell Hull, and Harry Hopkins all agreed that if the president's authority to determine compensation was overridden, lend-lease would become a "political football" with Congress very likely to require payment in dollars for aid rendered.[10] Confronted with the prospect of a resurrection of the old war debts issue, Britain and other members of the anti-Axis coalition would be extremely reluctant to accept additional lend-lease unless and until they were "so desperately in need of aid to avoid a present military noose that they would not hesitate to stick their heads into an economic noose which our Congress might pull tight in the future."[11] There would be a tendency, Hawkins asserted to Hull, to delay receipt of aid with the consequent risk that battles might be lost and the war prolonged.[12]

Deciding that the best defense was a good offense, State Department spokespersons immediately began circulating among the prickliest of congressmen and senators, promising that, if they left Roosevelt free to establish the principles governing final terms, Congress would have "several chances" (e.g., renewal of the trade agreements legislation) to support or reject measures designed to implement Article VII. In the end, both houses passed the lend-lease extension bill by overwhelming margins, but they had served notice that Congress intended to assert itself in postwar foreign policy-making and convinced the administration that economic isolationism was far from dead in the United States. Roosevelt would have preferred to ignore Congress—he once told Charles Bohlen that the Senate was a bunch of obstructionists and the only way to get anything done in the American government was to bypass them—but he could not.[13]

In the wake of this congressional onslaught and despite the advice of his internationalist associates, President Roosevelt began to retreat from the common pooling concept and to reintroduce the dollar sign into lend-lease. From spring 1941 through August 1945 when lend-lease was abruptly terminated, the administration of United States aid to Great Britain was punctuated by periodic debates over whether the program should operate on the pooling principle or the deficit principle. The British, not surprisingly, argued for the pooling theory: each nation contributed what it could in tanks, food, planes, cotton, petroleum, shipping, and so forth to a common Anglo-American pool. The combined chiefs then distributed these commodities to British and American military and civilian authorities according to need. At war's end, surplus items would be allocated to each country on the basis of its overall contribution to the war effort. Whitehall rejected the notion that Washington was subsidizing or making up a deficit in Britain's war production and the corollary ideas that the United States was entitled unilaterally to control the destiny of lend-lease, that all surplus at war's end belonged to America, and that Britain owed America compensation for lend-lease.

Roosevelt, Hopkins, and other American officials had paid periodic lip service to the pooling theory during the course of the war. In his fifth report to Congress on lend-lease delivered in June 1942, Roosevelt declared:

All the United Nations are seeking maximum conversion to war production in light of their special resources. If each country devoted roughly the same fraction of its national production to the war, then the financial burden of war is distributed equally among the United Nations in accordance with their ability to pay. And although the nations richest in resources are able to make larger contributions, the claim against each is relatively the same. Such a distribution of the financial cost of the war means that no nation will grow rich from the war effort of its allies. The money cost of the war will fall according to the rule of equality and sacrifice.[14]

FDR and other American leaders seemed to accept the approach because, as one official put it: "The common pool theory lends itself easily to inspiring statements that arouse the loyalties of men to a common cause."[15] In fact, as the State and Treasury departments repeatedly pointed out in internal memos, lend-lease was consistently administered according to deficit rather than to the pooling concept.

The foreign policy establishment rejected the notion that the pooling principle involved equality of sacrifice. The idea of "maximum conversion to war production" was not a fiscal concept but a political one based on willingness to sacrifice. The maximum in a politically realistic sense was determined by the revenue the government could raise from the public by taxation, borrowing, and inflation, and still stay in power. On this basis, a pooling was obtained if each country, with maximum conversion, met the financial cost of its own production, making no charge to its allies for production turned over to them. In practice, this meant all transfers would take the form of subsidies—no war debts—and national authorities were free to determine, through their taxation, rationing, and manpower controls, how much of their productive capacity would be made available to the pool; pooling in practice, then, meant simply that each country put into the pool what it decided to put into the pool. Franklin Roosevelt did indeed intend to eliminate the dollar sign from lend-lease, but neither he nor any other American official was willing to share control equally with British officials over a "common pool" of supplies and munitions to which the United States contributed 85 percent and the empire 15 percent. Article V of the British Master Agreement drawn up after the United States entered the war clearly implied a deficit theory: "The Government of the United Kingdom will return to the United States of America at the end of the present emergency, as determined by the President, such defense articles transferred under this agreement as shall not have been lost, destroyed, or consumed."[16]

Nonetheless, the White House for propaganda purposes continued to lead the British and the American people to believe that it was operating on the pooling principle. As late as August 25, 1943, in a cover letter to the administration's report to Congress, Roosevelt asserted: "The Congress in passing and extending the Lend-Lease Act made it plain that the United States wants no new war debt to jeopardize the coming peace. Victory and a secure peace are the only coin in which we can be repaid."[17] The resulting isolationist rumblings on Capitol Hill alarmed the president. At a press conference held in early September 1943 a few days after the White House had submitted its lend-lease report to Congress, FDR told reporters that the cover letter had not had his approval and was "a condensation of truth which might lead to misunderstanding."[18] He also said that, while the United States did not necessarily expect repayment in dollars of lend-lease advances, it was his thought that the recipients would repay all they possibly could.

FDR's defenders claimed subsequently that he was preoccupied with the course of the war. He would make whatever concessions necessary to Congress to keep supplies flowing to America's allies. But Roosevelt was concerned with more than the fate of the war effort. Congress, after all, overwhelmingly approved the extension of lend-lease in 1943 and again in 1944. Because 1944 was an election year, the president undoubtedly wanted to convince the electorate that he was running the war on a businesslike basis. As one American official told Richard Law during the Washington conversations, the theory of pooling and mutual aid was "very bad politics" in America.[19]

Rejection of the pooling concept by Washington raised grave doubts within the British Treasury and Foreign Office about the Roosevelt administration's commitment to the economic well-being of postwar Britain. Reinforcing that concern was continuing controversy over British gold and dollar reserves. The White Plan, the United States Treasury believed, was more than adequate to prevent perfidious Albion from draining Fort Knox in the postwar period. But in the meantime, according to Henry Morgenthau and Harry White, there was considerable danger that Britain, relieved of the burden of purchasing munitions, food, and raw materials by lend-lease, would be able to use American aid to build up its gold/dollar reserves.[20]

In fact, the British Treasury hoped to do just that. Chancellor of the Exchequer Sir Kingsley Wood wrote Anthony Eden in spring 1942, explaining the gold/dollar reserve situation. The United Kingdom could pay for current orders in the United States with the annual gold production of South Africa, but the issue was not the availability of gold to cover dollar commitments; the issue was security against sterling indebtedness. With overseas obligations increasing at a rate of $400–500 million a year, while purchases of newly mined gold would not exceed $100 million a year, "we need an adequate gold reserve in view of the large obligations which we are incurring to countries other than the United States, including those in the Sterling Areas."[21] The willingness of Britain's sterling partners to accept blocked balances in lieu of payment depended in part on their faith that sterling would be ultimately convertible. That faith, in turn, was dramatically affected by the size of Britain's reserves. Moreover, Treasury wanted to maximize British gold/dollar holdings in order to be in the best possible position to bargain with the United States over the shape of the postwar economy.

In the matter of dollar balances, as with almost every other issue, the British found the Roosevelt administration split, with the Treasury determined to hold down British gold/dollar reserves while the State Department took a much more understanding attitude toward Britain's need for a stash. Morgenthau and White held that lend-lease was essentially a wartime measure designed by Congress to furnish America's allies with the material they needed to defeat the Axis. Nothing in the act empowered the Treasury to use lend-lease to build Britain's dollar balances beyond an absolute minimum.[22]

Hull and Acheson regarded finance purely as a means to a commercial end, and they were not nearly as interested as Morgenthau and White in making the United States Treasury the arbiter of world monetary affairs. Large British assets, in their opinion, were indispensable to the proper functioning of a system of multilateral trade. Adolf Berle's International Reserve Bank had not been nearly as concerned as White's stabilization fund with holding down foreign reserves. In addition, the State Department tended to be less sensitive to congressional prerogatives than did Morgenthau and his minions. Unfortunately for Britain, Treasury rather than State had been assigned the overall responsibility for lend-lease, and Congress, jealous of its authority over appropriations, did in fact have to renew lend-lease every six months.[23]

The first significant discussions on British balances occurred in fall 1942. In October, Morgenthau and White took an extended trip to England to tour United States military installations, to talk with General Dwight D. Eisenhower's staff about currency problems in liberated areas, and to hold unofficial discussions on postwar finance with Keynes, Wood, and other British officials. Roosevelt was enthusiastic about the trip. "The President said that he was very glad I was going, and wanted me to find out certain things which he thought should be observed in England," Morgenthau noted in his diaries. "He said that he had heard the English would not let certain other Nationals trade in certain territories, and he wished that I would find out about it . . . the President wants all these Colonies, et cetera, open to all the world."[24] But the issue that would dominate the trip was the level of British gold/dollar balances.

Keynes and the Treasury believed Morgenthau to be more emotional and sentimental than White, and they decided to take advantage of his presence and his obvious sympathy for Britain's suffering on the home front to try to persuade him to liberalize the United States Treasury's position on Britain's reserves. To his English host Morgenthau was something of an enigma. "He certainly is a difficult chap to deal with," Keynes wrote. "I have seldom struck anything stickier than my first interview. One seemed to be able to get no human reaction whatever, which is, I suppose, his method of protection until he discovers what you are after." Morgenthau's acutely suspicious nature led to constant misunderstandings, "while fits of jealousy and depression made one tread on eggshells in his presence." The secretary of the Treasury was not, however, fundamentally unfriendly to Britain, Keynes observed, and he seemed to be remarkably free of "wrong motives." Keynes believed there was much truth in his wife Lydia's evaluation: "He is a good man and will do you no harm *on purpose*."[25]

At a dinner for Morgenthau given on the fifteenth, Wood, fully briefed by Keynes and his other subordinates, raised the issue of gold/dollar balances, thus beating, so he thought, his counterpart to the punch. It was always advisable, Keynes had told the chancellor, to mold the thinking of Americans before those thoughts had crystallized on their own.[26] After dinner Wood thanked Morgenthau for the invaluable service he had rendered in helping secure passage of a wartime aid program for Great Britain. Because of lend-lease, United States assumption of prior commitments, reciprocal aid (British lend-lease to America), and United States expenditures for troop pay and other purposes in Great Britain, gold/dollar balances had reached $400 million and would, unless the United States cut back on lend-lease food or other items, continue to rise. Wood pled with Morgenthau to allow that to happen. Britain had no dollar problem with the United States; lend-lease had taken care of that. But the sterling indebtedness was rising, Wood exaggerated, at an annual rate of $550 million. "We are having to meet the major part of the sums I have referred to [war expenditures abroad] . . . merely on tick without any provision of how they are ultimately to be paid, but with the liability to find the money when called upon, not only in this country itself, but for the post-war expenditure of these countries in the United States and elsewhere."[27]

What Wood did not tell Morgenthau was that a number of officials, including Sir David Waley, had expressed the opinion that the sterling debts would never have to be funded, that the Dominions could be persuaded to forgive them as their contribution to the war effort. However, they advised, if it became apparent that Britain *could not* fund them and *could not* make sterling convertible into gold/dollars, the more perverse and intractable members of the imperial family might demand funding. At the least, rumors of a default on the sterling debt would undermine Dominion confidence in sterling and reduce Britain's ability to borrow during a future international crisis.[28]

Morgenthau was unmoved. On January 3, the day after his return to Washington, he reported to the president. The United Kingdom had accumulated nearly $1 billion worth of gold in dollars, more than enough, he said. Through its control over lend-lease, United States purchases in England, and dollar expenditures for troops there, America could and should keep those reserves down to between $600 million and $1 billion. Congress and the American people were not sacrificing to enrich Britain. Roosevelt agreed.

Despite the United States Treasury's concerted efforts at obstruction, the British managed to rebuild their gold/dollar holdings until they reached $1.2 billion in July 1943.[29] These reserves, as Lord Cherwell reported to Winston Churchill, were likely to reach $2 billion within the next year as American troop concentrations in Britain, Australia, and India increased and as these soldiers spent their wages. Meanwhile, in January 1943 the president had reaffirmed Treasury's proposal that the United States manipulate lend-lease aid so as to hold British balances between $600 million and $1 billion, and had appointed a committee headed by Morgenthau to guide lend-lease policy to this end. In September during the Washington conversations, Keynes submitted a memorandum on the dollar balance issue to State, Treasury, and the Lend-Lease Administration; and at the first Quebec Conference, Churchill presented a similar document to Roosevelt and Hopkins. The arguments were familiar. Britain would face the postwar period with external liabilities of not less than $10 billion. If British gold/dollar balances were allowed to rise to $2 billion, they would still constitute but one-fifth of Britain's assumed liabilities and its only "quick assets" against those liabilities. On the whole, British indebtedness was increasing five or six times as rapidly as its reserves.[30]

As had been the case in 1942, the State Department and the Lend-Lease Administration were sympathetic to Britain's position; Treasury was not. Edward Stettinius, Oscar Cox, and Dean Acheson readily admitted that Washington could not allow British agencies or private British exporters to redistribute lend-lease goods for political or commercial profit, but there was no need to use lend-lease to hold British gold and dollar balances to a certain level. Morgenthau, however, remained adamant. After returning in late October from a trip to Italy and North Africa, he wrote FDR calling for an adjustment of lend-lease with a view to reducing British reserves to the $1 billion level the president had approved in January.[31]

Morgenthau's campaign to restrain the growth of Britain's gold/dollar holdings received a decided boost when the head of the newly created Foreign Economic Administration, Leo Crowley, joined the debate on Treasury's side. FEA was a product of the White House's decision to put an end to the wrangling between the feuding Reconstruction Finance Corporation and the Board of Economic Warfare by creating a new agency.

The man whom Roosevelt and Hopkins chose to head this new bureaucracy was a Wisconsin utilities executive and banker who had gone to Washington in 1934 as chairman of the Federal Deposit Insurance Corporation. From the White House's perspective, Crowley was particularly well suited for his new post. Identified with none of the major factions then contending for control of American foreign policy, Crowley was also a prominent Catholic layman who could and did serve as liaison with Irish Catholics during the 1944 campaign.[32]

A number of factors combined to make Crowley and the FEA bureaucratic allies of the Treasury Department on the British reserves question. For much of his life the new FEA head had been a professional Irishman; Anglophobia came naturally to him. He was a bureaucratic entrepreneur and as such was intensely aware of Congress's determination to influence foreign economic policy. If he could please the House and the Senate, he could survive, and his empire would flourish. According to Harold Ickes, Crowley had made a lot of money in banking in the 1920s only to lose it during the 1930s. His scrape with bankruptcy had made him insecure and cautious. Finally, Crowley and FEA found themselves almost immediately at odds with the State Department and hence with its lenient attitude toward British reserves.[33] Shortly after his confirmation, Crowley warned Dean Acheson that FEA had "clear authority from Congress to act in all matters relating to economic warfare."[34]

Throughout late October and early November, the British pressed the White House for a final decision on the balances issue, "a decision which is of absolutely vital importance to our financial capacity to get through the transitional period and, indeed, to our diplomatic independence during that time," Cherwell wrote Churchill.[35] Congress and certain elements of the administration seemed to be moving toward the view that, however great Britain's external liabilities, "We are not entitled to lend-lease as long as we have a dollar in the till." London complained to Washington that its position ignored Britain's contributions to the war effort before Pearl Harbor, the ravages caused by the Battle of Britain, and the United Kingdom's smaller resources. Besides, muttered Whitehall, Washington's insistence on limiting Britain's gold/dollar holdings would constitute a gross violation of British sovereignty. Officials in the United Kingdom were particularly outraged because America apparently proposed to link lend-lease to gold/dollar holdings only in the case of Britain. Russia held almost $2 billion in gold with no external liabilities, but the Roosevelt administration was not proposing to enforce an arbitrary limitation on Russian reserves.

On November 14 Morgenthau called in Lord Halifax and gave him the bad news: $1 billion was to be the maximum. The Lend-Lease Administration would begin cutting specific items such as sugar, steel, and cotton—nonmilitary items—until Britain's gold/dollar holdings reached the proper level. Moreover, if British Embassy and Treasury officials did not stop lobbying with the State Department behind Treasury's back, Morgenthau warned, Congress might abandon lend-lease altogether. The secretary admitted that liquidity in the transitional period was going to be a problem, but lend-lease was not the answer. If Britain would agree to cut down its balances, "I would be glad to tackle your other post-war problem of what you're going to do with your big sterling balances."[36]

Vague magnanimity, however, was not enough for the British. It seemed to Whitehall that not only the health of Europe's economy but also that of the United States required more, not less, wartime and postwar aid. But how could Britain keep the American cornucopia intact and fight off attacks on the Exchequer's gold/dollar reserves? Playing one American bureaucratic entity off against another was dangerous, but the situation seemed to demand it. Dollar balances and the administration of lend-lease involved the fate of multilateralism and the postwar security of Europe, and were much too important to be left to a bureaucratic megalomaniac and a professional Irishman.

London's chief bureaucratic ally in the lend-lease and dollar balance issues continued to be the State Department. Fall 1943 witnessed something of a comeback by Cordell Hull and his associates. The secretary had convinced himself that the department's principal wartime task should be to lay the groundwork for an enduring peace in the postwar era. Just as he considered multilateralism as the only alternative to neo-mercantilism in the economic sphere, internationalism in the form of a collective security organization was the only alternative to militarism and nationalism in the political sphere.

In October 1943 Joseph Stalin agreed to a foreign ministers' meeting in Moscow as a prelude to a gathering of the Big Three scheduled for Teheran in November. Hull was thus presented with an opportunity to sell his program directly to the British and the Russians. The trip, given the secretary's previous isolation from strategic decision making, was something of a triumph. It followed hard on the heels of a major bureaucratic victory. The president had finally given in to Hull's pleadings in September and asked for the resignation of Sumner Welles, whose independence and power had been an ever-increasing source of anxiety for the secretary. Rejuvenated, the aging Tennessean traveled to Moscow and negotiated energetically with Anthony Eden and Vyacheslav Molotov. The Russians wanted to talk only of the proposed second front in the West and the British of political arrangements in Italy. Nonetheless, Hull won his colleagues' endorsement of the Moscow Declaration, which pledged the three nations to work for the establishment of a postwar collective security organization and to consult and act jointly in the meantime to maintain law and order around the world.

It became clear to the secretary in Moscow that Britain could not and would not be able to accept multilateralism or shoulder its fair share of the burden in a revamped League of Nations if it, the only one of the Allies to emerge from the war with a large debt, was forced to expend its gold and dollar reserves. Back in Washington, he, Acheson, Hawkins, and Pasvolsky plotted against Treasury's scheme to hold down British balances, and for a time the Tennessee-Thames connection succeeded in blocking any and all cuts.[37]

With British gold/dollar balances steadily rising, Morgenthau and Crowley decided to go directly to the president. They described the growth of British assets, reviewed the mood of Congress, and cited the Truman Report specifically. "Neither Britain's international financial position outside the United States nor its postwar needs were among the considerations which prompted Congress to pass the Lend-Lease Act," they observed, and they asked permission to reduce some parts of nonmilitary assistance to the United Kingdom—fish, sugar, paper, and tobacco.[38] On January 5 the president wrote his warring subordinates, ordering a final round of discussions with the British with "the distinct understanding that I will be given a final report within 30 days, i.e. February 7, 1944."[39] Hull, Acheson, and their counterparts in the British Embassy reasoned that the only way they could stave off nonmilitary lend-lease cuts was to expose Treasury's true motive—a desire to arbitrarily hold down gold/dollar reserves—and in the process provide Churchill with an opportunity to protest directly this infringement of British sovereignty.

The president's directive produced a meeting of Anglo-American officials on January 7 in Hull's office. Thirty minutes before the British arrived, Acheson and White had a heated exchange. The British would want to know if the United States was trying to suppress their dollar balances by chopping away item after item from nonmilitary lend-lease all the while citing domestic political pressures as justification, Acheson observed. The United States ought to have the object of the cuts clearly in mind and tell the British. White said he did not understand how the two aspects of the problem could be kept distinct. What might be regarded as politically feasible when British reserves stood at several million would not when they reached several billion. Why was Acheson insisting on an either/or interpretation? Instead of answering, Acheson brought up another issue. Was the present list of proposed cuts definitive or did Treasury and FEA intend further reductions if British reserves did not shrink to some "pre-conceived level?" Morgenthau replied testily that he did not intend to make any statement now that would tie his hands in the future.[40] With the arrival of the British delegation, Acheson and Morgenthau sheathed their swords—but only for the moment.

On February 2, Morgenthau, as chairman of the Interdepartmental Committee on Lend-Lease, approved a program he believed would keep British dollar balances within reasonable limits and yet be palatable to the British themselves. The compromise cut nonmilitary lend-lease by $288 million annually, leaving $288 million worth of aid intact.[41] While State believed that this reduction was too much, FEA insisted that it was not enough. With Morgenthau ill with influenza, Crowley raised the dollar balance issue at a February 18 cabinet meeting and proposed further cuts. Roosevelt ordered the three interested agencies to draft a letter to Churchill on the matter for his signature. Undersecretary of State Edward Stettinius (Hull, too, was ill) asked for the task of drafting the letter and was given it. State had volunteered because it saw an opportunity to bring the Treasury-FEA stratagem out into the open and to either persuade FDR to repudiate it or allow Churchill to protest directly.

On February 22 Stettinius gave the president a draft of the telegram to be sent to the prime minister. It mentioned the recent discussions on elimination of items from lend-lease "which have proven to be embarrassing and no longer required," and included a request that the British hold down their dollar reserves to the $1 billion level. "What are your views as to what should be done," the draft asked Churchill bluntly, "and what do you think can be undertaken?" Attached was a cover letter written by Dean Acheson asking that the telegram not be sent. The British had been acting in good faith in lend-lease negotiations, he argued. They had agreed to cuts in deliveries that were proving a political embarrassment to the administration. How in good conscience could Washington make cuts in lend-lease and expect Britain to carry out its responsibilities in the Near East and Far East and make sterling fully convertible in the postwar period? "If the financial side of the war is run in such a way as to keep British balances at or about $1 billion, we thereby reduce our chance to achieve the basic economic policy we want and need," Acheson concluded.[42]

Roosevelt rejected State's advice and sent the telegram, but the undersecretary and his colleagues won a secondary victory. The message to Churchill, which had not been cleared with either FEA or Treasury, made it clear that the administration was determined to limit British dollar balances and would use lend-lease to do it if necessary.[43] As State anticipated, the telegram produced an indignant and effective reply from the prime minister.

Thus bolstered, Churchill told Roosevelt that British gold/dollar balances were off-limits as far as Washington was concerned. Of course, the Exchequer would keep the United States Treasury informed, he told FDR, but this was all that relations between two sovereign nations required. The prime minister ended with a parting shot at Morgenthau; reopening the issue of lend-lease cutbacks in the face of promises to the contrary and linking them to Britain's dollar balances was bad form to say the least.[44]

Not surprisingly, Morgenthau was furious at being outmaneuvered by the State Department. Stettinius and Acheson's machinations had momentarily stalled efforts to further cut nonmunitions lend-lease and, more importantly, put London and the United States Treasury openly at odds. Morgenthau moved quickly to reassume control of foreign financial policy. Calling a meeting of the lend-lease oversight committee, Morgenthau insisted that the United States make it clear to Great Britain that Washington reserved the right to curtail lend-lease when further deliveries became redundant or otherwise unnecessary. Cowed, Hull agreed. The Treasury chief said that henceforward dollar balances should be handled by Treasury alone. Did FEA agree? Crowley nodded. Did State? Hull said that he thought the responsibility ought to be Treasury's and told Morgenthau to ask Dean Acheson what he thought. Acheson, according to White, "appeared slightly embarrassed and seemed hesitant to make the response" but then reluctantly assented. Giving the screw one more turn, Morgenthau said that he had learned Stettinius was going to London in April on a trip to discuss a wide range of subjects and that he wanted Hull to order him specifically to exclude dollar balances from the talks. Hull replied that he had only learned of Stettinius's trip on his return to Washington. He would find out what the undersecretary intended to discuss and order him to stay away from dollar balances.[45]

Cordell Hull and Henry Morgenthau dwelt in a world of power and status. Ideological and even strategic and economic considerations ranked far down their list of priorities. Influence and the appearance of it ranked near the top. Fresh from his trip to Moscow, Hull was intoxicated by the attention that he was receiving. The president had gone so far as to assemble the cabinet and meet him at the airport on his return. Never a match for Morgenthau anyway, the secretary of state now found his momentary sense of euphoria made it easier for him to give way on the matter of Britain's dollar balances.

The drive to hold British monetary reserves to a minimum was a product of the bureaucratic power struggle between Treasury and State and of fiscal conservatism and residual isolationism in Congress. The political and strategic corollary of that policy was a refusal to condone an Anglo-Soviet spheres-of-interest agreement coupled with intermittent attacks on British imperialism. Forced to hold the United Kingdom at arms length, Washington then sought to avoid a postwar clash of superpowers by appeasing the Soviet Union.

During the first six months of 1943 certain political and strategic imperatives began to take shape in the minds of British officials, imperatives that were inextricably intertwined with Anglo-American financial and commercial negotiations. Hitler's invasion of Russia in June 1941 was, as numerous historians have pointed out, a decisive moment in World War II and in modern world history. Germany's surprise attack drew the Soviet Union irrevocably into the war and thrust upon it a life-or-death struggle that would end either with the Wehrmacht in Vladivostok or the Red Army in Berlin. That Operation Barbarossa was of immense significance was readily apparent to the British even if the eventual outcome was uncertain. Assuming that the Allies achieved unconditional surrender, the resurgence of German power was still a distinct possibility; France would probably be unable to serve as an effective counterweight to Germany for years after the war, if ever. But Germany was not the only cloud that loomed on the horizon. The Bolshevik Revolution had done nothing to diminish Russia's traditional desire to control Eastern Europe and the eastern Mediterranean. World War II, Whitehall realized, might present Moscow with the opportunity to achieve those objectives, even to the point of upsetting the European balance of power. Both the German and Russian threats seemed to call for a policy of friendship and cooperation with the Soviet Union, especially given Russia's historical tendency to collaborate with Germany.[46] An early agreement with the Kremlin on spheres of interest could forestall an Anglo-Soviet clash in the postwar world and successfully contain Germany.

The chief advocate, along with Lord Beaverbrook, of an Anglo-Soviet rapprochement in 1941–42 was Anthony Eden. Handsome, vain, ambitious, and able, Eden was a moderate Conservative. Both Churchill and Eden were enthusiastic about extending aid to Russia after Barbarossa; but whereas the prime minister's empathy for Moscow was to prove a temporary phenomenon, the foreign minister "entered a prolonged phase of near infatuation," according to his principal biographer. Churchill wanted to move quickly to head off the " 'Munichers' " within the Conservative party who were staunchly anticommunist and secretly harbored hopes for a compromise peace with Germany. The prime minister was aware that all-out Anglo-American aid could lead to the communization of all or part of Europe, but he was willing to aggrandize Russia in order to defeat Hitler. Eden, at least until 1944, appears to have viewed the Soviet Union as a genuine ally of liberal democracy and as an agent of progress. His hatred of the followers of Chamberlain and his increasing difficulties with Churchill over Soviet issues caused such an overreaction that his political and social views from 1941 to 1944 were more leftist than during any other period in his life. By June 1941, Beatrice Eden noted that her husband had ceased to feel like a Conservative and was getting on exceptionally well with Ernest Bevin.[47]

Yet Anthony Eden was not naive. He had no desire to grant the Kremlin carte blanche; indeed, his proposals for a rapprochement with Russia were designed as much to contain Soviet expansion as to prevent a resurgence of German power. This "realism," of course, reflected the prevailing consensus within the British Foreign Office. Russia, Eden's underlings believed, would take as much of Europe as the Western democracies would allow it.[48]

Following a visit to Moscow and lengthy talks with Stalin and Foreign Minister Vyacheslav Molotov during the opening days of 1941, Eden summed up the situation, as he saw it, for his cabinet colleagues. Russia was determined that the West recognize its pre-1941 claims to the Baltic states and to eastern Poland. To that Britain should not, because it could not, effectively object. Russia's claims to these areas were ancient, and Moscow's domination of them would not constitute a serious threat to the postwar balance of power in Europe. Britain should define the limits of Soviet expansion while the Red Army still remained in Russia, the foreign secretary advised.[49]

While in the Kremlin Eden had raised the possibility of a specific Anglo-Russian treaty whose object would be the containment of Germany and the maintenance of a balance of power in Europe after the war. Stalin and Molotov had been receptive, but they had a price—British endorsement of the annexation of the Baltic states and parts of Finland, Rumania, and Poland. According to one scholar, the USSR was more than willing to pursue a spheres-of-influence policy in 1942. Such a course would, Stalin and Molotov hoped, make impossible a revival of German military power and prevent the formation of an anti-Soviet bloc in Europe, thus maximizing Soviet security and Soviet influence abroad. If Britain and the United States acquiesced, the Grand Alliance could be continued indefinitely.[50] In his report Eden advised paying Moscow's price, and he subsequently convinced Churchill to agree to a twenty-year treaty of alliance that recognized pre-1941 Russian claims in Eastern Europe.

But as both the foreign secretary and the prime minister recognized, any lasting political arrangement would have to be backed by American power. Even with the conclusion of an early spheres-of-interest deal, there was likely to be a massive power void on the Continent at war's end. Potential Russian aggression could be contained through one of two methods—either massive economic aid to all of Europe, including Russia, which would eliminate the socioeconomic roots of totalitarianism in noncommunist areas and induce the Kremlin to pursue a conservative, status quo foreign policy; or massive economic and military aid to non-communist countries alone that would allow them simultaneously to eradicate unemployment, hunger, and the other causes of political extremism and to defend themselves from Soviet armed aggression.[51] Both plans required money and resources—food, oil, machinery, and other raw materials—which only the United States would be in a position to provide. "Unless the Great Powers, particularly those best able to give, i.e., the creditor ones, are ready to make such a sacrifice, it will be a waste of time to bother our heads further about the formulation of post-war plans," concluded Nigel Ronald.[52]

Not surprisingly, there was in 1942 and early 1943 a profound difference of opinion within the British government concerning America's willingness to make a commitment to the security of postwar Europe. Many within the Foreign Office distrusted Roosevelt, the American people, and American institutions. The careerists had a particularly difficult time in perceiving FDR as anything but an old-style Wilsonian. The Atlantic Charter, they condescended, was vague and senti-mental. Roosevelt's insistence on holding down British dollar balances and the administration's refusal to follow up on the monetary and commercial talks seemed to call into question the president's commitment to European security and stability. He appeared weak and too eager to do the bidding of the crowd. Even if the president was willing to provide the resources for the reconstruction and rehabilitation of war-torn Europe and to maintain a balance of power on the Continent, there was real doubt among Foreign Office officials as to whether intentions could be translated into national policy. The Democrats were in power and had been since 1932, but the results of the 1942 congressional elections were not lost on Sir Alexander Cadogan, Oliver Harvey, J. G. Donnelley, Nigel Ronald, and other Foreign Service officers. The GOP had been the majority party in America since the Civil War, and World War II seemed to be giving a fillip to conservatism in the United States. And, Wendell Willkie aside, Republicanism had always meant isolationism, at least as far as Europe was concerned.

Worries existed, too, about the strong strain of idealism in American foreign policy. "There is bound to be difficulty in practice in harmonizing day-to-day Russian cooperation with Anglo-American cooperation," Eden told his cabinet colleagues. "Soviet policy is amoral; United States policy is exaggeratedly moral, at least where non-American interests are concerned."[53] Despite the assurances of such luminaries as Felix Frankfurter, Harry Hopkins, and Cordell Hull, the Foreign Office remained skeptical, then, that the United States would help police Europe.[54]

But the foreign secretary and his advisers were not without hope that America would come around and endorse a specific territorial settlement with the Rus-sians. "As the U.S. becomes more realistically minded under the stress of war, this feeling [repugnance at Russia's territorial aims] may be gradually modified, especially as Russian assistance may be of great assistance in the Japanese war," Eden asserted.[55]

The empire isolationists were convinced that the problem of American isola-tionism was insurmountable, and that the only viable defense against Russian domination of the Continent was a British-led federation of Western European states. "The gyroscopic tendency of nations to revert to their normal course after the violent deflections of such a crisis as the present war is bound to assert itself," insisted Leo Amery. The swing in America away from the "Roosevelt–Cordell Hull"—that is, interventionist—policies had already begun and would inevitably gain momentum. The United States would continue to dominate Latin America and to extend its empire in the Pacific, but it would "wash its hands as quickly as it indecently can of Europe and the Middle East." Russia under Stalin's "elementary realism" would be less interested in peace in Europe than self-aggrandizement.[56] Britain, weakened by the war and preoccupied with empire affairs, should foster and work through a federation of strong, democratic European states. Anglo-American solidarity as a bulwark against the spread of Bolshevism, the empire isolationists insisted, was a pipe dream.

In sharp contrast to Amery and Beaverbrook, Churchill insisted that American isolationism was dead and that Anglo-American solidarity was the best hope for a stable and secure Europe in the postwar era. He believed that the United States was being educated out of isolationism and would be ready at war's end to share Continental responsibilities with Britain.

Shortly after America's entry into the war, Churchill proposed to Roosevelt the establishment between V-E and V-J Day of a "Council of Four." These powers—Russia, the United States, the United Kingdom, and China (included only out of deference to the United States)—would disarm the aggressors and maintain enough military power to police the world. Below the Council of Four would be a series of regional councils for Europe, Asia, Latin America, and the other principal areas of the world. The regional councils would do their best to settle disputes and halt aggression; situations beyond their control would be referred to the Council of Four. It subsequently became clear that what Churchill really envisioned was a "Council of Three" composed of Russia, China, and Anglo-America. By May he was urging, for example, the establishment of joint Anglo-American citizenship and the pooling of all British and American bases. Russia and Britain would be the dominant factors on the European council, but America would tip the scales in favor of Britain, democracy, and free enterprise in case an insoluble problem arose between the two European powers.[57] "None can predict with certainty that the victors will never quarrel amongst themselves, or that the United States may not once again retire from Europe," Churchill wrote Roosevelt, "but after the experiences which all have gone through, their sufferings and the certainty that a third struggle will destroy all that is left of culture, wealth, and civilization of mankind and reduce us to the level almost of wild beasts . . . it is believed that the United States will cooperate with her [Great Britain] and even take the lead of the world."[58]

Churchill and the Foreign Office wanted America to play a strong but not necessarily independent role in world affairs. Whitehall still fancied itself as arbiter of the international community and did not want to relinquish that role. While the English trusted America's instincts and goodwill, they did not trust its intellect or its ability to translate philosophy into action. Inexperience coupled with a problematical constitutional setup could lead to gross mismanagement. Without counsel from London, the Roosevelt administration could wreck relations with Russia—too much carrot or too much stick—and in the process provoke a resurgence of isolationism within the United States. The task ahead, given Europe's certain dependence on American aid in the postwar era, was to manage America—to mold and shape the republic's diplomacy—without letting it know it was being managed.

But the United States would not be managed, at least not in 1943. As the empire isolationists had predicted, the chief obstacle to an Anglo-Soviet rapprochement turned out to be not the anticommunism of British Conservatives, but the scruples of the Roosevelt administration. In fact, by the time Molotov arrived in London on May 20, 1942, to sign an Anglo-Russian pact, Washington had informed both London and Moscow that discussions concerning postwar boundaries were premature; they distracted from the war effort. Under the Atlantic Charter, moreover, the affected peoples of the Baltic and Eastern Europe would have to be consulted. Frustrated, Molotov and Eden had to settle for a pact of peace and friendship only.[59]

Franklin Roosevelt craved freedom of action to pursue his own unique foreign policy in the postwar period. He, Harry Hopkins, Oscar Cox, William D. Leahy, W. Averell Harriman, and his other closest advisers were acutely aware of the fact that the deadlock between the executive and legislative branches in the United States following World War I had hamstrung Woodrow Wilson and prevented him from making his peace program a reality.[60] Roosevelt was determined to avoid Wilson's mistakes; he intended to manage Congress and in so doing prevent an isolationist resurgence. To the White House, congressional control of foreign policy was synonymous with isolationism. While Churchill revered the House of Commons and was scrupulous in observing its prerogatives, Roosevelt regarded Congress and particularly the Senate as an obstacle, a nuisance.

Roosevelt was just as much a pragmatist in foreign affairs as he was in domestic. He was not an internationalist in the pure sense; he did not envision United States participation in a world government in which each nation relinquished part of its national sovereignty for the common good. His guiding principle throughout the war was the Four Policemen. Roosevelt explained to the Joint Chiefs of Staff in 1943 that he wanted "Four Policemen to stand guard against aggression on behalf of the future international organization." Should the "predatory animals, of the world" threaten the peace, the United States, Great Britain, Russia, and China would deter them from aggression even to the point of blockade or bombardment.[61] The Four Policemen were, of course, the Council of Four by another name. Furthermore, Roosevelt and his Advisory Committee on Post–War Foreign Policy believed that air power would be the key force after V-J Day and that America's position as the preeminent manufacturer of long-range aircraft would make the Big Four, and through them the United Nations, dependent on the United States.

The Four Policemen concept, subsequently ensconced in the charter of the United Nations, was actually harmonious with the tenets of American isolationism. In dividing the world into quadrants and relegating the United States to the Western Hemisphere, Roosevelt's strategy merely refined the two-spheres clause of the Monroe Doctrine. Yet because the Four Policemen implied spheres of interest, balance of power, and empire, not only isolationists but also Wilsonian internationalists adamantly opposed the idea.

Cordell Hull and Wendell Willkie were the principal advocates of the new internationalism, a vision of the future based primarily on lessons of the past. In November, after his return from the Moscow Conference, the secretary of state told a joint session of Congress that, given the Moscow Declaration, "there will no longer be need for spheres of influence, for alliances, for balance of power, or any of the other special arrangements through which, in the unhappy past, the nations strove to safeguard their security or to promote their interest."[62] The applause was thunderous. By war's end, the internationalist movement had come to encompass most of the informed public. Americans self-consciously learned the lessons World War II had to teach. Wilson had been right: internationalism and collective security were the only alternatives to appeasement and aggression. As interpreted by its heirs, Wilsonianism called for collective security, disarmament of aggressors, elimination of barriers to trade, anticolonialism, and self-determination of peoples.[63] Gradually, a legislative-executive consensus began to develop around the concept of international cooperation based on a revived League of Nations. Passage of the Fulbright and Connally resolutions by the House and Senate in 1943 and adoption by the Republican party of the Mackinac program the same year were hailed by internationalists as major breakthroughs.

The White House probably secretly agreed with Claire Booth Luce (R-Conn.) that world government was so much "globaloney," but Roosevelt and Hopkins were much impressed with Hull's popularity and the strength of the internationalist movement. Imperialism, spheres of interest, power politics—all had been the bêtes noires of isolationists for a generation, they realized. It was fear of this group and its residual strength inside and outside Congress that had largely been responsible for Roosevelt nixing the 1942 Anglo-Soviet spheres-of-interest deal. But the White House quickly came to realize that internationalists would have been as repelled by the deal as isolationists. In the end, however, the president decided that the United Nations concept could be modified to incorporate the Four Policemen mechanism. In fact, the former could serve as a mask for the latter. The White House became an ostentatious convert to Wilsonian internationalism in 1944, but its underlying commitment to collective security implemented by four great powers within specific geographic regions remained intact.

From the vantage point of the White House, there were two things that could destroy the bridges recently built to Congress, open the way for an isolationist resurgence, and thereby destroy the president's freedom of action in the postwar period: too close an identification with Great Britain, still linked in the minds of the public and Congress with imperialism and the "old diplomacy," and an aggressive, expansionist Soviet Union. By 1943 FDR and his White House advisers perceived America's immediate foreign policy goals to be to envelop the Soviet Union in a blanket of friendship and trust while holding Britain at arm's length.[64] The stakes were high. As Oscar Cox wrote Hopkins, "If we play our cards badly, there will be a revulsion abroad and a counter-revulsion at home, and we'll be back a long way."[65]

Hitler's declaration of war four days after Pearl Harbor made the United States and the Soviet Union allies, and the president never looked back. Lend-lease to Russia, which had begun in 1941, was accelerated. The president's promise to Molotov of a second front in 1942 was made in earnest if also in error. The White

House recognized early on that Russia and America would emerge from the war as the world's strongest powers. If they could maintain their relationship, no third force could prevail against them. Roosevelt realized that vast differences in culture, language, and ideology separated the United States from the Soviet Union. He had no illusions concerning the nature of Stalin's domestic rule, a dictatorship no less pervasive and oppressive than Hitler's. But he believed the Russian form of totalitarianism to be less dangerous than the German because the Kremlin had not yet sought world conquest through military aggression. The president operated on the assumption that he could obtain Stalin's postwar cooperation by meeting legitimate Russian needs for economic and military security, and in turn win a promise from the Soviet Union to give up any notion of forcing communism on the rest of the world.[66]

But how could this policy be implemented? Convinced that World War I diplomats had erred in not agreeing on war aims before hostilities ended, Roosevelt attached great importance to reaching an early understanding with Stalin. But it could not be a spheres-of-interest deal in the tradition of the "old diplomacy."[67] Thus, although the White House endorsed Eden and the Foreign Office's analysis of the problem, it could not endorse their solution. Roosevelt became persuaded that, in the absence of a specific agreement on boundaries, he could convince Moscow of America's good intentions through personal diplomacy. "I know you will not mind me being brutally frank," he wrote Churchill in 1942, "when I tell you that I think I can personally handle Stalin better than either your Foreign Office or my State Department. Stalin hates the guts of all your top people."[68]

In May 1943 Roosevelt sent Joseph E. Davies, an uncritical admirer of Stalin and the Soviet Union, to Moscow to suggest to Stalin that the American and Russian leaders meet alone, free from the embarrassment of Churchill's presence. Stalin demurred—the necessity of directing the battle against Germany prevented him from leaving Russia, he said. Churchill subsequently got wind of the offer and protested bitterly to Washington. Hitler would revel in the assumption that he had succeeded in dividing the Allies, he wrote Roosevelt. FDR denied he had tried to arrange a bilateral meeting, and Churchill let the matter drop when the president subsequently joined him in trying to arrange a Big Three meeting. Clearly, however, Roosevelt was trying to build a direct bridge to Moscow by bypassing London.

The Russian leader continued to put off his allies, and throughout much of 1943 relations between Moscow and Washington grew worse instead of better. Russia continually complained that America was holding back on lend-lease deliveries. Stalin refused to accept the United States' explanation that German submarine packs were sinking much of the material destined for Murmansk and Archangel via the Arctic Ocean. Admiral William H. Standley, the American ambassador, complained to Roosevelt that Russian officials were rude and surly in their relations with lend-lease officials and refused to provide basic information on Russian resources. Stalin remembered Roosevelt's promise of a second front in 1942. When it was announced at the Trident Conference in 1943 that the cross-channel invasion would not take place until the next year, he implied that Britain and the United States were guilty of deliberate bad faith. Finally, Soviet suspicions were aggravated by the manner in which the United States and Great Britain conducted negotiations for Italy's surrender. The Russians resented the fact that they were not consulted in detail, and they expressed uneasiness over the lenient treatment accorded the reactionary regime of Marshall Badoglio.[69]

Grave doubts existed in certain quarters in the United States about Soviet intentions as well. The Nazi-Soviet Nonaggression Pact of 1939 and the winter war with Finland in 1939–40 made Stalin seem an unprincipled adventurer to many Americans. Conservatives in the United States continued to regard Marxism as an anathema. But the event that caused more concern than any other was the deterioration in 1943 of Russian-Polish relations. Hitler's invasion of Poland in 1939 had brought the Nazi-Soviet Nonaggression Pact into play. Russia invaded from the east and the two conquerors divided Poland between them. The Polish government-in-exile, which subsequently settled in London, regarded Stalin and Hitler as equally pernicious. After Hitler's invasion of Russia and the formation of the Anglo-American-Soviet coalition, the Poles established diplomatic ties with Moscow and attempted to forge a rapprochement. The matter of a postwar boundary between the two remained unsettled, however, with the Poles claiming the line established following a successful war with the Soviet Union in 1921 and the Soviets the line of 1941 as it existed prior to Barbarossa. In April 1943, a major crisis erupted in Soviet-Polish relations when the Germans announced to the world that they had uncovered mass graves in the Katyn Forest containing the bodies of 8,000 Polish officers allegedly murdered in 1940 by Russian occupation forces. When the Polish government-in-exile called for a Red Cross investigation, Moscow abruptly broke relations with the London regime and began to organize within its own borders a Communist-dominated clique of Poles to assume power when the Red Army should liberate their homeland.[70]

Wartime propaganda portraying Russia as America's ally and Roosevelt's determination to build bridges to Moscow notwithstanding, there existed as of 1943 a group within the Roosevelt foreign policy establishment whose view toward the Soviet Union ranged from mistrust to hostility. Standley was one. "I am becoming convinced," he cabled Washington, "that we can only deal with [the Russians] on a bargaining basis, for our continuing to accede freely to their requests . . . seems to arouse suspicions of our motives in the Oriental Russian mind rather than to build confidence."[71] Standley was a military man, reacting to an immediate situation, but there were Russophobes among the State Department careerists as well. These so-called realists learned at the feet of Robert F. Kelley, head of the Division of East European Affairs in the late 1920s and early 1930s. Kelley had consistently argued that the Soviet Union posed a serious ideological and political danger to the United States, and that, unless Moscow agreed to cooperate with the

West and act in accordance with accepted Western standards of international behavior, Washington should not grant diplomatic recognition or promote trade between the two countries. Kelley established a training program in Russian affairs for foreign service officers who subsequently became members of the Roosevelt foreign policy establishment. George F. Kennan, Charles E. Bohlen, and Elbridge Durbrow were all graduates of the Kelley school. In addition, by 1943 both Dean Acheson and Adolf Berle were deeply suspicious of Soviet intentions.[72]

The pessimism of these naysayers was offset by a broad coalition of personalities and interests, including the White House, that looked to Soviet-American friendship as the key to postwar peace. They reasoned that, given the strength of residual isolationism in the United States, appeasement of the Kremlin might be the only alternative to Soviet domination of the European continent. Averell Harriman, though he was later to become a hardliner, won the post of ambassador to Russia in 1943 because of his positive attitude toward Russian-American collaboration. "As you know," he wrote Roosevelt in July, "I am a confirmed optimist in our relations with Russia because of my conviction that Stalin wants, if obtainable, a firm understanding with you and America more than anything else . . . he sees Russia's reconstruction and security more soundly based on it than any other alternative."[73] Also joining the White House in perceiving Soviet-American cooperation to be one of the cornerstones of a secure and prosperous postwar world was Henry Wallace. The United States must ally itself with progressive forces, disarm the understandably suspicious Soviets, and let the air out of British imperialism, he argued. "An Anglo-American alliance would lead inevitably to war with Russia," he wrote in his diary in September 1943.[74] Like Davies, Wallace was regarded in many quarters as a wild-eyed liberal whose judgment was suspect, but not so Henry Stimson. A former Bull Mooser and secretary of state under Herbert Hoover, "the Colonel" was widely perceived as an experienced, practical statesman. Stimson firmly agreed with those who argued that, next to defeating Germany and Japan, the forging of a sound relationship with Russia was America's chief task during and after the war. He, along with William D. Leahy, Roosevelt's chief of staff, led the attack on Churchill's beloved war of attrition. Failure to launch a major cross-channel assault would poison relations between the Soviet Union and the West for a generation, the secretary of war insisted.[75]

Nor was the American military anti-Soviet during 1943–44. As historian Michael Sherry points out, the assumption of an identifiable enemy has traditionally provided the basis for long-range strategic planning in the United States. But crystal ball gazers in the army and navy ignored tradition during World War II. In the preparedness ideology that prevailed in planning circles, the primary danger to American security arose from fundamental changes in the conduct of war and international relations, not the transient threat posed by a particular nation. Not surprisingly, when military officials did speculate in 1942 and 1943, they looked as often as not toward Germany or Japan as the most likely threat to world peace.[76] By summer 1944, however, the primary concern among military planners seems to have been that the United States would become trapped between Russian imperialism and an enfeebled but still grasping Great Britain. Russian policy would be moderately expansionist, they asserted. The Soviets would dominate, but not necessarily communize Eastern Europe and Manchuria, and would succeed Germany as the strongest power in Europe. The consensus among America's service chiefs was that traditional nationalist objectives and fear of Germany rather than a lust for world domination fueled Russian expansion. Though intelligence experts anticipated a clash between Russian and American interests, they doubted the Soviet Union would soon have the capability or inclination for war with the United States.[77]

As if to reinforce Roosevelt and other American advocates of rapprochement with the Soviet Union, Stalin began to soften his tone in late summer 1943. He suggested a foreign ministers' meeting as a preliminary to the first Big Three gathering at Teheran and he made no demands, imposed no conditions. A clear and heartening sign of good faith, the White House enthused.

The Roosevelt administration's determination to increase the distance between the United Kingdom and the United States and decrease it between the United States and the Soviet Union became apparent first at the foreign ministers' meeting and subsequently at Teheran. At Moscow in fall 1943, Molotov, Eden, and Hull agreed to the establishment of a European Advisory Commission (EAC) to sit in London and consider problems arising out of the liberation of Europe from Nazi domination. The responsibilities and powers of the EAC remained largely undefined and they did so primarily because Hull and other American officials, namely Stimson and his assistant secretary of war, John J. McCloy, saw a London-based EAC as part of a broader movement by the British to control political and economic developments in liberated Europe. Stimson bemoaned its establishment. "They make it with advisory powers only," he confided to his diary, "but I am afraid of its being more important."[78] In November the War Department learned to its distress that at Teheran the British were going to propose a Combined Civil Affairs Committee (CCAC) that would direct the occupation of Europe from London, thus bypassing the combined chiefs in Washington. The combined chiefs already had a Civil Affairs Committee that he chaired, and that body was adequate to the task, McCloy wrote Hopkins. "It is essential that the people of America become used to decisions being made in the United States. Over every cracker barrel in every country store in the U.S. there is someone sitting who is convinced that we get hornswoggled every time we attend a European conference."[79] Roosevelt and Hopkins were impressed by the War Department's arguments. As a result, the EAC's jurisdictional limits remained vague and a London-based CCAC remained a British dream.

When the Big Three finally assembled at Teheran in November 1943, the president not only acted the role of mediator, but also in private talks with Stalin he placed much emphasis on areas of disagreement between Britain and America. He invited Stalin, for example, to join him in a general liquidation of British and

French colonialism. FDR subsequently sided with his host rather than his British colleague on a number of issues. He refused to recognize De Gaulle's French Committee of National Liberation as the government for liberated France. Churchill's support for De Gaulle, Roosevelt charged, merely reflected a desire by Britain to have French military might at its disposal in any future crisis. On Germany, Stalin called for dismemberment while Churchill pushed for moderate reorganization and economic rehabilitation. The president seemed to side with Stalin. Finally, America's decision at Teheran to postpone discussion of the political life of postwar Europe was tantamount to acquiescence in Russia's demands: the Baltic states, the eastern one-third of Poland, and "friendly" governments throughout East Europe. When Stalin reaffirmed his pledge to enter the war against Japan, moreover, Roosevelt agreed that Russia might acquire all of the Kuril Islands and the southern half of Sakhalin from Japan.[80]

These concessions contrasted sharply with the Roosevelt administration's attacks on British imperialism in late 1943 and 1944. The president's invitation to Stalin to dismantle the British Empire at Teheran appeared to be more than idle chatter. Indeed, the White House believed that a refusal by the imperial powers to grant independence to the dependent peoples under their control was far more likely to produce a third world war than anything Russia might do. As William Roger Louis points out, FDR held essentially the same outlook toward the great colonial empires as Woodrow Wilson had two decades earlier. Both preferred reform to liberation. Roosevelt and Wilson believed that the colonizing powers should be held accountable for the political development and socioeconomic progress of its colonies. Although FDR envisioned independence for colonial peoples only after a period of tutelage by the parent state, he was quite certain that independence should be the destiny of all colonies. As the war progressed, Roosevelt and many other Americans came to the conclusion that the United States should actively wield the principle of self-determination to hasten the evolution of independent states out of colonial empires.[81] While Churchill labored under the impression that Article III of the Atlantic Charter would be applied only to areas liberated from Axis tyranny, Roosevelt and his advisers intended the clause to apply to Allied empires, including the British and the French.

The administration's anticolonialism was undergirded by widespread anger among the public and Congress over British "abuses" in specific areas. None of the United Kingdom's dependencies attracted more attention during the war than India. The world's second most populous country and the core of the British Empire, India was a polity to which Americans, generally uninformed, became increasingly attracted during World War II. Mahatma Gandhi's nonviolent struggle for independence won the hearts of many an American who thought of India as a land of elephants, maharajahs, and turbaned Sikhs. They knew little of the caste system or the blood feud between the Hindu majority and the large Muslim minority. The Indians were not willing participants in World War II.[82] Indian leaders, especially in the dominant Congress party, argued that Britain had dragged India into the conflict without its consent. Gandhi stepped up his campaign of nonviolent civil disobedience, and by late 1942 the situation from the American point of view had reached an intolerable state. On October 12, the editors of *Life* magazine published an "open Letter . . . to the People of England": "One thing we are sure we are *not* fighting for is to hold the British Empire together. We don't like to put the matter so bluntly, but we don't want you to have any illusions. If your strategists are planning a war to hold the British Empire together, they will sooner or later find themselves strategizing all alone."[83]

Even more troubling to Americans and to Roosevelt personally than India were Britain's vast imperial holdings in the Pacific. David Reynolds has eloquently described the extent of Britain's specific interests: "North and West in a vast arc around the Bay of Bengal stretched her South Asian empire from the Malay states—sources of vital tin and rubber—through Burma to India. Singapore also commanded another arc of interest running south and east through the oil-rich East Indies to Australia and New Zealand."[84] The interests of Britain and the United States in the Pacific were of a different type—Britain's were tangible and real, America's largely romantic and imaginary if no less compelling. Except for the Philippines the United States had no major territorial possession that was scheduled for independence, whereas Britain's possessions included India, Burma, Malaya, and Singapore. The United Kingdom's commercial interests in the area were also enormous. Shanghai and Hong Kong were two of the world's leading entrepôts and business centers. China attracted some 6 percent of total British overseas investment, compared with a figure of 1 percent for the United States.[85] Many Americans, particularly those who belonged to the Republican party, traditionally held the belief that America had a special role to play in the Pacific, a civilizing, Westernizing role. Influenced by the China lobby and Madame Chiang Kai-shek, more and more Americans during the 1930s and 1940s came to view China as America's agent or proxy in the Far East. Franklin Roosevelt either shared or reflected that perspective—a distinction always difficult to make in the president's case. In his scheme of things a strong, unified, democratic China would take its place as one of the Four Policemen, fostering self-determination of peoples and squashing incipient aggression wherever it appeared.

The collapse of British defenses in the wake of the Japanese onslaught in 1942 glaringly revealed British weakness in the Far East and created a void that the United States hoped to fill either directly or with its Chinese proxy. The fall of Singapore and Hong Kong followed by the Japanese invasion of Burma and Malaya caused Australia to press for the creation of a Pacific War Council in Washington. At first the Churchill government would agree only to the establishment of an agency in London that would act as an advisory group to the combined chiefs in Washington. But the fall of Singapore forced Britain to accept overall American control of the war in the Pacific, and Douglas MacArthur assumed command of Allied forces in the South Pacific. Commonwealth and British forces fought in New Guinea and Burma but, as M. A. Fitzsimons writes, "The major fight against Japan was an American show in which the British were barely welcome."[86] Churchill, however, made Roosevelt well aware of the fact that Britain intended to reclaim every inch of territory and every prerogative in Asia after V-J Day. Roosevelt feared that Hong Kong in particular would jeopardize relations with the Chinese and heighten Asian suspicions regarding Western imperialism in the postwar era. In Churchill's view, China was incapable of successfully administering Hong Kong, much less of playing the larger role FDR and Whitehall envisioned.[87]

Roosevelt's anti-imperial campaign in the Pacific and his efforts to build China's confidence climaxed at the Cairo Conference in November 1943. On his way to Teheran the president met with Chiang Kai-shek in the shadow of the Pyramids. Roosevelt promised that, upon Japan's unconditional surrender, every foot of territory taken from China since the 1850s would be returned. The Cairo Declaration issued at the close of the meeting promised that after the war China would be welcomed as an equal of the Big Four.[88]

A series of factors and forces combined in 1943–44 to diminish the intensity, or rather the specificity, of America's anticolonial drive in Asia. Increasing sympathy in the United States for the plight of colonial peoples tended to crystallize around a trusteeship program within the projected United Nations, and that body was still a dream. And after 1943, Roosevelt's cheerful faith in China began to waver somewhat. Finally, the administration's increasing willingness to accommodate Soviet territorial demands in Eastern Europe and the Far East undercut its denunciations of British, French, and Dutch colonialism. But if Washington's attacks on British colonialism abated somewhat, its efforts to build bridges to Russia did not.

The White House and Harry Hopkins, in particular, were convinced that, if the United States could make a start in satisfying Russia's postwar reconstruction needs, a giant step would have been taken toward allaying that nation's mistrust of the West. In mid-September 1941, three months after Germany invaded the Soviet Union, British and American delegates had journeyed to Moscow to promise Stalin long-range, large-scale aid. The principal negotiators, Lord Beaverbrook and Averell Harriman, spent three days in talks with Vyacheslav Molotov and then signed the First Soviet Supply Protocol. That document laid the basis for an extremely generous unilateral aid program to Russia. Although the American service heads, the State Department, the British ambassador to Russia, Sir Stafford Cripps, and much of the War Cabinet wanted to take a tough, hardbargaining line with Moscow, both Churchill and FDR picked emissaries who were more interested in dispensing supplies than trading statistics. Unable to go, Hopkins selected Harriman to be his surrogate. Britain and the United States promised to make available some seventy items from aircraft to cocoa beans. No mention was made of repayment or compensation.[89] Subsequently, Hopkins used his influence with the president to block the recommendation of American lend-lease agents in Russia that Moscow be required to justify certain of its requests with detailed statistics. "Thus far our policy has been to assume good faith on the part of the Russians and to help them to the maximum," he told Roosevelt. "I personally think that this policy should be continued." In addition, on February 3, 1944, Hopkins wrote Harriman expressing the view that lend-lease could and should be used to facilitate Russian reconstruction: "The United States should undertake to supply, and the U.S.S.R. should undertake to accept materials and supplies to be mutually agreed upon which are useful for both war and reconstruction purposes and which are contracted for but not shipped before the cessation of hostilities against the common enemy."[90] Moscow would have to make a commitment to repay in cash and/or goods, but the United States could subsequently relieve Russia of this burden by extending a large credit.

The contrast between American policy toward Britain on the one hand and the USSR on the other during the last half of 1943 continued to puzzle and alarm the Churchill government. At the same time that Roosevelt, Wallace, White, and Hull lambasted British imperialism in Asia, American diplomats bent over backward to accommodate Russian territorial demands in Eastern Europe and the Far East. While State and Treasury worked overtime to cut back nonmilitary lend-lease to the United Kingdom, haggling over each item and repeating again and again that Congress intended lend-lease as a measure of economic warfare only, Hopkins plotted how to convert the aid program into a mechanism for the postwar reconstruction of Russia. With Roosevelt's full support, Morgenthau and White labored to hold Britain's gold/dollar reserves at or below $1 billion while Russia's reserves stood at $2 billion with nary a peep from Washington. But London comforted itself with the knowledge that Britain was crucial to the operation of any postwar multilateral trading system; Russia was not. From the British perspective, the Roosevelt administration's efforts to simultaneously disarm isolationists, Wilsonian internationalists, and the Soviet Union by circumscribing British power would be disastrous to Washington's long-range plans. A Britain deprived of financial reserves and overseas assets would have to turn to bilateralism, and an impoverished Britain could not continue to maintain its military presence in Greece, Egypt, and liberated Europe; it could not take its place, in other words, as one of the Four Policemen. To many within the Churchill government, the great task ahead seemed to be to convince America that British weakness was as great a threat to postwar peace and security as American isolationism and Russian paranoia.

5. Birth or Stillbirth of a Monetary System? The Bretton Woods Agreements and the Triumph of the United States Treasury, 1944

THE CROWNING diplomatic achievement of the Roosevelt administration in 1944 was the Bretton Woods Conference. Britain, America, Russia, and the other nonfascist trading nations of the world came together in New Hampshire and agreed to establish after the war an International Monetary Fund and an International Bank for Reconstruction and Development. These institutions, it was claimed, would guarantee exchange stability, provide the liquidity necessary for a system of multilateral payments, and produce resources sufficient for the reconstruction of Western Europe. Bretton Woods marked the pinnacle of Henry Morgenthau and Harry White's professional careers. The fund and the bank, they were certain, would not only guarantee a healthy global economy following defeat of the Axis but also ensure the United States Treasury's control of international finance. To them Bretton Woods constituted a major triumph over isolationists and economic royalists in the United States, and economic imperialists in Great Britain.

The structures designed at Bretton Woods placed Washington in a position to control exchange rates and the circulating medium, but failed to guarantee creditors adequate liquidity. Treasury won its battle over Wall Street, but succumbed to its own nationalist tendencies and pressure from isolationists and fiscal conservatives in Congress. The Bretton Woods Conference unfolded in the midst of intense opposition from American bankers, both commercial and investment, who wanted to perpetuate Wall Street–City of London control over international banking. They were seconded in their opposition to the bank and fund by Robert Taft and other congressional figures who not only favored private control of international finance but were determined to keep American resources at home as well. While they were not able to sabotage the New Hampshire conference, conservatives and isolationists could take comfort from the fact that the scope and reserves of the IMF and the IBRD were severely limited.

But the constituency that should have been most opposed to the establishment of the Bretton Woods institutions was the British government and people. In signing the protocols, the Churchill government took a giant step toward embracing multilateralism. But neither the IMF nor the IBRD was capable of supplying Britain and its West European neighbors with the liquidity necessary for them to abandon trade protection and exchange controls. Far from using its leverage as a prospective lynchpin in a multilateral trading system to secure a United States commitment to the physical security of postwar Europe and acquiescence in the maintenance of the British Empire, London negotiated an agreement that had in it the seeds of the financial empire's destruction.

The Churchill government's acceptance of Bretton Woods was a product of John Maynard Keynes's vanity and his immense power within Whitehall, and of the determination of a segment of the foreign policy establishment to forge a formal link with the United States that would transcend the Grand Alliance. Keynes, in his desire to see an exchange stabilization mechanism established after the war, accepted an American-dominated scheme. He convinced himself and his colleagues that, under the Bretton Woods proposals, Britain would retain sufficient freedom of action to impose trade and financial controls during periods of disequilibrium and that the bank would provide the financial resources for the reconstruction of Western Europe. His enthusiasm was in turn shared by Frederick Lindemann and others who saw in the bank and fund a first step toward an Anglo-American alliance in the postwar period. Britain retained a degree of flexibility under the Bretton Woods accords, but it did not acquire the resources necessary for either its own rehabilitation or that of Western Europe.

By the time the Washington conversations drew to a close, Henry Morgenthau and Harry White had settled on a rigid agenda that called for publication of a Joint Statement of Principles by Britain and the United States and the convening of a general monetary conference no later than May 1944. That agenda, which had as its goal the establishment of a United States–dominated, publicly controlled world financial system, galvanized opponents of multilateralism and of the United States Treasury into action. The Republican party, which Treasury was sure would win control of the House of Representatives in 1944, seemed determined to advance an international monetary scheme of its own while criticizing the Anglo-American plan for being too liberal with American tax dollars. At the very least, the Republicans hoped to delay the calling of a conference until after the 1944 election campaign got underway.[1] The New York financial community plotted with both the Republicans and the Bank of England to undermine the Anglo-American plan and substitute for it a massive private loan to Britain as a prelude to restoration of the gold standard, with the gold/dollar rate set rigidly at $4 to £1. At the same time the State Department, jealous of the giant strides being taken by Morgenthau and White in the field of international cooperation, worked to delay any general conference. But the biggest threat to Treasury's agenda was the continued lack of an Anglo-American consensus on the structure and function of an international monetary system. British multilateralists in the Exchequer, the Foreign Office, and the War Cabinet Secretariat gradually reconciled themselves to the White Plan, but the Bank of England, directly and through Lord Beaverbrook and Leo Amery, mounted a vigorous counterattack.

The close of the Washington meeting in fall 1943 found White and Keynes at loggerheads. Keynes had refused to sign the draft purporting to be a record of their conversation. White had not initialed the revised version that was subsequently circulated. Keynes, who left for London with his wife immediately after the meeting, was much annoyed: "During the war I have altogether spent five months in close negotiation with the United States Treasury and on no single occasion have they answered any communications of mine in writing or confirmed anything in writing which has passed in conversation. My experience is not unusual. I doubt if any one has seen Harry White's initials."[2] On November 19, White sent Keynes a letter with a Draft Statement of Principles revised to reflect his latest views. He proposed that copies of the joint statement be handed to the Allies and published immediately; then, without further discussion, the United States would call a conference to be held in Washington in May.

Substantive issues aside, the American agenda presented the Churchill government with certain constitutional and political problems that were not pertinent for the Roosevelt administration. The American government could publish the joint statement and allow Congress to hold hearings and debate any Anglo-American scheme for international monetary stabilization. The executive would not be committed until Congress took action. Given the strength of the opposition in both the House and the Senate and the relative lack of discipline within American political parties, there was a good chance Congress would significantly modify any proposal presented to it. In Britain publication and presentation to Parliament of a Joint Statement of Principles would signify to all that the Churchill government was committed to the agreed-upon scheme and, given the government's majority in the House of Commons and Britain's tradition of party discipline, passage of the plan intact was virtually assured. Thus, publication of a joint statement would be a far more significant step for London than for Washington. For this reason Whitehall pressed the United States Treasury to delay publication until after further Anglo-American negotiations and the full-scale interallied conference.

White, however, when presented with this constitutional conundrum, remained unmoved. The British government would simply have to make a commitment. The United States had bent over backward to meet the British on the issue of flexibility of exchange rates, obligations of creditor countries, size of quotas, and strength of governing board, he said. Either the United Kingdom supported multilateralism as it had pledged in the Atlantic Charter and Article VII of the Lend-Lease Master Agreement, or it did not.

In the weeks following the return of Keynes and the British delegation to London, British multilateralists reconciled themselves to the White Plan. The international pool of credit—liquidity—was not as large as that envisioned by the Clearing Union, advocates of multilateralism argued, "but it is enough to give the scheme a good start and can be increased later on if it is necessary and the scheme is working well in other respects." How reserves were to be increased "later on" they did not explain. Moreover, the Americans had been reasonable on the issue of gold subscriptions, set at the close of the Washington talks at 25 percent of a nation's quota or 10 percent of its reserves, whichever was least.

In other areas the Americans had proved equally tractable. Concerning exchange rates, the 10/10/10 provision coupled with the right of unilateral withdrawal would protect Britain's interests. No one in the British Treasury or War Cabinet Secretariat seems to have articulated the obvious truth that political and strategic considerations would make unilateral withdrawal difficult if not impossible. Although in Washington a wide divergence of opinion emerged regarding the powers of the governing board, the Joint Statement of Principles was sufficiently vague to enable British multilateralists to interpret the International Monetary Fund as "an instrument, entirely passive in all normal circumstances, for the facilitation of international settlements."[3]

What troubled British officials most when they departed Washington were the clauses dealing with the transitional period. Specifically, they wanted to make sure that Washington understood that London was not committed unconditionally to free convertibility in the immediate postwar period and that the fund would not satisfy Britain's reconstruction needs. Back in London they quickly redrafted the transitional period provision, which became Clause 11 of the draft statement, and sent it together with a letter of interpretation to White. In the opinion of the multilateralists, the redraft preserved "full freedom of action" for Britain to control exchange rates during the transitional period before equilibrium had been reached. White and the United States Treasury accepted both the redraft and the explanatory letter without comment. Acquiescence did not, however, signify a willingness to allow Britain to control the length of the transitional period. Even if Treasury would have wished otherwise, Congress would insist on early and free convertibility as the price of American aid, inside or outside Bretton Woods.

British multilateralists had closed ranks around the modified White Plan in part because they believed that it was the best that could be had from the Americans and in part because they anticipated opposition from the empire isolationists. The response of British Conservatives to the delegation's report submitted to the cabinet the first week in February 1944 was more than the multilateralists had bargained for, however. During the month of intergovernmental debate that ensued, the Bank of England and its voices in the cabinet mounted a last-ditch, desperate attack on the whole concept of monetary stabilization through international agreement. That backlash threatened to sweep dubious Labour leaders along with it and doom multilateralism once and for all.

The first week in February the cabinet prepared a series of questions concerning the proposed stabilization scheme. Will we be able to ensure full employment and safeguard Britain against the "inevitable American collapse?" asked Ernest Bevin. Would not the plan undercut government pledges to protect domestic agriculture, Robert S. Hudson inquired? What of the sterling area? Leo Amery demanded. Surely the stabilization fund scheme would destroy sterling as the dominant currency in the world and end any chance the City of London had of regaining its former position as arbiter of international financial affairs.[4]

The English multilateralists had worked hard to have Richard Law chosen minister of state in the British Foreign Office and believed him to be the ideal spokesman for the Joint Statement of Principles. On his shoulders rested the burden of rebutting the naysayers. The youngest son of Bonar Law, Richard had first come to Churchill's attention as a young Conservative M.P. in 1938 when he spoke out courageously against further appeasement of Hitler. He, along with Churchill, had been one of the thirteen Conservatives who remained seated when the House of Commons divided on the results of the Munich Conference on October 13. A former reporter for the *Morning Post* and *New York Herald Tribune*, Law had first been elected to the House in 1931. After serving as financial secretary in the War Office, he was named minister of state in 1943. A leading figure in the reform wing of the Tory party, Law fully shared the views of both the economic and the political multilateralists in Great Britain. To his mind, it was all rather simple. If Britain broke off financial and commercial talks with the United States, it would have embraced a form of isolationism itself, given isolationism in America a tremendous boost, and opened the way for the triumph of totalitarianism in Europe even before the ashes of World War II had cooled.[5]

Law's lengthy report, in which he summed up the views and recommendations of the multilateralists regarding the Washington talks, spurred the empire isolationists into a frenzy of action. "This is the Gold Standard all over again," Beaverbrook proclaimed in a memo to the War Cabinet, "and at a moment when the U.S. has all the gold, and Great Britain has none of it."[6] The amount of liquidity promised Britain under the Currency Stabilization Plan was insignificant. Exchange rates would be allowed to vary by only 10 percent, the "Beaver" charged hysterically—and falsely. Sterling was still the strongest currency in the world and had a chance to remain so after the war. The government should devote itself to upholding the worldwide use of sterling and "not allow the United States to lasso [*sic*] us this time."[7]

In mid-February the Bank of England submitted its own memo on the Washington talks to the War Cabinet. Hugh Dalton, who admittedly saw things through multilateralist eyes, summed up the Bank's perspective in his diary:

> The Bank of England, who were hauled before us at Beaver's insistence made, I thought, a quite deplorable impression. Catterns, the Deputy Governor, came and Cobbold also. They obviously hated the very idea of any kind of international bank. Its assets, they held, must inevitably deteriorate until it was all filled up with lenas and dinars—and perhaps that would be the intention. The proposed fund could not possibly be "passive" because no active-minded banker could disinterest himself in the fate of his assets . . . it would all, they thought, be under the influence of foreigners. Assumed that it would be located in Washington. This would mean break up of the sterling block and decline of sterling as a currency. When asked if he would like to see it in London Catterns exclaimed "Oh, good gracious no! We don't want the thing here."[8]

Prestige and power, not social justice, were the main concerns of the Bank and the empire isolationists. Essentially, they took the position that the sterling area could maintain its economy in the postwar period without massive outside help from the only available source—the United States. They refused to accept the reality that any attempt to go it alone would require the severest possible austerity measures in Great Britain. The Board of Trade would have to virtually eliminate imports and Treasury would have to devalue the pound to make British exports more competitive abroad; consumption levels and living standards would fall below wartime levels. Other members of the sterling bloc would be forced to take similar measures. Opponents of multilateralism refused, moreover, to address the question of how New Zealand, Australia, India, and even countries like Egypt could be persuaded to abjure trade with the United States and other members of a dollar bloc. The United States, with its technology and resources, would be able to tempt even the most loyal member of the sterling area.

Keynes and through him Sir John Anderson, Anthony Eden, Richard Law, Lord Cherwell, and the other multilateralists began to bombard Labour leaders and Churchill with these and other arguments in March 1944. Do the ministers appreciate the consequences of the Bank plan? Keynes asked Anderson, who subsequently posed the same question in a cabinet meeting. "Do they appreciate that this alternative, whether it is right or it is wrong, would require them, as an act of ordinary prudence to reverse . . . a good many of the post-war decisions which they are now engaged in making? It is no good favoring currency arrangements seriously inconsistent with other branches of their post-war policy."[9] Cherwell subsequently wrote Churchill:

> We shall end the War owing nearly £3,000 m. abroad. Nobody expects us to pay all these, at any rate, for a very long time. Canada is outside of the Sterling Area; South Africa, which must sell gold, will certainly cut loose; whatever else may happen the sterling balances of India and the Middle East will certainly be very greatly scaled down. What hope is there in these circumstances of getting countries to join a sterling bloc knowing that it will involve indefinite austerity and that their pounds will not be available to buy outside the area save with permission of the Bank of England? Would they not rather join a sterling bloc enjoying American goodwill, a gold credit of £325 m., an American loan, the right of converting freely the pounds they earn into any currency in the world? The Bank's "plan" is about as substantial as a dream and attractive as a nightmare.[10]

Despite the intensity of their assault on the Bank of England and its arguments, the multilateralists did not favor unconditional acceptance of the modified White Plan, however. Britain should and would have something in return for recognizing the gold/dollar as the dominant currency in the world and accepting a monetary system run by the United States Treasury. By early April, the Treasury, Foreign Office, and Economic Section of the War Cabinet Secretariat were all advocating acceptance of the White Plan—that is, publication of the Joint Statement of Principles—on the following conditions: that the United States government agree that the International Monetary Fund was designed "primarily for the long-term" and could not function unless some agency to finance reconstruction in war-damaged countries was established; that the fund be implemented in stages during the transitional period, allowing Britain and other debtors to retain controls for a time; and that the United States provide to the United Kingdom, through a loan, modified lend-lease, or some other mechanism, adequate liquidity in the transitional period.[11]

But the political situation in America made White and Morgenthau increasingly unwilling to make further concessions to Whitehall. Actually, the opposition to financial multilateralism that developed in the United States in late 1943 and early 1944 in many ways closely paralleled that in the United Kingdom, although the opposition of American nationalists to the scheme was somewhat ironic since it would ensure the supremacy of the dollar and make the United States arbiter of international financial affairs.

The Washington conversations on finance and commercial policy that took place in fall 1943 were accompanied in the United States by the first public debate on currency stabilization. The main American criticism of the Keynes and White Plans issued from a coalition of midwestern isolationists and New York bankers. Robert Taft continued to be the leading spokesperson for fiscal orthodoxy and economic self-sufficiency. The junior senator from Ohio was the eldest but not the favorite son of William Howard Taft. He worshipped his father, who much preferred Robert's handsome, outgoing, athletic younger brother Charles to the dour, intense young man that Robert became. "Big Bill's" eldest devoted himself to pleasing his father, a task doomed to failure. Whether Robert's sobriety and humorlessness were responsible for, or a product of, parental rejection is unclear. Following his graduation from Harvard Law School, he returned to Cincinnati to a career of law and politics. The embodiment of Republican orthodoxy, Taft rose through the ranks to occupy a seat in the Senate and became a regular challenger for the presidency from 1940 to 1952.

Taft shared his father's reverence for the Constitution. The greatest threat facing the United States in the late 1930s, he believed, was not disintegration of the international order, but growth in executive authority. The primary reason he opposed an active foreign policy was that such a course inevitably augmented the power of the executive. Congressional acquiescence in Rooseveltian "internationalism," which he correctly identified as merely a desire by the president for complete freedom of action in foreign policy-making, was a threat to the balance of power within the federal system and to the liberties of the people. In 1939 he tried to cut funds for the Export-Import Bank, which he said "could finance a European war without Congress knowing anything about it." As early as January 1942 Taft was complaining about the postwar expectations of what he referred to as the "war crowd." He railed against Wendell Willkie, Thomas E. Dewey, and the other members of the eastern establishment who wanted to "out-intervention" the Democratic interventionists. The GOP should no more do this than it should try to "out–New Deal" the New Dealers. He ridiculed the idea of a world federation: nations would never surrender their sovereignty. His answer, like his father's, to international problems was legalism. The Allies, he said, should concentrate on developing a code of international law.[12]

In 1943–44 Taft was much feared in the Roosevelt camp, primarily because he advocated congressional independence and opposed bipartisanship in the area of foreign policy. As a matter of general principle, Taft proclaimed, there could be no doubt that criticism of the administration in time of war was essential to the maintenance of any kind of democratic government. "The duties imposed by the Constitution on Senators and Congressmen certainly require that they do not grant to the President every power that is requested . . . they require that they exercise their own judgment on questions of appropriations to determine whether the projects recommended have a real necessity for the success of the war," he told a reporter.[13] Some of his opponents attributed his hypercriticism to obtuseness. Dean Acheson once accused the senator of being a "re-examinist," "like farmers who pull up their crops each morning to see how they had done during the night."[14] Others gave him credit for being bright but insisted that he was virtually devoid of a social conscience. Of Taft, Felix Frankfurter said: "A man may have a very fine reasoning machine and yet have disastrous premises. That's true of Bob—plus a total want of what I call the poetic sensibility, sensitiveness to the feelings and wants of other people. He is not the only high-standard product of our school [Harvard Law] of first-rate reasoning capacity, but without insight into the nature of man and the great current of society."[15]But Taft regarded himself as the true guardian of conservatism, the most humanitarian of all doctrines because of its emphasis on individual liberty.

Taft's commitment to congressional independence was rooted not only in his own background and education but also in a broader philosophy that encompassed the conservative Republicans' commitment to the putative halcyon days of yesteryear. Their attachment to the nineteenth-century political and economic system as they perceived it dictated their whole posture on foreign policy. It aligned them against big government and a strong executive, which they feared would result in dictatorship and destroy political and civil freedom; against large-scale expenditures, which would hand the government the opportunity of imposing "socialist" controls over prices, wages, and the free enterprise system in general; and against high taxation, which crushed the initiative of the private sector. Yet, as John Spanier and others have pointed out, internationalism in the 1940s, even more than the New Deal, required all of these things—a powerful government capable of negotiating with other powerful governments; a strong president, who could act decisively and vigorously; and huge outflows of cash to sustain military establishments and finance foreign aid. According to orthodox Republican philosophy, active participation in world affairs was incompatible with the preservation of political democracy and free enterprise. Thus did the Taft Republicans oppose the view touted by the Churchill government—that Europe was vital to American security; and that both Great Britain and the nations of the Continent, devastated by the war, had to be nursed back to health and strength by the United States.[16]

These views were to prompt Taft to become the most articulate and effective opponent of multilateralism in the United States. "The Capital is full of plans of all kinds," the Ohioan told a group gathered to celebrate William McKinley's one hundredth birthday in January 1943. "Every economic panacea any long-haired crank ever thought of is being dusted off and incorporated in a magnificent collection of glittering landscapes supposed to lead to Utopia. Nearly every one of them rests on the huge expenditure of Government without telling us where the money is coming from, when we already face a debt of over $200 billion."[17]

In spring 1944 he attacked currency stabilization specifically. The proposed International Monetary Fund and International Bank for Reconstruction and Development were based on the fallacious assumption that underlay all administration foreign policies, "that American money and American charity shall solve every problem." Both institutions, he explained to the War Veterans Republican Club of Ohio, were to be funded in their entirety by the United States. And America's liability would be unlimited. If the fund and bank used up America's initial contribution, as surely they would, the taxpayers would be called upon once again to come to the rescue lest the whole structure collapse. "Like most spending solutions for domestic problems it resembles the pouring of money down the sewer."[18] In the area of international finance and stabilization, the United States had always retained its freedom of action. Cash (gold/dollar) shortages in foreign nations "should be dealt with on a case by case basis, preferably by direct loans in reasonable amounts on definite conditions imposed by us." The Clearing Union–stabilization fund schemes, then, should be rejected on two grounds: attempts to stabilize exchange without first forcing irresponsible nations to put their budgetary houses in order would be putting the cart before the horse, and the plan proposed to put the resources of the United States at the disposal of "boards controlled by the financially weak and borrower nations."[19]

The argument that it was pointless to have a fund until Europe and especially Britain's reconstruction problems were solved was somewhat disingenuous. Both the administration and conservative nationalists knew that direct bilateral aid to foreign nations would be much harder to sell to Congress than foreign aid appropriations wrapped up in a scheme designed to save international capitalism. Therefore, both liberals and conservatives reasoned, if multilateralism could be defeated, Fortress America would rise from the ashes of World War II.

The other chief source of opposition to Anglo-American stabilization schemes came from New York bankers. Wall Street investment houses longed for the days when the world's financial problems had been worked out in a private, civilized manner by Ben Smith of the New York Federal Reserve Bank and Montague Norman, head of the Bank of England. There was no reason why the two nations' leading financiers, backed by their countries' great countinghouses, should not continue to settle such matters as the ratio between pound and dollar, the amount and terms of credit available to developing countries, and the size of the money supply, both domestic and international. The heads of the great New York banks took a dim view of the movement on both sides of the Atlantic to establish clear-cut public control over the Anglo-American financial community. The Labour party had made it clear that one of its first moves when it came to power would be to nationalize the Bank of England. Morgenthau, with Roosevelt's blessing, had spent much of the 1930s trying to shift the financial center of the United States from New York to Washington. Wall Street financiers perceived that the stabilization fund was just another scheme to establish public (Treasury) control over what should be a private function.

In addition, both commercial and investment bankers opposed the Keynes and White plans because they believed each to be inimical to their interests narrowly defined. During and immediately after World War I the American financial community divided into two camps. One consisted of investment bankers and large investment houses in New York plus their affiliates across the country led by the House of Morgan and the Chase National Bank. This group believed that United States economic supremacy abroad could be best achieved through cooperation with Great Britain and the takeover of foreign banking and commercial operations through investment. American capital would "Americanize" existing concessions, plants, banks, and other enterprises. Opposing this position was the National City Bank of New York, controlled by the Rockefellers and supported by leading export manufacturers such as United States Steel and General Electric. This group wanted to invest directly in areas long controlled by the British, French, and Germans, building plants, establishing branch banks, and exploiting markets in direct competition with the great imperial powers. To a large extent the division within the United States banking community survived the Great Depression and carried into the 1940s. Both camps looked askance at any international stabilization scheme, however.

The Morgan–Chase Manhattan clique believed that either the Keynes or the White Plan would lead to a situation where an international agency rather than American investment houses would supply capital for multinational businesses and concessions. In this connection, it should be noted that Morgenthau and White were no less nationalistic than Wall Street. The question here was not whether America should control the international financial system but who in America should control it—the United States Treasury or Wall Street?

Commercial bankers and American exporters were as opposed as overseas investors to the White and Keynes plans. The commercial bankers were afraid that internationally monitored loans would be used for purposes inimical to them and their industrial clients. Credit and loans for reconstruction in developed countries would stimulate demand for American exports, but developing countries would seek and obtain loans that would enable them to build their own economic infrastructure, thus eliminating opportunities for American commercial and industrial establishments to operate directly in the countries involved.[20]

The first signs of overt political opposition to Anglo-American plans for currency stabilization began to appear in early 1944. In February Representative Frederick

C. Smith (R-Ohio), a medical doctor and an archconservative who abhorred the New Deal, delivered a major address in Congress on the "Keynes-Morgenthau Plan." It was clearly a "British plot to seize control of United States gold . . . and unload upon the United States an immense volume of debts owed by Britain to other countries."[21] Other Republican defenders of the faith subsequently rushed to respond to Smith's clarion call. He had been shocked to read in the *Washington Star* the previous evening that the Allies were near agreement on a postwar fund to stabilize exchange, Congressman Charles Dewey (R-Ill.) declared in a speech delivered on the floor of the House on March 16. The United States government ought to at once put friendly nations on notice that all war legislation would terminate with the cessation of hostilities and that in matters of finance sole authority rested with Congress. The "Keynes Plan," as Dewey called the stabilization fund, proposed to turn the economic destiny of the United States over to an international bureaucracy.[22]

This, the first phase of the GOP attack on financial multilateralism, culminated the last week in March 1944 when Congressman Dewey introduced his own plan for monetary stabilization. House Resolution 226 recognized the need for action in the area of exchange stabilization and proposed the establishment of a revolving fund of not more than $500 million. The board that would control Dewey's fund would be headed by a chairperson appointed by the president and confirmed by the Senate. It could make short-term loans to help foreign nations stabilize their currencies and longer-term loans for "wealth-developing activities." Dewey referred to his proposed agency, appropriately enough, as an international RFC. Some administration officials suspected that his proposal was a stalking horse. But privately Dewey confided to Alvin Hansen that Republican opposition to the stabilization fund was entirely political; the GOP was not out to stop currency stabilization per se.[23] It wanted part of the action and part of the credit. Nonetheless, the Dewey Plan and congressional opposition to the Anglo-American exchange stabilization scheme were components of the rising conservative tide in the country.

Congress's objections to financial multilateralism also stemmed from a specific and bitter bureaucratic encounter in late 1942 and early 1943 between two battle-scarred veterans of the Washington wars, Henry Wallace and Jesse Jones. After America's entry into World War II, Wallace set about building a bureaucratic power base in the area of overseas procurement of strategic raw materials and supplies for the war effort. Partially as a result of the vice-president's urgings, FDR on December 17, 1941, established the Board of Economic Warfare (BEW) and placed it under Wallace's control.[24] Wallace and his chief assistant, Milo Perkins, were determined to use their agency to control every aspect of overseas purchasing, from planning to financing. This self-defined mission inevitably brought BEW into conflict with the State Department, a conflict that stemmed both from bureaucratic competition and from philosophical differences between the leaders of the two organizations. At first Cordell Hull was not alarmed by the formation of BEW because similar cabinet boards and committees had proven to be paper tigers. To his dismay, however, Perkins and Wallace aggressively siphoned off congressional funds and created their own organization staffed by their own people.[25]

But the real bête noire of the BEW was the Reconstruction Finance Corporation, under the powerful and conservative Texas financier, Jesse Jones. Until Wallace and Perkins came on the scene, Jones's control of his empire was complete. His colleagues on the RFC board regarded him with awe—and so did most members of Congress. "I think Mr. Jones more generally holds the confidence of Congress than any other member of the Roosevelt administration," asserted Senator Arthur Vandenberg.[26] Jones, who paid careful attention to pet congressional projects, was particularly attractive to conservatives of both parties. Under his direction, RFC had established a unique position in government. Existing largely outside of the budget, financed by its own revolving fund and by its power to sell notes to the public through the Treasury, the agency enjoyed unprecedented freedom of action. From bailing out businesses during the depression the RFC had, following Pearl Harbor, moved to financing war production and procurement, first at home and then abroad. Jones, who frequently bragged that the only book he had ever read was *Gone with the Wind*, was dedicated to the concept of private enterprise, a view that was repeatedly reflected in the editorial page of the *Houston Post*, which he published.[27] "It is my belief," he wrote Carter Glass, "that Government should seek to preserve private business, use it whenever possible in the war effort, and operate directly only when necessary."[28]

From BEW's inception, the State Department had infuriated Wallace and Perkins by vetoing every BEW project that threatened to affect the international political situation, while, from his vantage point in RFC, Jones relinquished funds for BEW programs only after he was convinced that they would not damage private United States economic interests. To Wallace and Perkins, the State Department was a bureaucratic tar baby; Jones was a penny-pinching reactionary; and BEW was the only agency capable of bringing efficiency and speed to foreign procurement.[29]

In spring 1943, BEW, in an attempt to seize control of the financial apparatus through which RFC funded overseas procurement, began to press the White House to transfer supervision of the United States Commercial Corporation from Jones to Wallace. When Roosevelt procrastinated, the vice-president issued a public statement intimating that Jones cared more about the fiscal integrity of RFC than about winning the war. Jones retaliated by attacking Wallace through the press and through his conservative allies in the Senate. "As far as the charge which Wallace appears to regard as a major crime, that I have attempted to safeguard the taxpayer's money," Jones wrote Carter Glass, "I must plead guilty. Squandering the people's money even in wartime is no proof of patriotism."[30] The situation had obviously reached the point, the president decided, where he had no choice but to intervene.

In May, Budget Director Harold Smith and James F. Byrnes, director of the Office of War Mobilization and presidential troubleshooter, suggested that a solution to the Jones-Wallace feud might be consolidation of all foreign economic procurement and warfare functions in State under Dean Acheson.[31] Roosevelt concurred and on June 3 wrote Cordell Hull: "Since you are and have been responsible for determining the policy of this Government in relation to international problems, I shall rely on you to unify all foreign economic activities to the end that coherent and consistent policies and programs result."[32]

Incredibly, Hull refused. Assuming a classic dog-in-the-manger pose, a pose that was becoming increasingly familiar to those in charge of personnel matters within the Roosevelt administration, Hull complained bitterly about the tendency of other departments to meddle in foreign affairs, the impudent independence of Sumner Welles within his own department, and the president's apparent encouragement of both situations. But the secretary refused to take control. What evidence was there, he asked Smith who had been sent to make the proposal, that the president would support him if he accepted responsibility for coordinating all foreign economic activities? "The Secretary was very indiscrete [*sic*] in frankly telling me his problems internally and externally," Smith recorded in his diary.[33]

It was at this point that Byrnes and Roosevelt decided to create the Foreign Economic Administration under Leo Crowley, giving it many of the duties pertaining to economic warfare that had previously been performed by the State Department, BEW, and RFC. Harold Ickes, the former Bull Mooser and Chicago progressive, urged Wallace to fight to the bitter end. Wallace demurred, but he nurtured his hatred of Jones and other business people and financiers who had "penetrated the New Deal." Wallace was convinced, for example, that Will Clayton, the man in charge of RFC's foreign-related activities and William L. Batt, vice-chairman of the War Production Board, were fronts for German-dominated international cartels seeking to control key points in the American economy.[34]

The outcome of the Wallace-Jones feud dismayed liberals. When, subsequently, the president announced in the closing weeks of 1943 that "Win the War" had replaced "New Deal" as the administration's slogan, Harold Smith and Wayne Coy were so depressed that they considered resigning.[35]

To conservatives, however, the demise of BEW marked the beginning and not the end of the battle against "creeping socialism" and "dictatorship of the executive." Jones, as Ickes had observed, was a vengeful person. He and his colleagues in Congress were determined to keep foreign economic policy free of "wild-eyed radicals." If America was going to erect structures to stimulate international finance and commerce such as a stabilization fund, they were not going to be run by men like Wallace and Perkins. And, in spring 1944, as Britain and the United States debated dates for the release of the Draft Statement of Principles and for the calling of an international monetary conference, Washington was full of rumors that Wallace or Perkins would head the proposed IMF. The Dewey Plan was an effort by congressional conservatives to state their philosophy and slow down the movement for economic internationalism until they could gain control of it.[36]

Congressional concern over who would head the proposed international financial institutions both reflected and was reinforced by attitudes on Wall Street. As Edward E. Brown, president of the First National Bank of Chicago and one of the few big bankers favoring the fund, told Randolph Feltus, the banking community's opposition to the stabilization plan stemmed not so much from fear of anything in the agreement but from a general distrust of the Roosevelt administration. They were most frightened about who would be appointed to head the fund. "It is the old Teddy Roosevelt argument presenting itself again."[37] For the bankers as for congressional conservatives, the Wallace-Jones controversy had assumed major significance. According to Brown, all were solidly behind Jones. If Roosevelt was crazy enough to appoint Wallace head of BEW, he would be crazy enough to appoint him or some other "crack-pot" to manage the fund.[38]

In mid-April 1944 Morgenthau, with full White House support, began pressuring London to accept publicly and unconditionally America's version of the stabilization plan. On April 10 he wrote Sir John Anderson that sometime during the next week he would have to appear before congressional committees and explain where negotiations on the stabilization fund stood. It would be most embarrassing if he could not announce that British and American negotiators had been able to agree on a Joint Statement of Principles. "Unless we hear immediately that the Joint Statement can be published next week," Morgenthau concluded, ". . . it is my personal opinion that we shall not be able to hold a conference this year."[39] Delay might doom multilateralism and end any hope of an American commitment to Europe's postwar economic and strategic security.

Morgenthau's barrage stirred Whitehall to action. On April 11, Anderson submitted a memo to the cabinet arguing that Britain could safely agree to the next steps in the monetary scheme without waiting for commercial policy to catch up, as Hudson and Amery had been arguing."[40] The multilateralists' hand was greatly strengthened by the replacement in April 1944 of Montague Norman as head of the Bank of England by Lord Catto, a figure much more favorably disposed toward the idea of currency stabilization. Led by Hugh Dalton, Labour cabinet members began to come around.[41] "Many of our colleagues," Dalton told Richard Law, "look with the sourest suspicion on all proposals for international cooperation. They always think the other people will catch us out, never the other way around."[42] In the days that followed, Dalton's speeches and those of his colleagues began to emphasize the economic phase of internationalism and its potential contribution to postwar peace.

At a stormy cabinet meeting during the third week in April, the empire isolationists found themselves outmaneuvered. Beaverbrook shouted and pounded the table, nearly overturning Churchill's brandy; if his colleagues wanted any more proof that White's fund was a return to the gold standard, all they had to do was read the speeches of administration spokespersons in Congress. Moreover, the commercial plan should be published at once. "You want to strangle the one plan at birth and do an abortion on the other," Bevin interjected. In fact, it was the Beaver's opposition to the fund that probably most recommended it to the minister of labor. Churchill, who had already made up his mind, was genial. "I really cannot be expected at my age to start to get up all these currency questions which I have thought nothing about for nearly 20 years."[43] After several hours of debate during which everyone restated their position, the cabinet voted to approve publication, the only condition being that the United Kingdom be allowed to state at the time of release that publication in no way committed the government to the plan.[44]

Although Russia had shown little interest in plans for an international stabilization fund, the Roosevelt administration felt it important for political reasons that Moscow associate itself with the Joint Statement of Principles. On the seventeenth, four days before publication was scheduled, Treasury, still waiting for an answer from London, telegraphed Harriman in Moscow requesting him to call on the people's commissar for finance. Britain had agreed to publication of the joint statement, Morgenthau lied, and it would be highly desirable if a copy could be released in Moscow. White warned Morgenthau: "This says we have received an agreement and we haven't." The secretary retorted: "I thought you had graduated from being a professor and technician."[45] Still the Russians procrastinated. On April 20, Anderson cabled that plans were going ahead for joint publication in London on the morrow. Finally, on the morning of April 21, 1944, the day of publication, while Morgenthau was giving testimony before the relevant Senate committees, he received word that the Russians would go along.[46]

The multilateralists were overjoyed. Britain was in the bag. The Soviet Union had given further evidence of its desire to cooperate with the West. "They want to be associated with us in the eyes of the world," Morgenthau told FDR. "State and Treasury both think this is highly significant, as I am sure you will also." To top things off, as Morgenthau left the Senate hearing room, Vandenberg whispered to him that the fund and monetary conference would have his full support.[47]

Morgenthau had reason for jubilation. The world's need for American capital would ensure his role as one of the principal architects of the postwar order. Through the fund and other United States–dominated financial agencies, Treasury could do nothing less than force Britain and Russia to embrace collective security. "I feel that in this year," he said to White,

England and Russia have to make up their minds on two vital things for them: Is Russia going to play ball with the rest of the world on external matters which she has never done before and . . . is England going to play with the U.N. or she going to play with the Dominions? Now, both of these countries have to make up their minds and . . . I am not going to take anything less than a yes or no from them. I am not, because this . . . is a terrifically important thing, not the monetary conference as such but what is their position going to be? And once they come in they have crossed that bridge.[48]

On the bureaucratic level, Morgenthau was sure that publication of the principles had tipped the balance of power once again in favor of Treasury. The prestige of Cordell Hull and the State Department had grown alarmingly throughout 1943. Hull, always popular with Congress, had succeeded in wrapping himself with the mantle of Wilsonian internationalism. In part because of his antiplanning, conservative views on domestic affairs, Hull's advocacy of political internationalism was acceptable to the public and Congress.[49] Morgenthau and Treasury's frantic efforts to press forward with financial multilateralism in 1943–44 stemmed in no small part from a desire to implement the economic phase of multilateralism before Hull and the State Department could make concrete the political aspect. State realized this, and in the opening weeks of 1943 Leo Pasvolsky, special assistant to Hull for international planning, had labored mightily to prevent or at least delay publication. To Treasury's enragement, he posed objections throughout February and March to Morgenthau's timetable: there were problems with the proposed IBRD, commercial policy discussions had not reached a sufficient level of maturity, and so forth. But Morgenthau carefully bullied Hull into accepting his agenda and then used his acquiescence to undercut the secretary of state's own underlings.

Victory seemed to increase rather than diminish Treasury's animosity toward State. Ansel Luxford, one of Morgenthau's assistant secretaries, wrote Pasvolsky's objections off to jealousy—he was in charge of postwar planning but had nothing to show for it.[50] "Acheson doesn't fight in the open," Harry White blurted out in one departmental meeting; "if he did, we would be able to meet him. He is a throat-slitter of a very vicious kind." But no one could approach Morgenthau's hatred of State. He accused its leadership of being nothing less than a tool of the transatlantic financial and banking community that had worked to perpetuate plutocratic rule in both countries and to guarantee American subservience to Britain in both the economic and the military spheres. At the same meeting in which White attacked Acheson, Morgenthau exclaimed: "Just as long as they [State Department and British imperialists] could keep London the center and keep the English fleet on a basis of two to one for ourselves, they had the world trade and kept us in a second place." That may be Britain's objective but not the State Department's, White interjected; interdepartmental rivalry was one thing but representing the interests of a foreign power was another. Morgenthau was adamant. This was the same crowd in State that kept advocating all those disarmament conferences in the 1920s and 1930s; "It was the same crowd that kept our fleet small and kept us as a second-class nation in the international monetary field."[51]

The Joint Statement of Principles, published simultaneously in Washington, London, and Moscow on April 21, 1944, in essence summarized Anglo-American negotiations over the International Monetary Fund. A number of issues were left unsettled. Under the terms of the document the fund could urge countries to remove currency restrictions after a three-year transitional period, but no member country was bound to comply, and national governments would decide if and when to undertake free convertibility.[52] This open-endedness was totally unacceptable to American multilateralists; the type of trading world they envisioned could never come to pass unless and until all currencies were freely convertible. In addition, as public and legislative debate following publication would indicate, the document meant different things to different people. Terms such as "gold-convertible exchange" and "fundamental disequilibrium" were not precisely defined. These issues, as well as the questions of membership, quotas, and the precise structure and function of the IMF, remained to be settled. In the view of the United States Treasury, the proper forum for addressing them was an international monetary conference. The smaller nations, whose dependency on America was even greater than the United Kingdom's, would help overwhelm British objections to an American plan. Moreover, this first great international gathering of the war would undercut Republican conservatives, Wall Street bankers, and economic nationalists in the United States, and ensure Treasury a prominent place in the foreign policy establishment.

Meanwhile, the principles made front-page news in papers throughout Britain. The tabloid *Daily Mirror* and Beaverbrook's *Daily Express*, two papers with a huge combined circulation, blasted the fund as a return to gold. "One hundred experts want world back to gold," declared the *Mirror* on the twenty-second. The more respected journals, those with a small but elite readership, expressed conditional approval. *The Times* congratulated the experts on their achievement thus far but warned that "much as stability of exchange rates is desired, too high a price would be paid for it if it involved tying the supply of currency to a rigid international standard." Both *The Times* and the *Financial Times* agreed that the great desideratum was a stable and prosperous United States "without the alternate booms and slumps which spread havoc far outside the American boundaries."[53] *The Economist* observed that the envisioned fund might provide currency stabilization, but it did not of itself promote trade expansion. And that was a prerequisite if Britain was to participate in any kind of multilateral system. The liberal *Manchester Guardian* was most enthusiastic: "No one can predict what the trading position of this country in the world will be after the war, and we are undoubtedly taking risks if we become part of a relatively free and automatic international system. But that risk must be taken if we are to remain a trading nation . . . there may be safety in isolation, but it will prove as short-lived in the commercial as the political field."[54]

The Joint Statement of Principles was submitted to Parliament on May 11, 1944, for its debate and approval as a basis for further discussion. Anthony Eden persuaded Colonel Walter Elliot, a Conservative and a staunch supporter of imperial preference, to introduce the measure. Nearly all members, including those sponsoring and supporting the motion, were cautious and critical toward one or more aspects of the joint statement. Above all, M.P.s appeared deeply concerned with the postwar role and attitude of the United States. British legislators repeatedly expressed anxiety that the United States would not be willing to maintain full employment after the war or to permit imports on a scale sufficient to avoid international disequilibrium.[55] Without really having studied the plan, many M.P.s seemed violently against it for no other reason than that the Americans had agreed to it.[56]

Ten days after the Commons discussion, the Joint Statement of Principles was brought up for debate in the House of Lords. Here John Maynard Keynes could get at critics of the fund directly. When Lord Addison raised all the familiar objections, stressing particularly the charge that the scheme was a return to the gold standard, the economist asked incredulously how he, Keynes, who had spent most of his adult life trying "to persuade my countrymen and the world at large to change their traditional doctrines and . . . remove the curse of unemployment" could support a return to the gold standard. He continued: "Was it not I, when many of today's iconoclasts were still worshippers of the Calf who wrote that 'gold is a barbarous relic'? Am I so faithless, so forgetful, so senile that at the very moment of the triumph of these ideas when, with gathering momentum, Governments, Parliaments, Banks, the Press, the public, and even economists, have at last accepted the new doctrines, I go off to help forge new chains to hold us fast in the old dungeon? I trust, my Lords, you will not believe it."[57] As impressive as Keynes's rhetoric was, critics remained unmoved and unconvinced.

The House of Commons approved further international consultations on financial matters, but only after Anderson gave some rather far-reaching assurances, assurances on which the government was not at all sure it could deliver.

On April 28, 1944, FDR approved Morgenthau's proposal to send out invitations to "the United Nations Monetary and Financial Conference" to be held at Bretton Woods, New Hampshire. The first plenary session was scheduled to begin on May 26, well before the opening of party conventions in June.[58]

On May 24, White called together representatives of the Russian and British embassies and informed them that the United States was going to call an international monetary conference the first week in July. It would be necessary to hold a preliminary drafting meeting. In addition to the Big Three, White proposed Mexico, Brazil, France, and Belgium as participants in the preliminary meeting. Did Britain want Canada or Australia? Australia, Redvers Opie, the Exchequer's representative in Washington, replied weakly. In the days that followed, the British groused and grumped to the United States. The meeting, which would involve the departure from London of not only dozens of Britons but also representatives of the governments-in-exile, would constitute a grave security risk on the eve of the cross-channel invasion. Why was there a need for both a drafting meeting and a general conference? The newspapers were predicting several weeks of negotiations. "It would seem that acute alcoholic poisoning would set in before the end," one British official remarked.[59] Keynes subsequently wrote White that he would consider it a hostile act if he were forced to come to Washington in the stifling heat of July. Treasury accommodated the economist by naming Atlantic City as the site for the preliminary meeting. Anderson's advice to Churchill given in mid-April—"It is clear to me that we cannot afford at this stage either to fall out with Mr. Morgenthau or to risk being saddled with the responsibility for a break-down"—continued to prevail.[60]

The Mount Washington Hotel, one of the nation's most luxurious summer resorts, was selected as the site for the first major international conference of World War II. Nestled in the middle of the one-million-acre White Mountain National Forest, the hotel was a self-contained community with its own beauty parlor, power plant, and stock market ticker tape. Seclusion was guaranteed. The clear, cool mountain air was a welcome relief after the suffocating heat and humidity of Washington and Atlantic City. The climate also partially compensated for the initial mass confusion that confronted the seven hundred–odd delegates, staff people, and reporters who made the trip. The hotel had been closed for two years and was woefully understaffed. With the help of military police units, however, the management was eventually able to assign everyone rooms, and the way was thus cleared for the opening of the plenary session. The seventy members of the press who attended were exiled to the Twin Mountain House some five miles away. All forty-five of the United and Associated Nations were represented at Bretton Woods. The largest delegation was, of course, the American, numbering more than two hundred. Sixteen finance ministers were present.[61]

Bretton Woods would be the first in a series of international meetings that would usher in a new age of global collaboration that would have as its objectives an enduring peace and an ever-rising living standard. If Harry White did not mismanage the conference, it would give birth to an International Monetary Fund that would establish a mechanism capable of achieving and maintaining currency stabilization, guarding American interests, and ensuring Treasury's preeminence within the worlds of finance and diplomacy. And, if matters turned out as Henry Morgenthau expected, Treasury would have given the man in the White House a powerful weapon with which to vanquish isolationists and nationalists in the forthcoming fall election. Given America's anticipated monopoly of both credit and industrial production in the postwar era, how could the conference fail? Morgenthau, elected president of the gathering, reminded the delegates that they were not there to conclude binding, definitive agreements, but to hammer out proposals that would be submitted to their respective governments to be accepted or rejected. He exhorted the delegates to approach the coming negotiations as colleagues and coworkers, not as bargainers.[62] Though few would admit it, America's allies, with one notable exception, had little choice; they had nothing to bargain with.

For approximately two weeks the committees and commissions met at Bretton Woods and reviewed the provisions before them, making suggestions, recommending changes, and advancing new proposals. At the close of each day the American secretariat, overseen by Harry White, would add to the "journal" of the conference, which was established to keep the delegates abreast of day-to-day developments. But as is true of most conferences and conventions, the major decisions were worked out behind closed doors among key delegates—usually in Morgenthau's suite of rooms.[63]

By far and away the most glamorous personality at Bretton Woods was John Maynard Keynes. According to one of his American admirers, he proved himself once again to be "one of the brightest lights of mankind in both thinking and expression and in his ability to influence people." He, like Morgenthau, operated out of his suite of rooms, and delegates filed in and out by day and by night to receive enlightenment from the great man. Or at least they did so until in the midst of the conference Keynes suffered a mild attack of angina. Thereafter, the faithful Lydia made her spouse retire early to mustard plasters and cold packs.[64]

Henry Morgenthau was the key political figure. He and he alone was plugged into the White House power plant. The secretary was intoxicated by the conference. Bretton Woods propelled him to the front of the Washington pack. It would give him, Morgenthau believed, the right to lay claim to undisputed leadership in the field of postwar planning and international cooperation. The Treasury had been the first to deliver and consequently should have first crack at solving future international problems, he reasoned.

But the conference itself was Harry White's show. If he did not bestride it like a colossus, then he enveloped it like an octopus. The former radical economist approached Bretton Woods as a problem in management. He had the power—America's wealth and FDR's political position were his trump cards—but large meetings such as this could easily get out of hand and become diverted, disorganized. The object was to secure a draft agreement for the IMF and IBRD before the American political conventions opened in late July. That did not allow much time.

In White's view the real force to be contained at Bretton Woods was the Keynes-led British delegation, not domestic isolationists. Because of his intellect and persuasive powers, the Cambridge economist posed far more of a threat to the fund, as White envisioned it, than did United States politicians. White decided to appoint Keynes chairman of the commission on the bank, thus occupying him so that he would not have time to interfere with the fund commission and its various committees. As it turned out, by the time the British delegation reached the New World, the establishment of a bank was first on its list of priorities.

For White, the International Monetary Fund was the be-all and end-all. The International Bank for Reconstruction and Development would be a sop to the British, the devastated countries of Western Europe, and the developing nations of Asia, Africa, and Latin America. He wanted nothing in the institution's charter that could possibly offend Congress, thereby endangering the IMF. Thus, he opposed a provision in the covenant of the bank enabling it to borrow currency from the fund. The dollar would be the only fully gold-convertible currency in the postwar era, the bank would borrow primarily dollars from the fund, and nationalists in Congress would attack both institutions as mechanisms to put more dollars in the hands of irresponsible debtor countries. In addition, White favored making all IBRD loans tied, that is, requiring that the money loaned be spent in the country in whose currency the loan had been made. In fact, according to his proposal, international bank loans would be doubly tied. First, the borrower after being granted a loan could not convert the proceeds into other currencies. Second, every transaction of the bank in any currency would be subject to the prior approval of the country whose currency was involved.[65] Finally, he insisted, no loans should be made by the bank that would otherwise be made by private financial institutions at reasonable rates.

In contrast to White, State and FEA argued that the bank ought to enjoy maximum latitude to make loans as well as to guarantee them. Why should private loans be freely convertible—that is, able to be spent anywhere—whereas the bank's credits could not? asked Ben Cohen of FEA and Emilio Collado of State.

The British delegation, headed by Keynes and including Sir Wilfrid Eady (secretary of the Treasury), Nigel Ronald (assistant undersecretary in the Foreign Office), Lionel Robbins (head of the Economic Section of the War Cabinet Secretariat), and Dennis H. Robertson (economic adviser to the Treasury), arrived by ship in New York on June 22. They were met by Redvers Opie and Leo Pasvolsky and escorted to Atlantic City. During the brief train trip, Keynes told Pasvolsky that His Majesty's Government had concluded that establishment of a bank for reconstruction was absolutely essential to the postwar well-being of Western Europe. UNRRA had already proven itself inadequate for the task ahead. Conversations with representatives of the Czech, Polish, Norwegian, and Belgian governments-in-exile on the boat over indicated that a bank to funnel capital to war-devastated areas would be their number one priority as well. It was with delight, then, that Keynes on his arrival in Atlantic City learned that White intended to turn the entire bank matter over to him.

Keynes's new-found interest in an institution for reconstruction and development and his willingness to leave the fund in White's hands stemmed from a number of considerations. Already displaying the excessive optimism for which he would later be criticized, Keynes insisted that agreement on outstanding issues relating to the IMF would be easy. He found White uncharacteristically "hospitable, benevolent, and complacent."[66] Keynes's superiors had already decided that Britain would have to go along with White's version of the fund anyway. If Britain's needs during the transitional period were not met, as Whitehall fully expected they would be, Britain could simply refuse to participate or withdraw, the renowned economist reasoned. By this point the British Treasury perceived the bank as a potential backup to the fund; if the latter institution was unable or unwilling to provide the United Kingdom and other debtor nations with the liquidity necessary to participate in a multilateral system, perhaps the former could and would. Keynes's enthusiasm for the bank was shared by the Churchill government as a whole. Whitehall probably hoped to curry favor and gain influence with the governments-in-exile and the developing nations by playing midwife to an institution that would meet their needs. The decisive factor in Britain's enthusiastic response to the division of labor proposed by White, however, was the fear that America would proceed without the United Kingdom and establish a financial institution that would funnel tied loans to devastated and developing countries. If Britain did not take the lead, Cherwell wrote Churchill in late June, the bank could become a mechanism for shutting English exports out of formerly rich markets. Loans there would have to be, the United States would be the only source, and Whitehall must do everything in its power to see that they were untied.[67]

As the conference opened, Harry White set about establishing control of the United States delegation, which included in addition to Brent Spence (D-Ky.) and Jesse Wolcott (R-Mich.) from the House, and Robert F. Wagner (D-N.Y.) and Charles Tobey (R-N.H.) from the Senate, Dean Acheson from State; Marriner Eccles, chairman of the Federal Reserve Board; Fred Vinson, director of the Office of War Management and Production; Leo Crowley from FEA; Edward Brown, the Chicago banker who had acted as a go-between for the Treasury with Wall Street on previous occasions; and Mable Newcomer, an economics professor at Vassar. Acheson was assigned to the same division as Keynes—the IBRD. This would mean that Treasury would have to surrender on the question of tied loans; but if the bank was to be primarily a guarantor of private investment abroad, with its capacity to make direct loans remaining very restricted, there was little danger in this. Giving up tied loans was a small price to pay, moreover, if it would prevent the State Department from influencing deliberations on the IMF and gaining partial credit for what would surely be the principal achievement of Bretton Woods.

White presided over a series of daily delegation meetings to explain the United States' position on various aspects of the fund and bank. His justifications were usually economic or ideological; they could not, of course, be political. Both institutions would restore damaged economies, generate socioeconomic progress in backward areas, and raise living standards everywhere. The United States would benefit in two ways from this generalized prosperity, he told Tobey, Wolcott, and company. Economic and social security would prevent Europeans, Asians, and Latinos from embracing "some kind of 'ism'—Communism or something else."[68] Massive unemployment, runaway inflation, extinction of exports, and the general deprivation that would follow would breed totalitarianism and totalitarianism bred war. In addition, the United States would have available for its exploitation vast new markets as a result of exchange stability and adequate international credit. There was little overt opposition to either the bank or the fund within the United States delegation; discussions centered primarily on how to sell the institutions to doubters in Congress, to an apathetic and uninformed public, and especially to Wall Street.[69]

Prospects for accommodating the New York bankers did not appear bright. Publicly and privately they fought to prevent the holding of an international monetary conference and then, once it got underway, to sabotage the fund. In early June White had met in Washington with a delegation of bankers that included Leon Fraser, Leonard Ayres, Fred Kent, and W. Randolph Burgess. When White's efforts to allay the fears of his adversaries failed, Randolph Burgess made a last-ditch appeal to Morgenthau. Though his letter to the Treasury secretary was marked "personal," Burgess, a director of the New York Federal Reserve Bank, claimed to speak for the American Bankers Association (ABA) and, indeed, for the entire United States banking community. Financiers and business people were "distrustful of any program for giving away American gold; they are distrustful of all spending programs, especially when sponsored by Keynes." The fund would surely become a political football and would immerse the administration's entire program for international cooperation in partisan politics. All the old hostility and suspicion of Great Britain would come to the fore, and isolationism would have received a new lease on life. "The success of the peace which we all deeply desire," Burgess declared, "so that our grandchildren will not be risking their lives as your and my boys are, depends on building up continuing international cooperation."[70] Morgenthau did not even bother to answer the letter.

Undeterred, Wall Street decided to undertake a direct lobbying effort with various delegates, both United States and foreign, and to launch a publicity campaign. En route to Bretton Woods the official Australian delegate was lavishly entertained in New York by Thomas Lamont of J. P. Morgan and Company and Winthrop Aldrich, chairman of the board of Chase Manhattan Bank and president of the International Chamber of Commerce. Following an unsuccessful attempt to win the Australian's opposition to the proposals, the two bankers told him that Congress would reject whatever plan the conferees came up with anyway. After the conference opened, Tobey and Wolcott began to complain that they were being pressured by ABA lobbyists. "I speak of it," Tobey told the other American delegates, "because that kind of vermin is here and they will do their poisonous work." Because the two Republicans had been in opposition to the administration so long, Wolcott confided, the bankers thought that they would oppose anything. "All of the opposition spearheads on us," he said and appealed to White and Morgenthau for support.[71] In addition to applying pressure to individual delegates, the bankers worked through their press allies at the conference. Among the most notable was Sam Crider of the Hearst Papers and his brother John of the *New York Times*; the two began a smear campaign against the IMF while the conference was actually going on.

White and his cohorts agreed that there would be no compromise with the bankers over the fund. The two Republicans in the United States delegation recommended that the Treasury strike back through the media, and a counterattack was just what Morgenthau and White had in mind.[72] Public opinion polls conducted during the conference indicated that citizenry and press alike were ignorant of the administration's monetary plans. "There is virtually no public opinion about the Bretton Woods Conference," declared one of the pollsters. "There is no general discussion of it because there is no interest; and there is no interest because there is no comprehension of the issues involved and the plans proposed, or of their importance. Bankers and business circles are believed to be more informed than the general public, yet even these are often 'surprisingly ignorant' of the subject."[73] Anglo-American discussions on monetary stabilization and postwar recovery had been held in virtual secrecy. The determination of the British and American treasuries to keep the negotiations free of public discussion and, hence, hopefully, political controversy had created a void which if advocates of the fund did not fill, opponents would. White immediately convened a series of daily "seminars" at 3 P.M. for all members of the press during which he "explained" various aspects of the fund.[74] The United States staff at Bretton Woods began deluging the press with statistic-laden articles on the virtues of the institution. American exports would automatically increase from $3 billion to $10 billion a year if the bank and fund were established, declared one typical piece that White's staff wrote and the *New York Times* reprinted.[75]

The propaganda fight, however, would not be won or lost during the conference, White and company perceived. The real battle would come when Congress prepared to consider the Bretton Woods bill. The principal task of the American delegation, therefore, was to ensure that the conference produced a plan for Congress to consider and that that proposal conformed as closely to White's scheme as possible. The two chief obstacles to the White Plan were Britain and Russia; to many people's surprise, the latter turned out to be more formidable than the former.

An issue that proved to be one of the least important economically and the most important politically at Bretton Woods was that of quotas. The United States envisioned a total commitment by all members of $8 billion to $8.3 billion, with the American contribution not to be larger than $2.75 billion. The British Empire share would be a little less, with Russia third at $80 million and China fourth. A firm consensus existed within the American delegation that the total voting power of the British Commonwealth as determined by quota should not exceed that of the United States. This still left the field open for a scramble among the lesser powers, with Britain pushing for increased quotas for various Commonwealth members and the United States advocating larger shares for Central and South America. White was convinced that pandemonium would ensue if the question of quotas became a topic of general discussion at the commission meetings. Privately, he, Keynes, and Vinson agreed to an increase in the total to around $10 billion. The committee charged with establishing quotas for each country did not report to its commission until the United States, working behind the scenes, had worked out each country's quota with that country's delegation. During the negotiations, the smaller nations insisted that quotas and voting power not be linked, arguing that each member should arbitrarily be assigned one hundred votes. The United States with British and Russian support made it clear that those who supplied the resources would control policy, and the movement for an international version of the New Jersey plan quickly collapsed.[76]

A related issue was what percentage of a nation's quota should be in the form of gold. The Joint Statement of Principles called for each member to contribute one-quarter of its quota in gold or one-tenth of its total gold reserve, whichever was less. Early in the conference Russia moved to have the total reduced by 50 percent for those nations suffering "war devastation." The American delegation believed the issue to be fairly significant because of the extent to which the governing board could purchase scarce currencies—mainly dollars. There was also a political aspect. A reduction of gold contributions by other countries would proportionately increase the United States' contribution, thus playing into the hands of members of Congress who would charge that the fund was a scheme by the poorer countries to drain Fort Knox. Some American officials who placed a premium on Soviet participation in any international agreement favored granting Russia's request, even though its gold reserves stood at $2 billion. Nonetheless, because the plan could not afford a general reduction, the United States opposed reduction for anyone.[77]

The British once again raised the issue of exchange rates but the United States held firm. Under the charter of the IMF as finally agreed upon at Bretton Woods, each member country was obliged to establish a par value for its currency fixed either in terms of gold or of the dollar, and to peg the exchange rate of its currency against other currencies within a range of 1 percent above or below that par value. In addition, members were to be allowed to vary their exchange rates by 10 percent. Anything exceeding that would have to be approved by the fund, and the member would have to prove that the change was required to correct "fundamental types of disequilibrium."[78]

Moreover, White and his colleagues won the battle over whether the IMF was to be active or passive. The joint statement of 1944 provided for a passive fund in the sense that it could not buy and sell foreign currencies on its own initiative, but would have to accept requests from member counties. But did the fund have discretion in accepting those requests? If it did not, in the United States Treasury's view, the fund would be without an important sanction to force members to adopt free and nondiscriminatory currency practices. Under the agreement reached, members would have an automatic right to draw up to the level of their gold contribution. To obtain a larger drawing, the member would have to gain the permission of the IMF. Both the 1944 principles and the Bretton Woods proposals required that members use borrowed currencies "in accordance with the purposes and objectives of the Fund." The governing board was to decide what those guiding principles were. In White's opinion, it was the duty of the fund to withhold its resources from nations that failed to adopt "corrective factors" to bring their payments into equilibrium and that resorted to unsound, stop-gap measures such as commercial restrictions or unilateral inflation.[79]

Another related issue, which pitted the United States against not only Great Britain but most of the other delegations as well, was the relative pressure to be applied to debtors and creditors during long-term periods of disequilibrium. Here the British and their allies did quite well. Most of the other nations, White explained to his delegation, were afraid that in less than ten years America would apply tremendous pressure on the monetary system by developing huge export surpluses in goods and services, services that would drain away the gold and dollars of other nations because—through tariff barriers and other devices—the United States would prevent them from paying in goods and services. America's potential victims were arguing for penalties or interest charges on creditors when they accumulated export surpluses. "We have taken the position of absolutely no on that," White told his colleagues.[80] Britain and other debtor nations were eventually appeased, however, by a scarce currency clause. The Bretton Woods proposals stipulated that, when widespread drawings made a currency scarce in the fund, additional supplies of it could be obtained from the scarce currency country in exchange for gold or by borrowing the currency from the member country. Alternatively, the fund could declare the currency scarce, whereupon other member countries would be allowed to impose exchange controls on their dealings with the creditors, and the fund would take steps to ration its meager supply of that currency. These sanctions were to continue until the offending member took measures to eliminate its chronic trade surplus. Under scarce currency conditions, then, nations running a deficit and nations not running a deficit could discriminate against American exports. Whether or not the governing board would have the political will to declare dollars scarce over the objections of the United States remained to be seen.

There was surprisingly little Anglo-American friction over retention of exchange controls into a transitional period. Britain insisted on that right and both State and Treasury Department officials apparently recognized the validity of its claim. According to the charter of the proposed International Monetary Fund, members were to refrain from imposing new exchange restrictions on current account transactions after the war and to avoid practices that discriminated against any currency. But recognizing that exchange controls might be imperative in the early, difficult years of the postwar period, the fund provided for a transitional period of readjustment ending in 1952. After that date, members still retaining exchange restrictions were to consult with officers of the IMF about their continuation.

The Treasury's posture toward Britain at Bretton Woods—a successful United States–dominated IMF was in Britain's interest and the Churchill government should be made to accept it whether it liked the scheme or not—stood in sharp contrast to its solicitous and conciliatory attitude toward the Soviet Union. The position of Russia at the monetary conference was anomalous. In general, the Soviets regarded the monetary fund as designed to solve problems peculiar to capitalist countries. According to Russian economic theory and practice, the value of the ruble was determined by the intrinsic laws of the socialist economy and as such was a managed internal unit, completely divorced from foreign monetary markets. Russian trade balances were not affected by external monetary conditions; the government achieved a favorable balance of trade by establishing a stringent monopoly of foreign trade and a comprehensive national economic plan. The Russians did not keep ruble accounts for foreigners; rubles were not convertible into another currency. The Soviet government bought and sold goods abroad using gold and foreign currencies.[81]

Under the American plan, countries trading with the Soviet Union would be paid in rubles, which could be exchanged for dollars or pounds or any currency the seller preferred. Moscow was already planning a series of bilateral barter and trade agreements with Eastern Europe that would have been impossible under the Bretton Woods regime.[82] Edward Brown, the Chicago banker, recognized the apparent paradox: "Russia doesn't need to be in the Fund. It has a complete system of state trading—state industry. It doesn't make any difference to them whether the ruble is five cents or five dollars."[83] It was illogical to expect a nation with a system of state trading and absolute government controls over exports and imports to want to become a member of an organization that would not allow restrictions on current transactions and that was designed to deal with massive trade imbalances caused by the purchasing patterns of a nation's individual citizens, acting freely. Indeed, United States pressure on Russia to join Bretton Woods seemed analogous to Alexander I's asking the sultan of Turkey to join the Holy Alliance. Nonetheless, United States multilateralists clearly believed that Soviet participation in any scheme for stabilization and reconstruction was crucial.

Despite the awkwardness of their position, the Russians not only came to New Hampshire but also proved quite tractable once there. At a negotiating session on the night of July 11, the Kremlin delegation indicated to White and Morgenthau's secret delight that they wanted their quota increased from $800 million to $1.2 billion, a figure that made their voting power equal to that of the British. And they volunteered to lower their demand for a reduction of their gold contribution from 50 percent to 25 percent. On the thirteenth, the United States agreed to $1.2 billion but would grant only that Russia's newly mined gold would not have to count as part of Russia's gold/dollar reserves in figuring what percentage of its subscription had to be paid in gold. The Russian representatives, to no one's surprise, indicated that they would have to ask Moscow for instructions. Bargaining with the Russians at any international conference at which Stalin and Molotov were not present was difficult. On July 22, the last day of the conference, Molotov cabled Morgenthau that, in order to demonstrate its desire to cooperate with the United States, his country would go the full amount in spite of the tragic devastation to the motherland. The secretary proclaimed the concession to be a diplomatic victory for the United States and a breakthrough of great political significance.[84]

Why was the Treasury committed to mixing oil and water, to trying to fit a basically mercantilist system into a multilateral framework? When not only Brown but Eccles and Acheson objected to concessions to Russia, and indicated that the only reason the Soviets were at Bretton Woods was to obtain loans and credits for reconstruction, White angrily rejected their arguments and defended Russia's inclusion on economic grounds. Moscow would surely borrow exchange from the IMF for a short period until its economy was rebuilt, but the Soviet Union probably would be in a position to repurchase its rubles (traded for currency required to purchase imports) sooner than other countries. Russia's great agricultural and industrial potential, coupled with its gold production, would put the Soviet Union on a sound commercial and financial footing within five years.[85] White, while an American nationalist, was far from being a doctrinaire capitalist. Socialism and capitalism could be blended; there was no reason why nations whose external economies were based on state trading and those whose economies were based on private enterprise could not exchange goods and services through an established medium.

But Morgenthau and White wanted Russian participation in the Bretton Woods structures above all because the Treasury leadership had begun to see the fund and bank in political rather than primarily economic terms. First, the two institutions would be the cutting edge of the Roosevelt administration's campaign to disarm Soviet suspicions and continue a working relationship among the Big Three into the postwar period. Treasury fully expected Russia to make use of the fund and bank's resources for reconstruction purposes, and, though it would not admit as much to Tobey and Wolcott, hoped it would do so. Second, the two institutions would be the president's sword and shield in his forthcoming election struggle with economic nationalists and Republican isolationists. And without the Soviet Union, neither the IMF nor the IBRD could claim to be truly international.

In keeping with the scenario developed at Atlantic City, White diverted both Keynes and the State Department from the fund by placing them in charge of the bank. Keynes headed the commission on the bank and Acheson was the chief American representative. To Acheson's (and everyone else's) immense annoyance, the Englishman, whose ardor for the bank continued undiminished, ran the proceedings of the commission like the intellectual aristocrat he was:

> He [Keynes] knows this thing inside and out so that when anybody says Section 15-C, he knows what it is. Nobody else in the room knows. So before you have an opportunity to turn to Section 15-C and see what he is talking about, he says: "I hear no objection to that," and it is passed. Well, everybody's trying to find Section 15-C. He then says, we are now talking about Section 26-D. Then they began fiddling around their papers and before you find that, it is passed.[86]

Acheson also complained that White had short-changed him when it came to staff. Commission II was ill-informed and disorganized, particularly compared with the efficient team White had put together to deal with the fund. Morgenthau and White must have thought it fitting to assign their State Department adversary to a project directed and controlled by the British.

The International Bank for Reconstruction and Development finally approved at Bretton Woods was to have a capital of $9.1 billion, subscribed by forty-four nations with 10 percent paid in immediately and that sum plus another 10 percent on call, available for direct loans. Quotas for the bank differed perceptibly from quotas for the fund. The fund provided that the larger the quota of a nation, the larger the vote of that nation and also the larger the line of credit available to it for the purpose of stabilizing its own currency. In the bank, the vote of a country also depended on the size of its quota, but the opportunity to borrow was based not on quotas but on need. The poorer nations, those with the smallest quotas, would borrow the most; while the wealthier nations, those with the largest quotas, would accept the greatest risk. The very countries that had scrambled for larger quotas in the fund tended to demand smaller ones in the bank. The United States wound up subscribing $3 billion and Britain $1.3 billion; the other nations pledged amounts set in accordance with their gold/dollar reserves, trade volume, and other factors.[87]

There was some debate on the percentage of the bank's assets that could be loaned and/or guaranteed. The conservative Dutch pressed for 75 percent, while the devastated and developing countries advocated 200 percent. Within the American delegation White favored the maximum, Brown and Eccles the minimum. "After all, this isn't a commercial business," White burst out at one point in the debate. "We are not a board of directors here thinking how to invest our money in order to make money. You are dealing with a world cataclysm here. Sure, you have to take risks. We are spending eight billion a month on a war—My God, what is it to risk a matter of a half a billion or a billion over a period of 30 years?"[88] The commission settled on 100 percent.

Essentially, the bank was to be an underwriting and guaranteeing institution that would supplement rather than supplant private international investment. After the war, if the governments of Greece or Yugoslavia wanted to rebuild their railway system or restore bombed-out port facilities they could approach American banks or other private institutions for a loan. The two parties would then ask the IBRD for a guarantee. If the loan met bank guidelines for financial soundness and contributed to the general economic health of the country in question, it would be approved. The ensuing private loan would be guaranteed by both the bank and the borrowing government.

Clearly, however, the international bank meant different things to different people. For White and Morgenthau the institution would serve three financial purposes. First, it would provide the capital necessary for reconstruction of war-devastated areas, and in the process reap the accompanying socioeconomic and political benefits. Second, the bank guarantee would serve as an inducement to American financiers to invest in war-devastated areas. Moreover, the multilateral nature of the institution meant that United States taxpayers would not have to bear the entire burden in case of default. Finally, the bank would be in position to exercise a supervisory role over foreign loans. Transactions backed by the IBRD would be "what we call good loans—productive loans," White observed. A borrowing government would have to make full financial disclosure "to make certain you wouldn't have a repetition of what happened in the '20s."[89] Such a mechanism would also protect the United States from charges of imperialism if it became necessary to pressure a defaulting debtor.

Keynes was euphoric over the bank charter. The proposed institution, he wrote Richard Hopkins, "has quite extraordinary possibilities" and "Britain was not assuming undue burdens." On the other hand, "the Americans are virtually pledging themselves to untied loans on a vast scale, which can be expanded in whatever appears to be the cheapest market. They showed no indication whatever to get back to a tied loan philosophy, and genuine liberalism in this matter seems to be part of their conviction." The United States government, Keynes observed, was, insofar as the bank was concerned, embracing true multilateralism; that is, "they're coming to realize that the only possibility of equilibrium in the balance of payments depends on their furnishing credits for exports from third countries."[90]

Perhaps so, but White clearly led the legislators on the United States delegation to believe that virtually all IBRD loans would be spent in the United States, thus stimulating American exports. In a sense, he could make that promise while still claiming that the loans were untied. Where else would the world go for machine tools, furniture, airplanes, locomotives, and the other necessaries of life? For the bank charter to overtly tie its loans was unnecessary.

Both the United States and British delegations were far too optimistic about the bank and its ability to solve the world's reconstruction problems. Borrowing countries and the bank were still going to have to convince Wall Street to extend credit, and there was no guarantee that American financiers would cooperate if higher profits were to be realized from investing their capital elsewhere. New York's repeated offers to extend a loan to Great Britain stemmed from a desire to keep international banking entirely in private hands. Finally, if the United States alone was spending $8 billion a month destroying the world, how could the bank reconstruct the world with a total of $9.1 billion? Both Keynes and White were brilliant and experienced economists; they must have realized the shortcomings of the international bank. In all likelihood they perceived the institution as a selling point for economic internationalism in general and currency stabilization in particular. In Keynes's view, any United States commitment to the economic and military security of Western Europe was better than none.

The Russians, who were always less subtle in seeking to advance their national interests than the Western democracies, attacked the proposed bank like a group of children bashing a piñata at a birthday party. Disappointed by the defeat of their campaign to have the contribution to the fund reduced for war-devastated countries, Stalin's minions insisted that their subscription to the bank be smaller than nations untouched by the war. They argued that they needed gold and other resources to pay for rebuilding cities, factories, and bases ruined by the Nazis. The Soviets did not succeed in obtaining special status for war-devastated countries but their contribution to the bank was not commensurate with their quota in the fund.[91]

There was one last, inevitable Anglo-American conflict at Bretton Woods—a squabble over the location of the bank and fund headquarters. At Atlantic City White had indicated to Keynes that he wanted the central offices to be situated in the United States; Keynes said no. At Bretton Woods the Englishman argued that this highly political question could be solved only by the governments involved, not by the conference. White and Morgenthau, with the full support of the congressional delegates, disagreed. If the dollar was to be the "gold convertible" currency of the new international monetary system and if the United States was to be the largest contributor to both the fund and the bank, then Washington would have to be the fulcrum of the new mechanism just as London was of the old. Taking advantage of widespread jealousy among other delegations of London's past financial ascendancy, the United States was able to secure conference adoption of a motion placing the headquarters of the bank and fund in the nation having the largest quota. Keynes, who wrote Anderson that "we are on a losing wicket here," decided not to make a fight of it.[92] Rather foolishly, Acheson tried to intervene at the last moment. Keynes's argument had force, he volunteered at a delegation meeting; the matter ought to be settled between governments. You mean foreign offices, Morgenthau interjected. Well, yes, Acheson admitted. "The financial center of the world is going to be New York [physically, not politically]," the secretary declared hotly. "The advantage is ours here, and I personally think we should take it."[93] This, of course, was Treasury's motto at Bretton Woods, and it was applied successfully in the case of both Britain and the State Department.

The conference ended in a flurry of activity—and tragicomedy. The date scheduled for closing was July 19, but last-minute wrangling over quotas and a dispute between the Russians, who wanted the lion's share of the bank's resources earmarked for reconstruction, and the Latin American delegates, who insisted that the institution focus on development, required a three-day extension. Dave Stoneman, president of the Bretton Woods Company, which owned the Mount Washington Hotel, protested against postponement. Under the contract he had signed with the government, the conferees were to clear out on Wednesday; the management, he declared, could not accommodate its requests for an extension through Saturday. When Morgenthau threatened to "nationalize" the hotel temporarily, Stoneman caved in. He did not, he said, want to be carried out of his office like Sewell Avery.[94]

A formal dinner highlighted the closing plenary session. Long after everyone else had been seated, Keynes's chair remained empty. He came in late, "tired, pale as a sheep," and walked around the long table to his chair. Spontaneously, the delegates stood and applauded. Keynes had been asked to address the conference a last time and to move acceptance of the Final Act. It was a "signal honor" for him to do so, he said. He paid tribute to Morgenthau, White, teamwork, and, reluctantly, lawyers. The real struggle, the political one, was still ahead: "I am greatly encouraged, I confess, by the critical, skeptical, and even carping spirit in which our proceedings have been watched and welcomed by the outside world. How much better that our project should *begin* in disillusion than it should *end*."[95] In turn, the Canadian and French chairmen hailed the proceedings, with Morgenthau, the president of the conference, delivering the farewell address.

Press releases, interdelegation debates, closing statements, and subsequent public justifications portrayed the IMF and the IBRD as institutions that would establish and maintain financial equilibrium in the postwar world. At the economic level they were widely perceived, especially in the United States, as panaceas. They were not. The International Monetary Fund, as Richard Gardner has pointed out, provided only a mechanism of exchange clearing, not a mechanism for dealing with the problems of long-term investment or with chronic trade imbalances. An ambitious program of reconstruction would be needed to repair production facilities and build a new trade pattern in which equilibrium could be restored. If long-term economic problems were not solved outside the monetary organization, the limits of its resources would soon be reached. The situation facing the IMF, in fact, would be analogous to that confronting the Federal Farm Board created during the Hoover Administration. Congress established the board and authorized it to loan $500 million to agricultural marketing cooperatives. The object was to subsidize a private mechanism that would hold farm products off the market during periods of surplus and release them during times of scarcity. The board would have worked during a time of relative economic stability, but in 1929 massive surpluses and declining prices overwhelmed the board and bankrupted it within a year. The IMF would face a similar situation—a period of imbalance in payments caused by wartime devastation and destruction, so gross that, lacking an unprecedented program of reconstruction, the fund's reserves would be consumed under a situation of free convertibility within a matter of months. And the IBRD, primarily a guarantor of private loans, was not the answer to the world's reconstruction needs. In future negotiations over modifications in the bank's charter, the Latin American republics would succeed in having the institution's functions extended to cover development loans, eroding its capacity to satisfy reconstruction needs.

Moreover, the founders of the IMF and IBRD were naive in thinking that they could separate economics and politics. National governments were not going to allow an international agency to use its resources or those of its citizens for purposes perceived to be inimicable to the national interest. The United States would surely object to development loans to Latin American governments that had nationalized the property of United States citizens; Britain would oppose credits to any European power bent on territorial aggrandizement and probably to food-producing nations that wanted to industrialize a portion of their economy. The Soviet Union would certainly block loans to East European nations to finance long-term commodity agreements to nations other than the Soviet Union. In outlining arrangements for postwar loans under which the borrower, the bank, and private capitalists reached agreement, White ignored a fourth partner, the government of the lender. Even in nontotalitarian societies, central governments would block private financial transactions considered counterproductive to the nation's foreign policy goals.

For members of the Churchill and Roosevelt governments who had been most vitally involved with the creation of the fund and bank, however, the two institutions provided political benefits that would outweigh their economic shortcomings. Morgenthau could furnish his chief with the first tangible achievements of the internationalist movement. Thus armed for the coming electoral battle, FDR could indeed vanquish the forces of Republicanism, nationalism, and financial autocracy—all particular enemies of the Morgenthau-White regime. In addition, the IMF and IBRD could serve as screens for postwar credits to Russia, credits that were perceived by both the White House and Treasury to be essential to the success of the Four Policemen concept. The fund and bank would, finally, give Treasury another leg up in its struggle with the fast-fading State Department for a full partnership with the White House in the making of American foreign policy.

The true British architect of the monetary system constructed at Bretton Woods was not Keynes but Frederick Lindemann—and for him the benefits were certainly as much political as economic. Had Britain not cooperated at the New Hampshire meeting, he reasoned, the resulting split between the United Kingdom and the United States would have been well nigh inevitable and absolutely disastrous from Britain's point of view. The economic health and military security of Western Europe hinged on American aid. Britain, in Cherwell's view, was the cultural and historical bridge linking the Old World and the New. The fund and bank would indeed enable FDR to defeat isolationism and help him and Churchill forge an Anglo-American union that would save Western civilization. Lindemann, who peppered Churchill with memos on foreign economic policy throughout this period, also saw the fund and bank, and multilateralism in general, as important aids in the battle to save capitalism. Nationalization of industry and finance in Great Britain as well as state trading in foreign commerce would be impossible, Lindemann believed, under the regime envisioned by the fund and bank.[96]

After the banquet and Morgenthau's farewell address, the delegates boarded special trains for Washington. Keynes was so euphoric that he penned a poetic tribute to the conference entitled "Ode to the Ninth Floor."[97] Everyone had worked in harmony and the British "team" had been "wonderful," he wrote Whitehall. Dennis Robertson had been particularly effective. He had completely overwhelmed the United States Treasury's Edward Bernstein, "who adores Dennis," and had won every major battle. "My only real complaint has been the gravely excessive number of cocktail parties. I am decidedly of the opinion that they do no good and that the British delegation should set a good example on future occasions by having few or none. The flow of alcohol is appalling, and they cost from about 30 pounds sterling to 50 pounds sterling each, with about half a dozen of them going on every evening."[98]

Though no one was willing to admit it, the Bretton Woods Agreements pointed toward a flawed, or at least incomplete, multilateralism. The forces of nationalism were unwilling to accept even this half loaf, however. Robert Taft—who had issued a contemporary version of the Republican Round Robin Note during the conference—and Charles Dewey were waiting in the wings. They believed that the administration was assuming the existence in America of a consensus on foreign policy that did not exist. No one really knew what internationalism meant. If it meant world government, they were sure that the United States public did not want that. If it meant an international New Deal, they were certain the people did not want that. If internationalism meant pulling British chestnuts out of the fire, the populace would reject it out of hand. If it meant financing "communism," Americans would never put up with that. Even if internationalism did not mean all or any of these things, it was incumbent on the GOP to force the administration to define exactly what it did mean.

Bretton Woods had hardly spiked the guns of opponents of multilateralism on the other side of the Atlantic either. More than ever Leo Amery and Lord Beaverbrook believed that the fund and bank were American-owned and -operated juggernauts that would be used to penetrate and conquer the British Empire. If empire isolationists could play on the fears of the parliamentary Labour Party and reform conservatives that multilateralism would make social security and full employment policies in the immediate postwar period impossible, the battle might yet be won.

6. Competition and Cooperation: American Aid to Britain, 1943–1944

NO SOONER HAD the ink dried on the Bretton Woods accords than Great Britain and its American friends began to cast about for ways in which the United States could directly supplement the United Kingdom's income during the latter stages of World War II and the early postwar period. In spite of John Maynard Keynes's euphoria, cooler heads in the British Treasury, Board of Trade, and Economic Section quickly perceived that the resources of the International Monetary Fund and the International Bank for Reconstruction and Development—even if Britain had been willing to avail themselves of them—were inadequate for British participation in a multilateral system and the economic rehabilitation of Western Europe. What was needed was a generous American loan program in the form of direct credits or lend-lease.

In response to mounting pressure from Whitehall and in anticipation of the liberation of Italy and parts of Western Europe, certain figures in the State and Commerce departments and the White House pushed for adoption of a liberal American loan policy. Led by Harry Hopkins and his informal network of advisers, this group arrived at the conclusion that there was no substitute for a direct American subsidy to Great Britain. Given the American people's apparent unwillingness to tolerate a permanent United States military presence in Europe after the war, Washington would have to have a proxy and Britain was the logical choice. That logic was reinforced by the need to provide the United Kingdom with the liquidity necessary to participate in a multilateral trading system. Acting on these assumptions, the White House sent Edward Stettinius on a semisecret mission to England in April 1944 during which he offered the Churchill government a huge loan. Stettinius's proposal came to naught, however. Britain made clear its opposition to an interest-bearing credit in lieu of a continuation of lend-lease. And in the United States ideological conservatives, opposed to government intervention with the trading process, and fiscal conservatives, determined to prevent the squandering of American resources, objected to the notion of foreign subsidies. FDR was unwilling to challenge Congress and American isolationists so close to the 1944 presidential election.

British resistance to an interest-bearing credit of any sort, the progress of the war, and the lack of bureaucratic consensus in both Washington and London on a comprehensive postwar foreign economic program tended to focus attention on immediate matters—specifically the nature and extent of United States lend-lease aid to the United Kingdom during the period of the Pacific war. But it quickly became apparent to all concerned that the time had passed when the short term could be separated from the long. The degree to which Britain could reconvert to civilian production and compete for export markets—primarily with the United States—depended in large part on the lend-lease aid it received during Phase II. If the nation could not begin reconversion in 1944, British economists advised, Britain would lose its old markets and new ones as well to aggressive American exporters. With no means to pay for vital imports, the promise of work, food, and homes—already the political battlecry of Labour and reform Conservatives—would become impossible. Living standards would decline, and the social and political unrest that would surely descend on the Continent at war's end would threaten Britain as well. The option to fight the last stages of the war against Japan partially mobilized was still open to Great Britain, but the strategic and political costs of such a move would be enormous. To recover its empire in the Pacific and to retain American friendship, Britain would have to make an all-out effort.

The Hopkins group and the multilateralists in the State Department were more than ready to manipulate lend-lease to Britain's advantage, but they found themselves constrained by the same forces that obstructed a liberal loan policy. The use of public funds, especially in the form of lend-lease, by the United States to rehabilitate its principal competitor for the export markets of the world was no less problematic in 1944 than it had been in 1943. Congress remained unalterably opposed to the use of the wartime aid program as a tool of reconstruction, and it found a stubborn and powerful ally in the United States military. These factors coupled with the administrative decentralization characteristic of lend-lease, the bureaucratic competition for control of lend-lease policy, and the distractions associated with the presidential election of 1944 caused Anglo-American officials to postpone decisions on the amount and nature of lend-lease during Phase II until Churchill and Roosevelt met at the second Quebec Conference in October 1944.

Churchill arrived at Quebec sobered by a realization of how desperate his country's financial plight was and how precarious that predicament rendered his political position. As a result, he sought to commit Washington to a lend-lease policy that was so liberal that it would allow the United Kingdom to undertake a partial reconversion of its economy during Phase II and launch an export drive. In return for his endorsement of the Morgenthau Plan, Churchill won FDR and Morgenthau's approval of such a scheme only to see it undermined in the months that followed by a bureaucratic coalition consisting of the War Department, the State Department, and FEA.

Strategic considerations dovetailed with the Roosevelt administration's economic objectives in a way that made aid to Britain seem doubly logical. Multilateralists had come to realize that a system of foreign loans and credits was essential to the emergence and proper functioning of an interdependent world economy in the postwar era at the same time that strategic planners accepted the importance of a strong Britain to a secure Europe. In a "strictly confidential" memo written to edify Dean Acheson in 1942, Emilio Collado, Harry Hawkins, and Clair Wilcox noted that "battlefield" countries like Great Britain were seeing their export capacities greatly reduced and their import needs greatly increased. The "arsenal" countries within the anti-Axis coalition, such as the United States and Canada, were developing enormous surpluses of exports over imports. If there were not to be strict trade and exchange controls imposed by the battlefield nations and severe economic dislocation accompanied by high unemployment in America, there would have to be a net flow of goods from arsenal countries to battlefield countries. "This can take place," Acheson's colleagues advised him, "only if it is financed by loans or gifts from net exporting to net importing countries, that is to say, by 'capital movements' taking place in the same direction as the net flow of goods." An active foreign loan policy was essential, in the view of the multilateralists, to achieve their twin objectives of social justice and free enterprise.[1]

In 1943 and 1944 strategic multilateralists were beginning to regard foreign aid as a tool with unlimited possibilities. Averell Harriman, joined by the new leadership that took control of State in late 1944, saw the offer of a reconstruction loan to Russia as a means of obtaining concessions on specific territorial and political matters, while Roosevelt, Hopkins, and Morgenthau viewed such a credit as a means for improving the atmosphere of East-West relations generally. In addition, a system of loans and credits was an integral part of the new dollar diplomacy advocated by Adolf Berle and others of like mind within the foreign policy establishment. The former brain truster called in 1944 for a wide-ranging loan program directed toward the countries of Eastern Europe and the Near East and funded by "international organs such as the proposed Reconstruction Bank as well as purely U.S. instrumentalities of both public and private character." He emphasized that these credits would be "essential to the maintenance of political stability and national independence in those regions."[2]

The figure who was, however, most responsible for developing a foreign aid program in general and support for Great Britain in particular was Harry Hopkins. Though ill throughout much of 1944 and intermittently absent from Washington for trips to the Mayo Clinic in Rochester, Hopkins remained a seminal figure in the administration. As indicated by his advocacy throughout 1943 of a postwar reconstruction loan to Russia, Hopkins was well aware of the political and economic possibilities of an active foreign loan policy. In spring and summer 1944 Hopkins's informal network of advisers scattered throughout the bureaucracy began to articulate a variety of justifications for massive aid to Great Britain during Phase II and into the transitional period after Japan's surrender. William L. Batt, a senior official on the War Production Board, Lauchlin Currie, deputy administrator of FEA, and Charles Taft of the State Department all assumed that "the condition of the economy of the United Kingdom is a matter of direct concern to the United States, and that our overall policy will take the U.K.

welfare into consideration, in our own best interest," as Batt wrote Hopkins. America would have to recognize and acknowledge, it followed, that Britain must expect "to maintain her balance of trade and feed her people."[3] In normal times the United Kingdom had to pay for $4 billion worth of imported goods a year— including 60 percent of its food supply, Currie pointed out to the White House. If Britain was not able to resume imports at this rate after the war, "she must either reduce her populations, or cut her standard of living or both."[4] Statistics indicated that Britain could not resume imports at this rate.

Hopkins's advisers pointed out to him that Germany's economic fate was still very much up in the air. If, as Henry Morgenthau, Bernard Baruch, and other Germanophobes wished, the Ruhr and the Saar were shut down, the economic rehabilitation of Europe would become much more difficult. If the Allies adopted a harsh policy toward the enemy, an economically healthy Britain would be all the more crucial to the creation of a prosperous and secure Europe in the postwar world.

In addition, failure to aid the United Kingdom in a substantial way would prolong and even stimulate British imperialism. Britain, Currie reported, was very dubious about the possibility of receiving loans or subsidies from the United States. In fact, London feared that lend-lease would be sharply curtailed, even during Phase II. Morgenthau and his lieutenants had done everything they could to force England to "disgorge the relatively modest hoard of dollars she had saved up during the course of the war." Under these circumstances, England would have no alternative but to maintain the Ottawa Agreements and launch a vigorous effort to monopolize the colonial and Indian markets for British trade.[5] Credits and loans from the United States would not only make it possible for Britain to set its dependencies free, but also Washington could demand that it do so as the price for such aid. The United States would benefit directly and indirectly, politically and economically, from a loosening of the imperial bonds. There were even domestic political rewards: "We could . . . display sympathy for Indian independence and the gradual industrialization of India, with some hope of success." These objectives could be accomplished "relatively simply and inexpensively by continuing loans or subsidies to the United Kingdom for the five or ten years immediately after the war."[6]

It was essential, moreover, that Britain participate to the fullest extent possible in the war against Japan after Germany surrendered. There were those in England, Ambassador Gilbert Winant reported to Hopkins, who wanted to hold back and convert portions of the British economy from a military to a civilian basis so that Britain might begin recovering part of its export trade. In fact, plans were underway in Whitehall to return as much as 35 percent of British industry to civilian production, although the officials in charge were going to the greatest possible lengths to keep these plans secret from the American people. All agreed, Hopkins concluded, that a half-hearted effort in the final stages of the Pacific struggle would be impossible to keep secret and would generate an unprecedented wave of Anglophobia and isolationism in the United States.[7] Such a development,

Charles Taft warned, would "destroy the basic requirement for the success of all of the plans for peace, namely a cordial and cooperative partnership between the United States and Great Britain." He urged "with all the force at his command" that the United States maintain and even increase lend-lease during Phase II so that Britain could both fight the Japanese and make a start at reconversion in its export industries.[8] Emphasizing that the United Kingdom was America's "bridge-head" on the European continent, others even insisted that a refusal by the United States to come to Britain's financial and economic rescue would drive the United Kingdom into the arms of Russia, the only other power in the world capable of providing the former mother country with the economic and military security for which it so thirsted.[9] In these arguments Hopkins's counselors accomplished what so many other components of the Roosevelt foreign policy establishment failed to do—relate strategic considerations to economic factors.

In addition, Hopkins's advisers and multilateralists inside and outside the United States foreign policy establishment recognized something that economic nationalists would never admit—that the structures of the British and American economies were vastly different. A study by the State Department carried out in late 1943 showed that if World War II ended in 1944 the United States would emerge from the conflict a negligible net creditor (excluding lend-lease and World War I debts), while the net creditor position of the United Kingdom would range from $4.7 billion to $4.8 billion. The latter figure was down from the prewar total of $15.9 billion, but Britain was still very much in the black. Economic nationalists and Anglophobes would make much of this figure (which failed to take into account sterling balances), but in so doing they would ignore the fact that whereas America was economically self-sufficient, Britain was not. Britain had to import and export to eat and to maintain a minimum standard of living. The United States did not. Earnings from overseas capital investments were essential to pay for necessary imports. United States overseas investments were icing on the cake.[10]

Hopkins and his advisers were convinced that if Congress could be brought to endorse a credit to Britain it would want something in return, probably something tangible and valuable. Some believed that a loan, if that was the eventual form that United States aid took, would have to appear to be commercially profitable "in order to demonstrate to the American electorate that we are not . . . Santa Claus."[11] The truth is, declared the *New York Times*, which acted as mouthpiece for the New York banking community throughout this period, "that there is no more magic to bad foreign loans than bad domestic ones."[12] Others believed that Congress and the public would demand permanent United States sovereignty over the islands and bases acquired in the Destroyers-for-Bases Deal.[13] The multilateralists, not surprisingly, hoped and believed that the people and their legislators would be satisfied with British acquiescence in the liberal commercial policy envisioned in Article VII. Harry Hawkins, Clair Wilcox, Henry Wallace, and Will Clayton all were convinced that they could justify aid to Britain on the grounds that it would raise living standards the world over, hasten the demise of

British imperialism, and provide America with tangible economic benefits. The fact that they actually believed this to be true lent conviction to their arguments.

As of spring 1944, then, it was clear to the strategic and economic multilateralists that Britain would have to have massive aid both during Phase II and Phase III and that certain conditions would be attached to that aid. The form and amount of the subsidy and the nature of the strings attached were still unclear, however.

The first mention of a possible postwar credit to Britain made by an American official came during Edward Stettinius's mission to London in April 1944. Morgenthau succeeded in barring the undersecretary from discussing dollar balances, but Roosevelt and Hopkins had no intention of allowing Treasury a monopoly in the foreign economic field. As 1944 opened, it seemed to the White House that there were pressing political, strategic, diplomatic, economic, and constitutional reasons for discussing postwar aid to Britain with the Churchill government. Hopkins's advisers were pushing their arguments with greater intensity; the presidential election, in which multilateralism might prove a very useful weapon, was approaching; and Congress, suddenly, was threatening to formulate and even implement a foreign loan policy. The Dewey bill had been introduced in the House in March. That measure, the White House was convinced, clearly involved the exercise of executive functions by the legislative branch.[14] As a result of these diverse factors, Stettinius, whom Morgenthau thought was off to Europe for an innocuous photograph session, was authorized by FDR to discuss "any financial matter" with the British and to broach the subject of a postwar loan.[15]

As a Hopkins protégé and White House loyalist, Edward Stettinius was the perfect choice. Although the son of a J. P. Morgan partner, Stettinius as a young man had at first rejected a future in the business world and decided to go into the ministry. His four years at the University of Virginia were characterized by missionary work among the hill people, active participation in the YMCA, and failure to gain sufficient credits for graduation. Sensing that Stettinius had at least a kernel of managerial ability, John Lee Pratt, a vice-president of General Motors (GM) and a family friend, persuaded him to reject the cloth and carve out a career in the business world. Beginning in the stockroom of the Hyatt Roller Bearing Division of GM at forty-four cents an hour in 1924, Stettinius rose to become chairman of the board of United States Steel by 1938 with an annual salary of $100,000.

Throughout his rise to the top of the corporate heap, Stettinius managed to retain a sense of mission toward humankind and, as a result, was sympathetic to many of the Roosevelt administration's relief, recovery, and reform efforts. Due to his position in industry and his enthusiastic support for the work of the National Recovery Administration (NRA), Stettinius was named to the Business Advisory Council (BAC), a group of business people who were not overtly hostile to the New Deal and who served as advisers to Harry Hopkins while he was secretary of commerce from 1938 through 1940. While serving on the BAC, the thirty-eight-year-old executive caught Roosevelt's eye, and in 1939 the president called him to Washington to head the War Resources Board.[16]

In this and subsequent jobs, "Stet" as he was known to his friends and colleagues ("Junior" to his detractors) impressed the White House, and particularly Hopkins, with his social skills, administrative ability, and loyalty to the president. He was clearly a team player. Edward Stettinius was not an intellectual but neither was he an air-headed narcissist as his critics charged. As lend-lease administrator, Stettinius had come under the influence of Oscar Cox, a brilliant lawyer with an encyclopedic mind and, like Stettinius, a protégé of Hopkins. Along with Cox and many of his new colleagues in the State Department, the undersecretary was an internationalist in the broadest sense; only through multilateralism and collective security could a stable and prosperous world be achieved. Both programs required a Great Britain that was militarily and financially strong.

The British government had already decided to use the Stettinius mission to make its first formal statement of Britain's present and future financial predicament. Whitehall wanted to plant a seed that would hopefully bear fruit somewhere down the line. To its surprise, the undersecretary proposed a solution to problems arising not only during Phase II but Phase III as well. Stettinius arrived in London on April 7, 1944. Following a brief interview with Churchill, who told the former GM stock boy that Britain would be the "debtor nation of the world" after the war, he was driven to Sir John Anderson's private residence for a formal review of the United Kingdom's financial situation.[17] By the end of 1945, the chancellor estimated, British balances would have shrunk to about $1 billion and overseas liabilities would have risen to about $15 billion. Britain would be broke. For the time, Anderson left the implications to Stettinius's imagination.[18]

Stettinius spent the following weekend at Chequers. Neither Churchill nor Anderson were able to go, but the American held lengthy discussions with Richard Law. Stettinius complained about the lack of progress in Article VII talks; it was imperative from a political point of view to make headway on commercial matters. If important international issues in Anglo-American relations were not decided before the November presidential election, they might remain unresolved indefinitely. A Republican administration, he told Law, was unlikely to pursue policies "helpful" to the British unless it was committed to those policies before the election. Given the prevailing mood in the United States, the GOP could not oppose President Roosevelt's policies in the international field without incurring the stigma of isolationism. Therefore, the Republicans would go along until the election was over. If they won without being fully committed to international cooperation beforehand, they would surely "revert to type." The undersecretary expressed the opinion that it was still possible "to get Congress formally and irrevocably committed over a wide field" between April and November. Law, who personally favored cooperating with the Americans over Article VII but who had not been able to break the cabinet deadlock caused by the opposition of Churchill and the empire isolationists, was noncommittal.[19]

On Sunday the Law-Stettinius talks resumed. He had been thinking about economic matters, Stettinius said. Article VII was remote and theoretical. A problem that was more concrete and immediate was the certainty that lend-lease would come to an abrupt halt the moment the war ended. Britain's plight would then be desperate. He told an astonished Law that the president would be able to "get approval of Congress during the summer for an interest-free reconstruction loan of a kind which would tide us over the difficulties of the transition." But, again, the administration would have to act while the opportunity existed.[20]

Stettinius's offer, or what appeared to be his offer, rekindled the debate within the British foreign policy establishment over whether or not and how far Britain should go in participating in America's multilateralist schemes. In addition, it sparked a new controversy over the advisability of accepting a postwar credit from the United States. Not surprisingly, Law and Anthony Eden were enthusiastic about Stettinius's "proposal." Immediately after the Chequers weekend, Law wrote Churchill that he and his boss believed that "Mr. Stettinius's suggestion may be of supreme importance." Most opposition in Britain to implementation of Article VII stemmed from fear that the United States would not help its ally in the transitional period. The promise of a postwar loan might be just the thing to draw the teeth of the naysayers. Rather naively asserting that "no shrewder judge of Congressional possibilities existed than Stettinius," Law advised accepting the American evaluation of the political situation at face value and beginning negotiations on all fronts at once. "If we cannot get from the United States the kind of assistance that we need," he concluded, "there will be very little Food and not much in the way of Homes or Work." It was even possible that the policy of "fraternal association" would be wrecked as well.[21]

Churchill was dubious about the whole thing. The Stettinius proposal seemed much too vague and offhand to warrant any concrete action by Great Britain. It could all be a ploy staged by "a good party man" designed to help FDR get reelected. However much the War Cabinet might wish for that eventuality, there was no possibility, the prime minister told his young Conservative colleague, that the present Parliament would agree to any modification of imperial preference. He was impressed enough, however, to ask to see the undersecretary of state personally.

The principal opposition to a quick followup to Stettinius's suggestion came, somewhat ironically, from the Exchequer. There were all kinds of problems with the Stettinius proposal, John Anderson advised Churchill. Would a loan carry interest or not? Stettinius had not mentioned interest initially, but then did so during his meeting with Anderson. Would the terms of the Johnson Act continue to apply? That measure did not officially bind the United States government, but Roosevelt, like his Republican predecessors, had promised to abide by it. Surely the Americans would tie a large part of the loan to purchases in the United States. But prices on American foodstuffs were likely to be higher than on commodities from other sources, and, hence, it would be economically untenable for Britain to buy in the American market. How would the United Kingdom repay such a loan? America was not traditionally one of England's best customers. That tradition coupled with continuing high tariff rates meant that it would be very difficult for His Majesty's Government to earn dollars with which to repay a loan. In that case, the United Kingdom would confront the specter of default, and with it poisoned Anglo-American relations and a shot in the arm for isolationism in both countries. Although Anderson, who was speaking for the Treasury and for his special economic advisers, did not say so, his remarks clearly implied that a hurry-up credit might erode the fraternal association rather than cement it, as Law was claiming.[22]

By mid-June 1944 the British Treasury had developed a response to Stettinius's proposal, which it clearly considered both an opportunity and a trap. In his brutal analysis of Britain's postwar financial condition rendered for the cabinet, Keynes acknowledged that "Food, Homes, and Work" would require massive aid in the transitional period; otherwise, Britain would have to circle the wagons around the sterling area.[23] Without such aid, moreover, the United Kingdom would have to severely reduce its military presence overseas, even possibly in the Middle East and eastern Mediterranean. The Stettinius initiative afforded an opportunity to open negotiations on the whole subject of Anglo-American financial, economic, and strategic relations during Phase III, but London must be wary. In the first place, Phase II and Phase III should be separated. Britain could not endure a reduction in lend-lease aid during the period between Germany and Japan's surrender. Munitions could be cut but nonmunition supplies, including food and raw materials, would have to be increased. In the second, Great Britain must resist the substitution of a loan for lend-lease during Phase II. Reflecting on Stettinius's various statements, Treasury officials had concluded that that was just what he was suggesting. Far from being a magnanimous gesture, the undersecretary's proposal, insofar as it applied to Phase II, was designed to get the administration off the hook with Congress.[24]

Even if Whitehall had decided to accept a loan from the United States with minimal interest, there would still have been no agreement in 1944 because by summer the White House had decided that such a transaction was politically impossible. Harry Hopkins continued to believe that a healthy and vigorous Britain was essential to the maintenance of American interests, not only in the short run—the Japanese war—but in the long term as well. As always, however, Roosevelt's right-hand man tended to equate the welfare of the nation, if not the world, with the political well-being of his boss. It was essential, Hopkins told Winant, "that great masses of people must approve our policies." "Internationalism" in the strategic and political sphere and multilateralism in the economic, both of which required a strong and healthy Britain, had political appeal. But internationalism, multilateralism, and their corollary, massive economic aid to Britain during Phases II and III, were fraught with political danger as well.[25]

As 1944 progressed, the American people seemed increasingly to divide their attention between domestic issues, especially their postwar standard of living, and the war. A report, entitled "Suggested Procedure to Make the Administration's Post-War Policy Acceptable to American Public," prepared by Sam Rosenman and his staff, advised FDR that recent surveys showed that the average citizen was almost twice as much interested in domestic as international affairs. Two-thirds of those polled believed that the United States should not furnish aid to foreign countries after the war if such aid would lower the standard of living in America, and almost half of those questioned were convinced that such aid would do just that. Consequently, the Rosenman report advised, the administration should "tie all references to international cooperation clearly and closely to the public's own self-interest here at home."[26]

Further restricting the administration's freedom of action in foreign economic policy-making was the ongoing bipartisan jealousy in Congress over its prerogatives in foreign affairs generally, and finance and economics specifically—jealousy that became more intense as the war approached its climax. When Congress expressed itself on war and postwar policy, which it did increasingly during late 1943 and 1944, it gave notice of its intention to guard the nation's sovereignty and to prevent the establishment of any kind of "international New Deal." "More and more," Robert Taft declared during the debate over UNRRA, "there seems to be an assertion on the part of the President that he has a right to determine economic policies . . . by a series of executive agreements which . . . may gradually . . . extend the existing relations among nations to such a point that we finally reach an international settlement without any consultation of Congress."[27]

Suspicion of America's two major allies remained strong within the conservative coalition. So great did it become, in fact, that several times during the year Speaker Sam Rayburn felt it necessary to warn his colleagues to tone down their Anglophobe and Russophobe diatribes. In addition, by spring 1944 Congress had gotten wind of the fact that British gold/dollar balances were rising. Why, Congressman Frederick Smith of Ohio asked the administration, were British balances increasing? If the United Kingdom could accumulate resources, why did it need lend-lease? Could England once again be exploiting its gullible cousins and converting wartime aid into cash? Traditional anxiety concerning British gains at American expense was also stimulated by an ill-advised junket to the war's battlefronts undertaken by five members of the Senate Military Affairs Committee. Reports of waste and mismanagement in lend-lease aid were true, the committee proclaimed on its return. This was especially the case where the British were concerned. The senators accused Britain of using lend-lease supplies to promote its economic and strategic interests, particularly in oil-rich areas in the Middle and Far East.[28]

Congressional Anglophobia was further fueled by news that British and American officials had in 1944 begun renegotiating the British Export White Paper, which had since 1941 put severe restrictions on the volume and kind of goods the United Kingdom could sell to its customers. If British prosperity was in America's interest and if that prosperity depended on Britain's ability to increase its exports, Whitehall had protested to Washington, then the restrictions would have to be eased. A number of officials in the State Department and the Hopkins network agreed, but the talks that ensued gave the impression to many Americans that John Bull was going to use lend-lease goods to compete with American merchants for control of foreign markets. Later in the year the *N.A.M. News*, the official publication of the National Association of Manufacturers (NAM), published a controversial article charging that the administration planned to continue lend-lease aid to Britain into Phase II and Phase III and that that would allow a portion of British industry to convert to civilian production. Such a process would speed conversion in Britain, retard it in the United States, and give the United Kingdom a head start in the race for postwar markets, the business journal charged.[29]

So great was public, congressional, and particularly special-interest anxiety in 1944 that Treasury and State joined hands to block any significant change in the old 1941 policy. "I do not believe that we could justify, from a domestic political point of view, a procedure whereby the British, without our agreement transfer to third powers, often for political purposes . . . items similar to those which they have received from us under Lend-Lease," Cordell Hull wrote FDR in July.[30] Henry Morgenthau's advice was identical. Hugh Dalton, who as president of the Board of Trade was responsible for planning Britain's postwar export offensive, despaired at "all the wretched underlings who have been making so much trouble for us at Washington."[31]

When lend-lease came up for renewal again in 1944, a number of senators, particularly Republicans, were highly critical. Much of the aid was unnecessary and it was crippling the American economy, they insisted. As had been the case in 1943, State Department representatives had to reassure both houses of Congress that the measure did not take away from them any of their authority over economic policy, either domestic or international, and that the administration would scrupulously observe constitutional procedures in this area. As was also the case in 1943, many legislators supported the renewal bill, which passed by wide margins, because they understood lend-lease to be limited to items of wartime necessity and confined to the period of actual fighting.[32]

Throughout these debates Congress repeatedly reiterated its determination to guard free enterprise at home and foster it abroad if possible. Representative William M. Colmer (D-Miss.), appointed chairman of the House Postwar Economic Policy and Planning Committee in January 1944, told the House that his group would seek immediately after the cessation of hostilities to bring to an end "war-time regimentation of the people and to guarantee the continuation of free enterprise."[33] Speaking to the Sales Executive Club of New York, Senator Joseph C. O'Mahoney (D-Wyo.) warned in February 1944 that the end of hostilities would force the United States to choose between a capitalistic system of free enterprise and maximum production that guaranteed a job to all who sought employment, a totalitarian regime dominated by centralized governmental planning for industry and individuals, and a system of managed economies in which cartels would fix prices and regulate production without governmental control. The latter two, he declared, would "destroy the freedom of the individual in this country"; he, O'Mahoney said, would work untiringly for the first option.[34]

By mutual consent Democrats and Republicans agreed to keep "foreign affairs" out of the 1944 presidential campaign. Cordell Hull and John Foster Dulles, Republican nominee Thomas Dewey's foreign policy adviser, had actually reached a specific agreement to that effect in the fall. Dulles and Arthur Vandenberg had decided that any effort by the GOP to criticize the administration in this area would backfire and allow FDR and his supporters to brand Republicans as disloyal. By foreign affairs the GOP clearly meant strategic, territorial, and collective security issues, not economic and financial ones.

While Dewey remained aloof and always moderate in his statements, other more extreme Republican orators hammered away at executive usurpation and the threat of a pervasive "New Deal" at home and abroad. After warning at a Lincoln's Day banquet that the Democratic party was in danger of being taken over by a group of "Nazi New Dealers" headed by "Vice President Wallace and his fellow travellers," former presidential candidate Alf Landon insisted that rumors that the administration was going to use lend-lease for postwar relief and reconstruction were true. The administration was indulging in "mystical dreams" of raising the living standard of all the "heterogeneous" peoples of the world at the expense of the American taxpayer.[35] Landon's views were more characteristic of the congressional than the presidential wing of the Republican party; but since Congress would have to approve and fund any type of foreign aid package, the latter would be more important than the former to the implementation of a foreign loan policy.

In fact, while the GOP had essentially incorporated the Mackinac Declaration into its 1944 platform, it remained strongly nationalistic in economic affairs and unilateralist in political matters. Grave doubts continued to exist—especially regarding the wisdom of ongoing American intervention into European affairs. The Mackinac Declaration and Republican foreign policy planks strongly emphasized the need to protect the nation's sovereignty and its freedom of action. Ironically, Vandenberg saw the United Nations much the same way as did FDR— a mask for global domination by the Big Four; he praised the Dumbarton Oaks Conference and the Yalta Conference for establishing an absolute veto. "In my opinion," Vandenberg wrote Dulles in July 1944, "it [the Mid-West] is, way down under, more isolationist than ever. Yet, it is fully ready to cooperate internationally on the basis of the Mackinac formula as translated into our formula."[36]

In the end, Harry Hopkins and his brain trust decided that Congress and the American people were not ready for an explicit program of foreign loans justified on strategic and multilateral grounds. Or, at least, the White House was convinced that 1944 was not an opportune time to do domestic battle over a large loan to Great Britain. The attention of those bureaucrats and politicians on both sides of the Atlantic concerned with American aid to Great Britain shifted, inevitably, back to lend-lease.

Typically, the White House devoted most of its efforts in the area of lend-lease to seeing that no one in the foreign policy establishment took action until it did. And when action was forthcoming, it was as much a product of the moment and the immediate situation in which FDR found himself than of any well-thought-out policy. Moreover, because of Roosevelt's administrative style, the search for a clearly defined, well-reasoned, and yet politically feasible lend-lease policy for Phase II was accompanied by a bureaucratic struggle for control of that policy.

The State Department was acutely aware of the need to establish a central body to formulate United States foreign aid policy toward Europe for both the short and long term. Late in 1944 Charles Taft, director of the Office of Wartime Economic Affairs, lamented the absence of both a policy and a policy-making agency to his colleague, Roy Stinebower, who replied that he personally had been getting together "a Stinebower version of Fantasia, a document on American Foreign Economic Policy."[37] State, of course, wanted to be the architect of both form and substance and wished to construct an edifice that was Treasury-proof. Morgenthau would surely want Harry White to have the chairmanship of such a committee, but State favored Warren Lee Pierson, head of the Export-Import Bank.[38] Hull's subsequent attempt to obtain White House approval for the type of governing body his subordinates wanted was feeble and unsuccessful, however.

Nonetheless, by spring 1944 Harry Hopkins had become alarmed at Henry Morgenthau's growing stature. Riding the crest of Bretton Woods in 1943 and early 1944, the Treasury secretary seemed to be threatening the bureaucratic balance of power that Hopkins and the president had worked so long and hard to maintain. Moreover, as Hopkins's advisers pointed out to him, the IMF and IBRD were irrelevant to the problems of Phase II and would probably be so for Phase III. In addition, Morgenthau and White's hard line over the British gold/dollar balance raised some question as to Treasury's underlying goodwill toward Britain, or lack of it. As a result, Hopkins, after consultation with William Batt, Lauchlin Currie, Charles Taft, and various members of the British Embassy and Supply Mission, moved to contain Anglophobe elements in the executive branch, maintain the bureaucratic balance of power, see that Britain's needs were met, and ensure that all developments would redound to the political benefit of his chief.

From Hopkins's perspective, the first priority seemed to be to distill a foreign aid formula from the mixture of assumptions that existed within the Hopkins group. Those assumptions were that a healthy Britain was vital to America's economic and strategic interests, British prosperity depended on the nation's ability to export, the United Kingdom would have to shoulder its full share of the burden in the Pacific, and lend-lease aid in Phase II to achieve these goals would have to be ultimately palatable to Congress and the American voter. The plan that initially seemed most feasible provided for synchronized Anglo-American reconversion during the period following V-E Day and before Japan's surrender. According to estimates by the combined chiefs and the combined boards, the Allies could reduce total munitions production during Phase II by 30 to 35 percent.

Some United States officials wanted to take all or most of the cut out of United States production on the assumption that America had supplied its allies with the lion's share of the tanks, guns, and bullets needed to win the war. (As of mid-1944, the United States was furnishing Britain with approximately 25 percent of all its equipment needs.) According to the synchronized reconversion plan developed by Hopkins and associates, however, military production would be reduced in both countries by roughly the same percentage. This approach would permit each country to convert to civilian production the same percentage of its facilities then being devoted to war production. The deficiencies in British military requirements would continue to be met by lend-lease, reduced in amount, however, by reason of the overall reduction in the program. To protect the administration from criticism that it was supplying the United Kingdom with some of the same goods its civilian sector was manufacturing and exporting in direct competition with American exporters, the plan called for elimination of all nonmilitary lend-lease except food.[39]

But problems with the percentage plan quickly cropped up. While politically feasible, synchronized reconversion would be of greater benefit to American export industries than British. This approach would not enable Britain to expand its exports if it participated fully in the Pacific war because synchronized reconversion called for elimination of nonmilitary lend-lease items except food. Much of the production capacity freed by the cut in military requirements would have to go to meet domestic civilian requirements generated by the cut in nonmilitary lend-lease. Britain and the United States, moreover, were not starting at the same point. Whereas United States exports excluding lend-lease had stayed at prewar levels from 1941 to 1944, British sales had declined by two-thirds.[40] The War Production Board estimated that if the synchronized reconversion plan were implemented, nonwar production in the United Kingdom would be increased by 20 percent from the current level but would remain 16 percent below the prewar (1938) level.[41] By contrast, resources made available for nonwar purposes in the United States would allow an increase of 20 percent from the 1944 level of nonwar production and would represent an increase of 15 percent over the prewar (1939) level. Finally, because the United States's contribution to the common Allied pool of munitions was much larger than that of Great Britain, a percentage reduction would be of much greater benefit to the United States than the United Kingdom in absolute terms.

The drawbacks in the synchronized reconversion plan were readily apparent to the British. In fact, the percentage approach, which London got wind of almost as soon as it was suggested to Hopkins, prompted the United Kingdom to develop and sell its own plan.

Whereas the substance and timing of American aid during Phase III had sharply divided the Treasury and Foreign Office, the issue of lend-lease during Phase II saw them working in harness once again. This unanimity was a product not only of the importance and immediacy of the problem, but also of the continued refusal of the empire isolationists to accept Keynes's stark forecast for the United Kingdom's economic and financial future and to acknowledge the need ultimately to cooperate in the proposed American multilateral system. True, British and American representatives had agreed on the desirability of establishing an International Monetary Fund and an International Bank for Reconstruction and Development, but so strong was the Beaverbrook-Amery group that not until after the war was over would Parliament ratify the Bretton Woods proposals. Talks over tariffs, Article VII, and the Mutual Aid Agreement had broken off at the end of 1943 and remained moribund throughout the next year. Far from being discouraged by Britain's financial position, Amery was convinced that the sterling area was on the rebound. "I don't believe that even you realize what we have made out of the sterling area during this war," he wrote Beaverbrook. "At this moment the reserve banks in the sterling area countries hold about two thousand million of sterling paper." Ignoring the fact that Britain's sterling partners were responding to the exigencies of war and to British political coercion, he declared: "Thanks to the credit we have established in the world, our paper is being treated as good as gold, and we have an almost unlimited gold mine in our printing presses here at home." If the "present Dick Law policy" were followed, it would bankrupt the country financially and the Conservative party politically.[42]

As Anderson, Cherwell, and Law attempted to deflate these arguments, tensions rose. "The whole thing develops into the worst pandemonium I have ever seen in the Cabinet," Dalton reported after one confrontation. "Towards the end four or five Ministers are often shouting at once."[43] As a last resort, the British multilateralists had turned to the august person and intellect of Lord Keynes.

At the beginning of July Keynes presented a "gay and most vigorous" memo, as Sir Wilfrid Eady termed it, on Britain's postwar financial position. Only the prose was gay and vigorous. Dalton termed it a brutal and hopefully successful attempt "to shake up the complacent." Keynes marshaled his figures and belabored the cabinet, albeit with velvet-gloved fist, for refusing to come to grips with reality. The country's overseas liabilities, he pointed out, now amounted to $8 billion and were increasing at a rate of over $2.4 billion annually. In addition, the United Kingdom would experience a deficit of about $4 billion during the early postwar years, the result of the difference between what could be earned by the export of goods and services and what would be needed to cover the import of raw materials. To reconvert its economy from a wartime to a peacetime footing and to meet its deficit on current account, Britain would need massive lend-lease aid during Phase II and a substantial interest-free loan after V-J Day. Without it, the country would quickly pass from the scene as a world power.[44]

Throughout July and August the British position on lend-lease during Phase II began to crystallize. Britain would "fight the Japanese to the maximum of our ability," as James Meade put it. But full participation would be based on two conditions: "that we should begin to put a stop to the rake's progress of living on our external capital assets which are still deteriorating as a result of the war, and to start to replace and repair our productive capital equipment, our houses and our depleted stocks of durable consumers' goods such as clothing and furniture."[45]

London decided to press for acceptance of the principle that the proportion of Britain's total munitions supplies furnished on lend-lease during Phase II would be the same as it had been for 1944. If the end of the war in Europe made possible a reduction of Allied munitions needs of, say, one-third, the amount of munitions furnished the United Kingdom under lend-lease should also be reduced by one-third. On nonmunition supplies, Churchill should persuade Roosevelt to accept the same principle or set a fixed amount. British needs for lend-lease munitions for the first year of Phase II would total $4 billion and nonmunitions $3 billion.[46]

The British alternative proved acceptable to Hopkins, and in early August he and his advisers together with representatives from the British Treasury began to develop a strategy for winning the approval of the American foreign policy establishment.[47] There were a number of tactical obstacles to overcome. Hopkins's advisers began to warn him as early as June of disastrous results if the United States military was allowed to shape policy for Phases II and III. The decision on whether or not to continue lend-lease and at what levels "is of relatively little importance from the standpoint of the drain on our Treasury, but the decision may be of vast importance to us both politically and economically," F. M. Eaton of the War Production Board wrote Hopkins. "Such a decision is of an order of magnitude well beyond military competence."[48]

The United States military became aware of the dimensions of British lend-lease requests for Phase II and of White House support for the British position the first week in July. The National Association of Manufacturers again charged in the *New York Times* that a secret plan was afoot to lift the 1941 White Paper on Exports and that there were those in the administration who wanted to use lend-lease to facilitate British reconversion to civilian production during Phase II.[49] On August 11, 1944, the Joint Chiefs of Staff (JCS) pointed out to the rest of the foreign policy establishment that the president had already approved a lend-lease policy for the post–V-E period. In fact, FDR had initialed a strategic document, the appendix of which contained the military's plan for Phase II. "Upon the defeat of Germany," it read, "assignment of Lend-Lease munitions will be limited to the materials which are not available to the Allied Nations concerned and which are necessary to support that portion of the forces of such nations as, in the opinion of the United States Joint Chiefs of Staff, can and will be profitably employed against Japan in the furtherance of our agreed strategy."[50] American representatives "at all levels of the assignment machinery" were bound by this provision and orders to that effect were being issued, the joint chiefs declared. On September 5 agents of the Army Service Forces received orders to halt shipment of all lend-lease military equipment on Germany's surrender. The joint chiefs even went so far as to instruct United States military representatives in Europe to notify lend-lease recipient nations that, as soon as Germany was defeated, all unused lend-lease items were to be returned to the continental United States or to the control of the United States government. Only Hopkins's last-minute intervention with Chief of Staff William D. Leahy prevented implementation.[51]

The joint chiefs's position on lend-lease during the Pacific phase of World War II was apparently contradictory. In the short run, anything Washington could do to strengthen Britain's combat capabilities would save American lives and hasten the end of the war. In the long run, only an economically healthy and prosperous Britain could help police Europe and the Near East. But, as has been noted, the United States military did not trust Britain to look after America's interests in the postwar world and did not believe that it would possess the power to do so, no matter what its inclination or the amount of aid America made available.

In the opinion of many of America's top soldiers, the British Empire had by 1944 entered a stage of rapid and irreversible decline. Reflecting a widely held view among both officers in the field and War Department analysts, General Joseph Stillwell commented on several occasions that the British simply did not want to fight in Burma and they did not want to reopen communications with China. "The more I see of the Limies, the worse I hate them," the general commented with typical Stillwellian bluntness; "the bastardly hypocrites do their best to cut our throats on all occasions."[52] Americans must abandon their traditional view of British military power as a dominant force in world affairs. "Except for the elimination of Germany as a threat and rival," read a JCS memo on the subject, "nearly all the essential factors of national power in the postwar era will have altered, to the disadvantage of the British Empire. Both in an absolute sense and relative to the United States and Russia, the British Empire will emerge from the war having lost ground both economically and militarily."[53] Henry Stimson, traditionally regarded as a friend of Great Britain, wrote in April: "I have come to the conclusion that if this war is to be won, its [*sic*] got to be won by the full strength of the virile, energetic, initiative-loving, inventive Americans, and that the British really are showing decadence—a magnificent people, but they have lost their initiative."[54]

The opinion prevailed among many within military circles that the United States must and would replace Britain as the "dominant" power in the Pacific basin. (That opinion, of course, incorporated Britain's low estimation of Chinese power in the postwar era.) Early in 1944 Admiral William Leahy, in behalf of the joint chiefs, informed Cordell Hull that the Japanese-mandated islands should be placed under the sole control of the United States: "Their conquest is being affected by the forces of the United States and there appears to be no valid reason why their future should be the subject of discussion with any other nation."[55] Indeed, Leahy and others argued that it might be better if America did the lion's share of the fighting in the last stages of the war against Japan. "There is developing in America," Australian Ambassador John Curtain wrote Churchill in August 1944, "a hope that they will be able to say they won the Pacific war by themselves. . . . I am deeply concerned at the position that would arise in a Far Eastern Empire if any considerable American opinion were to hold that America fought a war on principle in the Far East and won it relatively unaided while the other allies including ourselves did very little toward recovering our lost property."[56]

If lend-lease could not be withheld, reasoned the military, it could surely be used as leverage to force the British to turn over its bases in the Pacific and, in addition, to convert the ninety-nine-year leases in the Atlantic into permanent transfers, to secure unconditional landing rights for United States military and commercial aircraft at British bases around the world, and to ensure that Britain would not block United States access to strategic materials in the Middle and Far East. The military's objectives and its plan to use lend-lease as leverage to attain them were set forth in a remarkable document prepared by General Brehon Somervell, chief of supply services for the United States military. If the military's blueprint for lend-lease aid to Britain after V-E Day were followed, he pointed out, the volume of supplies going to Britain would "dwindle so rapidly" that London would grant America's every demand. Those demands should include return of all unused or unexpended lend-lease items, indefinite extension of rights acquired under the Destroyers-for-Bases Deal, "rights of the same or similar kind in any part of the world under British control," and assurances of "full commercial rights" for the United States and its nationals to purchase "without unfavorable discrimination in respect to price or opportunity" strategic items such as petroleum, metals, and rubber, in areas under British control.[57] "The hard fact is," wrote Mountbatten's chief of staff in 1944, "that the Americans have got us by the short hairs. . . . So if they don't approve, they don't provide."[58]

The military's plan for lend-lease in Phase II seemed nothing less than disastrous as far as the British and their allies in the Hopkins network were concerned. The military wanted, essentially, to halt lend-lease shipments to Britain after V-E Day except for items that the United Kingdom could not produce for itself—which amounted to a tiny percentage of the total lend-lease picture. According to one survey done for Hopkins, under the Somervell plan, United Kingdom and empire munitions production would have to remain constant or even increase during Phase II in order to make up for the lack of lend-lease shipments from the United States. War expenditures in Britain would amount to about 38 percent of the total gross national product, as compared to 32 percent under the plan for continuing lend-lease on a proportional basis.[59] If the theory put forward by the American military authorities were to hold sway, Robert H. Brand wrote Hopkins, Britain would not fare as well in peace as the liberated countries, the neutrals, and even Germany, which would have no occupying role and which would be free to turn to "the arts of peace." Britain was "the only nation which has been in the front line from the first to the last day of the German war."[60] Its citizens deserved better. Lauchlin Currie, G. D. H. Coe, Charles Taft, Harry Hawkins, William Batt, and F. M. Eaton agreed that the military solution was no solution at all and that the military should not and must not have the last word.

The only individual powerful enough to contain the military and assure Britain adequate aid during Phase II was Franklin Roosevelt. But the president faced a delicate situation, Hopkins told Halifax on July 25. The military and its allies in

Congress and narrow-minded exporting groups such as the National Association of Manufacturers were powerful. Initially Hopkins envisioned a mission to the United States in mid-August headed by the chancellor of the Exchequer to explain Britain's plight directly to the president. But the NAM press release carried by the *New York Times* the first week in August frightened Hopkins and forced a change of plans. A special Anderson visit, he decided, would provide the president's political enemies with new ammunition. Though there was some risk of strengthening Treasury's already strong hand within the foreign policy establishment, the White House instructed the British Embassy to use Morgenthau's previously planned trip to England to state Britain's case. Morgenthau would in turn present it to Roosevelt. Hopkins readily agreed that Treasury was not and should not be concerned in any important way in the making of lend-lease policy, but, given the political climate, he had no choice but to use the secretary. Besides, Hopkins told Halifax, Morgenthau had much influence with the president. His previous hard line toward British gold/dollar balances would give added credibility to the British case if he pled it with FDR. After Morgenthau's report, Hopkins would secure a general directive from Roosevelt freezing lend-lease at current levels until a comprehensive decision could be reached by the two Allied leaders at the second Quebec Conference.[61]

In accordance with Hopkins's scheme, John Anderson made a formal, detailed presentation of Britain's economic and financial situation to Henry Morgenthau on August 11. The chancellor, in effect, summarized the statistics contained in the Keynes memo. There were, he told his American guest, two great desiderata as far as Britain was concerned: that "we should not emerge from the war as applicants for Poor Relief" and that there should be no repudiation of Britain's liabilities.[62] Only adequate gold and dollar balances would allow Britain to attain these objectives.

Morgenthau listened quietly and intently. If Britain expected Treasury's help in this matter, it must understand one matter clearly: Whitehall must not seek to play one United States agency off against the other, as had been the case in the past. The Treasury chief then revealed why he had taken such a hard line on the matter of British gold/dollar balances during the past year. Before Churchill's departure for the Cairo Conference in January 1943, the chancellor of the Exchequer, Sir Kingsley Wood, had handed Churchill two memos on the gold/dollar balance question. One, intended for transmission to the Americans, set forth Britain's position and called for relief. The second, intended for Churchill's eyes only, had sharply criticized Morgenthau's handling of the matter, insinuating that he was playing to the galleries. A more sympathetic hearing might be had at the State Department or FEA, Wood had suggested. Churchill had read only the first memo to Roosevelt and Hopkins, but then handed them both to the Americans. And they in turn eventually found their way into Morgenthau's hands. If the British would not trust him, he told his white-faced listener, they could expect no help.

But Morgenthau admitted that Britain's position was desperate. Congressional opposition to the use of lend-lease for reconstruction and reconversion problems, whether during Phase II or Phase III, was strong. What was needed was a "new name and a fresh approach." A solution might be for the president and the prime minister to name a committee of two, consisting of himself and Sir John Anderson, to frame lend-lease policy for Phase II. From that time forward, all aid would flow through and be approved by the United States Treasury. If all this came to pass, the British could count on the whole-hearted support of the Treasury. Morgenthau's conciliatory posture was merely that—posturing. He wanted to gain bureaucratic control of lend-lease, secure British ratification of the Bretton Woods Agreements, and obtain the Churchill government's endorsement of the Morgenthau Plan.[63] As events were to prove, he remained convinced that a stick rather than a carrot was the best method to attain his objectives.

On August 18 Hopkins met with FDR and told him that the British were requesting a continuation of lend-lease aid into Phase II. "In effect," Hopkins declared, "the British are asking us to produce munitions for them at a very high rate while they would turn many of their factories over to consumer production— much of it for export." It was a politically controversial proposal, to say the least, he observed. Most ominously, the matter was then being discussed "at a low level within our army and navy," a level that was not competent to decide such matters. The White House should put an end to this by ordering a continuation of lend-lease aid at current rates until the president and the prime minister could meet at Quebec. Roosevelt assented and subsequently issued the necessary orders.[64]

The next day, Morgenthau delivered his report to Roosevelt. Churchill had made a strong case to the effect that England was broke. "What does he mean by that?" FDR asked. "Yes, England really is broke," Morgenthau replied. Roosevelt seemed surprised, Morgenthau recalled. The secretary made his proposal regarding the committee of two to frame Phase II policy. FDR was noncommittal. "This is very interesting. I had no idea that England was broke. I will go over there and make a couple of talks and take over the British Empire."[65] Franklin Roosevelt knew perfectly well that his principal ally was in desperate financial straits, but he intended, as always, to play his cards close to the vest.

In mid-September Roosevelt, Churchill, and the Combined Chiefs of Staff gathered once again in Quebec for a meeting that was billed as primarily military in nature. According to official press releases, the two Allied leaders and their military chieftains were coming together to plan the last stages of the war against Germany and to discuss strategy for Phase II—the war in the Pacific.

Winston Churchill recalled in his memoirs that he became quite conscious of a power shift in the Anglo-American partnership following the successful Normandy landings in June 1944. Up to that point the two nations had made strategic, political, and economic decisions as equals. After that date, America was clearly the dominant party, the "booted rider" to use F. M. Eaton's phrase. The change was evident in the president and prime minister's posture toward each other before and during the Quebec Conference. As Christopher Thorne has noted, the Roosevelt-Churchill personal relationship, always rather superficial, had deteriorated by Quebec. Increasingly, the president regarded Churchill as hopelessly out of touch with the times—in his attitudes toward domestic policy, toward Russia, and toward colonialism. Through his actions and policies, the president seemed to indicate that Churchill was not worth taking all that seriously—certainly not compared to Stalin. Churchill continued throughout late 1944 and early 1945 to be as positive and complimentary toward Roosevelt as he had always been, expressing "indescribable relief" at the president's reelection in November. But the prime minister was nervous, irritable, and fidgety before and during the conference—primarily because he realized that Britain's fate no longer rested in its own hands. Lend-lease during Phase II was of vital importance, Cherwell told Churchill before the British delegation sailed aboard the *Queen Mary* for the Quebec Conference, "not only because it will determine the scale of our effort against Japan and the part we play in Europe, but also because our whole economic and political future depends upon the arrangements we make now."[66]

During the week before the conference, each side attempted to map its strategy. Roosevelt announced that he was taking only military advisers because purely military matters were going to be discussed. He even went so far as to forbid Churchill to bring Anderson and Oliver Lyttleton, the British minister of production. The limited nature of the president's entourage reflected Hopkins's desire that Roosevelt and Churchill, and those two men alone, would determine lend-lease policy for Phase II. But there was another reason. Hopkins wanted Roosevelt to appropriate multilateralism as his own, to preempt Hull who more than any other American was identified in the public mind with "economic liberalism." "I think it is important in Quebec," he told Roosevelt, "that you tell the Prime Minister how strongly you feel about kicking down some of the trade barriers to get somewhere in terms of world trade." Churchill, like many Americans, "thinks that the genius of this program . . . lies with Secretary Hull, while the thrust of the matter is that it is a program that, from the beginning, has been pushed by you."[67]

Franklin Roosevelt went to Quebec determined to use the leverage of lend-lease to secure British agreement on a number of specific points. He expected a commitment to cooperate fully in the final stages of the Pacific war. In the short run, American lives were at stake; in the long run, Anglo-American cooperation in the postwar world was on the line. In addition, the president still entertained hopes for Russian-American cooperation after the war and so continued to favor the harsh policy toward Germany he had outlined at Teheran. If Churchill wanted liberal aid during Phase II, he would have to endorse the Morgenthau Plan. Although Roosevelt was anxious to commit Britain to a multilateral trade and payments system, there was no need at that point, he believed, to press the British for specific assurances over Article VII.[68] The United Kingdom would still need massive aid from the United States after Japan's surrender, and that need would supply more than enough leverage to compel Britain to eliminate imperial preference and exchange controls.

Shortly before Roosevelt departed for Quebec, Cordell Hull, exhausted by years of bureaucratic infighting, refused a last-minute invitation from the president to go to Canada and wrote a long memo urging a generous lend-lease program for Phase II, but only if "accompanied by vigorous British efforts to join us in pressing a world-wide program of multilateral reduction to barriers to international trade." Specifically, Britain must promise to ratify the Bretton Woods Agreements and to implement Article VII.[69]

Despite his positive response to Anderson's presentation in London, Morgenthau urged Roosevelt to adopt a policy at Quebec that was closer to that advocated by the military than by the Hopkins clique. "We do not agree with the recommendation that the American and British reconversion programs should be synchronized nor that Lend-Lease can be reduced by only about one-third over-all," Morgenthau wrote the president on the day before his departure. Washington should discontinue the lend-leasing of all industrial materials. The United States should furnish to Britain only those munitions it needed for the Pacific war and "of which she does not have an exportable surplus within the Empire."[70] The secretary still rankled at the Cairo incident; he was convinced that the Churchill government was soft on the German question; and he wanted ratification of the Bretton Woods Agreements.

The British delegation arrived in Quebec in something of a stew. Churchill and his military advisers had fought nearly all the way across the Atlantic. Senior British military leaders were virtually unanimous in advising that Great Britain's air and naval forces should now concentrate their full strength in the Pacific against Japan. Churchill was unenthusiastic. For him, World War II seemed to consist entirely of the war against Germany. He still talked of giving the Nazis a "stab in the Adriatic armpit." Only when his advisers began talking of British military operations in the Far East as necessary to save the Crown's imperial outposts did the prime minister show any interest.[71] All the while, Cherwell labored to impress on Churchill the absolute necessity of obtaining $4 billion in munitions and $3 billion in other supplies for Phase II. A loan was out of the question. Britain must acquire these supplies under lend-lease. Moreover, "we cannot accept American supplies on conditions that would hamstring our export trade, by which alone we can begin to pay our way." Britain's future as a "Great Power" was at stake.[72] It appeared that Churchill was going to have to beg and he did not relish the prospect. Finally, he feared that FDR would continue to insist on the dismemberment and deindustrialization of Germany. How was Europe to be reconstructed and revitalized, thus preventing the Soviets from fishing in troubled waters, with the Ruhr and the Saar out of commission? There seemed to be no alternative to a resurrected Germany, particularly given the uncertain prospects of a generous American loan to Britain during Phase III.

The British and American delegations assembled in the fortress city of Quebec, the site of their 1943 meeting, on September 12, 1944. As Cherwell had pressed him to do, Churchill made lend-lease during Phase II the first order of the day. The prime minister emphasized that $4 billion and $3.5 billion were the minimum necessary for Britain to participate fully in the final stages of the Japanese war and hammered away at the theme that a solvent Britain was in America's economic and strategic interests. There must be no loan terms and no export restrictions, he added, lest United States aid during Phase II be counterproductive. At the very least, FDR should establish a joint committee to make recommendations and should order lend-lease to continue at present levels until after the election.[73]

During Churchill's presentation Roosevelt repeatedly tried to turn the conversation to the subject of Germany's political future, much to the Englishman's annoyance. According to one observer, the prime minister blurted out after one of FDR's soliloquies on Germany: "Is this what you brought me over here for?" After another presidential digression, he threatened: "If you do not do something for Britain then the British simply will have to destroy gold and do business largely within the empire."[74] Finally, in an effort to cheer up the former naval person, Roosevelt offered him "the steel business of Europe for twenty or thirty years." That afternoon the president cabled a surprised and delighted Morgenthau: "Please be in Quebec by Thursday, 14 September, noon. Roosevelt."[75]

Morgenthau arrived early the next day and lend-lease talks between him, Cherwell, and the two chiefs of state resumed at once. Cherwell and Morgenthau were instructed to take notes on the talks and then work out a joint memo for the signatures of the president and the prime minister. According to a transcription in James Forrestal's papers, Churchill declared that "he hoped that the President would agree that during the war with Japan we should continue to get food, shipping, etc. from the United States to cover our reasonable needs." Roosevelt "indicated assent." The British leader then asked his counterpart to agree that lend-lease munitions continue on a proportional basis "even though this would enable the United Kingdom to set free labour for rebuilding, exports, etc., e.g. if British munitions were cut to three-fifths." Again FDR "indicated assent." At this point Morgenthau jumped in. It would be better to establish definite figures for the first year of Phase II. The British had suggested, he believed, $3.5 billion in munitions and $3 billion in nonmunitions. The president agreed that it would be better to work on set figures than a proportional basis. Would this aid be lend-lease and not in the form of an interest-bearing loan? Churchill inquired. Naturally so, Roosevelt replied. Britain would not export or sell lend-lease items for profit, the prime minister conceded, but "it was essential that the United States should not attach any conditions to supplies delivered to Britain . . . that would jeopardize the recovery of her export trade." The president "thought this would be proper." The two agreed on a joint committee to implement the agreement. Morgenthau would be chairman, FDR declared, but Edward Stettinius, "who had taken such a large part in Lend-Lease," should also be a member.[76] Churchill believed that he had gotten everything he had asked for. The prime minister was so overcome, one observer recalled, that he had tears in his eyes.[77] They were to dry quickly.

The same evening, following a state dinner, Roosevelt asked Morgenthau to read his paper on the future of Germany. The plan that he outlined called not only for the denazification of Germany, but its deindustrialization as well. Britain and America's enemy would be converted into a nation "primarily agricultural and pastoral." There is some evidence that Roosevelt had been influenced, as Morgenthau apparently had, by Bernard Baruch's idea that the fate of German industry and the future of the British economy were bound up together. When Henry Stimson went to the White House on September 6 to object to the Morgenthau Plan, Roosevelt declared that Britain was going to be in very "sore straits" after the war. If the Ruhr was put out of commission and the coal of the Saar turned over to the British steel industry, the United Kingdom could grow healthy by supplying Europe's steel needs. In vain did Stimson argue that the future of Europe's economy was a complex question meriting detailed study and that FDR "should not burn down the house of the world for the purpose of getting a meal of roast pig."[78]

Churchill was, to put it mildly, hostile to the American proposal. The United States was asking Britain to chain itself to a dead German, he said. Morgenthau, who tended to be oversensitive to criticism, recalled Churchill's response: "He was slumped in his chair, his language biting, his flow incessant, his manner merciless. I have never had such a verbal lashing in my life."[79] During a break in the talks, Cherwell went to work on his friend. "The Prof" harbored "an almost pathological hatred for Nazi Germany," according to one of his associates.[80] He was emotionally attracted to the Morgenthau Plan. He had, moreover, accepted the Baruch-Morgenthau argument that the elimination of the Ruhr and Saar would make possible a geometric expansion of British exports. Cherwell forcefully recounted the advantages that would accrue to Britain after Germany was laid waste and also reminded his chief that FDR had not yet initialed the memo on lend-lease; he probably would not do so until Britain agreed to the swords-into-ploughshares plan. Britain's future, he repeated for the hundredth time, depended on lend-lease in Phase II.[81]

The next morning, Churchill was positively bubbling with enthusiasm for the Morgenthau approach. He even dictated the contents of the deindustrialization and pastoralization memo that was ultimately signed by the two Allied leaders. Anthony Eden, who had not been privy to the Cherwell-Churchill confab of the previous night, was appalled. Morgenthau recorded the scene in his diary: "When Churchill got through, Eden seemed quite shocked at what he heard, and said, 'You can't do this. After all, you and I publicly have said quite the opposite. Furthermore, we have a lot of things in the works in London which are quite different.' "[82] "Then Churchill and Eden seemed to have quite a bit of argument about it. . . . Churchill's main argument was what this meant in the way of trade; they would get the export trade of Germany. So Eden said":

> "How do you know what it is or where it is" and Churchill answered him quite
> testily, "Well, we will get it wherever it is." I was quite amazed and shocked at
> Eden's attitude; in fact it was so different from the way we talked when we were
> in London. Finally, Churchill said, "Now, I hope, Anthony, you're not going to
> do anything about this with the War Cabinet if you see a chance to present
> it. . . . After all, the future of my people is at stake, and when I have to choose
> between my people and the German people I am going to choose my people."[83]

Though disturbed and somewhat puzzled by the vehemence of Eden's opposition, Morgenthau and Roosevelt were pleased with the outcome of the talks. The prime minister had been adroitly manipulated. Roosevelt, who was capable of petty cruelty at times, could not resist showing off his boots and spurs. The day wore on, and still FDR put off initialing the memo on lend-lease. After a string of inane Rooseveltian stories, the exasperated Churchill burst out: "What do you want me to do? Get on my hind legs and beg like Falla?" As Roosevelt signed, he whispered to Morgenthau that the only reason Britain was willing to get into the war against Japan was to get Singapore back.[84]

Given his objectives, Franklin Roosevelt had managed Great Britain quite nicely on the issues of postwar Germany and lend-lease. He was not as successful with his own foreign policy establishment. Not only did State, War, and Navy blast the Morgenthau Plan, they attacked the lend-lease settlement as well. Hull and his advisers wanted commercial policy strings attached to lend-lease aid during Phase II; the service departments and joint chiefs wanted bases; certain high-ranking military officials wished to restrict Britain's role in the Pacific to a minimum; and all departments, including FEA, were angry that Treasury had stolen a march on them. Even Morgenthau worked to undercut the Roosevelt-Churchill understanding. During the discussions at Quebec, he had insisted on reserving to the United States the right to "recalculate" lend-lease aid to Britain during Phase II "in the light of the decisions on military matters reached at the Conference."[85] Morgenthau wanted to ensure continued British support for a harsh policy toward Germany, and he was determined to retain control of the administration of lend-lease during the period between V-E and V-J Day.

Almost as soon as the presidential entourage returned to Washington, Roosevelt's political enemies began to circulate rumors that he had let Britain off the hook concerning compensation for lend-lease; worse, he had made a massive commitment to underwrite civilian reconstruction in Britain through direct aid and through the immediate expansion of British export trades. A contingent of Republican members of Congress returned from a tour of England to report that the United States would receive no payment for lend-lease aid to Britain but instead would be billed by the British for wartime aid to America. In addition, they charged, the British were keeping records of all man-hours of labor used to move American troops and equipment. These labor costs would be added to the bill that, when all was said and done, would more than wipe out the British debt of both world wars. In a special bulletin to its twelve-thousand-member companies, the National Association of Manufacturers charged that a clique of policymakers in Washington was plotting to cancel all lend-lease accounts and even continue the program under another name after the war. Arthur Krock ran a story to the effect that Morgenthau had promised a huge United States subsidy to the British economy in return for Churchill's approval of the Morgenthau Plan.[86]

Rumors concerning a sellout at Quebec circulated in the midst of an intensifying xenophobia and Anglophobia in the United States. "The Washington atmosphere," ran a political report by the British Embassy, "is mainly determined by the 1944 election and by the general belief that the end of the European war is at hand."[87] Both factors redounded to Britain's detriment. Anticipation of the war's end meant closer scrutiny by Congress of governmental expenditures, particularly lend-lease. It also meant a general decrease in the public's willingness to sacrifice, and a growing eagerness for consumer goods and an end to controls. Above all, criticism of Great Britain was more than ever politically popular. A British officer assigned to the Joint Chiefs of Staff building on Constitution Avenue hailed a taxi after leaving work one day. Once the Englishman was inside, the driver said that he wanted to ask a question that had been on his mind a long time: what was the little stick British officers carried and why did they carry it? A swagger stick, the Englishman replied, and he and his fellows carried it, he guessed, to improve their military bearing by being forced to keep their hand out of their pocket. The driver responded: "In that event it would be a fine idea if you carried two swagger sticks so you'd keep your other hand out of Uncle Sam's pocket."[88]

Roosevelt's own foreign policy bureaucracy was almost as obstreperous as his political enemies and the average American. The military establishment—from Stimson, Forrestal, and the joint chiefs to the officers who sat on the various combined boards and supply missions—was outraged that Roosevelt agreed to lend-lease aid for Britain in Phase II well beyond the United Kingdom's anticipated battlefield needs, that he had required nothing—that is, bases—in return, and that the military had been excluded from the joint Anglo-American committee to be chaired by Morgenthau. After meeting with Hull on September 20 to discuss rumors of the Quebec settlement, John J. McCloy reported to Stimson: "I gather that all the Lend-Lease discussions with the British which have been conducted by the State Department and which were leading up to obtaining international rights, of one sort or another, have pretty much been cut under, there being little scope left as to what we want from them for the $21 billion already given to them or the additional Lend-Lease which may be given hereafter."[89]

Not surprisingly, the military took the position that all the talk about reconversion that was surfacing in London and Washington in late 1944 was grossly premature. Donald Nelson and the WPB had been trying to persuade Congress and the president to agree on a specific date at which civilian manufacturing could be resumed in America. The joint chiefs had fought him every step of the way. If the United States allowed the United Kingdom to resume civilian production during Phase II, political pressure on the government to allow United States manufacturers to do the same would be irresistible. Relaxation, James Forrestal told Paul McNutt, would open the way to "numerous pressure groups sponsoring local projects." Indeed, if the government permitted the expenditure of labor and materials on nonwar-related projects, some concerns might be encouraged to turn down war contracts in the hope of getting back into peacetime production ahead of their former or potential competitors.[90]

The State Department was no less unhappy with the results of the Quebec Conference than the armed services. On September 15, Roosevelt cabled Hull a copy of the lend-lease memo he and Churchill had initialed. He informed his by now continually exhausted secretary of state that a joint Anglo-American committee had been set up to administer lend-lease during Phase II. United States membership would include Morgenthau as chairman, Edward Stettinius, and Leo Crowley. Hull and his subordinates read the president's directive with sinking hearts. The secretary's plan for Germany, in their opinion, was idiotic and would certainly lead to another war. Moreover, Morgenthau clearly seemed to be winning the struggle for preeminence within the foreign policy establishment. Finally, the lend-lease memo Roosevelt had initialed promised the British $6.5 billion in lend-lease with no multilateral strings attached.

After reflecting on the matter, however, State perceived an opening, a contradiction of which it might be able to take advantage. The committee, FDR's directive to Hull declared, was to decide the amount of lend-lease during Phase II. Immediately Hull began to bombard the White House with memoranda arguing that, although the promise of aid had not been tied to British concessions on commercial policy, the actual extension of that aid should be.[91]

The Quebec memo on lend-lease even suffered from subterraneous burrowing by the Treasury Department. It was Morgenthau who had inserted the escape clause stipulating that exact amounts would have to be recalculated in light of the developing strategic and military situation, an escape clause about which he subsequently boasted to Forrestal. It was his intervention, he told the navy chief, that had prevented the British from getting approval at Quebec of their requests on a "frozen" basis.[92] The directive and accompanying memo, Morgenthau reassured Hull and Stimson on September 20, could be interpreted in such a way as to permit the United States "flexibility of decision" in the amount of lend-lease extended. By keeping the lend-lease issue open and by ensuring his personal control of its administration, Morgenthau believed he had placed himself in a position to apply pressure on Whitehall to continue its support for the destruction of Germany and to proceed with ratification of the Bretton Woods Agreements.

Of course, FEA was angry that Roosevelt had been so "charitable" to the British at Quebec. Aside from Crowley's Irish-Catholic Anglophobia, the agency took a proprietary view of lend-lease. Oscar Cox, deputy director, had been the author of the original act. Following abolition of the lend-lease agency under Stettinius, administration of the aid program had been one of FEA's principal functions. Crowley and Cox had repeatedly gone on record before congressional committees assuring members that lend-lease monies would be expended for war-related purposes only. And those did not include socioeconomic conditions capable of being taken advantage of by some future enemy. Like the commercial section of the State Department, FEA had to bear the brunt of complaints from American exporters concerning real and imagined advantages accruing to their British rivals in various parts of the world. As a result, a majority of FEA administrators, Lauchlin Currie being the primary exception, opposed any relaxation of restrictions spelled out in the Export White Paper and thus any significant

British reconversion during Phase II. Cox wanted a strong Britain but opposed using lend-lease to achieve that goal.[93]

Just as he was to do over the Morgenthau Plan, FDR caved in to bureaucratic and public pressure over lend-lease. A few days after his return to Washington Roosevelt called Crowley into his office to discuss aid to Britain during Phase II. Over the past several months the FEA chief had been telling Hopkins that a strong and vigorous Britain in the postwar period was vitally important to the United States and simultaneously whispering to the War Department that Britain should receive nothing under lend-lease that could not be justified under the congressional mandate. Crowley was just Roosevelt's sort of person. He could not recall exactly what he had signed at Quebec, the president told the foreign economic administrator. Regardless, Crowley was to "take charge of this thing and handle it in accordance with my commitments to Congress." (Incredibly, Roosevelt also told Crowley to "make a study of the German problem under the direction of the State Department.")[94] The president subsequently told Hopkins to prepare a public letter to Crowley regarding lend-lease that would satisfy everyone. The letter ordered FEA to relax export controls after Germany's surrender so as to "encourage private trade." Crowley was to furnish lend-lease supplies in such a way as to ensure the defeat of Germany and then Japan in the shortest time and with the least loss of life possible. "The amount and nature of the aid necessary after the defeat of Germany," the president added, "is closely tied up with the . . . program for reconstruction and reconversion of industry to civilian needs which we and our Allies work out on a basis of mutual understanding."[95] The presidential directive promised everything—and nothing.

The only things that were clear from all this were that, despite what Churchill believed, the matter of lend-lease for Phase II had not been settled as an issue in Anglo-American relations and the outcome would be determined as much by the bureaucratic power struggle within the Roosevelt foreign policy establishment as by any rational evaluation of the two countries' national interests.

Meanwhile deep divisions over postwar financial and economic policy continued to roil the political and bureaucratic waters in Great Britain. But as the various components of the coalition government came to grips with the hard realities of the postwar era, the empire isolationists were driven into grudging retreat, and the uneasy alliance between the parliamentary Labour party and reform Tories grew stronger.

Winston Churchill left Quebec dispirited and disheartened. His concessions to the Americans, made to protect the financial position of his country and the political position of his party, depressed him. "I have a very strong feeling my work is done," he confided to Cherwell and Cadogan after Quebec. "I have no message. I had a message. Now I only say, 'Fight the damned socialists.' I do not believe in this brave new world."[96] Yet he had staved off temporary disaster. The

United Kingdom would have to defend its financial independence against American pretensions again, he acknowledged, but not until Phase III, the period following Japan's surrender. For the time being, he was convinced, all was well on the economic front. "In very agreeable conversations yesterday between me and the President and Cherwell and Morgenthau," Churchill cabled Anderson from Quebec, "all our desires were met on both munitions and non-munition supplies."[97] Churchill proposed leaving Cherwell to represent Britain on the committee he and FDR had agreed to, to be joined or replaced later by Sir Robert Sinclair.

Anderson and the cabinet were gratified by the Quebec memo but were realistic about the commitment it involved. They had become increasingly aware of the bureaucratic situation in Washington and by September 1944 were very skeptical of any Rooseveltian promise. A number of ministers suspected that some hard bargaining lay ahead. Nor was the cabinet impressed with Churchill's personnel choices. Although men like Eden and Law—and to an extent Bevin and Dalton— agreed with Cherwell's point of view, they distrusted him and resented his personal influence over the prime minister. Anderson and the Treasury, moreover, felt him unsophisticated and likely to give away more than was necessary to the Americans.

The reality of British dependence on the United States and the emerging consensus within the British cabinet played into the hands of the Treasury and specifically John Maynard Keynes. England had to have aid but Washington would want something in return—at the very least full participation in the multilateral system the State Department had been pushing for so long and that the president had recently adopted as his own. Because Britain's future was so intimately tied to economic and financial questions, it seemed to the cabinet that only the Treasury and Keynes had the expertise to negotiate an agreement with the Americans that obtained what Britain needed and at the same time preserved as much freedom of action as possible in the postwar world. The cabinet could lay down principles and act as watchdog, it thought, but the great economist, the architect of the International Monetary Fund, the preeminent translator of statistics and financial jargon, would have to do the spadework.

In late September, John Maynard Keynes began building a consensus within the foreign policy establishment by setting out the imperatives that would control British diplomacy for the foreseeable future. Keynes called upon the cabinet to recognize that financial factors were now and would continue to be paramount. He lambasted Hugh Dalton and the Board of Trade for inactivity and the British military for overactivity. He pointed out that Britain would enter Phase III running an overseas deficit "at the fantastic rate" of £1.5 billion per year. Even to keep its deficit at this level Britain would have to have an income of £450 million from exports for 1945, a figure that Keynes called "preposterously optimistic." Britain must have a major export drive and begin at once.[98] At the same time, the United Kingdom would have to tighten its belt; the chief spendthrift in the projected budget for 1945 was the military. It was asking £550 million for overseas expenditures, excluding Europe. Most of this money would be used to maintain huge military establishments in Egypt and India, and to preserve imperial lines of communication. Under the plans being considered by the European Advisory Commission, a large number of occupation troops were to be kept in Germany for an indefinite period.

The United Kingdom, Keynes proclaimed, could no longer afford prestige and empire for their own sake; German occupation should be left to Germany's immediate neighbors. "We cannot police half the world at our own expense when we have already gone into pawn to the other half," he argued.

We cannot run for long a great programme of social amelioration on money lent from overseas. Unless we are willing to put ourselves financially at the mercy of America and then borrow from her on her own terms and conditions sums which we cannot confidently hope to repay, what are we expecting? Are we looking to a spectacular bankruptcy (not, altogether, a bad idea) from which we shall rise next morning without a care in the world? Or are we following some star at present invisible to me?

He concluded with a quote from Milton: "War has made many great whom peace makes small. If after being released from the toils of war, you neglect the arts of peace, if your peace and your liberty be a state of warfare, if war be your only virtue, the summit of your praise, you will, believe me, soon find peace most adverse to your interests."[99]

In this same vein, Keynes opposed a substantial reparations burden for Germany. If the victorious powers were allowed to drain Germany dry, those with a stake in the political and economic stability of Western Europe would have to prop it up—and that would require a massive diversion of resources. Keynes viewed the Morgenthau-Baruch Plan as nothing less than absurd. Britain would not profit from the elimination of German competition for export markets. Some of the United Kingdom's best customers would be the economically rehabilitated nations of Western Europe. Britain could not replace the Ruhr and Saar in Europe's economy. More importantly, the United Kingdom would not be able to fill the power vacuum that would result from the impoverishment of Germany, and that would constitute an open invitation to another would-be Napoleon or Hitler to seek European hegemony.

Following a barrage of Keynes memos to various ministers, Anderson persuaded Clement Attlee to convene the cabinet, which, if less entertaining in Churchill's absence, was more efficient. On September 18, the ministers duly approved an official British delegation headed by Keynes to go to America and hammer out the details of the Phase II agreement. As he could not arrive in Washington before September 28, they stipulated that all discussions up to that date were to be strictly informal.[100]

Meanwhile, in Washington a flurry of inter- and intra-governmental negotiations unfolded, with State and FEA conspiring to wrest control of the Phase II committee from Morgenthau and reintroduce commercial policy considerations into Stage II lend-lease negotiations. As soon as word of the Quebec committee's existence began to circulate in Washington, Charles Taft, Harry Hawkins, William Batt of WPB, and Charles Denby of FEA began to plot its capture. In their minds, the American representation was a disaster, Morgenthau was the enemy, and, of the other two (Stettinius and Crowley), "one is emotional and the other can't make up his mind," as Taft put it. On the positive side, the State Department was represented, and the loophole in the Quebec memo offered an opportunity to attach multilateral conditions to any aid that was forthcoming. Taft subsequently persuaded Stettinius, who was at Dumbarton Oaks, to name him as his stand-in. The multilateralists would have preferred Acheson, but all agreed that Morgenthau would have vetoed his selection. So it was Taft.[101]

The Republican internationalist immediately got on the phone with Lucius Clay. What was all this talk about $3.5 billion for munitions; had not the British request in August been for $2.5 billion? That was the figure he had seen, Clay said. Taft then called Denby and had the same conversation. The FEA official responded appropriately; $3.5 billion sounded like a figure "taken out of the air by higher ups."[102] Taft's calls were designed to leave a paper trail in support of the position that he would take with the British—namely, that the lend-lease figures mentioned at Quebec were still negotiable.

State Department officials anticipated from the outset that they would get no help whatsoever from Treasury in attaching a commercial policy pricetag to Phase II lend-lease, and they were right. No sooner had the combined committee had its initial meeting than Henry Morgenthau set about circumventing his American colleagues. The secretary was at the peak of his power in the foreign policy establishment in fall 1944. He felt that he had even eclipsed Harry Hopkins: "I think he resents that I am going to be the number one man in lend-lease because he said in the final analysis I'll have to decide what the British get and what they don't get, and I think he resents that, because up to now he has been the person. Whether he will play ball time will only tell."[103] Morgenthau was now willing to take a liberal posture over lend-lease but only on the condition that the British agree to deal with Treasury and Treasury alone.

On September 27, State and FEA learned that Morgenthau had "given instructions to the British to talk to no one concerning lend-lease except Harry White."[104] How could they "bust this thing up"? Taft asked his confidants.[105] Although Hull did not like to stand up to Morgenthau, the situation seemed to call for the secretary to intervene directly with the White House. On September 30, the Tennessean appealed to FDR to take advantage of the forthcoming Keynes visit to secure a firm commitment on Article VII. Moreover, argued Hull, State rather than Treasury should be in overall charge of negotiations with the Keynes mission and of subsequent implementation of agreements. "I am afraid," he wrote, "that we are courting disaster unless the whole subject is handled as a matter of foreign policy rather than solely or predominantly a matter of finance."[106]

Thus it was that when John Maynard Keynes arrived in Washington—sent, he told Anderson, as any good ambassador was, to lie abroad for his country—the bureaucratic pot was boiling. Despite this and the fact that fears were expressed among some administration officials that Thomas Dewey would try to exploit business and conservative prejudice against Keynes during the last stages of the election campaign, the great economist was, as always, optimistic about his ability to manage the Americans. Characteristically, he chose to ignore the incipient Anglophobia in the United States and to accentuate the positive. The atmosphere in Washington, he wrote Anderson, was one of the "greatest possible friendliness and good will." The Americans were inclined to be "intolerably tiresome in method and detail and with the execution of plans and in the mode of pressure they bring to bear," but one can and should approach them as a band of "friends and brothers." Like Britain, the United States was one of the few surviving nations that was inspired with "some measure of altruistic motive, and are prepared to sacrifice something for a better order in the world." More incredibly still, he observed, "all this applies not least to Congressmen, irrespective of party."[107]

Keynes's strategy for the forthcoming talks consisted of, first, getting rid of Cherwell; second, cultivating Morgenthau; and third, negotiating over the specifics of lend-lease while giving vague assurances on commercial policy and flatly refusing to talk about territorial concessions. Cherwell's presence was "a little embarrassing," Keynes wrote Anderson, since the paymaster general, insisting that Churchill had put him in complete and permanent charge, attempted to dictate strategy to Keynes and the new delegation. He and Cherwell had no personal difficulties (Keynes never admitted personal estrangement from anyone), but it would be better if he returned to London. Representatives of the British supply mission and the embassy were confused about who was in charge.[108] Cherwell remained for a time, but the physicist quickly took a back seat to the economist.

Keynes found Morgenthau and Harry White still obsessed with the Morgenthau Plan and still convinced, despite Stimson and Hull's bitter hostility, that they could win. In their first meeting, Morgenthau broached the subject, obviously trying to gain Keynes's endorsement. The Englishman was noncommittal. How were the Germans to feed themselves? There would have to be bread lines on a very low level of subsistence, the Americans replied. Of one thing he was certain, Keynes said. Britain could not pay for the pauperization of Germany. Not to worry, White interjected; the United States would foot the bill. In a subsequent report to Anderson on the interview, Keynes commented: "So whilst the hills are being turned into a sheep run, the valley will be filled for some years to come with a closely packed bread line on a very low level of subsistence at American expense." Keeping a straight face, he confided to Anderson, might be one of his principal tasks in the days ahead. "I try to prepare and sustain myself by repeating every night the three vows which I always make before a visit to America, namely, one, that I will drink no cocktails, two, that I will obey my wife, and three, that I will never allow myself to be betrayed into speaking the truth."[109]

What followed was a maze of negotiations between Keynes and the United States delegation, overlayed by the ongoing power struggle between State and FEA on the one hand and Treasury on the other. Morgenthau continued to assume a magnanimous posture. The Quebec memo tied their hands, he told Taft, Currie, Cox, and White. In negotiations over lend-lease for Phase II, no attempt should be made to hold down Britain's gold/dollar balances. "Now the best way I can describe it," he said, "is that here is a client or customer or friend who is broke, but who is a good moral risk, and we should ask this friend to state his entire problem . . . we should then do a good job for England to make it possible for her to stage a comeback and gradually meet her obligations, which are all over the world. And, therefore, I don't consider that the dollar balances are yardsticks anymore."[110] Treasury's new-found generosity scotched State's hidden agenda and fueled FEA's fears of congressional reprisal. "The arrangement in effect [the Quebec memo]," John Orchard complained to Stettinius, "would constitute a loan of three billion dollars to expend as they [the British] please except that there would surely be a Congressional rebellion when the Hill learned lend-lease was being used to refurbish Britain's civilian economy."[111]

At this point Harry Hopkins intervened and sided with State and FEA both as to who should control Phase II negotiations and whether or not conditions should be attached. Echoing Hull, Hopkins told Roosevelt that the administration and the United States would be "courting disaster unless the whole subject is handled as a matter of foreign policy rather than solely or predominantly a matter of finance." Financial assistance to Great Britain beyond its immediate military needs should not be divorced from "discussion of other extremely important matters." As all of these issues were of fundamental importance to the nation's foreign policy, they should be handled by the State Department with the advice of Treasury and FEA.[112]

On November 3, State fired a final salvo at Morgenthau and his campaign to seize control of American foreign policy. That day, on the eve of the presidential election, Arthur Krock ran a long article in the *New York Times* charging that Morgenthau at Quebec had traded the lend-lease memo, which, he claimed, called for unconditional underwriting of British economic reconversion, for Churchill's endorsement of the Morgenthau Plan. Morgenthau and White were furious, but there was nothing they could do.[113]

Claiming a prescience that did not exist, Keynes reported to London the last week in October on the new bureaucratic configuration in Washington. "What some of us expected from the outset" had turned out to be true, he wrote, namely, "that Morgenthau would have no authority to settle anything, and that our several demands would be referred almost immediately to the Departments primarily concerned with them. When it came to a question of action, Morgenthau inevitably had to accept the role of almost completely passive transmitter."[114]

Morgenthau's eclipse helped persuade Keynes not to hold out for the Quebec memo. Given Roosevelt's backsliding, of course, he had little choice. Accusations to the effect that the president had welched on a deal, no matter how true they might have been, would be counterproductive. Increasingly, Keynes was of a mind that Britain's balance-of-payments problems during the transitional period could best be taken care of through a new mechanism, separate from lend-lease. In private conversation with Cherwell and Keynes, Morgenthau indicated that "some novel way" needed to be found to provide Britain "with a large lump sum of money." Keynes agreed; "it would be vastly better to replace half-dead cats with a new live dog."[115] In this mood, then, Keynes settled down to some hard bargaining over specific issues with State, FEA, and the military.

One of Keynes's principal goals when he went to Washington was to have the White Paper on Exports lifted as of December 1, 1944. A year earlier British officials had become aware of an aggressive government-corporate campaign by the United States to capture overseas markets. A "large and influential American delegation . . . under the United States Government auspices" was at work in China, Whitehall reported to the cabinet. Another group was on its way to Ethiopia, and rumors were circulating in the British petroleum industry that "American interests have secured large and probably very important oil concessions in Arabia."[116] The Egyptian government, with several lucrative civil engineering contracts for irrigation projects in hand, was then dealing with Washington rather than London. In addition, the Board of Trade received reports that UNRRA was attempting to persuade recipients of its aid to buy American; South Africa and China had been told to purchase electrical machinery and cables in the United States. That agency had also forbidden the export by Britain of similar items to Australia and New Zealand, leaving America as the only possible supplier. The United States government, in other words, was using lend-lease and its position on various international boards to help American exporters take over former British markets. By mid-1944 British exporters were screaming their heads off, and rumblings in Parliament became correspondingly louder. The attitude of the Churchill government appeared to be "supine" and even "negative," its critics charged. The government had actually refused passports to a British delegation that wanted to go to China and compete with the Americans. Why, everyone was asking, did the government have no export policy?[117] The War Cabinet could hardly admit that it had none because Washington would not let it have one.

But even those American officials most anxious to see Great Britain get to its feet quickly were alarmed when Keynes suggested ending restrictions on British exports. A lifting of the white paper, announced with much brouhaha to the House of Commons while Britain was still receiving massive lend-lease aid, would give rise to the impression that the United Kingdom was using lend-lease goods, directly or indirectly, to capture new and old export markets. "We feel that since the discussions at Quebec were based on Stage II," Oscar Cox wrote Hopkins, "it would be safer not to allow Britain to announce or to create the impression that there will be any substantial increase in their export business until after the defeat of Germany."[118] Bring the matter up again after V-E Day, the Americans told Keynes.

Moving from one impasse to another, British and American negotiators quickly deadlocked over the breakup of the dollar pool. The commercial policy division of State and the FEA came under increasing pressure from United States manufacturers and exporters in 1944 to do something about their exclusion from empire markets. Bitterness over the "discriminatory" application of dollar and import license controls, reported one State Department official, was particularly sharp because exporters felt they were being circumscribed all the while Britain was using lend-lease items to supply markets that could be serviced by private American firms. In addition, United States agencies were being inundated with documented cases in which British manufactured goods had been exported to empire markets that traditionally bought such items from the United States, while lend-lease products were being utilized to meet British military and civilian requirements for these same articles.[119] The conviction persisted among American officials that at best the dollar pool was a mechanism designed to ensure, as one diplomat put it, that the members of the sterling area continued to "Buy British." At worst, the pool was a means to preserve Britain's political domination in the empire and throughout the sterling area. Thus, to the extent that the United States furnished lend-lease aid above and beyond Britain's immediate military requirements during Phase II, and did not require abolition of the dollar pool, it would be subsidizing British imperialism.

It would be helpful, Lauchlin Currie suggested to the British delegation, if the United States could obtain some written assurance from the British that the sterling area dollar pool would not be used to limit American competition. He then submitted a draft statement to that effect.[120] When Keynes and company balked, United States representatives suggested linking British concerns over the white paper with the United States desire for access to the sterling area; in other words, let's compete![121] Keynes, Brand, and the other British negotiators feigned interest but no one on their side of the table was willing to risk a free-for-all with a vastly superior adversary. For the time being, both the dollar pool and the white paper would remain in place.[122]

Finally, American negotiators attempted to use British needs for lend-lease during Phase II to force London not to sign a long-term meat contract with Argentina. On October 31 Keynes and Cherwell called on Morgenthau at his request. Stettinius had warned him, the Treasury secretary said, that the State Department's willingness to approve any lend-lease agreement depended on Britain's willingness to suspend at once its negotiations for a long-term meat contract with the "Fascist and pro-Axis" government of Argentina. Morgenthau indicated that he agreed with State's position except that, personally, he would go much farther. State was willing to countenance British purchases of Argentine beef on a month-to-month basis. What he proposed was a complete Anglo-American boycott of Argentina immediately after the November election.

As the presidential election approached, Anglo-American negotiations over lend-lease and related issues ground to a halt. In the early stages of the campaign FDR's physical condition was the major issue, its prominence a result of Thomas E. Dewey's electioneering and of an actual decline in the president's health. Roosevelt suffered an attack of angina pectoris during a speech to a group of shipyard workers in San Diego. During pauses at the Chicago nominating convention his face had been shadow-filled, his jaw slack. Dewey hammered away at the tired administration and one-man rule. Roosevelt countered by posing as chief of state above the political fray and by signing popular legislation like the GI Bill of Rights. He called for a Missouri River development plan modeled after the TVA and for a study of the Arkansas and Columbia river basins. It was during this campaign that Roosevelt conspired with Wendell Willkie to meld liberal Republicans and the mainstream of the Democratic party into a new political organization, leaving Republican conservatives and Democratic "reactionaries" out in the cold. The scheme, however, was stillborn.[123]

The principal issue during the final stages of the 1944 election campaign was the structure of the postwar world and America's role in it. The president could point to a host of United Nations collaborative efforts in which the United States had taken, or appeared to take, the lead: UNRRA, Bretton Woods, the International Civil Aviation Conference at Chicago, and Dumbarton Oaks. The president's philosophy seemed to be that the nations of the world would learn to cooperate with each other by actually cooperating. Dewey's position on foreign and domestic policy typified the presidential Republican tradition—moderate liberalism, moderate internationalism; but Roosevelt chose to campaign not against Dewey but the congressional wing of the party, against Robert Taft, Joseph Martin, and Hamilton Fish, against isolationism, and against economic nationalism. As in the past, he appealed to liberal and internationalist Republicans over Dewey's head, accusing his opponent of being controlled by the reactionaries of his party. He sought at the same time to hold the allegiance of his Democratic followers, particularly in the South, and to mobilize the voting power of the big cities.[124] In the end Keynes became caught up in the election fever; his prejudices, reported to Richard Hopkins, were probably typical of most Britons:

> At the moment there is a lull in our affairs on account of the Election; everybody is away voting; and everybody is in such a dither of nerves and excitement that they cannot concentrate. So it is only after Thursday that negotiations . . . will finally come to a head. . . . It has been impossible not to give a good deal of attention to the election. Dewey is one of the most miserable rats ever brought to birth and falls lower and lower even in the estimation of his supporters every time he opens his mouth. It would be the greatest possible disaster if he were to get in.[125]

Anglo-American relations threatened to play a minor role in the election. Krock's story to the effect that Morgenthau had traded Phase II lend-lease for British approval of the Morgenthau Plan broke on November 3. In his press conference the next day, Roosevelt denied this and other reports that the United

States had pledged at Quebec to give the British at least $2.5 billion in non-military supplies for resale and export. Administration opponents screamed that Keynes was at that very moment ensconced in the White House and the giveaway was proceeding apace. They recounted Morgenthau's promise to Congress in 1941 that not a nickel in aid would be given to Britain until and unless its financial reserves were completely exhausted. But the uproar was too little too late. Roosevelt swamped Dewey, 432 electoral votes to 99.[126]

With the political cauldron merely simmering rather than boiling, the principals in the lend-lease discussion could get back to business. John Anderson and Oliver Lyttleton made a last-ditch appeal to Morgenthau as chairman of the joint committee not to go back on the Quebec agreement. Keynes, too, fired off a final salvo, resorting in the end to passion rather than reason. Britain had "thrown good housekeeping to the winds" early in the war and totally subsumed financial policy to military necessity. "No doubt the above," he wrote Morgenthau, "makes up collectively a story of financial imprudence which has no parallel in history. Nevertheless, that financial imprudence may have been a facet of that single-minded devotion without which the war would have been lost. So we beg leave to think that it was worth while—for us, and also for you."[127] But most of the real negotiating had already been done. Lend-lease for Phase II was not, in the end, a matter for Anglo-American agreement but for unilateral decision by the United States. Washington recognized only London's right to be consulted.

The agreement on United States aid to Britain during the first year after Germany's surrender took the form of an executive order issued on December 2, 1944. The author of the directive was the same man who had played midwife to the original lend-lease bill—Oscar Cox. Acting in the name of FEA and State, Cox recommended a nonmunitions program—consisting of food, raw materials, miscellaneous manufactured goods, shipping, and petroleum—totaling $2.6 billion for the year following the defeat of Germany. His committee recommended $2.6 billion in military aid for the same period. These figures would allow a moderate easement in British living standards and make possible a limited resumption of the nation's export trade prior to V-E Day and a more substantial increase afterward. Britain would not be allowed to free its exporters from white paper restrictions in December or even January, however. Accordingly, the executive order stipulated that the white paper issued on September 10, 1941, would continue in effect as long as the United States furnished Britain with lend-lease aid. Articles that no longer obtained under lend-lease and for which Britain paid cash would be available for commercial export after Germany's surrender, subject to the availability of war shipping and to the principle that neither British nor American exporters should gain undue competitive advantage over the other as a result of the war situation. Surplus lend-lease articles stockpiled in England would not be exported but set aside for military purposes. Great Britain would reaffirm its intention to devote full production to the defeat of Germany and Japan, and to not attempt any general reconversion of industry or expansion of exports before V-E Day. In brief, the executive order that Cox drafted and FDR signed in December would allow Britain to return a portion of its manufacturing plant to civilian production, but goods produced as a result of this reconversion could only be stockpiled and not exported.

In an article entitled "New Lend-Lease Phase Aims to Bolster British," Arthur Krock wrote: "The agreement culminates a period of secrecy, intra-government controversy and rumor, and at the end of it all the participants expressed satisfaction."[128] And, for the most part, all parties were satisfied. On his return Keynes reported to Anderson and Dalton that the negotiations, as was always true with the Americans, had been tedious. The situation was typically "anarchic." They all tend to say just what comes into their heads and to say it to the press, he observed. Stettinius, while well meaning, had been very disappointing. He was simpleminded and inconceivably press conscious. These were minor irritations, however, and as always Keynes was optimistic. "We have really got all the export freedom we can use and we have not, as has been suggested, had our Lend Lease supplies cut down, but are really getting more than before."[129] Again, Keynes was stretching the truth. Though the United Kingdom had obtained more from the United States than the hardliners in the military and FEA had wanted it to receive—that is, nothing—London had certainly lost ground since the Quebec Conference. What the British delegation had avoided was making additional concessions in return for Phase II lend-lease aid.

The primary components of the Roosevelt foreign policy establishment were reasonably content with the outcome of the Phase II talks. FEA had not gotten everything it wanted in the area of exports, but at least Britain did not have as free a hand as it would have had under the Quebec memo. Nothing had been said about commercial policy, but State could take comfort from the fact that Phase II lend-lease had been cut down to such an extent that Britain would still be vulnerable during Phase III. The military was consoled by the same realization and by the fact that it had been at least consulted in the Phase II talks. Treasury had every reason to feel defeated. The secretary and his underlings, responding to the pro-British position taken by the Hopkins group and Roosevelt, had done an about-face and come out in strong support of a liberal lend-lease policy, only to have its philosophical and bureaucratic position undercut by the State-War-FEA coalition, backed as it was by congressional and public opinion. But resilience and persistence were what made Morgenthau such an effective bureaucratic guerrilla. Britain's need for massive financial assistance after Japan's defeat might allow Treasury to once again seize control of Anglo-American relations and with it United States foreign policy.

Despite its subsequent watering down, the lend-lease agreement signed by British and American negotiators in late November 1944 constituted a victory for strategic multilateralists on both sides of the Atlantic. In principle and in dollars, the accord seemed to ensure that Britain could play a full part in the Pacific war and simultaneously begin to reconvert a portion of its economy to civilian production. That it could not use goods produced as a result to hold or recapture foreign markets was not as important as it might have been, given the fact that domestic demand for nonmilitary items was so great. The multilateralists' victory was made all the more complete by the fact that both the president and the prime minister quickly abandoned the Morgenthau Plan on their return home. But England was far from out of the woods. At best it would be able to avoid losing any additional ground to its chief competitor during Phase II. It was obvious to Acheson, Taft, and Hawkins, Eden, Law, and Cherwell that Britain's long-range health—the nation's ability to export, earn exchange for necessary imports, and thus operate in international trade without a deficit on current account—would require massive United States aid in Phase III, the period following Japan's surrender.

The Quebec memo and subsequent negotiations on Phase II lend-lease constituted a severe setback for the empire isolationists. The imminence of Phase II forced the War Cabinet to at long last come to grips with Britain's short- and long-range economic plight. To the reform Tories and Labour party leadership Keynes's memo represented reality—the Amery-Beaverbrook position, nostalgic illusion. Though he had deluded himself into thinking the Quebec understanding was firm, Churchill too had confronted reality in fall 1944. Faced with the prospect of having to implement an unparalleled austerity program, the prime minister had endorsed the Morgenthau Plan in return for a promise of continued lend-lease aid after V-E Day.

Although Beaverbrook, Amery, and Hudson were in retreat, the British multilateralists, especially those in the Treasury, could take small comfort from the fact. The vanquishing of the forces of empire isolationism meant only that Britain would be able to accept American aid with a number of conditions attached. The extent of that aid and the strings attached depended on the struggle between multilateralists and economic nationalists in the United States, and on America's perception of the larger international picture. The ability of British multilateralists to control these two factors in the 1940s was as questionable as it had been during the preceding century and a half.

7. Multilateralism Interpreted: The Debate over Full Employment and Foreign Trade, 1943–1944

BY LATE 1944 and early 1945 progressive elements within the Churchill government and the Roosevelt administration had embraced multilateralism. After the Quebec Conference, the State Department succeeded in reinserting itself into negotiations over lend-lease and in linking United States aid to Britain during Phases II and III to elimination of preferences, quotas, and other trade barriers. The ultimate goals of commercial multilateralists in America were negotiation of an agreement to outlaw unfair trade practices and establishment of an International Trade Organization (ITO) to police that agreement. British officials endorsed these objectives but worked frantically to see that whatever commercial policy Congress adopted would provide the United Kingdom with the export opportunities necessary to maintain a favorable balance of trade.

The debate over commercial policy was accompanied in both countries by a national dialogue over full employment. Whereas multilateralists in the British government saw a full employment policy at the domestic level as a prerequisite for a liberal trading system, the White House viewed multilateralism as an alternative to planning and countercyclical deficit spending. World War II witnessed the triumph of Keynesian principles in the United Kingdom as forward-looking Conservatives and the parliamentary Labour party agreed that planning and countercyclical deficit spending were political and economic necessities. The vast majority of British multilateralists operated on the assumption that a tariff- and quota-free international economy would work only if nations adopted and maintained measures of full employment within the domestic sphere. Franklin Roosevelt and Harry Hopkins eagerly and openly embraced multilateralism in 1944, but they failed to see or refused to admit that despite the laissez-faire rhetoric associated with it, multilateralism would require planning and full employment policies at the national level. In 1944–45 the White House stood idly by as conservatives in Congress cut off funds for the National Resources Planning Board (NRPB) and emasculated the Murray-Patman full employment bill. Roosevelt and Hopkins, ever-sensitive to the rising conservative tide in the country, actually perceived multilateralism as an alternative to planning and countercyclical deficit spending at the domestic level and to a massive, and perhaps permanent, aid program in the international sphere.

In February 1944 *The Economist* ran an article entitled "The New Liberalism" in which it made a classic plea for pragmatism in commercial policy. The overriding goal of foreign trade, the editors argued, must be expansion—an increase in volume of production and quality of goods all over the world coupled with an increase in consumption and markets. In essence *The Economist* was calling for an application of Keynesian economics to international commercial policy, a comprehensive effort to first maintain and then increase aggregate demand. "The driving force behind the philosophy of Adam Smith and his successors was a strong belief in the national tendencies of the economic system toward material expansion. In this expansion they saw—and rightly so—the hope of rescuing mankind from penury," proclaimed Britain's foremost journal of political economy. But Smith and Ricardo recognized what many of their contemporary advocates did not—that free trade was a means to an end, not an end in itself. This was true of bilateralism as well. If bilateral pacts increased the volume of trade in one area and for one commodity without reducing it for other regions and other products, they were good; if not, they were bad. It was for this reason that the Ottawa Agreements were deplorable, not because they were ideologically impure. "But we have learned," asserted the editors, "that freedom of commerce may not be so completely synonymous with expansion, nor planning with restriction." Humankind, they declared with fearless certitude, had made up its mind to control its economic environment, "to prevent great depression, mass unemployment and poverty in the midst of potential sufficiency," and it must utilize whatever means were available to attain these lofty objectives.[1]

Those in the State Department and other agencies concerned with plotting postwar trade strategy did not equate planning with restriction; they just believed that the British were planning restriction or, more accurately, that the inevitable outcome of British plans would be restriction of international trade. Before 1929 it was possible for leaders in government and business to believe that economic expansion could be maintained simply through the encouragement of individual initiative abroad, disarmament agreements, antiwar pacts, and a minimum of unilateral political or military intervention. The depression and World War II destroyed this illusion.[2] By the 1940s the assumption that business could take care of itself was not considered practical by many policymakers and corporate executives.

The acceptance by the business community of a larger governmental role in its affairs was nicely reflected in the philosophy of William H. Culbertson, businessman, United States ambassador to Chile in the 1930s, and troubleshooter for the Roosevelt administration in the 1940s. In 1930 he had declared: "In spite of competition or even propaganda, American business will more than take care of itself. Our efficiency in production and distribution will excel. . . . I've every day evidence that the expanding forces of our economic life will give us first place in South America whether we consciously promote trade and finance or whether we indifferently leave them to take their upward course."[3] Fourteen years later he conducted a fact-finding tour of North Africa and the Middle East for

Cordell Hull. His mission was to investigate the degree to which British governmental agencies—namely, the United Kingdom Commercial Corporation and the Middle East Supply Center—were attempting to control the trade of the area and protect British markets. Lauding Hull's "fight for sound international economic policies," Culbertson claimed to be as much an Adam Smith liberal as he had always been. "It is my earnest hope," he wrote, "that international economic conditions and policies will exist following this war which will enable resumption of international trade and international production on the basis of free enterprise without the active participation of government."[4] But he was not optimistic. Hull's plans could succeed only with the enthusiastic cooperation of Britain, Russia, and France. That cooperation was not likely to be forthcoming. British agencies were particularly guilty of engaging in bulk-purchasing, encouraging maintenance of trade barriers, and exerting political pressure in behalf of British commercial interests in the Middle East, Culbertson reported. According to him, the United States would have to fight fire with fire. If American nationals were to control their fair share of world commerce and industry, he advised the State Department from Paris in December 1944, "the American government must lend affirmative support sufficient to create conditions of equality in the face of policies now pursued by other major powers." Specifically, he urged the conversion of the United States Commercial Corporation into a powerful agency that would not only extend "traditional protection" to United States business abroad, but also aid them in their operations.[5]

But the Culbertson approach ran the risk of offending domestic opinion—conservative ideologues and small business people who feared that "the Corporation" would become another National Recovery Administration—and undercutting America's campaign to return foreign trade to private channels. Americans voiced their opposition to collectivism in foreign as well as domestic commerce throughout late 1944. In October Charles Taft had felt compelled to write Claire Booth Luce denying allegations that the government was planning an "American Amtorg" and that a secret agreement had been forged with the British to divy up the markets of the world.[6] The government had no intention of "embarking on a totalitarian control of Government trade," Taft repeatedly asserted in other letters and speeches.[7] Free enterprise would be the watchword. Conservatives remained skeptical. Bernard Baruch continued to warn publicly and privately of "totalization"; industry and finance must be stimulated and freed up, not choked and regulated to death.[8] An American businessman who had served as a commercial attaché in Latin America during the war wrote Will Clayton: "I was impressed by a tendency in many countries for wartime government monopolies to continue after the war. It seems to me this tendency is adverse to American interests and detrimental to a sound economic development of this hemisphere."[9] The Division of Commercial Policy in State eventually rejected "the Corporation" approach not only because it ran counter to the prevailing domestic ideology, but also because foreign nations could use the existence of such an agency to resist multilateralism and justify continuance of restrictive controls.[10]

Instead of the nationalist-collectivist approach advocated by Culbertson, the multilateralists adopted a mechanism designed by Percy Wells Bidwell, a Yale economist who had headed up the research activities of the Council on Foreign Relations since 1938.[11] Preaching to the converted, Bidwell called for trade policy to become the heart of the administration's planning for peace and prosperity in the postwar world, and he put forward a blueprint for action.

Bidwell called for two types of international action: multilateral agreements to reduce tariffs and limit the use of quantitative restrictions on imports and exports, and to eliminate discriminatory practices; and the establishment of an administrative body to supervise operation of the agreements and to make recommendations to the United Nations organization regarding their enforcement. International rather than purely national action was required because different nations would emerge from the present war with different types of economic organization, he asserted. Only an international agency could facilitate the coexistence and participation in world trade of both "liberal" and "planned" economies. Moreover, Bidwell asserted, "experience shows that we cannot rely in either the transitional period or the later period upon national states, separately, to adopt tariff policies which, in the long run, will further either their own interest or that of the community of nations; the effect of their policies may prove quite the opposite."[12]

Among the duties of the proposed International Trade Commission would be the following: to consult with national tariff-making bodies to prevent unreasonable increases; to supervise international agreements to lower barriers; to monitor and report "dangerous" changes in exchange rates; to supervise the operation of most-favored-nation clauses in commercial treaties; and to prepare a Code of Fair Trade Practices for International Trade. In the multilateral accord, member states would agree to begin immediately a gradual reduction of import and export duties and the progressive elimination of licensing systems and quotas. (Exceptions were possible when necessary to facilitate trade between a planned and liberal economy and to protect legitimate infant industries.) Member states would further agree that within a specified period—five or ten years—they would aim at complete elimination of all tariff discriminations and base their commercial policies thereafter on the principle of equal treatment. Furthermore, they would undertake to abolish all export subsidies and to "take appropriate measures to suppress the practice of unfair methods of competition." Bidwell's program, then, was a kind of international combination of the Federal Trade Commission and the Clayton Anti-Trust Act. It proposed an amalgam of outlawing "unfair practices" and the establishment of a friendly agency to advise and assist national governments in eradicating these practices.[13]

Bidwell's plan for realizing multilateralism grew out of the philosophy of the State Department's commercial policy division and in fact was a distillation of its views. The multilateral agreement–international trade organization approach had by late 1944 been taken over lock, stock, and barrel by the economic multilateralists. From London where he and E. F. Penrose were preparing for commercial policy negotiations with the British, Harry Hawkins wrote a recommendation for implementing the Bidwell plan that became the basis for United States policy during trade negotiations throughout 1945 and 1946. "We should seek now international agreement on a code of rules to govern trade relations," he wrote. "An international trade organization should be established to harmonize trade policies of nations and to study the techniques whereby trade policies can be made mutually helpful rather than mutually destructive, and to formulate and supervise the operation of inter-governmental arrangements having these ends in view." Hawkins pled with the White House to make such a program the heart of its postwar economic policy. "If the President of the United States," he asserted, "should take the lead in advocating well-thought-out policies and concrete proposals in the field of international trade policy, public opinion throughout the world might well fall in behind him, and plans for reconversion to peacetime production might in large measure be made in the light of the principles and policies enunciated by him."[14]

Bidwell and commercial multilateralists in general had come to realize by 1944 something the British had known all along—that before a multilateral convention could be signed and an effective International Trade Organization inaugurated, the major trading nations would have to adopt legislation that virtually guaranteed uninterrupted full employment. Indeed, Bidwell took great pains to make it clear that his scheme rested on the assumption "that measures of national and international scope will prove reasonably successful in maintaining employment at a high level in the United States and in other great industrial countries, thus lessening the pressure to exclude goods of foreign origin from national markets."[15] In other words, labor and advocates of social justice should accept competitive imports in return for government action through currency manipulation, public works projects, and other devices that protected those who were thrown out of work by foreign imports. In fact, Bidwell's plan for commercial multilateralism, which was in no small part dependent for its success on national action to maximize employment, emerged just as the campaigns in the United Kingdom and United States for full employment were reaching a climax. The outcome of those struggles indicated clearly that, while Britain had accepted the "new liberalism," the United States had not.

During an interview in 1942 Sir Stafford Cripps, the radical aristocrat who served Churchill first as ambassador to Russia and then as privy seal, told Herbert Feis that Britain was in search of a new ideology. His country thirsted for something more "creative," vigorous, and productive than the official program then being sponsored by the Labour and Conservative parties. Parliament was now six years old and did not, could not, reflect current opinion. The two major parties basically represented special interests: the programs they framed and the policies they advocated were designed to benefit only that party's constituency.[16] Cripps's reading of the climate of opinion in Britain was quite accurate. It was clear from public opinion surveys, government investigations, and the private reports of *Mass Observation* that the British people wanted a better world after the war than the one they had known in the 1930s, though they were not in most cases very optimistic about getting it.

The bombing and mass evacuation of London brought to middle- and upper-class householders throughout England a consciousness for the first time of the deplorable conditions in the slums that still existed in the country's great cities.[17] Britain's very involvement in the war, moreover, both in auxiliary forces at home and in the armed forces, meant that people became better educated and more aware of themselves. They had, as Arthur Marwick puts it, "heightened consciousness."[18] "I think it is Fear that dominates nearly everyone's life in varying degrees," R. F. Hazell wrote Ernest Bevin. "Fear of illness, fear of old age and fear of unemployment. This fear . . . prevents people enjoying this life as it should be enjoyed—and in a world of plenty, this, in my opinion, is entirely wrong."[19] William Temple, archbishop of Canterbury, became an outspoken advocate of social reform. Sir Richard Acland founded Common Wealth which, though in the beginning was mainly a collection of intellectuals, gradually attracted rank-and-file members of the Labour party who were frustrated with the wartime political truce. This organization popularized the idea of a people's war and a people's peace. Heavy taxation, rationing, a positive nutrition policy, and wartime wages produced a leveling of standards—up as well as down. As the war progressed, the majority developed a clear picture of what it expected from the modern, industrialized, civilized society: a decent living standard, employment security, and comprehensive health insurance. Partly as a result of this intense interest in a better future, the Churchill government in 1941 appointed an interdepartmental committee under the chairmanship of Sir William Beveridge to survey existing national schemes of social insurance and allied services. In June 1942, after completion of the first draft of the Beveridge Report, John Maynard Keynes and Beveridge began to meet regularly. Over lunches and dinners at the West End Club, the renowned economist persuaded Sir William to divide his report into two parts—a definition of ultimate goals and a less ambitious statement of gradual stages by which these goals might be attained. Keynes subsequently played a key role in selling the report to the cabinet. In the final analysis, however, Beatrice and Sidney Webb and G. D. H. Cole exerted more influence on Beveridge's thought than Keynes. They and the war convinced Beveridge that comprehensive state planning in a democracy was in fact possible.[20]

The Beveridge Report on Social Security, ready by late summer 1942, recommended the establishment of a national health insurance program that covered all classes, that provided minimum benefits, that covered all contingencies, and that was financed with public funds. More importantly, implementation of a national health insurance program should be only one component of a "comprehensive policy of social progress" encompassing the institution of children's allowances, an all-embracing health service, and "maintenance of employment."

The Beveridge Report provoked a storm of controversy. It was suppressed for a time by Conservatives in the cabinet and not debated in Parliament until February 16, 1943. Not surprisingly, the insurance and medical professions were vehemently hostile, but critics had to be careful and work indirectly. The director of the Federation of British Industries expressed his opposition—privately. Conservative members of Parliament and Sir Kingsley Wood insisted that the plan would promote mass idleness and that it was the old Poor Law immensely magnified. Churchill was as negative about the report as the British people were positive. He suggested that because the government derived its authority from a Parliament elected in 1935 under different circumstances, it would be "unconstitutional or at least improper" for the War Cabinet to implement decisions on postwar policy. Clement Attlee, however, pointed out to him with effect that there was "a remarkable consensus of opinion . . . between people of different political parties and different economic and social backgrounds" on the need to take action on matters pertaining to homes, work, and food before the war ended.[21] Two weeks after publication, a national opinion poll indicated that 95 percent of those interviewed showed some knowledge of the report and 88 percent approved the idea of universal doctor and hospital services. However, while the Beveridge Report provided a blueprint for comprehensive health care, it merely urged the adoption of measures to create full employment.

Articulation of these policies was the work of yet another academic cum bureaucrat, James Meade of the Economic Section of the War Cabinet Secretariat. Significantly, Meade would become by war's end the chief architect of British commercial policy. For Meade, 1944 marked a turning point in his personal career and in the ongoing campaign against the "Treasury view" by advocates of a "liberal-socialist economy." Meade wanted very much to return to Oxford and finish work on *The Economics of Welfare*. But when Edward Bridges in November proposed to make him director-designate of the Economic Section in anticipation of the retirement of the aged Sir Richard Hopkins, Meade decided to stay on. He believed that the need for pragmatic economists to translate theory into action would be even more pressing in the early postwar period than it had been during the war.

The former don had had much to do with shaping the middle way. In 1944 he had met with Captain Peter Thorneycroft, chairman of the Tory Reform Committee, and several of his associates. Meade, a devout Christian, believed that unemployment was morally wrong and that civil servants and enlightened politicians must persuade the government and people always to place the general welfare above that of private interests. The state should intervene in the economy in three main ways, he told the reform Tories: (1) implement financial policies (public expenditure, tax policy, etc.) that would lead to high employment but curb inflation, (2) leave production in private hands where possible but nationalize industries where a large number of competing units was impractical, and (3) redistribute income through taxation and measures of social security. A true believer in the new liberalism, Meade preached to all who would listen that "the purpose of economic policy should be to make the economic calculus work and that the particular uses of planning or of *laissez-faire* should then be judged as means toward this end."[22]

Meade, like Keynes, believed that multilateralism could not work unless all of the trading countries adopted effective full employment policies at the national level. He was certain as well that the Treasury view, which stressed above all an annual balanced budget, was alive and well in both America and Great Britain. Meade agreed with the protectionists that another depression was certain in the United States but, with the 1929–31 experience to go on and Harry Hawkins's enlightened leadership, the federal government would take necessary measures to restore employment. ("God help the rest of us if it [an American depression] really gets out of hand," he confided to his diary.[23])

In Britain public opinion was more informed than in the United States; here Meade feared the shallowness and inconstancy of his colleagues in the civil service rather than the popularity of fiscal conservatism. Bridges, in his estimation, was very able and competent but without technical expertise in economics. Richard Hopkins, or "Hoppy," was "wise and learned as the elder statesman," but clearly losing his grip. Wilfrid Eady was muddled and uncertain while Keynes was "perverse, brilliant and wayward."[24] Above all, Meade did not trust Keynes to be true to his own principles. Whereas Meade was convinced that in a full employment economy, the government must use higher interest rates, higher taxes, and direct controls over prices and production to control inflation, Keynes wanted to rely on controls alone. High interest rates and high taxes were an anathema to the politicians in the cabinet, and apparently Keynes was willing to tailor his theories to their interests.[25] But Meade was confident that he could hold the cabinet and Keynes's feet to the Keynesian fire.

Wartime discussion of employment policy per se began with Meade's "The Prevention of General Unemployment." Echoing Keynes, he argued that the budget must be more than just a financial statement; it was an instrument available to government to stimulate employment by countercyclical deficit spending and to curb inflation through wage controls. Hopkins of the Economic Section and Eady and Hubert Henderson of the Treasury responded that public works were an inefficient method of stimulating demand. They preferred reduced taxation and interest rates as weapons with which to combat depression and they clung to a balanced budget. In 1943 the War Cabinet established the Reconstruction Priorities Committee under Sir John Anderson to examine the Beveridge Plan, including its recommendations on employment. The two principal staff people for the committee were Meade and Hopkins. The debate raged on, with Hopkins and the Treasury view gradually losing ground.[26]

When the White Paper on Employment Policy was published in mid-1944, it aroused far less controversy than had the Beveridge Report on Social Security promulgated some eighteen months earlier. Employment was a subject the average Briton was even more willing to see the government take action on than social insurance. The Tory Reform Committee had succeeded in making planning and government action to maintain full employment palatable to the rank and file of the Conservative party. Conservatives such as Winston Churchill and Oliver Lyttleton were finding it harder and harder to hold out for pure laissez-faire and free enterprise. In addition, with the end of the war "in sight," Ernest Bevin and his colleagues felt freer to challenge Churchill and the Conservatives on postwar domestic issues. Even before the Normandy invasion Labour leaders began to press for a clear, public commitment to maintain employment through currency manipulation and public works.

Moreover, it seemed to many Britons that the fate of Western and Central Europe was tied to the United Kingdom's willingness to embrace full employment strategies. The people of the Continent, reported a French friend of Hugh Dalton, had not yet coalesced into political parties, but he predicted that they would be ready for radical change after the war, particularly in the direction of European federation and socialism. Public ownership of heavy industry, for example, would be virtually universal. If Britain did not take the ideological lead, there was considerable risk that much of Europe would gravitate toward the Soviet Union. London's allies warned that its paens to free enterprise and unfettered capitalism would not be accepted as substitutes for homes, food, and work.[27]

In the end, the white paper enjoyed broad support in the cabinet. "It is wonderful that 'the maintenance of aggregate demand' had become official government policy," Dalton observed in his diary. "I find that Cherwell is as good on this as any of my colleagues."[28] In August Lord Beaverbrook wrote Bernard Baruch: "This conception of stability of employment which goes along with the philosophy of planning, has a wide acceptance here at present."[29] By the time a draft of the white paper had been approved during the last week of May, only Churchill seemed a bit sour. Dalton remembered: "The P.M. says he understands that what is proposed for public authorities is the exact opposite of what would be done by private persons—that when things look bad, they should not draw in their horns but push them out and launch forth into all sorts of new expenditures. . . . I suppose that at such times it would be helpful to have a series of Cabinet banquets—a sort of Salute to the Stomach Week?"[30]

The white paper proclaimed that "the Government [would] accept as one of their primary aims and responsibilities the maintenance of a high and stable level of employment after the war." The document paid deference to expansion of exports in a multilateral context but then devoted itself to outlining specific domestic policies to guarantee every Briton a job. The government would have to keep economic controls in place throughout the transitional period, including consumer rationing and price controls. It would have to impose restrictions on capital transfer, allocate labor and raw materials in accordance with a priority system, and oversee disposal of government plants and stocks. Special areas of chronic unemployment, such as the cotton- and coal-producing regions of Great Britain, would undergo a "diversification program" in which the government would direct "suitable new industries" to these areas and retrain the local population. The government promised to intervene at the "earliest possible stage to avert

a threatened slump" in the national economy. Intervention would include variations in social insurance contributions, manipulation of interest rates, and funding
of public works projects. The paper closed with a promise that while doing all
this, the government would keep in mind "the need for a policy of budgeting
equilibrium such as will maintain the confidence in the future which is necessary
for a healthy and enterprising industry";[31] that is, it would try to balance the
budget.

The government's program was a compromise between Keynes and Treasury
conservatives such as Hubert Henderson, and between Richard Hopkins and
James Meade in the Economic Section. References to the need to fund the debt
and balance the budget coexisted with warnings that there would be a tendency
toward increasing deficits. It should be noted that by 1944 Keynes had become
concerned about inflation and was himself only a moderate "Keynesian." He fully
supported the Economic Section's belief that total government expenditures
would have to exceed total government revenue to achieve full employment. This
would be necessary, however, for only a five- to ten-year period after the war. He
accepted, moreover, a permanent 5 percent unemployment rate. Despite all this
caution the unemployment white paper was still a remarkable statement of governmental responsibility. Its authors noted with pride that, while the conception
of an expansionist economy and the broad principles governing its growth were
widely accepted in the industrial countries, they had never been systematically
applied as government policy.[32]

During World War II America no less than Britain experienced a groundswell of
concern about the shape of the economy in the postwar period. Multilateralism
was in no small part a product of that concern. "How can democratic freedom,
economic efficiency and social welfare," economist Lewis Loring asked, "be
welded together under the new technical and intellectual conditions of the twentieth century, so as to do away with the two scourges—depression and war?"[33] The
prospect of a postwar depression was considered very real and Loring along with
Harry Hawkins, Clair Wilcox, Harry Dexter White, Wendell Willkie, Eleanor
Roosevelt, and thousands of other Americans searched for ways to extend wartime prosperity into the peace that would follow. The pure multilateralists hoped
to realize the twin goals of individual liberty and social security by linking
domestic prosperity to the elimination of trade barriers, nondiscrimination, and
currency stabilization. Another group of liberal New Dealers and economists,
some of whom paid lip service to multilateralism and some of whom did not,
offered a different and primarily domestic solution to the problem of economic
instability and unemployment. These survivors of the institutionist school outlined a planning procedure incorporating Keynesian fiscal principles. These principles would be developed and implemented by a central staff agency armed with
broad coordinative power over the entire federal bureaucracy. Through planning,

government would integrate and coordinate its economic activities and thus be in a position to combat instability. Between 1939 and 1946, liberals attempted to use three Executive Office agencies—the National Resources Planning Board, the Bureau of the Budget, and the Council of Economic Advisers—to coordinate economic planning, social welfare, and resource development programs to stabilize the economy at full employment.[34]

The movement for postwar economic planning at the domestic level was an extension of prewar efforts by institutional economists to achieve a planned economy and stemmed generally from their acceptance of Alvin Hansen's secular stagnation thesis. With the closing of the frontier, the decrease in the rate of population growth, and an end to technological innovations, Hansen concluded, the economy had reached a stage of maturation. Insufficient outlets for investment had caused the depression. Hansen did not believe this to be a temporary aberration, and the only alternative to continuing depression lay in a government economic policy designed to increase consumption and supplement deficiencies in private capital formation. The stagnation thesis not only constituted the principal assumption that underlay the National Recovery Administration, the First Agricultural Adjustment Act, and the administration's work relief and currency manipulation schemes, but it also enjoyed a good deal of support in the early 1940s. The nonstagnationist liberals, heirs of the Brandesian tradition, believed a postwar depression would occur, but its cause would be due not to economic maturity but a downward swing in the business cycle and the transition to a peacetime economy. Like the stagnationists they favored deficit spending to stimulate the economy, but only on a temporary basis.[35]

As a sop to the stagnationist-planners, President Roosevelt, who believed planning should be a sharply limited exercise and generally disparaged attempts at a "grand reshaping of the nation," established the National Resources Planning Board in 1939. While Roosevelt felt uncomfortable with long-range planning, he shared to some extent the liberal's fear of a postwar depression. He was certain of the inability of the private sector to guarantee full employment and social security; he was aware of the need to provide a propaganda, if not a real, alternative to fascism and communism; and he was increasingly sensitive to the rising public demand that the administration develop a scheme during the war for fending off depression and unemployment after the shooting had stopped. Late in 1940 Roosevelt met with the NRPB and told it that the federal government had a responsibility to plan for the inevitable economic maladjustments that would follow the emergency period. Deferred, nondefense public works projects would provide employment opportunity, and the president directed the board to prepare a variety of programs to be ready when economic conditions dictated. To ensure that the expansionary efforts of public spending were not neutralized by regressive taxation, FDR also authorized the board to explore unorthodox methods of financing, that is, deficit spending. Finally, he said, he wanted the board to develop plans in the areas of social security, public assistance, and relief.[36]

To formalize the relationship between planning and democracy, the NRPB drew up an economic and social bill of rights. The document asserted a citizen's right to work, to fair pay, to adequate food, clothing, and shelter, to economic security, to a free enterprise system, to education, and to rest and recreation. To ensure that all benefited from the advances of a modern industrial society, the board asserted that it should be the "declared policy of the United States Government to promote and maintain a high level of national production and consumption by appropriate measures." The government should, moreover, "underwrite full employment for all employables" and even underwrite when necessary security, education, nutrition, and housing.[37]

The bill of rights and the board's much more widely debated report published in 1943 encapsulated the philosophy of wartime liberals and their view of the postwar period. Henry Wallace, Eleanor Roosevelt, and Harry White by late 1942 had themselves become active and articulate in advocating postwar planning for full employment. The cessation of active hostilities would bring a sudden and complete end to the need for more armaments, White wrote Morgenthau in 1942. "But sudden, wholesale cancellation of war contracts would create a bad situation unless steps are prepared ahead of time to take care of the millions of men and women that would be precipitously thrown out of work."[38] The military-industrial complex would use the unemployment issue to try and force a continuation of arms production. In the case of both disarmament and social justice, the federal government would have to develop a game plan to deal with reconversion and the specter of unemployment, and it would have to do it quickly. Wallace had already begun work on the *Century of the Common Man*, a clarion call for full employment at home and abroad. Eleanor Roosevelt, David Lilienthal, and Harold Ickes urged the president to use his incomparable political skills to forge a consensus for postwar full employment and social security.

Publication of the Beveridge Report created a major stir in the United States. In the words of R. L. Strout of the *Christian Science Monitor*, Britain's scheme of social insurance served to highlight the fact that "something very basic is going on, the search for a better postwar world that will justify to the common man all the sacrifices and hardships he is now making."[39] It provoked widespread comment among conservatives and liberals, and really marked the beginning of the public debate over a full employment policy in the United States. Moderate-to-conservative oracles seemed to be somewhat relieved. There had been a certain amount of advance publicity connected with the report, highlighted by a statement attributed to Beveridge himself that his plan went "half way to Moscow." Underlying several of the comments was a feeling of surprise that "practical and realistic" Britain had commissioned a report from just such a representative of the "long-haired, starry-eyed enthusiasts" as were then being attacked in Washington.

More extreme conservatives, particularly business people and corporate executives, reacted much as Churchill and the high Tories had. Realizing that the humanitarian appeal of the plan made open opposition dangerous, they resorted to flanking attacks. The measure was not to be taken seriously; it was designed to keep the working population in line for the duration of the war. Americans needed no such cradle-to-grave sop, capitalist ideologues declared. Free enterprise would create a postwar world so prosperous that there would be no need for such schemes.

Liberal opinion, as articulated by the *Nation*, the *New Republic*, and *Newsweek* was, of course, positive, if somewhat jealous. "Perhaps we had better hurry," commented one. "Great Britain has thought up a system so far advanced in social thinking as to make us catch our breath." Finally, according to the *Christian Science Monitor*, publication of the report convinced liberals and New Dealers that the issue of social security not only could but should be taken up during wartime.[40]

Despite his penchant for pragmatism, Franklin Roosevelt as 1943 opened was also a man in search of a plan—a formula for prosperity. Allied fortunes on the battlefield had definitely taken a turn for the better. The North African campaign was going well, the air war in Europe had shifted from the British Isles and English Channel to French and East European skies, and plans were under way for an all-out offensive in the Pacific. On the propaganda front, however, the Axis still held the initiative. By 1943 a principal issue in the ongoing debate between Hitler and Roosevelt was the meaning and application of the term "freedom." Hitler once interpreted freedom as lebensraum for Germans, but he steadily shifted its meaning before and during the war years to freedom for the masses to enjoy security and the good things of life. Freedom in America he denounced as freedom for democracy to exploit the world and freedom of the plutocrats within this democracy to exploit the masses. Indeed, by spring 1943 the German propagandists were taking a distinctly Marxist line. The two great tools of American imperialism, Berlin alleged, were the Atlantic Charter, an "American political instrument for domination of non-American countries," and lend-lease. That measure was not one of "foolish magnanimity" but a shrewd maneuver to facilitate the takeover of British markets in South America and penetration of the Commonwealth and empire by United States businesses and financiers. While lend-lease was being used to expand plants in the United States, according to Joseph Goebbels, Washington successfully demanded economic concessions around the world from its "beneficiaries."[41]

Roosevelt, feeling Berlin's indictment of lend-lease too absurd to refute specifically, sought instead to take the initiative across a broad front. He repeatedly assailed Hitler's freedom as not freedom to live but simply as freedom for the Nazis to dominate and enslave the human race. The president, who considered himself an expert on mass psychology, tried to relate the concept of liberty to human problems and social conditions. "There can be no real freedom for the common man without enlightened social policies," he declared. "In the last analysis, they are the stakes for which the democracies are fighting."[42] But what policies was he referring to? When the hostilities ended millions of people would be homeless, starving, diseased. Even if the United States possessed the will and the ability to reconstruct war-shattered economies and restore the status quo ante bellum, what would prevent the reoccurrence of the events and circumstances that led to the first two world wars? America was singing the praises of internationalism but to what end, the peoples of the world were beginning to ask.

This demand for action, for specific planning, existed at home as well as abroad. Public opinion polls in late 1942 and early 1943 showed that American attitudes regarding the coming peace were still largely unformed on specifics but definitely in favor of an immediate start to postwar planning. But Roosevelt was not one to plot the future in a political void, and, as he tested the congressional waters in early 1943, he was chilled to the bone. The tribunes of the people were definitely not in a liberal frame of mind.

In his state-of-the-union address in 1943, FDR outlined his vision of postwar America, a vision characterized by freedom from want and by economic and social security. Immediately afterward the National Resources Planning Board released its response to the Beveridge Report, the *Security, Work and Relief Policies Report*. Begun in 1939, the paper recommended expanded social insurance and public assistance programs in education and health care. It called for unemployment relief and public works to guarantee a minimum standard of living, raise consumer purchasing power, and keep prices up. Responsibility for funding these programs was to belong to the federal government. The most controversial aspect of the NRPB's report was its recommendation that during demobilization after the war certain basic industries such as aluminum, chemicals, aircraft, and magnesium be forced to accept mixed public-private ownership.[43]

Congressional response to the report was overwhelmingly negative. Representatives Gerald Landis (R-Ind.) and John E. Rankin (D-Miss.) denounced it as a threat to the free enterprise system. Another conservative legislator derided the "womb tomb security illusion" as fanciful, illogical, and the product of the socialist thinkers staffing the NRPB.[44] Some conservatives in Congress agreed with the *New York Times* which claimed that, in laying the groundwork for the welfare state, the *Report* paved the way for the rise of fascism in America. "The fundamental basis of totalitarianism is an exaltation of the state which takes command of the individual from cradle to grave," proclaimed the *Times*.[45] In June 1942 Isaiah Berlin of the British Embassy reported to the Foreign Office that increasing numbers of representatives and senators had been complaining in public and in private about the mounting arrogance of the bureaucracy and the consequent erosion of their own powers. Not coincidentally, he wrote, the National Association of Manufacturers had just initiated a nationwide publicity campaign to tout its services to the country and to warn against a postwar social order that curbed free enterprise.[46]

Western Europeans, who had long since recognized that with the coming of the Industrial Revolution and the concentration of wealth in the hands of private financiers and industrialists, laissez-faire policies led to a diminution and not an increase in economic democracy, were mystified by America's seemingly infantile views on social and economic policy. Conservatives in the United States appeared to be either minions of the powerful and privileged or incredibly naive dupes.

Members of Congress were in some cases both, but they also reflected a growing conservatism among the general populace. The war had virtually ended unemployment in America and elevated a large segment of the working class to middle-class status. It had instilled in them a desire for protection from another depression and the determination to keep what they had. High taxes and inflation—these were the worries of bourgeois America. Ironically, while memories of the depression lingered, the war had brought economic security and a rising level of expectation.

Not surprisingly, Congress refused to take any action on the NRPB report. Moreover, in June it voted a $50,000 appropriation to be used to terminate the agency itself. The board was ordered to cease all operations on August 31, 1943, and Congress stipulated that the "function exercised by such Board shall not be transferred to any other agents."[47]

Liberals remained undaunted, however. With the demise of the NRPB in 1943, the Keynesian torch passed to the Fiscal Division of the Bureau of the Budget, still a New Deal stronghold under Harold Smith. The broad outline of a new postwar plan for full employment began to crystallize in the United States in summer 1944. Before 1941 the highest level of employment attained in the United States was 46 million. That figure was reached in 1929, 1937, and 1940. As of 1944, approximately 52 million people were employed in the United States with another 12 million or so in the armed forces. The Labor Department estimated that the labor force would grow at about 750,000 a year. Full employment advocates decided, therefore, that a goal of 60 million jobs was not unreasonable. But how to realize that goal?—that was the problem that preoccupied liberal economists.[48] Admitting that it could do little without a wholehearted commitment from the White House, the Fiscal Division and its allies in other departments nevertheless began to plan their political strategy.

In early July 1944, Alvin Hansen approached Marriner Eccles about the possibility of developing an "American White Paper on Employment Policy" and including it in the Democratic platform. Jobs were going to be on everyone's mind and Thomas Dewey had already taken the offensive. FDR needed to take a strong stand on full employment, Hansen said, both in order to win and to create the impression of a political mandate so that he would be in a better position to implement the policy once victory had been won. Eccles sounded out Harold Smith, and the two men subsequently approved the convening of an informal committee of government economists to draft a white paper on postwar economic policy. The group quickly agreed that the federal government would have to directly underwrite aggregate demand if private expenditures and investment fell below a full employment national income. Political considerations, however, made it necessary to play down the spending role of the government and instead emphasize those policies that encouraged and stimulated private investment. In early October the committee completed the final draft of the "Report on Postwar Employment." The authors prepared a summary and forwarded it to the White House, suggesting that the president use it in his campaign speeches and, if he so desired, as a basis for detailed postwar employment policies.[49]

Moving independently of this group, Henry Morgenthau urged FDR to make employment a primary issue in the campaign. "I have been working for three weeks to try to sell the President the idea that he should do a discussion on jobs, and I finally succeeded the other night," the secretary told Robert Nathan. "He has been very loath to do it," he added. Morgenthau urged Roosevelt to recapture the spirit of 1932–33. The administration must be able to convince people "that we have plans, [that] there are jobs, that we want a high level of productivity." The British white paper had recently been published and "it is a darned good plan of postwar England." Dewey, Morgenthau reminded the president, had been harping on the ten million unemployed before the war and was scaring "the death out of people." According to Morgenthau, FDR directed Treasury to prepare a speech for campaign use. Harry White enthusiastically complied.[50]

Two subsequent addresses by Roosevelt—the Soldier's Field speech of October 1944 and the state-of-the-union message in January 1945—outlined a postwar economic policy that reflected the influence of the "Report on Postwar Employment" and the United States Treasury. Roosevelt, however, never followed up his liberal economic goals with specific legislative programs. The president sounded like a Keynesian, but in his private conversations with Harold Smith he appeared very much the fiscal conservative. He told the budget director, as the two prepared the president's annual message to Congress, that he wanted to commit the government to a program of debt retirement. The country could not and should not carry such an enormous burden. If Herbert Hoover had cut the public debt, it might have dampened the economic boom of 1929. Smith, a thoroughgoing New Dealer, observed with distress in his diary that the president seemed to share some of the common citizen's concern over public indebtedness.[51]

The fact that the president had not learned the lessons of the depression of 1929–36 or the recession of 1937–38 was not readily apparent to liberals. Most chose to regard FDR's reelection as a triumph for their cause and a mandate to move ahead in the areas of social security and full employment. Four days after the election, Eleanor Roosevelt told her husband that if he did not want to lose the support of the United States public for his foreign policy he had better follow through on his promises regarding domestic policy. He had placed himself under a moral obligation to organize the nation's economic life so as to give everybody a job.[52] From England Harold Laski urged Roosevelt to make this "the Lincoln-term of your four terms" and transform the Four Freedoms into living realities for all people.[53]

The full employment bill was introduced in the Senate on January 22, 1945, by Senator James Murray (D-Mont.). A companion measure was placed in the House hopper on February 15 by Congressman Wright Patman (D-Tex.). The bill declared it to be the national policy of the United States to foster free enterprise and private investment while recognizing the right of every citizen to "useful, remunerative, regular and full-time employment." In modern society, the Murray-Patman proposal proclaimed, it was the government's duty to plan a consistent and coordinated economic program to ensure that sufficient employment opportunities existed for all Americans.[54]

Under the proposed law, the president would prepare and submit to Congress annually a national budget for the next fiscal year. It would project the estimated size of the labor force, the total national output required to employ that labor force, and the expenditures and investments necessary to purchase total production. The budget would survey current and future economic trends and decide whether production, investment, and income levels would exceed or fall short of full employment requirements. If they were deemed subpar, the bill authorized the president to utilize a variety of tools—fiscal policy, resource development, social insurance—to stimulate the expansion of nonfederal and private investment. If these proved insufficient, the president would recommend an increase in federal expenditures and investment to close the deflationary gap. Conversely, in the event of an inflationary spiral, the national budget would outline a program for discouraging nonfederal and private spending and investment and adjusting federal policies so as to cool off the economy.[55]

Almost as soon as it was introduced into Congress, the full employment bill ran afoul of a major political blowup within the Roosevelt administration, an explosion that linked full employment with the "radical New Deal" element in America in the minds of many conservatives. The episode also demonstrated the breadth and depth of conservative sentiment in America as the last year of the war opened.

FDR had never liked or trusted Jesse Jones. He was too powerful, too conservative, too independent. But Roosevelt had needed his political support in 1943 and 1944 in various disputes with Congress. Consequently, despite the rantings of Wallace, Sidney Hillman, Eleanor Roosevelt, and other liberals, the president had left him alone. Roosevelt's patience evaporated during the election of 1944, however, when Jones agreed to campaign for the Democratic ticket only at the last moment, subsequently making one weak and ineffective speech in the president's behalf. In fact, Jones's nephew, George Butler, headed an anti–fourth-term movement in Texas. As a result, when (after the election) Jones routinely turned in his resignation, Roosevelt accepted it. Indeed, FDR stripped Jones not only of his post at Commerce but at the Reconstruction Finance Corporation as well. Furthermore, the president subsequently nominated none other than Henry Wallace to succeed the wealthy Houstonian as secretary of commerce and head of the RFC. When told that Jones was going to be ousted from the cabinet, Morgenthau, who hated and feared the Texan, asked: "Mr. President, are you going to cut off the entire dog's tail or are you going to do it in pieces?" Roosevelt said: "No; I'm going to do it all at one time. Wallace says that he doesn't want him around Washington making trouble. . . . I am going to let him go entirely out of government."[56] The dismissal and nomination touched off a firestorm of controversy inside and outside Congress.

Liberals and some moderates who looked on Wallace as both willing and capable of promoting schemes of full employment and of propping up small business against the large conglomerates were enthusiastic. But conservatives and the business community were furious. They flooded the capital with telegrams, letters, and lobbyists. "Can't *you* or somebody start a backfire in time to prevent the travesty of imposing this bastard Democrat upon the business interest of America," J. W. Cunningham of Toledo wrote Senator Robert Taft.[57] Infuriated over a comment attributed to Henry Wallace in the press that America was going to have a revolution and he, Wallace, hoped it would be a bloodless one, H. R. Cullen wrote the Iowan demanding to know against whom the revolution would be directed. The orphans and widows who constituted the bulk of the nation's stockholders seemed to be the only logical targets. America was tiring of "unscrupulous labor leaders and politicians who resorted to demagoguery at every opportunity."[58] Men and women of property could not forget Wallace's 1944 comment about the need to seize business by "the scruff of the neck." Editorials in the Scripps-Howard press portrayed Wallace as a scatterbrained dreamer who would squander the nation's resources with breakneck speed.

Jones's power and prestige within the business community and among congressional conservatives stemmed not only from his conservative philosophy—what is good for business is good for America and vice-versa—but also from his utilization of the RFC to implement that philosophy. By 1944 that agency and its lending subsidiaries controlled between $30 billion and $40 billion. From 1932 through 1944 RFC had loaned $45 billion. As director, Jones had great influence in seeing which private and public ventures received money and which did not. The RFC chief also headed vast wartime government corporations such as the Metal Reserves Company, Rubber Reserves Company, and Defense Supplies Corporation. As Jones himself said, this financial and corporate empire "is bigger than General Motors and General Electric and Montgomery Ward and everything else put together."[59]

When the White House submitted Wallace's nomination to the Senate Commerce Committee, Senator Walter George (D-Ga.), a target of FDR's unsuccessful purge campaign in 1938 and a staunch friend of Jones, introduced a bill separating RFC from the Commerce Department. George claimed that the vast powers vested in the RFC, then generally regarded as the governmental agency freest of congressional control, and the Commerce Department should not be vested in one person, and that lending should be brought under more direct legislative control. Before the Commerce Committee could vote on Wallace, it first held hearings on the separation question. George called Wallace and Jones as expert witnesses on the issue.[60] The press predicted a confrontation as potentially significant as the Bryan-Darrow encounter of a generation earlier.

Wallace made it clear that he would accept the Commerce post even if RFC were divorced from it and made a characteristically sincere speech about his goals—expansion of private trade, with special emphasis on small business and creation of more regional development projects like the TVA. He and Senator Claude Pepper (D-Fla.) attacked Jones frequently and by name. Wallace referred to Jones's failure to accumulate strategic stockpiles from 1940 to 1942. It was not his lack of experience that should trouble Congress, the Iowan exclaimed, but the nature of Jones's long experience.

It was clear from the debate over separation and then confirmation that Jones and big business controlled the committee. Although he only named his rival twice, Jones converted his testimony into an anti-Wallace diatribe. Committee members followed his lead. "Mr. Wallace is the leader of the most radical group in America," Senator Harry Byrd (D-Va.) declared. "He is the close friend and coworker of Sidney Hillman and the extreme elements of the CIO. The maintenance of free enterprise means the preservation of our American way of life. It may well be that the action of the United States Senate on this appointment will have a decisive effect on the future of the free enterprise system."[61]

In a sudden ballot the Commerce Committee declined to confirm Wallace by a vote of 14 to 5 and adopted George's scheme for the separation of power by 15 to 4. Many observers predicted the Iowan's defeat, but, in the end, the traditional view that the president is entitled to whatever cabinet he appoints outweighed the repugnance conservatives felt for Wallace. He was confirmed by both chambers in February. Commerce came without RFC, however. One of Wallace's first moves, significantly, was to appoint a committee of orthodox businessmen to advise him.[62]

Among other things, the controversy over his confirmation as commerce secretary fixed Henry Wallace in the eyes of the public as the chief spokesperson for measures guaranteeing full employment. The full employment campaign did not benefit from the association, although it is probable that animosity toward Wallace and subsequent criticism of the Murray-Patman bill stemmed from the common roots of wartime prosperity and fear of postwar deflation.

Throughout the last year of the war, the full employment bill was gradually diluted. Anti-Keynesian forces in the United States including the National Association of Manufacturers, the United States Chamber of Commerce, and the National Industrial Conference Board mounted a broad and persistent attack on the concept and the bill. They pointed out that while employment had grown during the war, so had the national debt—from $43 billion in 1940 to a projected $270 billion by war's end. Moreover, these business organizations told their constituents that defeat of the Employment Bill of 1946, as it eventually came to be known, provided another opportunity to strike a blow against the "fiscal irresponsibility" and "socialistic tendencies" of the New Deal. In early 1946 Congress passed a wholly new bill that declared it to be the national policy of the United States "to attain and maintain a high level of employment, production and purchasing power" by promoting free enterprise, encouraging business expansion and individual initiative; adopting sound fiscal measures; and avoiding government competition with the private sector. Instead of a national budget, the president would submit an economic report describing current economic conditions and making recommendations to combat either inflationary or deflationary conditions. The government's stabilization activities were restricted to adjusting the volume of public construction expenditures and loans to cyclical fluctuations in the economy. This was essentially a timing procedure involving the implementation of normal public construction activities, and it did not envision the use of a compensatory program. Additional expenditures had to be accompanied by recommendations for financing these projects.[63] "It may truly be said," Donald Winch has written, "that the United States walked backward into a commitment to promote maximum (not full) employment."[64]

What then was left to FDR in his efforts to placate domestic liberals, calm the fears of the security-conscious American people, and win the propaganda war against fascism and communism? How was the administration to guarantee jobs and social security without undertaking massive public works programs and permanent deficit spending? What possible mechanism would allow the United States to underwrite the economic and social security of Western Europe without launching a massive foreign aid program? Multilateralism, answered Wilcox, Hull, Acheson, and Hawkins.

Hopkins and Roosevelt responded enthusiastically. The president was more than ever concerned about raising living standards abroad as the war entered its last year. "All around the world there are millions of people who have no purchasing power . . . the world must concern itself with these areas where the people cannot buy anything at the present time," he remarked at Yalta. "That is another reason why the U.N. should organize as soon as possible and there should be a world-wide study made of helping those nations that have no purchasing power today, to get some."[65] In addition, as he had stated so often during the 1944 election campaign, he was committed to full employment in the United States. If multilateralism could secure prosperity at home and peace and stability abroad without antagonizing the conservative majority in America, it was indeed a panacea.[66] In December 1944 Franklin Roosevelt, on the recommendation of Harry Hopkins, signified that he had accepted multilateralism as the cornerstone of American foreign and domestic policy by naming William L. Clayton assistant secretary of state for economic affairs.

Will Clayton grew up in Mississippi, the son of transplanted Virginians who had moved to the Deep South and prospered as cotton planters. At the turn of the century young Clayton went to New York to seek his fortune, having to settle at first for a job as a clerk and secretary for the American Cotton Company. In Mississippi and New York Clayton became acutely aware of America's status as a commercial and financial colony of Great Britain and of the South's position as a colony of both. The United States was then in the process of accumulating the capital necessary for it to control the terms of trade with its foreign partners. Clayton hoped his native region could do likewise and thus emancipate itself from the City of London and Wall Street.

With barely $9,000 in capital, the aspiring young entrepreneur and two associates established Anderson, Clayton and Company in Oklahoma City in 1904 while Oklahoma was still a territory. The partners gambled that times were right for United States cotton growers to seize control of their own marketing process. Their venture paid off: by late 1944 the company could boast sales of $272 million and was the largest cotton exporting firm in the world. At the same time the corporation diversified and spread throughout the world. Anderson, Clayton and Company built fourteen cotton oil mills and seventy-five cotton gins in Brazil, Mexico, Argentina, Peru, Paraguay, and Egypt.

Discouraged by early New Deal Agricultural Adjustment Administration restrictions, Clayton joined the Liberty League in 1934. After FDR stopped trying to achieve domestic prosperity through currency inflation and tariff protection and, with Cordell Hull, launched the trade agreements program, Clayton abandoned Herbert Hoover, Al Smith, and the du Ponts, and became an administration supporter.[67] Roosevelt called him to Washington to serve as war surplus property administrator, and he subsequently campaigned for the president's reelection in 1940 and 1944.[68]

Tall (six feet six inches), handsome, silver-haired, with a reputation for integrity and civility, Clayton was an evangelist in the cause of multilateralism. "Will Clayton was one of the most powerful and persuasive advocates to whom I have listened. Both qualities came from his command of the subject and his conviction," Dean Acheson observed. On one level the Texan was an exporter who coveted foreign markets. During World War I the federal government had stimulated domestic cotton production through loans and price supports, and foreign output through bulk purchasing and preemptive buying. By 1914 there was a glut of raw cotton in both the domestic and foreign markets. An expanded volume of world trade would absorb this surplus, Clayton believed, and make cutbacks unnecessary.[69]

But, like Hawkins and Wilcox, Clayton was committed to multilateralism as a general theory. In 1944 the Texan wrote Hopkins reporting on a meeting of the Committee for Economic Development he had recently attended in Chicago. There, Dean Calvin Hoover of Duke University had delivered a lecture, arguing that foreign trade was irrelevant to high employment and domestic prosperity in the United States. The expansion of foreign trade through across-the-board tariff reductions might alleviate unemployment in export industries, but the resulting prosperity would be more than offset by unemployment created through loss of protection for industries producing primarily for the home market. At best the two would balance each other out. For a country like the United States that was virtually economically self-sufficient, foreign trade was an ornament.

Calvin Hoover's reasoning was absurd, Clayton commented to Hopkins. How was the American economy to take up the slack if and when industrial exports were cut from the present level of $15 billion to the prewar level of $3 billion? The United States could achieve full employment without multilateralism only through emulating either the German model which involved slave labor, militarism, and regimentation or the Russian method which involved total collectivism.

"Is CED's objective merely employment," Clayton asked, "or employment at satisfactory wages in a free economy?" He went on to repeat familiar arguments about the need of war-devastated and developing nations for capital and consumer goods in the postwar era and America as the only possible supplier of these goods. Touching on the chief appeal of multilateralism, Clayton argued that America had a unique opportunity to serve itself and the world simultaneously. Unlike the professional economists in the State and Treasury departments, Clayton did not readily admit to Hopkins that the United States would have to import in order to export. The United Nations and other leading agencies would supply the world with credits initially. Later, income from United States travel and investments abroad would generate the dollars foreigners would need to buy American goods. It might eventually be necessary for the United States to take imports, he admitted, but because seventy cents out of every dollar spent on imports were for handling, distribution, rent, taxes, and labor in the United States, foreign goods would not necessarily cause unemployment. Foreign trade, Clayton concluded, would promote prosperity at home, raise living standards abroad, and establish the basic conditions in which democracy and peace could prevail.[70]

Clayton's appointment symbolized the White House's determination to use multilateralism to achieve all of these objectives. In addition, it was designed to bring order out of bureaucratic chaos. Clayton was to be the new high priest of the creed and the czar of foreign economic policy, putting an end once and for all to the bureaucratic struggle between State, Treasury, FEA, and other agencies.

More out of a desire to end the internecine warfare than to see a comprehensive foreign economic policy formulated, the White House in March 1944 created the Executive Committee on Economic Policy with the secretary of state as chairman, and including the secretaries of Treasury, Agriculture, Commerce, and Labor; the attorney general; and the director of the FEA. That body did nothing to end the backbiting or produce a unified policy.[71]

Immediately following Quebec, Morgenthau and the Treasury Department strongly recommended to the president the creation of a Foreign Financial Policy Board, with Morgenthau as chairman, to coordinate the various aspects of United States financial policy including lend-lease. Such a body would allegedly prevent situations whereby "foreign governments exploit and intensify the differences between agencies and officials of this Government for their own advantage."[72] Of course, State and FEA immediately cried foul. The Executive Committee on Economic Foreign Policy was functioning very nicely, Hull wrote FDR."[73] Harold Smith agreed; it was impossible to separate financial from economic policies and both from overall foreign policy considerations. If anything, he told the president, all these activities ought to be consolidated in State.[74]

By the eve of the 1944 election, Roosevelt had lost patience with the squabbling over foreign economic policy. He told Harold Smith that he liked the unity with which the British Foreign Office worked. The members of its staff had terrible arguments among themselves; but once a decision was made, they stuck together. Our people "would blurt out their disagreements." Hull was always "in the stratosphere" where administrative detail was concerned, the president complained.[75] Roosevelt and Hopkins wanted to centralize foreign economic operations in the State Department but, ironically, the chief stumbling block to that plan had been Hull. The Tennessean had spent much of the fall in the hospital, however, and in November he acquiesced in FDR's wish for a change of leadership in the department. Rumor had it that James F. Byrnes, passed over the for the vice-presidential nomination, was in line for the job, but he never was. Hopkins and through him Roosevelt intended to retain as much power as they could. To this end they selected Edward Stettinius to succeed Hull.

"Junior's" tenure as undersecretary had not improved his reputation. John Maynard Keynes termed him a publicity-conscious "bubblehead," while Harold Ickes likened him to a YMCA director.[76] Charles Bohlen, part of the new regime in the department that appeared after Stettinius's appointment, wrote of the new secretary:

> Stettinius was a decent man of considerable innocence. All of his impulses were correct. He was certainly no intriguer, no fighter, no politician. He had a pleasant, outgoing personality and brought a Boy Scout enthusiasm to his job . . . but he made some awkward slips. Just before the founding conference of the United Nations, he told the Polish Ambassador, who represented the London emigre government and was therefore opposed by the Soviet Union and barred from attending the meeting, that he looked forward to seeing him in San Francisco. The Ambassador dryly said he did not think so.[77]

Hopkins and Roosevelt intended to continue to control the details of American foreign policy by relying on a network of second-level officials in FEA, WPB, and State who were loyal to and in communication with the White House, and who shared its views. Stettinius, even more than Hull, would be a front man.

To strengthen State's hold on foreign economic policy and to convince friend and foe alike that the administration was serious about multilateralism, Roosevelt and Hopkins asked Clayton to join Stettinius's team as assistant secretary for economic affairs. Stettinius had prepared the way for Clayton by consolidating all economic and financial functions within the assistant secretary's bailiwick.[78] Both Adolf Berle and Dean Acheson would have liked to have had the job but neither was seriously considered. Acheson was persona non grata with Morgenthau, and Berle with virtually everybody in his own department. Hopkins gave the former brain truster a special assignment in civil aviation and named Acheson chief liaison officer with Congress. "The State Department is unquestionably the place for Clayton," Hopkins told Roosevelt on November 28. "I think he would get in difficulty in the domestic scene, but be a great success in the foreign field. In this area his views are identical with yours and Hull's."[79] The next day

Roosevelt wrote Clayton: "Am most anxious to strengthen the State Department higher command and feel that we really need your services as Assistant Secretary of State for all economic affairs."[80] On December 9, Harold Ickes remarked enviously to Henry Wallace that Harry Hopkins and Will Clayton were now the two strongest men in Washington. Leo Pasvolsky was right in observing that Clayton's appointment was the most important administrative change that had been made since the election.[81]

Though the White House had seemingly embraced multilateralism, it had not accepted the new liberalism. As had been the case with Cordell Hull, multilateralism for Roosevelt, Hopkins, and Clayton was an alternative to collectivism and specifically to countercyclical deficit spending to finance public works. After the war, the United States would boast the greatest industrial plant and the largest and most skilled work force in the world. If these resources and this energy were not absorbed, unprecedented surpluses would glut the domestic market and depression would follow. Unemployment and social unrest would threaten domestic stability and vital institutions. But unlike the nations of Western Europe, America was unwilling in 1944–45 to abandon laissez-faire and free enterprise for social security. Roosevelt, Hopkins, Byrnes, and their advisers persuaded themselves, indeed, that, by expanding America's overseas markets, multilateralism could guarantee full employment at home without additional collectivist measures or further deficit spending. To the White House multilateralism seemed the only available method for reconciling the political and economic realities of the day.

The Roosevelt administration, including Harry Hopkins, seems never to have realized that the effective functioning of a multilateral system depended on the participating nations adopting fiscal and social policies designed to guarantee full employment. Instead, the White House in late 1944 and 1945 embraced and advocated multilateralism primarily as an alternative to countercyclical deficit spending to stabilize the domestic economy and guarantee full employment. In viewing multilateralism as an international means to a national end, it put the cart before the horse. The administration's inability or unwillingness to see that planning, control, and deficit spending at the national level were complementary rather than contrary to an interdependent, expanding world economy diverted America's move toward economic internationalism. Apparently, the United States did not understand the implications of its own creed and, as Great Britain was to learn, a flawed multilateralism was a dangerous thing.

8. Heads I Win, Tails You Lose: Congress, the Reciprocal Trade Agreements Act of 1945, and the Ratification of Bretton Woods, 1945

IF THE ROOSEVELT administration's perception of multilateralism as an alternative to collectivist measures at the national level was not enough to convince Britain that Washington's view of economic internationalism was flawed, its abandonment in 1945 of simultaneous, horizontal tariff reductions in commercial policy and its stance over ratification of Bretton Woods should have been. The emerging consensus in the United Kingdom in behalf of the Beveridge Report and social security strengthened the hand of British multilateralists in their conflict with the empire isolationists and the left wing of the Labour party. Following a protracted struggle that saw Lord Beaverbrook, Leo Amery, and company invoke the need to maintain aggregate demand at home as justification for protection and a groundswell of support for empire preference within the Conservative party, Richard Law and his colleagues persuaded the cabinet to reopen negotiations with America on commercial policy. Britain entered the new round of talks, which opened in January 1945, ready to accept a multilateral accord to reduce trade barriers and an international organization to police such an accord.

But just as Britain prepared to embrace commercial multilateralism, the United States recoiled from it. During the Anglo-American negotiations, Harry Hawkins and E. F. Penrose put forward a version of the Bidwell Plan in which states with tariffs would be bound to an across-the-board reduction whereas nations with preferences would be committed to total elimination. When London balked, the Roosevelt-Truman administration made the Reciprocal Trade Agreements Act the centerpiece of its foreign commercial policy. That measure as renewed by Congress in spring 1945 guaranteed national control over United States tariff rates and protected special interests in every case. RTAA precluded a simultaneous, horizontal cut in tariffs and preferences and thus made impossible a meaningful agreement between the United States and Great Britain on the reduction of trade barriers during World War II.

At the same time the Roosevelt administration backtracked on commercial multilateralism, it negotiated an arrangement with Congress over ratification of the Bretton Woods Agreements that left United States control of a postwar international system intact but that provided for increased input from Wall Street and Congress. During spring 1945 American bankers agreed to drop their opposition to the International Monetary Fund and the International Bank for Reconstruction and Development if one of their number were made a member of a National Advisory Council (NAC) that would oversee the foreign loan policy of the United States, if Congress were empowered to set guidelines for the governance of the IMF and IBRD, and if the two institutions were headquartered in New York. Henry Morgenthau and Harry Dexter White decided to appease Wall Street out of fear that Congress would not otherwise approve the Bretton Woods proposals and because the secretary of the Treasury would chair the proposed NAC. The terms of ratification clearly tied the Bretton Woods institutions more closely to Congress and American special interests than either Treasury or the Exchequer would have liked.

Despite the fact that the Bretton Woods proposals were not capable of providing the United Kingdom with sufficient liquidity in the postwar period and the fact that Washington continued to make clear its determination to force Britain to accept full convertibility at war's end, John Maynard Keynes endorsed the IMF and IBRD after his return from New Hampshire. He continued to urge his beleaguered country to accept the two institutions even after they had been further modified by Congress. Determined to see his creations, no matter how malformed, come to life, he convinced himself and his compatriots that the United States would provide the credit necessary for Britain to participate in Bretton Woods.

British observers initially believed that the campaign for sixty million jobs, the Murray-Patman bill, Roosevelt's reelection, and Will Clayton's appointment signaled not only the final triumph of multilateralism in the United States but also acceptance of the fact that full employment policies at the national level were prerequisites for the proper functioning of any multilateral system. "To the liberal economic thought of the country the New Deal by any other name would smell as sweet," a British official in Washington reported to London.[1] But Whitehall soon learned that economic nationalism and fiscal conservatism were alive and well in the United States.

In Britain as in America, the debate over domestic social and economic policies was accompanied by a wide-ranging discussion of commercial policy. But whereas in the United States outside multilateralist circles commercial policy was perceived to be icing on the cake of economic self-sufficiency—a politically expedient way to smooth out bumps in the economic cycle—in Britain it was seen as the key to national survival. In an article entitled "Export or Die," *The Economist* proclaimed that "if there is one matter which, second only to victory, should be regarded as vital to the future welfare of the British community, it is the restoration of international trade."[2] But how was it possible to revive foreign commerce? After the inconclusive Washington conversations on commercial policy in fall 1943, the debate continued between those who insisted that multilateralism, with all its pitfalls, was diplomatically and economically inevitable and those who insisted that it contained the seeds of destruction for the British Empire.

Early in 1944 Richard Law urged his colleagues to reopen commercial policy talks with the Americans and to allow good-faith negotiation to parallel talks over monetary policy.[3] His recommendation, in turn, touched off a stormy cabinet meeting which saw the empire isolationists invoke Keynesian economics as part of their frantic effort to head off what they considered to be Britain's economic Armageddon. Once again Hugh Dalton's diary sets the scene. Although Law had provided "a good statement, quite brightly written," the meeting at No. 10 Downing Street, he wrote, was long and grueling. "The Beaver put in a ludicrous paper" making a direct frontal attack on Law's position, claiming that the Clearing Union was the gold standard all over and that the American commercial plans were designed to destroy imperial preference. All this was the "sheerest piffle," Dalton remarked. Ernest Bevin, "who is always a little difficult on this point," was warned that if he did not cooperate he would be isolated along with Beaverbrook and the Bank of England. Lord Cranborne, secretary of state for dominion affairs, confirmed that the Dominions were no longer "much interested" in imperial preference. "Why not sell it in return for a good multilateral arrangement," argued Dalton, Cranborne, and Oliver Lyttleton, who as minister of production was desperately dependent on American supplies.[4] Cherwell spoke strongly for renewed negotiations. At this point, according to Dalton, Beaverbrook began to wave his arms and rant. Canada could be persuaded to enter into bilateral barter arrangements. When told that the MacKenzie government fully supported multilateralism, Beaverbrook declared that when the Canadian people found out there would be a revolution.

"It is incredible how these rambling discussions succeeded one another, every few months, with no new arrangements and no one changing sides and never any really firm decisions," Dalton observed. "The P.M., a little torn between Cherwell and the Beaver, says that he knows nothing about these things and has not had time to pass this paper through his mind, but it is clear that a majority of the Cabinet are in favour of going forward with the negotiations on the lines suggested." The ministers wound up appointing a committee of Lyttleton, Dalton, Law, Cherwell, and Beaverbrook with Sir John Anderson as chairman to report back on steps to be taken in the commercial area.[5]

The committee met almost continuously from February 14 through February 17. Hugh Dalton quickly emerged as the spokesperson for commercial multilateralism. He was departmentally so disposed; as the official in charge of reviving Britain's postwar export trade, he believed there was no alternative to lowering trade barriers and working with the Americans for an expanded volume of world trade. He was certain that Labour would sweep to victory in the first postwar election and that subsequent government policies and programs would enable Britain to compete with the United States. And it was Dalton who more and more bore the brunt of Beaverbrook's ire and guile:

When I have spoken a few sentences he shouts, "Have you finished." I shout, "You will know soon enough when I have finished. You have talked a great deal more than I have for the last few days and now you had better listen to me for a change." Through all this J. A. [Anderson] sits immobile and expressionless in the chair. But at the end of this scene the Beaver invites me to lunch alone at Arlington House. It is a very good lunch with some very good Rhine wine of which he makes me drink the larger part, a wing of chicken, some dates from Marakesh, some rather good Canadian cheese, and a large brandy. He says, "I think you are doing very well in this Committee. You are putting your case very clearly and with great good temper." He also says, "I think you are doing your job very well at the Board of Trade." I say, "You used not to think that when you were attacking me every day in your paper." He says, "Oh, there was nothing personal about that."[6]

In the face of the multilateralist onslaught Amery, Beaverbrook, and Robert Hudson began to tack frantically. The empire isolationists decided that they had to whip up popular support for their cause, and the only way they could do that was to champion all the latest social programs and denounce multilateralism as the preeminent threat to them. Sounding almost Keynesian, Beaverbrook wrote in "A Policy of Expansion": "Let us keep plainly before us that our first purpose must be expanded employment and rising standards of living . . . if this becomes our aim as a nation, with all other financial and economic policies subordinated to it, we shall achieve some measure of prosperity in our domestic economy." Beaverbrook called for an international project to "challenge the concept of the Free Traders with its idealism," namely, an agreement among nations to pursue policies that would promote and ensure high wages and full employment within their own borders.[7] The Keynesian revolution was indeed pervasive. Apparently, if Beaverbrook had to choose between free enterprise and imperialism, imperialism would win every time.

As a result of agitation by the empire isolationists, the rumblings in Parliament against commercial policy concessions to the Americans grew louder and louder as 1944 wore on. The balance-of-power, multilateral payments system operated by Great Britain in the nineteenth century had worked magnificently, Leslie Hore-Belisha declared. But it was no more. America had destroyed it. The United States had rallied to the Allies' side too late during the Great War and had taken advantage of Britain's resulting decline to horde all the world's gold, removing it from circulation and making impossible a global payments system linked to gold.[8] Sounding the keynote of the high Tory program, Hore-Belisha told Parliament that the government must end domestic controls over business while protecting it from unfair foreign competition. Responding to the argument that the United States would never provide financial aid to a nation that proved uncooperative in the commercial field, Ivor Thomas declared: "If I understand the Americans, I think that they have one characteristic which they share with the Deity; the Americans help those who help themselves."[9] But the person who more than any other embodied the parliamentary revolt against multilateralism was both a long-time supporter of Winston Churchill and a prominent reform Tory—Robert Boothby. The Americans, he said,

> seem to think that non-discrimination means doing away with all forms of preference, all forms of long-term purchase contracts, exchange restrictions, and reciprocal trading or payments agreements. If that view were to prevail, it would be the end of us. After the war we shall have only two assets, our productive capacity and our internal market. Unless we retain the necessary powers to enable us to trade those assets, I cannot see how we can get through, unless we choose to live indefinitely on charity, which I do not think anyone in this country would wish to do.[10]

Despite Britain's deteriorating international position, left-wing Labour figures like Emmanuel Shinwell, Aneurin Bevan, and Jennie Lee continued their vehement opposition to multilateralism. Whereas Roosevelt and Hopkins saw export trade as a mechanism to achieve full employment at home, the doctrinaire socialists saw full employment through the maintenance of aggregate demand as a prerequisite for a healthy export trade. If Britain was forced to pursue monetary and commercial policies that prevented the government from implementing plans for comprehensive social insurance and full employment, exports were irrelevant. "To reduce the purchasing power and lower the standard of life of your own people, is to injure export trade," declared a Labour backbencher. "The basis of health of the export trade is the health of your own economy."[11] Others argued that planning was as necessary in international economic matters as in domestic, particularly for Britain which was so dependent on international trade. "A fully employed America," declared Labour M.P. S. S. Silverman, "could be attained at the expense of an unemployed world quite easily, and that would be a violent world. . . . There is no place for this country . . . in any uncontrolled, unplanned scramble for markets . . . our salvation depends on a planned economy at home [and] a planned economy in the world."[12]

To their delight, opponents of multilateralism managed to create enough outcry over the threat to imperial preference to paralyze Winston Churchill. After the cabinet committee's report, the prime minister laid down principles that he felt should govern Anglo-American economic and financial relations: "no fettering of our country, direct or indirect to gold . . ., no abandonment of Imperial preference unless or until we are in the process of a vast scheme of reducing trading barriers in which the United States is taking the lead . . ., and no artificial dearness or scarcity of basic foods by tariffs or quotas."[13] In early April Churchill addressed some fifty-two rebellious Conservative M.P.s concerning Article VII. So hostile was the reception that he vowed not to go back again and ordered Anderson to take his place in future caucuses.[14] "All this frantic dancing to the American tune is silly," he told Anthony Eden.[15] Buoyed by this show of grassroots support, Amery threatened to resign if Britain gave in to United States demands. So violent was the backlash among Conservatives, both traditional and reform, that even Cherwell was momentarily intimidated. "On rereading these notes [regarding the Law memo] I feel I must apologize for having succumbed to the revivalist fervour which has recently been imported into the dismal science of economics."[16]

But there was a central truth that the Churchill government and Parliament simply could not ignore. The United States was economically self-sufficient and could act with virtual independence in world affairs; Britain was vitally dependent on overseas trade and its empire was crumbling. Like it or not, Britain's economic and military security and that of all of Western Europe depended on the United States. Consequently, in the jumble of political and economic interest groups, bureaucratic empires, ideologies, and personalities that competed for control of Anglo-American relations, those originating in the United States would ultimately be controlling. What Franklin Roosevelt, Henry Morgenthau, Will Clayton, and the Congress wanted mattered more than what Leo Amery, Emmanuel Shinwell, or Parliament wanted. Richard Law put the chips on the table in a candid memo to the Foreign Office. His visits with Hopkins and his interviews with the president had convinced him that Roosevelt's attitude toward Britain and commercial policy went something as follows:

It's essential to increase U.S. exports. If this is to be done without great damage to other people, in particular to the British, we must get some kind of settlement along the lines of Article VII, which will tend to increase the total of international trade. The British seemed determined on suicide. I'm prepared to do everything I can to stop them, short of having long arguments with Winston on the subject neither of us understand. My position has been made abundantly clear. If the British refuse to see it, I'm sorry. But it's their funeral after all.[17]

The illusion created at the Quebec Conference that Britain could get what it wanted from the United States with no strings attached was quickly shattered during the Phase II negotiations that followed. In addition, when Britain opted for the Keynesian alternative in domestic policy in 1944, it had at the same time to confront the question of how jobs, homes, and food were to be paid for. For a time Labour clung to a belief that its victory at the first general election after the war and the socialization of Britain's economy that would follow would solve the nation's economic problems. Similarly, high Tories tried to rely on free enterprise and reform Tories on the middle way. But given Britain's dependence on overseas trade and its indebtedness, prosperity could not be achieved through mere domestic policy or unilateral action. And because the empire was disenchanted with imperial preference, Britain would have to increase its exports with the world at large. The United Kingdom would have to compete, and it would have to have a loan or a credit from the United States to get in shape to compete.

The realization that Britain would have to sacrifice pride and prejudice for food and homes produced in early 1945 a grudging, reluctant decision by the Churchill government to enter into informal discussions on commercial policy with American representatives in London. The British delegation was instructed "to studiously refrain from discussing stage III financial questions." The need for a postwar loan was one of the prime reasons the British Cabinet was willing to reopen commercial talks with the Americans, but Britain would labor frantically to prevent the formal linking of the two. Any trade policy agreement that was reached must appear to stand on its own merits. If a free trade convention were tied to a loan or the promise of one, it would appear that the British government had sold its birthright (imperial preference) for a mess of pottage.[18]

Meanwhile, the State Department had been hard at work developing its commercial policy strategy. The first week in March the Secretary's Staff Committee submitted and Stettinius approved a statement of principles for the expansion of international trade. Its main features were a multilateral pact providing for a simultaneous, horizontal reduction of tariffs and elimination of preferences and quotas, and an international organization to enforce the provisions of such an agreement. These principles were subsequently discussed and finally approved in May by the Executive Committee on Economic Foreign Policy. The department and the Executive Committee endorsed the Hawkins-Penrose stratagem of proposing negotiations among as many countries as possible, but including at least a nucleus of the major trading nations, looking toward the conclusion of a multilateral commercial policy agreement. It also adopted a standby plan. If in the course of the negotiations it appeared that a consensus was impossible in one or more of these areas, the United States and other participants should be free to negotiate "individual, bilateral trade agreements on a most-favored-nation basis."[19]

The "alternative strategy" endorsed by the Executive Committee was in fact the policy that the United States adopted in 1945, and that strategy marked a significant deviation from commercial multilateralism. Despite administration rhetoric, the economic internationalists in the White House and the State Department were not willing to wage a major battle with the forces of economic nationalism in 1944–45.

The first week in January 1945, Hawkins secured State Department approval to discuss with the British what was essentially the Bidwell Plan for a multilateral trade agreement and an international trade organization to enforce it. What the multilateralists envisioned was a scenario whereby United States and British technicians would hammer out a set of principles that would govern the code-writing process and sketch the structure of the body that would administer it. The president would then approach Congress and, without mentioning Great Britain, advocate adoption. After congressional acquiescence, Washington would call a United Nations conference which would endorse the principles and create an interim ITO to translate generalizations into detailed multilateral conventions.[20]

In the London conversations that followed, both Harry Hawkins, E. F. Penrose, and their British counterparts agreed that the convention should provide for a simultaneous, horizontal cut in tariffs and preferences. The British, however, proposed some exceptions. They wanted a guarantee that the empire could retain a minimum, or "residual," tariff rate of 5 percent. They argued that the codes should impose a greater obligation to reduce rates on nations with high duties than on those with low ones. Sir Wilfrid Eady and his colleagues went so far as to propose a specific mathematical formula that would achieve greater reduction of high rather than low tariffs. The British also argued that under the guidelines proposed, America would be agreeing to lower only tariffs, whereas everyone else would be obligated to eliminate quotas and other devices. Finally, they expressed their opposition to subsidies, devices for protecting vulnerable sectors of a nation's economy that were dear to the hearts of American politicians and technicians.

The British were correct in pointing out that a simultaneous, across-the-board *reduction* of tariffs was not equivalent to *elimination* of preferences; the administration's plan to achieve commercial multilateralism would in fact give the United States a tremendous trade advantage over the United Kingdom. But in the end, Washington was not even willing to commit to a horizontal reduction of tariffs. The main weapon in the administration's trade arsenal turned out to be the Reciprocal Trade Agreements Act. That measure, as modified, was an instrument to protect vested interests while expanding American exports.

The Reciprocal Trade Agreements Act, first passed in 1934, was scheduled to expire on June 30, 1945. The measure was administered by an interdepartmental trade agreements committee that formulated recommendations for the president and negotiated commercial treaties provided for under the act. Participating agencies were State, Treasury, Commerce, and the Tariff Commission. Under RTAA, the executive branch had the authority to lower tariff rates on items imported into the United States by as much as 50 percent in return for a comparable reduction on an American export to that country. According to the most-favored-nation principle, the reduced rates would apply to all items of the same class for countries with whom the United States had signed trade agreements. As required by law, the government gave advance public notice of its intention to negotiate each agreement and provided full opportunity through public hearings and other means for individuals and businesses to object. After the program began, Congress added the "peril point" provision authorizing the Tariff Commission to recommend higher rates to the president if tariff rates in any case endangered the well-being of an American industry.[21]

As originally conceived, the trade agreements program was a mechanism designed to increase United States–Latin American trade. United States exports to that area had fallen from $5.240 billion in 1929 to $1.675 billion in 1933. During the same period the other principal trading nations of the world took control of their external commerce and advanced it by means of bilateral agreements. Under pressure from the business community, the State Department persuaded Congress to pass the Reciprocal Trade Agreements Act. Cordell Hull's liberal conscience was salved when the measure's authors added a most-favored-nation clause. It should be noted, however, that Latin America wanted reciprocal agreements without most-favored-nation arrangements. By 1939 only three republics had signed trade pacts with the United States.

Between 1939 and 1941 self-styled economic internationalists within the State Department touted RTAA as an American alternative to "Schachtism," the German practice of forcing unfavorable bilateral economic pacts on other nations through economic, political, or military coercion.[22] In fact, renewal of the measure in 1943 was part of the broad program of action on the international economic front recommended by the State Department in response to Republican "protectionism" as embodied in the Dewey Plan. That program included repeal of the Johnson Act and expansion of the lending authority and capital of the Export-Import Bank.

Although Stettinius, Clayton, Hawkins, and Charles Taft insisted on portraying RTAA as an internationalist measure, a weapon with which to fight the forces of economic nationalism in the United States and abroad, it was, as modified, an act of economic nationalism. The most-favored-nation clause notwithstanding, the trade agreements program was designed to expand American exports without exposing American enterprises to potentially destructive foreign competition. Hull and his heirs tended to equate any device that promised to reduce a trade barrier with "internationalism." They were never willing to admit that mechanisms such as RTAA could be made to protect special interests while promoting the expansion of American foreign trade.

The campaign for renewal of RTAA officially began in mid-January 1945. On January 17 John W. McCormack, House majority leader and a close administration ally, wrote FDR reminding him that the measure was due to expire June 30. He proposed that, in view of "the war and changed conditions, and particularly future permanent peace," RTAA be continued indefinitely. Responding to this invitation, the State Department and the White House decided not only to ask that the measure be made permanent but that Congress also increase the president's authority to reduce rates. If RTAA was to be an important bargaining tool in reducing trade barriers between the United States and its principal trading partners, the president would have to be able to go beyond the 1934 limitations, the State Department reasoned. Duties on 90 percent of the items in Anglo-American trade had already been cut by the 50 percent allowable under the original act. Therefore, the administration decided to propose that the executive be free to negotiate a 50 percent reduction in tariff rates as they existed on January 1, 1945, not June 30, 1934.[23] The original legislation also proposed congressional approval for a broad offensive by the president in the field of international trade to remove barriers and facilitate the flow of goods and services among countries.

The first week in March State Department representatives met with Sam Rayburn, John McCormack, Robert L. Doughton (D-N.C.), chairman of the House Ways and Means Committee, and Jere Cooper (D-Tenn.), a member of both the Ways and Means Committee and the Special Committee on Postwar Economic Policy and Planning. The legislators told the diplomats, in effect, that, if they wanted freedom to reduce rates by an additional 50 percent, they would have to relinquish their objectives of permanent renewal and broad authority in the commercial policy field. Congress was much too jealous of its prerogatives to give the president carte blanche. As a result, the bill that was finally introduced into Congress empowered the president to negotiate reciprocal reductions for an additional three years beginning June 12, 1945. It authorized him to make a 50 percent reduction on 1945 rates but made no mention of broad authority in the commercial field. Rayburn referred the measure to the Ways and Means Committee, which scheduled hearings to open April 18, 1945.[24]

Ironically, the person the State Department assigned to shepherd RTAA through Congress was Charles P. Taft, brother of the chief opponent of the administration's foreign economic policy, Senator Robert A. Taft. Charles Taft was in many ways the opposite of his sibling—athletic, outgoing, handsome, and cheerfully optimistic. Like Robert, he was a Yale Law School graduate and like all the Tafts interested in politics. While Robert's law partner in Cincinnati in the 1920s, "Charlie" became involved in a revolt against the regular party machine. His insurgency ended a budding political career, opening the way for the orthodox Robert's rise to power. During the same period, Charles became involved in the national YMCA movement and in the process met Edward Stettinius. An early advocate of aid to Great Britain and a staunch member of the internationalist wing of the GOP, Taft caught Roosevelt and Hopkins's eye, and they readily agreed when Stettinius proposed to bring him into the department in 1943 as director of the Office of Transport and Communications Policy.[25]

Charles Taft's internationalism was in no small part a product of his religious conviction. He along with John Foster Dulles took the lead during World War II in combating "perfectionists," those Christians who argued that all human institutions were by definition compromised and tainted and that those who supported or participated in them ran the risk of contamination. His compassion for humanity coupled with his innate conservatism caused Taft to embrace multilateralism as the hope of the world. "A productive job for every individual able and willing to work, affording an income sufficient for the basic needs of food, clothing and shelter, recreation and cultural pursuits," should be the ultimate goal of United States foreign policy, he asserted.[26] Bretton Woods and commercial multilateralism, he believed, were the means to attain that goal.

A number of State Department officials, including Taft and Harry Hopkins, recognized that a bilateral approach to tariff reduction contravened multilateralism and that RTAA was designed in part to protect domestic interests. Nevertheless, with an eye to Anglo-American negotiations, administration spokespersons continued throughout the debate to portray the act as a measure to end discrimination and reduce trade barriers worldwide, that is, as the commercial phase of internationalism. They, no less than John Maynard Keynes, believed that a flawed multilateralism was better than none at all.

Shortly before the hearings opened, Charles Taft began to try to line up Republican support for renewal of RTAA. Passage of the trade agreements bill was essential if the European countries were to be kept away from "a state managed foreign trade" and the Latin Americans prevented from trying to industrialize behind high tariff walls, he wrote Alf Landon.[27] Two days after the Ways and Means Committee convened, Taft appealed to Thomas E. Dewey. Opponents of the bill were taking the preposterous position that the United States should not help other nations increase their domestic production of any product—agricultural or industrial—that was at all competitive with an American product. "It is obvious," he wrote Dewey, "that somebody is going to ship these goods anyway if we don't and that you can't stop the industrialization of the rest of the world but this bunch seems to be sitting back in the chair of George III."[28]

Initially, economic nationalists took the administration at its word and equated the reciprocal trade program with multilateralism. After all, had not Cordell Hull struggled since 1934 to identify himself with Adam Smith and reciprocity with free trade. What ensued in spring 1945 was a debate in which State, Treasury, and Agriculture officials attempted indirectly to persuade representatives of special interests that RTAA was no threat to them while at the same time hailing it as the beginning of a tariff- and preference-free world. At first, spokespersons for special interests and self-appointed guardians of the national sovereignty were not impressed.

As in England, the special interests most opposed to renewal of RTAA, and to multilateralism in general, were not American industrialists fearful of raising up competitive economies abroad, but certain sectors of American agriculture. Indeed, the opposition of rural America to what it called "free trade internationalism" began after World War I and grew more intense during the interwar period. Farmers, particularly those in the Midwest, opposed free trade because it meant increasing imports into the United States of cheap raw materials, thus glutting the commodities market and driving prices downward.[29]

Nonetheless, because the administration claimed that a main purpose of RTAA was to expand the export market for farm commodities, farmers initially had been willing to give Roosevelt's trade program a chance. In fact, free trade had had a historic appeal among some segments of the farm community. Southern agricultural interests, especially cotton and tobacco, which were traditionally dependent on British and other overseas markets, fondly remembered the Wilson-Gorman and Underwood tariffs. Many of these heirs of William Jennings Bryan and Woodrow Wilson viewed free trade as a philosophical and political as well as an economic article of faith. In practice, however, the trade agreements began reducing tariffs on agricultural imports and not expanding markets for agricultural exports. Sentiment began to shift in 1935–36 and then a storm of protest erupted in the Midwest when in 1939 FDR proposed a trade agreement with Argentina, a major exporter of beef and wheat.

Leading the opposition was Carl H. Wilken and the Raw Materials National Council.[30] Wilken, an Iowa farmer and president of the 7,000-member Progressive Farmers of Iowa, was one of the founders of the council (composed largely of farmers and rural business interests) which was incorporated in Sioux City in 1936. Wilken derived his ideas from the "institutional economists" (i.e., Thorsten Veblen, John R. Commons, and Wesley Mitchell), men who prized observation over theory. He took the position that farmers made money out of production and not out of trade. In his judgment, free trade could not stimulate economic recovery because a mere "5 percent increase in our domestic buying power is equal to all foreign trade."[31] Wilken opposed the trade agreements program because it increased the importation of cheap commodities and failed to expand agricultural exports.

However economically unsound Wilken's ideas seemed to the multilateralists, he was more than a crackpot to a substantial segment of the agricultural community. So strong was midwestern and southern farm opposition to the trade agreements program that the administration was forced to abandon its plans for an agreement with Argentina. In 1940 RTAA barely mustered enough support to gain a three-year extension from Congress.[32]

Joining farm bloc representatives in opposing commercial multilateralism were GOP senators and representatives who took advantage of the RTAA renewal debate to hammer away at the issue of executive usurpation. During the brouhaha over repassage in 1943, Senator Arthur Capper (R-Kans.) boasted that he had maintained "a consistent record in opposition to the reciprocal-trade treaties, miscalled 'trade agreements.' " Similarly, Senator William L. Langer (R-N.Dak.) railed against "governmental bureaucrats determined to make treaties." William P. Malony (R-Conn.) offered an amendment proposing that no foreign trade agreement take effect until ratified by two-thirds of the Senate. Others claimed that the measure not only encroached on Congress's treaty-making powers, but challenged its control over revenue and the regulation of commerce as well.[33]

Of course, the Republican party was traditionally the party of protection, the principal advocate of self-sufficiency and economic nationalism for the United States. The object of American foreign economic policy, Martin J. Gillen wrote John A. Ritchie, should be "self-sufficiency for the nations of the world and the right of every nation to build up manufacturing facilities with their own people within their own borders."[34] Under the benign influence of the Republican tariffs of the late nineteenth and early twentieth centuries, America had achieved that universal goal. Barely 6 percent of United States commerce consisted of foreign trade, GOP policymakers emphasized again and again. Republican tariff policy, based as it was on the principle of equalization of costs of production, had enabled United States industry to pay its labor the highest wage in the world which, in turn, created a prosperous home market for United States agriculture. Other nations ought to be free to use any device they felt necessary to achieve self-sufficiency.[35] The Republican platform in 1944, largely the work of Robert Taft, called for each separate trade agreement to be ratified by Congress.

Labor was split over renewal. Representatives of various trade unions—the potters, glass blowers, cigar makers, hatters—opposed passage of the expanded trade agreements measure. Matthew Woll, president of the American Wage Earner's Protective Conference and of the Union Label Trades Department of the American Federation of Labor, argued that the measure had exposed United States industry to unfair competition from cheaply produced foreign goods and would continue to do so. But representatives of the Congress of Industrial Organizations enthusiastically supported renewal. The division was logical; skilled workers in the AFL were worried about competition that would produce either lower wages or unemployment, or both, while the generally unskilled assembly-line workers in the CIO were concerned about surpluses. If foreign markets were not found for automobiles, machine tools, raw steel, and other mass-produced products, unemployment in the postwar period seemed to them to be a certainty.[36]

Administration officials scheduled to testify in behalf of renewal encountered a rough reception from critics of the trade agreements program. Harold Knutson (R-Minn.) led off in the House Ways and Means Committee. "It will be necessary for the administration," he declared to Will Clayton, "to advance something more concrete than scintillating fallacies, glittering generalities, glittering absurdities, and the same sort of promises that were used in 1934, again in 1937, 1940 and 1943."[37] Specifically, he wanted to know why the depression of the 1930s was never ended until the war economy intervened, and how exactly, given the current "unpleasantness" in Europe and the Far East, the trade agreements program prevented war. Knutson and his principal ally in the Senate, William Langer, accused Clayton and Henry Wallace of trying to sell Congress a "pig in a poke," and they refused even to admit that dollars held by foreigners had ultimately to be spent in the United States.[38] Hostile members of Congress accused Wallace of being a socialist and argued that if any doubt existed that RTAA was a long stride down the road to totalitarianism, Wallace's support of it cleared that away. Before the hearings ended, Carl Wilken, Robert S. Palmer of the Colorado Mining Association, F. E. Mallin of the National Livestock Association, Arthur Bene of the National Association of Wool Manufacturers, and dozens of other special-interest representatives testified against passage.

When the vested interests and congressional nationalists had fired their final salvo, government spokespersons set about the laborious task of convincing critics that their goals and those of the administration were totally compatible. In fact, they argued, the reciprocal trade program was just what the members of Congress and their constituents had been looking for, a policy that would protect special interests from foreign competition and at the same time leave those interests unencumbered by permanent regulation and interference in the domestic sphere. The White House promised that the new authority would not be used to endanger any segment of American industry, agriculture, or labor, and Edward Stettinius assured Congress that "the trade agreements should be employed to expand our foreign trade by a process of hard-headed and business-like bargaining."[39]

What was particularly attractive about RTAA, the administration told senators and representatives, was that it promised to expand trade and foster free enterprise at the same time. During the debate, opponents had declared that they were fighting to preserve individual initiative in foreign trade as well as in domestic commerce, that government manipulation of foreign trade via RTAA would stimulate collectivism at home and, indeed, was part of an effort by the New Deal bureaucrats to regiment and "totalize" the domestic economy. The administration responded to the arguments of the laissez-faire enthusiasts who opposed public works and deficit spending by pointing out that reciprocal trade offered what they wanted—domestic, economic, and social stability without Keynesian economics at the national level. Indeed, RTAA and other mechanisms designed to promote international commerce were the only alternatives to countercyclical deficit spending and collectivization. During the debate on the Murray full employment bill, which overlapped consideration of RTAA, Edward Stettinius wrote Senator Robert F. Wagner (D-N.Y.) that continuing full employment could best be achieved by an increase in foreign trade rather than permanent public works projects and an unbalanced budget. Any full employment policy should "rely substantially on trade and investment," and those ends would be dramatically advanced by renewal of RTAA and passage of the Bretton Woods bill.[40] "The core of our whole post-war foreign economic program is the expansion of private trade and the encouragement of private enterprise," the secretary told the Chicago Council on Foreign Relations.[41]

The Reciprocal Trade Agreements Act was renewed by record margins in both houses, with the vote cutting across partisan, geographic, and ideological lines. After trying and failing to force the administration to admit that it was parading about a nationalist animal in internationalist clothing, Robert Taft voted for it. So did a number of other conservative Republicans. That vote was made possible not by the conversion of economic nationalists and the guardians of special interests to the cause of internationalism, but by their realization that RTAA was a servant rather than an enemy of United States economic interests, narrowly defined. In fact, RTAA was itself a concession to these forces.

Congressional conservatives and protectionists were reassured by the knowledge that the measure as renewed guaranteed national as opposed to international control of the tariff-making process. The United Nations and other multinational organizations notwithstanding, major decisions on economic matters would continue to be made by national governments, as Clayton correctly assured Congress.[42] Any regime that wished to stay in power was not going to negotiate a series of agreements that exposed important sectors of the economy to competition it could not meet, particularly in view of the fact that exports constituted but a small fraction of the total production of the country.

Not only did RTAA ensure the protection of domestic interests by guaranteeing national as opposed to international control of tariff rates, but it also ensured that agreements with other countries would be concluded on a bilateral, item-by-item basis. What Republican nationalists like Robert Taft feared most of all was a simultaneous, mass reduction in United States rates. In fact, a rumor to the effect that the administration was negotiating an "arbitrary reduction of American tariffs by 75 percent from existing rates" had prompted the senator to openly oppose the administration's trade policy.[43] RTAA provided for selective reductions on individual products, not across-the-board percentage cuts dictated by a multilateral convention or authority.

In addition, the renewal legislation required the administration to demonstrate that each reciprocal treaty promoted the expansion of American exports and that it did not seriously injure a domestic industry.[44] During lunch with Raymond L. Buel of *Fortune* magazine at the Cosmos Club a month after passage, Charles Taft admitted that reciprocal trade was a device that protected special interests. Buel congratulated Taft on his success in shepherding RTAA through Congress but remarked that he thought the act was of no possible further use. "The President and the Government witnesses in agreeing not to injure any American industry" seemed to preclude meaningful tariff reduction, he observed. The measure would protect uneconomic industries; the administration had apparently abandoned its long-held goal of seeing them shut down. Government agencies could never get away with such action, Taft replied testily. Any attempt to change the pattern of American industry was totally unrealistic; the assurances to which Buel objected "constituted the very basis of the success in getting it [RTAA] through Congress."[45]

Moreover, RTAA did nothing to redress the commercial and financial imbalance that had plagued international trade since World War I. Theorists of multilateralism had long pointed out that because the United States would have a monopoly of the world's gold supply and of its productive capacity at war's end, the nation would have to pass through an extended period during which imports exceeded exports. "Unless this is done," declared a State Department position paper on postwar commercial policy, "the balance of payments situation of other countries, notably the United Kingdom, would become critical, perhaps desperate."[46] RTAA contributed nothing toward the realization of this objective, toward generating imports in excess of exports. Because other nations would receive concessions for the concessions they granted to America, it could be argued that RTAA was not a mechanism for the unilateral expansion of United States exports. But while the legislation would strike a balance between the value of goods received and goods exported, it did nothing to remedy past imbalances and redistribute the wealth of the world.

Finally, as John Maynard Keynes had pointed out in 1942, bilateral treaties with most-favored-nation clauses did not always make for a freer flow of trade at a greater volume. As a number of Latin American countries had begun to complain in the late 1930s, the trade agreements did not encourage diversified investment or provide protection for new industries but kept developing nations locked into single-crop production for export, thus making them practically economic slaves to the world markets of whatever crop happened to be their specialty.[47] The trade agreements did not raise up balanced economies overseas capable of competing with the United States; to the contrary. In this sense they were no different from or better than the bilateral treaties British officials had threatened to conclude and of which American multilateralists claimed to be so frightened. When Philip Reed termed the trade agreements a "series of government cartels," which had as their purpose controlling and allocating the markets of the world, Henry Wallace concurred.[48]

The renewal of RTAA in May 1945 marked a dramatic turning point in the commercial policy of the United States. Shortly before Harry Hawkins returned to Washington to hold Will Clayton's hand during the congressional hearings, Clayton wrote him of the change. The informal discussions Hawkins and E. F. Penrose had been conducting with the British had been very helpful and must continue. It would be well to keep in mind, however, that the introduction into Congress "with Administration support" of the Trade Agreements Act "has now determined the line of policy which the Executive Branch of Government favors." Under RTAA the government would negotiate agreements in which selective tariff reductions would be made on a commodity-by-commodity basis after careful study. "This is a quite different idea from the horizontal, non-selective reduction of tariffs by a uniform percentage, which has been looked into here during the past year." In fact, the government could not implement a horizontal, percentage cut under RTAA. "I suggest," Clayton concluded, "that in your discussions in London you try to influence the thinking of your British colleagues toward a policy that would be practicable under the pending act."[49]

What ensued was an ironic turnabout in the Anglo-American dialogue over commercial policy in which the United States pressed for the selective bilateral approach—essentially the approach advocated by Hubert Henderson and for a time by John Maynard Keynes in 1941 and 1942—and Great Britain and the Commonwealth countries for a simultaneous, percentage cut by all countries. The Churchill government had decided by mid-1945 that if Britain wanted United States help in rehabilitating its own economy and that of Western Europe, substantial reductions in imperial preference were unavoidable. Nonetheless, the sine qua non of any reductions in British preferences was a simultaneous, horizontal cut in the American tariff. But now the United States seemed to be denying the truth it had been touting since 1941—that all trade barriers were bad and their reduction benefited the nation doing the cutting as well as its trading partners.

On June 28 in London, Harry Hawkins broached what he called the multilateral-bilateral approach to reduction of trade barriers. RTAA ruled out horizontal nonselective cuts, but the same objective could be achieved if all the major trading nations enacted their own set of trade agreements. Bilateral pacts with most-favored-nation clauses would soon effect a general reduction, he announced. No, they would not, retorted the astounded British. Such an approach would require an army of technicians and would commit participating nations to a process the outcome of which would be impossible to judge. But most importantly, it was "psychologically" necessary that all parties make sacrifices at once. "Psychologically" was Whitehall's euphemism for "politically."[50]

The multilateralists in Washington were not charlatans. Will Clayton, Harry Hawkins, Clair Wilcox, and even Charles Taft would have preferred a straight multilateral approach to commercial policy. Like his father, who had convinced himself that the highly protective Payne-Aldrich tariff of 1909 was really a low-tariff measure and was the best that could be gotten out of Congress, Charles Taft was given to wishful thinking and self-deception; but he remained a multilateralist. Special interests and the forces of economic nationalism were simply too strong. Ironically, the administration had been forced to introduce RTAA renewal legislation and wage an all-out struggle for its passage because the trade agreements program was closely identified, thanks to Cordell Hull and Franklin Roosevelt, with both economic and political internationalism. Congress's failure to sustain the trade agreements program would everywhere have been viewed as a defeat for the administration's foreign policy.

There is also a distinct possibility that the political leadership in the Roosevelt foreign policy establishment did not understand RTAA and its commercial implications. Hull, Gilbert Winant, and Edward Stettinius argued at one time or another that renewal of RTAA was necessary to reassure Great Britain about the willingness of the United States to reduce its tariffs.[51] Hawkins, Wilcox, Emilio Collado—the experts—were basically economists with no political base. Their foothold in the bureaucracy was tenuous. For them to have suggested that the trade agreements program was not 100 percent multilateralist and internationalist could have led to their quick exit from public service. As FDR indicated when he passed over Hawkins in favor of Thomas Blaisdell to head the London Economic Mission, he still liked team players.

Carl Wilken, Robert Taft, the CIO, Bernard Baruch, and certain mining and industrial interests had won a perverse victory. But the multilateralists believed that there was still hope. The multilateral-bilateral approach was cumbersome, inefficient, and not nearly as dramatic as the straight multilateral approach, but it had possibilities for achieving significant reductions in trade barriers, they believed. It even had its apologists on technical grounds. In mid-July 1945 the Executive Committee on Economic Foreign Policy adopted the "selective nuclear-multilateral" approach as its official position in all future negotiations with the British.[52]

Passage of RTAA in 1945 and the consequent need to abandon a horizontal, simultaneous approach to tariff cutting confronted the commercial multilateralists in the State Department with a dilemma. If the United States could not offer Great Britain and other trading nations a commercial inducement to abandon their trade barriers, what could it offer? In search of an answer to this problem, they turned, ironically, to finance. If debtor countries were convinced that the IMF and IBRD, then awaiting congressional approval, would provide sufficient liquidity, they might do away with preferences and quotas after all. The danger to the State Department in placing all its multilateralist eggs in a financial basket was that such a move would facilitate Treasury attempts to dominate foreign economic policy. Dean Acheson, Clayton, Wilcox, and Hawkins decided they had little choice, however. As a result, State Department officials joined ranks with their Treasury colleagues in summer 1945 to do battle with special interests and the forces of economic nationalism over ratification of the Bretton Woods Agreements.

As has been noted, Henry Morgenthau and Harry White were jubilant at the outcome of the Bretton Woods Conference. They were not naive enough to believe that the IMF and IBRD were panaceas, but they were steps in the right direction. The institutions would be particularly helpful as multilateral masks for United States aid to Russia and other war-devastated areas. More importantly, the agreements promised immense political and bureaucratic benefits. Morgenthau anticipated that Bretton Woods would serve FDR well in the 1944 campaign. In addition, the structure of the fund and bank ensured that the United States

Treasury and not Wall Street would control international finance. But the Bretton Woods meeting, like the Versailles Peace Conference, would be a hollow victory indeed if Congress failed to act.

To coordinate the campaign for Bretton Woods, Treasury hired Randolph Feltus, a public relations executive who quickly developed a strategy for selling the agreements to Congress, special interests, and the American people. Feltus's approach called for an appeal to conservatives. The left, he argued, was solidly behind the plan; and to impress moderates, powerful elements on the political right would have to be brought around.[53] The key to the success of this strategy seemed to be the American banking community. Through their work in various war bond drives, American bankers had slowly but surely begun to win back some of the public trust they had lost by their irresponsibility and selfishness in the 1920s and 1930s. Without their support, or at least acquiescence, there was little chance that conservatives in Congress would vote for the IMF and IBRD. What the bankers were interested in was control. They had recognized early on that the fund was in part a mechanism to transfer control of international finance from New York to Washington. The bank, essentially a multilateral tool for guaranteeing private United States investments abroad, was a sop and a very attractive one to Wall Street, but initially it was not enough.

It will be remembered that both investment and commercial bankers with substantial overseas operations had opposed the Keynes and White plans. Investment bankers led by the House of Morgan and the Chase National Bank feared they would lose control over the value of the money they loaned and invested abroad. They, in conjunction with the great banking institutions of London, had been accustomed to setting exchange rates and controlling the international money market. If they could not manipulate the market and take advantage of fluctuating exchange rates, a great source of profit would be closed off to them. The commercial bankers were afraid that loans made or controlled by an international agency would be used to enable governments of developing and war-devastated nations to establish their own indigenous industries, thus closing out these countries as areas of operation for General Electric, Ford, United Fruit, and other important clients. Despite Marriner Eccles and the Federal Reserve Board's support of Bretton Woods, the Federal Reserve Bank of New York led the opposition. The New York institution was, in fact, little more than a front for Wall Street.

No sooner had the last trainload of delegates left the New Hampshire woods than a joint committee of the American Bankers Association and the New York Bankers Association (federally chartered banks in New York) set to work "studying" the IMF and IBRD and preparing their own alternative. The group included George Whitney, president of J. P. Morgan and Company; Eugene Stetson, chairman of the board of Guaranty Trust; Gordon Reutscher of City Bank; William Potter, president of the New York Bankers Association; Randolph Burgess, head of the ABA; and E. E. Brown, representing the Federal Reserve Advisory Council.[54]

Before the committee could make its report, however, Winthrop Aldrich of Chase Manhattan and a bitter enemy of Henry Morgenthau, launched a full-scale public attack on the Bretton Woods proposals. Both the fund and bank were unnecessary, he insisted. London and Washington should work out a joint agreement to "shun totalitarian tactics in international trade and to adopt economic liberalism,"[55] and then the United States should provide England with a grant-in-aid large enough to establish stability between the dollar and the pound. At this point Anglo-America could turn its attention to stabilizing other currencies.

The Treasury Department's response to the Aldrich Plan was simple. On the day his report appeared, Morgenthau phoned the attorney general and pressed him to get busy on an antitrust suit then pending against Chase Manhattan. In addition, the Foreign Funds Control Board began accusing the bank's representative in occupied areas overseas of mismanagement.

There is some evidence that Wall Street knew of Aldrich's broadside and withheld its report while he fired it; that is, that the New York banking community was using Aldrich as a stalking horse. His extremism would act as a lightning rod, eastern bankers believed, and prepare the way for a compromise with Treasury. By early January 1945 the ABA and the Reserve Advisory Council had their report ready; but before going public, the joint committee presented it to Morgenthau and company. The report disapproved of the IMF because it would automatically give credit to nations that were not credit worthy. It recommended that the fund be merged with the IBRD without increasing that institution's capitalization beyond the $10 billion figure set at Bretton Woods. The governor of the bank should be American, and he and the United States directors ought to be appointed by the president with the consent of the Senate. Finally, the report recommended that the capital of the Export-Import Bank be increased to $2 billion. The bankers' initiative had two objectives. Their report, hopefully, would torpedo the whole arrangement or, failing that, would modify Bretton Woods into a channel for virtual risk-free overseas lending for American bankers. Morgenthau told Burgess and Potter that their objections were superficial and did not warrant the diplomatic negotiations that would be required.[56]

The day the bankers' report appeared an enraged Morgenthau began plotting his own strategy. Because Wall Street had gotten the propaganda jump, it clearly had the momentum. As Oscar Cox had written Morgenthau, the American press and public were almost totally uninformed on Bretton Woods. Other than the bankers' report, the only study of note had been an article in *Foreign Affairs* by John Williams, Harvard economist and member of the board of directors of the New York Federal Reserve Bank, and it had anticipated the bankers' report almost exactly.[57] The only East Coast paper really to have come out in favor of Bretton Woods was the *Washington Post*. Ansel Luxford remarked that he doubted that any major paper would write an editorial attacking the bankers' critique because members of the press would be unsure of themselves and "there is quite a galaxy of names in the report." Herbert Gaston, Morgenthau, White, and the other officials who regularly gathered in the secretary's office decided to take the low road in the forthcoming struggle and denounce at every opportunity the effort by "a few New York bankers" to control the exchange rates and investment capital of the world. Any attempt to approach the problem at the technical level would be dull and time-consuming "because the public is never going to examine the merits of this proposal."[58]

Treasury also decided, as it had done in summer 1944, to mobilize bankers outside New York, individuals whose primary customers were United States industrialists who feared overproduction in the postwar period and who craved overseas markets capable of absorbing surpluses. This stratagem, of course, allowed Treasury to exploit the widespread jealousy of Wall Street that existed in financial circles outside New York. Edward E. (Ned) Brown, chairman of the board of the First National Bank of Chicago, again agreed to head the drive for Bretton Woods within the banking community. In April, Ralph Flanders, president of the Federal Reserve Board of Boston, established the Business and Industry Committee for Bretton Woods, Inc.[59]

As was true of the campaign for renewal of RTAA, the heart of the administration's effort to win congressional approval for Bretton Woods was an attempt to build bridges to the presidential, internationalist wing of the Republican party. Treasury Department officials initially wanted the Bretton Woods Agreements submitted to Congress immediately after the conference ended and made an issue in the campaign of 1944. "We are at great advantage now because opposition is disorganized and political leaders do not know which way to turn," Luxford argued. Nevertheless, FDR ordered Morgenthau to hold up on Bretton Woods until after the election. The reason became clear when on September 20, 1944, Ned Brown informed Morgenthau that Thomas Dewey and John Foster Dulles wanted desperately to keep the issue out of the election. If he was forced to take a stand on the IMF and IBRD, which he favored, Dewey would forever alienate Robert Taft, thus splitting the party right down the middle and making possible a takeover by the congressional, isolationist wing. The Republicans promised to restrain the banking community and see that it kept Bretton Woods out of the campaign if the administration showed similar restraint. Except for Winthrop Aldrich, the GOP made good on its pledge.[60]

With the election over, there was little reason for the Republican internationalists to kowtow to Robert Taft and his fellows. Leading members of the presidential wing openly declared their support for Bretton Woods. After a visit at Harvard with Alvin Hansen, who convinced him that congressional approval of Bretton Woods was crucial to the success of the San Francisco Conference, Harold Stassen agreed to go to Washington and lobby for passage.[61] For somewhat the same reasons, John Foster Dulles publicly endorsed the fund and bank.

Dulles was not particularly enthusiastic or knowledgeable about multilateral mechanisms for exchange stabilization or international economic development, but he was unwilling to challenge the contention that Bretton Woods was the economic phase of collective security. By World War II collective security had taken on a significance for Dulles that was both diplomatic and moral. In 1940

Dulles agreed to chair the Commission on a Just and Durable Peace of the Federal Council of Churches in the hope, shared by members of both the British and American Protestant communities, that future wars could be averted by the creation of a viable international collective security organization. In 1943 the commission published its postwar program, entitled the "Six Pillars of Peace," which asserted that the success of any future peace would depend not only on disarmament and restraint of aggressors but also on the victor's ability "to make provisions for bringing within the scope of international agreement those economic and financial acts of national governments which have widespread international repercussions."[62]

Republican support for financial multilateralism culminated the first week in June 1945, when Thomas E. Dewey publicly endorsed both the IMF and the IBRD and simultaneously called for cancellation of all prewar debts and an early and generous settlement of lend-lease obligations.[63] It should be noted, however, that neither Dewey, Dulles, nor any other prominent political figure advocated sacrificing American living standards to elevate those of foreigners.

Despite this GOP rallying to the internationalist and multilateralist banner, the ability of the Bretton Woods Agreements to survive congressional scrutiny still seemed very much in doubt in early summer 1945. None of the aforementioned Republican supporters of Bretton Woods held a seat in Congress. Many who did sit in the House and Senate were more attracted by the biblical passages that spoke of an eye for an eye and stressed that God helped those who helped themselves than those that emphasized universal fellowship. Moreover, as the fight over Henry Wallace's confirmation indicated, a sizable number of Republicans as well as conservative Democrats were fearful that the administration was still dominated by those who wanted to squander the nation's resources through establishment of a giant international Works Progress Administration. Representative Jesse Wolcott (R-Mich.), ranking minority member of the House Banking and Currency Committee, even linked his opposition to Wallace's confirmation with Bretton Woods. Declaring that "the people look to Congress to stop this excited move to the left," he observed that Wallace's nomination was "most unfortunate for the Bretton Woods proposals." As secretary of commerce, the Iowan could very well dominate the bank and fund with "his philosophy of global economic reform." Moreover, a survey of press opinion indicated that if there was any connection between editorial attitudes, public opinion, and congressional action, the vote on Bretton Woods would be close.[64]

On February 12 FDR asked Congress to take immediate action on the Bretton Woods proposals. Acknowledging Wall Street's criticism of the International Monetary Fund, the president admitted that the institutions envisioned were not perfect, but suggested that experience would produce necessary improvements. He linked Bretton Woods with RTAA, expansion of the Export-Import Bank, and future agreements on commercial policy, oil, and civil aviation. Robert Wagner and Charles Tobey (R-N.H.) immediately announced that they would introduce appropriate legislation in the Senate, and Brent Spence (D-Ky.), chairman of the House Banking and Currency Committee, and Jesse Wolcott did the same in the House. The administration took no chances with a two-thirds vote; the plans for the IMF and IBRD were submitted as executive agreements to be approved or disapproved by a simple majority of both houses. Also, the legislation required not a cent of new money. The total subscription of $2.75 billion to the fund and $3.175 billion to the bank was to be covered by the transfer of $1.8 million from the United States stabilization fund, with the balance to be financed through advances of noninterest-bearing Treasury notes, or IOUs, which would be deposited with the international bodies and replaced with dollars only as needed.[65]

Morgenthau and White knew that Congress would base its deliberations not on the technical perfections or imperfections of the agreements but on political considerations and the prevailing mood of the country. As Arthur Vandenberg told Morgenthau, the proposals were just "too damn complicated." The outcome of the vote would thus be influenced by the campaign for and against and, in particular, the arguments presented by witnesses at the hearings. Above all, the administration decided, it must try to link Bretton Woods to Dumbarton Oaks.[66]

The battle was joined a few days before the hearings were scheduled to open when Robert Taft convened a meeting of Republican legislators to consider the Bretton Woods proposals and asked Dean Acheson to appear and present the pros and Leon Fraser, president of the First National Bank of New York, the cons. Fraser, who took the Wall Street/ABA position, made "a very effective, very powerful and utterly unscrupulous misrepresentation of the thing," Acheson later told Morgenthau. "It was really a demagogic appeal to every prejudice they have. . . . And he did it very ably. He's no slouch." Acheson reported that he had counterattacked without getting personal and believed he had made some headway. Morgenthau was not above getting personal. He immediately ordered his staff to initiate a campaign to smear Fraser. They should let it be known that he had represented a German firm before the war and should try to label him as an "appeaser."[67]

Morgenthau opened the hearings before the House Committee on Banking and Currency by arguing that the Bretton Woods Agreements would benefit every American citizen. Stability and order versus insecurity and chaos—those were the issues.

Every member of the committee was given a chance to ask questions, but it quickly became apparent that the only congressman who had read and tried to understand the agreements was Frederick Smith, the conservative physician from Ohio. The agreements, declared Smith, were complex, technical, and, most importantly, ambiguous. To Harry White's embarrassment, Smith brought up the gray areas that remained after the New Hampshire meeting: the methods the fund would use to guard against deflation, the scarce currency provision, and the question of when and to what extent the members were committed to undertake convertibility. When White, who was loath to admit that there remained profound differences of opinion over the fund and bank, appeared confused, Smith rebuked him. "You are a monetary expert and you are supposed to know more about his proposition than most of us."[68]

Ned Brown represented those bankers who favored the agreements, while Randolph Burgess and Leon Fraser spoke for those who opposed them. Fraser again made a very effective speech, praising the objectives of Bretton Woods but calling for the absorption of the fund by the bank. By objectives of the agreements, of course, he meant currency stabilization, reconstruction, and development, and not control of international finance by the United States Treasury. Essentially the fund was a mechanism to enable nations with weaker currencies— "leis, lats, and zlotys"—to exchange them for dollars, he charged. Both Fraser and Smith sprinkled their statements with numerous sarcastic references to "Lord Keynes" and his "theories."[69]

The midpoint of the hearings in the House found Treasury officials depressed and pessimistic about the chances of approval for Bretton Woods. A consensus held that all of the Republicans and at least two Democrats would vote against the agreements.[70] Further contributing to Treasury's gloom was a visit to New York the first week in March by Robert Boothby. After conferring with leading opponents of the agreements, the Conservative M.P. wrote an open letter which appeared in the *New York Times*. Did the agreements mean that participating countries could not sign discriminatory trade agreements? Boothby asked. Lord Keynes had assured Parliament that Bretton Woods did permit such agreements. In addition, Keynes had assured Britain that Bretton Woods did not spell the end of the sterling area, but surely the area's survival depended on the maintenance of currency controls. Finally, did or did not the agreements require members to peg their currencies in relation to gold-backed dollars? If this was true, then the agreements did in fact reestablish the gold standard, a move the British people would never accept. "Nothing could be more deleterious to the future of Anglo-American relations," he concluded, "than the two countries should sign an agreement, each thinking that it means something quite different."[71] Immediately, opponents of Bretton Woods in the House used Boothby's letter to grill White.

It is quite possible that Boothby's trip had been arranged through Bernard Baruch and, moreover, that Baruch acted throughout 1945 and 1946 as go-between for the empire isolationists and Wall Street. Baruch and Lord Beaverbrook were intimates and, though he was somewhat indirect in public about his attitude regarding Bretton Woods, the financier worked behind the scenes to defeat the agreements. The fund and bank had been set up, in Baruch's opinion, to loan money to nations with unsound economies and unsettled finances. Ignoring the fact that the bank's primary mission was to guarantee private loans, Baruch disparaged the Bretton Woods Agreements because they provided for public as opposed to private lending. Credit has been extended by individuals ever since the beginning of time, he wrote with approval. But government lending was an offshoot of "totalitarianism and statism." "Government lending is unnecessary and hurtful," he asserted; "it is a reflex of fascism, communism, and nazism."[72]

Reluctantly, Morgenthau decided that Bretton Woods could not garner congressional approval while the banking community remained actively opposed. Therefore, when Randolph Burgess suggested a meeting to work out a compromise, Morgenthau agreed. The Treasury, he believed, could win at least Wall Street's acquiescence by making minor concessions. Besides, if Treasury refused to meet, the opposition could portray Morgenthau and company as intractable. Calling Burgess a "rattlesnake," White at first opposed the meeting but then gave in.[73]

On April 5 Ansel Luxford and Edward Bernstein met in New York with Randolph Burgess. The banker proposed first that management of the IMF and IBRD be overlapping, that the United States appoint one person to serve as governor of both institutions. If other countries followed suit, there would be a single board of directors for the fund and bank "able to integrate and coordinate their operations." The banking community, he added, would very much like to see Ned Brown appointed governor. To formulate American policy toward the fund and bank, Burgess suggested a board made up of the secretary of the Treasury as chairman, the secretary of state, the chairman of the Federal Reserve Board, the foreign economic administrator, and a president of a federal reserve bank elected by the open market committee of the Federal Reserve System. Alan Sproul as president of the Federal Reserve Bank of New York would "obviously fill the latter position." Above all else, however, the board should not include the secretary of commerce. Burgess insisted that Wallace would constitute "a red flag" in the eyes of the bankers and could singlehandedly prevent congressional approval of Bretton Woods. The board, in addition to laying down general policies for the governor and executive director, would also "coordinate the policy of the various United States agencies interested in international monetary and financial affairs." In other words, it would control the foreign loan policy of the United States. Certain that Wall Street still wielded considerable influence with Congress, Burgess also proposed that the House and Senate pass specific legislation laying down "rules of policy" to guide American representatives on the boards of the Bretton Woods institutions. Finally, in order to "reassure" the bankers that the fund and bank would not come under "undue political influence," their headquarters should be situated in New York. Luxford and Bernstein replied only that personnel matters were not proper subjects for discussion with the bankers, but left all other matters open to negotiation.[74]

Morgenthau eventually accepted Burgess's suggestions, and the Bretton Woods legislation approved by Congress included most of the banker's recommendations. Why did Treasury back down? Certainly Wall Street's clout on Capitol Hill was a factor, but also Morgenthau saw an opportunity to gain complete control of the postwar foreign aid policy of the United States. The banker's proposal for a board to oversee foreign lending provided Morgenthau with an opening to secure approval of a Foreign Financial Board with himself as chairman, a goal toward which he had been working for more than a year. Throughout fall 1944 he had pleaded with FDR to consolidate foreign financial matters under his control, but he had gotten nowhere.[75] Now at Burgess's suggestion, Congress would give Treasury a mandate allowing it to drive all its bureaucratic rivals from the field.

Although a number of Treasury staffers feared that the Burgess compromise would jeopardize passage of the Bretton Woods Agreements by encouraging opponents to demand fresh concessions, it seems to have been crucial in securing the endorsement of the Banking and Currency Committee. Opponents of the legislation had dominated the hearings, but the committee nonetheless endorsed Bretton Woods by a vote of 23 to 2 on May 24.[76]

The debate on the floor of the House was brief but colorful. The opposition banners were carried by the three Republicans who had voted no in committee: Jesse Sumner (R-Ill.), Howard Buffet (R-Nebr.), and Frederick Smith of Ohio. Buffet tried a bit of indirection, suggesting that his colleagues postpone consideration of Bretton Woods until satisfactory assurances were received that "the money thus made available in this scheme is not going to be used to make possible more killing of the common people everywhere."[77] He made a simultaneous, nonverbal comment on the agreements by waving a sheet of dollar bills caught in a mousetrap. Sumner, a female protégé of Colonel Robert McCormick, pronounced the Bretton Woods bill "the worst swindle in American history. . . . Why, the amateur diplomats who represented the United States at the conference last summer were babes lost in the Bretton Woods."[78]

Supporters responded by summoning the ghosts of Woodrow Wilson and the victims of the Nazi gas chambers. "After the last war," Brent Spence declaimed, "there was a statesman who had a vision—a vision of a federation of mankind; a vision of a world where the war drums beat no longer and the battle flags are furled in the parliament of man. . . . Now we have an opportunity to do what he wanted to do in a small way."[79] Congressman Albert Rains (D-Ala.), who had just returned from a tour of Buchenwald, described the corpses, the living dead, the crematorium, the experimental clinic, the lamp shades made of human skin, and argued that the fund and bank were integral parts of a peace program designed to ensure that history did not repeat itself.[80] "Most of Europe and Asia is in such a desperate plight," insisted William Barry (D-N.Y.), that anything can happen. "If one form of totalitarianism supplanted another—which was a distinct possibility in such an environment, most Americans will feel that sacrifices were not worthwhile and that our victory was a hollow one indeed."[81] After supporters beat back a Sumner amendment calling for membership in the bank but not the fund, the House approved the Bretton Woods legislation by a vote of 345 to 18 on June 7, 1945. As passed, the bill included nearly every exception suggested by the bankers except the stipulation that the governor and executive director of the two institutions be the same individual. The measure exempted all nations who became members of the bank and fund from the provisions of the Johnson Act.[82]

Significantly, a number of Bretton Woods supporters in the House pushed for the IMF and IBRD on the grounds that they would make direct postwar loans by the Treasury unnecessary. "If we participate in the Fund and Bank, and increase the funds of the Export-Import Bank, there will be no justification for the Treasury loaning a foreign country one single dollar," declared one congressman. Another supporter labeled Bretton Woods "a kind of international RFC."[83] Many members of Congress who supported Bretton Woods and viewed themselves as internationalists, then, saw the fund and bank as alternatives to publicly financed reconstruction and development overseas.

House approval by no means meant that Bretton Woods was home free. Primarily because it was led by Robert Taft, the opposition in the Senate promised to be more formidable than it had in the House. As Acheson, Clayton, Morgenthau, and White recognized, Taft had decided by spring 1945 to go along with United States participation in the United Nations, thus hopefully ridding himself of the isolationist label. Support for the United Nations, membership in which no way impinged on America's national sovereignty, would in turn allow him to oppose Bretton Woods and other specific internationalist programs.[84]

Not surprisingly, in the general debate that followed hard-core isolationists such as Kenneth Wherry (R-Nebr.), Henrik Shipstead (R-Minn.), and Owen Brewster (R-Maine) argued that the end of the war would find America in a most advantageous financial and commercial position and that Washington should use that leverage to improve its own position and that of its special interests. Brewster pointed to the recently issued Meade committee report, which emphasized America's strong bargaining position in relation to European countries. America should conserve its bargaining chips—its gold, dollars, technology, and industrial production—and not give them away through international organizations like the IMF.[85] In Brewster's Darwinian world, every nation was engaged in a bitter struggle for survival and only the fittest would prevail.

Robert Taft seconded the argument that the fund was merely a mechanism to give away American resources. While Brewster roamed the floor of the Senate waving 500-million drachma notes, Taft contended that under the agreements irresponsible nations would be able to trade their worthless currencies for gold and dollars. But Taft also recognized that the Brewster-Wherry-Wheeler position was too extreme. For reasons of both politics and principle, he was unwilling to identify himself with it. He readily admitted that the interests of the United States were to a degree bound up with those of other countries. Prosperity abroad promoted stability and security. Nevertheless, the United States should not cripple its own economy and sacrifice its own freedom in an orgasm of giving. Did the Senate know, Taft asked, that the administration had promised Britain a $3 billion loan and was in the late stages of negotiating a huge credit with the Soviet Union? The foreign aid to be furnished under Bretton Woods was just a drop in the bucket. The goal of America's policy should be to help other nations become economically self-sufficient.[86] Robert Taft seemed to take Bretton Woods almost personally. The Treasury Department, he charged, "has organized the most efficient propaganda campaign in behalf of Bretton Woods in the history of the nation." Taft pleaded with his colleagues to ignore "emotional propaganda" and judge Bretton Woods on its merits. "For some reason the Treasury was determined to have a fund, no matter what it was, so long as it was a fund," he told his colleagues. "Even though it is not able to solve the problems of the world, and though the time has not come for establishment of such a fund . . . they are willing to do anything in order to get the fund."[87]

In subsequent remarks, the Ohio senator argued that the Bretton Woods instrumentalities were basically mechanisms to subsidize alien socioeconomic systems. The Russian economy, for example, was based on state trading; the Soviets had no need for international trade and hence no interest in currency stabilization. They would use the resources of the IMF to finance internal reconstruction and would make no contribution to multilateralism. Russia and Britain were, in fact, the two most isolationist countries in the world in economic and financial affairs.[88]

After much tugging and pulling, coercing and cajoling, the administration persuaded the isolationist-cum-internationalist, Charles Tobey, to act as chief spokesman for Bretton Woods in the Senate. During his 1944 bid for reelection, Tobey had benefited greatly from the Bretton Woods Conference being held in his home state and his being a delegate. Treasury refused to let him forget his debt.[89]

By April 16 it was clear that the overwhelming majority of senators would vote for United States participation in the fund and bank. Taft's only hope, it appeared, was to attach an amendment or amendments to the Bretton Woods proposals that would make the fund and bank unacceptable to the other nations involved. The Ohioan began his onslaught on July 18. It was Taft rather than Wagner, who had introduced the legislation, or Majority Leader Alben Barkley (D-Ky.), who was the center of attention. Fearful of leaving the scene of battle for even a moment, Taft during lunch would retire to one of the swinging doors at the rear of the chamber and stand with one foot inside the Senate and one outside, eating a sandwich and monitoring the debate.[90] His first addendum would postpone consideration of Bretton Woods until November 15, 1945. Barkley interceded to remind the senators that the cutoff date for ratification of Bretton Woods was December 31, 1945. November 15 would not leave sufficient time for the United States and its allies to act. Postponement was tantamount to abortion. "I can think of nothing that would more embarrass the President of the United States, who is now engaged in negotiations at Potsdam, than for the Senate to take this action," Barkley told his colleagues. The Taft amendment was defeated by almost a straight party vote, 53 to 31. Taft then put forward his proposal that no member be allowed to draw upon the resources of the IMF until it had removed currency controls and lowered trade barriers. When Barkley accused Taft of trying to deny Britain its transitional period, he did not deny it. This second amendment was defeated by a vote of 53 to 13, with 19 abstaining. At this point Barkley announced that the Senate would remain in session throughout the evening or until final action on Bretton Woods was taken, whichever came first. Alarmed by the specter of a nighttime session, the upper house sprang into action. Following the defeat of a flurry of minor amendments, the Bretton Woods bill was brought up and passed by a vote of 61 to 16.[91]

Most of those who voted "yea" wished their constituents to believe that they had done so for altruistic reasons. One southern legislator declared that he had cast his ballot for Bretton Woods not as a business deal, not as something that would add to the military or material strength of the United States, but "as one more faltering step we are making as a Nation . . . on the road to a just and lasting peace."[92] But the overwhelming vote for Bretton Woods did not signify a congressional conversion to an internationalism that called for the United States to relinquish part of its national sovereignty for the common good or to institute a global foreign aid program designed to secure economic and social justice for all people. Congress had not even accepted the need to subsidize those nations deemed vital to American security. The conservative impulse that was so conspicuous in America in 1944 and early 1945 had not simply disappeared, swallowed up by the enthusiasm surrounding the San Francisco Conference. Such nationalists as Arthur Vandenberg of Michigan, Homer E. Capehart of Indiana, Kenneth McKeller of Tennessee, and James Eastland of Mississippi had voted yea. Surely these men were trying to avoid charges by their constituents that they were selling out the peace. Illinois Congressman Charles Dewey had been overwhelmingly defeated in 1944 by a candidate who made his support for and Dewey's opposition to Bretton Woods the main issue in the campaign. But most conservatives who voted for Bretton Woods were veterans of the Senate from safe districts. The fact was that the fund and bank did not impinge on America's sovereignty in the political or economic field and did not damage any significant American interest. Not only the CIO, but also the AFL, most American industries, and southern agriculture supported the agreements. It could be argued, in fact, that the IMF was a mechanism to secure United States control over the international financial system, and the IBRD a mechanism to protect private United States loans abroad. True, Wall Street would lose much of its power over exchange rates, but midwestern Republicans and southern Democrats were not sure that was a bad thing. Antipathy toward the New York plutocracy was a strain common to both progressivism and agrarian radicalism and was not contrary to economic nationalism.

American multilateralists wanted very much for the Churchill government to interpret the renewal of RTAA and congressional approval of Bretton Woods as indications that the United States intended to lower its tariff barriers and provide Britain and other creditor nations with the liquidity necessary for them to participate in a multilateral system.[93] And while the Britons' reaction to the approval of Bretton Woods was not as hostile as their response to renewal of the trade agreements program and its impact on commercial negotiations, they were more certain after congressional approval than they had been before that Bretton Woods was not sufficient to ensure the United Kingdom adequate credit and to protect it from foreign depressions.

Britain and John Maynard Keynes's position vis-à-vis the United States at Bretton Woods was somewhat similar to the United States and Franklin Roosevelt's posture toward the Soviet Union at the Yalta Conference; that is, it was constrained by circumstance. Moreover, the fragile state of Keynes's health and his optimism led him to misapprehend or underestimate the degree to which the Bretton Woods Agreements ensured United States financial hegemony and rendered Great Britain vulnerable. Shortly after the Bretton Woods Conference ended, Keynes wrote Sir John Anderson that "the fact that we have been able to work in such intimacy and for so long a period with the Americans and more especially with the American Treasury, more as colleagues on the same side of the table, helping them to common ends and to make a good job of a piece of work, than trying to get something for ourselves has, as I think all of us agree, produced a relationship of intimacy and confidence which has never previously existed."[94]

Whether through illness, fatigue, or excessive optimism, Keynes left Bretton Woods much too sanguine concerning the ability of the fund and bank to create an enduring system of multilateral payments in an environment of gross imbalance caused by war devastation and America's creditor position. Keynes had developed and advocated plans for a fund and bank as a means for redistributing the wealth of the world. The institutions, he believed, would provide creditor nations with the liquidity necessary to participate in a multilateral system. In his mind, the Bretton Woods Agreements were an alternative to a massive United States foreign lending program.

As soon as Keynes returned to England, critics of the New Hampshire conference brought him back to earth. Not surprisingly, the *Daily Express* and *Financial News* led the attack. Paul Einzig, one of Beaverbrook's top editorial writers, denounced the Bretton Woods Agreements as a lawyer's document, full of camouflage and tricky phraseology designed to conceal from the American and British publics that this was the second time in a generation that sterling was going to be linked to gold. The result would be the same—depression, first at home and then abroad. He charged specifically that the provisions in the agreements stipulating that currency transactions within a member country could not vary more than 1 percent from the rate set by the IMF meant that the British government would have to buy zlotys, drachmas, and other worthless currencies at par value if they were offered for sale in Great Britain—and no one would buy them.[95]

Much more serious were questions raised within the Treasury concerning interpretation of the agreements. Professor Dennis Robertson, not Keynes, had represented Great Britain on the fund committee, and his reading of that institution and its functions was quite different from Keynes's. The agreements imposed convertibility on all members; that is, no signatory could impose restrictions on payments or transfers for current international transactions. This rule was not to apply during the transitional period or at any time if a currency were declared scarce. Robertson held that this clause imposed absolute convertibility. The United States would be able to use its dominating position on the boards of the two institutions to limit the transitional period to an absolute minimum and to block efforts to declare the dollar scarce. Following the transitional period, Britain had to provide facilities to convert sterling held by residents and nonresidents. This would mean instantaneous funding of $13 billion worth of sterling balances—and instant bankruptcy. Moreover, Robertson contended, the obligation to convert continued even after a nation had exhausted its quota; a country in accepting this clause would be promising to maintain convertibility even after it had lost the power to do so by purchasing foreign currencies from the fund.

Keynes first made a very conciliatory and somewhat surprising reply to *The Times*. He declared that financial and commercial multilateralism were not the same, and the United Kingdom had made no commitment in the latter area. There was nothing in Bretton Woods to prevent Britain from requiring a nation from which it imported to take a certain amount of British exports, although he admitted that such a trading system would render Bretton Woods somewhat pointless. But Keynes confirmed that if Robertson's interpretations were correct, Britain could proceed no further.[96]

Desperately, Keynes turned to Washington for reassurances. On October 6, 1944, he wrote Harry White, setting forth his interpretations and asking his American counterpart to support them. White neither answered nor acknowledged the letter. The next month found Keynes back in Washington for Phase II lend-lease discussions. When told that Morgenthau intended to introduce the Bretton Woods Agreements into Congress and ram them through without amendment, Keynes believed it more important than ever to get a clarification of "ambiguities" from the Treasury. Consequently, he sought and was granted an audience with Harry White on the eighteenth. The two immediately reached an impasse over the duty of a member to assume an obligation of unlimited convertibility, especially after that country had exhausted its quota. White declared that the matter was unimportant. Anyway, the document must be submitted to Congress as it stood; if he agreed to an amendment now, the whole agreement would fall apart. Keynes became livid; the question had already been raised in England, and His Majesty's Government would have to respond to charges that membership could expose Britain to the possibility of having to choose between bankruptcy and international isolation. Repeatedly Keynes charged that under threat of forcible expulsion by the hotel management neither he nor the other delegates had had time to read the Final Act. When the other nations realized what they were risking, there would be a general revolt. White said he would have to have time to mull over the matter.

Keynes rightly perceived the convertibility clause to be crucial. Would Britain be willing to hand over to the fund the power to decide at what point the country would have to reduce its gold reserves, having already run through its resources with the IMF, before the obligation of free convertibility was suspended? Moreover, the government would have a tough time explaining to the House that membership carried obligatory convertibility because the British delegates had not been alert enough to notice that safeguards against had been negated. Keynes complained bitterly that those who drafted the Final Act had quietly "removed and cancelled out" the escape clause.

White and Keynes failed to reach agreement before the latter's departure. Back in England Keynes confessed his misgivings to Anderson, and on February 1 the chancellor wrote Morgenthau putting forward the British interpretation of convertibility. The nations currently struggling with Bretton Woods were having to deal with a document hurriedly and faultily drafted. If Britain and America could not resolve their dispute over the obligation of a nation to convert, then His Majesty's Government and the other governments would have to go public with their charges of sloppiness and imprecision.[97] Morgenthau's response was silence. The Bretton Woods Agreements that went to Congress in early 1945 remained free of amendment or clarification.

By summer 1945 the noose of circumstance seemed to be drawing around Britain's throat. Post–Bretton Woods talks between British and American officials in the spring had indicated that the United States was determined to force Britain to accept free convertibility following the transitional period. As ratified by Congress, the Bretton Woods Agreements established a monetary fund whose governing board would be dominated by the United States. The only way Britain could suspend convertibility, if and when it experienced a massive imbalance in payments, was with the permission of the IMF. There was certainly no guarantee that the American delegation to the fund, representing Treasury, Wall Street, and Congress, would be forthcoming. Unless the United States behaved in practice like a big creditor nation, Sir John Anderson told his cabinet colleagues, and imported goods from the rest of the world while at the same time lending money to finance reconstruction and restart stricken economies abroad, mechanisms for currency stabilization—Bretton Woods—would surly break down.[98]

Developments in the area of commercial policy were as alarming to Whitehall as those in finance. In the wake of renewal of the trade agreements program, American negotiators had abandoned their demand for simultaneous, horizontal tariff cuts by the principal trading nations of the world and insisted that commercial multilateralism could be achieved through bilateral treaties with most-favored-nation clauses. At the same time the United States continued to demand abolition of imperial preference, import quotas, currency pooling arrangements, and other "non-tariff" barriers to trade.

By mid-1945, then, many Britons had come to the inescapable conclusion that the United States wanted to protect its special interests while forcing its trading partners to expose the vulnerable spots in their economies. But the short term need by Great Britain and Western Europe as a whole for United States capital made it very difficult for London to escape the clutches of a one-sided multilateralism. The economic and political imperatives of Phase III—the period after Japan's defeat—seemed even more compelling in spring and summer 1945 than they had in fall 1944. Multilateralism aside, Britain would have to have direct and massive American aid to feed, house, and employ its people. Any political faction that did not offer a credible program for delivering on these items did not stand a chance in the forthcoming general elections. Moreover, if America abandoned Western Europe, the power vacuum there coupled with the economic and social distress of the general populace would almost guarantee that another totalitarian power bent on European hegemony would arise to threaten Great Britain and all of Western civilization. Despite congressional approval of RTAA and Bretton Woods, and in part because of these programs, Britain still faced the task of obtaining from America the resources necessary to ensure the security of the United Kingdom and all of Western Europe.

9. Mediation and Breaking the Cordon Sanitaire: *Great Britain, Russia, and the United States, 1944–1945*

GREAT BRITAIN was no more successful during 1944 and 1945 in providing for its military security in the postwar era than it had been in looking after its commercial and financial well-being, and once again the principal stumbling block for Whitehall was the United States. Despite their personal rivalry, both Winston Churchill and Anthony Eden, the two preeminent political figures in the British foreign policy establishment, believed that America could be successfully managed in strategic matters. They were wrong. From the Italian invasion through the Normandy landings, American power and influence within the Grand Alliance steadily increased while Britain's diminished. That shift stimulated America's determination to pursue a course independent of Great Britain and to control the shape of the postwar settlement. That impulse both reflected and was reinforced by a virulent Anglophobia. Britain's military and economic eclipse earned it not sympathy but contempt and aroused a latent imperialism among many Americans. Some were convinced that the "Limies" were not doing their fair share in the war and others that United Kingdom merchants were out to take over traditional United States markets. Virtually everyone viewed Britain as incapable or unworthy of leading the noncommunist world in the postwar period.

The rising tide of Anglophobia in the United States and Washington's resistance to a common Anglo-American strategy in 1944 angered Britons inside and outside Whitehall. They resented America's propensity for self-righteousness and marveled at the contradictions in their ally's foreign policy. With memories of interwar isolationism heavy on their minds, British officials searched for alternatives to an Atlantic security community. The only viable option was a British-led, Western European union. If such a confederation was to be economically and militarily successful, however, Germany, denazified and rehabilitated, would have to become a full-fledged participant. All the while the Churchill government made plans to create and dominate such a federation, British officials worked to forge a specific agreement with the Soviet Union delineating spheres of interest in Europe.

Unfortunately for Great Britain, its plans for a European union—including Germany and a precise agreement with Russia—ran afoul of American foreign policy. Although committed to the Four Policemen concept and to a pragmatic realpolitik, the Roosevelt White House continued to be intimidated by isolationist and internationalist opinion in the United States. Given the prevailing mood of the country, any overt spheres-of-interest arrangement in Europe seemed out of the question. Roosevelt and Harry Hopkins decided that the only way to achieve peace and security in the postwar world and simultaneously satisfy domestic opinion was to avoid even the appearance of Anglo-American solidarity and make unilateral concessions to the Soviet Union. Taking advantage of the Churchill government's desperate need for short-term aid during Phase II, Roosevelt forced the prime minister to approve the Morgenthau Plan, a scheme that was intended to win friends in the Kremlin but one that also made an economically strong Western European federation impossible. The following month Washington refused to approve the famous percentages deal hammered out between Churchill and Stalin in Moscow. The United States, and, by default, Great Britain, was left with FDR's personality and the promise of a postwar reconstruction loan to hold back the advancing communist tide in Europe.

For a brief period in spring and early summer 1945 during the last days of Franklin Roosevelt's life and the first weeks of Harry S. Truman's administration, British hopes that the United States might assume a more realistic stance toward postwar Europe and Soviet pretensions there rose dramatically. Frightened by its isolation, offended by the treatment of its representatives in Russia, and shocked by the brutality of the Red Army, the various elements of the British foreign policy establishment coalesced in favor of an all-out effort to persuade the United States to stand up to Russia. FDR responded positively to Churchill's frantic arguments and to those of the hard-liners within his own foreign policy establishment by insisting that the Soviets live up to their "commitments" under the Yalta accords. After Roosevelt's death, Harry Truman, wishing to preserve continuity in foreign policy, determined to appear decisive, and momentarily swayed by the get-tough advocates in Washington, confronted Russia over its policy toward Eastern Europe. He insisted that Moscow broaden the Polish government and allow Westerners to participate in the reconstruction of the Balkans. The new president quickly abandoned this initial attempt to prevent the construction of a closed Soviet sphere, however. America seemed dead set against maintaining a permanent military force in Europe, and popular hopes for a rapprochement with the Soviets remained high. As the limits on United States power became apparent, Truman fell under the influence of those American liberals who favored a policy of conciliation. In cooperation with Anglophobes and Russophiles within the foreign policy establishment, Truman attempted to pursue a "middle way" whereby the United States mediated between Great Britain and the Soviet Union in a tripolar world. To London's dismay, Truman and his new secretary of state, James F. (Jimmy) Byrnes, clung to the belief that Moscow's desire for security and stability plus the leverage of America's monopoly of atomic energy and reconstruction capital would render Stalin reasonable if not pliant. Thus, throughout summer and fall 1945 Washington, while holding Britain at arm's length, attempted to hammer out modus vivendi with Russia over occupation policy in Germany, Rumania, Hungary, Poland, and Japan.

As minister of defense and foreign secretary respectively, Winston Churchill and Anthony Eden dominated the making of British policy toward the United States and the Soviet Union during World War II. Personally and politically the prime minister and the foreign secretary enjoyed something of a love-hate relationship. While they were bound together by a common antipathy toward the "Munichers," Eden tried repeatedly to undermine Churchill's political position during the war in hopes of replacing him as prime minister. In addition, to Churchill's enragement, Eden undercut him with the Roosevelt administration on a number of occasions. From the start of the war, for example, the foreign secretary had favored an early cross-channel invasion, and he wasted no opportunity to tell Roosevelt and his chief of staff, General George C. Marshall so. Moreover, the two English statesmen differed over the Beveridge Report and the plight of the Jews, Eden being much less sympathetic to Zionist aspirations than Churchill. Yet they were both British nationalists. Eden resented attacks on British colonialism just as much as Churchill. In 1938 he had resigned as foreign secretary in the Chamberlain government in protest over the prime minister's policy of appeasement, thus endearing himself to the former naval person. After Churchill replaced Chamberlain, he sent Lord Halifax to Washington and gave the Foreign Office to Eden. In the trying years that followed Churchill frequently kept Eden up all night, summoned him at odd hours, and lectured him endlessly on trivial subjects, but there was no one whom he consulted more on foreign affairs.[1] On one subject the two men saw eye to eye. Both were certain that America was crucial to Britain's future, and both were initially optimistic that the United States could be managed to the United Kingdom's advantage.

Churchill believed more than ever in 1944 that postwar security depended on the Big Three. Inside or outside a United Nations, Britain, Russia, and the United States should divide the world among themselves and police their respective areas. By 1944, however, it appeared that Russia intended to encroach on part of Britain's bailiwick, Western and Central Europe. Churchill wanted to contain Soviet power through a combination of military force and hard bargaining. Committed to the idea that the nation that liberated a particular area of Europe should be free to occupy and control that area's economic and political reconstruction, he adamantly opposed, for example, including Soviet representatives on the Allied Control Council for Italy. As German resistance crumbled in early 1945, Churchill would press Field Marshal Sir Bernard Montgomery and General Dwight D. Eisenhower to occupy as much of Europe as they could as quickly as they could.[2] At the same time, he wanted to settle territorial and political issues with the Soviets before the Red Army and Anglo-American forces were cheek by jowl somewhere in Central Europe. Winston Churchill assumed, at least through fall 1944, that Anglo-American wartime cooperation would continue unbroken into the postwar period, that the two countries' identical interest in maintaining a balance of power in Europe was as obvious to Roosevelt and Hopkins as it was to him.[3] Britain was fighting for rugged individualism, private striving, and individual liberty. As a basically conservative country, the United States would recognize this fact and follow London's lead.

Anthony Eden, Richard Law, Harold Macmillan, and a host of second-level officials in the Foreign Office and Washington Embassy initially assumed a far less confrontational relationship with the Soviet Union than Churchill, Lord Cherwell, and Brendan Bracken. As of mid-1944 Eden still believed it possible to deal with Russia on a basis other than arms and power blocs. The foreign secretary argued that two schools of thought existed in the Kremlin, one "collaborationist" faction that was preoccupied with the looming tasks of reconstruction and anxious to resume the government's interrupted program of internal development, and the other, paranoid and aggressive, convinced that Russia should trust no one and acquire as much foreign territory as it could as quickly as it could. Stalin, Eden advised his colleagues, belonged to the first group, and it was still ascendant as of 1944. Britain must do everything possible to reinforce Stalin and the collaborationists.[4]

Eden and the reform Tories labored under no illusions, however. The devastation and suffering that would surely accompany the end of hostilities in Europe would make the Continent a ripe breeding ground for totalitarianism, either of the right or the left. To counter this threat Britain should assume the moral and political leadership of Europe, holding up the middle way as a means to peace, prosperity, and security. It was crucial to British interests that as many European nations as possible should "seek our friendship and guidance and should give us their confidence." Because Britain's financial power was ebbing, it would have to "compensate for that loss by winning the admiration of the European peoples for our way of life and for our achievements in social, economic, industrial, scientific and intellectual fields." Britain's influence in Europe after Germany's surrender "will much depend upon whether, in attempting to restore order out of chaos . . . these countries adopt . . . methods and regimes such as would be likely to seek inspiration in Moscow, or whether they will model themselves on methods of Western democracies, and especially Great Britain, because they judge from what they see here that these methods can command success in tackling the appalling social and economic problems of postwar Europe."[5] In short, Eden, Macmillan, Law, and their colleagues contended, Britain must couple a comprehensive program of full employment and social security with its democratic traditions in order to produce a progressive democracy that would serve as a shining example to the rest of Europe.

Unlike Churchill, the reform Tories at first assumed that New Deal progressives were ascendant in America and could be counted on to support Britain's efforts to rebuild Europe around the principles of English social democracy. Eden, Law, Macmillan, Halifax, and second-echelon officials in the Washington Embassy, Foreign Office, Treasury, and War Cabinet Secretariat included in their definition of American liberals such diverse individuals and publications as Henry Wallace, the *Nation*, the *New Republic*, Walter Lippmann, Dorothy Thompson, Raymond Graham Swing, the *St. Louis Post-Dispatch*, and the *Washington Post*. American liberals were committed to a comprehensive collective security organization and, consequently, Eden told Churchill, Britain would have to swallow its cynicism and participate enthusiastically in the United Nations. In addition, the reform Tories argued, the cousins would come to Western Europe's aid only if American liberals were convinced that Britain was committed to the same progressive policies in the domestic sphere (including the empire) that had characterized the New Deal. Thus did Eden and his colleagues welcome the release of the Beveridge Report in December 1942 not only as a scheme that would enable the Conservative party to steal some of Labour's thunder and help its chances at the general election that would follow the end of hostilities, but also as an initiative that would undermine Anglophobia among American liberals.[6] The reform Tories, then, believed that the Churchill government had a marvelous opportunity to seize the initiative at home and abroad by acquiescing in United States plans for a collective security organization and by pushing programs for increased social services and full employment within the context of a mixed economy. If the Eden group did not misread the nature of American liberalism, it certainly misperceived the degree to which liberalism pervaded American policy.

While the reform Tories wanted to ride the crest of a liberal democratic wave bankrolled by New Deal America to European domination, and the high Tories looked forward to the creation of an Anglo-American community of interest based on free enterprise and individual liberty, both factions agreed on the need to hitch the American horse to the British wagon. As recent students of Anglo-American affairs have pointed out, British cabinet officials from Anthony Eden to Hugh Dalton, career civil servants in both the Foreign Office and the Treasury, and the academic economists who had set up shop in Whitehall were determined to use America to advance British interests and those of Western civilization (frequently identical in the British mind).[7] Harold Macmillan most aptly summed up British strategy toward the United States in 1944: "We are like the Greeks in the late Roman Empire," he told Richard Crossman. "They ran it because they were so much cleverer than the Romans, but they never told the Romans this. That must be our relation to the Americans."[8]

Unfortunately for British designs on American power, there had developed in the United States by 1944 a broad consensus that Great Britain had not changed and was conspiring to use America for its own selfish interests. Nearly every major political group disliked one aspect or another of British society and politics. Liberal New Dealers led by Henry Wallace and Eleanor Roosevelt considered Britain—even with the Labour party playing a prominent role in the coalition government—too anti-Russian, too concerned about preserving its empire, too little committed to internationalism. Fiscal conservatives in the United States still could not forget that Britain had welched on its World War I debts. Moreover, business people believed that their counterparts were plotting a vast expansion of Britain's commercial and financial empire. For the English merchant, observed one American industrialist, "the war is not something to be gotten over with, it is an event to be utilized for the sake of Britain's future."[9] In addition, a "hard core of Anglophobes," as Edward R. Morrow told Harold Nicolson, comprised of Italian, German, and Irish Americans, continued to rail against perfidious Albion. Traditional isolationists still blamed John Bull for drawing the United

States into World War I, a conflict, they said, that had no real bearing on America's strategic and economic interests. And, of course, anti-imperialism continued to flourish. During a speaking tour through the Midwest, Edmund Wilson, a State Department information officer, found the average person particularly concerned about British policy in Italy and Greece. Prevailing wisdom had it that His Majesty's officials were more concerned with propping up reactionary monarchies in both countries than in advancing the cause of democracy and socioeconomic progress.[10]

These groups and attitudes had existed to a greater or lesser extent before the war, but British visitors to America in 1944 noted a new, more intense, more pervasive Anglophobia. Following a trip to the United States in late summer, Lord Beaverbrook told Halifax that, despite Allied military successes in Europe and the Far East, British perseverance in the face of the buzz bomb onslaught, and the Churchill government's "almost unfailing willingness to fall in with American desires in the political and economic spheres," American opinion was virulently anti-British. "I found an acute deterioration in our position in the United States compared with the summer of 1943. Feeling towards us in all save perhaps high Administration circles had gone back in an alarming manner. The impression is widespread that we are not playing our full part in the war. Our stand in 1940–41 seems to have been forgotten. And we are accused of looking selfishly to our own interests."[11] A perceived lack of effort, enthusiasm, and effectiveness in the war against the Axis was particularly prominent in the new Anglophobia. "Anti-British feeling appears to spring from three [sic] main sources," reported an Englishman who had lived on the West Coast for the preceding ten years: "(1) the belief that the British army doesn't fight, is officered by 'stuffed shirts' and has let America down in the Far East; (2) that America has given . . . all her aircraft to England; (3) that England has dragged America into war; (4) and that America is always the sucker, who starts by helping and ends up doing the whole job herself." Servicemen returning from the front spread stories of British cowardice and selfishness. According to one typical rumor, an American warship had had to fire a shot across the bow of a British destroyer that sought to flee from action during convoy duty.[12]

The contempt for Great Britain that had become apparent in the attitude of the White House in 1943 spread to press, public, and other parts of the foreign policy establishment in 1944. Given its declining power, the United Kingdom's pretensions to world leadership seemed to many to be preposterous. There was also a good deal of fear that London's unrealistic efforts to cling to the past, to control an empire on which "the sun never set," would plunge humanity into World War III. This perception was particularly prominent within the military, an institution that both molded and reflected popular opinion in the United States to a greater extent than at any other time since the Revolutionary War.

The pervasive desire in the United States to play a role in international politics independent of Great Britain—verging at times on Anglophobia—was in part a product of America's logistical domination of the Anglo-American alliance. As the fourth full year of the conflict in Europe drew to a close, American predominance in manpower and material became glaringly apparent. By the end of October 1943 Britain obtained from America 77 percent of its supply of escort vessels, 88 percent of its landing craft, 68 percent of its light bombers, virtually all of its transport aircraft, 60 percent of its tankers, all of its tank transporters and ten-ton trucks, and half of selected strategic materials such as magnesium. During 1942 alone United States ground forces grew from 37 to 73 active divisions, and air combat units from 67 to 167. Still, until July 1944 the British Empire had more soldiers in contact with the enemy than had the United States. Thereafter the balance shifted rapidly in the other direction.[13]

Not surprisingly, the English reacted to America's growing domination of the transatlantic partnership and its barely veiled contempt for the United Kingdom with resentment and consternation. To many Britons, the United States was still peopled by a collection of upstart colonials whose pretensions would have been amusing had it not been for the American monopoly on gold and gunpowder. Observed one American visitor to England in 1944: "I think that the Beaver alone of the governing group is inclined to regard the United States as an independent and rival nation with the others regarding us as merely a colonial dominion which doesn't happen to belong at the moment in name to the British Commonwealth."[14] Britons bridled at the tendency of the Roosevelt administration in particular and Americans in general to deprecate the United Kingdom's role in the struggle against the Axis. "Americans have a much exaggerated conception about the military contribution they are making in this war," Eden fumed to Halifax. "They lie freely about this, distorting figures on relative contributions to Overlord and the number of U boats sunk." Such exaggerations could easily play into the hands of members of the administration who wanted to make Washington the fulcrum of the transatlantic alliance.[15]

Halifax, for one, believed that Britain's vulnerability and its need to play the supplicant had eroded much of the respect it had traditionally enjoyed in America:

> Because since 1939 we have had to seek and accept American assistance, and because lately we have seemed to be pleading poverty, the Americans have got too much into the habit of regarding us as weak. Even our friends in the U.S. think we are compelled to make our economic and strategic position our first consideration, and tend to put this conception forward for all our actions. Critics naturally draw the conclusion that we are not interested in a sound world order.[16]

He also felt the United Kingdom was being singled out for special treatment. "Why is it that although it is known that the Russians are weak to the extent of needing great assistance in rehabilitation, they are considered strong?"[17] Washington's air of superiority, both real and perceived, produced in British ruling circles a degree of hostility toward Roosevelt personally. Anthony Eden was typical. "He regards Roosevelt as an astute politician," Harold Nicolson told a friend, "and a man of great personal vanity and obstinacy."[18]

Attacks in Congress, the press, and the executive branch on British imperialism infuriated Britons. Churchill, that relentless exponent of Anglo-American partnership, was moved by Edward Stettinius's rambling denunciations of British power politics to an uncharacteristic outburst. "Would you ask [Stettinius]," he wrote Halifax in 1944, "to give me a definition of 'power politics'? Is having all the gold in the world buried in a cavern 'power politics'? Is it giving all the bases in the West Indies which are necessary to American safety to the United States— is that 'power politics?' "[19] Six months later, angered at what he perceived to be hypocrisy in the American press regarding British motives and policy, Michael Wright, counselor of the British Embassy in Washington, arranged a luncheon showdown with a group of the "most hostile and critical" broadcasters and reporters. Why, Wright asked, was it permissible for the United States to create a special regional arrangement in the Western Hemisphere but "wrong that in other parts of the world neighbors should draw together for self-defence"? Why, after refusing to accept political and military responsibility in areas such as the Balkans, should America criticize others for attempting to build an exclusive sphere of interest there? There was much danger, Wright asserted, in foisting principles such as those contained in the Atlantic Charter on the peoples of the world without furnishing the economic and military aid that would make those ideals realities. "It had always been dangerous to believe that principles were enough," he warned.[20]

As Wright's comments indicate, America's domination of the partnership caused a number of Britons inside and outside the government to decide by 1944 that the United States was actively working to supplant the United Kingdom as the principal moral, commercial, and military force in the world. Richard Law, returning from a trip to Washington and New York in late 1942, was particularly struck with the revival of missionary diplomacy in the United States. There was very much an attitude abroad in the land that America had something that the rest of the world needed—whether it knew it or not—and that it was America's duty to export this commodity. From the Great Lakes to the Rio Grande, from New England to the Golden Gate there was a great mood of exhilaration and a determination to paint with a broad stroke. "Washington sees world problems through a telescope where we look at them through a microscope," he observed to his colleagues. "Washington is thinking in terms of centuries and continents when we are thinking of question time next Wednesday and the Free Austrian Movement." These people were not men of the world; "they are children playing with bricks and 'making the world over.' "[21] A 1944 Foreign Office report on American attitudes toward Great Britain declared: "Americans are slowly swinging towards the belief that since the British 'have made such a mess of the world' it is America's painful duty to take charge of everything."[22]

Other British students of American society claimed to see a more traditional type of imperialism burgeoning in America, an expansiveness advocated by a coalition of conservative nationalists and, ironically, isolationists. Ronald Campbell and Halifax warned as early as May 1942 of the emergence of a group centering around Wendell Willkie, Thomas Lamont, and Bernard Baruch. Such men see the world as a vast market for the American producer, industrialist, and trader, Halifax wrote. "They are believers in the American century, energetic technicians and businessmen filled with a romantic, . . . self-confident, economic imperialism, eager to convert the world to the American pattern." Isolationists such as Colonel Robert R. McCormick of the *Chicago Tribune*, despairing of a return to the nineteenth century, were becoming convinced that the only alternative to pulling Britain's chestnuts out of the fire was for America to find its own cat's paw. "There are among the isolationists," Campbell wrote, "a type of people who I can easily imagine proceeding from their isolationist reasoning to a stage where they will satisfy themselves that in order to isolate themselves properly the United States must rule the roost."[23]

Fear and resentment produced a secret desire in many Britons that America be brought low. Sir Gerald Campbell, a Foreign Office functionary who visited the United States in late 1944, was typical. America in 1944 reminded him in its "cock-sureness" of America in the 1920s. "They were as critical as they could be of us poor devils, pitied and blamed us in the same breath and thanked God they were not like other men." The thirties brought tribulation and with it humility and humanity. "What will happen when they are up against the problems that they fear—the negro question particularly—goodness only knows, but they may have coming to them that which will make them human. It is almost worth praying for as we are still more likely to be so in the future, Victim No. 1 of their present mood."[24]

Britain's eclipse within the Anglo-American alliance was accompanied, of course, by a dramatic increase in Russian power in Eastern Europe in 1944. According to Vojtech Mastny, the key to understanding Russian foreign policy during and immediately after World War II is Joseph Stalin. He transcended the "cooperationists" and the hard-liners within the Kremlin, if these two groups even existed. Faithful to the Leninist formula, Stalin thought in terms of minimum and maximum goals. When Russia's back had been up against the wall in 1942, his objectives were restoration of pre–June 1941 frontiers, prevention of an anti-Soviet bloc in Europe, and preservation of communist outposts abroad. Anything exceeding these minimums remained in the realm of wishful thinking until after Stalingrad. The Red Army's ascendancy in the East by 1943 opened new vistas to Stalin. He briefly considered concluding a separate peace with Germany in which the two would divide Europe between them or, alternately, spreading communism by force. He rejected both, however, and opted for the "orderly" growth of communism from a base in Eastern Europe. Britain's constant and America's intermittent willingness to divide Europe into spheres of influence abetted Stalin's quest for power and influence; yet his exact goals remained fluid and subject to negotiation with the Western democracies.[25]

The second front profoundly changed Stalin's outlook; his determination to seek a unilateral solution to the Polish question signified that change. The Anglo-American commitment embodied in the landings prompted Stalin to order his armies to move beyond the frontiers of June 1941 and conquer land that would eventually become part of the new empire. By the close of the year the Red Army was the most intimidating force on the Continent, attacking Germany with 13,000 tanks, 16,000 fighters and dive bombers, and 525 divisions totaling 5 million men.[26] By military action and inaction (the Warsaw uprising), Stalin had by fall 1944 secured Russian supremacy in all countries he regarded as vital to Russian security—and more. He showed a disturbing reluctance to define for the West the exact extent of his "security" needs. As German forces retreated from eastern Poland, Rumania, and Bulgaria in 1944, the Red Army and its entourage of political commissars followed in their wake, establishing martial law and laying the foundations for provisional governments that would be friendly to the Soviet Union.

Thus, ironically, as 1944—the decisive year of the war—progressed and victory at last appeared clearly on the horizon, Britain felt more and more crushed between the two superpowers, both of which seemed to be waiting in the wings, ready to fill the power vacuum created by German and Japanese aggression. "Political affairs—international ones, I mean—are not going very well," Percy Grigg wrote Field Marshal Montgomery. "I can't get out of my head the idea that the Americans and Russians are going to frame us in the end and that unless we make up our minds for a generation of hard work and self-denial (and no Beveridge) we shall be left in the position of the Dutch after Utrecht in 1713."[27]

While Whitehall and the War Cabinet worried about mounting Anglophobia and residual isolationism in the United States, and expansionism in the Kremlin, the Roosevelt administration attempted to make up its collective mind about what, if anything, it wanted to do in regard to Europe after Germany's surrender. There was no policy base on which to build.

Franklin Roosevelt knew little about diplomacy or decision making in diplomacy. He had abdicated in the area of foreign affairs throughout the 1930s, choosing to reassert the executive's constitutional prerogatives only after Germany invaded Poland. His knowledge of foreign cultures and politics was superficial. The president was aware of his shortcomings in the field and from 1933 through 1943 relied heavily on Sumner Welles, an expert practitioner of the diplomatic arts. If the Roosevelt administration may be said to have had a foreign policy prior to 1939, it was Welles's Good Neighbor initiative toward Latin America. The undersecretary's departure in 1943 left a void.

During World War II FDR immersed himself in strategy, but the political and territorial issues kept crowding in on him. By 1944 he could no longer procrastinate. Never an original thinker, the president turned initially to tried-and-true methods that were advanced by individuals inside and outside the foreign policy establishment. Among those receiving strongest consideration were collective security, dollar diplomacy, and traditional balance of power, spheres-of-interest realpolitik.

Partly as a result of the void in American foreign policy and partly as a response to German and Japanese aggression, the internationalist movement enjoyed a revival in the United States during World War II. Led by Cordell Hull, neo-Wilsonians denounced isolationism with all the vehemence they could muster and called on President Roosevelt to commit America to a revitalized League of Nations. All nations must surrender a portion of their national sovereignty for the common good and the United States was no exception, they proclaimed. Republican internationalists were no less vehement in their attacks on power politics than their Democratic counterparts. In March 1944 twenty-four first-term members of the House, who in obedience to the Mackinac recommendations had voted for the Fulbright resolution, put the administration on notice: "We believe that the great majority of American people is badly confused by the seeming emergence of embryonic spheres of influence on a regional basis—the domination of small nations by great. Those who like ourselves have supported the efforts which . . . appeared to bear fruition at the Moscow Conference are now wondering whether they were being led up a blind alley."[28] True converts to world government were, however, a tiny minority in the United States. Congress and the average person applauded Wilson and Wendell Willkie's *One World* without having any intention of limiting the nation's freedom of action within the context of a postwar collective security organization. Franklin Roosevelt was no exception.

Sensing the White House's lack of confidence in Hull's internationalist schemes, the secretary's subordinates in the State Department worked behind their chief's back to hammer out a European policy that would be acceptable to Roosevelt and Hopkins. One group, including Adolf Berle, John D. Hickerson (chief of the Division of British Commonwealth Affairs), and the heads of the Western Europe, Eastern European, and Middle Eastern area desks, called for an updated version of William Howard Taft's dollar diplomacy—the use of trade and investment for essentially political objectives. The United States, these officials believed, would have to act unilaterally to foster peace, to ensure the eventual establishment of "free and democratic governments" for both large and small nations, to promote liberal commercial policies, and to mold "a continent friendly to the United States."[29] Specifically, the United States should participate in control commissions and armistice commissions in liberated areas but then withdraw as rapidly as possible from such bodies in areas not directly occupied. In Southeastern and Central Europe and in the Middle East, however, the United States should offer continuous and implacable opposition to closed zones. The United States ought to demand and obtain the right of its journalists, merchants, airline operators, shipping interests, and tourists to move freely in and out of these countries. Such activities, Berle asserted, were not primarily commercial, although they were so conceived in the United States. "These thin lines," he wrote, "are likely to be the only lines through which we can maintain contact with and maintain some influence over the underlying situation . . . whether the work is forwarding the results of the Dumbarton Oaks Conference or forwarding a generalized good neighbor policy which may avoid conflict between the two major powers." Given the limits imposed on America's freedom of action by war weariness, neo-isolationism, Anglophobia, and popular prejudice against power politics, dollar diplomacy was the only answer. Again, politics was the dog, profits the tail: "Commercial interests, though they are important in some respects, are incidental to the maintenance of the general moral and diplomatic position which we should have and which we will need, if we are not to be caught between the unresolved British and Soviet forces in respect of which there is no accommodation yet in sight."[30]

Dollar diplomacy was a tempting alternative to Roosevelt and Hopkins. In the end, however, the White House was shrewd enough to realize that this approach promised to alarm both Russia and Great Britain without providing any tangible benefits.

A small minority within the State Department headed by Dean Acheson displayed a strong skepticism toward both Wilsonian internationalism and dollar diplomacy. Acheson was the grandson of the Episcopal bishop of Connecticut, an Englishman who had migrated to America just before the Civil War. Educated at Groton, Yale—where Averell Harriman was his rowing coach—and Harvard Law, this tall, handsome New England aristocrat developed during his school days the mental toughness and penchant for hard work that was to characterize his public career. A protégé of Felix Frankfurter and law clerk to Louis Brandeis, Acheson developed a skepticism toward panaceas and utopias and a commitment to pragmatic progress.[31] But the man who more than any other influenced Acheson's thought during the late 1930s and 1940s was the Protestant theologian and social critic, Reinhold Niebuhr.

Between 1939 and 1945 Niebuhr, like so many other American liberals, reverted to a type of conservative progressivism. He criticized liberal Protestants and communists alike for believing that history marched ever onward toward perfection. From the vantage point of Christian realism, he attacked American isolationists, denying that America represented virtue and Europe vice. All people were in the same boat. America must choose the lesser evil of war to defeat the greater evil of Nazism. He praised the founding fathers for wanting simply to preserve some relative decency and justice in society, and he denounced modern dictatorships for substituting their wills for God's. The defeat of Nazism, he was predicting by 1944, would clear the way for the rise of a new, more menacing threat to the principles of liberty and democracy—the Soviet Union.[32]

Dean Acheson was one of Niebuhr's pragmatic, nonideological warriors who felt called upon to struggle against antihumanist centralization. For Acheson, life was a series of small victories not a messianic crusade. Some members of the Roosevelt administration, Acheson warned Hull and Stettinius, wanted to send agents into economically and strategically crucial regions of the world to "convert the Russians from Communism" and "the British from oppressive imperialism." Apparently these individuals, "at no cost to us," were supposed to accomplish by their moral example a dissolution of imperialism and the creation of "government based on the consent of the governed, and of a system of free enterprise."

Denouncing such "messianic globaloney," Acheson argued that America's goal in Europe and the Middle East must be stability even if this meant working with native monarchies and right-wing dictators like Franco and Salazar. "If chaos prevails there," he insisted, "and the region becomes a military vacuum, tempting adventure, we shall face the same danger of war which accompanied the collapse of the Turkish and Austro-Hungarian Empires."[33] Acheson, of course, wanted to concede Eastern Europe to the Soviets and work closely with Great Britain to rebuild Central Europe and maintain the status quo in the eastern Mediterranean and Middle East. His day would come, but in 1944 realpolitik was still out of fashion in the United States.

Of the three ways open to him, Franklin Roosevelt favored realpolitik. Specifically, he wanted to divide the world into four spheres of influence each dominated and policed by its most powerful resident. In an effort to placate the Wilsonian internationalists and to satisfy the smaller powers, he agreed to blend the Four Policemen arrangement with the concept of a United Nations organization. But the key position occupied by the Security Council and its permanent members within the United Nations served to ensure that the Great Powers would continue to determine the contours of international relations. A problem with the spheres-of-interest approach—or one of the most important problems—was that the Big Four were not equal in strength. Inequality tempted the more powerful to encroach on the bailiwicks of the less powerful. As Churchill, Stalin, and the United States military recognized all along, China was a third-rate power that would in all probability grow weaker instead of stronger. In addition, Britain seemed to be slipping completely from the ranks of the great, a development few had anticipated or faced up to. Britain's decline and Japan's demise would produce a vacuum in Europe and the Far East. There existed some difference of opinion among the Big Four as to how those vacuums were to be filled. For example, it was becoming increasingly obvious that London and Moscow's perception of their spheres of interest overlapped considerably in Europe and the Middle East. The greatest danger to world peace in the postwar era, judged the joint chiefs, lay in either the USSR or Great Britain "seeking to attach to herself parts of Europe to the disadvantage and possible danger of her political adversary." In any war in the foreseeable future between the Soviet Union and Britain, the United States would most likely side with Britain, America's military planners argued. But so great was Soviet strength on the Continent that while the United States might be able to defend the United Kingdom, it could not defeat the Soviet Union. It was crucial, therefore, that the United States act energetically to prevent such a war by promoting a spirit of "mutual cooperation between Britain, Russia, and ourselves."[34]

But if the spheres were not to be self-regulating, how was the United States to maintain a balance of power and promote cooperation? FDR perceived correctly that the American people would be in no mood after the war to condone the permanent stationing of troops in Europe. The first week in February 1944 he wrote Churchill: "I am absolutely unwilling to police France and possibly Italy and the Balkans as well. After all, France is your baby and will take a lot of nursing in order to bring it to the point of walking alone."[35] Three weeks later he wrote the former naval person: " 'Do please don't' ask me to keep any American forces in France. I just cannot do it! I would have to bring them all back home. As I suggested before, I denounce and protest the paternity of Belgium, France, and Italy. You really ought to bring up and discipline your own children. In view of the fact that they may be your bulwark in future days, you should at least pay for their schooling now!"[36] Nor would the American public tolerate a common Anglo-American policy toward Europe. "It is clearly the policy of the Department to avoid as far as possible any situation in which the United States and the United Kingdom appear to have developed a party line," declared a State Department memo approved by the president.[37]

Roosevelt was convinced that, so great were the domestic restraints on his diplomacy, he could not even permit Churchill and Stalin to divide Europe into blocs or spheres through direct negotiation. Though the American people did not share the pure internationalists' willingness to relinquish part of the nation's sovereignty, they did share Hull and company's antipathy to spheres of interest and power politics. To maintain a working political consensus the White House believed that it had to cultivate Hull and the internationalists. Thus the president would have to appear to oppose regionalism and support national self-determination at every turn.

But what then was left? By late 1944 the White House had concluded that the only politically and diplomatically viable option available to it was appeasement of the Soviet Union. That is, FDR decided that he must convince the Kremlin of the West's good intentions and trust Stalin not to destroy the independence of those nations occupied by the Red Army. Averell Harriman recalled that the president believed he could explain to Stalin the positive world reaction he could expect from decent behavior on the part of the Russians, as opposed to the violent antagonism he would encounter if he seized certain territories "and that the Kremlin's fear of public opinion would restrain its actions."[38] More concretely, the White House's plan of rapprochement called for internationalization of the land and sea approaches to the Baltic, internationalization of the Persian Railroad, and American assumption of responsibility for the postwar reconstruction of Russia.[39] In addition, the West would require that the Soviets legitimize their occupation zones through holding plebiscites rather than multiparty elections. Assured of the economic and strategic security it had traditionally sought, Russia could then assume its rightful place among the Great Powers.

Above all, Roosevelt's strategy called for a harsh policy toward Germany. If Soviet suspicion of the Western democracies were to be allayed, Moscow would have to be assured that Britain and America did not plan to breathe life once again into the German military machine and unleash it on the Soviet Union. It was with these imperatives in mind that Roosevelt met Churchill at the second Quebec Conference in September 1944 and, using American aid during Phase II as leverage, persuaded him to initial the Morgenthau Plan. That stratagem called for the political dismemberment of the Third Reich and the destruction of the Ruhr and Saar. Designed to render Germany a land "primarily agricultural and pastoral," it threw a wrench into the Churchill government's plans to restore the European balance of power by quickly denazifying and rehabilitating its vanquished foe.

Spurred by the specter of a permanently enfeebled Germany, Churchill revived the spheres-of-interest issue in October during a face-to-face meeting with Stalin in Moscow. Although Poland was the primary purpose of Churchill's trip to Russia, he was determined to reach a temporary accord with the Soviet leader on southeastern Europe. When the prime minister arrived in Moscow, Soviet troops controlled Rumania and Bulgaria and had nearly completed their occupation of Hungary. The Germans were in full retreat in Greece and fighting for survival in Yugoslavia. All five countries were experiencing intense internal turmoil. In addition to propping up the pro-British monarchy in Greece, the Churchill government was then trying to hammer out a workable accord between Tito's powerful partisan forces and the Yugoslav government-in-exile in London. Churchill had gone to Moscow to define—and limit—the boundaries of Soviet influence. In a now-famous episode, the prime minister jotted down a proposed country-by-country division of power: Rumania—90 percent for Russia and 10 percent for others; Greece—90 percent for Great Britain "(in accordance with U.S.A.)" and 10 percent for Russia; Bulgaria and Yugoslavia to be divided evenly; and Hungary—75 percent for Russia and 25 percent for others. Stalin seemed to approve—he told his English visitor to hold on to the paper.[40]

Churchill subsequently asked FDR to concur in his latest effort to demark Russian and Anglo-American interests in this extremely volatile area.[41] A tripartite agreement was necessary, he said, "so that we may prevent civil war from breaking out in several countries when probably you and I would be in sympathy with one side and U.J. [Uncle Joe] with the other." Roosevelt continued to believe that Russian predominance in Eastern Europe was inevitable, and, as he indicated in a letter to Ambassador Averell Harriman in Moscow, he was determined to take "such steps as are practical to insure against the Balkans getting us into a future international war."[42] Nevertheless, although Roosevelt did not flatly denounce the percentages deal, he refused to endorse it, and he expressed the hope that such spheres-of-influence arrangements should not be conclusive but only preliminaries to postwar settlements agreed to by the major powers.[43]

But appeasing Russia proved more difficult than Franklin Roosevelt had imagined. Having blocked Great Britain in its efforts to lay the foundation for a strong West European federation through the rehabilitation of Germany, the White House expected the Soviet Union to give up any plans that it had to dominate Central and Eastern Europe. Those hopes were disappointed. The Warsaw uprising and Russian policy toward Eastern Europe generally in late 1944 raised doubts as to whether the Grand Alliance could be maintained into the postwar period and made it increasingly difficult for the president to justify his policy of stiff-arming the British and "disarming" the Soviets.

At the Yalta Conference in February 1945, the Big Three discussed four major questions: occupation zones for Germany, reparations, Poland, and the Far East. Roosevelt, Churchill, and Stalin, after awarding France a tiny zone in the west, ratified the recommendations of the European Advisory Commission which divided Germany into three zones, Russia controlling the eastern one-third, Britain the northwest, and the United States the southwest. Berlin, situated in the Russian zone, was to be a microcosm of Germany as a whole. Stalin, supported by Roosevelt, took a hard line on reparations while Churchill took a soft one. After much wrangling it was decided that an Allied commission would meet in Moscow after the war and take $20 billion, with half going to Russia, as a basis for discussion. Both Roosevelt and Churchill pressed Stalin to broaden the communist government he had installed in Warsaw and to hold free elections. Stalin finally agreed to include in a new Polish coalition noncommunist Poles from within the Resistance and from the exile government in London. The three leaders signed a Declaration of Liberated Europe, which committed the occupying powers to hold free but unsupervised elections in their zones at the earliest possible date. Finally, Stalin agreed to enter the war against Japan in return for Outer Mongolia, the Kuril Islands, the southern half of Sakhalin Island, and the opportunity to regain political and economic control of Manchuria.

Roosevelt, Hopkins, and Stettinius claimed to be much pleased with the results of the Yalta Conference. It proved, they asserted, that the Soviets were "reasonable and farseeing," as Hopkins put it, and that peaceful coexistence was a virtual certainty.[44] On March 1, 1945, the president, so sick and tired that he could not stand, addressed a joint session of Congress. Though not perfect, the Yalta accords provided the foundations for a lasting peace, he told the legislators. The Declaration of Liberated Europe had halted a trend toward the development of spheres of influence, and the compromise on Poland was the best chance that country had for freedom and independence. But, of course, the administration was overly optimistic.

Just as had been true in the mid-1930s, the White House in the mid-1940s gradually became a prisoner of the contradictory ebb and flow of public and congressional opinion. Quite simply, Franklin Roosevelt possessed neither the intellectual equipment nor the political clout to develop and implement a plan for ordering the postwar world. In the end, he could only view international relations in terms of domestic politics. Only belatedly did he discover that Joseph Stalin was not Ed Flynn, did not respond to "favors," and did not view FDR as "the boss."

Winston Churchill and Anthony Eden, Ernest Bevin and Clement Attlee were stunned by American foreign policy in late 1944 and early 1945. Like the imp of the perverse, Roosevelt seemed determined not only to remove the United States from the postwar balance of power in Europe but also to keep Britain from establishing any arrangement that would protect its vital strategic interests. The United States undermined the Churchill government's plans to quickly restore noncommunist power bases in Central Europe by forcing Britain to approve the

Morgenthau Plan, which called for a dismembered and deindustrialized Germany. In desperation Churchill attempted to reach a specific spheres-of-interest understanding with Stalin, only to have Roosevelt withhold his approval of such an accord. By the time the Big Three met at Yalta, it was too late to secure meaningful Western participation in the occupation of Eastern Europe. Moreover, nothing had been done at the Crimea conference to establish and protect the economic and military security of Western Europe.

In Britain there emerged during this same period a rapidly growing consensus in behalf of a policy of overt resistance to Soviet expansion in Eastern Europe and pressure in the eastern Mediterranean. Eden and his supporters continued to favor every possible effort at cooperation with Russia, but he, Richard Law, Harold Macmillan, and their followers were at the same time committed to the traditional British policy of seeing that no one power emerged to dominate the continent of Europe. As Moscow consolidated its position in Europe following V-E Day, as local communist parties successfully fished in troubled waters in France and Italy, and as the apparently communist-led revolutions in Greece and Iran (Azerbaijan) gained momentum, the Eden group's two objectives seemed increasingly to be mutually exclusive.[45] All the while, Churchill, Frederick Lindemann, and their followers persisted in viewing Stalin as a reincarnation of Hitler, and Soviet Communism as just another version of National Socialism. Despite the Quebec Conference, Roosevelt's scotching of the percentages deal, Yalta, and American efforts to impose a flawed multilateralism, both high and reform Tories were driven back to the truth that their country would be hard-pressed to maintain a balance of power in Europe without American power.[46] Both groups of Conservatives, it should be noted, continued to show little faith in the United Nations, viewing it as a placebo for the United States.

The Yalta Conference produced a brief thaw in Anglo-Soviet relations but it was brief indeed. Although on March 1 the House of Commons endorsed the Yalta accords by a vote of 413 to 0, some moderate and all right-wing Conservatives remained extremely dubious about the possibility of an East-West rapprochement.[47] These skeptics, who predominated in the Foreign Office, continued to assume that the Soviet Union was a totalitarian, expansionist power bent on establishing its hegemony over all of Europe.

Hardening attitudes in Whitehall were reinforced by mounting Russophobia among British personnel who came in frequent contact with the Soviets. Diplomats and soldiers stationed in Moscow, Leningrad, Murmansk, and Archangel were alarmed not only by official Russian policy but also by the suspicion and discourtesy they encountered at a personal level. Frustrated by months of bureaucratic red tape, electronic eavesdropping, rudeness, and ostracism by private Russian citizens fearful of reprisals if they were caught fraternizing with a Westerner, these soldiers and diplomats were portraying their host country in most unflattering terms by April 1945. After observing the Politburo, "the real rulers of Russia," at the opening session of the Supreme Soviet, Frank Roberts, Ambassador Alexander Clark-Kerr's deputy in Moscow, reported:

> The group at the back sitting with Kalinin are enough to make one shudder and fill one with considerable apprehension regarding future Soviet policy. Apart from Kalinin and Voroshilov none of them, I think, are old party Bolsheviks. They are all tough, fat, prosperous individuals who might equally well have come to the top in any other ruthless, totalitarian society such as those we are defeating in Germany and Italy. Zhdanov in particular might be a plumper and perhaps more humane version of Hitler himself. Beriya and Malenkov at the back give the impression of being at worst perverts and sadists and at best reincarnations of medieval inquisitors justifying every action of the principle of the end justifying the means.[48]

In spring 1945 Roberts, who as minister-counselor in the British Embassy in Moscow was George F. Kennan's counterpart, articulated what eventually came to be the Anglo-American policy of containment. He sensed that the foreign policy establishment, having worked so long and so hard to establish a viable relationship with the Soviet Union, was becoming frustrated, and he perceived two emerging attitudes among Britons. One equated Stalin with Hitler and saw Soviet power as potentially dangerous as Germany's had been. The other accepted the argument that Russia was simply immature and insecure, and advocated further patience in the expectation that Russian aggressiveness would pass. Each of these options was based on fallacious assumptions, and both were equally dangerous, he believed. History, ideology, and the nature of the present leadership made the second course naive. As long as the Politburo was comprised of "the tough, tricky and untrustworthy personalities" who then were in power, the efforts to conciliate the Kremlin would be counterproductive. Nor must Britain forget that the Russian people were acutely conscious of past national glories; they identified Russian greatness with the power politics practiced by Peter the Great, Catherine the Great, and even Ivan the Terrible. Finally, Roberts observed, "there is a fundamental divergence between the Soviet political philosophy and totalitarian practices, and the way of life of the outside world." What was called for was a policy of reasoned firmness, a quiet resistance to Soviet expansion built on strength:

> We have, above all, to show that there is a limit beyond which they cannot go. We must also show them that we are not bankrupt in political and economic leadership and that the Western world, under our guidance and with the vast economic resources of the Anglo-Saxon world behind it, remains strong and healthy enough to resist Soviet pressure tactics. . . . Since Europe had been divided by Soviet action into two parts, we had better lose no time in ensuring that ours remains the better and with the support of the outside world, the stronger half.

Such a policy would require semi-official campaigns to reeducate public opinion. It was not yet necessary to embark on an anti-Soviet campaign, he advised the Foreign Office, but "we should put a stop to the adulation of the Soviet Union which has been going on for the past three years."[49]

On April 3 Winston Churchill addressed an empire prime ministers' conference. Relations with Russia, "which had offered such fair promise at the Crimea Conference," had deteriorated sharply in recent weeks, he said. It was by no means clear that "we could count on Russia as a beneficent influence in Europe, or as a willing partner in maintaining the peace of the world." Yet the end of the war would see Russia in a position of "preponderant power and influence throughout the whole of Europe."[50] Churchill told the prime ministers that the British Commonwealth must unify and utilize its superior statecraft and experience to match the power of the United States and the Soviet Union.

Though increasingly pessimistic, the Churchill government did not give up trying to draw the United States into the European vacuum of power that would be created by Germany's demise. In March and early April 1945 Churchill bombarded the White House with telegrams generalizing from the Polish situation to all areas liberated by the Russians and arguing that British and American troops must push as deep into Central Europe as quickly as they could. Gradually, he began to make progress. Although there would be no race for Berlin— Roosevelt declared that he would not jeopardize Soviet-American relations for a few more miles of German rubble—by April Roosevelt's tone toward Russia seemed to be changing. He wrote Churchill that the West must be firm with Stalin and leave no impression that it operated from fear.[51]

On that soft, sunlit day in Warm Springs, Georgia, when Franklin Delano Roosevelt's heart finally failed him, Harry S. Truman was on Capitol Hill hobnobbing with Sam Rayburn, Alben Barkley, and other of his legislative cronies. Indeed, he was in Rayburn's office having a bourbon and branch water when he received an urgent message to go at once to the White House. There he learned the terrible news. After being sworn in as president of the United States, he told assembled reporters that he felt as if the stars and the moon had fallen on his shoulders. One of the reasons for Truman's feelings of inadequacy was his isolation from the various wartime conferences and from foreign affairs in general while he was vice-president. Roosevelt, who characteristically refused to confront the imminence of his own death, failed to give any on-the-job training to the man in line to succeed him. "He was an obscure vice-president who got to see Roosevelt much less than I did and who knew less than I did about United States foreign relations," Charles Bohlen recalled of Truman.[52]

As his most recent biographer points out, however, Truman may have been shut out of meetings and conferences on international relations while serving as Roosevelt's second-in-command, but he came to the presidency with knowledge and skills in other areas—budget, tax policy, and executive-congressional relations, for example. He was, moreover, gregarious, popular on the Hill, straightforward, unpretentious, and relatively candid. He was a skilled, methodical politician, schooled in the ways of compromise. The man from Missouri also had a short fuse and a large capacity for self-righteous indignation. After ten years in the Senate, he had put the Pendergast machine behind him, but as Robert Donovan observes, Truman still came from a world of two-bit politicians. He preferred mediocrity to brilliance in his friends and associates, and was given to cronyism. He could be intensely partisan and was stubbornly loyal to those who had been loyal to him. He was never able to rid himself of a deep-seated inferiority complex. Always anxious to appear the hail-fellow-well-met, his diaries are full of attacks on stuffed shirts and "prima donnas."[53]

Harry Truman was a New Dealer, but like his predecessor he tried to combine social justice with fiscal orthodoxy and the American creed of self-reliance and economic independence. He believed in a balanced budget. He distrusted theories and abstractions but took the position that the government had a responsibility to solve social and economic problems. Like most denizens of the American heartland he revered business and business people, but at the same time he distrusted concentrations of economic power. In brief, Harry Truman was a well-meaning, decent man without intellectual depth whose most comfortable mode was the world of big-city and then congressional politics.[54]

Though Truman had not been privy to high-level discussions regarding wartime strategy and the politics of the Grand Alliance, he soon became aware that a shift in the direction of a firmer line toward the Soviet Union had developed in the last weeks before FDR's death. Anxious to appear decisive and to reflect the most recent trend in the policies of his predecessor, the new president set about making Moscow toe the line. On his way to the United Nations Conference on International Organization (UNCIO) in San Francisco in late April, Soviet foreign minister Vyacheslav Molotov agreed to stop in Washington to consult with the new chief executive. This gave Truman less than two weeks to decide what position to take with the Russians, particularly over the Polish question, which, it was already clear, would be a major issue at the conference. Truman immediately closeted himself with Roosevelt's principal advisers on Soviet policy. As luck would have it, Averell Harriman was then in Washington for consultation. In private conversations with Truman, he warned bluntly that Russian occupation of any country would resemble a "barbarian invasion" that would result not only in Russian domination of that country's foreign policy but also the establishment of a totalitarian police state. A much firmer policy toward the Russians was called for. Harriman told Truman that the Kremlin would not dare react violently to a get-tough approach by Washington, for it still desperately needed United States economic assistance to repair its war-devastated economy.[55] Other presidential counselors echoed Harriman's call for a tougher line, especially Bernard Baruch, Admiral William D. Leahy, and Secretary of the Navy James Forrestal.

Truman's rhetoric began to reflect the influence of his Russophobe advisers. The Soviets were uncivil and untrustworthy, he proclaimed; their rhetoric was "insulting." The Russians, he told Henry Wallace, were like people from across the tracks whose manners were very bad. They did not keep their word. Moreover, the Soviets were wrong. Domination of other peoples against their will was immoral.[56]

By mid-April Truman's mind was made up—he would challenge Soviet efforts to dominate and communize. On April 17, after learning that the Russians intended to sign a treaty of mutual assistance with the Lublin government, the president resolved to "lay it on the line with Molotov when he arrived in Washington." To Harriman and Leahy's delight, Truman talked to Molotov "as he had never been talked to before" in a famous interview on April 23. He sharply reprimanded the Soviet foreign minister for Moscow's failure to carry out the Yalta decisions regarding Poland. A week after the Truman-Molotov encounter, the State Department, while privately acknowledging that Russian interests in Bulgaria and Rumania were more direct than those of the United States, demanded that the Soviets allow British and American representatives to participate in the political reconstruction of the two Balkan nations and that Moscow open them to Western business people.[57]

The United Nations Conference on International Organization, which opened with great fanfare on April 25, 1945, had the ironic effect of aggravating rather than alleviating international tensions; it revealed to the American public the full extent of the differences between Russia and the West. Two days after the conference began, Molotov demanded that representatives of the Lublin regime be seated immediately as the official Polish delegation. Senator Arthur Vandenberg, representing Congress and the Republican party in the United States delegation, insisted that Secretary of State Stettinius publicly reject the Russian ploy. Admission of the Lublin Poles would wreck any chance of ratification of the United Nations Charter by the Senate, he argued. Then, on May 4, the Soviet government finally acknowledged that it had arrested sixteen Polish underground leaders after having promised them safe conduct to Moscow to discuss broadening the Lublin regime. Leading American journals opened up on the Soviets. Even the left-wing *New Republic* observed that the Soviet Union seemed to be acting more out of a desire to safeguard its own interests than to make the United Nations work.[58] Not all press commentators blamed the growing East-West split on Moscow, but April and May 1945 did witness the first widespread press criticism of the Soviet Union since the Russo-Finnish War of 1939–40.

The United States delegation managed to block the seating of the Lublin government, but in the process it had to actively support admission of Argentina, whose right-wing government had broken with the Axis only weeks preceding the conference. Latin America agreed to oppose the Kremlin's Polish strategy on the condition that Washington sponsor Buenos Aires for membership.

More significantly, the delegates to the San Francisco Conference adopted amendments to the United Nations Charter that went far to protect the national sovereignty of member nations, amendments that at the same time dramatically eroded the democratic nature and collective security powers of the United Nations. The meeting ratified the understanding reached at Yalta giving each member of the Security Council an absolute veto on "substantive" matters. Section two of article seven reserved to member states those matters primarily domestic in nature. Finally, Arthur Vandenberg succeeded in shepherding through the conference his famous article fifty-two, which condoned regional collective security agencies (thus clearing the way for NATO, the Warsaw Pact, and the OAS).

Vandenberg, in many ways the most influential member of the United States delegation, was delighted with the results of the United Nations conference. "I might sum it up for your private ear," he wrote Robert Taft, "by saying that we have stopped any possibility that San Francisco might become another Munich. I think the track is now clear for us to go ahead on the real job we have at hand. From my own personal standpoint, the situation in this respect is entirely satisfactory. I find widespread hospitality for the Republican point of view."[59] The Michigan senator's satisfaction, which was shared by fellow delegate John Foster Dulles, stemmed from the fact that the Lublin Poles had not been seated, that the United States had publicly confronted the Soviet Union, that the principle of national sovereignty had been upheld, and that the groundwork was being laid for an all-out political assault by the Republicans on the Roosevelt-Truman administration's "sell-out" at Yalta.

If signs in both the international and domestic spheres seemed to point to a tougher line toward the Soviet Union, what policy options were open to the Truman administration? The Red Army continued to occupy Eastern Europe and the president was no more ready for an armed confrontation with the Kremlin than FDR had been. Some of Truman's advisers argued that the leverage of a postwar reconstruction loan would surely convert Russia into a responsible member of the international community.

Truman had no apparent qualms about using economic aid as a lever to pry diplomatic concessions from the Russians. When Averell Harriman briefed him on East-West relations in the days following FDR's death, he frequently mentioned economics and finance as areas where Washington could exert pressure on Moscow. Truman was enthusiastic. He intended to be "firm" but "fair" because "anyway the Russians need us more than we need them." During his confrontation with Molotov, the president reminded the Soviet foreign minister that Congress would have to approve any measures of foreign economic aid, and he implied that Soviet conduct in Eastern Europe would largely determine whether or not approval was forthcoming.[60]

A week after FDR's death the State Department—not the Treasury, it should be noted—began to move on the issue of a loan to the Soviet Union. The department's plan, subsequently approved by Truman, recommended that, following the conclusion of the San Francisco Conference, the administration should offer Moscow a $1 billion (not $6 billion or $10 billion as Henry Morgenthau had originally suggested in January 1945) loan through the Export-Import Bank at the bank's regular rate of interest. In mid-July FEA chief Leo Crowley asked Congress to raise the bank's loan ceiling from $700 million to $3.5 billion and to repeal the Johnson Act which forbade loans to defaulting governments. Though Robert Taft as well as other Republicans and some southern Democrats expressed reservations, a majority in both houses of Congress supported the granting of a nominal credit to Russia and voted for the export-import bill. Russian intransigence was not yet readily apparent to the American people and the United States still tended to associate internationalism with Soviet-American cooperation. The time was not yet ripe, Republican leaders felt, to open up on the administration over Eastern Europe.[61]

Armed with this new lending authority, President Truman left for Potsdam in July for his first face-to-face meeting with Churchill and Stalin. The State Department advised Truman not to broach the matter of a loan unless Stalin first inquired. But just as had been the case with Roosevelt at Yalta, Stalin said nothing about Russia's postwar reconstruction needs or an American credit. He concentrated instead on reproaching Truman for the abrupt cancellation of lend-lease in May. The Soviets wanted American credit to facilitate imports of much needed capital goods, but at the same time the Kremlin was convinced that Russia could industrialize on its own, and it was not willing to trade territorial or political concessions for American dollars. Thus, just as Yalta had, Potsdam ended without the Russian loan issue playing any overt role.[62]

Some historians have argued that the primary motive behind United States economic policy toward the Soviet Union during this period was the open door, that, above all, Washington wanted to pry open the markets of Eastern Europe for American exports.[63] It is true that those markets were becoming increasingly closed to Western exports in spring 1945. But most senior American policymakers were not overly alarmed by the economic consequences of the Russian trade initiative in Poland and the Baltic because the area was not a good prospective market for American products. The American officials and business leaders who were concerned about a depression in the postwar period wanted to acquire markets primarily for United States industrial goods. During World War II German occupation authorities had forced industrial development in Eastern Europe, thus making the economies of those countries competitive with rather than complementary to that of the United States. American policymakers worked to force Russia to allow Westerners to travel and trade freely in the area in the hope that such contact would prevent these countries from becoming Soviet-dominated, totalitarian societies antithetical to Western values and traditions. Quite simply, Washington wished to open up Eastern Europe for political and strategic rather than economic reasons.

Despite Truman's tough talk to Molotov and his willingness to use economic leverage to force Moscow into a more cooperative posture, there were obvious limits to the administration's confrontational strategy during these early, belligerent days. Washington was not willing to risk a military clash with Russia, and Truman's basic strategy was for the West to live up strictly to its obligations under the Yalta agreements, demanding, in turn, that the Soviets do the same. America's determination to avoid a military encounter with Russia became clear during the debate over how far Anglo-American troops should penetrate Central Europe during the last days of the war. In early April, as German resistance collapsed in the west but stiffened in the east, Anglo-American troops faced an opportunity to occupy Berlin and its environs ahead of the Soviets even though that area was clearly within the Soviet zone of occupation agreed upon at Yalta. Shortly before FDR's death General Dwight D. Eisenhower, Supreme Allied Commander in Europe, announced his intention to stop at the Elbe River.[64] Despite the energetic protests of Winston Churchill and the State Department Eisenhower, supported by Truman, stuck to his guns. Truman later wrote in his memoirs that he could see Churchill and Undersecretary of State Joseph Grew's point that the West should, like the East, take advantage of the military situation to occupy as much territory as possible, but there was another side to the coin. The best approach to securing Soviet cooperation and thus peace and stability in Europe appeared to be for the United States and the United Kingdom to observe the commitments on occupation zones they had made at Yalta.

Indeed, as numerous historians have pointed out, by June 1945 Harry Truman was beginning to pull in his claws as far as the Soviet Union was concerned. In the first place, a number of advisers and interest groups, alarmed by the influence that the hard-liners initially enjoyed with the new president, stepped forward to outline the implications of a confrontational stance toward the Soviets and the limitations on the president's ability to get tough. The alarmist outlook advanced by some in the military and State Department in regard to the Soviet Union in spring and summer 1945 was not shared by other influential members of the military's top command. While determined to resist Soviet penetration of Western Europe, many service leaders showed little concern in April and May over Soviet domination of Eastern Europe. More broadly, these leaders still clung, though with diminishing confidence, to their hopes for Soviet cooperation in the Pacific war and participation in the crusade for world peace.[65] Chief spokesman for the military moderates was Henry Stimson. The "Colonel," it will be remembered, was a traditional Republican nationalist in the Henry Cabot Lodge–Theodore Roosevelt tradition. The primary concerns of United States foreign policy should be, first, the security of the Western Hemisphere and, second, peace and stability abroad. Maintenance of the Monroe Doctrine and the regional security system that had grown up around it was the key to attaining the first objective, Stimson argued. Allowing the Soviets to have their own sphere of interest in Eastern Europe might be the key to the second.

Dwight Eisenhower and George Marshall shared Stimson's perspective. Much more than Marshall, Eisenhower recognized that all wars were fought for political ends, but he did not believe that eviction of the Soviets from Eastern Europe was a viable political goal. Given the manpower and material demands of the final stages of the war in the Far East, the United States could not afford confrontation with Russia over Eastern Europe. Indeed, if the United States wanted to protect Central and Western Europe and simultaneously demobilize, the best approach to protecting that area was for the West to strictly observe the Yalta accords while quickly concluding agreements with the Soviets for four-power control of disputed areas.[66]

In addition, a number of military leaders concerned primarily with the Pacific theater feared that despite the Quebec agreement of fall 1944 the British were going to allow the United States to bear the brunt of the final stages of the war, and then, once Japan was knocked out, step in and reassert their claim to empire and influence in the Far East. Douglas MacArthur and others argued that such a scenario would be disastrous for the security of the region and American interests there. MacArthur was already openly pleading for an Asia-first policy after the war. He argued that imperialism constituted a severe obstacle to Asia's self-realization, and, if the West attempted to restore the status quo ante bellum, it would create resentment and turmoil that would play directly into the hands of the Russians.[67]

Joining military moderates in urging a more flexible, realistic policy toward the Soviet Union was the coalition of individuals and publications that the British Foreign Office had labeled American liberal opinion. The *New Republic* and Eleanor Roosevelt were as alarmed by developments at the San Francisco Conference as Vandenberg had been gratified. Citing the drive to seat Argentina, they accused the United States–led Inter-American System and the British Commonwealth of ganging up on the Soviets and engaging in the worst type of power politics.[68] A very real danger, liberals warned, was that the Soviet Union would be driven out of the United Nations, and no international organization could work without Soviet participation. Many saw an English Machiavelli behind the Soviet-American confrontation. "Harriman and Stettinius . . . are taking orders from London," one of Henry Wallace's confidants wrote him, "AND I'M DUBIOUS ABOUT LONDON WHEN LONDON TRIES TO LAY DOWN A FOREIGN POLICY FOR US." Declared another Wallace correspondent: "Eden and Stettinius are Siamese twins out here—and the Russians know it."[69] Joseph E. Davies, wealthy Wisconsin businessman, former ambassador to the Soviet Union, and arch proponent of Soviet-American friendship, wrote Jimmy Byrnes on May 10 that the Russian situation was deteriorating to a frightening degree:

> It would be desperately tragic if after the Soviets had trusted us sufficiently to cooperate to win the war, they might not, from their point of view, be justifiably compelled to "go it alone" in a hostile ideological and religious world, and to create a *cordon sanitaire* not only in Europe but in the Pacific because of some of the crazy militarists and prejudiced fools who preach the inevitability of war between Russia and the United States, and are "sowing the dragon seed."[70]

Henry Stimson, George Marshall, Patrick J. Hurley, Joseph Davies, Henry Wallace, and other opponents of a get-tough policy made their views known repeatedly to Truman in late April and May, and had much to do with the decision to stop at the Elbe and not take Prague. The president continued to be irritated with Soviet behavior, but he was also increasingly suspicious of British motives and fearful of an anti-Soviet backlash among the American press and public that would tie his hands in dealing with the Kremlin.

Truman, no less than Roosevelt, tended initially at least to lump Britain and Russia together. Certainly no Anglophobe himself, the new president came from the section of the country least inclined to seek close ties with the British. He counted few friends among those intellectuals, financiers, and business people, most of whom resided along the eastern seaboard, who were traditionally Anglophile. Nor could he have been immune to the intense anti-British feeling that swept America in the months before his accession to office. The man from Missouri shared the midwestern progressive's fear of an international plutocracy, and he deplored colonialism. Even more than his predecessor, he was determined to give the United Nations a serious go, and Britain's traditional balance-of-power stratagem seemed antithetical to the whole idea of international cooperation. One of his major tasks during the first weeks of his administration, he later wrote, was "to get Churchill in a frame of mind to forget the old power politics and get a United Nations organization to work."[71] To Eleanor Roosevelt, he wrote: "I have been trying carefully to keep all my engagements with the Russians because they are touchy and suspicious of us. The difficulties with Churchill are very nearly as exasperating as they are with the Russians."[72]

Moreover, the American people, victims of their own government's propaganda, still regarded the Russians as gallant wartime allies. A Princeton poll taken in May 1945 showed that 80 percent of the American people felt that the United States should continue to cooperate closely with *both* Britain and Russia after the war.[73] In addition, demobilization threatened to turn into disintegration after V-J Day, leaving America's armed forces in a dangerously weakened condition. Tough talk and economic pressure had not worked; why not try to build bridges to Moscow and if necessary put some distance once again between British and American policies, the president reasoned. "Every time we get things going halfway with the Soviets," Truman confided to his diary the first week in June, "some smart aleck has to attack them. If it isn't Willie Hearst, Bertie McCormick or Burt Wheeler, it is some other bird who wanted to appease Germany, but just can't see any good in Russia. I'm not afraid of Russia. They've always been our friends and I can't see any reason why they shouldn't always be."[74] Truman managed to persuade himself that Soviet leaders were no different from Western political leaders with whom deals could be struck. In effect, he decided to resort to the approach that FDR had clung to so tenaciously and that Walter Lippmann was now espousing—mediation between Britain and Russia.

In mid-May Truman took three important steps to try to reverse the decline in Soviet-American relations. First, he finally responded favorably to Churchill's pleas for another Big Three Conference while rejecting the prime minister's demand for an East-West showdown at that meeting. Second, Truman decided to send the ailing Harry Hopkins to Moscow for private, conciliatory talks with Stalin. Third, he asked Joseph Davies to go to London to warn Churchill that America would not allow itself to be maneuvered into a confrontation with the Soviet Union. Halifax quickly perceived the meaning of Truman's moves. The administration, Halifax reported to the Foreign Office, was preoccupied with

Soviet-American relations. The president was moving to counter "Liberal and Left-wing" criticism that he had been "maneuvered by Britain into an anti-Soviet bloc."[75]

As the war in Europe wound down, Winston Churchill had repeatedly urged Truman to join with him in convening a Big Three meeting to settle specific questions relating to boundaries, occupation policies, reparations, and colonies. "The retreat of the American army to our line of occupation in the central sector, thus bringing Soviet power into the heart of Western Europe," Churchill wrote Truman, should be accompanied by settlement of the host of important matters that would constitute "the true foundation of world peace."[76] The British, of course, wanted to meet separately beforehand with American military and political officials to work out a common strategy. This the president refused to do, but he did agree to attend a summit in mid-July. In fact, it was Hopkins who broached the subject with Stalin. The Russian leader told his American visitor that he would be glad to meet with Churchill and Roosevelt at a site in or near Berlin.

Churchill, with Clement Attlee in tow, arrived at Potsdam in an anxious and confrontational mood. The prime minister and his advisers had quickly picked up on the changing mood in Washington and felt American power slipping through their hands. Jock Balfour, a member of the British Embassy staff in Moscow, wrote Halifax in late May:

> Coming from Russia, I can't help thinking that every ounce of Anglo-American cooperation will be needed if the Bear is to be brought to a halt in the game of squeezing his Allies out of any say in the settlement of that part of Europe into which he had waddled. . . . It is therefore most aggravating to find that high-minded pundits like Lippmann and Raymond Graham Swing are showing signs of scuttling like rabbits for cover and persuading themselves that the behavior of the bear is largely the fault of the naughtily provocative British lion and that . . . it would therefore be best for Uncle Sam to adopt an attitude of "wise reserve" toward developments in Europe.[77]

Joseph Davies seemed to be saying, Orme Sargent noted, that it "does not pay to be tough with the Soviets and it does pay to appease them." This was the language of 1938 and he hoped it did not reflect Truman's attitude; however, he observed pessimistically, "there is no smoke without fire."[78]

In fact, as the Hopkins and Davies missions indicated, the hope of Soviet-American reconciliation burned brightly in the hearts of both Harry Truman and his new secretary of state, James F. Byrnes. A South Carolinian of Irish stock, Byrnes began his long and illustrious political career in 1910 when he was elected to the House of Representatives.[79] In 1930 his constituents elevated him to the Senate, where he remained until 1941. So impressed with Byrnes's loyal support of administration policies was FDR that he appointed him to the Supreme Court in

1941 and then the next year asked him to manage the mobilization effort at home by becoming director of the Office of Economic Stabilization. A New Dealer who retained his standing with southern conservatives, Byrnes grew to be a force in Washington. "Charming and gracefully informal, yet with a professional knowledge of Congress and its workings and a zest for the political process, the South Carolinian was both useful and good company," writes Kendrick Clements. "His warm baritone voice with its lingering hint of Irish lilt could sing a song, tell a funny story, or cajole a reluctant senator all with equal grace and effect."[80] Above all Jimmy Byrnes was a compromiser, a horse trader, a power broker. Leslie Biffle, secretary of the Senate, called Byrnes "the smartest, most effective and most unobstructive operator" he had ever seen in action: "One Senator reportedly remarked: 'When I see Jimmy Byrnes coming I put one hand on my watch, the other on my wallet, and wish to goodness I knew how to protect my conscience.' "[81] The new secretary of state looked forward to applying the negotiating techniques he had found useful in these jobs to the problems of foreign affairs.

Truman and Byrnes had one overriding objective at Potsdam: to clear up remaining wartime problems so that United States military and economic responsibilities in Europe could be terminated as quickly as possible. Both men were able practitioners of the art of politics, acutely sensitive to the public's desire for a return to "normalcy" at home and abroad. At this point both tended to look upon the Russians as fellow politicians, with whom a deal could be arranged.[82] "The smart boys in the State Department, as usual, are against the best interests of the U.S. if they can circumvent a straightforward hard-hitting trader for the homefront," Truman confided to his diary. "But they are stymied this time. Byrnes and I shall expect our interests to come first."[83]

Of all the topics discussed at Potsdam, none was more compelling than Germany. United States policy toward postwar Germany had been in a state of flux since Roosevelt's death. The army was initially prepared to implement JCS 1067, which incorporated Morgenthau's plan for dismemberment and pastoralization of the German economy. But for a variety of reasons, by mid-1945 the joint chiefs and the State Department had come to strongly favor the quick rehabilitation of the Reich. Keeping Germany weak and divided would perpetuate a power vacuum in Central Europe which, given Britain's debilitation and America's determination to demobilize, the Soviets were sure to exploit. It was becoming increasingly apparent that the rehabilitation and hence stability of other war-torn Continental countries depended on the Ruhr and the Saar operating at full capacity. Finally, if the Germans and their neighbors were not able to feed and clothe themselves, American taxpayers would more than likely have to do it for them. Truman proved responsive to his diplomatic and military advisers. In a conversation with State Department officials on May 10, the president said that he "entirely disagreed" with Morgenthau's recommendation that synthetic oil plants in Germany be destroyed. Later he rebuked the Treasury secretary for wanting to dispense with legal procedures in meting out punishment to Nazi war criminals. Early in

July, just before leaving for Potsdam, the president finally asked for Morgenthau's resignation. In his memoirs, Truman claimed that he had always opposed the Morgenthau Plan.[84]

But the administration's decision to support rehabilitation made it imperative to work out a satisfactory agreement with the Soviet Union on reparations. If on the one hand the Russians were given free rein to take what they wanted in the West, they would strip the industrialized areas of western Germany, producing the economic chaos that Washington wanted to avoid. On the other, if the Russians did not obtain a satisfactory settlement, they would cut off badly needed food shipments from their zone to the West, making it necessary for Britain and America to initiate a costly reparations program in order to prevent starvation. The final protocol provided that the reparations claims of each victor would be met by removals from the territory each occupied, but that in addition the Russians would receive from the Anglo-American zones 10 percent of "surplus" industrial capital equipment. The Soviets could collect an additional 15 percent of such material from the Western zones in exchange for an equivalent value of food and raw materials from the Russian zone.

The British delegation saw eye to eye with Truman and his advisers on the German questions but quickly diverged over "enforcement" of the Declaration of Liberated Europe. It will be remembered that the British were of the opinion that Russian security and Marxist ideology were inextricably intertwined in Soviet foreign policy. The Kremlin viewed capitalist nations as not only ideologically incompatible with communist nations but also overtly hostile to their very existence. In their search for friendly governments on their boundaries, which included potentially the entire world, Moscow would ally with and give aid to political elements that would inevitably be communist.[85] Moreover, the British went to Potsdam determined to reveal for the Americans the extent of Soviet ambitions and their techniques of expansion. As J. G. Donnelley remarked: "the more intransigent they [the Soviets] are, the clearer it must be to the Americans that the Lippmann thesis is as absurd as it is dangerous."[86]

Churchill believed that Yugoslavia was a good case in point. Tito was nothing less than a Kremlin puppet in Whitehall's view. The Yugoslav leader's occupation of Venezia Giulia and his claims to Fiume, Trieste, and other areas in Greece and Austria, his suppression of criticism and opposition in areas under his control were tactics "all too reminiscent of those of Hitler and Japan," Churchill wrote Truman.[87] At the third meeting of the Big Three, Churchill brought up the Yugoslav situation in the context of the Declaration of Liberated Europe and insisted that the three nations act immediately and militarily if necessary. Stalin insisted that there was no proof of Tito's perfidy, and, to Churchill's dismay, Truman showed no interest in the matter.

Seeing an opportunity to take advantage of the rift between its allies, Russia immediately pressed for a series of concessions in areas of critical strategic importance: ownership of the Dodecanese Islands, the disposition of the Italian colonies, control of the Turkish Straits, and the continued presence of British troops in Greece. Specifically, the Soviets demanded at the Berlin meeting a share in the administration of Italian colonies and the right to build bases in the vicinity of the Straits and in northeastern Turkey.[88] At the same time the Russians showed little interest in evacuating Iran. Britain wanted to exclude the Soviets in every case. "If we were to talk generously to the Russians this time about access to the wider oceans," Churchill warned the Americans, "I fear that they would only regard it as an indication that we had not been shocked by their demands on Turkey, and would proceed to make more and more demands on Persia and on other countries in the Middle East."[89] United States support for a common Anglo-American front against Russia over these points was almost completely lacking. In the end, the Big Three agreed to establish a council of foreign ministers which would try to come to grips with these problems and would begin work on peace treaties with the former Axis allies.

The American delegation left Potsdam divided about the possibility of future cooperation with the Soviets, but Truman chose to be optimistic. Public opinion polls before the conference indicated that the American people felt that Big Three cooperation was deteriorating at an alarming rate but that they very much wanted the Grand Alliance to continue. Truman found Stalin frustrating to deal with but manageable: "Stalin is as near like Tom Pendergast as any man I know."[90] The president had not sided with the British, whom he regarded as openly provocative, while ensuring Soviet participation in the Pacific war and leaving the door open for compromise on virtually all outstanding issues. The policy of mediation was intact.

The foreign policy initiated by Franklin Roosevelt and Harry Hopkins in 1944 and continued by Truman and his advisers in 1945 was more threatening to British interests than even Whitehall or No. 10 Downing Street were willing to admit. While tripod or tripolar in name, the thrust of United States policy was to conciliate the Soviet Union while denying Great Britain the wherewithal to protect its own power base. State Department officials nixed the idea of a federation of Western Europe on the grounds that it would be a closed economic bloc and that its formation would stimulate Russian paranoia. Treasury, in its drive to make Washington the financial capital of the world, and the State Department, out of a desire to achieve commercial multilateralism, set about destroying the sterling bloc. Now, it seemed, the United States was not even willing to fill the power void it was helping to create.

10. *Alliance Renewed: British Labor and the Harnessing of America, 1945–1946*

IN JULY 1945 British voters went to the polls, turned Winston Churchill out of office, and elected a new Labour government by an overwhelming margin. The election had remarkably little effect on British foreign policy, however. The party's center, represented by Clement Attlee, Ernest Bevin, and Hugh Dalton, proved to be as committed to the preservation of British strategic and economic interests as the Conservatives had been. Alarmed by the rapid advance of the Red Army through Eastern Europe and by the police-state atmosphere in Russia, the Attlee government readily acknowledged the need to use the United States to redress the rapidly shifting balance of power in Europe. The new regime's determination to cling to its colonies and spheres of influence, and to resist Soviet expansion, served to further stimulate Anglophobia in the United States and to confirm the Truman administration in its conviction that mediation was the proper course.

A series of events and forces converged in fall 1945, however, to bring about a dramatic reversal in American diplomacy and propel the Truman administration toward a policy of Anglo-American solidarity and overt resistance to Soviet expansion. Soviet intransigence at the London and Moscow foreign ministers' conferences created doubt in the minds of Harry Truman and Jimmy Byrnes concerning the wisdom of appeasement, and subsequent Russian machinations in Iran drained the reservoir of goodwill Moscow had built up during the war. Meanwhile, the British Labour government adopted a new tactic that allowed the United Kingdom to resist Russian aggression without incurring charges from America that it was playing spheres-of-interest, power politics. Attlee and Bevin, mindful of the restraining effect of both isolationism and the new internationalism on American foreign policy, confronted the Kremlin over Iran and other issues within the context and in the name of the United Nations. A stance Americans found threatening and anachronistic outside the United Nations, they found not only acceptable but inspirational within. But perhaps the most important factor responsible for America's rejection of the policy of mediation was the Republican party's decision in late 1945 and early 1946 to openly challenge the Democrats over foreign policy. Arthur Vandenberg was able to unite the presidential and congressional wings of the GOP behind a policy of overt resistance to the Soviet

Union and criticism of the Truman administration for being soft on communism. His political fortunes already at a low ebb over domestic issues, Harry Truman became a convert to the hard-line cause and gave notice of his conversion by sponsoring Churchill's Iron Curtain speech and forcing Russia to back down over Iran in March 1946.

British foreign policy was in shambles by late July 1945. Whitehall had goals both general and specific—but not the power to realize them. Britain was willing to take up sword and buckler against the Soviet menace to Western civilization, but its American steed kept trying to gallop off in the opposite direction. Russian intransigence at Potsdam triggered feelings of uneasiness in the minds of American officials, but their misgivings had not produced a stampede in behalf of making common cause with the British. The British found the meeting as a whole both disheartening and galling. Not only had the Americans refused to join them in confronting Stalin, but also they had held themselves condescendingly aloof from their Western partner in the Grand Alliance. Clement Attlee, who accompanied Churchill and replaced him as head of the British delegation in mid-conference when the results of the general election became known, observed that United States officials were "inclined to think of Russia and America as two big boys who could settle things amicably between them."[1] Foreign Office officials complained that their American counterparts presented them with proposals on a more or less take-it-or-leave-it basis. In the week after Truman's return from Germany, Lord Halifax observed that, given the fact that Americans historically were wont to equate material abundance with moral rectitude, relations with the United States were likely to be rockier in the future than in the past.[2]

Confusion and uncertainty in British foreign policy in 1945 was a product not only of the nation's ebbing power and its increasing despondency over an erratic America, but of the disintegration of the wartime coalition as well. Sizable segments of the British population had been dissatisfied with the patchwork government Winston Churchill had put together. Its inability or unwillingness to address social and economic issues—a major achievement rather than a failure in Churchill's mind—rankled particularly with blue- and white-collar Britons. What influence the Conservative party enjoyed by 1945 stemmed from its traditions and identification with the empire, its entrenched wealth and power, and Churchill as the embodiment of the coming victory. The Right Honorable Member from Woodford had been able to establish by means of his broadcast addresses a remarkable degree of rapport with public opinion during the war. As a London tenant remarked to his housing manager during the Battle of Britain, Mr. Churchill "takes such an interest in the war doesn't he?"[3] What Americans seemed blissfully unaware of was that few Britons considered Winston Churchill an appropriate peacetime leader. He was perceived to be insensitive to the social needs of the working class—witness his clandestine warfare against the Beveridge Plan—and ignorant of the complex economic and financial questions that would confront the nation in the postwar period.

The only Conservative of prime ministerial timber in the party seemed to be Anthony Eden, who had tried to identify himself with the reform Tories without burning his bridges to the old guard. When forced out into the open, however, he chose Harold Macmillan and company. "Never again must we tolerate chronic unemployment, extremes of wealth and poverty, slums and the lack of opportunity for so many which disfigured our national life in the past," he declared; and again: "If there are three million unemployed in Europe, America and Asia, you will not get peace. If there is unemployment, malnutrition and animal standards of life, and poverty that can be remedied and is not remedied in any part of the world you will jeopardize peace."[4] Eden's speeches increasingly sounded as if he were paraphrasing *The Middle Way*.

The old guard remained committed to prewar conditions and wanted only to restore the status quo ante bellum. In 1941, at Churchill's behest, the party had established the Post-war Problems Central Committee. R. A. Butler headed this body, which by 1943 had ten subcommittees with Conservative M.P.s on each. It was made clear throughout the war, however, that the responsibility for formulating postwar policy lay solely with the leader of the party. The committee's *Forty Years of Progress* was merely a complacent review of the past. Meanwhile, Leo Amery and Lord Beaverbrook stuck to their imperial, sterling bloc guns.

As the war drew to a close, Conservatives were increasingly wracked by internecine warfare. In mid- and late-1944 Beaverbrook, the Astor's *Sunday Observer*, and the old guard launched a campaign to force Eden to give up the Foreign Office and devote his attention to being leader of the House of Commons. In December and January, however, when public opinion polls showed a marked increase in the foreign secretary's popularity in response to his handling of the Greek crisis, the "get-Eden" movement ceased.[5] Nonetheless, the Conservatives entered the final year of the war facing an inevitable electoral contest and deeply divided over policies and personalities.

By contrast Labour's program, calling as it did for nationalization of basic industries and full implementation of the Beveridge Plan, seemed much more capable of delivering on the government's promises of "Food, Homes, and Work," than did the Conservatives. In foreign affairs the Labour platform called for solidarity of the "international working class" and implementation of the Atlantic Charter. Compared to the Conservatives, Labour seemed far more united behind its program. The party's promise to offer an alternative to the "hard-faced" men who had controlled the peace following World War I struck a responsive chord with the electorate.[6] And yet problems existed. The prevailing wisdom was that the party suffered from a dearth of able and charismatic leadership. Its representatives in the War Cabinet—Bevin, Dalton, Attlee, and Herbert Morrison—were dull and nondescript, and its leadership in the House was aging and out of touch. Jennie Lee, the firebrand Scottish trade unionist, had commented in the *New Republic* as early as 1942 that Labour had been unable to attract the "great deal of restive unanchored, forward tending, namely middle class opinion" in Great Britain and the party would suffer for it at the polls.[7]

In addition, there was the ever-present split between the doctrinaire socialists headed by Harold Laski, G. D. H. Cole, Aneurin Bevan, and Lee, and the trade unionists led by Bevin. The ideologues accused the trade unionists of selling out to monopoly-capitalism, of acquiring a vested interest in the continuation of big business in private hands. But, of course, the unionists composed the rank and file of the party and controlled its finances. Wartime debates in Commons were notable for the frequency and venom with which Emmanuel Shinwell, Bevan, and other Labour M.P.s repudiated their representatives in the ruling coalition and accused them of abandoning their socialist principles. Attlee and the other Labour ministers who had grown up in the party and were accustomed to its looseness of discipline bore with these attacks as best they could, but Bevin, entering the world of parliamentary politics for the first time, found it hard to suffer in silence. He even talked of joining Churchill in a special capacity in the peace-making process and then retiring from public life.[8]

The Liberals, as always, billed themselves as the only alternative to a moribund conservatism and an unrealistic and dangerous radicalism. In foreign affairs the party conference called for implementation of the Atlantic Charter and declared its support for an "armed international organization" and the Bretton Woods program. The Liberals' domestic scheme was literally a British version of the New Deal, and was actually called "a Liberal New Deal for Britain."[9] If the party could draw the middle class away from the Conservatives and Labour—that is, co-opt Macmillan's middle way and the right wing of the Labour party—it might have a chance in the general election.

By the opening months of 1945 all parties were busy preparing for the electoral contest that everyone expected would follow the defeat of Germany. Nevertheless, the sudden end of the war in Europe took many in British ruling circles by surprise. Churchill himself wished to postpone dissolution of the government if possible until after the defeat of Japan which, early in 1945, was not expected to occur until some eighteen months after the fall of Germany. If relations with the Soviet Union should deteriorate, as they seemed most likely to do, his task would be less difficult with Labour in the government. Already he had received valuable support from Bevin in the British-backed struggle against the left-wing revolution in Greece. The military case for continuation of the coalition was good, but the task of postwar reconstruction was now becoming the nation's first priority. Moreover, Churchill came under strong pressure from influential colleagues such as Beaverbrook for a quick election in order to maximize his electoral appeal as the nation's great war leader. The prime minister overcame his own doubts and offered the Labour party the choice of a July poll or the continuance of the coalition until after the defeat of Japan. Attlee carefully put the pros and cons of these alternatives to Labour's national executive committee on May 19, 1945. It unequivocally instructed him to demand in return either an immediate end to the coalition or an October election. Telling Attlee that it was unthinkable that "we should go on bickering together till the autumn," Churchill on May 23 drove to Buckingham Palace and submitted his resignation. The election was set for July 5.[10]

In the campaign that followed, Labour bested the opposition in both content and style. The Conservatives dwelt on the "stark realism" of the present and tried to portray their opponents as hopeless visionaries. Party spokespersons accepted full employment and the Beveridge Report while at the same time emphasizing the virtues of private enterprise. But Conservatives relied too heavily on the personal stature of Churchill and the socialist bogey. The prime minister confirmed the suspicions of many Britons that he was still, underneath the garb of wartime leader, an intemperate reactionary when in one famous address he predicted that a Labour victory would usher in an era of totalitarianism with Harold Laski as head of a British Gestapo. As A. J. P. Taylor has put it: "The electors cheered Churchill but voted against him."[11]

Labour promised housing, full employment, social security, and a comprehensive health service. It was also careful to make a strong bid for those among the middle classes for whom private enterprise was not a sacred cow. Nationalization was not an issue—at least in Britain. Bevin's successor as general secretary of the Transport and General Workers' Union had moved from espousing the socialization of industry to the vaguer position of a planned economy with only selective nationalization. Such, too, were the views of Bevin, whose aim was "a humanized, modernized, but only partially socialized Britain," as C. J. Bartlett has put it.[12] Attlee was careful to emphasize the independence of the parliamentary party lest the more extreme ideas of Labour's current chairman, Harold Laski, frighten off support from the moderate center.

In terms of the British electoral system Labour won a great victory in 1945, but the system inflated the victory. Labour garnered a majority of 146 seats but with less than half the total vote. The party polled 3.5 million more votes in 1945 than it had in 1935 for a total of 12 million, while the Conservatives lost 1.5 million for a total of 10 million. The Liberals were still a force in terms of votes (2 million) but not in seats. The swing to Labour was impressive but not overwhelming. Moreover, the torrent of new Labour M.P.s who flooded the House included relatively few radical left-wingers; over half came from nonmanual occupations.[13] "In this day and age," *The Economist* had remarked during the peak of the campaign, "the best form of economic organization for a complex industrial country lies somewhere between the extremes of *laissez-faire* and bureaucracy, of full control and no control."[14] The British people wanted security rather than change for change's sake, and in the end believed the Labour party rather than Conservatives to have the flexibility and pragmatism to guarantee that security. But what did the Labour victory mean in terms of foreign policy? It meant relatively little, as it turned out.

Churchill and Attlee returned to London from Potsdam for announcement of the final results. (Collection and tabulation of the soldier vote had required almost three weeks.) By midday on July 25 a Labour majority was assured, and Attlee set about forming a new government. The leader of the party and Churchill's deputy was not a charismatic man. "He remained ill-at-ease on the platform and in Parliament," Michael Foot has said of him, "often giving an exhibition of feebleness or reducing great matters to the most meagre aspect."[15] Attlee first offered the Foreign Office to Hugh Dalton but then changed his mind, giving foreign affairs to Bevin and offering the Exchequer to a disappointed Dalton. These three together with Herbert Morrison, who became leader of the House of Commons, and Sir Stafford Cripps, who assumed Dalton's old post of president of the Board of Trade, constituted the inner circle that would rule Britain from 1945 to 1951. Of these, three—Attlee, Dalton, and Cripps—came from the British professional classes at a time when those classes were gaining ascendancy in Britain. The other two were, in different ways, political bosses. Morrison owed his rise to his domination of the London Council of Labour and Bevin to his leadership of the largest and most heterogeneous union in Britain.[16]

Clement Attlee had told Dalton that the main reason he had changed his mind about the Foreign Office was the necessity of keeping Bevin and Morrison apart. If one were concerned with the domestic scene and the other foreign affairs, they would be less likely to be at each other's throats all the time. But Dalton believed that Churchill had interceded with Attlee on July 26 and persuaded him to give the Foreign Office to Bevin.[17] The implication was that the tough-minded, pragmatic Bevin would be most likely to deal strongly with the Soviets and protect traditional British interests in the eastern Mediterranean and elsewhere, even if that meant utilizing balance-of-power tactics. Dalton's Germanophobia, it seemed, might blind him to the Russian menace. Indeed, the careerists in the Foreign Office were much reassured by Bevin's appointment. "He's broadminded and sensible, honest and courageous," Alexander Cadogan remarked—"the heavyweight of the Cabinet."[18] Bevin not only kept Cadogan on as undersecretary but Orme Sargent as well. Some of Bevin's more antiestablishment colleagues complained at year's end that Bevin had become very much devoted to the "Career Diplomat" and all the "Old Boys" in the Foreign Office.[19]

In the weeks following the general election and the Potsdam Conference, three primary approaches to foreign affairs were recognizable among British Labour leaders. Those on the far left—neo-Marxist intellectuals such as G. D. H. Cole and Harold Laski, and radical trade unionists like Aneurin Bevan and Jennie Lee—clung to the traditional "socialist" foreign policy which was compounded of a belief in the capitalist and imperialist origins of war, and the conviction that the internationalization of socialism would lead to perpetual peace. They were, before they came to believe Stalin had sold out the revolution, optimistic about the possibility of Anglo-Soviet solidarity. Bevan, who as minister of health, was part of the Labour government's outer circle, found talk of an Anglo-American combine to halt the Soviets alarming for two reasons. Such an association would certainly provoke the Soviets, and it would open the door to an influx of American power into Europe that could not be wholly advantageous to Britain.[20]

The bulk of the Labour party, including Cripps, Attlee, and Dalton, advocated the idea of a socialist "Third Force," freed from both American and Soviet influence and comprising Western Europe and the British Commonwealth, which should be able to hold a balance of power, if not to mediate between the two power blocs of capitalism and totalitarian socialism.[21] "If we and the Russians and the Americans can't maintain a triangular friendship," Hugh Dalton confided to his diary, "it were best for us that the failure, if there must be failure, should be in the maintenance of Russian-American friendship."[22] Then, of course, Britain could step into the void and mediate between the two superpowers. This third-way approach, of course, was not new and was essentially similar to the strategy put forward by Anthony Eden and Richard Law in 1943 and 1944. The third-force concept continued to attract strong support in 1945 in important circles outside Parliament.[23]

A third element in the Labour leadership, including Attlee and Bevin, was committed to the maintenance of the British Empire and resistance to Soviet expansion through Anglo-American solidarity. The members of this group claimed to see all problems in terms of the welfare of the British worker, and that welfare, as they saw it, depended on preservation of British interests throughout the world. In 1947 Bevin told a labor conference: "Reference was made by one speaker in connection with the Middle East to the fact that we ought to hand this over to an international concern. I am not going to be a party to voluntarily putting all British interests in a pool and everybody else sticking to his own. The standard of life and the wages of the workman of this country are dependent on these things."[24]

In fact, the new foreign secretary not only practiced but also embodied the third approach. Attlee gave the former TGWU leader a free hand, intervening only on specific issues and when Bevin needed support in the cabinet. As the prime minister put it: "When you've got a good dog, you don't bark yourself."[25] Standing in sharp contrast to his elegant, well-educated predecessor, Anthony Eden, Bevin was a short, fat man with a broad nose and thick lips; his suit was perpetually rumpled and his speech blunt and uncultivated. Rather than being a compromiser or bridge builder, he was a fighter. "Bevin did nothing to placate his critics," notes his principal biographer. "When he fought, he fought hard and to win. Conciliation was not in his nature; he was a 'good hater,' as the *Express* said."[26] When in spring 1946 left-wing Labour critics dared to attack his Greek policy, Bevin immediately branded them all "communists."[27] Increasingly, he focused his formidable capacity for confrontation on the Soviets. Phrases like "resistance to aggression" began to appear in his speeches. He met Soviet intransigence with an uncompromising logic of his own. His realism in dealing with the Soviets and protecting British interests was the product of years of experience at trade union negotiating sessions, his fight against communist infiltration of the trade union movement, his intimate association with Churchill and the wartime coalition government, his patriotism, and a strong sense of where the interests of his country lay.[28]

Bevin proved much more successful in manipulating the United States than had his predecessors. Winston Churchill later insisted that he would have broken up the Potsdam Conference before accepting the Byrnes-Molotov compromise, but his claim rings hollow. Britain's only sensible policy—as Attlee, Bevin, and Churchill well knew—was to put Britain's complaints on the record and then get back in step with the Americans. With one major exception, Bevin never strayed from that principle. Moreover, he believed even more than Churchill that it was essential to confront the Soviet Union—and to lead America into doing the same.[29] Most importantly he realized that unless Whitehall acted within the context of the United Nations, such a policy might well arouse latent Anglophobia and isolationism within the United States. The Labour victory in 1945 had done much to dispel fears among American liberals concerning British imperialism and power politics.[30] But suspicion that Britain was ever ready to use the United States as a cat's paw still lingered. Under Bevin, Britain became an enthusiastic participant in the United Nations and his tirades there against Russian totalitarianism and Soviet expansion had a telling effect in the United States.

Reaction in America to the outcome of the British election was mixed. Liberals and particularly the AFL-CIO were exultant. The Hearst-McCormick-Patterson press issued dire warnings, invoking Harold Laski as the new left-wing bogey. Hearst's *New York Mirror* called him "that sinister pro-Russian figure, the real Prime Minister of Great Britain."[31] Industrialists were negative, tending to see the election as a shot in the arm for planners when it was thought the "New Deal" tide was ebbing. Wall Street withheld judgment: nationalization of steel and coal would be tolerable; a takeover of the Bank of England would not. Moderate conservatives in the United States saw no real reason for alarm. British Labour, remarked one, was quite able to distinguish between liberalism, which emphasized preservation of individual freedom and civil liberty, and communism, which subordinated the individual always to the interests of the "State."[32] "As regards foreign affairs," read an embassy analysis of United States opinion, "it is taken for granted that there will be no sensational new departures."[33]

While the new Labour government attempted to put its house in order and consolidate its power, the Republican party decided that the time was right for a public attack on the Roosevelt-Truman policy of appeasement. Soviet behavior in Eastern Europe had alienated many Americans, as had the uncompromising position of Russian negotiators at San Francisco and Potsdam. The House Un-American Activities Committee (HUAAC) appeared to have died a timely death when its chairman and creator, Martin Dies (D-Tex.) of Fort Worth, decided not to stand for reelection in 1944. But when the Seventy-ninth Congress met in early January 1945, John E. Rankin (D-Miss.) succeeded in turning HUAAC into a permanent standing committee of the House with broad investigative powers.[34] In September it began its first postwar probe of American communism.

Shortly after V-E Day several congressional bodies began clamoring for the opportunity to evaluate Russian-American relations by visiting the Soviet Union. One of these, composed of seven members of the House Select Committee on Postwar Economic Policy and Planning, toured Russia and thirteen other European countries in September in an effort to decide whether or not the United States should make postwar loans to foreign governments. The Americans, led by committee chairman William M. Colmer (D-Miss.), were appalled by the police-state atmosphere they found in Russia and by the fear of Soviet domination they uncovered in Eastern Europe. Colmer subsequently told Byrnes and Truman that the Kremlin was in "desperate haste to build up a system so powerful that it could support the flood of the Red Army and pour [it] in the very near future." The United States, he declared, should end its "policy of appeasement" at once.[35] The Colmer committee subsequently was willing to endorse an American loan to Russia, but only if the Soviets met certain conditions—namely, reform of its internal system of government and abandonment of the sphere of influence it was so carefully constructing in Eastern Europe.

If it were to offer a credible alternative to Democratic foreign policy, one that would allow it to recapture the White House, the Republican party could not simply restate its traditional positions. Fiscal conservatism and even economic nationalism, if properly masked, were in vogue, but political and military isolationism were not. If the American people were opposed to the permanent stationing of United States troops overseas, they were not adverse to participating in a collective security organization. Arthur Vandenberg, Robert Taft, and their colleagues were not ready to embrace military intervention and certainly not Wilsonian internationalism. They could, however, rail at the menace of world communist revolution and Soviet imperialism, portraying members of the Roosevelt-Truman administration as appeasers and in the process appear to offer an "alternative" to Truman's "tripod" or "mediation" approach without alienating their conservative, isolationist constituents. Anticommunism was the only kind of internationalism conservative Republicans would buy because it was the only kind they could sell.

Joining Congress in demanding a harder, more intransigent policy toward Russia in fall 1945 were planners in the United States defense establishment who fastened on the policy of strategic deterrence as America's optimum defensive technique in the postwar era and who targeted the Soviet Union as the most likely threat to American security. In August and September 1945, United States military leaders reached speedy agreement on a strategy for postwar America when the Joint Chiefs of Staff and the service secretaries approved JCS 1496 and JCS 1518 respectively. In addition to the conventional goals of protecting the territorial integrity of the United States and its possessions and enhancing the nation's political, economic, and social well-being, the joint chiefs also defined a much more ambitious aim, one not previously assumed: "the maintenance of world peace, under conditions which insure the security, well-being and advancement of our country."[36] This new role coupled with advances in military technology presented unique problems. Not only had the modern airplane and warship rendered America's geographic defenses obsolete, but also there was an absence of strong allies to absorb the first blows of an aggressor. Recognizing the decisive role the United States had played in the first two world wars, any future enemy would not give America time to mobilize its forces and productive capacity—the United States would be attacked first. The only counter available was for the United States to maintain an overwhelming deterrent force and to plan for preventive war. In view of the military's ebbing confidence in the United Nations as a peacekeeping force, the JCS recommendation amounted to nothing less than a call for the United States to become the world's policeman and peacemaker.

At the same time the joint chiefs were embracing globalism, Army Intelligence (G-2) was drawing analogies between Russia in 1945 and Germany in 1938–39. Both operated as totalitarian regimes, engaged in propaganda and subversion, and maintained a closed economy. Both made temporary deals with their enemies to gain time; the Germans through the Nazi-Soviet Pact of 1939, the Soviets by adhering to the United Nations Charter. Both sought domination of Europe. Thus, a facile equation between Nazism and Stalinism made the USSR appear to military intelligence to be an ominous threat and fostered an expectation that history would repeat itself in the form of a Soviet bid for Continental or world domination.[37]

Pressure from the defense establishment and Congress seemed to the Truman administration to point toward a firmer Russian policy. At the same time, however, Congress and the American people were reluctant to pay the price—emotional and financial—for the policy of strategic deterrence envisioned by the JCS. One of the requirements the joint chiefs listed for implementation of their far-reaching plans was universal military service. But America was tired of arms and uniforms, of separations and the threat of sudden death. In the first year after V-J Day, America's military force of 12 million shrank to less than 3 million. In October 1945, Truman called for the continuation of selective service and the institution of universal military training. Both proposals aroused strong opposition in a nation that had never before known permanent conscription in peacetime. Moreover, with the war over, many Americans hoped for relief from the crushing burden of taxation that a large military program would require. Congress, particularly isolationist Republicans, reflected popular opinion; like the Republicans before the War of 1812, they simultaneously advocated frugality and confrontation with a powerful and dangerous enemy. Perhaps they believed that a continuation of the American "monopoly" on atomic energy would be enough.

Even if he had been willing to capitulate to demands from certain segments of Congress and the foreign policy establishment in fall 1945 for a hard line with Russia, the president did not have the muscle to back up such a policy, and he knew it. Consequently, he resorted to negotiation, hoping that the implied carrot of a postwar loan and the stick of America's nuclear monopoly would render the Kremlin pliable. As the London foreign ministers' meeting in September 1945 revealed, however, the administration was wasting its time.

Harry Truman was vitally interested in foreign affairs, but he had no intention of being his own secretary of state. Unfortunately he filled that post with a man who duplicated rather than complemented his strengths and weaknesses: wisdom and experience in political and domestic matters but ignorance and inexperience in foreign affairs. Moreover, James F. Byrnes was a politician with an immense ego who came to the State Department with something to prove. He rather than Harry Truman should be sitting in the White House, Byrnes felt; and if FDR had not unfairly passed him over for the vice-presidency in 1944, he would have been. The South Carolinian, in short, was determined to be his own secretary of state, indeed to be the chief architect of American foreign policy. As John Carter Vincent told B. E. F. Gage, the new head of the North American Department in the Foreign Office, it was Byrnes—not the department heads like John Hickerson and Leo Pasvolsky—who made policy.[38] In a now famous incident at the London foreign ministers' meeting, the new secretary came across Theodore Achilles who was typing a report to be sent back to the department and asked "What's this?" When Achilles explained, Byrnes exclaimed, "God Almighty, I might tell the President sometime what happened, but I'm never going to tell those little bastards at the State Department anything about it."[39]

Adding to Byrnes's problems as secretary of state was a misunderstanding between him and Truman as to how well versed the South Carolinian was in the previous president's foreign policies. The president believed his new appointee to be bright and honest, his only fault being a tendency "to look for hidden motives behind everything he was told."[40] Truman later recalled that he had appointed Byrnes because Edward Stettinius lacked ideas and because Byrnes had been cruelly treated by FDR. But, as Robert Messer points out, there was another reason. Roosevelt had pointedly taken Byrnes along to Yalta. Truman, thinking Byrnes was privy to the various conferences and strategy sessions there, named him secretary in hopes of bringing some continuity and expertise to foreign policy-making. As Byrnes's notes indicate, however, he was allowed to attend only those conferences that Roosevelt wished Congress and the public to hear about. Byrnes led everyone to believe that he knew more than he did. His ignorance also led him to portray the Yalta accords in a far more favorable light than they deserved. When the truth emerged and the president began to uncover the nuances of the agreements, the revelation embarrassed both men and strained their relationship.[41]

Though Byrnes was committed to seeing that the Soviet Union lived up to the Yalta accords in regard to Eastern Europe, that is, that occupation authorities there permit free elections and free access to Westerners, he was not a hard-liner. He was determined to be independent of the military and those who had so influenced Roosevelt during his last days in the presidency and Truman during his first. In early August he remarked to a subordinate that Admiral William Leahy still thought he was acting secretary of state as he had been under FDR, but he, Byrnes, would show him differently. The new secretary was also a close friend of Joseph E. Davies. For Byrnes, diplomacy, like politics, was more process than substance. Diplomacy consisted of identifying respective positions and then fashioning a compromise. And, just as Roosevelt, Byrnes believed in personal diplomacy. Soviet-American differences could be worked out through dialogue between him and Molotov or him and Stalin. Unfortunately, Byrnes had the same amount of luck FDR had had with this approach. For the hot-tempered Irishman from South Carolina, frustration bred aggression.[42]

The avowed purpose of the London foreign ministers' conference attended by representatives from the USSR, the United States, France, China, and Great Britain was to draw up peace treaties for Germany's wartime allies: Finland, Hungary, Rumania, and Bulgaria. Moscow seemed willing to tolerate democracy in Finland and possibly Hungary, but American observers in Bucharest and Sofia accused Soviet occupation forces of trying to set up puppet governments in Rumania and Bulgaria. Truman, Byrnes, and their advisers realized that the United States lacked the power to influence events in Rumania and Bulgaria directly, but hoped that, by delaying the signing of peace treaties and withholding diplomatic recognition, they could force the Kremlin to at least hold plebiscites and agree to admit Western correspondents.

As numerous historians of the Cold War have noted, Byrnes went to London with the expectation that Russia's fear of the bomb and its need for a postwar reconstruction loan from the United States would be the hands that would part the iron curtain that separated Bulgaria and Rumania from the West. Late in August the secretary of state told John J. McCloy that he intended at London to negotiate with the implied threat of the bomb in his pocket, and on September 4 Henry Stimson recorded in his diary a similar conversation with Byrnes. In addition, remarks Byrnes made to Ernest Bevin during and after the London meeting indicated that the State Department was still considering a postwar loan to Russia and that economics continued to be an important area for exerting pressure on the Soviet Union.[43]

To Byrnes's dismay, however, the Russians were more stubborn than ever at London. Soviet Foreign Minister Vyacheslav Molotov repeated Stalin's Potsdam claim for Russian control of former Italian colonies in Africa and accused the Americans of supporting anti-Russian elements in Eastern Europe. Russia's chief diplomat made his government's position clear; unless the British and Americans signed peace treaties with the Groza government in Rumania and the left-wing regime in Bulgaria, both of whom were "friendly" to the Soviet Union, he would not accept the Anglo-American draft terminating hostilities with Italy. In an effort to conciliate the Russians, Byrnes on September 22 gave in to their demand for the exclusion of France and China from further discussion of the satellite peace treaties. Two days later, Molotov demanded establishment in Japan of an Allied Control Council composed of representatives from the United States, the Soviet Union, Great Britain, and China to supervise occupation policies. Byrnes refused to surrender Italy's former African possessions and to allow meaningful Soviet participation in the reconstruction of Japan. After Truman issued a futile appeal to Stalin, the conference broke up in early October.[44]

The London foreign ministers' meeting disappointed and angered Jimmy

Byrnes. He later told the cabinet that in his opinion Moscow had no intention of living up to the Yalta accords and its word was not to be trusted. Yet, though frustrated, Byrnes was not ready to call it quits. When Walter Brown remarked that America was going to have to fight another war to prevent Russian domination of Europe, Byrnes responded that war was out of the question. Moreover, though he despaired of Molotov, Byrnes still had hopes for Stalin. The only solution to the Soviet-American impasse, he declared, was to have another meeting in Moscow in the very near future where he could deal with Stalin personally and directly.[45]

Despite the tough stance he took in his widely publicized Navy Day speech of October 27, Truman had not yet given up hope of reaching an accommodation with the Russians either. Stresses and strains such as those that had appeared at the London Conference were bound to occur among allies who had fought a long war, he told himself. Serious differences existed but they could be worked out if everyone was patient. On October 15 he met with Henry Wallace and told him that Stalin was "a fine man who wanted to do the right thing." Wallace observed that the primary goal of British foreign policy was to promote an "unbreachable break" between Russia and the United States. According to Wallace: "The President said he agreed. I said Britain's game in international affairs has always been intrigue. The President said he agreed. I said . . . we must not play her game. The President agreed."[46]

On November 25 Byrnes proposed another foreign ministers' meeting to take place in Moscow before Christmas. The secretary of state recorded in his memoirs that he had called the conference in part because he found it difficult to press for more authority for American representatives in Rumania and Bulgaria while denying Russian requests for a role in the occupation of Japan. Moreover, he realized that as long as the Rumanian and Bulgarian peace treaties remained unsigned, the Russians would have an excuse to keep troops in these countries. In his proposal to Molotov Byrnes had deliberately excluded the French and Chinese and, even more astonishingly, he did not consult with Bevin beforehand or even make the proposal simultaneously to London and Moscow.[47] Indeed, Bevin first learned of the proposed meeting from the British ambassador to the Soviet Union.

The foreign secretary was hurt, angry, and incredulous. The British had been dismayed by the Hopkins and Davies missions and the Truman administration's willingness to embrace the Lippmann-Swing strategy of mediation, but the Foreign Office was outraged at Byrnes's sudden, independent action in calling the Moscow Conference. In the first place, Bevin had chosen to make a major issue of Molotov's effort to exclude the French and Chinese from the London deliberations. In a policy address to the House of Commons on October 9, he had asked how Molotov's suggestion could be reconciled with the United Nations Charter, which "lays upon the five Powers as permanent members of the Security Council a special responsibility to maintain the peace of the world," and blamed the breakup of the meeting on Molotov's ploy. Now Byrnes was proposing to meet on virtually the same issues without France and China. Bevin and the Foreign Office feared, moreover, that at the Moscow Conference British interests would become the sacrificial lamb in a new United States effort to appease the Soviet Union. "Mr. Truman and his associates," Halifax wrote Bevin, "are disposed to chart their course in the manner best calculated to propitiate what they conceive to be the prevailing sentiments of Congress and of important pressure groups," and he assumed that this sensitivity would produce appeasement and isolationism.[48] Hugh Dalton offered a typically blunter evaluation: "I have the sensation that the Democratic Party in the U.S.A. is reverting to what it used to be before Roosevelt's time, with a strong Irish-American flavor, and not much sympathetic understanding towards us."[49] Byrnes in particular was perceived to be a shallow politician who was dedicated to compromise for compromise's sake, just the sort of person who would make concessions to the Soviet Union in areas of vital concern to Great Britain merely for the sake of an agreement. But one suspects that the most important element in the British reaction was a fear of being deserted during a period of weakness and insecurity. Bevin had not ruled out compromise with Russia, as he made clear in his speech to the House. Byrnes's independent action had hurt his official feelings and deepened Whitehall's sense of isolation.

Bevin's efforts to divert Byrnes from his independent ways before the Moscow meeting proved fruitless. On November 6 Ambassador Gilbert Winant cabled Byrnes from London: "Situation serious. Unilateral action deeply resented by both Bevin and Cabinet. Bevin refuses to talk tonight or attend conference Moscow."[50] When Byrnes made no response, Bevin cracked first. Several days later Winant reported that the foreign secretary was "desperately anxious" to talk with Byrnes. If the secretary of state would stop off in London on his way to Moscow and discuss an agenda, Winant advised, Bevin would probably attend. Byrnes rejected what he considered to be a proposal to gang up on the Russians and implied that he was going to meet with Soviet leaders with or without the British. Bevin and his colleagues knew, of course, that their attendance at the Moscow Conference was a fait accompli. If Britain stayed home, it ran the risk of assuming the role played by the Czechs at the Munich Conference. The foreign minister and the rest of the cabinet consoled themselves with the thought that anything was preferable to United States isolationism.[51] Nonetheless, Bevin arrived in Moscow on December 15 in a foul mood. George F. Kennan, then minister-counselor to Averell Harriman, recorded in his diary:

Bevin looked highly disgusted with the whole procedure. It was easy to see from his face that he found himself in a position he did not like. He did not want to come to Moscow in the first place and was well aware that nothing good could come of the meeting. The Russians knew his position and were squeezing the last drop out of it. As for Byrnes, Bevin saw in him only another cocky and unreliable Irishman, similar to ones that he had known in his experience as a docker and labor leader. Byrnes, as the British saw it, had consistently shown himself negligent of British feelings and quite unconcerned for Anglo-American relations.[52]

After the opening session Bevin asked for a private conversation with Byrnes, and on December 17 they met at the American Embassy. Bevin declared that the Kremlin was busily trying to undermine Britain's position in the Middle East. Moscow refused to withdraw its troops from northern Iran and was fomenting revolution in Azerbaijan, that country's northernmost province.[53] Moreover, Stalin was demanding that Britain withdraw its troops from Greece and pressing Turkey for permission to construct a naval base on the Bosporus. The Kremlin, Bevin warned, was building a "Monroe area"—sphere of influence—that would stretch from the Baltic to the Adriatic in the West to Port Arthur in the East.

What Bevin wanted, of course, was a common Anglo-American front to halt the Soviet advance. But it was not yet to be. Byrnes was determined to work out an agreement, and he saw not consensus but conflict in overt Anglo-American cooperation against the Russians. Given United States coyness, Bevin felt he had no choice but to approach the Russians alone. In discussions between the foreign secretary and Molotov on the eighteenth and Stalin on the nineteenth, the two powers quickly outlined their differences but made no progress toward resolving them.

Russian intransigence and American aloofness frayed Bevin's nerves to the breaking point. Charles Bohlen recalled that the former dockworker, after liberally imbibing at dinner one evening, returned to a plenary session in a belligerent mood. When Molotov attacked Britain for past sins in international affairs, Bevin rose to his feet, his hands knotted into fists, and started toward Molotov, saying, "I've heard enough of this, I 'ave," and for a moment it appeared that the two foreign ministers would resort to fisticuffs.[54]

The stage was now set for Byrnes to perform his political magic; he met privately with Stalin on Christmas Eve. Byrnes's chief objective in Moscow was to resolve the impasse over Rumania and Bulgaria so that work on the peace treaties with Germany's former satellites could begin; to his surprise and delight, the Russian leader immediately began giving ground. Stalin emphasized his country's determination to have only friendly governments along its border. He then conceded that it might be possible to broaden the governments of both Bulgaria and Rumania in such a way as to "satisfy Mr. Byrnes." It was subsequently agreed that a three-power commission organize, go to Rumania, and advise the government to take in two additional ministers. The Soviet government itself would assume the initiative in expanding the Bulgarian regime. In return, the secretary of state agreed to make token concessions on the issue of Japan. The United States would establish an Allied Council made up of representatives of the United States, the British Commonwealth, China, and the Soviet Union, which would consult with and advise General Douglas MacArthur on occupation policies.[55]

Byrnes was jubilant. He believed he had ended the impasse created at the London Conference. But Stalin's concessions in Eastern Europe no more weakened Soviet influence in that area than Byrnes's gestures in the Far East undermined American authority in Japan. And when the secretary of state returned to the United States, he quickly learned that a variety of powerful groups and individuals in Britain and the United States considered his "achievement" at best a superficial compromise and at worst appeasement of a totalitarian power bent on world domination.

Between September 1945 and November 1946, Republican criticism of American foreign policy approached pre–Pearl Harbor intensity. In October James Reston reported mounting GOP dissatisfaction with Byrnes's failure to ask its advice before formulating policy. Chief articulator of that dissatisfaction was John Foster Dulles, the Republican party's unofficial spokesman on foreign affairs. Byrnes had taken Dulles to the London Conference but had not consulted him, thus leaving the impression that Dulles was along just to provide a Republican rubber stamp. On his return, Dulles reported to a closed meeting of the Council on Foreign Relations that the United States delegation had "set sail for the Conference without proper preparation and that the policy which it put forward at the meeting had not been discussed with the Foreign Relations Committee of the Senate or the Foreign Affairs Committee of the House, nor did it have a firm root in American public opinion."[56] But Dulles's disaffection did not stem from personal pique alone. The New Yorker distrusted Byrnes's tendency to "compromise" and he favored a stiffer line toward the Soviet Union. As he told Charles Halleck, the United States ought to seek to make common cause with the other great powers but repudiate "great power domination of the world" and reject the thesis that world peace required America "to endorse alien doctrines or to abandon efforts to seek justice for the weaker peoples of the world."[57]

In addition, Dulles was very much a part of the movement within the GOP to offer an alternative to Democratic foreign policy in 1946 and again in 1948, an alternative that would go beyond the Democrats in calling on the United States to confront the Soviet Union. What made the movement within the Republican party for an alternative foreign policy so powerful was that it was supported by both the congressional and presidential wings. GOP zenophobes from the heartland joined Dulles in criticizing Byrnes and Truman. American policy toward Russia, Karl Mundt (R-S.Dak.) and Francis Bolton (R-Ohio) wrote the president, "is lacking on the side of firmness." The United States should approve in Eastern Europe and the Middle East only those Russian policies that conformed to an American standard of political morality. They even called for Harriman's replacement since "he served as our ambassador during a period when the approved American policy followed the appeasement line toward Russia."[58] Herbert Brownell, chairman of the Republican National Committee, declared to his constituents in October 1945 that the London Foreign Ministers' Conference had been "a failure" and called for a clear and comprehensive statement of foreign policy.[59] In a speech he prepared for delivery on the floor of the Senate, Robert Taft predicted that if World War III—most certainly an atomic war—came, it would be due to mistakes in American foreign policy. Appeasement of aggression did not work in the 1930s and it would not work in the 1940s or 1950s either. "Munich led to World War II," he wrote. "Yalta, Potsdam and Moscow may well lead to a war which may destroy civilization."[60]

The GOP foreign policy initiative in fall 1945 represented something of a personal and political triumph for Arthur Vandenberg. He had been trying to forge an alliance between the two wings of the party throughout the war. The congressional faction, however, continued to express disgust at the "me-tooism" of Thomas Dewey and Dulles, while eastern liberals chafed at the isolationist albatross their heartland colleagues had draped around the party's neck. The advent of Harry Truman and Soviet expansion in Europe and the Far East opened the door for a rapprochement that Vandenberg hoped would lead first to a Republican majority in Congress in 1946 and then to a Republican president in 1948.

Meanwhile, the period of mediation culminating with Byrnes's unilateral calling of the Moscow Conference had plunged the British foreign policy establishment into a pit of despondency and provoked a variety of theories as to why America was once again refusing to recognize that Anglo-American strategic and economic interests were inextricably intertwined. And, of course, it provoked an equal number of stratagems as to how to get the cousins to see the light. None of those stratagems recognized that the Truman administration's freedom of action was being increasingly circumscribed by a conservative Congress in which the balance of power was held by Republicans committed to a strident if toothless Russophobia. Some denizens of Whitehall fell back on the familiar and comfortable explanation that the Truman administration was basically midwestern and that Midwesterners—Republican or Democratic—were parochial, agricultural, undereducated, introverted, zenophobic, and paranoid—in other words, unalterably isolationist.

J. G. Donnelley, who had spent eight years in America, six in the Midwest, claimed that sibling theory was more appropriate in explaining American behavior than geography. He argued that there was no real difference among regions in their views on international relations generally and Great Britain specifically. "A leading psychologist told me the other day," the head of the North American section told his colleagues, "that in his quite considerable experience of treating Americans, mostly persons of intellectual attainment, he had never found one who did not have a feeling of inferiority in relation to Europe generally and most acutely in relation to Britain." Britain, Donnelley declared, is the elder sister who inspires feelings of both close dependence and resentment. As long as the younger sibling perceived her elder to be prosperous and strong, she acted with aloofness and even hostility. But when Britain faced serious difficulties, as after Dunkirk, "they feel sympathetic, rather conscience stricken and most anxious to help." The problem, he concluded, was how to bring out this more helpful side of the American mind without being actually obliged to stage an obvious crisis.[61] Jock Balfour, counselor in the British Embassy in Washington, shared Donnelley's views. "Old attitudes of mind about the ability of the British to outsmart the innocent Americans in international negotiations still enter into the emotional makeup of this people," he wrote, "and we must consequently . . . make allowance for [a] latent inferiority complex in our dealings with them."[62]

Others continued to trace the "fickleness" of American foreign policy to the United States Constitution; it provided for too much public input into the decision-making process and too little cabinet responsibility. "My own theory is that 140 million experts on international affairs is too many even for the U.S.," Halifax wrote.[63]

Though some continued to suggest that Britain act as mediator between the superpowers, such a course was out of the question by late 1945. Britain's lifeline in the eastern Mediterranean and its strategic and economic position in the Middle East were being threatened. Gradually a consensus began to emerge within the British foreign policy establishment that the best course was to be realistic. Britain should not dwell on historic grandeur and past achievements but should set about putting its own damaged house in order, defining its interests in various parts of the world, and frankly sharing power with the United States in areas where those interests were being threatened by the Soviets. "The more we can stress our vigor and vitality and our determination to win back what we have sacrificed," Paul Mason wrote, "the better hearing we shall secure in America. . . . Americans appreciate realism even if they do not always display it in themselves."[64] That consensus, of course, paralleled the thinking of the dominant element in the Labour party.

These speculations did not, however, provide a solution to the central dilemma in British foreign policy: how to overcome a deep-seated Anglophobia and persuade the United States to join Britain in containing the Soviet Union. Following extensive explanations by the Washington embassy, Bevin and other decision makers in London began to recognize that it was possible for those in charge of American foreign policy to practice realpolitik only within the context of an international collective security organization. Initially, British officials had despaired of America's apparent obsession with the United Nations, seeing it as a form of escapism. "There seems to be a tendency to regard the UNO as a *deus ex machina*, which will relieve the U.S. of some of the responsibilities arising from her position in the world, rather than thinking of it as an experimental structure, which must be tested for strength before heavy burdens are laid on it," noted Foreign Office analyst Dennis Brogan.[65] America's penchant for "universalizing" their "humanitarianism" had only increased with mounting international tensions, Donnelley noted.[66] Balfour and Halifax repeatedly urged Whitehall to turn this vice into a virtue and work within the United Nations. The United Nations Charter was the Truman administration's general authority from Congress to "involve or entangle" the United States in questions not previously regarded as American concerns, they argued. Moreover, by working through the United Nations and especially the Security Council, Britain could make the United States less apprehensive about appearing to "gang up" with it against Russia.[67] "Americans," Balfour told London, "are aware in their heart of hearts that the continuity of their country's moral values is inseparably bound up with the welfare of Great Britain."[68] By defending the charter and using it to indict Soviet imperialism, Britain could raise this sublimated truth to the level of consciousness. The opening session of the United Nations General Assembly, scheduled for London in early 1946, provided Whitehall with an opportunity to test this strategy.

The dawn of the new year found the average American frightened and confused. As George Marshall told Halifax, "the American people are passing through an emotional crisis." The United States had learned the folly of appeasement and unpreparedness, but it wanted nothing so much as to enjoy the fruits of victory. The bomb made confrontation with the Soviets a terrifying prospect. Yet the existence of repression and totalitarianism in areas occupied by the Red Army could not be denied. "In articles that resemble nothing so much as the strophe and anti-strophe of a funeral dirge," the British Embassy reported to Whitehall, "Lippmann and Dorothy Thompson have played Jeremiah and Cassandra to one another."[69] Truman and Byrnes's reassurances that the Soviets could be reasoned with, that peaceful coexistence was possible, were seductive, but what if the Republicans were right? Only with the greatest effort had Hitler been stopped; if the United States allowed Stalin to go too far, the democracies might not win a third world war. In desperation, the American people looked to the United Nations for an answer.

The inaugural session of the United Nations General Assembly opened in January 1946 amid pomp and ceremony, but quickly degenerated into a bitter Anglo-Russian dispute over Iran. In mid-December 1945, Moscow Radio had announced the formation of an autonomous Republic of Azerbaijan in northwestern Iran. Government troops sent to crush the revolt were turned back by Soviet occupation forces. Bevin had confronted Stalin at Moscow with accusations of Soviet interference in Iranian internal affairs but had gotten nowhere. Byrnes had completely dissociated himself from those representations. Not only did he want agreement with Russia over Eastern Europe, but he also feared that if the United States identified itself with British interests in Iran—specifically the United Kingdom's oil concessions including the invaluable refinery at Abadan—it would sacrifice its influence in countries of the Middle East that were struggling against European imperialism. Ignoring advice from the United States and Britain to remain silent for the moment, the Iranian government brought formal charges at the United Nations meeting against Russia for instigating the Azerbaijanian revolt. Convinced that Whitehall was behind the Iranian move, the Russians retaliated by calling on the United Nations to denounce Britain for retaining troops in Greece. Andrei Vyshinski and Ernest Bevin minced few words in the terrific row that followed. Bevin took the high ground, asserting that there was a tremendous moral difference between a nation that kept its troops in a country against the government's will, as was the case with Russia in Iran, and one that stationed troops in a nation with the consent of its government, as was the case with Britain in Greece. The United States, hoping to spare the United Nations the stigma of a Russian or British veto, played its mediator role for what would be the last time. Byrnes worked out a compromise whereby Russia and Iran agreed to bilateral talks to be held in Moscow.[70]

Americans were shocked by what they perceived to be the Kremlin's efforts to torpedo the United Nations just as it was being launched. Piecemeal aggression by a large and powerful totalitarian state against a defenseless neighbor was all too familiar. Bevin's defense of Iran in the name of the United Nations Charter struck a responsive chord in Americans of virtually all political persuasions and geographic locations. Resistance to Soviet expansion in defense of the Suez Canal was one thing but a tough stance in the name of self-determination and collective security was quite another. "In making a stand in defense of the fundamental principles of international conduct," J. G. Donnelley correctly noted, "Mr. Bevin appears to Americans not just as a British statesman but as a champion of the Charter which is not only based on the same fundamental principles but is a declaration of American policy which both Houses of the American legislature endorsed with a degree of unanimity rare in their country's history."[71] After Bevin's speeches at the London United Nations meeting, Whitehall officials became positively euphoric for a time about the possibility of seizing leadership of the Anglo-American partnership. B. E. F. Gage pompously observed: "America will always see their relationship with us in truer perspective when they can compare consistent, constructive, and principled statesmanship on our part with vacillation and lack of principle on the part of their own international politicians. We can exert considerable influence on American thought this way."[72]

By January 1946 British officials were noting that Americans were finally perceiving that in the "power and inscrutability of Russia, there may be a threat to the 'one world' upon which they had been relying in order to be free to continue their own secure, prosperous, and pleasant way of life."[73] Contributing to that perception was a rare public address delivered by Joseph Stalin on February 9, 1946. Stalin's speech, a "pre-election" address designed to galvanize the masses into a 99 percent plus mandate for his regime, dealt primarily with domestic affairs. The Soviet leader boasted about the wartime accomplishments of the Red Army, the rapid industrialization of the Soviet economy, and the unity of the Soviet Union's heterogeneous population. More ominous, however, was Stalin's declaration that both world wars had been caused by "contradictions" in capitalism and until and unless these contradictions were eliminated, the world would continue to have wars. To prepare for any "eventuality," Stalin called for three consecutive five-year plans to increase Russia's annual steel production from twenty to sixty million tons by 1960.[74]

Some Americans, like liberal journalist Vera Micheles Dean, considered the speech merely a chauvinistic appeal to the Russian people to make further sacrifices to complete Moscow's five-year plan, but most took a much more pessimistic view of the address. Eric Severeid and the influential Walter Lippmann believed that the Soviet leader had acceded fully to the "two-camp thesis" and was saying in effect that permanent peaceful coexistence was impossible. H. Freeman Matthews, head of the Division of European Affairs, told Dean Acheson and Jimmy Byrnes: "Stalin's speech constitutes the most important and authoritative guide to post-war Soviet policy. It should be required reading for everyone in the Department. It will henceforth be the communist and fellow-traveler Bible throughout the world."[75]

Perhaps the most important byproduct of Stalin's two-camp speech was George F. Kennan's famous long telegram of February 22. Kennan, a career foreign service officer with a reputation as a Kremlinologist, believed that the United States committed a dangerous error in not making clear what its interests and wishes were in Eastern and Central Europe. "Why could we not make a decent and definitive compromise," he wrote ". . .—divide Europe frankly into spheres of influence—keep ourselves out of the Russian sphere and keep the Russians out of ours." In refusing to place any limits on Russian expansion, the United States had confused Stalin and his associates, "causing them constantly to wonder whether they are asking too little or whether it was some kind of trap."[76] Britain and the United States, Kennan wrote from Moscow, should give up their hopes of a permanent resolution of issues with the Soviet Union. Internal political necessity, not Anglo-American policy, determined Stalin's foreign policy. Kennan therefore concluded that the West must reject "one worldism" and accept the harsh reality of "two camps." Rather than continue the futile search for a postwar settlement with Russia, the Western democracies should move toward making their camp a model of liberal principles and economic prosperity.[77]

The reaction in Washington to this explanation of Soviet behavior was, in Kennan's words, "nothing less than sensational." President Truman read it, the State Department sent Kennan a message of commendation, and Secretary of the Navy James V. Forrestal had it reproduced and made required reading for the entire upper echelon of the United States officer corps. The telegram arrived just as pressures were converging from several other sources to "get tough with Russia."[78] In the week following Stalin's speech, H. Freeman Matthews, Elbridge Durbrow, and Dean Acheson met with Lippmann and other advocates of mediation and used Kennan's arguments to persuade them that the Kremlin was implacably hostile to capitalism and democracy.[79]

The anti-Soviet trend in American opinion was, then, a product of Soviet rhetoric, the Republican search for an alternative foreign policy, and also the growing influence within the foreign policy establishment of a clique that had taken charge of the State Department in 1944 and whose views were shared by Averell Harriman and his staff in Moscow. This faction was directly and indirectly cultivated by British diplomats. "With a weak presidential leadership, an oscillating public opinion and constantly harassed by pressure groups," Donnelley observed to his colleagues, "the task of the stubborn men in responsible quarters in evolving a consistent foreign policy suitable to deal effectively with the all important problem of the Soviet [*sic*] is no easy one."[80] But with a little help from their British friends, they might succeed. Frank Roberts and George Kennan, as has been noted, frequently compared notes, and their views on Soviet foreign policy developed in parallel.[81] Who was leading whom was not exactly clear, but the British certainly felt that Bevin's stand in the United Nations and private contacts between British and American diplomats had been responsible for the new backbone apparent in American attitudes toward Russia. Responding to Kennan's long telegram, Roberts observed to his colleagues in London that for the time being the Americans seemed willing to take the advice of "the embassy here to eschew wishful thinking, and to take a more realistic line in regard to the Soviet Union."[82] Whether he meant the British or the American Embassy was unclear. What is clear is that the British foreign policy establishment no less than the Republican party and Soviet bellicosity played a role in Truman's decision to get tough.

As Soviet policy toward Germany, Eastern Europe, and Iran became more intransigent, and as bureaucratic and political pressure mounted on the White House to pursue a more aggressive policy, Harry Truman became less and less happy with the results of the Moscow Conference and with Jimmy Byrnes. Byrnes's reputation as a compromiser, which seemed to be borne out by the Moscow agreements on Rumania and Bulgaria, became not only a target for the GOP but also a matter of concern and discussion among members of the foreign policy establishment and Truman's advisers. Admiral Leahy, who by late 1945 had come to regard almost anyone who would consider agreement with the Russians as an appeaser, compared the Moscow accords with what Chamberlain had done at Munich. Byrnes had, moreover, alienated both Harriman and Kennan at Moscow. Harriman complained that Byrnes was "stiff and unwilling to listen" to advisers, and Kennan noted that during negotiations Byrnes had not set objectives, was often unprepared, and relied instead on his mental agility.[83] Harry Truman was clearly disenchanted with the Moscow agreements. After reviewing the negotiations, the president put his thoughts down on paper. He objected particularly to Byrnes's failure to secure concessions from Russia on the international control of atomic energy and on the withdrawal of Russian troops from Iran. He charged that the Russians intended to invade Turkey and seize the Black Sea straits. Truman recorded his determination not to recognize the governments of Rumania and Bulgaria until their composition had been radically changed. It was unwise, he wrote, for the United States to attempt compromise with the Soviets any longer. There was only one posture that would work—firmness backed by military force.[84]

The president was also aware that the prevailing political winds had set sharply against Soviet-American rapprochement. Opinion polls showed that at the time of Japan's surrender, 54 percent of the American people polled in a national survey had been willing to trust the Russians to cooperate with the United States in the postwar world. By the end of February 1946, the number stood at 35 percent. Truman fully realized the importance of this shift, especially in view of the clear indications that the Republicans intended to capitalize on it in the midterm elections in 1946.[85]

Opinion polls showed further that as popular distrust of Moscow increased, so did public disapproval of the president and his policies. Polls taken before Potsdam while Truman was still in his honeymoon period indicated an 87 percent approval rate for the way the president was handling his job. A year later that figure had halved to 43 percent.[86] "Mr. Truman's present situation is distinctly unsatisfactory," noted J. G. Donnelley, that outspoken observer of the American political scene. "Each successful new experiment naturally reduces the likelihood and the corresponding hopes that by his method of trial and error he will eventually learn how to provide the strong leadership which the United States obviously needs."[87]

Sensing that the time had at last arrived to seize the initiative in foreign policy, Arthur Vandenberg rose on the floor of the Senate on February 27, 1946, to deliver one of the most famous speeches of the Cold War era. "What is Russia up to now?" he asked. He went on to review Soviet activities in the Balkans, in Manchuria, and in Poland. Two rival ideologies, democracy and communism, now found themselves face to face. Peaceful coexistence was possible only if the United States was as vigorous and firm as Russia in defending its interests. The United States should establish limits beyond which it would not compromise. Vandenberg went on to praise the work of every major participant in the Moscow Conference except Jimmy Byrnes. The galleries gave the Michigan Republican a standing ovation and his colleagues lined up to congratulate him.[88]

It should be noted that, in calling for a policy of resistance to Soviet expansion, Vandenberg was not declaring his support for an Anglo-American alliance—tacit or otherwise. He wanted the United States, he said, to uphold the United Nations Charter and exert "moral leadership." The former isolationist made it plain that he would tolerate no power politics, no special relationships. The United Nations was the place and the means: "Mr. [Andrei] Vyshinski," said Vandenberg, had used the Security Council to defend Russia's interest and Bevin had used it on more than one "eloquent and courageous" occasion.[89] Clearly, Jimmy Byrnes should do the same.

The Truman administration responded almost immediately. Speaking to the Overseas Press Club on February 28, Byrnes outlined America's new get-tough policy. Some observers believed Byrnes's speech to be a hastily prepared response to Vandenberg's address—"the second Vandenberg concerto," one reporter dubbed it—but the Press Club speech was more than that. It marked the culmination of forces—political, bureaucratic, and diplomatic—that were impelling the Truman administration toward a policy of confrontation with the Soviet Union. Byrnes declared that any nation that kept troops on another nation's soil without its consent, that prolonged unnecessarily the peacemaking process, and that seized enemy property before a reparations agreement had been worked out violated the charter of the new world organization. Byrnes called on America to perform its duty as a great power and act not only to ensure its own security, but the peace of the world as well.[90] America could not and would not permit aggression "by coercion or pressure or by subterfuges such as political infiltration."[91]

This "new departure" in American foreign policy did not have as its objective the eviction of the Soviet Union from Central and Eastern Europe. Although it could not admit so publicly for political reasons, the Truman administration was no more willing to challenge Russia's domination of its sphere of influence in Eastern Europe than the Roosevelt administration had been.[92] While Truman and Byrnes might, in response to mounting GOP criticism, rhetorically roll back the iron curtain, their real goal was to hold the line in Europe and to protect British interests in the eastern Mediterranean and Middle East. These interests were now regarded as vital to America's own well-being.

The Economist accurately posed the dilemma facing Washington in spring 1946:

If they [the Americans] genuinely regard Britain as a valuable partner, they cannot afford to see a steady weakening of Britain's position in the world. They are traditionally blind to this point, until war and imminent collapse drive home the lesson. In wartime they recognize their own vital interest in British security. But in peacetime they are so obsessed with the need to "avoid playing Britain's game" that they run the risk of lending themselves to everybody else's game. Can they be persuaded to anticipate a little the last ditch and to realize that the Middle East is as vital to Britain as the Far East to America or Eastern Europe to Russia and that it is an American as well as a British interest to see that the position is not whittled away?[93]

The answer to *The Economist*'s question, given in Washington's response to the final stages of the Iranian crisis, was a resounding yes.

The appointed day for Soviet troop withdrawals from Iran—March 2—came and went. Moscow announced that it would remove some of its personnel, but others would stay until the situation had been clarified. The Soviets continued to insist on autonomy for Azerbaijan and the right to maintain troops in the north, but now added a demand for the formation of a Soviet-Iranian Oil Company in which Russia would own the controlling interest. On March 5 the State Department charged Moscow with violating the Teheran Declaration and called for an immediate withdrawal of all Soviet troops.[94] Instead, on the morning of March 6, 1946, the State Department received word from its vice-consul in Azerbaijan that "exceptionally heavy troop movements" were taking place, not toward the Russian border, but in the direction of Turkey, Iraq, and the Iranian capital of Teheran.

Meanwhile, the Soviet-Iranian bilateral negotiations had gotten nowhere and, with the encouragement of the United States, the shah's ministers decided to submit the issue of Soviet troop movements to the United Nations Security Council, which was scheduled to meet again in New York on March 25. When the delegates to the world organization gathered at Hunter College, the Russians tried to keep the Iranian complaint off the agenda. Seeing that he could not succeed, Andrei Gromyko dramatically walked out of the chamber. His departure was a parliamentary and propaganda ploy, but one that backfired in the United States.

To the American people it seemed that Russia was thumbing its nose at the last great hope of mankind. In a dramatic reversal of events, the Iranian and Soviet governments one week later announced a formal agreement calling for the withdrawal of Soviet troops by early May and the recognition of Iranian sovereignty over Azerbaijan.[95]

Truman's most recent biographer argues that the Soviets backed down in the 1946 Iranian crisis because the prospect of a breakdown in international relations so soon after a devastating war was too much to contemplate. But there is another explanation. In his recently discovered secret diary, the man from Missouri recorded that the Russians decided to be cooperative because he threatened to use military force to defend Iranian sovereignty. Whether Truman actually menaced the Soviets or merely contemplated such action, he had clearly decided to take extreme measures to defend Anglo-American interests around the world.[96]

The Iranian crisis put the Russians on notice that henceforth Washington would regard the Middle East as an Anglo-American sphere of interest. The Truman administration notified the American people and the rest of the world of that intention by sponsoring a bellicose speech by Winston Churchill, a speech delivered just as the Iranian situation was reaching a climax. In October 1945 the president of Westminster College in Fulton, Missouri, learned that Churchill planned to visit the United States in winter 1946. Westminster had a fund to attract famous speakers and perhaps the college could use the Missourian in the White House to capture the most famous orator of all. Truman subsequently endorsed the invitation and offered to introduce Churchill if he accepted.[97]

As both Churchill and Truman knew, the former prime minister's talk would be read by virtually every literate American with an interest in foreign affairs. The public was frightened and insecure. Russia's shadow did indeed hang heavy over the world, and, though the United States was sole possessor of the atom bomb, the very existence of a doomsday device seemed to make the shadow far more menacing than it otherwise might have been. Innate Anglophobia aside, Winston Churchill was probably America's favorite foreigner and his defeat in 1945 had come as a profound shock.[98]

Thus it was that Harry Truman introduced Winston Churchill to a much wider audience than the students and faculty at Westminster College on March 5, 1946. "I know," Truman said, "that he will have something constructive to say to the world." Churchill made the obligatory reference to Westminster and began. "War and Tyranny," he asserted, were threatening the world once again. An iron curtain had descended over Central Europe and behind that curtain Soviet power was stamping out liberty and democracy. "It is not our duty at this time when difficulties are so numerous to interfere forcibly in the internal affairs of countries whom we have not conquered in wars," he declared. But Anglo-America had a right, indeed a duty, to defend Western civilization against further totalitarian incursions. He called for a strengthening of the "fraternal association" of English-speaking peoples as the surest safeguard against future wars. "If the population of the English-speaking Commonwealth be added to that of the United States," he said in conclusion, "with all that such cooperation implies in the air, on the sea and in science and industry, there will be no quivering precarious balance of power to offer its temptation to ambition or adventure, on the contrary, there will be overwhelming assurance of security."[99]

The response to Churchill's address in the United States was swift and much of it was negative. "Why did you lend yourself today as a sounding board for Churchill to preach from?" Fred Arkin asked Truman. "Who on earth gives a good damn what British imperialists would like us to do," he said, adding: "I keep telling myself you can't be as unenlightened and inane as you seem."[100] Nonetheless, Americans could not forget that Winston Churchill had sounded the clarion call against Hitler. The prophet had spoken again and, though his vision was frightening, a large number of Americans felt that it must be taken into account. Among the American press, only left-wing writers and broadcasters denounced the speech as war-mongering and imperialistic. Even those declared that it was the "bad" rather than the "good" Mr. Churchill speaking. More moderate opinion was willing to admit the validity of Churchill's statements regarding Soviet imperialism, the iron curtain, and America's global responsibilities but to recoil from the remedy prescribed: an Anglo-American alliance. Asserting that no other statesman—American or foreign—could have gotten away with such a speech at so little cost, Halifax wrote Bevin that all but extreme Anglophobes and isolationists "concede that there is something wrong with the tooth in question; some are inclined to suspect that the condition may be grave indeed; but almost all shy with real or simulated horror from the idea of a drill and complain that the dentist is notorious for his love of drastic remedies, and that surely modern medicine had provided more painless methods of cure."[101] The reaction in Congress was much the same—with Republicans and southern Democrats on the whole approving the attack on communism and warning against appeasement while expressing varying degrees of skepticism about the prospect of an Anglo-American alliance. Liberal Democrats such as Claude Pepper attacked the speech as a disservice to the United Nations and a piece of reactionary imperialism. The only out-and-out support came from extreme right-wing, anti-Soviet legislators.[102]

Truman and Byrnes had known what was in the speech, had approved, and had taken the political risk of associating themselves with it. On March 5, Henry Wallace and his wife attended a dinner given by Dean Acheson and his wife at which Richard Casey, Australian ambassador to the United States, and Charles Bohlen were present. "We then got to talking about Russia again," Wallace recorded in his diary, "and it was apparent that Bohlen, Acheson and Casey all think that the United States should run the risk of immediate war with Russia by a very hardboiled stand and being willing to use force if Russia should go beyond a certain point."[103] Soviet foreign policy was a dangerous amalgam of traditional Russian imperialism and Marxist/Leninist ideology, so the United States foreign policy establishment was convinced. Churchill could articulate publicly what Truman, Byrnes, Acheson, and Bohlen could say only privately. The administration could use Churchill to prepare the public for a course it had already decided upon, namely the defense of British interests in the eastern Mediterranean and the Middle East. How better to gain public support for a policy than by using a surrogate who would absorb the political fallout? Truman had acted shrewdly to steal the anti-Soviet thunder of the political right in the United States without exposing himself to attacks from Anglophobes on both the right and the left.

Thus, although enunciation of the Truman Doctrine was nearly a year away, it was already in force by March 1946. In August 1944, the Joint Chiefs of Staff had portrayed the Soviet Union as a war-devastated nation whose moves in Eastern Europe and the Far East were defensive in nature and based on an overriding desire for military security. By 1946, they were writing that world domination was the primary objective of Soviet foreign policy. Moscow had decided that peaceful coexistence with the capitalist countries was impossible. "The USSR was concentrating therefore on building up its war potential and doing everything it could, short of open warfare to subjugate the satellite nations, to gain control of strategic areas, and to isolate and weaken the 'capitalistic' nations militarily," declared a JCS report to the president. The Soviets were making frantic efforts to overcome the United States lead in military technology and were receiving much help from French communist scientists. They were openly trying to sabotage the United Nations and were busy undermining pro-Western governments from France to Indonesia.[104]

During his first eight months in office, Harry Truman had tried to treat America's wartime partners equally, to mediate between them, and especially to avoid giving Moscow the impression that there was a Washington-London axis directed against Russia. The Soviets had proved intransigent and had clumsily provoked the United States over one issue after another, while under its new Labour government Britain had shrewdly confronted Russia and defined its interests within the context and in the name of the United Nations. Meanwhile, the resurgent GOP, deciding that it had to offer an alternative to Democratic foreign and domestic policy, called for a get-tough policy abroad and retrenchment at home. Responding to stimuli in both the political and diplomatic environments, the Truman administration decided in winter and spring 1946 to pursue a harder line toward the Soviets. Like the interventionists in 1940 and 1941, Truman and his advisers concluded that it was better to deal with aggression on foreign soil and to act in concert with allies rather than alone and isolated in the Western Hemisphere. That perception in turn led American policymakers to once again identify Britain's strategic interests with those of the United States. The Soviet Union, B. E. F. Gage noted with delight, "is busily forging a strong demand in the United States for a strong foreign policy and arousing universal sympathy for the British position, which many thinking Americans are beginning to have an uncomfortable feeling is their own."[105] In his Overseas Press Club speech, Jimmy Byrnes had denounced the Soviets for gnawing away at the status quo. The British were convinced that it was essentially an Anglo-American status quo— British in the Near and Middle East and American in the Far East—that Byrnes referred to, and they were right.

11. *Ends and Means: The Termination of Lend-Lease and the Origins of Anglo-American Financial Negotiations, 1945*

UNFORTUNATELY FOR Great Britain, the United States's willingness to recognize a mutuality of interest in Europe and the Middle East, and to identify the Soviet Union as a mortal threat to that interest, was not matched by a willingness to provide the United Kingdom with the means to become a strong and effective partner. Instead, the Roosevelt-Truman foreign policy establishment saddled Britain with a flawed multilateralism that helped to bring that country to its knees. United States policy toward Great Britain in the economic sphere roughly paralleled its demarches in the strategic and political spheres through the end of the mediation stage in late 1945. In August Washington abruptly terminated lend-lease to the United Kingdom, and then in the winter of 1945–46 forced the government of Clement Attlee to accept a loan whose multilateral conditions contributed to a disintegration of Britain's international financial position and drastically reduced its ability to defend its interests around the world.

The Truman administration did not consciously seek the diminution of British power during 1945, but for both diplomatic and political reasons it was determined not to show any "favoritism" toward Great Britain and to extract a pound of flesh for every pound of aid extended. America's lend-lease and foreign loan policies in 1945–46 reflected the continuing strength of conservatism and nationalism in America, Harry Truman's political vulnerability, continuing bureaucratic confusion, and contradictions inherent in the concept of multilateralism itself. Thus, the abrupt cutoff of lend-lease and the imposition of a loan inimical to the United Kingdom's interests were consistent with Washington's previous efforts to hold British gold/dollar levels to a minimum, to prevent early reconversion, to destroy empire preference, and to accelerate decolonization within the British Empire—with its campaign, in brief, to hold Britain at arm's length. But these actions were totally inconsistent with the burgeoning anticommunism in Congress and with Truman and Byrnes's decision in late 1945 and early 1946 to get tough with the Kremlin.

Britain was more than just a passive victim of its powerful but inept partner. A primary objective of the British Treasury during World War II had been to prevent Britain from becoming financially dependent on the United States, and thus having to endure a humiliating repetition of the war debts–reparations imbroglio.

John Maynard Keynes and his colleagues believed that Britain's "indebtedness" from the Great War and the necessity to default had poisoned Anglo-American relations in the interwar period and contributed importantly to the ascendancy of isolationism in the United States. Not counting lend-lease, London had managed to wage World War II without accumulating any significant indebtedness in foreign currencies. But by 1945 the goal of financial independence had come into sharp conflict with the need to defend Britain's sphere of interest from Soviet aggression and subversion. It also threatened the pervasive political objective— shared by Labour and reform Conservatives alike—of providing homes, food, and work to the British people. In the final analysis, Britain had to drastically reduce its overseas expenditures and go hat-in-hand to America for a massive dollar loan. Whitehall's negotiating team succeeded in obtaining a credit but theirs was a Pyrrhic victory. Britain's pursuit of its short-term political and strategic objectives together with Keynes's determination to see established a new system of international finance, no matter how flawed, led to a sacrifice of those mechanisms that had kept the sterling area intact.

Great Britain had been able to fight and defeat the Axis powers without incurring massive indebtedness in foreign currencies. But it appeared as 1945 opened that London could not long avoid a trip to the international installment loan department. In the first place, British overseas military responsibilities would not cease with the end of the war in Europe and the Pacific. The have-nots in Greece and Indonesia had taken up arms against their conservative, pro-Western governments; Turkey and Iran were vulnerable to Russian attack; and the Middle East from Egypt to Palestine was seething with anticolonialism. Britain would be no less dependent on these areas for food, strategic materials, markets, bases, and lines of communication during the postwar period than it had during the prewar era. Conservative estimates were that it would cost Britain £500 million sterling a year minimum to maintain a one-million-person army and adequate naval and air forces abroad to sustain the status quo.[1] In addition to causing budgetary problems, protection of British interests would require massive amounts of foreign exchange. The cost in foreign currency of maintaining four divisions for a year in Egypt, Persia, Palestine, and Iraq was £30 million. That meant that Britain would have to ship this value in unrequited exports to these four countries each year. Moreover, not only would Western Europe be unable to supply Britain with the trade and materials to enable it to fulfill its responsibilities in other parts of the globe, but also it was likely to constitute an additional drain on British resources.[2] France was weak and would remain so for the foreseeable future.

Britain could not replenish its cupboard and its armory by stripping its defeated enemy of food, machinery, and forced labor as Russia was planning to do and as Henry Morgenthau and Bernard Baruch wanted it to do. The United States, with a large Italo-American population, had already gone to great lengths to "rehabilitate" and, in fact, protect Italy. West Germany was all that was left. Moral considerations aside, that area did not have what England needed—food, rubber, and iron ore. Moreover, Britain required markets and, while the German economy was competitive with and not complementary to Britain's, its health was crucial to the economic rehabilitation of Western Europe. Also Western Europe was a prime potential customer for Great Britain. Finally, to strip West Germany of plant and resources would further weaken the region and invite communist adventurism.

On the domestic scene, His Majesty's Government estimated that German bombs and missiles had destroyed four million dwellings. A white paper on the British war effort presented to Parliament in November 1944 reported that the nation's meat consumption was down one-fourth from prewar levels; butter consumption was off two-thirds; and fruit, tea, eggs, and sugar levels were all significantly lower.[3] Statesmen cannot be statesmen without being politicians first, and the people demanded food, homes, and work.

Labour's smashing victory in 1945 was viewed by both left and right as a popular mandate for governmental action to guarantee social security. For generations the Conservative party had been fundamentally the party of property and privilege—business people, landed gentry, industrialists, and bankers—but it also included a number of dependent allied groups such as farmers, rural employees, white-collar workers, and members of the professional classes. Labour was primarily the party of the organized working classes, whose political arms were the trade unions, with allies in the cooperative movement and among the less economically secure professions such as teaching. Labour was underrepresented in Parliament during the war and had lost the last general election in 1935 badly. The Conservatives were powerful and entrenched. Labour had to attract voters at a time when British labor was becoming increasingly professionalized, that is, a larger and larger percentage of British workers were white-collar workers employed in government or service rather than basic industry where the trade unions were strongest. Indeed, when the white collars had voted, they had generally voted Conservative. It had become clear to the Labour leadership that if it were going to win in 1945 and retain power for any length of time thereafter, it would have to add the service and professional classes to its rolls. These classes, more than any other, had experienced a rising level of expectations during the 1930s and 1940s, and it was they who were least likely to accept a policy of "austerity" in the postwar period. Labour captured this crucial voting bloc by making a convincing argument that it could provide homes, food, and work within the context of a mixed economy. The millions of Britons who had voted Labour in 1945, and especially white-collar converts, expected Attlee and company to deliver.[4]

Britain's ability to emerge from World War II virtually free from indebtedness in foreign currencies was due to three factors: lend-lease, the imposition of a strict rationing system which carefully limited and controlled civilian demands, and the willingness of the Commonwealth and empire to accept blocked sterling as payment for goods and services rendered to the United Kingdom. By spring 1945 it was obvious that London could not count on these three mechanisms to continue into the postwar period.[5] Few British officials expected lend-lease to last beyond the end of the war in the Pacific, and no British politician was willing to risk the wrath of the electorate by extending wartime austerity programs into the postwar period. Not only would the Commonwealth and empire refuse to put up with a continuation of the blocked sterling mechanism, but they also would demand funding of existing debts as soon as possible. In the past Britain had been able to make reconstruction loans to war-torn allies, to finance proxy armies, and to extend virtually unlimited credit to finance overseas trade. Those days, though some might not admit it, were clearly over.

Some wishful thinkers such as Anthony Eden argued that Britain could get by on the appearance of power, but Sir Wilfrid Eady, who more than any other person in the British Treasury was responsible for reconciling defense requirements with political and budgetary realities, disagreed. "No defense is weaker than one that seems to be stronger than it is," he wrote. Eady was not sure Britain could afford the appearance of strength on all fronts: "We cannot simultaneously *seem* to be strong in the Navy and the Air by reference to U.S.A. standards, and on the land by reference to Russian and possibly French standards, or maintain sufficient strength for all contingencies in the European center and also at the periphery of British possessions."[6]

Franklin Roosevelt, Henry Morgenthau, Harry Hopkins, Henry Stimson, and Edward Stettinius were not insensitive to Britain's plight. Throughout much of the war the Roosevelt White House had presumed the existence of a strong and vigorous Great Britain able to police and protect its sphere of interest in Western Europe and the Middle East, and during the early weeks of 1945 it felt the need more than ever for a proven and trusted ally in an increasingly uncertain world.[7] In 1944 the president and his advisers began to try to come to grips with the fact that Britain would be financially—and thus militarily—crippled after the war. And in April of that year the president, through Stettinius, told the British of his desire to help. But that desire and Roosevelt's ability to aid the United Kingdom were circumscribed by a number of factors, including Anglophobia and a deep-seated fiscal conservatism. Public opinion polls indicated clearly that the American people were not willing to extend postwar aid to other nations if it meant a reduction in their own living standards.[8] As 1945 dawned, multilateralism seemed once again to be the solution to a number of domestic and international problems. By promising to expand American markets and reduce domestic unemployment, it appeared to be a context in which aid could be extended to Great Britain without raising conservative hackles in the United States.

Britain had made it abundantly clear that it would not venture forth on the uncharted seas of multilateralism unless and until it was able to achieve a balance on current account in the transitional period. The United States Treasury and the White House acknowledged the United Kingdom's need and no more wanted to saddle Britain with a debt that it could not repay than Keynes and Eady wanted to undertake such an obligation. During congressional debates over the Bretton

Woods proposals, Harry Dexter White had portrayed the International Monetary Fund and the International Bank for Reconstruction and Development as the only alternatives to special reconstruction loans or credits to Great Britain. But the Treasury, elements in the State Department, the Hopkins ring, and, of course, the British themselves quickly recognized that the fund and bank could not and would not solve Great Britain's problems during the transitional period. Even if the IMF and IBRD had possessed sufficient resources, the British were determined not to be a supplicant of the Bretton Woods institutions. Prestige considerations aside, a British claim on their resources would take funds away from developing nations on whom Britain depended for food and from the war-devastated nations of Western Europe on whom Britain depended for markets and security. If multilateralism was to become a reality, the United States government would have to initiate a massive program of foreign loans whether it be through lend-lease, direct credits, the Export-Import Bank, or some other source. Multilateralists were confident as of late 1944 that conservatives and nationalists in the United States could be placated by the arguments that these loans were not welfare and would not drain the resources of the Republic, but rather were a stimulant to foreign trade that would provide jobs at home and forestall the need for public works and "collectivism" in general.[9]

But, like Congress, the White House remained unwilling to undertake the second prerequisite for a viable system of multilateral trade—an across-the-board slash in United States tariffs. Like Cordell Hull, Roosevelt actually believed that the Reciprocal Trade Agreements Act had fulfilled the American commitment to reduce tariffs. More sophisticated officials in the State Department and Treasury, and among the Hopkins group, recognized that RTAA did not put the United States on a free trade or limited free trade basis, that it provided ample opportunity for vested interests to protect themselves, that it was a mechanism whereby a basically self-sufficient nation could bargain for those few items it needed to import and export. Some salved their intellects by arguing that tariffs were in a different category from preferences, quotas, and other barriers to trade, while others—Dean Acheson, for example—equated RTAA with multilateralism because it was the best that could be had from Congress and because the president and the political leadership in the State Department had bought into it.

Despite the fact that British commercial policy experts and certain English politicians repeatedly pointed out that the United States had not actually embraced multilateralism and could hardly ask London to abolish its trade controls until it agreed to an across-the-board cut in tariffs, the Roosevelt administration continued its assault on British quotas, preferences, exchange controls, and state-nurtured monopolies. At the Yalta Conference FDR dashed off a note to Churchill, who was ensconced in the Vorontsov Villa. He did not want to miss this opportunity, Roosevelt said, to emphasize the importance he attached to implementing Article VII. He suggested the "prompt naming of full delegations on both sides to be headed by a Chairman with the rank of Minister" to meet and hammer out a liberal commercial policy.[10]

Churchill recoiled from Roosevelt's initiative as if from a serpent. The coalition government was disintegrating beneath him. Ernest Bevin and Oliver Lyttle-ton had fallen into bitter quarreling, Bevin charging the Conservatives with turning the question of maintaining economic controls in the transitional period into a political football and Lyttleton hotly denying it. Commercial policy questions seemed just as certain to polarize the cabinet in 1945 as they had in 1944. Lord Beaverbrook and Leo Amery were no less convinced in spring 1945 that multilateralism was a Yankee plot to steal British markets than they had been in the previous years. Bevin continued to suspect that Bretton Woods and Article VII would sacrifice the right of national governments to manipulate their currencies and control overseas commerce—in the name of full employment—to the cause of international currency stabilization. All the while, right-wing Conservatives like Lyttleton and Lord Cherwell, and moderates such as Richard Law and Anthony Eden continued to support multilateralism, some for ideological and some for strategic reasons. Thus Churchill cabled Roosevelt in mid-February that the time was simply inopportune for sending a high-powered delegation to Washington.[11]

The United States would not be put off, however. The Roosevelt administration intended to help Britain whether Britain liked it or not. No doubt Roosevelt and Hopkins were determined to avoid a repetition of the events of 1940–41, as they read them, in which the United Kingdom was forced to deal with a colossal Continental aggressor while America wallowed in isolationism. Lend-lease had arrived in the nick of time. Multilateralism, supplemented by a loan, might not make a future lend-lease program unnecessary, but it would certainly rehabilitate the United Kingdom, enabling it to take its place as America's most important European ally, and it would help dispel Anglophobia among exporters and bankers. In early February Roosevelt asked his trusted friend and chief speech writer, Samuel Rosenman, to visit London and other European capitals to explore the supply requirements of the liberated countries of northern and Western Europe and to analyze the United Kingdom's need for financial assistance from the United States during Phase III. Although the political leadership in Britain wanted to delay a discussion of commercial policies, which they knew would be intimately connected with any financial assistance, until after the general election, and although Treasury experts were still very leery of any kind of financial arrangement with the United States, London had no choice but to receive Rosenman and make the best of a bad situation.[12]

Like other visitors to London before and after him, Sam Rosenman was stunned by the devastation he encountered and was inspired by the cheerful stoicism of the British people. He wrote Roosevelt:

> Here in London . . . which is a great distance from the actual fighting front, the impact of the war on the civilian population is most significant. The dreary black out at night which has gone on for five-and-a-half years, grim evidence of the damage by the blitz, buzz bomb, and V-2 bomb, an occasional explosion of a V-2 bomb at a distance . . . with the much reduced ration and monotonous diet (including the ever-present brussels sprouts—boiled not broiled)—all of this which

has been going on for so many years makes one's admiration for the British people increase. Last night, I went down into the underground to watch the people at sleep and I assure you it is a moving experience to see workers, mothers and children who have either been bombed out of their houses or have become nervous about bombs, trying to get some rest in spite of the lights and noise. The underground ceases operation only between 12:30 and 5:30 A.M.[13]

In a sense, the Rosenman mission marked the beginning of Anglo-American negotiations over the British loan of 1946. As experienced horse traders the British staked out their most extreme position. Rosenman met with Keynes and Eady at Keynes's room in Whitehall on March 7, 1945. As he had told Roosevelt the last time he was in Washington, Keynes said, what was needed was "for the President to have a 'brainwave' out of which would come some new financial arrangements which would be successful in placing the world economy in a position to function in a manner satisfactory to both the British and American governments." If the United States could not help the British government quiet its anxieties regarding the transitional period, empire isolationism and bilateralism might well come to dominate British trade policy. Britain's total indebtedness from the war, he noted, was of the same magnitude as the amount of reparations Russia had suggested at Yalta that Germany be made to pay ($20 billion with half going to Russia). In effect, what Keynes and Eady told Rosenman in early March 1945 was that Britain's prospects in the immediate future were bleak and that only the United States could help. Any aid that was extended, however, would have to be on Britain's terms.[14]

After Rosenman's departure for Washington, Eady, Keynes, Sir David Waley, and the other permanent civil servants and economists in the British Treasury concerned with international finance decided that the time for delay was over. Because Treasury alone could understand the complexities of international trade and finance, because it was the government agency that in the end would have to reconcile defense needs with budget realities, because the coalition government was increasingly fragmented and was unable and unwilling to deal with social and economic matters, and because America would not wait, all agreed that the Exchequer would have to develop a policy and act both internally and externally to see that policy adopted.

Eady, Keynes, and their colleagues decided that the best time to approach America for aid during Phase III was immediately after V-E Day. Roosevelt, they reasoned, would be at the height of his power then, but that power would surely decline rapidly thereafter. Above all, Britain should be careful to avoid an agreement under which the United States had been "generous" to Britain and Britain had to be "grateful" for that help. Nothing would do more to poison Anglo-American relations and to "make impossible the realization of that humdrum conjugality between them and us to which we look forward," Eady subsequently wrote Keynes.[15] Keynes and Eady tentatively settled on an arrangement whereby the United States would provide Britain with a $3 billion grant-in-aid and make available for the purchase of food and industrial machinery in the

United States an additional $5 billion in credit that London could call up as it needed. Even with this, Treasury experts reasoned that it would be at least two years before Britain could undertake free convertibility on current account.

The question of how Britain was planning to handle its sterling indebtedness was sure to come up in any loan negotiations. The president, Congress, and American people would not want to give money to Britain if they thought the funds would be used to pay India, Egypt, Persia, and other members of the Commonwealth and empire. Why, they would ask, should these regions not have to bear part of the burden of their defense? Of course, many within the British foreign policy establishment and the cabinet were asking the same question. Various officials from Keynes to Eady to Lord Catto to Churchill agreed that blocked sterling should not be treated as a standard debt to be paid for in gold and/or dollars. Churchill wanted to write them off unilaterally. The Board of Trade took a more moderate but still tough position. But others saw just how tenuous were the threads that bound the empire together. Lord Catto, the new, more liberal head of the Bank of England, agreed with Keynes and Eden that if Britain attempted to block sterling balances indefinitely or to write them off unilaterally, the sterling area members would revolt. India and Egypt were already convulsed with discontent. Conciliation not provocation was necessary if Britain was to maintain its influence in these strategically and economically crucial areas. Thus, Treasury settled on a plan whereby, with the help of financial aid from the United States, Britain would achieve convertibility on current account within two years, and, through voluntary, multilateral agreement with its sterling creditors, it would write off one-fourth to one-half the debt and fund the rest. In this way and this way alone would Britain be able to restore confidence in sterling and hold all or part of the sterling bloc together.[16]

After much discussion, Keynes and Eady decided, additionally, that Whitehall should abandon its attempts to separate commercial and financial discussions. Eady was of the opinion that it was unwise either tactically or on its merits to persist in these efforts. "If we do not mention it, they [the Americans] will mention it, and they will be suspicious of our reasons for not mentioning it," he told Keynes.[17] After all, Britain and the rest of the trading world believed that it was essential "to have a world in which America imports," and the United Kingdom could make sure that the United States lowered its tariff barriers across the board in any Phase III agreement. In the forthcoming negotiations Britain should take the line that it wanted the kind of liberal trading environment that multilateralists were calling for as much as America did, but that only the United States could speed the United Kingdom along the path. In a multilateral world, commercial policy and financial policy were inextricably linked. Creditor nations had to pursue both a liberal loan policy and a program of tariff reduction.

Thus, by late March 1945, the general outline of British strategy was set. Whitehall would take the initiative in linking commercial and financial policy. It would ask for a grant and credit based on justice, agree to pursue separate negotiations for a settlement of blocked sterling, and use whatever leverage it possessed to reduce United States tariffs to the lowest possible level. But the strategy was fraught with danger, great danger. "If the U.S.A. goes back on imports and free lending," Eady asked, "is there not a risk that this temporary financial solution might result in our position being worse?"[18]

Treasury officials knew how delicate was the balance of power within the War Cabinet, how distracted were their political officials with the war and the forthcoming general election, and how divisive socioeconomic questions could be for the Conservative-Labour team Churchill had put together. But diplomatic and defense matters cannot always wait on politics. Keynes and his colleagues embarked at once on a campaign to persuade the cabinet to authorize the arduous financial and commercial negotiations that now seemed essential to Britain's survival. To Amery, Beaverbrook, and the empire isolationists they declared that the only alternative to multilateralism was rationing at home, strict economic controls, and state-run foreign trade—all enemies of free enterprise. "Barter trade is the very antithesis to individual enterprise. If this breaks down as it may, it is probably to the Russian model that we shall have to look," Keynes announced. Moreover, a loan from America, crucial to early, free convertibility, was the only way to preserve the financial empire.[19] Treasury representatives pointed out to both reform Tories and the Labour contingent in the cabinet that there were far-reaching political implications if Britain continued to operate in the red on international account, namely, rationing, overcrowding, unemployment, and inadequate health care. The cabinet had promised much, and woe to those politicians who did not deliver. Again and again Keynes and his colleagues frightened and then reassured doubters. In the process they led the cabinet to believe that a free gift from the United States was not only a possibility but also the only thing the Treasury would settle for.[20]

A little over a month after Judge Rosenman's return to the United States, Franklin D. Roosevelt died and Harry S. Truman took the oath of office, assuming, in the process, control over the end of the war in Europe, atomic diplomacy, Soviet-American relations, implementation of plans for a collective security organization, and the fate of multilateralism. Reactions to Truman's accession to the presidency among those with an interest in international trade and finance varied. New Dealers were impressed by Truman's voting record. They were pleased by his promise, subsequently fulfilled, to press Congress for an extension of Social Security, an increase in the minimum wage, additional regional development projects similar to the TVA, and establishment of a national health insurance system. Conservatives were heartened by his obvious reverence for business and free enterprise in general. Progressives liked the fact that he was from the Midwest and had no obvious ties with monopolies or the eastern establishment. Reactions in Britain were similarly mixed and for equally diverse reasons. Lord Beaverbrook and Brendan Bracken were enthusiastic: "Men from Missouri,"

Bracken wrote, "are from birth reared in the belief of freedom of the individual and the rights of individual ownership of property."[21] Hugh Dalton, Ernest Bevin, and Clement Attlee anticipated a continuation of the New Deal. So did Harold Macmillan, Richard Law, and Robert Boothby who predicted that the Rooseveltian program under Truman's guidance would become an American version of the "middle way"—as if it had not been in its original form.

Truman, like Roosevelt and a majority of American liberals, took a basically conservative approach to social and economic policy. The new president believed that in modern society the federal government had inescapable obligations to provide employment for all who wanted it, to care for the dependent and disadvantaged.[22] He believed in a countervailing economy whereby the government helped weak and disorganized sectors of the economy and society and restrained those interests that were unduly strong and privileged. Like Roosevelt, he was in order to achieve social justice willing to endorse deficit spending—but of a temporary nature only. He did indeed admire business and business people, but he opposed private collectivism and championed fair and open competition.

Actually, the major issue on the domestic front turned out to be inflation, not unemployment. The relatively affluent workers and middle-class Americans wanted the government to protect their purchasing power and not to pursue expansionist policies that would overheat the economy. With much of their constituency dedicated to preserving the status quo, Truman and the Democratic party would have been courting political suicide by advocating ambitious schemes of planning and control, even if they had been so inclined.

Not surprisingly, the president was in international economic matters a multilateralist. No sooner had the man from Missouri taken the oath of office than he ranged himself squarely behind the Bretton Woods legislation then pending in Congress; this, despite the fact that the House Banking Committee was reported at the time to be divided 13 to 13 over recommending passage without revision. Believing it to be a crucial component of the multilateral scheme, he also threw his weight behind the broadened Reciprocal Trade Agreements Act. Liberals were ecstatic. The *Baltimore Sun* wrote: "In a very few minutes he disposed of the hopes of a few short sighted industrialists and a few confused bankers that he could be persuaded to assist in the destruction of these two essential parts of the new international structure which the peoples of the world are now attempting to erect."[23] Truman's principal advisers on foreign economic matters—Will Clayton, Dean Acheson, Fred Vinson (head of the Office of War Mobilization), Oscar Cox, and later Thomas Blaisdell—were all outspoken multilateralists.

The new president, like his predecessor, acknowledged that, for multilateralism to work, the United States would have to pursue a liberal loan policy and accept foreign imports on a massive scale. At the same time he convinced himself that existing institutions and programs coupled with a series of limited bilateral loans would make a tariff-and-exchange-free world possible. He and his advisers bought into the idea that the reciprocal trade program as renewed by Congress would bring enough imports into the United States to create an eventual trade balance and that the program would constitute sufficient proof to Britain and other potential participants in a multilateral system that America had abandoned protectionism.[24] At Potsdam Truman would announce to the British with great satisfaction that under RTAA United States tariffs had been cut by 50 percent and he had just been given authority to reduce them an additional 50 percent.[25] While Harry Truman understood generally that the economic recovery of war-devastated areas and their ability to participate in an American scheme for multilateralism would require infusions of American capital, he did not initially perceive the extent to which Britain had been damaged financially by World War II and the consequent amount of aid the United Kingdom would require from the United States. He assumed that the IMF, the IBRD, and a limited credit would suffice. The new chief executive's misconceptions were a product of his own intellectual limitations, his and Congress's economic nationalism, and the powerful presence of Bernard Baruch.

Baruch's influence survived the Roosevelt-Truman transition intact. He continued to play the role of adviser, confidant, and financial supporter to Jimmy Byrnes. An old political favor assured continued access to the White House. In 1940 when Truman was involved in a hard-fought campaign for reelection to the Senate, Byrnes persuaded his friend Baruch to contribute $4,000 to Truman's campaign. Baruch's long-time interest in questions of international trade and finance increased sharply as the war's end approached, and he made known his desire to be accorded a key role in the formulation of postwar policy. From London Rosenman sent Baruch a confidential copy of his talk with Keynes.[26] Almost immediately afterward, the White House asked Baruch to go to England and discuss postwar problems with Churchill and his colleagues.

Bernard Baruch was opposed in principle to government loans, whether domestic or international. "Under proper conditions," he wrote, "government lending is unnecessary and hurtful . . . it is a reflex of fascism, communism and nazism for the State to seek to get hold of everything so that an individual has to bow . . . to the State."[27] In his opinion private American loans and investment were more than sufficient to take care of the capital needs of foreign countries.[28] After returning from England, the financier reported to Truman that the United Kingdom's difficulties were more psychological than financial. Admitting that a strong Britain was crucial to America's security, Baruch insisted to Truman that the chief problem facing the British was a breakdown in morale, a pervasive sense of pessimism. Their fears were groundless, he declared, and he had told everyone so. With the disappearance of Germany as an economic force in Europe, Britain would have all the markets it needed. At the very most, Britain would require a $1 billion "cylinder head" loan to get its economy started again. He was pleased to report, he told Truman, that after he had made these facts clear to Churchill, Attlee, Keynes, Beaverbrook, and Catto, their anxieties and fears had evaporated like the mirages they were.[29] Truman was not as simple-minded or sanguine as Baruch, but he was still subject to his spell.

Before the executive branch of government could deal with the matter of a loan to the British, however, it had to come to grips for a final time with the increasingly politicized issue of lend-lease. The way in which Washington handled the wind-down and termination of its wartime program of aid to Great Britain in spring and summer 1945 made many Britons think that Truman had taken Baruch's position as his own. In August the Truman administration declared its Phase II commitments at an end and abruptly terminated lend-lease.[30] That deed not only set the stage for the final round of negotiations on the British loan, it also brought the forces of economic nationalism in Congress and the bureaucracy into sharp relief and foreshadowed the fate of Anglo-American multilateralism.

As of November 30, 1944, the United States had extended a total of $25,048,800,000 in lend-lease aid to the British Empire. This sum represented 73.5 percent of the total American wartime aid provided to all countries, and it included the value of items procured from appropriations made directly to the president and the service departments. Of the total, 88.2 percent had been in the form of goods transferred and 11.8 percent represented services rendered. Munitions items, including ordinance, aircraft, tanks, and other vehicles, totaled $10,518,900,000. For fiscal 1945 (July 1944 through June 1945), FEA asked for and received an appropriation of $3,904,900 for the British Empire.[31]

At the second Quebec Conference in fall 1944, Roosevelt had agreed to Churchill's proposal that the United Kingdom continue to receive lend-lease assistance after the defeat of Germany on the basis of a British reconversion from wartime civilian production that would be "on a proportional basis" to reconversion in the United States (synchronized reconversion). The American committee of Morgenthau, Stettinius, and Leo Crowley set up after Quebec subsequently reported to the president on November 25, 1944, that the recommended figures for the British Commonwealth of $2.7 billion for munitions and $2.8 billion for nonmunitions "will make it possible for Britain and the United States to release some manpower and resources for reconversion, easement of living standards, and a partial revival of exports." United States officials, however, made it clear to the British at Quebec, and the American committee reaffirmed, that the program approved was not a commitment and was "subject to changing demands of strategy as well as to supply considerations and the usual considerations of procurement and allocation."[32] Despite the escape clause that Morgenthau had succeeded in inserting into the Quebec accord, Churchill had departed Canada with the impression that Britain could at least begin reconversion of its wartime economy to a peacetime basis and still receive lend-lease aid.

In late 1944 and early 1945 multilateralists in the State Department who wanted to use present and future aid to compel Britain to abandon trade barriers and exchange controls joined forces with economic nationalists in Congress, the FEA, and the military to force FDR to denounce the concept of synchronized reconversion and deny that lend-lease could be utilized by the British government for reconstruction purposes. After much discussion and fruitless negotiation in Washington, Keynes and his colleagues failed to move the Roosevelt administration. Keynes remained optimistic in part because he anticipated a presidential "brainwave" for Phase III. Members of the War Cabinet and particularly the British joint chiefs were not nearly as sanguine, however.

As has been noted, Congress chose to exert itself in the area of foreign economic affairs during the hearings on the renewal of lend-lease in spring 1945 not by blocking its extension but by ensuring that the executive branch did not use the measure as an instrument to dispense postwar foreign aid. Charges that the British were profiting from lend-lease by expanding their commercial export markets and reconverting their economy from a wartime to a peacetime footing were explicit and implicit in the speeches of various senators and representatives. During an executive session of the Senate Foreign Relations Committee, Arthur Vandenberg charged that British gold/dollar reserves had risen to $2.5 billion and insisted that the previous administration had pursued a firm policy of holding these reserves at $1 billion or less. In fact, unexpected revenue from expenditures by United States troops in the British Isles had caused the Exchequer's gold/dollar holdings to rise to $1.744 billion net by January 30, 1945. This increase had occurred even though the British had predicted a decline to $1.3 billion by that date. Even pro-administration defenders of lend-lease on the committee like Claude Pepper were shocked. They had assumed that British balances still hovered near the 1941 level. Both Crowley and Acheson promised the House Foreign Affairs Committee that lend-lease would not be used "for the purposes of post-war rehabilitation and reconstruction." The House wound up voting 354 to 28 in mid-March to extend lend-lease and the Senate followed suit a month later with a unanimous voice vote. Nonetheless, the upper house narrowly defeated an amendment offered by Robert Taft that would have prohibited the president from using lend-lease for postwar relief, rehabilitation, or reconstruction—even through outright sale of materials and services. Taft's initiative was turned back following a 39 to 39 tie by the vote of the presiding officer—Harry Truman.[33]

Those who would construe the Lend-Lease Act literally were not limited to Congress. Leo Crowley's promise had been made enthusiastically. "The test of our administration of the Lend-Lease Act," he wrote Baruch, "depends on our making certain that we do not get the cart before the horse. What I mean by this is that we must make certain that Lend-Lease is not used indirectly for post-war reconstruction. I am firm in my conviction that Lend-Lease should cease at the end of the war."[34] The Catholic and conservative Crowley was intimidated by the grilling he had had to endure at the hands of the House and Senate committees and, as always, was eager to do Congress's bidding. As the war's end approached, the FEA chief had felt more and more insecure because his was a temporary agency; Congress could choke off its appropriations in the twinkling of an eye. The liberal Phase II commitment made at Quebec had infuriated Crowley because it was the result, he believed, of State and Treasury Department meddling in what should have been purely an FEA affair. There were liberal Anglophiles within FEA such as Oscar Cox and Charles Denby who fought for a flexible interpretation of America's wartime program of aid to Britain. Unfortunately for the United Kingdom, summer 1945 would witness Cox and Denby's bureaucratic demise.

In addition, the military continued to advocate a tight-fisted administration of the program, a position that was at most ironic and at least short-sighted. Virtually all military figures concerned with postwar matters and strategic planning were by spring 1945 beginning to see the Soviet Union as a threat to America's interests and Britain as America's first line of defense. But in many ways the military was as bureaucratized and compartmentalized as the civilian sector of the federal government. For instance, General Brehon Somervell, who was in overall charge of supply for the army, and Admiral William D. Leahy did not trust the British and believed that the United States would unilaterally have to assume the defense of the free world. They and like-minded military officials wanted to supplant Great Britain in the Pacific, literally taking possession of their bases. Leahy, moreover, was an intense conservative in economic and social matters. The admiral, a straightforward disciplinarian who had served as FDR's military aide, endeared himself briefly to Truman by showing him the same loyalty he had shown Roosevelt. The United States, Leahy argued, could not afford welfare either at home or abroad. Every nickel was needed to keep the nation's defenses strong. Somervell, meanwhile, began to display the parochialism so characteristic of supply chieftains. Exposed to constant demands and complaints from United States military officials in charge of the Pacific theater that they were being short-changed and to sometimes blatantly inflated requests from the British, Somervell became rigidly tight-fisted. In addition, he and officers with a wider view such as George C. Marshall were angered by British efforts to lobby Congress directly. Despite objections by high-ranking American officers, the British at their expense flew members of Congress to various theaters (in lend-leased planes) throughout 1944 and 1945.[35]

Harry Hopkins's failing health also had an important impact on the way in which lend-lease was administered. Under his guidance the Munitions Assignment Board (MAB) had at least paid lip service to the pooling principle whereby Anglo-American resources would be combined and then distributed in light of strategic needs. Hopkins, in the view of the British, had acted as an entirely neutral chairman, deciding the claims of various parties on their merits. In his absence, the representatives of the War and Navy departments came to dominate the distribution process. The British claimed in spring 1945 that MAB was now operating on the assumption that United States production and resources should be allocated primarily to meet American needs. "In tight times," complained British service representatives, "only the crumbs that fall from the rich man's table are available for assignment to foreigners." All the Americans had to do to obtain necessary munitions was to say what they needed, while the British had to submit "elaborate strategical data and full operational briefs."[36]

There would seem to be little doubt that the president was aware of the relationship between Britain's ability to achieve equilibrium in its balance of payments and continued lend-lease assistance from the United States. On April 24 Lauchlin Currie, who had been asked by Roosevelt and Hopkins to go to Great Britain and evaluate the financial and economic situation there, made his report to Truman. "In general," he declared, "the possibility of Britain achieving equilibrium without assistance from America or the International Monetary Fund or Bank is dependent upon (a) the quickness with which exports can be built up, (b) the length of the Japanese War, (c) the magnitude of Britain's contribution in that war, and (d) the magnitude of Lend-Lease in this period." Nonetheless, when the president met with Harold Smith on April 26 to go over the lend-lease budget to be submitted to Congress, he agreed with the strategy of asking less from Congress than had been requested the previous year. (FEA had cut its total requests from $6.59 billion to $4.5 billion, with much of this earmarked for relief for liberated Europe.[37]) The isolationist spirit was still very much abroad in the land though it was wearing various disguises, Truman told Smith. Excessive lend-lease requests might provide the old guard with the opening it needed. "The President was very clear," Smith recalled, "that Lend-Lease could not be used for rehabilitation purposes. For the present such needs would be met with the resources of the Export-Import Bank and the International Bank."[38]

After consulting with Crowley and Joseph Grew, who was then acting secretary of state, Harry Truman decided to hew the line laid down by his predecessor and consequently on V-E Day, May 8, signed an order authorizing the FEA and State Department "to take joint action to cut back the volume of Lend-Lease supplies." Crowley immediately "placed an embargo on all shipments to Russia and to other European nations." Soviet and British protests quickly persuaded the president to rescind the directive. For the benefit of both allies, the White House on May 23 "explained that the article . . . was intended to be not so much a cancellation of shipments as a gradual readjustment to conditions following the collapse of Germany. . . . all allocations provided for by treaty or protocol would be delivered and every commitment fulfilled."[39] Truman's "clarification" was designed more to placate Russia than Britain. On the twenty-third he told Henry Morgenthau that he had never favored giving Britain all they asked for.

Truman's actions and attitudes should not be viewed as a conscious repudiation of multilateralism. Indeed, he had told Harold Smith that it would be essential for the United States to make loans to nations whose economies were crippled and not all of these loans could be paid back. Nonetheless, during this period Truman appeared to believe that he would have to sacrifice economic internationalism—a liberal interpretation of lend-lease and a generous loan policy—to political and strategic internationalism—United States participation in the United Nations and the maintenance of a strong military presence overseas. That is, the White House seemed to think that its advocacy of a comprehensive program for the rehabilitation of Europe in general and Britain in particular would stimulate isolationism and make United States intervention to preserve a European balance of power impossible. These assumptions boded ill for Great Britain's economic and strategic interests during both Phase II and Phase III, and pointed to considerable confusion at the highest levels of the United States government about the relationship of means to ends.

The British, of course, objected to the crimp being put in their lend-lease umbilical. Above all, insisted the Treasury, Britain should resist the War Department argument that the United States was bound only to supply items that were essential to the war effort and that the United Kingdom could not produce for itself. Such an interpretation would be a clear repudiation of the Quebec agreements and an act of bad faith.

As always, however, Whitehall's success in securing what it wanted from the United States depended on its ability to read the shifting bureaucratic balance of power in Washington. Ever since the blowup in 1944 over gold/dollar balances and Morgenthau's charges that the British were going behind his back to State and other agencies, Whitehall had been careful to work through the Treasury. In late April and early May 1945, Brand and Chancellor of the Exchequer John Anderson appealed repeatedly to Morgenthau to intervene with FEA, the United States military, and the White House, and they simultaneously worked to revive the lend-lease committee that Morgenthau had been named to chair at Quebec.[40]

But Henry Morgenthau's star was in rapid decline. Truman probably did not like being told what to do and being implicitly compared to Roosevelt at every turn, as Morgenthau was wont to do. Moreover, since his old friend's death, "Henry the Morgue" had lost much of his verve and ambition. In mid-May Treasury learned indirectly and accidentally that FDR had decreed that no action to implement the Phase II agreement should be taken without the expressed approval of the Office of War Mobilization, then headed by Jimmy Byrnes and now run by Fred Vinson. Truman continued that practice and relied more and more heavily on Vinson for advice on financial and economic matters.[41] Morgenthau made one feeble attempt to have Truman convene the Quebec lend-lease committee and then abandoned himself to the luxury of self-pity. "I am waiting for the President," he told his underlings on May 29, "to tell me whether he wants me in on it. . . . I want it in writing and I want it made public . . . the French are starving and freezing, and I'm the one who's holding this up, and this is wrong, and Churchill gets on the floor in Parliament and thanks Lord Keynes for the wonderful job he did, and I never get a line."[42] Morgenthau was also discouraged by the slow pace of denazification in Germany. Moreover, both Harry White and Morgenthau realized that, from spring 1945 on, lend-lease was going to be a politically thankless task and whoever handled it would be subject to massive public and congressional criticism.[43]

Meanwhile, despite Truman's promise to fulfill all past commitments on lend-lease, shipments remained at a fraction of their pre-1945 rate. On May 25, the United States Air Force informed the British Ministry of Production that it could not supply any of nearly nine hundred transport aircraft that had been promised in fall 1944 at Quebec.[44] Three days later Churchill appealed directly to Truman. The War Department was clearly violating the Quebec agreement initialed by

President Roosevelt and himself, Churchill asserted. The "machine" had come to a standstill and British war production for the final stages of the Pacific conflict was in danger. "I hope," he concluded, "that your people can be told that the principles your predecessor and I agreed to at Quebec still stand."[45]

Officials in the State Department favored a policy of mild deprivation. Given the ascendancy of those who supported a get-tough policy toward the Soviet Union—Joseph Grew, for example, had favored a constriction in the flow of lend-lease supplies in order to exert pressure on Moscow, not London—and given past State Department support for Whitehall's effort to maximize aid from the United States, it was logical for the British to have expected help from the denizens of Foggy Bottom. In fact, Acheson and Clayton went to Crowley and urged FEA to live up to the Quebec accords. They were told, however, that the Phase II figures had been accepted for planning purposes and in no way constituted a commitment. They were able to persuade Grew, who was still acting secretary, to release a statement to the press on May 14 to the effect that until Japan surrendered America and its allies were still at war. Consequently, Britain and the other nations involved in the Pacific theater would continue to qualify for lend-lease assistance. But the multilateralists in State did not want Britain to get all that it had asked for. They had been furious with what they considered to be the unilateral concessions the United States had made to Great Britain at Quebec, not because they wanted Britain to bleed to death, but because the president did not obtain a firm promise to abolish imperial preference, quotas, and other trade barriers. In other words, the multilateralists in State occupied a position halfway between the British on one hand, and Crowley and Somervell on the other. Clayton, Collado, Acheson, and Wilcox wanted to continue to supply Britain with lend-lease on a restricted basis. If the tap were either turned all the way on or all the way off, Washington would lose its leverage.[46]

By June, any semblance of a coherent lend-lease policy in Washington had disappeared. The bureaucracy was in chaos. Even FEA was divided against itself. Unbeknownst to Crowley, Charles Denby, Al Davidson, and other liberals in the agency had been holding extensive talks with their opposite numbers in the British Supply Mission in an attempt to implement synchronized reconversion. They totally disagreed with Crowley's parsimonious approach and felt betrayed when he submitted the reduced 1945–46 budget to Congress. So discouraged was Denby, in fact, that he resigned on June 23, much to the dismay of the British. "If there were not ten righteous men in FEA, there was at least one," Brand wrote Keynes, and he asked the famed economist to write Denby a secret letter of appreciation.[47] By June the leadership in the War Department, particularly Undersecretary John J. McCloy, an Anglophile who perceived Great Britain to be America's one dependable ally in the postwar period, was trying to loosen the bonds placed on lend-lease by Somervell. Meanwhile, Treasury waffled.[48] Brand wrote Keynes: "I pointed out to Oscar [Cox] that it looked as if the different Departments were making it impossible for the President to send a satisfactory answer to the Prime Minister's cable."[49]

At Truman's behest Fred Vinson called a meeting of all concerned parties in his office on June 5, 1945. Confusion ensued. Vinson announced that he had memoranda of the Quebec conversations and a letter from Stimson on implementation of the Phase II agreements. Everyone seemed to have documents that the others had not seen. Crowley brandished a letter from the joint chiefs, while Assistant Secretary of War Robert Patterson seemed completely lost. When Vinson proposed referring the whole matter back to the committee Churchill and Roosevelt had created at Quebec, Crowley hit the roof. Lend-lease was an FEA affair, he said, and declared that if the committee were formed he would not sit on it. Vinson promised to get out a directive on implementation of lend-lease, but later the same day Truman told Edward McKim, a Treasury Department representative, that he had decided that lend-lease to Great Britain between V-E Day and V-J Day was strictly an FEA matter and would be handled by Crowley.[50]

When after a month had passed and the bureaucracy had failed to disgorge a lend-lease policy, Admiral Leahy decided to take the bull by the horns. On July 5 he intervened personally with Truman and persuaded him to issue through the joint chiefs a directive to all concerned agencies stipulating that military lend-lease would be extended only to facilitate direct participation by America's allies in the war against Japan. The directive was interpreted by Somervell to mean that the United States should not provide supplies to British and French occupation forces even though the presence of Allied troops in liberated and ex-enemy areas made possible the redeployment of American troops to the Pacific theater. By the time Vinson, Clayton, and Patterson realized what had happened, Truman had left for Potsdam. On July 12, Vinson sought Byrnes's aid. Everyone was confused, he said. Moreover, the July 5 directive was threatening the buildup of United States troops for the final assault on Japan, not to mention poisoning Anglo- and Franco-American relations. Byrnes, in turn, appealed to the president to adopt a lend-lease policy that would "permit a partial and equitable reconversion in the United Kingdom."[51]

Truman was willing to give some reassurance to the British but was afraid that the public and Congress simply would not tolerate use of lend-lease as an instrument of peacetime foreign aid. In late June, Joseph Grew had sent Truman a Gallup Poll showing that nearly two-thirds (64 percent) of the American people thought that Britain should pay America in full for lend-lease. Twenty-five percent favored partial repayment, while 58 percent continued to advocate repayment even after it was pointed out that lend-lease goods were used in the common defense. When Truman finally responded to Churchill's note of May 28, he made no mention of the United States commitment to aid British reconversion. The United States recognized its commitment to provide munitions and nonmunitions lend-lease but only as the strategic situation dictated.[52]

At lunch with Truman at Potsdam, Churchill briefly recounted Britain's economic and financial plight, including sterling balances, exports, and convertibility. Britain would have to have as liberal a settlement of lend-lease as possible during Phase III. "Until we get our wheels turning properly once more," he told

Truman, "we could be of little use to world security or any of the high purposes of San Francisco." Truman listened attentively, Churchill recalled, and was sympathetic. He spoke of the immense debt the United States owed Great Britain for having held the fort at the beginning. "If you had gone down like France," Churchill recalled him as saying, "we might well be fighting the Germans on the American coast at the present time." This fact alone justified America in viewing lend-lease and postwar aid as more than just matters of finance. But, significantly, the American leader made no promises.[53]

The British Chiefs of Staff, led by General H. L. "Pug" Ismay, quickly let Churchill know that they needed more than a sympathetic hearing from Truman. In deference to congressional sensitivities, the services in the United Kingdom had trimmed their requests for Phase II from $2.8 billion to $1.8 billion; they had gone as far as they could in appeasing the tightwads in the United States, Ismay informed Churchill. Commonwealth forces all over the world were equipped with American products, and they could obtain replacements only from the United States. Moreover, the inability to secure machinery from America would severely hamper production in the United Kingdom. Finally, Britain simply had no means to produce transport aircraft and long-range bombers; the RAF was completely dependent on the United States for these types. The final figure for British lend-lease munitions decided on at Quebec—$2.8 billion—was considerably less than three-fifths of the wartime lend-lease level Britain was then receiving. And now, apparently, the United States was not even prepared to come across with a paltry $1.8 billion. The service chiefs asked Churchill to submit their specific complaints to Truman, to request him to withdraw the July 5 directive, and to ask that he permit lend-lease to Britain for occupation purposes. "What we want," Ismay wrote, "is for the President to get down to the solid case put forward in our memorandum, in consultation with his advisors, and to give the Prime Minister a personal reply."[54]

Finally, on July 24, the day before his departure for England to await the general election returns, Churchill communicated the specific requests and complaints of his military advisers directly to Truman. This time the president was less sympathetic. He was trying to give the Lend-Lease Act the broadest possible interpretation, he told Churchill, but Congress had, after all, insisted that it be used for war purposes only.[55]

At this point, internecine fighting broke out within the American delegation. At dinner with the president at Potsdam on July 26, Somervell announced that he had made up his mind that supplies of lend-lease munitions should be limited to the requirements of units in the Japanese theater or designated for action there and that the Japanese theater should be defined as the area east of Calcutta. The next day Clayton, McCloy, and Byrnes met with Leahy, and argued for acceptance of the British munitions requests excluding supplies for British occupation forces. Leahy finally agreed.

Truman subsequently notified Clement Attlee, who by this time had replaced Churchill at the conference, of America's final position on lend-lease during

Phase II and assured him that, aside from those dealings with occupation forces, the specific complaints voiced by the British military chiefs would be satisfied. After obtaining Truman's assurance that Will Clayton would stop off in London on his way home to discuss arrangements for a general Anglo-American conference on lend-lease and Phase III in Washington in September, Attlee indicated that he could not ask for more. Good as his word, Truman on August 1 issued a new directive replacing the controversial July 5 document.[56]

Two weeks later the war in the Pacific came to an abrupt halt. On July 22 from Potsdam, Harry Truman issued top secret orders to the United States Air Force to select appropriate military-industrial targets in Japan and to bomb them until the emperor surrendered unconditionally. On August 6, the *Enola Gay* dropped a single atomic device on Hiroshima. Eighty-five thousand people died from the immediate blast, but still Japan did not surrender. On August 8 Russia entered the war. On August 9 a second nuclear device obliterated Nagasaki. Japan finally succumbed on the fourteenth. World War II was over, and Phase III had begun.

British officials in Washington had acknowledged several times during spring and summer 1945 that, given the mood of Congress and the American public, and the apparent awe in which the new resident at 1600 Pennsylvania Avenue held them, lend-lease would not and could not survive V-J Day. But at the same time various statements by Rosenman, Clayton, Morgenthau, and others to the effect that the United States was committed to providing Britain with financial assistance during Phase III encouraged some in Whitehall to believe that lend-lease would not be shut off abruptly and that, in order to ensure a comfortable transition for Britain from Phase II to Phase III, material in the pipeline would continue to flow. Moreover, some hoped that among America's allies Britain would be singled out for special treatment. They were wrong.

Contributing to the hasty if temporary demise of lend-lease was the fact that two of its champions within the United States foreign policy establishment were out of pocket when the decision on aid to Britain was made. From London, where he was engaged in detailed talks on Phase III with Eady and Keynes, Will Clayton appealed to Crowley and Acheson not to make any change in lend-lease policy regarding nonmunitions until he had a chance to return and report. Lend-lease, its continuation, and its final settlement were intimately tied up with Britain's postwar economic health, he pointed out.[57] But unbeknownst to Clayton, Dean Acheson, the administration's preeminent strategic multilateralist, was out of town as well. Having just been named undersecretary of state by Byrnes, he and his family were in Canada for a brief vacation when the final decisions concerning lend-lease were made. Thus, the field lay open for Crowley.

Leo Crowley had decided some weeks earlier that when the opportunity presented itself, he would make a clean break with the British over lend-lease and then leave government service. On August 14 the FEA chief asked his legal counsel, Walter N. Thayer, to develop an opinion on whether or not the chief executive had the authority to continue lend-lease aid to Great Britain after V-J Day. Thayer replied that the president did if he and FEA deemed such aid to be in the interest of national defense. Under the law lend-lease could be used for mopping up operations, occupation of former enemy countries, "or some other appropriate post–V-J Day purpose." It could continue as a free gift or as a loan. Post–V-J Day aid would have to stop if and when (1) the president determined it was no longer essential to national security or (2) July 1, 1946, arrived and Congress had not passed a concurrent resolution stating that such aid was necessary to national security.[58] Thus, the chief executive clearly had the authority to continue lend-lease if he wished. Moreover, Crowley was well aware of the economic benefits that accrued to the United States as a result of its massive program of overseas aid and of the possible negative impact on employment levels sudden termination might have.[59] Nonetheless, he decided to shut down the lend-lease machine at once. Anglophobia and hypersensitivity to congressional opinion aside, the Irishman was irritated with Whitehall for conspiring behind his back with members of his own staff.

Fear of Congress and resentment at perceived British opportunism made the president receptive to the arguments put forward by lend-lease hard-liners. On August 17, Crowley, Leahy, and Byrnes met with Truman at the White House to discuss termination. The administration had repeatedly informed Congress that lend-lease would be discontinued at the close of the war, Crowley and Leahy pointed out. To protect themselves against charges that they were misusing public funds, FEA and the military would have to close out aid to Britain immediately. Truman and Byrnes sympathized with this position for obvious political reasons. Moreover, America's two top foreign policy decision makers also believed that Britain had lately been reneging on its "obligations" under Article VII. On August 8, Byrnes had reported to Truman that the United States legation in Bern, Switzerland, had learned from several sources that the British were in the process of negotiating modifications to existing currency and financial agreements with some eight or nine European countries. "It is understood," Byrnes reported, "that in several cases these agreements contain secret clauses which are contrary to the Bretton Woods resolutions and intended to bring the countries concerned within the sterling orbit."[60] Consequently, the White House issued a directive to all concerned agencies that immediately on cessation of hostilities with Japan (1) no new contracts were to be entered into except for items the joint chiefs might approve out of military appropriations, (2) all countries with 3(c) agreements would take and pay for items under contract, (3) countries without 3(c) agreements might obtain goods in the pipeline on payment terms to be set by the United States government, and (4) all uncompleted contracts would be reviewed to determine if completion would be in the best interest of the United States. At the time of the directive, FEA estimated that lend-lease goods contracted for but not yet delivered amounted to about $2 billion and that lend-lease supplies in stockpile abroad were worth between $1 billion and $1.5 billion.[61]

Both strategic and economic multilateralists claimed to be much upset by Washington's "abrupt" decision to terminate lend-lease. Hugh Clayton and Emilio Collado, who had also made the trip to London, deluged Washington with protests. At least, that is what they told their British hosts.[62] Dean Acheson later claimed in his memoirs that if he or Clayton had been in Washington, the sudden cut-off would not have happened. The decision to terminate, he wrote, was the work of Grew and Crowley: "Made even before the surrender of Japan had been signed on board the *U.S.S. Missouri*, when millions of our own and our Allies' troops still had to disarm our enemies and occupy their territory and to stabilize an as yet unplumbed situation in Europe, Asia, the Middle East, and Africa, it [the cut-off] knocked the financial bottom out of the whole Allied military position."[63] But the order was not wholly a surprise to the multilateralists, nor were they that displeased. The White House had consulted closely with the commercial policy division of the State Department before and during formulation of the directive. The cut-off of lend-lease would put definite and immediate pressure on the British to sign a multilateral commercial policy agreement, while the multilateralists could make Crowley and Leahy scapegoats.[64] What Acheson, Clayton, Hawkins, and Winthrop Brown did not like was the manner in which aid was terminated. Crowley was unnecessarily rude. In notifying Brand of termination, he had also demanded an inventory of all lend-lease goods in Britain's possession not consumed or destroyed and put the Englishman on notice that the United States would expect compensation. "Negotiations," he had written in conclusion, "will be carried on in Washington and you will be advised of developments."[65]

Public comment in the United States on termination of lend-lease to Britain was mixed but generally favorable. Some twitted Truman for his "supremely gauche international bad manners."[66] Union members and liberal internationalists tended to be critical, the former because they reasoned that an abrupt cut-off of aid to England would increase unemployment and the latter because they tended to favor a continuation of economic aid to all victims of Axis aggression.[67] But others seemed to agree with Nathan Cropper, who wrote:

> The decision to discontinue Lend-Lease to Britain is a thoroughly sound and essentially just determination. . . . In the midst of a savage war for survival, the British utilized the major forces at their disposal to murder Greeks who fought the Nazis and Italian enemies; to intimidate the French in Syria and Lebanon; to annihilate the helpless Jews in Palestine; . . . through incitements throughout the Near East, Balkans, and Europe all for imperialistic and financial advantages.[68]

Soldiers in particular tended to applaud the move, as did economic conservatives. American Zionists were positively euphoric. "Can't tell you how happy I am with your statement over Lend-lease," Rabbi Stephen Wise wrote Truman.[69]

Crowley tried to persuade Truman that neither Britain nor any other country violently objected to the sudden termination. "While the various governments would have liked to have had it continued," he wrote the president, "their reaction on the whole was quite favorable."[70] He was, of course, misrepresenting the facts.

The reaction in the United Kingdom was at worst vitriolic and at best confused. Some were shocked and frightened. "The dollar sign is back in the Anglo-

American equation," proclaimed one official, "and the ghost of Mr. Coolidge seems to be hovering near the White House."[71] Wilfrid Eady was angry and acutely concerned about Britain's immediate gold/dollar situation. "From now on," he announced to his colleagues, "H.M.G. would not permit a single article to be imported into this country unless it was absolutely unavoidable." If necessary, the government would impose severe new restrictions on civilian consumption. Such a course was essential to preserve British monetary reserves and to demonstrate to the Americans the folly of their ways. The Labour cabinet was particularly concerned about food. Britain was heavily dependent on the United States for cereal, meat, and dairy products, the Ministry of Food informed the Treasury, and it would be at least three months before a shift from a lend-lease to a cash basis would be possible. The central question that lurked in every Briton's mind was whether the sudden termination of lend-lease marked a reversion to isolationism and a declaration by the United States that it intended to withdraw from Europe, or whether termination was a clearing of the decks preparatory to the launching of a new aid program for Phase III. In the end, the British had little choice but to bite their tongues and press Washington to convene a meeting on financial and commercial policy as quickly as possible, that is, to assume that the severance of their lend-lease lifeline was but a prelude to a new foreign aid program.[72]

On April 20, 1945, Henry Morgenthau informed Harry Truman that "the British are more worried about their post-war financial position than almost any other subject," and that Sir John Anderson wanted "to dispatch a top financial mission to the United States immediately after V-E Day to discuss the whole question of financial assistance to the United Kingdom."[73] The two men suddenly realized that Anderson's request found the United States without a consistent, comprehensive foreign loan policy; there did not even exist a political or bureaucratic consensus that the country should have one. In fact, negotiations over the Anglo-American Financial Agreement of 1946 proceeded simultaneously with the evolution of an American foreign loan policy.

After passage of the Bretton Woods Agreements in summer 1945, more than a dozen channels existed through which the United States could extend financial assistance to other countries. These included loans by the Export-Import Bank, the World Bank, the Reconstruction Finance Corporation, congressionally approved direct loans, the operations of the IMF and the United States Stabilization Fund, United States contributions to UNRRA, lend-lease aid, purchases of foreign materials for strategic stockpiles, and expenditures in overseas areas for United States military operations. Until the Bretton Woods institutions were operational, which required British as well as American ratification, the Export-Import Bank continued to be the principal means for financing foreign orders for American goods. The federally funded bank had been created in 1934 to finance trade between the United States and the Soviet Union, but it was never used for that purpose; instead, Washington employed the reserves of the bank primarily to make commercial and development loans to Latin America. Largely because of the size and comprehensiveness of the lend-lease program, Congress did not add significantly to the capital of the Export-Import Bank during the war. Consequently, by V-E Day, May 8, 1945, the bank had only $150 million available for loans. As has been noted, the Truman administration persuaded Congress in 1945 to reconstitute the bank and increase its total lending authority from $700 million to $3.5 billion. The Export-Import Bank Act of 1945 authorized the institution to expend its funds for short-term credits to American exporters of agricultural products, medium-term dollar loans to foreign nations to enable them to purchase American goods, medium- and long-term credits to foreign nations for the purchase of specified United States equipment and technical services, and direct loans to American firms exporting industrial products. In other words, Export-Import Bank loans were tied absolutely to the purchase of American goods and services. Notwithstanding the bilateral nature of the loan agreements, the United States insisted that all recipients of loans from the Export-Import Bank pledge to organize their trade along multilateral lines. Jacob Viner, a distinguished University of Chicago political economist, described the bank's foreign loan policy as "double usury" because it charged interest on loans and also required recipients to adhere to America's international trade program.[74] The transfer of control of the Export-Import Bank to Leo Crowley and FEA by Congress at the time of the institution's modification was further proof that senators and representatives defined the institution in conservative and essentially nationalist terms.

Not surprisingly, the State Department took the position that foreign loan policy was an integral part of the nation's overall foreign policy. Although Cordell Hull had adopted a dog-in-the-manger stance toward lend-lease, his underlings continued to believe throughout the war that control of foreign aid was the prerogative of the nation's diplomatic corps. When Congress modified the Export-Import Bank and transferred it to FEA, Jimmy Byrnes, now secretary of state, wrote Crowley that it was more important than ever to coordinate—he meant subsume—the activities of the bank to the nation's overall foreign policy as determined by the president and the Department of State.[75]

By June 1945 the secretary of state's Staff Committee had laid down the basic principles and objectives of the department's postwar loan policy. The United States should (1) continue to provide lend-lease in order that its allies be able to prosecute the war against Japan to the fullest; (2) participate fully in relief and rehabilitation activities; (3) cooperate in the management of international exchange mechanisms through the IMF, supplemented "by bilateral arrangements with the United Kingdom and perhaps other nations"; and (4) promote public and private dollar investment in reconstruction and development abroad during the next decade "to the extent of 25 to $30 billion."[76] The last objective was, of course, the most significant. It seemed to indicate a realization on the part of the State Department that a liberal loan policy was essential to the proper functioning of a multilateral system and an assumption that private institutions could and would provide a substantial part of that capital.

As negotiations over Article VII indicated, State Department officials expected recipients of United States largesse to embrace multilateralism. But, in addition—and this became clear during negotiations over the British loan—the State Department expected actual repayment in dollars. "It is essential," Byrnes wrote Crowley, "that financial aid for reconstruction go hand in hand with creation of commercial conditions which will permit repayment by stimulation of international trade so necessary to the prosperity of America's expanded industrial potential."[77] Insistence on repayment grew not out of financial considerations but rather out of the department's belief that Europe's default on its World War I debt had stimulated isolationism in America. Nonetheless, the economic repercussions of State's position would be immense. Moreover, as it turned out, the State Department was not committed to supplying those nations who were to be principal participants in America's multilateralist schemes with the capital necessary to enable them to achieve equilibrium. American diplomats were determined to drive a hard bargain and if possible get more than they gave. "In bilateral dealings with Britain," Halifax remarked presciently of United States policy in 1945, "a tough, business-like and 100 percent American line will be kept to the fore."[78] As a result, the amount of money doled out to Britain and other prospective trading partners of the United States was much too small and the conditions attached made the loans economically, not to mention strategically, counterproductive. Washington attached other price tags to its foreign loans—American domination of Pacific bases and American control of civil aviation, but those demands were implied and secondary to general commercial and monetary considerations.

The bureaucratic in-fighting that had marred the formulation of lend-lease policy for Phase III continued into the postwar period and dramatically affected the shaping of a coherent loan policy. The Bretton Woods Agreements, enacted into law by Congress in mid-1945, contained a mechanism designed to centralize the making of foreign loan policy and ensure that it was responsive to both the legislative and executive branches of government. The legislation established a National Advisory Council on International Monetary and Financial Problems consisting of the secretary of the Treasury (chairman), secretary of state, secretary of commerce, chairman of the Federal Reserve Board, and chairman of the Export-Import Bank. The NAC was not only to recommend policy for the IMF and IBRD to the president, but it also was to coordinate the foreign lending and international monetary activities of all federal agencies. For a variety of reasons, however, the NAC did not move to formulate a general loan policy until January 1946. Until that date, it did little more than approve loans recommended to it by the Export-Import Bank.[79] Thus, neither the State Department nor the NAC moved to grasp firm control of foreign loan policy prior to negotiation of the British loan in fall and winter 1945.

In March 1945 following the Rosenman mission, the British Treasury acknowledged the necessity of obtaining a postwar loan from the United States but decided to wait until after V-E Day to approach Washington. In June and July, John Maynard Keynes and his colleagues in their roles as contemporary England's Jason and the Argonauts set about planning to wrest the golden fleece from America. But it was Britain who would be fleeced. The British Embassy in Washington warned Whitehall that the political atmosphere was not conducive to a request for postwar aid. Crowley, a blatant Anglophobe and conniving politician, was temporarily in charge of America's foreign aid program, such as it was, and Congress was choosing to flex its muscles in the area of foreign economic policy. That meant that parochialism, nationalism, and special interests would be in temporary command of any foreign policy requiring a substantial appropriation. United States newspapers were still sprinkled with editorials and columns charging that Britain was not doing its fair share in the war against Japan. But Treasury decided that, given the imminent demise of the war in the Pacific and the termination of lend-lease that would accompany it, Britain had little choice but to press for comprehensive Phase III talks at the earliest possible date.[80]

As usual, it was difficult to know with whom to deal. Leo Crowley's ascendancy was surely a temporary aberration. The British originally believed that Henry Morgenthau was still the key figure on the American financial scene, and Robert Brand in Washington tried several times to get Harry White involved in secret, preparatory talks in anticipation of a general conference on Phase III. Whitehall, though aware of the NAC and its statutory clout, still believed it was best to prepare the way first with Treasury and then the White House. The British government also wanted initial talks to be held in London. There were fewer American bureaucratic toes to step on there and much less likelihood of a leak to Drew Pearson. If Congress and the American people learned that Britain was asking for a large grant-in-aid before the executive branch had time to prepare and educate them, an anti-British backlash would make meaningful assistance in Phase III well-nigh impossible.

Eventually, Whitehall decided to rely on its allies in the State Department. To London's consternation, Harry White refused an invitation to fly over for confidential talks. The time was not right, he told Brand; Bretton Woods was still up in the air and Congress's mood was volatile. This uncharacteristic circumspection on the part of the United States Treasury and reports that Will Clayton's star was on the rise in the foreign policy establishment finally convinced Whitehall to try and make their case to Clayton when he visited London in August in his role as United States delegate to the UNRRA Conference.[81]

After digesting advice from the Board of Trade, the Bank of England, and other interested parties, Keynes and his colleagues decided to ask the United States for a $4 billion free gift, appealing simultaneously to America's sense of justice and its self-interest. Britain would make it clear that it could not take part in any multilateral schemes without such aid and would in fact refuse to ratify the Bretton Woods Agreements until it was forthcoming. British negotiators should convince the Americans that, distasteful though such a course might be, Whitehall was prepared to tighten its belt and cling to wartime controls rather than enter into a financial agreement that could go sour. "What we shall be aiming at," Keynes noted, "will be American assistance as a basis for a joint handling of the problem with a view to a liquidation, so far as possible, of the financial consequences of the war in so far as they affect and distort future international relations."[82] In addition, the British delegation should indicate to the United States in very general terms that it was preparing to undertake immediate negotiations with its sterling creditors looking toward settlement of the sterling debts. Under no circumstances should the final agreement mention the United Kingdom's sterling obligations, lest Britons accuse the negotiators of concluding an agreement that violated Commonwealth sovereignty and Americans charge them with using American money to pay off Britain's empire and Commonwealth partners. Keynes proposed that immediately after informal talks with Clayton in August 1945, the chancellor of the Exchequer should lead a delegation to Washington to present Britain's case directly to the president.[83]

It should be noted that Keynes and his colleagues believed that the number one item threatening Britain's balance-of-payments position in the postwar period was military expenditure overseas. Cash outflows for arms and troops had to be reduced, as Eady put it, because "we could not both police the world and have homes on an adequate scale." And Treasury believed that in the months immediately following V-J Day, the United States would object to subsidizing British military installations in the Far East, Middle East, and Europe.[84]

In the United States, meanwhile, a heated debate over reconversion reinforced the Truman administration's conviction that multilateralism constituted a promising solution to its political and economic problems and that any financial agreement with Great Britain should hasten the demise of the financial empire. When Japan surrendered on August 14, 1945, Truman was caught high and dry without an immediate, clear policy on reconversion. In both the Roosevelt and Truman administrations, economic planners, knowing nothing about the atomic bomb, had accepted military estimates that the war with Japan would continue well into 1946. Thus, they visualized reconversion as a process that could be dealt with gradually over many months. Notorious for temporizing, Roosevelt had in any case been preoccupied with the war. The National Resources Planning Board, to which he had sometimes looked for ideas about reconversion, was dead, killed by conservatives in Congress. Truman likewise became absorbed in military and diplomatic problems after taking office and was away from home at the Potsdam Conference at a critical time in the domestic planning process. No one knew whether the end of the war would bring deflation and unemployment, as huge war contracts were canceled, or whether it would bring inflation, as consumers with unprecedented savings rushed into the market to compete for scarce goods.

In July Truman decided to send Congress a message on postwar problems—in effect his first state-of-the-union address. Conservatives and liberals maneuvered to influence the presidential recommendations. John Snyder, a midwestern banker and old friend of Truman who had replaced Fred Vinson as director of the Office of War Mobilization and Reconversion, was one of the most outspoken. Private initiative was Snyder's ideal. He thought FDR had gone too far toward federal control of business and he distrusted deficit financing. Jesse Jones, who had once been Snyder's employer, Bernard Baruch, and Herbert Hoover called on the president to put his trust in free enterprise and the private sector. Truman probably agreed with Snyder, if not with Jones, Baruch, and Hoover, yet he could not ignore liberal sentiment entirely. His political career had been based in no small part on the support of organized labor. And he believed not only that the federal government had a responsibility to care for those who could not care for themselves but also a mandate to protect ordinary citizens from the vicissitudes of an unregulated economy. Economic forecasts for the immediate postwar period were not encouraging. Secretary of Commerce Henry Wallace warned him on October 19 that 1946 payrolls would be about $25 million below the 1945 level. "The situation," he wrote, "may be very serious by the Spring of 1946, particularly in light of the estimated volume of 8 million unemployed which will confront us at that time." Without "aggressive action under administrative leadership," America could experience a postwar depression of major proportions.[85]

Into the reconversion breach stepped Fred Vinson and his Treasury staffers. They put together a comprehensive program calling for modification of Social Security to cover additional workers and to increase unemployment compensation, a raise in the minimum wage, additional regional development projects like the TVA, permanent farm price supports, a housing program, and enactment of the full employment bill. The program was designed in the long run to ensure the survival of the private sector and to dampen the fires of inflation. If the government did not take action to prevent depression before it happened, "we shall face an unmanageable problem of deficit financing," declared the Treasury report on postwar policy.[86]

But Vinson's recommendations, subsequently embodied in the president's message to Congress, failed to consider the increasingly conservative mood of the country. Basic New Deal reforms, notably Social Security, were accepted by most people, and the existence of labor unions had become a foregone conclusion, but a majority of Americans wanted to stop there. Republicans and southern Democrats had banded together to block further extension of the New Deal; indeed, the Roosevelt administration had not been able to get a major domestic bill through Congress since 1938. The conservative coalition refused to enact a single major recommendation of Truman's September address. Once again the multilateralists stepped forward to offer their stratagem as a panacea for the administration's domestic and international problems.

The preeminent champion of the multilateralist cause within administration councils and the man who would subsequently shape and orchestrate strategy in the Phase III discussions was Will Clayton. Leo Crowley's ascendancy was a product of circumstance—primarily the confusion surrounding the transition from Roosevelt to Truman and the end of World War II. Vague as he was on the issues involved, Harry Truman wanted to support Britain in the immediate post-war period and Crowley had no plan whatever to offer for Phase III. By summer 1945, Will Clayton's role as chief spokesman for commercial and even financial multilateralism was widely recognized. He combined the ideological fervor of Cordell Hull with the economic sophistication of Clair Wilcox and the political acumen of Dean Acheson.

In June 1945 Clayton moved to fill the bureaucratic void that had developed in the area of foreign economic policy. He succeeded in persuading Vinson, and through him Harry Truman, that multilateralism was a politically feasible way for the United States to aid its allies and to subsidize the domestic economy, a way to achieve full employment without collectivization. Emphasizing Britain's pivotal role in the economic system of the noncommunist world, he told the new leadership that, without aid during the transitional period, the United Kingdom could not embrace multilateralism.[87]

Clayton, Vinson, and their subordinates realized on the eve of the Phase III negotiations that a large credit to Great Britain to enable it to achieve free convertibility was of more importance to the United States than the United Kingdom. They recognized that a large deficit in Britain's international balance of payments might force it to maintain and even increase wartime financial and trade controls in order to provide minimum essential imports for itself and the empire. Given Britain's need to increase exports as much as 50 percent over prewar levels, the world could look forward to a continuance of the dollar pool, empire preference, and quotas. Such practices threatened multilateralism and hence United States prosperity. "The United States interest in dollar loans to the United Kingdom is greater than the United Kingdom interest in such loans in spite of the United Kingdom's need for dollars because our immediate and long-range interests are at stake and could be protected to some extent by a generous loan policy to the United Kingdom," one official wrote. Great Britain, he added, had "only the choice of shifting creditors and she does not particularly trust the United States in the creditor role."[88]

The State Department and Treasury anticipated that Britain would want as large a credit as possible and would want it as a grant-in-aid. But Clayton in particular believed that the political situation in the United States was so volatile that any aid that was extended must carry the trappings of a commercial transaction.[89] He proposed to offer Britain "a dollar credit of as much as 2 or 3 billion as required," repayable over thirty years. The United States would have to charge interest but should grant the most liberal rate; 3(c) arrangements under lend-lease carried a rate of 2⅜ percent but the United States should be prepared to go as low as 2 percent. British reluctance to incur a dollar debt could be met, Clayton argued, by including a provision in the financial agreement that waived payment in any year that Britain experienced a deficit in its balance of payments. In return for this loan, the United States would require the Exchequer to undertake free convertibility of sterling at once. Washington would also insist on "substantial funding" of the abnormal wartime sterling balances.

In the area of commercial policy, United States negotiators would insist on the elimination of empire preference, "probably as one term in a new reciprocal trade agreement reached under the strengthened act or as part of a multilateral trade convention." State Department officials acknowledged, however, that given the fact that empire preference was a highly emotional and politicized issue in Britain, the most the United States could perhaps hope for was a scaling down of preference rates. Clayton recognized that Britain would have to retain import controls on essential items to reduce the strain on its balance of payments. But these would have to be nondiscriminatory barriers that would apply equally to all of Britain's trading partners and would not, like imperial preference, impose restrictions on third parties.

The terms of the financial agreement the foreign policy establishment proposed to foist on the British were brutal. Their main effect would be to secure British compliance with the Bretton Woods Agreements as soon as the war ended rather than at the end of a five-year transitional period. "It is of the utmost importance," Clayton concluded, "to accelerate Britain's reconversion to multilateralism in this way, both because of the danger that bilateralism and restrictionism might otherwise become imbedded in British policy during the transition, and because the American business public will demand early evidence that Britain is going to go along with us in our post-war trade policy if they are to continue to support it."[90] In addition, the United States would not only demand repayment of the principal but also charge interest on a loan that was admittedly more to the advantage of the United States than Great Britain. The waiver clause was a financial loophole but, as the British were to point out, one that could turn into a political noose for them. Any time Britain invoked the clause, it risked setting off a wave of Anglophobia and isolationism in the United States. Finally, Washington seemed determined once again to force the world to embrace commercial multilateralism without being willing to do so itself.[91]

At this point and throughout succeeding negotiations, United States officials refused to acknowledge the fundamental truth that America's economy was basically a national one whereas Britain's was international. The United States, as Robert Taft so frequently pointed out, was still virtually self-sufficient, producing within its borders nearly all of the raw materials—food, fiber, minerals, energy—and finished goods that it required. Great Britain depended more than ever on overseas sources for food, iron ore, petroleum, and certain finished products. Its trading system required international interdependency. Areas of the empire were analogous to various economic regions of the United States; it could even be argued that the interstate commerce clause in the United States Constitution was comparable to the Ottawa Agreements, at least insofar as both were designed to ensure the freest possible flow of goods and services among the several states and members of the union and the sterling area respectively. Imperial preference was also comparable to the American tariff system in that it attempted to protect an economically integrated whole from more powerful entities outside the community that could force unfavorable terms of trade on the various constituents of the community.

Except for a brief six-week period after his accession to the presidency, Harry Truman operated throughout 1946 on the assumption that Joseph Stalin and his associates were reasonable men with whom deals could be struck, leading to a prolonged period of peaceful coexistence. Part of the United States' strategy for building bridges to Moscow called for it to avoid any appearance of an Anglo-American combine directed against the Soviet Union. In its self-assumed role as mediator between the two European rivals, the Truman administration abruptly terminated lend-lease in August 1945, developed a loan policy that promised Great Britain only token aid, and worked out an arrangement with the Soviets over Eastern Europe at the Moscow Foreign Ministers' Conference without even consulting the British. At first glance, American strategies in the economic and strategic spheres during 1945 would seem to be consistent. The policy of mediation, however, looked forward to the restoration and maintenance of a balance of power in Europe and that condition, in turn, called for a strong and healthy Great Britain and a fully developed rather than flawed multilateralism. As had been true in the past, inconsistencies in American foreign policy in summer 1945 were a product not so much of the Roosevelt-Truman administration's insensitivity to or ignorance of Britain's need as to the strength of Anglophobia and economic nationalism in the United States, and to bureaucratic conflict within the foreign policy establishment.

12. The Tie That Binds: The Anglo-American Financial Agreement, 1945–1946

THE BRITISH government entered into negotiations with the United States over a postwar credit in fall 1945 anticipating an agreement generous enough to enable Britain to safely participate in a multilateral trading system. It was to be sadly disappointed. During three months of tense and at times bitter negotiation, both within and between governments, London made concession after concession and in the end accepted an arrangement that provided only token aid and that required Britain to surrender its financial safeguards within a year.

Britain agreed to accept what was clearly an imperfect agreement for several reasons. John Maynard Keynes saw the loan as the last and crucial stone in the international financial structure on which he had been toiling since the beginning of World War II. His charisma, persuasive powers, reputation, and mastery of detail exerted a powerful influence on the new Labour government; but in the end, the Labour leadership, which recognized that the Anglo-American Financial Agreement was dangerously flawed, endorsed it for reasons of its own. Clement Attlee, Hugh Dalton, and Ernest Bevin—the liberal socialists—urged on by Keynes and James Meade, were determined to keep the party and the government from being dominated by Labour's left-wing, the "Gosplanners" of Meade's nightmares, and they became convinced that a credit from the United States in whatever form was necessary to attain that objective. If the government could not meet the British public's immediate need for housing, food, and employment, either the Conservatives would take over in an early general election or, what was more likely, the Labour government would be compelled to undertake radical, socialist experiments in domestic policy. Such policies were not only an anathema to Attlee, Bevin, and Dalton but they were also sure to permanently alienate the United States at a time when Britain desperately needed a powerful ally in Europe.

During the financial and commercial negotiations that transpired in Washington from September 11 through December 6, 1945, the Truman administration insisted not only that the amount of any loan granted to Britain be kept to a minimum but that it also bear interest and require full and early convertibility. In their defense of these requirements American negotiators made much of congressional parsimony and nationalism together with anti-imperialism and Zionism, and no doubt public and legislative opposition to a liberal postwar aid program weighed heavily on the minds of American decision makers.

The flawed multilateralism that Washington forced on the United Kingdom in the form of the financial agreement was also a function of the foreign policy bureaucracy's inability to reconcile divergent objectives. The Treasury Department proved to be more interested in United States domination of the international financial structure provided for in the Bretton Woods Agreements than in commercial or financial multilateralism. Consequently, the Treasury Department succeeded in limiting the amount of the loan and structuring its repayment in such a way that Britain could not build up its monetary reserves.

Will Clayton, Harry Hawkins, and other advocates of a more liberal aid package tried to block the efforts of Harry Dexter White, Fred Vinson, and Marriner Eccles to restrict the credit proffered to the United Kingdom, but they failed. Yet, when the nationalists insisted on cutting the amount of the loan and making it interest-bearing, American multilateralists were not willing to relinquish their demand that Britain make an immediate and complete jump to full and free convertibility. Modified multilateralism seemed preferable to none at all.

In the process of accepting what was clearly a flawed agreement, the liberal socialists within the Attlee government had first to overcome their own misgivings and then the objections of their more radical colleagues, the Gosplanners. Keynes's prestige and persuasiveness played a role in converting the cabinet, but by the final stages of the negotiations Dalton, Attlee, and Bevin acknowledged that the financial agreement was a spear aimed at the heart of the financial empire. They accepted Washington's terms partly out of fear of an open breach with the United States but primarily in response to the perceived political need to meet the British public's immediate material requirements.

Clayton and Emilio Collado reached London from Potsdam on the morning of August 3, 1945, and, even before checking in at the American Embassy, sat down with Keynes, Sir Wilfrid Eady, and Robert Brand, who was in England for consultation on the ominous financial situation. Both parties agreed that Phase III talks should begin no later than September 15 and be held in Washington. This would give little time to permanent officials in Whitehall to acquaint the new Labour ministers with the complexities of the situation, but Britain had to know which way to turn in international finance and commerce, and the direction would be determined largely by American generosity in Phase III—or the lack of it. Challenging conventional wisdom in Whitehall, Keynes insisted that the talks be held in America where he would have greater freedom of action. If he were subject to constant buffeting by the political storms of London, the results could be disastrous. Moreover, both Clayton and Keynes agreed that it was imperative that the real purpose of the negotiation—that is, extension of a credit—be masked until the conversations had actually produced a financial agreement. The British and American publics would be told that the United Kingdom delegation was in Washington to discuss the cleanup of lend-lease and related matters.

Will Clayton was optimistic, even expansive. Congressional and public opinion in the United States had changed considerably on questions of international economics and finance, he assured his hosts. He pointed to the success of Bretton Woods in Congress, the ease with which the Export-Import Bank received additional funds, and the margin by which Congress had renewed RTAA even though many observers had originally predicted its defeat. Official opinion, he said, seemed to be coalescing around a $3 billion credit for the United Kingdom. The cotton broker–turned–diplomat made no mention of either interest or repayment of principal. In return the United States would expect immediate convertibility of sterling on current account and an end to the dollar pool, that great bogey of American business.

Britain was grateful that America was willing to help its friend and ally, Keynes said, but if Britain were "but a shilling better than bust, we shall be bust."[1] He then told the Americans that Whitehall had been thinking more in terms of a free gift of from $5 billion to $6 billion. Any financial agreement, moreover, would have to include a final settlement of lend-lease. Keynes and his colleagues made it clear that a 3(c) arrangement would not be an acceptable basis for such a settlement.

The next day, the United States Treasury representatives in London, Harold Glasser and William Taylor, who were miffed that they had not been included in the initial discussion, took Clayton and Collado to task for not mentioning that the United States expected any loan to be repaid in full with interest. Clayton was sanguine. It would not do to lay one's cards on the table all at once; the British would come around to the idea of a repayable loan in time. Glasser and Taylor were not so sure, and they let it be known that they were providing summaries of the London discussions to their superiors in Washington.[2]

By the time the next major round of talks was held on August 17, Japan had surrendered, Phase III was no longer a matter of conjecture, and Will Clayton had decided to take a tougher line on what Britain could expect from America. Clayton, Collado, Glasser, and Taylor met with representatives from not only the Treasury but also the Board of Trade and the Ministry of Food. The United States delegation made it clear that an agreement on commercial policy was a sine qua non for a loan and that a loan was exactly what the United States was prepared to offer—one that was not only repayable but that carried interest. In return for its generosity the United States expected elimination of empire preference, discontinuance of the dollar pool, immediate convertibility for currency transactions on current account, and continuation of nondiscriminatory economic controls for no more than three years. Moreover, his government, Clayton asserted, was not prepared to pay the empire and Commonwealth's share of the cost of World War II. A loan would depend on London working out a suitable funding arrangement for blocked sterling.

In what was to become a pattern, Keynes took a hard line with the Americans in negotiations while privately assuring his colleagues of the reasonableness of the United States position. A loan would be history repeating itself, he told Clayton. If the Truman administration could not come up with an "inspired" solution to Britain's economic and financial woes, His Majesty's Government would have to embrace state trading. Keynes went on to argue that financial and commercial issues had to be kept separate since the United States had reneged on its commitment to a simultaneous, horizontal tariff cut. The sterling balances, moreover, were a matter solely for the Commonwealth to decide. The meeting ended without a hint of an emerging consensus.[3] Several days later, however, Keynes was all sweetness and light. "A very large part of the American policy," he told Eady and Edward Bridges, "is in our interest as much as in theirs and that they are urging it on us sincerely and believing that we also have much to gain from it" was a very good sign. "We can safely walk with them a very long way. There are only a few elements in their projective [*sic*] policies which are dangerous to us."[4]

Significantly, Sir Wilfrid Eady was more pessimistic than Keynes. Eady was fond of his colleague and had great respect for his intellect. But sometimes Keynes could be all sail and no anchor. "I am always a bit anxious when he is about being idle and ingenious," Eady had written Sir Richard Hopkins in February during a lag in Anglo-American negotiations.[5] "The present Administration," he subsequently told Bridges, "was more likely to start from guessing what they could get past Congress and then making that their policy than from formulating their own policies and selling them." "I found Mr. Clayton's attitude on the financial talks ominous on two aspects," he added: "that he clearly thinks in terms of a credit which is to be serviced . . . and that he clearly expects sufficiently precise assurances about our policy to enable him to say that the multilateral world . . . would follow."[6]

Sir Richard Clarke, a high ranking Treasury official, shared Eady's skepticism. According to Clarke, Keynes exhibited from the first complete optimism that "justice would rule America's postwar policy toward the United Kingdom." He was almost consumed with fear that British procrastination would make a satisfactory Phase III settlement impossible. But in Clarke's opinion lingering Anglophobia and economic nationalism in Congress, the advent of Labour to power, and the unwillingness of both London and Washington to decide long-range financial policy made Keynes's optimism inappropriate. Clarke argues that Keynes was simply in a hurry. A financial agreement with the United States that committed both countries to currency convertibility would be the capstone of the multilateral system on which he had been working since 1941. Keynes did not expect to live more than another year or two; not only did he want to see his edifice complete, but also he believed no one else could bring the matter to a successful close.[7]

By the time Clayton arrived in London for initial negotiations on Phase III, the results of the general election had been published and the civil servants in Whitehall had a new set of political bosses to deal with. The Conservative party contained perhaps the most strident opponents of multilateralism in all of Britain—Leo Amery, Lord Beaverbrook, and Robert S. Hudson—together with some of its most ardent supporters—Sir Richard Law, Sir John Anderson, and Lord Cherwell. The Labour party was initially as split as the Conservatives. The far left, represented in the new government by Aneurin Bevan and Emmanuel Shinwell, continued to see multilateralism as a capitalist plot to force free enterprise on the world and a blatant attempt to restore the gold standard, a mechanism it equated with deflation and depression. Dalton remained a multilateralist for economic reasons and because he anticipated the dismemberment and deindustrialization of Germany. Bevin shared the left's misgivings but inclined toward accepting multilateralism for strategic and political reasons. Attlee saw modified multilateralism as inescapable. Labour's promises to provide homes, food, and work had secured their victory at the polls. This, coupled with its determination to protect the empire and stand up to the Russians, made the Attlee government perhaps more responsive to American financial and economic demands than a Churchill regime would have been. Multilateralists were encouraged when Dalton showed no hesitation in keeping Keynes as his adviser. Nonetheless, the new government's tractability was not clear or certain in the first days of its existence.[8] The ministers were an unknown quantity to their underlings. Moreover, it could be expected that Britain's new leaders would move with extreme caution until they got their feet on the ground and until or unless they understood the complex issues involved.

After Japan's surrender, Treasury multilateralists supported by the Economic Section of the War Cabinet Secretariat had less than a month to "educate" the new Labour ministry. James Meade articulated the British Keynesians' perspective on the changed political situation:

> The effect of the Labour Government upon the external economic settlement will depend very largely upon whether the Liberal-Socialists or the Gosplanites win the internal struggle. If the Liberal-Socialists win out, an economic settlement with the U.S.A. *a la* Article VII would not be impossible. Prices and costs would exist and would be used to measure discrimination and protection in those trades which were controlled by the State; the rate of exchange would be a meaningful price and the Bretton Woods rules about exchange rates would be applicable; and much trade in fact would be left to private initiative. If the Gosplanites won, it would seem difficult to attach much meaning to the Article VII discussions, since there would be no internal system of prices and costs on which degrees of protection or discrimination could be measured. If the Liberal-Socialists win internally, the result of the elections might exercise a very wholesome effect in the international political scene. There will then be an alternative progressive socialist but liberal government to set against authoritarian Russia. The forces of the left in Europe will have a free as well as a totalitarian point of attraction. We might per-

haps even set a bridge between the United States, with which we should share all the fundamental English-speaking ideas about individual liberty, and the Russians, since we should not be a purely laissez-faire capitalist regime.[9]

Keynes, and to a lesser extent Meade, assumed the role of mentor to the new government. Their long-range goal was to strengthen the hand of the liberal-socialists. For their own good Keynes decided to scare Attlee and his colleagues into accepting a credit from the United States on whatever conditions Whitehall and Washington agreed upon, and to see to it that the delegation to Washington was not tied down by overly rigid instructions. In the process, consciously or unconsciously, he portrayed himself as a savior of the realm.

After reviewing the sterling balances situation, current and future balance-of-payments problems, export requirements, reconversion problems, and overseas military requirements, Keynes told the ministers that the nation could be saved only by (1) an intense concentration on exports, (2) drastic and immediate economies in Britain's overseas expenditures, and (3) substantial aid from America on terms that Britain could accept. On the last point the United States would likely require in return for a credit (1) repayment with interest, (2) British adherence to United States commercial policies, and (3) lease or cession of certain British bases. Clearly, if repayment terms carried any danger of default, Britain would have to refuse. "For the time being," Keynes declared, "Ministers would do well to assume that no arrangement we can properly accept is yet in sight; and that, until such arrangement is in sight, we are, with the imminent cessation of Lend-Lease, virtually bankrupt and the economic basis for the hopes of the people non-existent." In short, the nation faced a "financial Dunkirk," the consequence of which would be a British withdrawal from its overseas responsibilities with a resulting loss of power and prestige. The best the United Kingdom could hope for was second-class status "much like France is today." The government would have to seek what "charity" it could from the Dominions and initiate austerity policies at home harsher than any known during the war. "There would have to be indefinite postponement of realization of the best hopes of the new government," he observed unnecessarily. A successful conclusion of the forthcoming negotiations in Washington could avert such a bleak future, however. If the cabinet would authorize Treasury to work out the best deal possible with the Americans, then victory might be snatched from the jaws of defeat. Before the ministers dispersed, Attlee told Keynes that the figures and even the phrases in his report were political dynamite and should be held in the strictest confidence.[10]

The left wing of the Labour party adamantly opposed any arrangement that would tie Great Britain to either American domestic or foreign policy. The party's official position on foreign affairs consisted of a collection of philosophical generalities on the nature of international affairs that intellectuals and left-wing backbenchers called a "Socialist Foreign Policy." The three major tenets of this approach were (1) that socialist countries inevitably had similar interests, (2) that armies and navies caused rather than deterred wars, and (3) that capitalism was a major cause of international tensions. During the year following Potsdam, the rank and file of the parliamentary party gradually came to the realization that Bevin's foreign policy, which was based on maintenance of the British Empire and quiet development of an Anglo-American strategy to block expansion of communist Russia, cut across all three tenets of a socialist foreign policy. Throughout 1945 left-wingers relentlessly pressed for a more sympathetic attitude toward Russia, for complete independence from American political and economic influence, for state trading and bilateralism in foreign trade, for drastic reductions in the military services, for a pro-Zionist policy in Palestine, and for major reductions in Britain's costly overseas commitments. Left-wingers were, however, extremely reluctant to press any disagreement on international stratagems to the point of threatening Labour's majority in Parliament.[11] The ideologues and radical socialists had waited too long for this opportunity to send their domestic "revolution" on its way.

The man to convince, as Keynes surely realized, was Ernest Bevin, not only because he was foreign secretary but also because he was the bell cow and weather vane of the Labour party. For Bevin, the overriding objective of Britain's foreign economic policy was improved living standards for the masses. He preferred establishing limited objectives and shaping policy to achieve those goals rather than forcing events and circumstances to conform to a rigid formula, he told a group of visiting American members of Congress in late August 1945. He was convinced that a partnership in international trade and finance between the United States and the United Kingdom, with each being free to follow independent policies in regard to domestic socioeconomic matters, would save "Middle Europe" and raise the "purchasing power of the peasantry of the world."[12]

Nonetheless, the foreign secretary initially took a very cautious view of the Phase III negotiations. Britain should ask America for the financial resources to cover the transitional period, but His Majesty's negotiators should not agree to any monetary or commercial arrangements, "not even Bretton Woods," until Britain's economic picture came into sharper focus. "I should never be a party to any international agreement which . . . would prevent me from insulating the home market from the violent repercussions . . . when wide fluctuations take place on the international price level,"[13] he announced.

When Treasury made it clear that the Truman administration would require concrete commitments with a specific timetable, Bevin had to choose between political and economic logic, between theory and practice. Predictably he chose to take what he could get in the short run. Ironically, a loan from the United States would be necessary to keep Labour's left wing relatively happy or at least prevent it from entering into a cabal against the government with the empire isolationists. Moreover, a loan agreement would facilitate Labour's plans for domestic reform and make possible an Anglo-American posture of resistance to Soviet expansion. In a sense, then, Bevin had to buy off the left wing of his own party with American money and buy off the Truman administration with concessions to multilateralism in order to pursue a policy of realpolitik in strategic and political matters. Prompted by Keynes's arguments and by his own reading of the domestic and international situation, the foreign secretary took the lead in August 1945 in persuading his cabinet colleagues to allow financial negotiation with the United States to begin as soon as possible.

At Hugh Dalton's suggestion, the cabinet approved a negotiating team that included Keynes, Halifax, Brand, and S. L. Hall-Patch of the Foreign Office. Noticeably absent from the British delegation were commercial policy experts Percival Leisching and Lionel Robbins. Keynes, now clearly obsessed with breathing life into Bretton Woods at all costs, did not want the International Bank for Reconstruction and Development and the International Monetary Fund held hostage to trade issues. But Meade and officials in the Economic Section, who suspected that if given a chance, Keynes would sacrifice the Commercial Union to his schemes for international monetary stabilization, would be heard from again.[14]

As usual, the putting together of an American team was accompanied by a flurry of bureaucratic sparring. The rivalry between State and Treasury never assumed the proportions that it had when Henry Morgenthau and Cordell Hull were in the saddle, but Jimmy Byrnes and Fred Vinson were old Washington hands and were not afraid to stick up for themselves. It had been "Assistant President" Byrnes after all who told Harry Hopkins to mind his own business. Treasury's representatives in London, William Taylor and Harold Glasser, had not been at all happy about Clayton's stopover. No sooner had he arrived than they began bombarding the home office with complaints that Clayton was treading on financial ground. He was, moreover, giving up too much too soon. "It is scarcely dignified," Edward Pritchard observed to Fred Vinson after reading their complaints, "for American officials to remain in London for a month begging the British to accept a loan."[15] Treasury representatives suspected that Whitehall intended to hold Bretton Woods hostage until it got the kind of aid package it wanted for Phase III. Because they perceived that the State Department did not hold the IMF and IBRD in the same esteem as did Treasury and in fact might compromise on the Bretton Woods Agreements, Vinson and his assistants maneuvered to have the negotiations transferred at once to Washington and placed under their general supervision.[16]

But State had the initiative and was not going to relinquish it willingly. While Clayton was in London, Byrnes authorized him over the phone to formally invite the British to send a delegation to Washington to begin discussions by September 10. The talks would revolve around four topics: financial problems, lend-lease termination, commercial policy, and disposal of surplus property abroad. In briefing Truman on what he had done, the secretary of state remarked, "obviously, these negotiations will be the primary responsibility of the State Department."[17] According to Byrnes's game plan the talks would be handled by four subgroups, Vinson chairing the financial task force, Clayton the commercial, Leo Crowley, lend-lease, and Stuart Symington, surplus war property administrator, the committee on overseas property disposal. The four subgroup chairmen would report periodically to a United States top group including the chairmen plus the secretary of commerce (Henry Wallace) and the chairman of the Federal Reserve (Marriner Eccles). The secretary of state would preside over the top group. Clayton, Byrnes advised Truman, would fill in for him until he returned from the London Foreign Ministers' Conference. The State Department would, of course, keep the White House posted from time to time. Vinson tried to block Byrnes by invoking the name of the National Advisory Council of which he was chairman, but Treasury was too late with too little.[18] Byrnes and the State Department had moved first to fill a void and that was crucial to bureaucratic success during the early stages of the Truman administration.

Keynes and his colleagues arrived in Washington on September 10, 1945, and the first meeting of the British and American top committees took place the next day. Even the elegance of the board room of the Federal Reserve could not compensate for the sweltering heat of Washington. Keynes expressed regret that Jefferson and Hamilton had agreed to so inclement a site. He was further irritated when literally dozens of Americans showed up for the talks. With such a large number of Yanks, the possibility of leaks increased geometrically, he grumbled to London. Moreover, the small British delegation felt besieged. The situation was somewhat relieved when Clayton asked the American departments to limit their observers to no more than three.[19]

From the beginning, Keynes and Halifax labored simultaneously to convince their opposite numbers that Britain did indeed have an alternative to dependence on the United States in the postwar period and that it was so destitute, a generous loan was a prerequisite to national survival. The "easy course" would be for the United States to offer and the United Kingdom to accept a large loan on commercial terms, they told the Americans. But such an arrangement, as every thoughtful observer agreed, would be short-sighted and would constitute a very real threat to future Anglo-American relations.[20] Keynes then presented a specific summary of Britain's financial situation—past, present, and future. British liabilities to overseas creditors stood at $13.4 billion at the end of June 1945 and were likely to increase to $14.5 billion by the close of the year. Against this, Britain had an estimated reserve of $1.9 billion in gold and dollars. During the sixteen months from the beginning of September 1945 to the end of 1946, Britain would face an additional overall deficit in its external transactions of approximately $4 billion. A deficit on current account would continue for two more years but at a sharply declining rate. These estimates were based on the following assumptions: "The British imports would be held at 85% of the pre-war volumes; exports would reach 75% of pre-war levels by the end of 1946; net income from overseas investments would have declined by 40% over pre-war levels; and overseas military expenditures would decline, but gradually."[21]

Neither White nor Clayton was impressed. One was determined not only to see that the United Kingdom accept the Bretton Woods institutions, but also that it not challenge United States domination of the IMF and IBRD by building up its gold/dollar holdings. The other was determined to use Britain's need for a loan to force Whitehall to abolish the dollar pool and embrace free convertibility. Between these two positions Keynes and company did not have much room for maneuver.

Although the figures presented by Keynes and Halifax almost exactly paralleled those prepared in an independent study by the staff of the National Advisory Council, Harry White and the United States Treasury representatives took the position that the British estimates were much too "pessimistic" and implied that Keynes had inflated the statistics for bargaining purposes. Whereas the British estimated their net deficit for the first three years of the transitional period at $5.3 billion, the Treasury working group put it at $3.3 billion. Moreover, Britain's sterling indebtedness was not as imposing as it seemed: $2 billion could be handled through "miscellaneous arrangements" with Britain's South American and European creditors, an additional $2 billion would be necessary for ordinary working balances, and the empire and Commonwealth could be persuaded to write off an additional $4 billion as their contribution to the war effort. Thus, the real problem was about $5 billion. White and the financial committee suggested to the top group that Britain's problems could be completely taken care of by at most a $4 billion credit.[22]

Clayton, who despite the prearranged division of labor, attended virtually all the finance committee meetings, together with Vinson and Eccles, quickly made it apparent that he would settle for nothing less than an end to the dollar pool, early and free convertibility of sterling, and a scaling down of the sterling balances. On the nineteenth the Americans demanded a specific plan from the British for scaling down, eliminating, and/or funding the balances as a precondition to further negotiations. What Clayton wanted, of course, was to clear what he perceived to be major roadblocks to multilateralism and to ensure that United States merchants had access to closed empire markets. There were also political considerations. "I cannot for the life of me see what we will tell our Texas Congressmen who put us on the grill with questions about British blocked balances," John Hickerson had told Clayton but a week earlier. "What is the answer to this question? Why should Australia, India, and other parts of the Commonwealth get paid to any greater extent than the U.S. for goods, services, and assistance extended to the U.K. during the war?"[23]

London was ambivalent about submitting a specific plan. Leaks were always a problem with the Americans. News that Britain was discussing a funding plan with the United States without even consulting its sterling area partners would enrage them, particularly the more nationalistic like Egypt and India. On the other hand, a loan proposal would be very useful in applying pressure to Britain's sterling creditors. What Whitehall wanted was an indication from the Americans that assistance on a large scale would depend on the United Kingdom coming to an arrangement with each of its major creditors for scaling down and funding its credit. This would take the heat off London. The cabinet decided that the possible benefits of presenting a specific plan outweighed the potential risks and on September 26 authorized Keynes and Halifax to go ahead.[24]

In line with their intention to lead rather than follow the new Labour government, the two diplomats had already developed a scenario. On September 19 Halifax and Clayton arranged for the smallest possible group to hear the British out on sterling balances. Assuming that Britain's sterling debt was $12 billion at the end of 1946, His Majesty's Government would ask its creditors to write off $4 billion, in some cases perhaps in return for a surrender of British assets or claims in the country concerned. Britain would then agree to immediately free 10 percent of the remainder, or $800 million. This would take care of the needs of the nations concerned for four to five years. At the end of this period Britain would begin releasing 2 percent a year for fifty years, an action that would cost Britain about $145 million per year. For this scheme to work, Great Britain would have to obtain a $5 billion interest-free grant from the United States.[25] The Americans listened intently but did not respond.

By the end of the first week of talks, which had dealt almost exclusively with financial matters, a number of State Department multilateralists were predicting that the negotiations would end before they ever began. Vinson obviously did not like Keynes and was already complaining about his "filabustering [*sic*]" and his "threatening" in regard to the possibility that Britain would adopt a bilateral as opposed to a multilateral course. Everyone seemed to want to blame the "empire system" for all the world's economic difficulties, Emilio Collado told Clayton, and to refuse to admit that the United States would have to accept imports on a massive scale if multilateralism was going to work. There was, moreover, far too much preoccupation with the issue of a final settlement of lend-lease, including compensation.[26]

The Washington conversations that took place in fall 1945 not only determined the shape of American aid to Britain in the immediate postwar period, but also marked the final chapter in the debate over Article VII. Harry Truman attempted to confront the question of compensation directly in his August 31 report to Congress on lend-lease. World War II had cost America $280 billion, 15 percent of which or $42 billion had been in the form of lend-lease. Any attempt to collect for wartime aid would threaten the political stability of America's wartime allies and sow the seeds of a new world conflict, he told the legislators. "Debts of such magnitude would drive our chief fighting partners into desperate measures like those developed before the war by the Axis for the forcing of export surpluses in order to repay us," the president told a postaddress press conference. "In a world thus overburdened with unproductive debts, the sound expansion of United States foreign trade and investment abroad would meet with almost insuperable barriers."[27]

But the idea that America was being used as a cornucopia by an ungrateful and undeserving world still flourished in the United States, and economic nationalists immediately leaped on Truman's statement. Robert Taft, seconded in milder terms by Arthur Vandenberg, protested that the president's disavowal denied

America an important bargaining weapon in negotiations over the shape of the postwar world. Stung by such criticism, Jimmy Byrnes told reporters on September 1 that the president's statement notwithstanding, there were still lend-lease settlements to be made.[28]

There was never a real threat that the World War I war debts issue would reappear. Instead, various bureaucratic entities and special interests maneuvered once again to use Article VII and the proposed loan as leverage to achieve their strategic and economic objectives. Those officials within the State and War departments concerned with protecting and extending America's empire deluged the United States delegation in late September with conditions to be attached to the loan agreement and the lend-lease settlement. John Hickerson insisted that Britain agree to sign a "Five Freedoms' Civil Aviation Agreement" with the United States whereby the United Kingdom would provide free and unlimited fly-over and landing rights in British territory to United States planes. Britain had steadfastly resisted such an arrangement. Given the fact that the United States controlled the majority of the world's transport aircraft at the close of the war, the five freedoms' arrangement would enable America to monopolize commercial air traffic within the British Empire. In addition, the State and War departments insisted that, in return for writing off lend-lease and a postwar loan, London also agree to transfer ownership of certain telecommunication facilities in South America and the Pacific to American interests.

But the strongest pitch made by War and State department strategists was for the transfer of British-owned or claimed air and naval bases around the world. Repeating a recurrent theme in the speeches of House and Senate members, Hickerson and Assistant Secretary of War John J. McCloy suggested that the 99-year leases provided for under the Destroyers-for-Bases Deal be converted to 999-year leases. The War Department wanted to go even farther. No objective was more important, declared General G. A. Lincoln, chief of the Army Air Force and Policy Group, than obtaining air rights to bases not only under direct British jurisdiction but under their indirect control or influence. The Azores were particularly desirable. Considering the new United States concept of defense, namely, "striking at the source of the influence controlling future disturbances," possession of this strategically located, all-weather island group was considered crucial by American military planners. The third week in September, McCloy conveyed Lincoln's views to Clayton and enumerated specific locations: Teheran and Abadan in Iran, Baghdad in Iraq, Habbaniya in Kuwait, and Basra in Oman.[29] American marines, he noted, had just suffered 50,000 casualties in taking Tarawa, Iwo Jima, and Okinawa. Military strategists insisted that the only way to prevent repetition of that carnage was United States strategic domination of the Pacific. As a guard against future aggression, the United Kingdom should grant base rights to the United States in Rabaul, Tarawa, and Aden, all of which were clearly owned by Britain or a Commonwealth country, and Christmas, Canton, Penrhyn, and Funafuti islands, all under disputed ownership. In addition, War Department planners wanted very much to become the sole supplier of arms to

Latin America and to standardize all hemispheric weapons systems. To this end, they demanded that Britain withdraw all military missions from Latin America and refrain from any and all arms sales in the area. Finally, Britain should provide the United States with full access to critical raw materials under its control. McCloy concluded:

> Not only are some of these matters of deep interest from the military point of view to the United States but, I think, approaches along these lines may provide an avenue which will be subject to less criticism on both sides of the water than almost any purely financial arrangement which now can be made with England. The American people would feel that they had really gotten something of substance or substantial value; the British would have avoided a heavy debt, and, what is probably more important than anything else, our general partnership would be better cemented throughout the world.[30]

Clayton, Collado, Wilcox, and the other multilateralists in the State Department, of course, wanted to use the loan and lend-lease settlement to force Britain at long last to embrace their financial and commercial schemes. They opposed "tying" the loan to specific purchases—Britain should be free to spend the money anywhere and in any way it desired—and they wanted no "extraneous" conditions that could dilute Britain's commitment to multilateralism.[31] Other concessions were purely secondary. State Department negotiators decided to introduce Hickerson and McCloy's demands but quickly abandon them when the British resisted.

To ensure that he did not lose control of the negotiations, Clayton arranged for a series of special, secret meetings between him, Vinson, Keynes, and Halifax at Blair House. He also reported directly to Truman throughout the talks. "I am encouraged by the progress of the discussions," he told the president, "and the reasonableness of the British." Their proposal for dealing with blocked sterling seemed credible, as did their request for a credit of $5 billion. Discussions on commercial policy would begin at the end of the week when a "strong delegation" arrived from Britain. As soon as agreement was reached in this field, the two nations could conclude a financial arrangement as well.[32]

Clayton, Vinson, Keynes, and Halifax held their first meeting at Blair House on September 25. Free from the encumbrance of the two entourages, the Americans laid their cards on the table. The United States was entirely satisfied with the British suggestion for resolving the sterling balances problem. Assuming no hitch in the commercial policy talks, the two nations ought to be able to sign an agreement by October 25. Of two things the British should be sure, however. Congress would never accept an agreement that did not liberalize and facilitate international trade, and it would never embrace an interest-free grant-in-aid. The amount was no problem—$5 billion was not excessive—but the loan would have to be repaid with interest. Keynes and Halifax replied that His Majesty's Government would never agree to interest. During the heated exchange that followed, neither side gave ground.

In his official report, however, Keynes was optimistic almost to the point of being misleading. Although Clayton and Vinson took a firm line, he wrote the cabinet, "there is reason to think that their experts are carefully examining the question of a loan without interest . . . a proposal for a loan free of interest would not take the American public by surprise." The British government should discard the idea of a grant-in-aid and consider carefully the merits of an interest-free loan.[33]

His private communications were much more pessimistic. "Nothing could have appeared more Rhadamanthine than the poker faces of these two noble Roman Senators," Keynes embellished in a personal communication to Hugh Dalton. The real difficulty was with Clayton, Keynes mistakenly asserted. "He is not only deeply imbued with business analogies but suffers in my opinion from honest intellectual misapprehensions about the ease with which America's debtors can discharge their debts."[34] Moreover, in a simultaneous but separate letter to Eady, Keynes indicated that he knew the United States negotiators meant business about interest. In fact, he was already working on a plan that included interest payments. He confided to the Treasury that while he realized the political (prestige) problems that would arise if the government accepted an interest-bearing loan from the United States, there were no financial risks. The loan agreement could be "dressed up" to "camouflage" interest payments and it would cost Britain very little more. Of course, those in the Truman administration most worried about congressional and public opinion were not interested in masking interest payments—just the converse.[35]

Other British representatives found the first Blair House encounter uniformly discouraging. "We ran into some dirty weather yesterday," Hall-Patch wrote Michael Butler. He was not surprised, he said. "Congress and the outside world are blanketed in an impenetrable fog of ignorance and prejudice lit by fitful flickers of downright hostility." The White House seemed unwilling to exercise any leadership. In such an atmosphere, Congress was unlikely to make any "large concessions" and it was from Congress that concessions would have to come. "The people in London," he concluded, "will soon have to decide whether we are to stay here or if it would not be better tactics if we withdrew, make all preparations to tighten our belts, and then see, in say three or four months' time, whether the hard facts of life have penetrated sufficiently to curb ignorance and prompt discussions to be resumed."[36]

Unfortunately for this stratagem the British Empire was already starting to crumble around the edges. Just as the Washington conversations were getting underway, Clement Attlee told Hugh Dalton that it was no use pretending any longer that Britain could keep open its Mediterranean transportation routes in time of war. In view of Keynes's evaluation of the British economy, Britain would have to pull its troops out of the entire Middle East from Egypt to Greece. Nor could the United Kingdom hope to defend Turkey, Iraq, or Persia against the steady pressure of "the Russian land Masses."[37] Some Foreign Office officials believed that, economics aside, the Russian menace would convince the United States to provide liberal aid to Britain, while others questioned whether the United States was capable of identifying and acting on its vital interests.[38] In any case, breaking off negotiations would constitute a tremendous gamble.

Within hours of the first Blair House interview, Keynes had developed a plan for repaying a $5 billion interest-free loan. Payments would consist of $100 million a year for fifty years, the first payment to be made five years after the signing of the financial agreement. Annual installments on the debt to the sterling area might amount to another $150 million. The aggregate service for Britain's war debts would be less than 5 percent of the export target the Treasury and Board of Trade had set to enable Britain to break even on current account. "Either we can manage this, or we are sunk anyhow," he argued. Under an ingenious escape clause, none of Britain's creditors, whether the United States or a member of the sterling area, would be entitled to draw an installment in any year in which the United Kingdom's monetary reserves (as defined by the Bretton Woods plan) fell below its Bretton Woods quota and were decreasing. In such a situation, the installments would be deferred and the period of amortization would be extended. This formula would force the creditor nations to accept British goods and services in payment. Moreover, Britain's credit would in no way be impugned by deferment.[39]

When Keynes presented his plan to Dalton and Bevin, the two Labour ministers bristled. The United States must recognize that Britain's predicament stemmed from its sacrifices in the war, they proclaimed. How could having to lay out an additional $100 million a year, even in goods and services, help the United Kingdom attain the objective of balance on current account? Keynes should not, repeat not, broach his plan for repayment to the Americans. Could not he and Halifax revive the idea of the United States repaying Britain the $2 billion that it had to spend in the United States before lend-lease had gone into effect? Cabinet members and Labour backbenchers began grumbling that conservatives and special interests in the United States intended to use the loan negotiations to restrain the advance of socialism in Britain.[40]

In addition, the cabinet made it clear that under no circumstances should the delegates submit to "blackmail," that is, the attachment of conditions to the loan agreement that were unrelated to the agreement. Keynes, Halifax, and their colleagues had become acutely aware of War, State, and congressional demands in the areas of civil aviation and telecommunications, Hall-Patch wrote Butler, "but their underlings are certainly applying pressure, and once they have applied it apparently the honor of the great U.S.A. is involved and they have to be supported."[41] "The demands put forward in sundry quarters for bases or other aeronautical advantages . . .," advised J. G. Donnelley, "would in effect be surrender of sovereignty on our part without any reciprocal advantages."[42] Britain, the cabinet declared, would discuss these issues on their merits but not in connection with the loan. "The abrupt stoppage of Lend-Lease followed by these long drawn-out negotiations in Washington, in which Halifax and Keynes go on explaining but meet nothing but a row of poker faces across the table, are not encouraging," Dalton confided to his diary.[43]

The next Blair House meeting between Keynes, Halifax, Vinson, and Clayton took place on September 27. The Englishmen chose to act as if they had not received the cabinet's directive. Halifax offered to convert the 99-year leases to 999-year leases as a political "sweetener" to the forthcoming deal, and Keynes proudly outlined the escape clause he had devised. The Americans expressed interest in both suggestions.[44]

The conversations were partially eclipsed by the resignation of Leo Crowley on September 27. The British Supply Mission rejoiced that it would no longer have to deal with the FEA chief on major policy questions regarding lend-lease. "Things are much brighter," Hall-Patch wrote Butler, "one of the 'niggers in the wood pile' has departed, i.e. Leo Crowley."[45] "I should reckon that his departure should save us at least $100 million," Keynes wrote Dalton. Actually, Crowley's days had been numbered for some time. In late August Oscar Cox had resigned his post in FEA to take a position as unofficial adviser to President Truman. As Crowley felt himself increasingly isolated, his behavior became more erratic. He derided his colleagues without discretion and even abused the president personally. But as Michael Butler observed, the Irishman's departure was insignificant in the overall scheme of things because it had changed neither congressional nor public opinion a whit.[46]

Despite the obstinance of the Americans and the intransigence of the cabinet, negotiations over the British loan constituted for John Maynard Keynes the most exhilarating period in his life. The heat and humidity were oppressive, he wrote London, with the temperature exceeding ninety degrees every day. Nonetheless, in spite of the heat and his heart condition, the economist claimed to be enjoying his best health in years. The Americans were good-hearted if a bit dense, while the British delegation was "just about the finest group one could want to go into action with," he wrote Dalton. Everyone lived in a "blaze of limelight," he reported with obvious glee. The negotiations were tedious and exhausting, the social engagements endless but crucial to future congressional approval. "The Ambassador gave last week what I would think was a very useful, small dinner to half a dozen of the leading Senators on both sides," Keynes related. "They cross-examined me for three hours sitting on the porch of the Embassy on a tropical evening and seemed both interested and friendly, though incredibly remote."[47] Keynes did not particularly want the negotiations to end—he enjoyed having the fate of the British Empire in his hands. What the delegation needed from the cabinet, he wrote Eady, was general guidance. "You can rely on us to be very slow in making any concrete proposal. There will be at least another week or two of poker play."[48] And he certainly did not intend for the talks to end in failure. If London wanted something better than a noninterest-bearing loan repayable in fifty equal installments with an escape clause, he told Dalton, then negotiations would have to be broken off. "My advice would be to accept a settlement on these terms."[49]

Apparently unaware that Keynes and Halifax had suggested a deal on bases and a mechanism for repaying a $5 billion loan, Dalton, Bevin, and the staffs of the Foreign Office and Treasury huddled once again. At a cabinet meeting on October 5, Dalton told his colleagues the United Kingdom would have to have assistance in some form from the United States. If aid were to be sufficient to enable the world to move toward multilateralism, a minimum of $5 billion would be required. If Washington insisted on a smaller amount on commercial terms, His Majesty's Government would have to divert the channels of trade artificially and turn away from the United States as a source of supply. Strategic considerations aside, such a development would have a profound impact on British living standards. It would mean that during 1946, while bread and potatoes would continue to be available at wartime levels, the fats ration would be much reduced and there would be no more tinned milk or dried eggs. Meat rations would decline by 15 percent, and poultry production in the United Kingdom would drop off because of a shortage of maize. Timber supplies would fall off by 15 percent and plywood by 40 percent. Perhaps most importantly, there would be an 80 percent cut in tobacco.[50]

The cabinet decided, however, that, before it could opt for a $5 billion interest-free credit, the delegations should investigate the possibility of obtaining a two-tiered credit from the United States: a $2 billion grant-in-aid to be used to fund the sterling balances and thus open up the sterling area, and a $3 billion repayable loan for purchase of essential items in the United States. Eady asked Keynes to return to London to meet with the Labour ministers but he refused, arguing that, if he left, everything achieved in the negotiations to date would be lost.[51]

Meanwhile, a second British delegation whose primary expertise was commercial policy had arrived in Washington. In the conversations on commercial policy between the British and American committees that began on October 2, Clayton and his colleagues clung to the fiction that RTAA represented full and complete compliance by the United States with the principles of commercial multilateralism. In addition, the Americans once again insisted on distinguishing between tariffs, which, they claimed, were applied equally to all countries, and preferences, which, they alleged, were exclusive agreements between one or more countries to discriminate against the rest of the trading world. Although Clayton did agree to link preference reductions to reductions in the United States tariff secured through bilateral negotiations, he demanded that any agreement on commercial policy include a pledge by Great Britain to eliminate all residual preferences. He added that the administration would find it "virtually impossible" to secure congressional approval for a financial agreement without such a commitment.[52]

Whitehall's instructions on commercial policy seemed to leave the British delegation little room for maneuver. Imperial preference was political dynamite, the cabinet insisted. It carried emotional significance for most Britons far beyond its economic importance. Moreover, the Labour governments of Australia and New Zealand were committed to the preference system, and Attlee and his colleagues were loath to alienate their collectivist cohorts within the Commonwealth.[53] "You can explain that it is not too easy for me to find a basis of financial settlement acceptable to my colleagues and to Parliament," Dalton wrote Keynes, "and that my task would be made hopeless if anyone can represent that a financial pistol has been held at our head on the subject of Imperial Preference."[54]

Rather surprisingly, given the length and bitterness of the controversy over Article VII, American and British negotiators quickly narrowed the gap that separated them. It was agreed that the United States would call an international conference on trade and employment during summer 1946. Britain would support the United States invitations to the meeting and also the American proposals for the establishment of an international trade organization. In so doing the British would thereby undertake (1) to negotiate the reduction of empire preferences (without, however, agreeing to remove residual preferences); (2) to negotiate a reduction of import duties, export duties, and other barriers to trade; and (3) to curb cartel practices that restricted trade. It was generally assumed that whenever Britain experienced balance-of-payments problems, it would be free to retain or impose nondiscriminatory controls such as quotas and national tariffs. Moreover, Britain could continue to enter into long-term commodity-purchasing agreements with regular suppliers if it could prove that such suppliers were the cheapest source.

These agreements amounted to a capitulation by the United States. Clair Wilcox and the other commercial policy experts representing the State Department claimed to have extracted commercial policy concessions from Clayton and Vinson with great difficulty. The two had caved in only after a "tremendous struggle" in a very "stormy session." Exclaimed one American official to Percival Leisching: "My God, I was glad to get out of that room. I was afraid every minute that they would go back on what we had wrung out of them."[55] This may or may not have been true. A favorite American negotiating technique was for second-level officials to pose as friends and confidants to the British and to act as if they were making common cause with their counterparts against their superiors when, in fact, there was no division of opinion. Everyone realized, however, that significant as the statement of principles and the proposed International Trade Organization were, the Americans had really gotten nothing specific out of the British and were no nearer eliminating preferences, quotas, commodity agreements, and cartels than they had been in 1941. In part they were handcuffed by their commitment to Congress to stick to the bilateral, selective method for tariff reduction and in part by the logic of British arguments that this constituted a retreat from commercial multilateralism.[56]

But the most important factor in the United States delegation's sudden tractability was Clayton's growing conviction that the key to establishing a multilateral trading system in the noncommunist world was the free convertibility of sterling at the earliest possible date. At the same time United States representatives were making concessions in the matter of imperial preference, they demanded that Britain remove all restrictions on convertibility of sterling for transactions on current account. The order would be applicable to all members of the international trading community as of June 30, 1946. Britain would agree to make sterling partially convertible for the sterling area only and insisted on a deadline of December 31, 1946. Increasingly this would become the crucial financial, strategic, and political issue in the Anglo-American negotiations.[57]

Meanwhile, two touring congressional committees returned to Washington to make their reports and submit their recommendations regarding a postwar foreign loan policy for the United States. One, the House Subcommittee on War Department Appropriations, passed through London in late September on the last leg of a trip around the world. The members had interviewed various European heads of state, including Stalin, and the finance ministers of the major trading nations. On its arrival in Washington, the subcommittee had recommended to President Truman that foreign countries, which seemed to look upon the United States as a land of milk and honey from which vast sums of money would be forthcoming merely for the asking, be informed that American prosperity was the product of hard work and frugality, and that loans, if made, would be expected to be repaid. The second body, the House Committee on Post-War Planning chaired by William Colmer, paused briefly in London in mid-August on its way to the Continent. Having visited France, Belgium, Germany, Denmark, Norway, Sweden, Russia, the Middle East, and Italy, the legislators stopped again in London for a brief round of talks with the Labour government before returning home in early October. Representatives Jesse Wolcott (R-Mich.) and Clifford Hope (R-Kans.), the two most outspoken members of the committee, told Truman, the State Department, and the press that based on conferences they had had with Stalin and Attlee the committee was very dissatisfied not only with Russia's views on international relations, but Britain's as well. Attlee apparently had not paid the Americans the deference they believed they deserved. Among other things, the Colmer committee recommended that any nation applying for a loan from the United States would have to prove need beyond a shadow of a doubt and agree to terms set by Congress.[58]

While Colmer and company warned their fellow Americans that an alien and unsympathetic world was looking for a handout, Anglo-American financial negotiations remained on dead center. The "secret" meetings at Blair House continued but with no perceptible benefit. On October 9 Keynes and Halifax renewed their plea for a combination grant-in-aid and loan. Vinson insisted that the bottom line was a $5 billion credit at 2 percent, payment to be made in fifty equal annual installments of $150 million.

The British knew well that some special interests in the United States very much wanted to see Britain the beneficiary of a liberal aid program, interests that ranged from members of labor unions who lived on or hoped to live on exports to Great Britain to Wall Street bankers who had invested with Britain in joint concerns. A poll taken in early October among leaders of American industry, labor, and the press indicated that between 70 percent and 80 percent of those questioned approved of financial aid to Britain. The embassy considered lobbying directly with these groups in hopes that they in turn would shake Clayton and Vinson from their perch, but decided in the end not to. In America a charge of meddling in domestic affairs was one of the most devastating that could be leveled against a foreign country.[59]

Both the British and the Americans did spend an inordinate amount of energy during the Washington conversations trying to manipulate the press. After an Anglophile article appeared on the op-ed page of the *Washington Post* on October 24, Hall-Patch wrote Michael Butler: "One sometimes wonders whether all the time and effort spent on people like Eugene Meyer is worth it and along comes an article like this."[60] To the dismay of the British, the Americans virtually negotiated in public. Every time either side advanced a position, the State or Treasury Department leaked it to a pet reporter such as John Crider or James Reston who then printed it. In this way, the administration attempted to gauge congressional and public opinion before proceeding any further.[61] The technique lent further credence to the British perception that the policy of the Truman administration "is to keep in close touch with the opinions and desires of Congress, following rather than leading, and flavoring to taste any pill which is indispensable to administer."[62]

By mid-October Keynes's nerves and his logic were becoming frayed. Having to negotiate with the cabinet on the one hand and the United States delegation closely wed to an ever-present "Congressional and public opinion" on the other was almost too much for even his psyche. If the United Kingdom delegation held out long enough, the administration's will might, in fact, break and a financial agreement to London's liking would be forthcoming, wrote Keynes, reciting a familiar litany. But, more likely, this would not happen. "In this business country," he observed somewhat bitterly, "where it is a moral duty and not merely a self-regarding act to make any money which the traffic will bear and the law allow, some imitation of a normal banking transaction is necessary if the moral principles of the country are not to be affronted." If Roosevelt were in the White House, the administration might be willing and able to overcome this counting-house mentality, but he was not. Moreover, there were strategic considerations— not only the security of the United Kingdom was at stake but that of all of Western Europe. If Britain chose to end "our present friendly and intimate relations" with the Americans by announcing that it was tired of being pushed around, "so much will be disastrously changed over so wide a field and for a period to which no one can set a term, that we cannot bring ourselves to contemplate it."[63]

As Keynes and company hoped, argument and circumstance at last forced the cabinet to bite the bullet. Early in October, the Labour government had arranged for Clement Attlee to visit Washington. The new prime minister wanted to clarify

Anglo-American policy over atomic energy and to indirectly smooth the way for a financial agreement. It was important, all concerned Britons believed, that the financial and commercial negotiators have a realistic proposal before them during Attlee's stay in Washington. To this end, the cabinet held a series of frantic meetings culminating in a lengthy night session on November 5 and two day meetings on the sixth. Dalton, Cripps, and Bevin took the position that Great Britain had no choice but to propose a financial agreement that would be acceptable to Congress and the American people. If the United States negotiators would not accept the two-tiered proposal, then Keynes should be authorized to ask for $4 billion at 2 percent with an option for another $1 billion at the same rate of interest. In both cases, interest would start after five years and repayment would stretch over fifty years.[64]

Not surprisingly, most of the objections to this proposal came from Aneurin Bevan and Emmanuel Shinwell, the Gosplanites of James Meade's nightmares. Bevan was opposed to the Bretton Woods proposals and the proposed International Trade Organization—that is, to multilateralism per se. The loan agreement was just a means to a multilateralist end, he proclaimed. Bevan refused to acknowledge Keynes as the great economic prophet of the new age. The ideas expressed in the *General Theory* were mere palliatives designed to save capitalism and were no substitute for a fuller socialist critique of American society. The free trade doctrines that Keynes and the Americans were conspiring to foist upon the world might just destroy socialist Britain. The new liberalism took no more account of rich and poor among the nations than the old liberalism did of rich and poor within nations, Labour's left wing argued. The whole concept of writing off part of the sterling debts was an anathema to Bevan. Britain's creditors were among the most wretchedly poverty-stricken nations of the world. The various schemes put forward for funding sterling balances smacked to him of plans hatched by Anglo-American capitalists to exploit the poor.

Gradually, however, the objections of the left-wing ministers were overwhelmed. Dalton's boast that "nothing much can be done in this cabinet when Bevin, Cripps and I are in firm coalition," was generally true. "We take the assault in successive waves and help each other very effectively," wrote the chancellor in his diary, and in due course the cabinet voted to instruct its delegation as he had suggested.[65] Shinwell and Bevan had it recorded that they were most unhappy and apprehensive about the future, but they went quietly in the end, never even threatening to resign. They were, after all, junior ministers, and did not want to split the Labour party before it had had a fair chance to rule.

Heartened by this sudden thaw in the cabinet's position, Keynes, Halifax, and company pressed the $2 billion/$2.5 billion proposal with renewed vigor through both official and personal channels. "We are seeking something which will benefit not only the U.K. but the whole of the world, and not least the U.S.A. itself." It was therefore not right that Britain should have to pay interest on the whole amount, Keynes wrote Vinson.[66]

There was, of course, never any chance that the United States delegation would proffer a loan without interest paid on the whole amount. Except during Clayton's exploratory talks in London in August, neither he nor Vinson had indicated otherwise. In fact, the dynamics of the decision-making process within the British foreign policy establishment and the various positions put forward by the British delegation did not have any significant impact on the American decision-making process. Each of the principal actors on the United States side decided early on what Britain needed and what the administration could afford politically and financially to give.

On November 10 Clayton and Vinson turned down the two-tiered proposal flatly and Keynes and Halifax for the first time indicated that Britain would accept $4.5 billion at 2 percent, including lend-lease, with payment to be deferred for five years. Britain would pay interest only on the amount drawn, the two Englishmen declared. The financial agreement would commit Britain to fifty payments of $31,800 for each $1 billion of principal drawn. The Americans countered by offering $3.5 billion at 2 percent including a final lend-lease settlement, and they insisted on Britain's assuming full convertibility on current account as of June 30, 1946.[67] Keynes did not even bother to notify Dalton of this latest exchange.

Despite the optimism of their communications, many within the British delegation were expressing doubts by mid-November about a successful conclusion to the financial negotiations. The forces of nationalism and imperialism seemed to pervade not only Congress and the American people, but the foreign policy establishment as well. During a discussion of waivers, the British had objected to an American proposal that would bind the United Kingdom too tightly. To their objections Marriner Eccles replied: "But we would then have no safeguards if some of our money was used to raise your standard of living or to meet military expenditures." "What else would the loan be used for?" the British asked incredulously. America, the British were beginning to feel, was determined to reduce Britain to a third-rate power. Hall-Patch, for one, never believed that Clayton, Vinson, and their subordinates were the great friends of Britain that Keynes and Halifax made them out to be. "I am becoming steadily more worried," he wrote. The "smoke-filled room" approach with no witnesses and no record—the Blair House meetings—was suitable only if one's counterparts were strong and trustworthy. "With the rabbits with whom we are dealing," he concluded, "I am not sure it is the right technique, and I am not at all sure that what will emerge from the smoke-filled room will be at all palatable to London."[68]

While the battle raged in Washington, Conservative leaders in the United Kingdom rather ingeniously attempted to use Britain's need for a loan and America's attachment to the tenets of free enterprise to block the Labour government's collectivist experiments in domestic policy. Referring to the cabinet's putative plans to nationalize coal, steel, and banking in Great Britain and to the socialist M.P.s' frequent attacks on capitalism, Oliver Lyttleton declared on the floor of the House of Commons: "May I say . . . that if you need assistance from a country—and how we need it—the best way to obtain it is not to affront, on every possible occasion, the opinion of that country by criticizing and sneering at things in this field which they hold most dear, namely, the overriding contribution which private enterprise has to make if the world is to be rebuilt."[69] Lyttleton specifically advised the government to reign in "Prof. Laski" and his firebrand colleagues. Labour backbenchers fought back, accusing Lyttleton and the Conservatives of wanting to appease the United States just as they had wanted to appease Germany before the war. They pointed out that the American economy was dominated not by the principle of private enterprise but by private collectivism. Nevertheless, Attlee, Bevin, and Dalton knew Lyttleton had a point.[70] The prevailing political atmosphere in the United States was conservative, and Britain would have to genuflect periodically to the American creed.

The new regime did adopt a markedly moderate posture during the loan negotiations. Bevin had told the visiting congressional deputation from the United States on August 22 that Americans really had no reason to fear the new Labour government. Its objective, like the Truman administration's, was full employment, and it would utilize private enterprise and public control to achieve that goal. "Coal and the Railways had let us down," he told them, but the cotton industry was being given another chance to reorganize.[71]

Clement Attlee's trip to the United States in mid-November 1945 was designed primarily to convince America that he and his colleagues were level-headed devotees of the middle way. Before the prime minister's departure, Dalton had presented a budget to Parliament that won almost universal praise from Conservative as well as Labour M.P.s. Rather than calling for radical schemes of currency manipulation and higher taxes, it prescribed a 40 percent cut in excess profits tax and reduced the sales tax on some items by as much as 33 percent. Impressed as they were, British business people and bankers left no doubt at the Lord Mayor's Luncheon in London on the eve of Attlee's departure that they expected the prime minister to reassure the United States that in loaning Britain money it would not be underwriting "radical" experiments by a "red" regime.[72] Arriving on November 15, he spent the next five days trying to convince members of Congress, bankers, and administration officials that he and his colleagues were Christian democrats first and socialists second. "I sat on the left of Prime Minister Attlee at dinner," Henry Wallace recorded in his diary. "He is a rather mousey little man who speaks without spark." Style aside, the prime minister gratified Wallace by telling him that English socialism was derived from William Morris and that it had a Christian base in contrast to the Marxian socialism of the European continent. "On the whole . . . ," Wallace later remarked, "Attlee's administration will probably be more conservative than Winston Churchill's would have been."[73]

Did Britain's need for financial aid from a predominantly conservative United States retard the advance of socialism in 1945–46? Left-wing ministers and Labour backbenchers believed that it did and that preservation of free enterprise in the United Kingdom was the overriding goal of the Truman administration in the financial negotiations. More than likely, the government's dependence on United States aid made it more conservative than it otherwise would have been. But in terms of socioeconomic policy the real struggle in 1945–46 in Britain was not between a conservative America and a radical Great Britain, but between

James Meade's "liberal-socialists" within the Labour party who wanted to preserve a modicum of free enterprise and Gosplanners who aimed at the elimination of the private sector. Leftists like Aneurin Bevan recognized the conservative predilections of Bevin, Dalton, Attlee, and Herbert Morrison at the outset of the new Labour government's tenure. The party's leadership was hard on the inside but soft on the outside, they charged. Attlee and his cohorts were just another example of working-class leaders who "curtsied to Tory dominance" once they assumed power.[74] Clearly the United States was a tacit ally of the liberal-socialists in 1945–46 as they fought to preserve a mixed economy at home and to offer an alternative to Russian communism to the social democrats of Western Europe.

Meanwhile, that adviser to presidents, Bernard Baruch, had once more leapt into the fray. On October 10, 1945, the very day Clayton and Vinson rejected, finally, the $2 billion/$2.5 billion proposal, Baruch published a letter he had written to Representative Albert Gore (D-Tenn.). The financier once again expressed his fear that loans to other countries might be used to nationalize their industries, deny America overseas markets, and eventually destroy free enterprise. A loan to Great Britain under prevailing conditions would constitute a subsidy to "totalization," he proclaimed. Britain must pull itself up by its bootstraps and revitalize its industry. Private striving and the entrepreneurial spirit were the keys to British recovery. What harm could a $3 billion loan to America's best customer do, Thomas Lamont subsequently wrote Baruch, especially in view of the fact that the United States spent $300 billion waging the war. "It is not 3 or 4 billions, Tom, it is pretty close to 28 billion," Baruch wrote back with typical illogic.[75] Given the timing of the Gore letter, Walter Lippmann charged, Baruch was deliberately trying to disrupt the loan negotiations during their most crucial point.

The "great financier" was certainly conservative and opposed to collectivism, but personal pique at not being continually consulted by the Truman administration probably had more to do with his outburst than ideology. "Twice when visiting Washington," he wrote Will Clayton, "I left word with your office that if you cared to see me you could."[76] But Clayton had had no time for him. Baruch may have been inane and irrational—he told Clayton, for example, that America's greatest mistake of the war had been not to "reestablish the producing and distributing agency that was once Germany"—but he was a dangerous and formidable opponent because of his inflated reputation and because his arguments appealed to the ingrained prejudices of the American people. "It [his argument] incites the very suspicion on both sides of the Atlantic which stand in the way of a constructive compromise," Walter Lippmann noted, "namely the American fear of being rooked into giving away our patrimony to foreigners and the British fear of becoming subservient debtors of the United States."[77] At one point Robert Brand actually called on Baruch and asked him to stop ruining Britain's chances of getting a loan.

While American conservatives recoiled from British socialism during the loan negotiations and attempted to use the nationalization program to block a loan, both liberals and conservatives criticized the Attlee government's dalliance with imperialism. By the time Clement Attlee visited Washington in November 1946, the Palestine question in particular had become an issue in the loan negotiations. "The squall on the horizon now is the Jewish question," Hall-Patch wrote Butler. "I hope we shall be able to give the appearance of *doing* something, as opposed to talking about something."[78] The massacre of several hundred Polish Jews en route to their homes from German concentration camps prompted a bipartisan coalition of House members headed by Leverett Saltonstall (R-Mass.) and Edwin C. Johnson (D-Colo.) to urge Truman to save displaced Jews before they all fell victims to a "hostile people who are already playing an encore to the Nazi plan of extermination."[79]

While Keynes, Clayton, and their colleagues wrangled over interest rates and conversion dates, Truman's congressional cronies urged him to place his stamp of approval on the Wagner-Taft Palestine Resolution which called for unlimited Jewish immigration into the British mandate and the eventual establishment of a Jewish national homeland. Although Wagner told the White House that it had better get on board lest the Republicans garner all the credit, the State Department and Joint Chiefs of Staff, still strongly opposed to an overtly pro-Arab policy, managed to restrain Truman. Citing pending negotiations and national security, the State Department temporarily arrested the advance of the Wagner-Taft Resolution.

American Zionists subsequently vented their frustration on the impending British loan. Congressman Emmanuel Cellar (D-N.Y.) took a most critical and most public interest in the loan negotiations. Moreover, there is a good bit of evidence that Baruch's attempted intervention into the loan proceedings was the product of Zionist pressure. "I enjoyed tremendously your statement in the public press on the subject of loans to foreign nations," Rabbi Abba Hillel Silver of Cleveland wrote Baruch in November. "President Truman must be 'stiffened up' to insist upon the admission of one hundred thousand immigrants into Palestine which he requested."[80]

Further complicating loan negotiations was a deadline that if not met promised to spell the final doom of multilateralism. According to the Bretton Woods Agreements, the government of the United Kingdom would have to ratify plans for the IBRD and IMF by December 31, 1945, or the entire scheme would become subject to renegotiation and repassage by Congress. The United States Treasury above all wanted to keep the agreements from lapsing and had let the United Kingdom delegation know that, without approval of Bretton Woods, Britain could forget about aid during Phase III. As they had been told to do, Keynes and his colleagues had tried to hold Bretton Woods hostage. The catch was that the political leadership in the United States believed that it held the chips, that Britain needed both Bretton Woods and a loan far more than the United States. Clayton, Vinson, and company refused to budge and the British had broken first. Parliament would adjourn on December 20, 1945, and, if it were to have time to act, Bretton Woods would have to be introduced the first week in December.[81] There was general agreement within the British foreign policy establishment that Keynes's advocacy would be required to secure parliamentary ratification. In fact, Keynes booked passage aboard the *Queen Mary* for November 30 in order to lobby for Bretton Woods. But then on November 24, the British delegation received a telegram from Attlee that seemed to make a loan agreement within the foreseeable future impossible.

His Majesty's Government, Attlee wrote, was willing to settle for a loan of not less than $4 billion, including lend-lease, at 2 percent to be repaid over fifty years beginning after five years. The United States would extend such a credit in return for liberalization of the sterling area on terms previously agreed, liberalization of commercial policy as previously agreed, and recommendation to Parliament of Bretton Woods "as soon as we reach a financial agreement." The British government was not prepared to agree (1) to complete negotiations with its debtors by the end of 1946, (2) to adopt free convertibility at the end of 1946, and (3) to formally rank the American debt ahead of all other obligations. Hugh Dalton had convinced the cabinet that American demands for (1) and (3) constituted interference in British affairs and would cause a Commonwealth revolt. The second demand was "impossible" because it would bankrupt Britain with the blinking of an eye. London had originally agreed to consider convertibility in 1946 only because it expected to receive a $5 billion grant-in-aid, Dalton insisted.[82] The cabinet, it seemed, had at last perceived the implications of early convertibility. At the same time, Attlee, in behalf of his colleagues, rejected the waiver and deferment plan being offered by the United States.[83]

The cabinet's latest missile exploded on the British delegation in Washington, shattering its morale and unanimity. Keynes complained bitterly: "The thought that anyone in London could suppose that this [the cabinet telegram] was a starter suggests that dangerous and indeed demented advice is abroad." Did London not believe its representatives? Did it not trust them? Keynes asked Dalton and Eady. If the negotiations were to be brought to a successful conclusion, the British representatives must have London's permission to settle for $4 billion inclusive of lend-lease. The cabinet's cavalier attitude toward a waiver, moreover, was unconscionable; $3.5 billion in new money was cutting it dangerously close, and under these circumstances an escape hatch was essential. He and his colleagues, the famed economist declared, would give up an objective waiver only on explicit instructions and ask to be excused from any responsibility for relinquishing it. Robert Brand seconded Keynes. A most favorable opportunity for settling the "whole business" with the Americans was at hand, but it was fading fast. London tried to soothe the delegation. "Please believe that we are not trying to sabotage your efforts by being more stupid than nature has made us," Eady told Keynes over the phone.[84]

To the horror of multilateralists within the British foreign policy establishment, Ernest Bevin at this point suggested sending Eady to Washington to replace Keynes. For many advocates of the middle way, Eady had become the principal threat to an Anglo-American financial settlement and hence to liberalism in Great Britain. His argument that Britain could survive without an American credit and endure a prolonged period of austerity seemed to Labour's left wing and the empire isolationists to offer a tempting alternative to a loan laden with dangerous and unpopular provisions. But there was no alternative, James Meade and others argued. Without an American credit liberal-socialism in Britain would fail. The Gosplanners would take over and regiment every phase of Britain's economic life with an accompanying loss of individual freedom. Meade, who was now convinced that it was Eady rather than Keynes who had attempted to downgrade commercial policy and exclude the Economic Section from postwar planning, had Sir Edward Bridges intervene with Dalton. As a result, on November 27 the cabinet dispatched not Eady but Bridges to assess the situation in Washington and pour oil on troubled waters.[85]

While Bridges was winding his way across the stormy North Atlantic, Will Clayton continued to struggle against what he considered Vinson and Eccles's oversensitivity to Congress and their consequent nit-picking. "We are in danger of allowing the numerous points of detail in the negotiations to obscure the main purpose, which is to ensure that the loan brings about the maximum development of international trade on a non-discriminatory basis," he warned Vinson. Specifically, the purpose of the credit was to bring about the convertibility of the pound and all other considerations should be subsumed to this. But Clayton's arguments fell on deaf ears. Vinson and Harry White were as determined as ever to hold Britain's gold/dollar reserves to a minimum.

Treasury was aided and abetted in its campaign by conservative nationalists in Congress who opposed a liberal loan policy. On the evening of December 2, Byrnes, Vinson, and Eccles hosted a dinner for congressional leaders in which the main topic of discussion was the loan. Arthur Vandenberg declared that he was against it; if America granted a credit to England, it would have to make a loan to Russia, and he was opposed to that. If the United States extended a credit to Britain and not to Russia, the Kremlin would be so offended that rapprochement would be impossible. Tom Connally declared that Britain would no more repay this loan than it had its World War I debts. Walter George announced he was for a loan but on the installment plan and in return for a series of concessions. Dean Acheson subsequently remarked to Henry Wallace that he never saw such stupendous ignorance in his life as that displayed by the senators. At a meeting of the United States Financial Committee on November 28, Vinson and Eccles cited congressional intransigence and refused to budge from $3.5 billion in new money, a tough waiver clause, and a deadline for sterling area negotiations.[86]

On Sunday, December 2, Byrnes, Vinson, White, Clayton, and Acheson met with the full British delegation, including Bridges, and restated the American position. Three days later at noon, the British cabinet met in emergency session.

Dalton reviewed the situation for his colleagues and moved that His Majesty's Government accept the latest American offer, including a provision that would require Britain to undertake free convertibility at the end of a fifteen-month period.

Once again Emmanuel Shinwell and Aneurin Bevan, the Gosplanners, led the opposition while Dalton, Cripps, Bevin, and Attlee patiently reviewed the alternatives to a breakdown in negotiations. Britain with antiquated and inefficient export industries would be exposed to cut-throat competition with the United States for the export markets of the world; the sterling area would disintegrate when Britain was unable to supply its needs for finished products, machine tools, and other items; and finally, and most importantly, Britons would throw the Labour government out on its ear as sources of American food and tobacco dried up. The two left-wing ministers grumbled but finally agreed that a loan on American terms was inevitable. The cabinet then voted unanimously to instruct the Washington delegation to proceed.

On December 6, 1945, at 10:30 A.M., the British and American delegations signed the Anglo-American Financial Agreement at the State Department. The United States extended to the United Kingdom a credit of $4.4 billion to be drawn upon as needed. Of this, $3.75 billion was new money, while the balance of $650 million was to come from existing congressional appropriations and to be used to pay for lend-lease acquired by Great Britain since V-J Day. The loan agreement constituted, then, a final settlement of lend-lease; the United States tacitly agreed not to seek any additional consideration for "the most unsordid act." Washington also renounced the right of recapture and in fact turned over to the United Kingdom all United States military and civilian supplies and installations in British territory that had been declared surplus. The dollar sign had indeed been removed from lend-lease.

The loan carried a nominal interest rate of 2 percent but, given the fact that payments were to be deferred until 1951, the actual rate was 1.62 percent. Principal and interest were to be repaid in fifty annual and equal installments of $140 million. The interest (but not the capital repayment) would be excused if in any year the income from the visible and net invisible income fell below $866 million (the average for the years 1936–38). In making this calculation the United Kingdom was entitled to deduct the normal amortization as well as the interest on the American loan, on any similar loans from nations such as Canada, and up to £43.75 million of any payment made to the sterling area in settlement of the sterling debts. Treasury experts calculated that Britain would have to increase its exports to a level of 60 percent above prewar figures before the Exchequer would have to pay interest on the American loan. The interest thus excused would not be added to the principal of the loan.

The British government was bound to invite its other creditors—not merely those in the sterling area, but also such "payments agreement" creditors as Argentina—to discuss an adjustment of the principal of the debts owed them by Great Britain. In return for a scaling down of the debts, London would offer a gradual unfreezing of the remainder of the sterling balances and complete convertibility for any balances accruing thereafter. In addition, the United Kingdom agreed to recommend passage of the Bretton Woods Agreements and to accept the full obligations of the system within a year of the effective date of the agreement. Because Congress eventually approved the pact on July 15, 1946, Britain was obligated to accept full convertibility of sterling on current account by midsummer 1947.

Finally, the Truman and Attlee governments joined in inviting the nations of the world to an early conference on commercial policy. At the same time the terms of financial agreement were released to the press on December 6, the British and American governments jointly published proposals for an International Trade Organization and principles to govern a multilateral convention on commercial policy.[87]

Clearly, Great Britain negotiated the Financial Agreement of 1946 for political and strategic rather than financial reasons. John Maynard Keynes convinced himself that the credit was the last stone in the great financial edifice that he had constructed, a structure that would expand the volume of world trade, raise living standards everywhere, and at the same time protect British interests. He was wrong, and, by the time the cabinet finally approved the loan, virtually everyone in the British government recognized that he was wrong. The Labour ministers agreed to expose Britain to the vagaries of financial multilateralism in order to buy time. Without a credit to take care of the nation's short-term needs, the government would not last out the year, Dalton, Bevin, and Attlee reasoned. Dalton's diary bears vivid witness to the government's fears had negotiations failed:

> We should go deeper into the dark valley of austerity than ever during the war. Less food—except for bread and potatoes—in particular less meat and sugar; little cotton and therefore, less clothes and less exports; and worst of all from the point of view of public morale, practically no smokes since 80 percent of our tobacco costs dollars. Very soon, after a tremendous patriotic upsurge, the tide of public opinion would turn. Everywhere the Tories would exploit the situation, attributing every shortage to the Government's incompetence. We should be on the downward slope, leading towards defeat at the next election.[88]

Whitehall and No. 10 Downing Street approved the agreement, in addition, because virtually all sectors of British political opinion, outside the extreme left, believed that a common Anglo-American front was necessary to contain Russian expansion. And in the face of the Truman-Byrnes tripod policy, Britons were willing to forge any kind of link with the United States, no matter how tenuous.

Something remains to be said of Keynes's role in this whole affair. Without his optimism, his tenacity, and his intellectual agility, there would have been no financial agreement. But it also must be said that Keynes harnessed his imposing talents to an agreement that was not worth having—at least in economic terms. It is as an economist—and a diplomat—that John Maynard Keynes must be judged for the period 1941–46. Those who believed at the time that he had sold out to American interests vis-à-vis the gold standard blamed variously his penchant for intellectual tinkering, his increasingly entrenched position within the establishment, his obsession (paradoxically) with financial multilateralism, and his desire to protect his stock market investments.[89] There may be a kernel of truth in all of these arguments. What is clear is that the author of *The Economic Consequences of the Peace* was guilty of the same political expediency that he had criticized Woodrow Wilson and David Lloyd George for practicing at the Versailles Peace Conference.

A great change came over Keynes's life during and immediately after World War I. He realized the possibilities that lay ahead for influencing public opinion and official policy, and he self-consciously devoted himself for the rest of his life to affecting history directly through the application of "passionate perception" to public policy, rather than indirectly through educating a new generation. Psychologically and emotionally, he could not afford for the Anglo-American negotiations to fail. It must be said, in addition, that Keynes was a creative artist rather than a social scientist or diplomat. He wanted to produce an economic system that would bring peace, prosperity, and social justice to a war-ravaged world. In the end, the beauty and power of his vision blinded him to the economic if not the political realities of the situation.

But why did the United States saddle Great Britain with a flawed multilateralism in the form of the Financial Agreement of 1946? In the first place, American officials concerned with the making of financial, commercial, and strategic policy never seemed to come to grips with the geopolitical imperatives of Britain's status as a densely populated island nation lacking in certain basic raw materials. American statesmen wanted to aid the United Kingdom in 1945 for both economic and strategic reasons. Multilateralism would never work without British participation and London would never participate without a loan. United States multilateralists did not cynically force Britain to accept an arrangement that would enrich America at the expense of the United Kingdom—though that would be its effect. Those in positions of power refused to analogize between an economically self-sufficient United States and an economically integrated, British-led sterling area. Instead they insisted, by their philosophy and their policies, that the United Kingdom was economically as well as politically sovereign. It was not.

The Financial Agreement of 1946 was, in the second place, a product of compartmentalization and conflict within the foreign policy establishment. Harry White and his new chief, Fred Vinson, were determined to force Great Britain to participate in an international financial system pegged to gold and dollars, and in which the United States controlled the lion's share of the dominant medium. Treasury supported a loan just large enough to tempt Britain, primarily on short-

range political grounds, to join the IMF and IBRD and to accept full convertibility, but not a loan large enough to enable the United Kingdom to survive full
convertibility and join the Bretton Woods institutions as a permanent, healthy
party. While Will Clayton and the State Department favored a much more generous aid package, they still insisted on early and full convertibility in order to
achieve commercial multilateralism even after Treasury succeeded in holding the
loan amount to a bare minimum. In essence, Great Britain and the financial
empire were ground between two powerful bureaucracies whose combined policies forced Britain to embrace multilateralism but denied that nation the liquidity
necessary to survive in such a system.

13. Politics and Diplomacy: Britain, the United States, and the Struggle for Ratification, 1946

FROM JANUARY through June 1946 Congress, the Truman administration, the press, informed public opinion, and a wide variety of special interests debated the pros and cons of the Anglo-American Financial Agreement. More than any other event of the early Cold War period, the British loan forced American decision makers and commentators to relate international financial and commercial issues to domestic politics, ideology, and national security. On one level, the financial agreement constituted an attempt by economic internationalists within the foreign policy establishment to sell a flawed multilateralism to the American people. In theory designed to create an interdependent world economy based on specialization and reciprocity, multilateralism had by 1946 been so modified by bureaucratic and conventional politics, by economic nationalism, and by fiscal conservatism that it had become a machine to enrich the United States at the expense of the rest of the trading community. Multilateralism's supporters, while acknowledging its flaws, continued to insist that it would create the best of all possible worlds in an imperfect universe.

On another level, the loan represented an attempt by increasingly Russophobe senators and representatives to aid America's principal ally in the burgeoning struggle against international communism. The perception of the loan as primarily a weapon in the Cold War against Russia emerged from a tangle of other political, ideological, and economic issues only gradually during the debate. Consideration of the financial agreement put the conservative coalition, especially its southern wing, to a severe test, involving as it did a conflict between fiscal orthodoxy and a get-tough posture toward the Soviet Union. In addition, the loan proved troubling because, while it was justified as a device to promote free enterprise in international trade, it seemed to many conservatives to be a subsidy to British socialism. Liberals were similarly confused. Will Clayton, Fred Vinson, and Dean Acheson depicted the loan as an integral part of the new internationalism, but its recipient was still one of the most blatantly colonialist powers in the world. Moreover, torn between fear of inflation and fear of depression, American progressives had to decide whether the credit would benefit the country by creating jobs in export industries or impair national prosperity by increasing demand for already scarce consumer and capital goods.

In the end, a majority of conservatives and liberals alike put questions of domestic economics aside and chose to evaluate the credit in terms of national security and ideology. The Soviet Union, rather than Great Britain, liberals decided, represented the forces of imperialism and autocracy. At the same time, conservatives concluded that communism posed a greater collectivist menace to free enterprise than socialism. Each group became convinced that both communist ideology and Soviet foreign policy so threatened America's national security that a common Anglo-American front was called for.

In fact, however, modified multilateralism undercut and was counterproductive of the goals of Cold War interventionism. At the very time Congress, the White House, and the State Department were concluding that a strong and stable Britain was America's first line of defense, they imposed on the United Kingdom a financial agreement that, in forcing early and complete convertibility, accelerated the breakup of the financial empire and contributed to the paralysis of the British economy by the summer of 1947.

In Great Britain the basic decisions regarding the loan had already been made by the time the financial agreement was submitted to Parliament. The Attlee government had chosen to guarantee its immediate future with a loan from America and to let the long run take care of itself. The only development that could have prevented passage—a renewal of the alliance between Labour's left wing and the empire isolationists—did not materialize. Even though it perceived the loan as a mechanism to save capitalism, the left was not willing to bring down the Attlee government. And while Conservatives sought to embarrass His Majesty's Government during the debate in the House of Commons, in the end only a handful voted against the loan. The need for a common Anglo-American front against Soviet communism seemed too compelling for them to do otherwise. Thus did Great Britain knowingly, if grudgingly, ratify an agreement that was to prove so detrimental to its interests.

Conservative Labour leaders were well satisfied with the outcome of the financial negotiations in Washington. "If we don't play our cards badly," Hugh Dalton wrote in his diary, "we and our successors should be in Office for many years."[1] The initial response of the British press and public to the financial agreement also was favorable. *The Economist* saw compelling reasons for parliamentary approval of the loan. Britain "(in this very uncertain world)" could not afford to be estranged from both of its principal allies at the same time. Without a loan from America, the United Kingdom would be unable to afford not only the machinery necessary for industrial reconversion but also the food and fiber necessary to feed and clothe its people. Of course, Lord Beaverbrook's *Daily Express* blasted the proposed transaction as just another chapter in the sordid story of America's conspiracy to return the world to the gold standard.[2] In the immediate aftermath of the agreement, it was a voice crying in the wilderness.

The positive attitude exemplified by *The Economist*, however, quickly gave way to widespread press criticism of the agreement pervaded by bitterness over the "harsh" terms America was forcing on its gallant ally. The left wing of the Labour party and its mouthpiece the *Weekly Tribune* accused American capitalists of driving a "savage bargain." After a war in which Britain had sacrificed more than any other ally, it was being forced to accept a loan on which the present generation's great-grandchildren would still be paying. Added the moderately conservative *Spectator*: "Unless the United States can learn to use the immense wealth and power she has acquired by the allied victory with greater magnanimity and generosity, and with greater understanding of the needs of others than she has shown on this occasion, then the 'American century' will prove an unmitigated evil to every country that cannot escape it." The moderate Labour weekly *New Statesmen and Nation* asserted: "As matters stand our conclusion is that we have been forced into a disastrous bargain."[3] Finally, a week after its laudatory stance, *The Economist* did a 180-degree turn. "We cannot accept the American doctrine of 'non-discrimination' and hope to get our exports up to the required level," Geoffrey Crowther declared; he went on to criticize the agreement by ruling out the possibility of a planned expansion of international trade.[4] Even multilateralists in the Treasury and Economic Section were uneasy. Sir Richard Clarke later remarked that the financial agreement was John Maynard Keynes's greatest success and his greatest failure. Britain's preeminent economist had negotiated "brilliantly but badly, over-complicating and finessing against London and himself." Clarke predicted that "we have not yet seen the beginning of the complexities and difficulties which this settlement has thrust upon us."[5] British business interests joined the chorus of naysayers by deploring the secrecy that had enshrouded the discussions and the indecent haste with which, apparently, the Attlee government was preparing to push both the loan agreement and Bretton Woods through Parliament.

With the financial agreement at long last inked, Dalton, Clement Attlee, Ernest Bevin, and Sir Stafford Cripps decided to present the loan, the IMF, and the IBRD as complimentary facets of an integrated plan to free up world trade and expand British exports. With Bretton Woods pending, the loan agreement was introduced in the House of Commons on December 7.[6]

At the time Parliament took up the financial agreement and Bretton Woods, the House of Commons was racked by partisan strife highlighted by bitter disputes over ideology. On the very day it introduced the loan, the Attlee government had to fight off a vote of censure. Winston Churchill and the Conservatives charged that the Labour government was neglecting urgent and immediate tasks and concentrating instead on long-term schemes of nationalization. The mainstream of the Conservative party headed by Churchill, Anthony Eden, Sir John Anderson, and Oliver Lyttleton had no intention of blocking the loan agreement; this group was convinced of the loan's strategic and economic value to Britain. But after the parliamentary Labour party met in caucus on December 9 and voted to approve the financial pact with the United States, the Conservatives were afforded a golden opportunity to play to the galleries, an opportunity they exploited with gusto.[7]

In the House of Commons on December 12, 1945, Hugh Dalton moved acceptance of the financial agreement, including final settlement of lend-lease, and approval of the proposals for an International Trade Organization, an International Monetary Fund, and an International Bank for Reconstruction and Development. He painted the same gloomy picture of no food, no homes, no shirts, and no smokes for the common Briton as he had for his cabinet colleagues. "Finally and perhaps most serious of all," he concluded, "the rejection of these Agreements would mean the dissipation of all hopes of Anglo-American cooperation in this dangerous new world in which we have moved."[8]

John Anderson, speaking for the majority of Conservatives, declared first that he believed that His Majesty's Government had secured the best terms available under existing circumstances; nevertheless, he personally was acutely disappointed. "There was clearly no evidence in the agreement to support the axiom that whenever the Americans and British get together, America is always outsmarted," he observed.[9] Anderson defended the IMF against charges that it constituted a return to the gold standard but attacked the requirement that Britain undertake free convertibility by December 31, 1946. Given the ambiguity of the financial agreement, he asked all Conservative members to abstain in the forthcoming division.

Robert Boothby immediately rose to challenge both Dalton and Anderson. Boothby, whom Keynes once described as "quite an intelligent fellow but thoroughly misguided," announced that he would not abstain but vote against the measures, and all patriotic members should follow suit.[10] He denied that the lend-lease settlement was evenhanded—the measure was an act to aid in the defense of the United States, and that was just what it had done. The Truman administration's decision to terminate in August was "like giving a man a lift in an aeroplane, taking him nine-tenths of the way across the Atlantic Ocean, and then when 200 miles from the shore, throwing him out of the aeroplane and telling him to swim for it."[11] Free convertibility would be disastrous for Britain. As soon as India and Egypt converted their sterling balances into dollars, they would go straight to the United States to spend it, not out of any special love of that country but because they could get from America more of the goods they wanted more quickly. The loan agreement coupled with the IMF would make gold the basis of worldwide credit; of $28 billion of monetary gold in the world, $23 billion was in the vaults of Fort Knox. As for the commercial policy proposals, multilateralism would work only if every country in the trading system maintained full employment; but the domestic policies of the United States were pointing in the opposite direction. He would speak bluntly, Boothby told his colleagues. The twin objectives of these schemes were to return the world to nineteenth-century laissez-faire capitalism and to "prise open the markets of the world for the USA."[12]

The same alliance between empire isolationists and Labour's left-wing that had cropped up during negotiations over Article VII and Bretton Woods surfaced once again during the Commons debate on the financial agreement. "There is no wisdom in this loan, and there is no kindness in it," proclaimed Jennie Lee, firebrand wife of Aneurin Bevan. "There is nothing in the terms of this loan which gives us any reason to suppose that an administration which could offer a niggardly, barbaric antediluvian settlement, such as this, can solve the unemployment problems in their own country, much less help the world." If Labour had to join forces with Conservatives such as Boothby to protect the world from the " 'hard-faced Businessmen's' Government" then ruling America, so be it.[13]

Churchill, appropriately enough, finished off the debate. He denounced the loan as unworkable, unfair, poorly negotiated, and dangerous to the nation's economic health, and then declared that Parliament could not afford to reject it. Consumer privation aside, the peace and stability of the world would not survive "a prolonged rough and tumble struggle in the economic and financial sphere between the United States and the British Commonwealth of Nations and the Sterling Area."[14] Therefore, since the measures before the House would obviously pass, the correct thing for the Conservatives to do was abstain.

Hugh Dalton recorded this scene as the final votes were taken: "The Tories presented a very poor aspect. Several of their front bench speakers advocating the loan but recommending—after great rows behind the scenes with Winston—their followers to abstain. When the vote was called 60 or 70 of those went into the lobby against the Government and some half dozen in favour, while the front bench, including Winston, Eden, Stanley and Lyttleton sat miserably on their backsides."[15]

In the end, the mainstream of the Labour party could not turn away from the short-run benefits that would accrue to it from an American loan, and it overwhelmed the antiloan coalition made up of empire isolationists, "conservative Marxists," and left-wing Labour leaders. Its members correctly perceived that, after they grumped and griped and self-righteously denounced the ungrateful Americans, the Manchester steelworkers, the public house operators, the Scottish sheep raisers, and the Welsh miners would support the loan and oust any government that did not because it meant bread and shirts and tobacco. The House divided 345 to 98 in favor of the agreement and 314 to 50 in support of Bretton Woods.[16]

Churchill and Eden clearly wanted the measures to pass. The fact that 79 out of 167 Conservative M.P.s present and voting refused to follow their advice and voted no was counted by some as a repudiation of the party's leadership, an event that seemed significant in view of the fact that there were 600 Conservative peers in the House of Lords compared to 30 Labour members and 50 Liberals. Under law, Lords could sit on money bills for thirty days; if the upper house exercised its prerogative in the case of Bretton Woods, the December 31 cutoff date for governmental approval of the IMF and IBRD would pass. Even before the Bretton Woods and loan proposals were introduced into Lords, Beaverbrook had announced that he would introduce an amendment calling for rejection of the measures on the grounds that they constituted a return to the gold standard. At this point the Attlee government let it be known that if the upper house balked, it would either introduce legislation in Commons to eliminate Lords from the legislative process altogether or create enough new Labour peers to obtain a majority. Faced with this logic and Churchill's persuasiveness, the Conservative majority decided to abstain en masse. At the last moment Keynes arrived to speak in behalf of the proposals, delivering an address that he naturally credited with turning the tide. With Conservative members either abstaining or absent, Lords approved the proposals 90 to 8.[17]

Both the Truman and Attlee governments anticipated a very tough time in securing congressional approval of the Anglo-American Financial Agreement; surveys of congressional and public opinion made in late December 1945 confirmed those fears. The State Department was pleased with the support expressed by editors, news commentators, magazines, and business executives. Some 87 of the 147 newspapers that commented on the Washington negotiations were extremely positive; only 30 editors had opposed the agreement. Except for the Hearst and Patterson writers, newspaper columnists generally supported the loan. In addition, the United States Chamber of Commerce came out early and strongly in favor. But a public opinion poll taken ten days before Christmas indicated that whereas 78 percent of the public had heard of the agreement, only 41 percent approved. Those endorsing the loan did so for primarily political or humanitarian reasons. One-third of those questioned who had heard of the agreement understood that the United States would be getting advantages or concessions other than interest, but most of these believed that they would take the form of bases— the Destroyers-for-Bases Deal being their primary frame of reference—rather than concessions to multilateralism. The poll indicated that the greatest opposition came from the Midwest where only 31 percent favored the loan, while 41 percent in the East indicated approval and 52 percent in the South responded positively. Generally, the better educated, particularly those with college degrees, approved the transaction while only 28 percent of the grammar school graduates favored it. Finally, a survey of Congress conducted by the Treasury in late December revealed that some fifty-four members of the House had either spoken against the loan in public or had been quoted in the press as being opposed, while some twenty-four others had been critical; only nine senators and twenty-five representatives had announced their support.[18]

Because time was short and because the American people were particularly uninterested in the arcane principles of international economics, Clayton, Vinson, and their colleagues decided to focus their time and efforts on Congress rather than on the general public. But Congress was no less resistant than the average person to issues revolving around commercial and financial diplomacy. As Dean Acheson and others have pointed out, the secretary of state nearly always comes to Congress bearing word of troubles about which Congress does not want to hear. Foreign affairs generally constitute an intrusion on the major preoccupation of senators and representatives—the internal affairs of the country and especially of the particular parts they represent. The most familiar aspects of diplomacy—war, relief, and trade—are nearly always threatening to members of Congress and the folks back home.[19] Despite World War II, this was as true in 1946 as it had been in 1936. Almost to a person, the Seventy-ninth Congress regarded the Anglo-American Financial Agreement as bad news, a piece of legislation that was loaded with political dynamite.

In large part the fate of the loan would be determined by the conservative coalition in Congress, that combination of southern Democrats and Republicans that had gradually been growing in numbers and power during World War II. The coalition could trace its roots back to small clusters of legislators who even during the first hundred days regarded the New Deal, in the words of Senator Carter Glass (D-Va.), as "an utterly dangerous effort of the Federal Government to transplant Hitlerism to every corner of the nation."[20] On the whole, these men and women opposed heavy government spending, especially if it involved deficits; they were also fearful of and hostile to the growth of the federal bureaucracy and loud in defense of states' rights and individual liberty. They tended with some exceptions to be anti-intellectual. As the crusty Glass complained: "The sooner Washington is rid of impatient academicians whose threatening manifests and decrees keep business and banks alike in suspense, if not in consternation, the sooner and more certain will we have a complete restoration of confidence and resumption of business in every line of endeavor."[21] Southern conservatives were not isolationists, but neither, as some have claimed, were they internationalists. Historically, they had favored free trade for economic reasons; but Southerners and their representatives were generally as xenophobic and parochial as Midwesterners were alleged to be. Their votes in behalf of lend-lease and other "interventionist" measures stemmed from the region's militarism and combativeness. When challenged, the nation must fight, but true internationalism in which nations surrendered part of their sovereignty for the good of the whole was an anathema to these Americans.[22]

The British loan posed a special dilemma for the southern members of the conservative coalition. Dixie legislators were deeply concerned about the state of the Republic: the federal bureaucracy had grown to monstrous proportions; a huge deficit incurred during the depression and World War II threatened the financial stability of the country, with inflation and the possibility of another depression lurking on the horizon; labor unions and consumers were demanding more and more. It was time, most believed, for the government to balance the budget, trim the bloated bureaucracy, restrain unions, encourage private enterprise, and leave Europe to the Europeans. In view of this philosophy, postwar credits for reconstruction and development, especially to nations with socialist governments, would seem to be out of the question. Yet the international situation was extremely uncertain. By early 1946 many southern senators and representatives were fearful of and hostile toward the Soviet Union whose actions in Europe and the Middle East conjured up images of Nazi Germany in the 1930s.

Senator Josiah W. Bailey summed up the dilemma facing southern Democrats over the loan. The British always looked after themselves, he wrote Henry

Wallace, and should continue to do so. He was alarmed, he declared, by the "unstable condition" of America: "I do not know what the taxes will be. I do not know at what point we will stop issuing evidences of debt. I do not know how we are ever going to balance our budget. I do not know when the American people will cease their cry day after day for more and more and more."[23] Russia frightened him as well. "It seems to me she means to have her way or no way at all."[24] If recent history were any criteria, Moscow was determined to dominate all of Europe. Bailey proclaimed that America's safety lay with a strong domestic economy and a strong military.[25] But his declaration of unilateralism rang hollow. Bailey and his southern colleagues were afraid of facing the future without a European ally, and Britain seemed the only available candidate.

In many ways, the views of the Republican members of the conservative congressional alliance paralleled those of their southern Democratic counterparts: worship of free enterprise, distrust of the federal bureaucracy, and America first. Within the congressional wing of the GOP there were still many outright isolationists. Individuals like William Langer of North Dakota, Karl Mundt of South Dakota, and Hamilton Fish of New York were not only opposed to "globaloney" but to unilateralism as well. Republicans were more distrustful of the military and military might as a solution to international problems than southern Democrats. With some major exceptions Republican conservatives were not as anti-intellectual as their southern counterparts. Nor were they as opposed to bigness in business or federal support for business activities. Nonetheless, the congressional wing of the Republican party would have to choose between its fear of fiscal "irresponsibility" and collectivism on the one hand, and its fear of Russia on the other.

Throughout World War II the Republican leadership in the Senate had divided responsibilities, with Arthur Vandenberg taking foreign policy and Robert Taft domestic. The loan involved both. Due to his interest in and knowledge of finance and economics, Taft quickly eclipsed his Michigan colleague and, just as he had done with Bretton Woods, became the principal spokesman for the GOP. By late 1944 Taft was reaffirming his opposition to alliances—with Britain, with Russia, or with anyone else—and he denounced universal military service. "The very purpose of this war," he told the War Veteran's Club of Ohio, "is to prevent a condition in which America shall become an armed camp and be diverted from the progress, the liberty, and the pursuit of happiness." He attacked the Roosevelt-Truman administrations for "loaning money directly and indirectly, and indiscriminately to every foreign nation that desired it in a fervor of international love."[26] Such a policy would mean inflation, debt, weakness, and bankruptcy. America should lead, Taft declared, but through example. It should spread democracy and free enterprise by practicing both to perfection. Putting one's national interest first was not immoral or unfair. As one of the senator's colleagues put it: "It is just as foolish to call a man names who wants to look after his own country as it is to condemn a father for regarding his family as his primary duty."[27] Robert Taft was much more of an isolationist than Vandenberg; he detested

Russian totalitarianism and distrusted Moscow's intentions, but he was not at all sure that what happened in Europe, the Middle East, and the Far East affected America's interests. He was determined to place all the Democratic "isms"— internationalism and multilateralism—under a magnifying glass, he said, and measure them by the standard of the nation's economic and strategic interest.[28]

By January 1946, with southern Democrats in daily, open revolt, congressional-executive relations were in shambles. Dixie members of Congress were disgusted with Truman's stand in favor of a permanent Fair Employment Practices Commission (FEPC). Discrimination in hiring was, after all, one of the keystones in the southern caste system. They were also angered by the refusal of the White House to support antiunion legislation. Senator John McClellan (D-Ark.) deplored Truman's "leftist tendencies" and proclaimed that he could not support him as long as he consorted with the likes of Sydney Hillman and Henry Wallace.

General disenchantment with the administration as well as Anglophobia, fiscal conservatism, and parochialism prejudiced Southerners against the Anglo-American Financial Agreement during the early days of the debate. But perhaps the most important element in the loan equation for the sons and daughters of Dixie was cotton, that same King Cotton that had played such an important role in Confederate-British relations during the Civil War. The British government had closed the Liverpool Cotton Exchange during the war in order to purchase most of its cotton from within the empire. Southerners feared that the Labour government would keep the exchange closed, thus adversely affecting their region's most important export. Senator James Eastland (D-Miss.) told James K. Vardaman (D-Miss.) that Southerners, unaware of the benefits to be reaped from the loan and angry over the cotton situation, were telling their legislators by a margin of 100 to 1 to vote against the financial agreement.[29] The southern Democratic leadership was itself split on the loan: Senate Majority Leader Alben Barkley (D-Ky.) and Speaker Sam Rayburn (D-Tex.) favored it, Kenneth McKeller (D-Tenn.) was uncertain but leaning away, and the influential Burnett Maybank (D-S.C.) seemed opposed.

With southern Democrats so alienated, the administration would, as the previous regime had so often done, have to seek support from the presidential wing of the Republican party. Vandenberg, Taft, party whip Kenneth Wherry (R-Nebr.), and Wallace White (R-Maine) were the chief GOP policymakers in the Senate. The eve of the loan debate found the Republican leadership divided and unsure. In mid-December, John Foster Dulles urged Vandenberg and his colleagues not to openly oppose the loan, but rather to require the administration to develop a detailed foreign loan program of which the British loan would be just one part and to explain specifically the impact of such a program on the domestic economy.[30] In subsequent conversations with Vandenberg, the churchman-lawyer-diplomat argued that the war for liberty and democracy had not yet been won, that Britain was an outpost of that freedom, and that without a loan the United Kingdom could very well succumb to regimentation at home and Soviet imperialism abroad. The Michigan senator agreed that there were valid economic, ideological, and strategic reasons for voting a credit to Britain, but he also saw reasons against it. The agreement itself was faulty—full of "side doors, back doors, and escalators"—and would not accomplish its multilateral objectives. Like all loans it would earn not friendship for the creditor but enmity. Left to himself, Vandenberg told Dulles, he would probably go along with the loan "for the sake of some nebulous affinity which the English-speaking world must maintain in mutual self-defense." But 1946 was an election year and the people of Michigan were going to be dubious. "About 90 percent" of his constituents, he declared, would insist on remembering what happened with the last British loan; would inspect, in vain, the new agreement for dependable collateral; would be unable to forget Harold Laski and his fellow fire-breathers; and would "impolitely remember our own near bankruptcy." In view of all this, he wrote Dulles, "I have not yet made up my own mind."[31]

Further contributing to the uncertainty of Vandenberg and other GOP legislators with "internationalist" leanings was the fact that they were tied much more so than normal in foreign policy matters to Robert Taft. At this point, he too was undecided. "I don't like it," he said bluntly. "I don't want to vote for it and I don't want to vote against it."[32]

For the Truman administration, then, the conservative coalition and residual isolationism in Congress made a bipartisan foreign policy absolutely necessary. The machinery for cooperation was already in place. Dean Acheson has described how it worked:

> In the Seventy-ninth Congress this [bipartisan coalition] operated in the Senate out of the Secretary of the Senate's office, and in the House out of Speaker Rayburn's "board of education" room in the basement of the Capital. Here "Mr. Sam" presided at a large desk over a select company ensconced in overstuffed sofas and chairs and refreshed from an immense refrigerator. The Secretary of the Senate's quarters, west of the Senate Chamber, were equally secluded from public view and inquiry . . . a long narrow room lined with chairs along two sides ended with Leslie Biffle's desk. A door to the left of it led into his private dining room, served from the Senate restaurant. Here the power structure of the Senate met and decided what at first appeared to be largely matters of procedure.[33]

Before dealing with Congress directly, however, the administration would have to get its own house in order and develop a coherent strategy. In mid-December Acheson, Emilio Collado, and Willard Thorp of State and Fred Vinson, Edward Bernstein, and Ansel Luxford of Treasury put their heads together. Wayne Taylor, head of the Export-Import Bank, Marriner Eccles, and other interested parties also attended. Will Clayton was ill and absent. After much debate, the group decided that the loan should be handled as a public debt transaction by the Treasury. That meant it would have to go to Congress. Depending on how it was written, the bill could be sent to one of three committees: Banking and Currency, Foreign Affairs, or Ways and Means. After careful consideration, administration officials decided in late December that the bill should be handled by the Banking and Currency Committee of both houses because of better leadership and because a majority of both committees favored the loan.[34] State and Treasury held the bill for six weeks before submitting it to Congress. The delay was intended to give proponents time to prepare their case, but opponents gained as much from the lull as supporters did.

Perhaps the most effective antagonist of the financial agreement in the days before its submission to Congress was Bernard Baruch. His most telling argument was that it would contribute to inflation by putting dollars in the hands of foreign consumers, thus adding to the demand for United States goods.

Economists and financial experts in the Treasury and Commerce departments dismissed the inflationary threat as of no consequence. A large portion of the market demand that would grow out of the loan to Britain, Randolph Paul reported to the NAC, would merely bring about fuller utilization of the nation's industrial capacity. The United Kingdom would not be buying goods in short supply but rather those in surplus such as railway equipment, machine tools, chemicals, synthetic fertilizers, and power equipment. The administration took the position that some of these industries would be forced to reduce their rate of output in the near future unless the United States loaned money to foreign customers. Reflecting this view, Truman remarked in mid-December that the loan would be principally of value to the United States economy and that other, foreign loans would have to be made.[35] Nonetheless, the inflation argument was hard to refute.

What made Baruch's reasoning all the harder to contend with was that his defense of consumer interests stemmed from more than a concern for the soundness of the economy or the welfare of the little person in America. Just as feelings of isolation and neglect by the establishment had caused him to oppose the loan during its negotiation, they prompted him to interfere with its ratification by Congress as well. He knew more than anyone else about reconversion and the relationship between domestic economic and international relations, he not overmodestly admitted to his old friend, Jimmy Byrnes. He had stood ready to go to Potsdam, London, and Moscow and to form a supreme council of economic advisers for the United States, but had anyone asked him? No. While Winston Churchill was vacationing in Florida before his Fulton address, Byrnes and Baruch went down to visit him. Baruch assured Churchill that he was most anxious to help Britain and would do nothing to jeopardize the loan. But, Churchill subsequently reported to Hugh Dalton, Baruch was extremely disgruntled at not being consulted, and several times during their Florida visit he accused Keynes of mismanaging the negotiations.[36] "It seems the height of ridiculous for us to lend money, either by banks or direct loans, to the English or other people without having any idea where the production is coming from," he wrote John Snyder on January 14. "We talk much about price and inflation control," he complained. "That is sheer nonsense unless you control all the component parts."[37] Shortly afterward, he went public and continued to hammer away at the inflation theme throughout the debate.

All the while the State and Treasury departments had to worry about United States public opinion, Congress, special interest groups, and Bernard Baruch, they had to be concerned with the international aspects of the loan debate. It was clear to diplomats on both sides of the Atlantic that other facets of the Anglo-American relationship could and would affect the outcome of the debate and that the course of the hearings could in turn alter Anglo-American relations. As a number of scholars have noted, British officials played a prominent role in writing the lend-lease bill, developing strategy for its passage, and even persuading various legislators to vote for it. After some thought, the Truman administration rejected a similar role for Halifax and his advisers in 1946. The American people were too xenophobic to take such a risk. "One of the most terrifying accusations which can be leveled against a public figure here is that he is generous to or sympathetic with anyone beyond our shores," Dean Acheson wrote Keynes.[38] Consequently, those in charge of shepherding the financial agreement through Congress urged the British to leave the job entirely to them. Whitehall should concentrate on reigning in anti-American sentiment in Britain and placating Anglophobes in the United States.

The State Department even went so far as to suggest that Britain go slow in reassuming control of its disintegrating empire, or, at least, mask its efforts. Stories of British military activity in Indonesia, Indochina, and elsewhere were feeding the fires of anticolonialism in America. London made no promises but in fact proved sensitive to the issue of public-to-public relations. For example, much of the loan had already been earmarked for overseas military expenditures and subsidies to Britain's allies, but Whitehall managed to conceal this fact throughout spring and summer 1946.[39]

In January President Truman named Fred Vinson and the Treasury to coordinate strategy for the forthcoming ratification struggle but designated State to handle publicity. Because various straw polls projected defeat for the financial agreement in the House, the administration pressed ahead with plans to have it introduced in the Senate first. The Justice Department declared that if raising revenue was the primary purpose of the measure, it must originate in the House; if it were secondary, the bill could originate in either chamber. Consequently, the joint resolution, written by Treasury experts and submitted first to the Senate Banking and Currency Committee, stated that the purpose of the loan was to further implement the Bretton Woods Agreements. The legislation authorized the secretary of the Treasury to carry out an agreement to promote stable and orderly exchange arrangements, to effect the prompt elimination of exchange restrictions, and to end tariff discrimination. An amount not to exceed $3.75 billion was therefore requested to execute the agreement between the United States and the United Kingdom.[40]

On the eve of the congressional debate on the financial agreement, a consensus existed within the State and Treasury departments that the loan must not be put to Congress as a commercial transaction designed to "profit" America in a literal sense. Rather, it must be portrayed as a transaction intended to rehabilitate international trade and promote peace and prosperity around the globe. "You cannot fool the American public into believing this is a 'commercial' loan, no matter what interest rates and other trappings may be employed," Ansel Luxford advised Vinson. "Experience indicates that they are willing to be the most generous people on earth as long as you put it on that basis," he said. "But if you attempt to put a commercial or bargaining front on the proposal, their Yankee business instincts will revolt at being out-traded."[41] Acheson agreed. "I think the whole tone for this business-like type of discussion is wrong," he told Charles Bunn. "This is not a transaction in which the United States engages for the purpose of making money."[42] But when push came to shove, administration officials could not resist posing as hard bargainers who had more than held their own with the wily British.[43]

Soon after Truman delivered his message to Congress urging passage of the loan as part of the Bretton Woods program, the legislation ran into problems. Because southern senators were then in the midst of a monster filibuster against the administration's Fair Employment Practices Commission bill, the managers of the loan measure would have to obtain unanimous consent of the upper house to suspend the rules and introduce their legislation. Alben Barkley, a moderate liberal who was an anathema to the conservative coalition, assumed that no one would object and had begun his speech when the isolationist senator from North Dakota, William Langer, rose and cut him off. Langer subsequently told some reporters he was against the loan and boasted that in blocking its introduction he had "done a good day's work because it will save a whole day's interest, which I estimate at $180,000, enough to cover my salary for the rest of my life."[44] The next day, however, Langer surrendered, Barkley made his speech, and hearings were scheduled to open before the Senate Banking and Currency Committee on March 5, 1946.[45]

The generally pessimistic mood that pervaded official circles in Washington soon spread to Whitehall. Keynes pointed out once again that the main casualty of rejection would be British overseas military expenditures. Because further reductions in the British standard of living were politically unfeasible, failure of Congress to approve the loan would mean that the United Kingdom would have to withdraw from its strategic outposts in the Far East, Middle East, and Mediterranean. Despite Washington's warnings to London to stay out of the debate, Whitehall's anxiety could not be contained. From Ottawa where he was negotiating for a $1 billion loan from the Canadian government, Sir Wilfrid Eady warned that if the United States government did not approve the loan to Britain, "it will mean an end to any participation in the Bretton Woods Agreement and all that."[46] The Foreign Office even went so far as to consider asking Eamon De Valera, the president of the Irish Republic, to make a public declaration in support of the loan agreement. Though such a statement might mollify Anglophobes among Irish-Americans, the British in the end could not force themselves to ask for help from the head of a nation they believed had collaborated with Adolf Hitler.[47]

British concern over the fate of the loan legislation did produce concessions in an area of growing concern to both nations—civil aviation. World War II convinced British and American soldiers and business people that the airplane would play the same role in the warfare and commerce of the future as the ocean-going ship had in the military conflicts and trade competition of the past. The nation that controlled the major airlanes and monopolized aeronautical technology would rule the world. Early in the war the Big Three had reached an agreement whereby the United States would concentrate on the construction of long-range bombers and transport aircraft and Britain and Russia would devote their efforts to building fighters and dive-bombers. As a result, at war's end the United States controlled the lion's share of the world's long-range transport aircraft. America made no secret of the fact that it wanted to become the principal supplier of commercial airliners to other nations, thus maintaining the world's largest and most advanced aircraft industry. Washington also applied pressure to other nations to sign so-called Five Freedoms agreements with the United States, granting the aircraft of both nations full and free access to the air space and airports of both countries. Such agreements would keep other nations from protecting their infant aircraft industries and airlines from United States competition.

From 1943 to 1946 Britain fought a losing, rear-guard action against United States efforts to control the airways. It refused to sign a Five Freedoms agreement and as a protest over resulting pressure from the United States cut Pan American flights to London from eight to two per week in December 1945. The aircraft industry's chief spokesmen in Congress, Senator Pat McCarran (D-Nev.) and Senator Owen Brewster (R-Maine), charged that this was part of a conspiracy to control international air routes. Later in the month England refused landing privileges to America civil aircraft at island bases built with lend-lease funds. Several members of the Colmer committee warned that British policy seriously handicapped American airlines and could jeopardize the pending loan. In February London, under intense pressure from the State Department, accepted the Five Freedoms. Shortly afterward the Air Ministry notified Lockheed Corporation and the United States Embassy that, if Congress approved the loan, the British government would buy thirteen Constellations for use by its external airlines.[48]

Meanwhile, in America the political skies had begun to clear for the administration; an opinion poll conducted by the Public Affairs Division of the State Department showed a majority of Americans—44 percent to 37 percent—favoring the loan, the first time a poll had shown more people in favor than opposed. The British were certain that deteriorating East-West relations were responsible.[49] Stalin's two-camps speech and the confrontation between Ernest Bevin and Vyacheslav Molotov at the opening session of the United Nations in London had frightened Americans. Whitehall noted with delight the various approving editorials that appeared in the United States following Bevin's defense of freedom and democracy, and his demand that the Soviets fulfill their agreements. It appeared that Soviet intransigence over Eastern Europe and Iran had scuttled Walter Lippmann's "mediation" strategy for good.[50] In observing that the burgeoning confrontation between East and West was "not likely to affect adversely the chances of our loan being passed through Congress,"[51] B. E. F. Gage undoubtedly had a point. Little had changed in administration rhetoric concerning the benefits of the loan, and there had been no overnight conversion to liberalism on the part of Congress and the American people. Senator Homer E. Capehart (R-Ind.), angered in particular by Harold Laski's attacks on American capitalism, had been one of the loan's most vocal opponents. The second week in February he confided to Halifax that recent developments in the United Nations and elsewhere had caused him to change his mind.[52]

But as Foreign Office analysts had so often noted, American public opinion was fickle. Moreover, despite their growing distrust of the Soviet Union, Republican legislators were determined to take advantage of the administration's political vulnerability over the financial agreement in the short term. A number of them were concerned about the forthcoming election and could not convince themselves that a yea vote on the loan would be an asset. Yet another Gallup Poll, taken on the eve of the congressional hearings, indicated that 57 percent of the American people had heard of the loan to Great Britain while 43 percent had not. Twenty-two percent of those who had heard of it said they favored it, whereas 29 percent opposed it and 6 percent remained undecided. Those in favor said they responded most enthusiastically to the argument that the loan would promote world trade and stimulate business, and those opposed flatly stated that England would not repay it.[53]

The hearings on the Anglo-American Financial Agreement before the Senate Committee on Banking and Currency opened in Room 301 of the Senate Office Building on March 5, 1946. Robert F. Wagner (D-N.Y.), a friend of organized labor, was chairman, but he was ill and absent. In his place, Senate Majority Leader Alben Barkley (D-Ky.) presided; from this point forward he would play a major role in the loan debate. FDR's decision to support the Kentuckian for majority leader following Joe T. Robinson's death in 1937 had not been popular in the Senate. In choosing him, the White House had passed over southern conservative, Pat Harrison. Carter Glass, James K. Vardaman (D-Miss.), and James Eastland (D-Miss.) resented the snub and insisted on treating Barkley as an exalted White House errand boy.[54] Although by 1946 Barkley was a veteran who had run up hundreds of favors, residual resentment toward him still lingered among southern Democrats.

The committee's membership reflected the various factions in the Senate. Carter Glass and John W. Bankhead II (D-Ala.) represented southern conservatives, while Barkley and freshman Senator J. William Fulbright (D-Ark.) spearheaded the liberal, proloan Democrats. Robert Taft and Homer Capehart (R-Ind.) spoke for the nationalists and neo-isolationists. Although a number of Republican members had reconciled themselves to the loan, liberal Republicans such as Warren Austin had no really strong spokesperson on the committee. Only former isolationist Charles Tobey (R-N.H.) could be so classified.[55] A Treasury survey of eleven members taken just before the hearings opened showed seven in favor, two opposed, and two undecided. Although the tally was encouraging, the issue, even for this carefully chosen body, was still very much up in the air.

The powerful opposition aroused by the British loan placed the Truman administration in a difficult position. It was not willing to present the loan as a generous measure in behalf of a wartime ally. Anglophobia, fiscal conservatism, and lingering resentment over lend-lease were still too strong for that. In addition, State and Treasury department spokespersons were unwilling at this point to portray the loan as a weapon in the forthcoming struggle with international communism.

It was not that policymakers failed to see the loan in the context of an East-West confrontation. In late January George F. Kennan wrote the State Department that Moscow was counting on an economic struggle between the United States and the United Kingdom to weaken the capitalist world and divide its enemies. In early 1946 a leading Communist party theorist had delivered a major address describing the rocky course of Anglo-American economic and financial relations during World War II and the inevitability of a clash between Britain and America, the world's two great imperial powers. Shortly afterward an article appeared in *Pravda* describing with glee the outrage and resentment expressed in Britain after publication of the financial agreement.[56] Failure by Congress to pass the loan, many United States officials believed, would seem to bear out the Soviet thesis and encourage an even more adventurist policy by Moscow.

Moreover, by the close of 1945 United States policymakers had come to view foreign loans as a stick rather than a carrot in their dealings with the Soviet Union. The State and War departments had abandoned hope of trading a massive reconstruction loan to the Soviet Union for "cooperation" in Europe and the Far East, and began advocating the extension of credits to America's potential allies as a means to counter communist subversion and Soviet expansion. Shortly before leaving his Moscow post, Averell Harriman called for the tendering of credits to the economically weak and disorganized countries that lay in Moscow's path. "Since we under no circumstances are prepared to involve ourselves in the internal political affairs of other countries by such methods [Soviet], our only hope of supporting the peoples of these countries who resort to totalitarian minority dictatorship," Harriman wrote on April 4, "is to assist them to attain economic stability as soon as possible. Lack of sufficient food and employment are fertile grounds for the subtle false promises of Communist agents."[57] James Forrestal, a former partner in the international investment firm of Dillon, Read, and Co., enthusiastically supported this view. In September the State Department opened negotiations in Washington with representatives of the Polish government for a postwar reconstruction loan.[58]

Nonetheless, the administration would run a great risk in justifying the British loan on anti-Russian grounds, for to do so would surely alienate such staunch liberal supporters of the agreement as Henry Wallace and Claude Pepper (D-Fla.).

Soon after testifying before the Senate Banking Committee, Wallace visited Truman at the White House. Senator Hugh Mitchell (D-Wash.) had asked Wallace if he thought the purpose of the loan was to bring about a military alliance between Britain and the United States. If he thought that were the purpose, Wallace told Mitchell, and subsequently Truman, he would oppose the loan. "I said," Wallace continued in his conversation with the president, "granted that Russia is wrong on every stand which she is taking at the present time, the fact still remains that the proper policy for the United States is to serve as an intermediary between Britain and Russia and not as a defender of England."[59] According to Wallace, Truman "swore up and down" that the United States was not going to enter into an alliance with England.

The consensus within the foreign policy establishment was, therefore, that the loan would have to be presented as a keystone in the arch of multilateral trade and, as such, a harbinger of world prosperity and world peace. But it soon became apparent that there were problems with this approach as well. The economic argument once again left State and Treasury department representatives sandwiched between economic internationalists and economic nationalists. Commercial policy experts estimated that for Britain to pay back the loan at $140 million per year, it would have to import at least an equivalent value of goods into the United States annually. In other words, if Britain were to live up to the terms of the agreement it would have to sustain a net trade surplus with the United States for years to come. But multilateralists in and out of government insisted that the principal benefit of the loan would be to expand export markets for American merchants in the United Kingdom and throughout the empire. The thrust of their argument to economic nationalists was that the loan would expand rather than shrink America's trade surplus.[60] Thus, as the date set for the opening of congressional hearings approached, the administration was unsure of itself, uncertain as to which justifications would open the door to congressional approval.

Robert Taft was the crucial figure in the Senate debate over the British loan. As with the Reciprocal Trade Agreements Act, he would eventually vote to approve but not because of any conversion to multilateralism. Rather, he became convinced that the agreement would benefit American exporters without exposing domestic manufacturing and agricultural interests to dangerous foreign competition. He also came eventually to view the loan as a subsidy to an ally, a diplomatic move to enable the Europeans to keep their own house in order. The Ohio senator's initial vehement opposition to the financial agreement was intended to damage the administration both by discrediting multilateralism and by demonstrating that either Truman and his colleagues had not made a commitment to multilateralism or they had made concessions that fatally flawed the stratagem they were touting as a panacea.

Fred Vinson led off for the administration; standing before an easel full of charts and reading from various tables, he presented the case for multilateralism and the British loan. Compared to those who followed, especially Will Clayton, Vinson was unsure of himself and ineffective. Taft immediately went on the attack and in a three-day tour de force demolished one administration rationale after another. It mattered little, he told Vinson, whether United States trade was on a bilateral or a multilateral basis. Britain and the sterling area would be able to import from the United States only to the extent that they were able to sell to the United States. Through the selective, bilateral mechanism contained in RTAA, the United States would be able to obtain whatever goods from foreign sources it needed. And those needs would continue to be relatively few. America was and would continue to be for the foreseeable future economically self-sufficient. He also made short work of the "safety valve" thesis. Testifying in behalf of the loan, former Supreme Court Justice Owen Roberts told Taft: "I have always understood that the 10 to 15 percent of our production that was exported was the safety valve that meant the difference between real prosperity and something else in this country."[61] That was the conventional wisdom, Taft replied, but it was hogwash. A nation had to import to export; it could not continue to maintain a trade surplus indefinitely.

At one point, in response to questions from Ernest K. McFarland (D-Ariz.) and George Radcliffe (D-Md.), Vinson defended the loan as a hard-headed business deal.[62] Taft at once interrupted. If this was a business deal, it was a very poor one. Based on its past record, Britain was a terrible credit risk and the interest, assuming it would ever be paid, was only 1.64 percent; Treasury generally had to pay 2.5 percent on the money it borrowed.

Shortly after Clayton made his opening statement, Taft attacked the administration's assertion that the agreement would promote free enterprise and facilitate private control of international trade. Clayton had proclaimed dramatically: "Lincoln said that this nation cannot exist half free and half slave. I think that applies to other things besides human beings. I don't think you can conduct your foreign trade on a closed economy. One or the other is going to have to change, and they will both have to be the same."[63] Where in the agreement, Taft asked Clayton, was state trading prohibited? Nowhere, Clayton admitted. Britain had a socialist government that was in the process of nationalizing the country's basic industries, Taft pointed out. How could the United States reasonably expect it not to nationalize its foreign trade if it so desired? And what difference, in economic terms, would it make to the United States? Could not nations with different economic systems exchange goods and services?

Mr. Republican next attacked the administration's assertion that multilateralism in general and the loan in particular would prevent war by retarding the development of rival trading blocs. Competition for control of markets and raw materials had always been a cause of war and always would be, but what difference would it make if the competition was between nation states or individuals? When trade was in private hands, governments would for political and strategic reasons act to protect the interests of their nations. Clayton could only reply that one was much more "vicious" than the other. There was one final question, Taft asserted. Administration spokesmen claimed that the development of rival trading blocs could and would lead to war. Russia, a nation with an alien social, economic, and political system, was forming a trading bloc. Whether or not this made war with Russia inevitable was a moot point. Certainly the administration was not claiming that the survival of the sterling bloc meant war with Britain. Clayton could only squirm in his chair.[64]

In part, multilateralism stemmed from the efforts of the business people and economists who were in charge of American foreign policy during World War II to reconcile the ruthlessness of free market competition with humanitarian concerns. Some critics charged that what the multilateralists were saying was that it was all right for one corporation or individual to crush another economically as long as they received no "artificial" help from the government. Moreover, the multilateralists appeared to be suggesting that in a world of expanding international trade there did not have to be any losers. Not only did Taft reject the idea that a proper goal of United States foreign policy was to raise living standards around the world, but he also dismissed the argument that multilateralism could achieve this goal without weakening America. One could not create something from nothing.

In succeeding days Taft and other GOP senators implied that a loan to Britain would open the doors of the United States Treasury to scores of other countries, especially Russia. Administration spokespersons had to be careful in responding. Clayton, Acheson, and Barkley had steadfastly denied that they were proposing to extend the loans on "political"—that is, strategic or ideological—grounds. When asked if the financial agreement was but the first in a series of loans to foreign governments, communist and noncommunist, Barkley waffled; if a credit would be mutually beneficial to the United States and another country, the United States should extend it to that country, regardless of its internal form of government. Privately, however, State Department spokespersons let Russophobe members of Congress know that the administration had no plans to proceed with the loan to Russia.[65]

After administration officials had completed their testimony, a succession of special-interest representatives paraded through Room 301 to urge passage. Edward A. O'Neal, president of the Farm Bureau Federation, led off, followed by William Green of the AFL. The head of the Textile Workers Union of America read CIO president Phillip Murray's statement in support. Various women's groups from the American Association of University Women to the League of Women Voters called on Congress to help Britain. American exporters were well represented, and the ubiquitous Eric Johnston, speaking in behalf of the United States Chamber of Commerce, endorsed the loan. The American Economic Association sent practitioners of the dismal science to testify and at the same time authored several letters to the editor of the *New York Times*, *Washington Post*, and other national newspapers. Unlike the Bretton Woods hearings, the present debate saw Wall Street solidly behind the loan. Winthrop Aldrich testified at length in favor of the agreement. Bankers had always preferred a one-time shot in the arm to stabilize the ratio between the dollar and the pound, although they would have preferred to give the injection. Indeed, as Henry Breck wrote John Maynard

Keynes: "It would have been much better to have had the present Anglo-American Agreement negotiated and approved at the time, and in the place of, the Bretton Woods exchange fund agreement."[66] Speaking for American manufacturers was Phillip D. Reed, chairman of the board of General Electric.[67] It made good business sense, he said, for America to aid its best customer.

As prearranged by the administration, Senator Fulbright assumed responsibility for bringing southern senators around. The task proved most difficult. After lunching with Theodore Bilbo (D-Miss.) and Alan Ellender (D-La.), he reported that these two flowers of Dixie were unalterably opposed to the loan. He and Eastland agreed that southern members of Congress would do an about-face if someone could persuade Oscar Johnson, head of the Cotton Growers Association, to testify. Will Clayton was in the process of enticing Johnson to go to Washington and lend his support when, on March 19, Sir Stafford Cripps announced plans to keep the Liverpool Cotton Exchange closed indefinitely, leaving cotton purchasing in the United Kingdom in the hands of the British government. Neither Johnson nor any other representative of the American Cotton Growers subsequently appeared to testify.[68]

Outright opponents of the loan were not well represented at the hearings— "three-hand picked lunatics with straw in their hair," according to Keynes.[69] Senator Eugene Milliken (R-Colo.) spoke for those western interests—sugar beet growers, cattle raisers, and metal producers—whose products were produced more cheaply in other parts of the world and hence felt threatened by multilateralism in general and the loan in particular. Bernard Baruch, Leo Crowley, and Jesse Jones had all let it be known that they would appear. In the end, both Crowley and Jones got cold feet, although the *Houston Chronicle* led a one-paper crusade in the South against the loan. Baruch also decided not to testify and instead submitted a long, rambling statement that criticized the loan but never explicitly recommended against passage. Baruch's sudden reticence stemmed in part from the persuasive powers of Jimmy Byrnes and Winston Churchill and in part from Truman's promise to name him to the Atomic Energy Commission.[70] March 20 was set aside for the opposition, but the best it could muster was Hamilton Fish, a former congressman from New York, and John B. Trevor, president of the American Coalition, "an association of over 80 patriotic societies."[71]

The notion that the loan was necessary to save Britain from communism was introduced explicitly at the hearings on March 14 by Ralph Flanders, head of a machine tool firm and a member of the Boston Committee for Economic Development. The Soviet Union did not want war, Flanders said, but there would be an intense rivalry between the Russian socioeconomic system and Western democratic capitalism. The criteria others would use to judge the two systems were living standards. Britain was the first battleground. That nation was torn between empire isolationism, the Russian model, and a "free world economy."[72] The loan would be crucial in helping the British people decide. Flanders was, of course, voicing a concern that had lurked continually in the background during the early stages of the debate. *Barron's*, a conservative financial journal that opposed multilateralism ("globaloney"), declared at one point early during the hearings: "At bottom what we are trying to do with that $3.75 billion is to assist the British because they are our allies. In other words the money is intended to help carry out the policies of Winston Churchill."[73] The *Wall Street Journal* warned more bluntly on March 8 that "without assistance Britain may have a very hard time holding her Empire together and she may lose strength and prestige to the extent that Russia will sweep over Western Europe and encompass the Mediterranean." Former ambassador to Britain Joseph P. Kennedy, an outspoken opponent of the Truman administration and of multilateralism, suggested publicly during the Senate hearings that the loan be an outright gift. "Britain is our best customer in foreign trade," he declared, "and their way of life forms a last barrier in Europe against communism."[74]

On the very day that Flanders introduced communism into the debate, Winston Churchill, fresh from his Fulton speech, arrived in Washington to lobby for the loan. At dinner with Arthur Vandenberg and other senators, he focused on the advantages of multilateralism and assured his listeners that the Attlee government was not being run by doctrinaire socialists.

After opponents of the loan agreement had completed their testimony, the hearings ended on March 20. The Senate Banking Committee endorsed the loan by a vote of 14 to 5. Ernest McFarland suggested that the United States be given permanent leases on British bases in the Western Hemisphere. His amendment was defeated 11 to 7, but only because Barkley commanded enough proxy votes (Wagner and Glass) to ensure its failure. Taft's amendment to the effect that Britain receive an outright gift of $1.25 billion lost 15 to 3, and Capehart's proposal that England be given $1.5 billion to offset an unfavorable trade deficit was defeated by the same count.[75] The motives of those who voted for the loan are, of course, impossible to define precisely. *The Economist*, as usual, had an opinion. "The opposition is deflated," it noted, "because, illogically, the twisters of the Lion's tail are even readier for a bear hunt. If the loan goes through, the balance will have been tilted in its favor by the belief that it represents an investment in security against Russian expansionism . . . the first fruits of Fulton."[76]

United Kingdom officials were encouraged by the Banking Committee's action but were still apprehensive. Shortly after the hearings closed, John Maynard Keynes returned to England and reported on the situation to Hugh Dalton. Prospects for passage in the Senate were bright. "I judge the American Loan to be quite safe unless some unexpected factor develops," he declared. Keynes attributed the improved situation to four factors: Russia, the pope, Winston Churchill, and good stage management by Will Clayton and Fred Vinson. Economic arguments had appealed only to the already converted, while fear of Soviet imperialism had swayed a number of fence sitters. After they had been instructed by the pontiff not to do anything to weaken British power to resist communism, the Conclave of Cardinals in Rome had officially appealed to the faithful not to oppose the loan. The Vatican had thereby effectively undercut Irish-Catholic opposition in the United States. Churchill had been instrumental in allaying fears that the loan would constitute a subsidy to socialism. "One can say that for the time being at least America is safely set on the course of trying to make a good job of international cooperation on the economic as well as on the political side," Keynes concluded.[77] As usual, the economist was overly optimistic.

The United States Senate took up the loan agreement the second week in April. Both opponents and supporters were unsure of themselves. While Clayton, Vinson, and their lieutenants lobbied intensively behind the scenes, nearly every senator of any prominence made a lengthy speech on the loan and related topics. During an extended address, Claude Pepper argued for passage in hopes that it might clear the way for a Russian loan. He had visited Russia in 1945, he said, and that nation's need was as great as England's. He insisted that granting the loan would lead to a less secretive Russia and the holding of free elections. Glenn Taylor (D-Idaho) and Harley Kilgore (D-W.Va.) strongly supported Pepper, but this trio of liberals constituted a distinct minority. Significantly, Pepper's oration took place against the backdrop of a vicious campaign in the conservative press designed to label him a fellow traveler and a traitor.[78]

In the early going, opponents of the loan chose to stress the cotton issue. Senator Thomas Stewart (D-Tenn.) charged that not only would the loan subsidize a government that had closed the Liverpool Exchange but also part of the credit would be used to purchase cotton from countries other than America. To counter such "propaganda," Clayton and Willard Thorp held a series of secret meetings with the cotton senators. Increasingly they focused their attention on Burnett Maybank, who had been active in the cotton export business all his life and who was well respected by his colleagues. The administration gave Maybank iron-clad assurances that no part of the loan would be used to purchase foreign cotton. It also showed him the results of the poll conducted in his native state which indicated that farmers in the Pee Dee area of South Carolina favored the credit by a ratio of 28 to 1. On April 29 he announced to the Senate his conversion to the cause and began working energetically behind the scenes to line up other Southerners in favor of the loan. But Maybank's support was offset by other factors. Angered by the administration's support for OPA and the FEPC, several sons of Dixie swore to use the financial agreement to get even with Truman.[79]

In fact, no sooner had the loan cleared the cotton hurdle than it fell afoul of parliamentary maneuvering against the pending FEPC legislation. Theodore Bilbo launched a tirade that lasted from April 18 through May 10 against not only the fair employment bill but the loan measure as well. If the Senate adjourned for the summer recess without taking action on the loan, Britain would be unwilling and unable to join either the IMF or the IBRD. Delay would be tantamount to Senate rejection of the financial agreement. Racists and isolationists made a powerful combination. "As the week [of April 18] progressed," the British Embassy reported to London, "the prospect of bringing the British loan to a vote in the Senate receded and prophecies of gloom multiplied."[80]

Antiloan forces hoped that the Senate, frustrated by the filibuster, would lay both measures aside by the first week in May and begin deliberations on the extension of the draft, due to expire on May 15. "Wild Bill" Langer spent the eighteenth and most of the nineteenth monotonously repeating all the old arguments against the loan. He reserved special vehemence for denouncing Lord Keynes, or "Kerns" as he called him, for his criticism of Woodrow Wilson and the *Economic Consequences of the Peace*. Eventually Langer yielded the floor to Clyde Reed (R-Kans.) to discuss wheat prices and to Stiles Bridges (R-N.H.) to criticize the army for taking the bust measurements of Wacs. Bilbo followed. "The Man" declared that he would summarize all of his ideas in the first ten minutes and spend the next ten days on "elaboration." During the ensuing forty-eight hours Bilbo declaimed on a number of favorite subjects and used the opportunity to take on lifelong enemies. He denounced "glamour girl" Claire Booth Luce and her husband, Henry Luce, for their attacks on him and charged that *Life* magazine was dominated by communists and blacks. But then, suddenly, Bilbo asked permission to return home. "I can never stay here when there are four peckerwoods down in Mississippi trying to take my job away from me," he said. Permission was quickly granted.[81] Bilbo's place in succeeding days was taken by Alan Ellender (D-La.), Langer again, and Olin Johnston (D-S.C.).

Alben Barkley, nearing the end of his patience, informed the Senate on May 2 that it had been debating the loan for nearly three weeks and it was time to vote. He grimly ordered the sergeant at arms to scour cloakroom and restaurant for senators driven from the chamber by the Bilbo-Langer tirade. With a quorum present he declared: "I now announce that I will not move at any time between now and the 15th of May to lay aside the pending measure in order to take up the measure to extend the draft law." The Senate would either vote first on the British loan or "By God the draft act will be allowed to expire."[82] Although efforts at cloture failed, Barkley was able to obtain unanimous consent for the Senate to vote on the McFarland amendment on May 8.

The War Department wanted desperately to gain formal control over British-owned or British-claimed bases in the Atlantic and Pacific, and the Truman administration was not adverse to using the loan as leverage to gain its strategic objectives. It recognized, however, that Britain would never accept explicit linkage of the two issues and therefore had labored frantically to obtain what it wanted through private diplomatic channels before Congress acted to make bases part of the actual loan agreement. Beginning in October 1945, the United States had pressed London to grant it full military and commercial access to American-built or American-funded bases in British territory in both the Pacific and the Atlantic as well as permanent leases on the ninety-nine-year bases in the Atlantic. The Foreign Office had adroitly procrastinated. They would consider such an arrangement, Bevin and his cohorts declared, if the United States would reciprocate. There were no British-built bases in American territory, however. What the British, together with Australia and New Zealand, wanted from the United States were regional defense arrangements in the Pacific and other areas to protect

American and British Commonwealth interests. Washington was not any more willing to embrace this version of an Anglo-American alliance than any other.

Throughout the spring United States pressure on London over the bases issue increased and became more specific, focusing on the Atlantic and Caribbean islands and Canton, Christmas, and Tarawa in the Pacific, islands that were jointly claimed by the United States and Britain. In April 1946 Byrnes, referring directly to the pending loan agreement and to the McFarland amendment, asked Bevin to cede the Pacific islands outright. After considerable delay, Bevin replied that he, personally, was sympathetic, but public opinion in the Dominions would never permit territorial giveaways while the loan was under consideration by Congress.[83] Despite frantic efforts, then, the State Department was unable by gaining concessions from the British to let the air out of the McFarland amendment before it came to a vote.

During the Senate debate over the bases proposal, such illustrious members of the conservative coalition as Richard Russell (D-Ga.) and Owen Brewster (R-Maine) spoke in favor. Fulbright, in what was certainly an ironic stance given his future role as watchdog of Congress's role in the making of United States foreign policy, appealed for the freedom of the executive branch to conclude agreements with foreign powers without having to worry about them being picked apart by Congress. Barkley closed the debate with an emotional appeal. He wondered aloud how Congress would react if the United States wanted to borrow money from England and it demanded territorial cessions. No senator would vote for such a transfer. Acceptance of the bases clause, the majority leader argued finally, "could drive an ally into arms into which we do not want her to be folded."[84] So threatened by the McFarland amendment did the administration feel that Byrnes actually approached Bevin during the foreign ministers' conference then being held in Paris and asked him to state publicly that London intended to meet some of America's base requirements. Bevin refused, however, and Byrnes dropped the matter. The much-feared amendment was defeated 45 to 40. The tally showed that twenty-eight Democrats and seventeen Republicans opposed the amendment, while nineteen Democrats, twenty Republicans, and one Progressive favored it.[85]

Rejection of the McFarland amendment unfroze the parliamentary logjam. The Senate unanimously consented to vote on all pending amendments and the loan itself by Friday, May 10. After rejecting a brace of alterations and substitute proposals, the upper house approved the financial agreement 46 to 34 with 16 not voting. A combination of twenty-nine Democrats and seventeen Republicans, including Robert Taft, voted yes, while fifteen Democrats, eighteen Republicans, and one Progressive voted no.[86]

Whether or not a majority of the members of the United States Senate voted for the loan out of fear of Russia is unclear, but it is fairly certain that the loan would not have passed had not the specter of international communism and Soviet imperialism been hovering over Europe. By March and April 1946, Americans had come to view the Soviet Union as a threat to Christianity, democracy, and Western civilization, and they were ready, albeit grudgingly, to accept foreign aid as a means to help their overseas allies. During this period significant changes occurred in the editorial opinions of moderate business journals such as *Business Week* and *Fortune*. Initially, both supported the loan as a prerequisite for multilateralism. By mid-March 1946, however, each was emphasizing the value of the loan as a symbol of Anglo-American solidarity against Russia. Benjamin Anderson, a California businessman who had testified against Bretton Woods before the Senate Banking and Currency Committee, called at the same time for a $3 billion loan to Great Britain, and he worked energetically for passage of the financial agreement. "I did not say what was in my mind, that we need the British Empire politically and to help offset Russia," Anderson wrote Will Clayton of his Senate appearance, "but that was in my mind."[87] The British loan is a vital step toward world reconstruction and peace, Reinhold Niebuhr wrote the editor of the *New York Times* on April 18. Isolationist and reactionary forces have been joined in their attack on the loan by communists and their supporters who are working to defeat it, he charged.[88] Walter George (D-Ga.) told a friend that "as an individual" he was not for the loan but he felt it was his "patriotic duty" to support it.[89] Harry Stanfill (R-Ky.) summed up the dilemma facing many conservative senators and the reasons they finally decided to vote for the loan. Anyone opposed to it, he said, was characterized in the "New Deal Press" as being "Anglophobe, old guard, standpatter, America firster, and an isolationist." He pointed out, however, that the loan could not be justified to the American people as a business deal. Britain had never made good on the billions of dollars in debts it still owed. Yet Stanfill decided to support the loan, he said, out of "enlightened self-interest," and because the British people were the "last barrier against communism."[90]

Senate approval of the British loan did nothing to decrease administration fears that it would fail in the House. The Democrats controlled the lower chamber 238 to 191 (the Progressive and American Labor parties held one seat apiece), but those in charge of the financial agreement were certain the voting would not correspond to party affiliation. Moreover, the House had been consistently more hostile to the loan in particular and to the Truman-Byrnes foreign policy in general than the Senate. Southern Democrats and Republicans had combined more frequently in the House than the Senate, and a powerful rural coalition had already given notice of its vehement opposition to the loan. Like their fellows in the upper chamber, House members were worried about the impact of a vote for the British loan on their chances at the forthcoming mid-term elections. While only one-third of the Senate members were going to have to put their careers on the line, all of the representatives would have to face the music. Republicans in particular were painfully aware of the lack of public support for the loan, and they privately criticized the administration for not conducting a Bretton Woods–type publicity campaign. They claimed that their constituents were apathetic and closed-minded when it came to the agreement.

In addition, general feeling against the administration was running high by early summer 1946. GOP legislators disliked and distrusted the State Department and had no respect for the Treasury. Citing the fact that legislators were excluded from the loan negotiations, more than one expressed the opinion that the State Department "will have to be taught a lesson about its high-handed manner."[91] A Treasury Department survey indicated that only 36 members of the House definitely favored the loan, while 66 opposed it. Another 4 were listed as leaning in favor, 14 tending against, and 309 uncommitted. A poll of the House Banking and Currency Committee showed 9 in favor, 6 opposed, and 10 uncommitted. Clayton, Vinson, and Acheson believed that Brent Spence (D-Ky.) was strong enough to get the bill through committee, but the House as a whole was a different matter. Everyone saw Jesse Wolcott (R-Mich.), a master parliamentarian who frequently hamstrung administration bills, as a key figure.[92]

The anticommunism that had played a major part in persuading key senators to vote for the Anglo-American Financial Agreement was sure to be equally important in the House. Nonetheless, those in charge of the loan remained reluctant to cash in on the burgeoning red scare. Fear of alienating liberal supporters was still a factor. But in addition, Clayton, Acheson, Vinson, Collado—and Truman, for that matter—were neither Russophobes nor capitalist ideologues. They perceived themselves to be internationalists. For Acheson, Truman, and others concerned primarily with strategic and political matters, that meant realpolitik—cooperation with one's friends and cajolement and coercion of one's opponents in the pursuit of peace and stability. It meant a pragmatic approach to world affairs, a willingness to deal with each situation on its merits; above all, it meant freedom of action for the executive to conduct foreign affairs. For those concerned with economic affairs, internationalism meant not the obliteration of socialism at the national level or even abolition of state trading. The multilateralists envisioned cooperation and trade between capitalist, socialist, and communist nations. Internationalism meant rather the creation of a worldwide system of trade and finance in which member nations agreed to abide by certain rules. Pure multilateralists such as Will Clayton were determined to sell Bretton Woods and the financial agreement as mechanisms that would end the economic distress and social insecurity that bred war at all times and in all places, not merely as devices to contain Soviet expansion. Oscar Cox, who was equally concerned with economic and strategic matters and who was at this time still a key adviser to Truman, supported the financial agreement but only with the multilateral strings attached. He also believed that a loan to Russia was still possible but that in the course of negotiating such a credit Washington "should try to persuade the Soviets to participate in a true world trading system, in which Soviet goods and Soviet citizens may not only move freely in non-Soviet areas . . . but in which Americans, British, Frenchmen, and other peoples may move freely and buy and sell in the Soviet Union and the areas which surround it."[93] The economic and strategic internationalists felt threatened by Soviet imperialism but even more by isolationism and economic nationalism—both at home and abroad.

The truth was, however, that isolationists and economic nationalists held the balance of power in Congress and hence were in a position to determine the destiny of the loan, a component the internationalists believed crucial to their program. For many of these legislators, anticommunism was the only grounds on which they could justify the transaction to themselves and their constituents.

Hearings before the House Banking and Currency Committee opened on May 14. Spence was prepared to use all of his powers to secure approval of the financial agreement, and the Democrats were in a majority. Moreover, southern representatives on the committee such as Brooks Hayes (D-Ark.) and Wright Patman (D-Tex.) tended to be more progressive than other spokespersons for Dixie. But the Republican minority included some of the most virulently isolationist members of either house: Frederick C. Smith of Ohio, Fred Crawford of Michigan, Howard Buffet of Nebraska, and *Chicago Tribune* darling Jesse Sumner. They immediately attempted to get administration representatives to depict the loan as a part of the struggle between Soviet communism and Western capitalism. When Fred Vinson defined the credit as a mechanism that would keep the world from being divided up into rival economic blocs, Crawford asked whether the loan would not create two rival blocs: Russian and Anglo-American. Vinson's answer was: "We've got to take the world as it is. No, we can't avoid the two economic groups at the present time." Playing further into Crawford's hands, Vinson expressed the opinion that the financial agreement was "in the interest of capitalism, free enterprise, and the kind of country, the kind of life we want here."[94] O'Connell and Ferguson subsequently tried to downplay the two-bloc image, asserting that it was Crawford's rather than Vinson's, but to no avail. The secretary's remarks, duly reported in the press, created a major sensation inside and outside of Congress.[95]

Mounting Russophobia, it should be noted, did not translate into Anglophilia, even among supporters of the loan. Shortly before the House opened hearings, Walter Lippmann had charged that British activities in Germany were concealed behind a "silken curtain." Within the British sector operated a German army, "a large and good one," which had surrendered to the British; presumably it was being used to maintain law and order, he speculated.[96] Moreover, anti-British feeling among American Zionists reached a fever pitch in spring 1946. In fact, American resentment of British policies in Palestine loomed as a major threat to loan passage.

From early January through late March 1946 the Anglo-American Committee on Palestine, composed of six Britons and six Americans, held hearings in Washington, London, various displaced person camps, and several European and Middle Eastern cities. In late January Ernest Bevin appeared before the committee and made a promise he would later regret. If the committee could unanimously agree on a set of recommendations, he would implement them, he said. The foreign secretary apparently believed that once the committee had all the facts, it would support his position, namely, continuation of strict controls on Jewish immigration into Palestine.[97]

At the end of April the Anglo-American committee delivered its report to

London and Washington. All twelve members agreed to the establishment of a binational state in Palestine, with the British mandate to be continued pending the establishment of a United Nations trusteeship. Their report downplayed the possibility of Jewish terrorism and Arab-Jewish violence, and advocated the immediate admission of 100,000 European Jews to Palestine. The committee made it clear that its recommendations were based on the appalling conditions in Europe rather than on a rational evaluation of the viability of a binational state. On the day the report was released the president, after acknowledging the advice of the State-War-Navy Coordinating Committee that "no U.S. armed forces be involved in carrying out the committee's recommendations," publicly endorsed the suggestions on immigration while reserving judgment on the remainder of the proposals.[98]

Truman's action infuriated Bevin. In fact, the foreign secretary had no intention of implementing the inquiry's recommendation.[99] When Truman continued to agitate publicly and privately for the immediate admission of the 100,000, Bevin blew up. At a speech delivered at the annual Labour Party Conference at Bournemouth, the foreign secretary declared: "The agitation in the United States and particularly in New York for 100,000 Jews to be admitted to Palestine is caused by the desire not to have too many of them in New York."[100]

Bevin's faux pas came a day before the Senate Banking Committee completed hearings on the financial agreement. The anger against Britain that had been festering for months among Zionists and their friends at once burst into the open and threatened to scuttle the loan for good. "This reckless and unjustifiable outburst with its alarming overtone of anti-semitic bias cannot but alarm and disturb me and millions of other Americans," Adolf Sabbath (D-Ill.), powerful chairman of the House Rules Committee, wrote Truman.[101] Taft and Wagner cranked up their machine again and began pressuring the administration to do something. "The case for the immediate admission into Palestine of 100,000 Jews who had been the victims of Nazi persecution is written in blood and suffering," read a senatorial petition to the White House.[102]

Liberals and conservatives, isolationists and internationalists sympathized intensely with the Jewish victims of Nazi oppression and had expressed varying degrees of resentment over Arab neutrality during the war. But even the most outraged proved in the end unwilling to commit American troops to the area. Nor did they intend to sacrifice postwar aid to Great Britain to the Zionist cause. Gradually it began to dawn on State and War Department strategists that the only way to overwhelm Zionist and pro-Jewish opposition to the loan was to cast the Palestinian crisis in light of the Cold War. The British were certain that the Russians were exploiting the volatile situation in the Middle East, even to the point of funneling Russian Jews into Palestine from Constanza, and they reported their suspicions to the State Department.[103] Using intelligence gained from the British and drawing parallels between Iran and Palestine, administration spokespersons subsequently argued to key members of Congress that, if America abandoned Britain, it would either have to replace British power in the Middle East or concede the region to the Soviets.

One of the greatest obstacles confronting wavering conservatives was the ideological inconsistency of voting a loan to socialist Britain in the name of defeating communism. Most were free enterprise ideologues and regarded socialism as a halfway house between Marxism and capitalism. Indeed, one asked, was not the United States fouling its own Anglo-American nest by subsidizing a socialist government in Great Britain? "The British and Americans are forming a partnership here split two ways: Socialist-Democrats [i.e., socialist-capitalists], with Russia on the other side of the fence with a Communistic form of government," Fred Crawford observed to Fred Vinson. "What is there in this agreement which will protect the people of the United States, in our form of government, in the event the Socialist government of Britain . . . proceeds in a very dangerous manner against the interest of our form of government?" he asked.[104] How could Britain nationalize its iron and steel industries and the Liverpool Cotton Exchange, demanded John Kunkel (R-Penn.), and still promise to promote free trade and free competition abroad?[105] "Well, of course," proclaimed Howard Buffet, "when one country goes National-Socialist [Britain], then the free enterprise area will move out of it." These assertions jibed perfectly with Bernard Baruch's frequent warnings against totalization. To make matters worse, the British loan had been negotiated by the man whom many conservatives had regarded as the creator of modern socialism, John Maynard Keynes. "You just love socialism," Jesse Sumner hissed at Marriner Eccles at one point during the hearings.[106]

Because they believed that Europe's viability as an investment area and market depended on the return of peace and stability in a noncommunist context, both investment and commercial bankers supported the British loan. American investment houses and bondholders had poured billions into Europe during the 1920s only to be wiped out by the coming of totalitarianism and World War II. From New York former Congressman Charles Dewey, who had bitterly opposed Bretton Woods, headed a committee of business people and bankers that planted pro-loan editorials, sponsored pamphlets, and applied pressure to opponents. When Dewey learned that Brent Spence intended to invite former President Herbert Hoover, Baruch, Jones, and Crowley to testify, he and his Wall Street associates intervened with each. At one point, Dewey assured Joseph O'Connell that Jesse Jones would be a good boy and stay in Houston. In fact, none of the men Spence mentioned appeared in person to testify. Dewey did, and he made it clear that the communist menace was responsible for his position. "I believe that the Western countries of Europe need our help in their difficulties in this day of famine and distress to fight the insidious doctrines that are produced by Communism in the Soviet Government, and this will bring them on our side," he told the House Banking Committee.[107]

By May 1946 both Republicans and Democrats were predicting victory for the loan bill. House Minority Leader Joseph Martin told the British Embassy that the final margin of passage would be between forty and fifty votes, with some fifty to sixty Republicans voting in favor. Democratic leaders also expressed confidence but were more cautious. Aside from the Midwest, only the West Coast and its spokespersons seemed solidly against the loan. The British suspected "Communists and fellow-travelers" of being responsible for western opposition, although there was no evidence to that effect.[108] Despite these forecasts, most members of Congress remained uncommitted. He was swinging back and forth like a pendulum, Jesse Wolcott told J. A. Judson of the British Embassy.[109]

Then on May 6 the influential syndicated columnists, Joseph and Stewart Alsop, openly advised the administration to sell the loan as a weapon against Soviet expansion. They criticized Alben Barkley and Will Clayton for failing to exploit the issue, and urged Truman and Jimmy Byrnes to explain the new Soviet imperialism and its implications to the American people. A public opinion poll and a Nebraska election seemed to support the Alsops's arguments. The poll, taken in late June, indicated that 58 percent of those questioned believed that Russia wanted to rule the world, 29 percent were of the opinion that the Soviets were concerned primarily with self-defense, and 13 percent had no opinion. In Nebraska on June 11, isolationist Senator Hugh Butler won an easy victory over Governor Dwight Griswold in the Republican primary. Griswold had enjoyed the support of Harold Stassen of Minnesota and had made Butler's vote against the British loan a major issue.[110] Administration officials interpreted the outcome to mean that isolationism was still quite strong in America and that anticommunism might be the only force powerful enough to overcome it.

The House Banking Committee reported the financial agreement out with a do-pass recommendation on June 13. The margin of victory was four to one. Bevin's Bournemouth speech had come too late to affect the committee vote, but it quickly became obvious that the Palestinian issue would play a major role in the floor debate. Emmanuel Cellar, Adolf Sabbath, and Sol Bloom (D-N.Y.), chairman of the House Committee on Foreign Affairs, told the administration that they would not only vote against the loan but speak against it as well. One of O'Connell's associates told him that Bloom's opposition would kill the bill.[111]

In an effort to counter Zionist-inspired Anglophobia, the administration with great difficulty persuaded Rabbi Steven Wise to speak out in favor of the transaction. The loan issue had caused moderate Zionists in the United States much soul-searching. Even the most temperate regarded the 1939 White Paper as British appeasement of Hitler. Jews had been further angered by the United Kingdom's intervention in behalf of the mufti of Jerusalem, the anti-Semitic and pro-Nazi Arab leader who had been charged with war crimes by the Allies. For many, Bevin's speech was the last straw. But after due reflection, Wise and his followers could not bring themselves to denounce the financial agreement. The first week in July seventy-four Republicans had issued a manifesto of opposition to the loan entitled "There Will Always Be a U.S.A. if We Don't Give It Away."[112] All were from the Midwest. All were former isolationists and "not one of them had ever raised his voice in favor of the Jews," Jacob Fishman, a prominent Zionist and columnist for the *Jewish Journal* observed. Even if Jewish opposition succeeded in blocking the loan, British policy toward Palestine would not change, he argued. Moreover, Zionists would find doors closed to them in Britain that were previously open. Jewish opposition would, in fact, stimulate anti-Semitism among Britons and liberal elements in the United States. If the loan failed, Anglo-American isolationists and anti-Semites would claim that American Jews were responsible for its demise. It seemed, then, that Wise and his fellows had no option. Consequently, after lengthy interviews with various State Department officials, the rabbi issued a public statement in support of the loan not "as a matter of favor to the British Government" but "to bring about a financially stable world."[113] In the end, Bloom and Sabbath supported the loan while Cellar remained opposed.[114]

By July 2 the loan was ready for full House debate, but Sam Rayburn postponed consideration for nearly a week because more than one hundred representatives were absent. In the meantime, Rayburn and John McCormack (D-Mass.), who embodied Catholic, anticommunist support for the loan, called House members to the "Board of Education" for quiet, heart-to-heart talks. Pleading for support, they reminded their colleagues that Britain was the one friend the United States could depend on in an uncertain world. They warned that with Russia marching through Europe at every open gate, Britain could not be allowed to go down to financial ruin. On the twelfth McCormack and James Wadsworth (R-N.Y.) took the anticommunist argument to the floor of the House. The fate of the world, they declared in separate speeches, depended on the final vote on the loan scheduled for the next day. If democracy was to survive at home and abroad, America must help it survive, and the British loan was a step in that direction. Was the United States ready to surrender world leadership to Moscow? both asked. When Wadsworth finished, both sides of the House cheered.[115]

The sixteen-hour debate on the British loan concluded on Saturday, July 13, 1946. Administration forces quickly beat back a series of amendments that roughly paralleled those that had been offered in the Senate. When the climactic roll-call vote had been taken, 219 voted yes and 155 no, with 1 abstention and 57 not voting. The division was more partisan than it had been in the Senate; 157 Democrats and 61 Republicans voted for the loan, and 122 Republicans and 32 Democrats voted against it. An analysis of the ballot shows that the Liverpool Cotton Exchange notwithstanding, the heaviest support for the measure came from the South with 44 of 54 Dixie legislators voting yes. As in the Senate, New England went strongly for the loan, 24 to 3. Only 76 out of 115 northeastern representatives voted yea, however. The strongest opposition, not surprisingly, came from the Midwest where 82 out of 155 voted no. What is unusual is how many heartland members of Congress, including Robert Taft, voted in favor of the financial agreement.[116]

The British Broadcasting Company interrupted its programming late Saturday evening, July 13, to report the results of the final vote on the loan. The average Briton's reaction was relief mixed with skepticism. The weeks of anti-British tirades by Anglophobe legislators were over, and the economic uncertainty clouding the immediate future had dissipated. Had Congress rejected the loan, everyone expected the Labour government to adopt extreme measures—strict food rationing, rigid quotas on imports from dollar areas, bilateral deals with nondollar countries to import essential supplies, and precipitate withdrawals from costly overseas commitments, perhaps even Greece and Germany. In fact, the Labour government had just recently decided to ration bread, a drastic step that had not been necessary even during war. In other words, a consensus existed that the loan had given Britain sufficient time to work out less drastic solutions to its problems. British skepticism rose from doubts about Congress's willingness to maintain price controls in an election year. Inflation in the United States could, by increasing the price of American exports, significantly reduce the value of the loan to Britain. A clever ditty in the *Daily Herald* neatly captured the ambivalence that characterized Britain's reaction:

> The credit (supposing they dole it)
> We must pay in equivalent pounds
> but inflation (unless they control it)
> will make it far more than it sounds.[117]

On July 15, 1946, President Truman signed the British loan legislation and issued a carefully drafted statement composed earlier by Averell Harriman, the new American ambassador to Great Britain. Since mid-May Harriman had been warning the State Department that if Congress rejected the loan, left-wing Labour leaders would force Bevin to dissociate Britain from America's get-tough policy and seek "rapprochement" with the Soviet Union. After Congress approved the agreement, Truman described it as a "move of mutual benefit" rather than merely a good deal for America. What Harriman wanted, of course, was the president to follow McCormack, Rayburn, Taft, Vandenberg, and Churchill's lead and openly justify the agreement with the "natural ally" argument. To a certain extent Truman followed his ambassador's advice, but the White House avoided invoking the Soviet bogey explicitly. The president's statement said that it was "fortunate and gratifying" that the loan simultaneously served Britain and America's interest. It would promote prosperity at home and abroad, and in particular help Britain overcome the economic problems that had arisen from its sacrifice in the common cause during World War II.[118]

In truth, the Roosevelt-Truman foreign policy establishment's seven-year struggle to maintain its freedom of action in world affairs was coming to a close. Internationalism did not carry the day for the British loan—anticommunism did. No significant segment of the population was committed to the concept of one world; no region or interest group seriously entertained the notion that America ought to relinquish part of its sovereignty and prosperity for the good of the international community as a whole. The South, which voted overwhelmingly for the loan, was militaristic, insecure, aggressive, and interested in selling its cotton and tobacco abroad—it was not internationalist. The congressional wing of the Republican party was still dominated by midwestern isolationists. Heartland farmers distrusted free trade and still clung to the Garfield-Blaine view of America as a self-sufficient economic entity. Robert Taft and Arthur Vandenberg's German and East European constituents rejected the economic arguments for the loan almost to a person. Public opinion polls in 1945–46 showed Americans to be clinging desperately to commercial and fiscal orthodoxy. They were worried about their own living standards and were generally committed to the idea that free enterprise and a balanced budget were the means for maintaining it. While multilateralism was in many ways a creed for conservatives, its subtleties were lost on the average person. Moreover, the loan was certainly not passed in a fit of Anglophilia. The image of Britain as a selfish, imperial power that had shirked its duties in the Pacific still prevailed among many Americans. The Palestine problem reinforced that negative image not only among Zionists but also among millions of non-Jewish citizens tormented by visions of the Holocaust. Whitehall was right; without the Soviet menace, the United States would never have approved the loan to Britain. Just as lend-lease was an emergency response to a perceived threat to United States security, so the British loan was a reaction to another foreign devil bent on world domination.

Ironically, Will Clayton, Dean Acheson, Jimmy Byrnes, and Harry Truman were reluctant to invoke that demon. Concern about possible adverse reaction among American liberals was partially responsible for their reserve, but there were other reasons. For Clayton and his lieutenants multilateralism, flawed though it was, was a mechanism that promised to create a new international order and eliminate the economic roots of war, not a device to contain a specific aggressor nation at a specific point in history. For Acheson, Byrnes, and Truman, internationalism meant not abstract one-worldism but the freedom for the United States to analyze each international problem as it arose and formulate a policy that would protect America's security and prosperity. These men were not ideologues; the fact that the governments of Clement Attlee in Britain and Leon Blum in France were socialist bothered them not at all. If aid to these regimes would serve United States interests narrowly defined, then it was in order. But it became clear during the loan debate that foreign aid would carry a price: United States participation in an aggressive anticommunist, anti-Soviet crusade. Would-be practitioners of realpolitik within the foreign policy establishment recognized that the most virulently anticommunist voices in America were former isolationists and xenophobes, but once again their hands were tied. The monster was out of its cage and it would do more to limit the freedom of action of future United States policymakers than Clayton, Acheson, Truman, and Byrnes could ever have dreamed.

Finally, modified multilateralism was counterproductive of the goals of Cold War interventionism. The British loan proved to be a distinctly mixed blessing for the United Kingdom. The Attlee government was forced by its terms to raise its trade barriers and relinquish its financial controls much too quickly. When in conformity to the agreement Britain made the pound freely convertible in July

1947, dollars and gold fled the country, destabilizing the economy. London had to freeze dollar assets, restrict imports to the absolute minimum, and embark on a long-range austerity program to achieve a balance of payments. And it had, finally, to reduce its overseas military presence and abandon many of its strategic outposts in the Near and Middle East. All this occurred at a time when the foreign policy establishment and Congress were concluding that Britain was America's only reliable ally in an unstable and threatening world.

Conclusion

THE GREAT CONFLICT that began in 1939 and ended in 1945 destroyed the European balance of power in both a strategic and an ideological sense. World War II was truly cataclysmic in its destructive power. Ten million Allied and six million Axis soldiers died. As many as twenty million civilians may have perished in the conflict. World War II cost more than $1.15 trillion. It left the world, but particularly Europe, battered, gasping for breath, and searching desperately for a new order that would usher in an era of physical, economic, and social security.

The Soviet Union had an answer to the Continent's problems. Relinquish your claim to individual liberty and subsume your national sovereignty to ours and we will guarantee you food, work, and peace. Britain was prepared to make a counteroffer in the form of the new liberalism. The concept, consisting of a pragmatic blend of state socialism, private enterprise, planning, and countercyclical deficit spending, transcended party lines in Britain, its Conservative adherents calling themselves reform Tories and its Labour advocates, liberal socialists. The stratagem seemed tailor-made for the war-damaged, postindustrial societies of Western Europe because it promised social security without undermining democracy or diminishing individual liberty. But alas for Britain, who hoped to ride the crest of the new liberalism to a position of leadership within the European community, only America could provide the resources necessary to make this healing nostrum available to the Continent.

Though a postindustrial society, the United States had not evolved ideologically to the point that Britain, Belgium, France, and the Scandinavian countries had. In the United States during World War II, a battle still raged between the new liberalism and the old. With the coming of World War II the New Deal had gone into remission in America. Even Brandesians, who advocated merely countercyclical deficit spending of a temporary nature to smooth out the bumps in the business cycle, were driven underground by the champions of laissez-faire and free enterprise.

Intimidated by the rising conservative tide within the Congress and among the American people, Franklin Roosevelt, Harry Truman, and their advisers searched for foreign policy stratagems that would placate conservatives and at the same time ensure social justice, economic security, and physical safety both at home and abroad. The answer to their dreams appeared out of the past: multilateralism, that British-bred and British-led system of payments and trade that had prevailed in the Western world during the last quarter of the nineteenth century. Those members of the Roosevelt-Truman foreign policy establishment responsible for economic matters embraced multilateralism as a technique that would raise living standards at home and abroad without accelerating collectivist trends, while those concerned with armies and boundaries viewed multilateralism as the economic phase of balance-of-power realpolitik. But so strong was the conservative impulse in America that nationalists, bureaucratic imperialists, and special interests modified multilateralism into a machine to enrich America. As such, it proved counterproductive of Anglo-American efforts to restrain Soviet imperialism and prevent the spread of communism into Western and Central Europe.

For a variety of reasons—economic, political, strategic, and ideological—powerful individuals and interest groups in the United Kingdom were committed to seeing multilateralism work. British domestic politics during World War II was dominated by a search for a viable social democracy. Within the Churchill coalition, the principal struggle was between Conservative proponents of the middle way and advocates of laissez-faire capitalism. Adoption of the Beveridge Plan and publication of the White Paper on Employment marked significant victories for Harold Macmillan, Anthony Eden, and the disciples of Keynesian economics. But the British electorate did not trust the Conservative party to achieve economic and social security, and it turned Winston Churchill and his cohorts out of office in 1945 in favor of Clement Attlee and the Labour party. In the wake of the general election the political center in the United Kingdom shifted to the left. In its early stages, the Attlee regime was dominated by a struggle between liberal socialists who wanted to nationalize major portions of the British economy while protecting individual liberty and preserving a portion of the private sector, and "Gosplanners" who advocated comprehensive planning and total government control over the economy. The liberal socialists, of course, triumphed over Harold Laski, Aneurin Bevan, and Emmanuel Shinwell, and work on the construction of a social democracy in Britain proceeded apace.

For Britons, social democracy was more than just an answer to domestic problems. Men such as Anthony Eden, Richard Law, and to an extent Ernest Bevin saw it as a third way between capitalism and communism. It would serve as an attractive alternative to the hungry, shivering, benumbed masses of Europe and catapult Britain once more into a preeminent position in European affairs.

The economists who served as architects of the new order in the United Kingdom, men such as John Maynard Keynes and James Meade, believed that multilateralism and democratic socialism were compatible. They were sure, in fact, that planned national economies geared to the achievement of full employment were a prerequisite for a sound multilateral system. But multilateralism as modified by the United States hindered the emergence of a viable social democracy in Britain and called into question the efficacy of the third way for many West Europeans. Under the influence of bureaucratic and congressional politics, multilateralism became the servant of capitalism and American special interests.

The first great obstacle to the realization of a rational international system of banking and trade was bureaucratic conflict within the Roosevelt administration. Henry Morgenthau and Cordell Hull were nonelected officials who lived in a world of power and status. They pushed forward policy options designed not so much to serve the national or international interest as to enhance their standing and that of their agency within the Washington milieu. Treasury's determination to secure control of international finance through mechanisms that were designed to preserve United States control over gold and credit would have alone doomed multilateralism to failure.

The second great hurdle proponents of the new economic order had to o'erleap was isolationism and economic nationalism in the United States. World War II did nothing to change the hearts and minds of those who for so long had advocated the continuation of economic self-sufficiency through trade and financial controls, and preservation of America's physical security through adherence to the Monroe Doctrine. It was these men and women who delivered the coup de grace to multilateralism by joining with Treasury in limiting the ability of the United States to provide the world with adequate liquid capital. Thanks in part to the efforts of congressional conservatives, neither Bretton Woods nor the Anglo-American Financial Agreement of 1946 was liberal enough to ensure a smoothly functioning system of international payments. In addition, through the mechanism of the Reciprocal Trade Agreements Act, opponents of multilateralism rendered a simultaneous, horizontal reduction of tariffs impossible. The United Kingdom and its sterling area partners proved unwilling to slash preferences, while special interests in the United States were protected through a system of bilateral tariff treaties that they controlled.

Clearly Britain failed in its effort to educate America. Keynes, Meade, and Law believed that the United States could be persuaded that the national as well as the international interest could be served by sharing its resources. Unlike the strategic sphere where the Foreign Office enjoyed some success in alerting the United States to the threat of Soviet imperialism, British multilateralists made no headway against the forces of economic nationalism. American conservatives insisted that business principles be applied to national and international affairs. That position had a clear logic which was to become painfully apparent to Great Britain. The essence of capitalism is competition and self-aggrandizement. The principles of American capitalism when applied to foreign affairs were incompatible with economic internationalism.

Multilateralism was more than just an irrelevant anachronism, as many of its critics charged. The goal of relatively free trade in which creditor nations provide liquid capital to debtor nations in order to maintain continual equilibrium in trade and payments is a worthy one. The architects of multilateralism in Washington and London erred not in designing their system but in continuing to press for its acceptance after it had been subverted by special interests, Congress, and the United States Treasury. In their determination to have half a loaf if they could not have a whole, Anglo-American multilateralists saddled Britain with a scheme that brought it to the verge of bankruptcy.

The failure of multilateralism had profound implications for the diplomatic and strategic realms. For Franklin Roosevelt, Harry Truman, and their foreign policy advisers, internationalism meant primarily freedom for the American executive to practice realpolitik, to react pragmatically to international crises. While not afraid to make moral judgments, they defined the national interest in strategic and economic terms; survival and prosperity were the ultimate goals of statecraft. They rejected Henry Wallace and Wendell Willkie's concept of one world in which, among other things, nations surrendered a portion of their sovereignty within the context of a collective security organization. Nor were they idealogues who saw foreign policy as a crusade to save capitalism and democracy from one form of totalitarianism or another. But the methods of realpolitik are balance of power and sphere of interest. Isolationists and Wilsonian internationalists joined together during World War II to declare those techniques mischievous and outdated. As a result, FDR refused to support Anglo-Russian efforts to reach specific territorial and political arrangements in 1942 and 1944.

Spheres of interest emerged, nonetheless, as German power receded and British and Soviet troops moved to fill the void. After Roosevelt's death, Harry Truman opted for a policy of mediation that not only allowed the Soviets to consolidate their enclave in Eastern and Central Europe but encouraged them to expand into the eastern Mediterranean and Middle East as well. The United States turned to a policy of confrontation with the Soviet Union only after GOP isolationists joined southern Democrats to become avid Cold War warriors. As had been the case in 1941, Anglo-American solidarity and resistance to aggression became possible only within the context of a global struggle of good against evil. Realpolitik failed during World War II not because it was flawed but because Congress and the American people refused to allow the White House and State Department to practice it.

There were those in the United Kingdom who were repelled by communism and Russian imperialism, and who were ready to take up sword and buckler in defense of freedom and democracy, but Eden and Bevin saw European affairs during and immediately after World War II through the eyes of Lord Castlereagh and Eyre Crowe. They wanted to restrain Soviet imperialism and maintain a balance of power on the Continent while protecting Britain's strategic outposts and economic lifeline in the eastern Mediterranean and Middle East. As had been true during the Great War, however, British diplomats had to call in the New World to redress the balance of the Old. Throughout the war the architects of Britain's foreign policy believed that they could educate America in the ways of realpolitik and, encouraged by White House and State Department rhetoric, mistakenly assumed that America's participation in the European conflict signified acceptance of the "realities" of European balance-of-power politics. One of those realities was a willingness to finance Britain's reconstruction so that it might contain Soviet military expansion and offer a noncommunist alternative to the war-devastated nations of Europe. Whitehall succeeded merely in obtaining a quick-fix loan at an exorbitant price and, unwittingly, in helping to plant the seeds of a rabid anticommunism in its erstwhile ally. Moreover, the United States refused to play the balance-of-power game by Britain's rules, at first blocking political and territorial agreements during the war and then attempting to arbitrate or "mediate" disputes among the contending parties without choosing sides.

The period from 1943 to 1945 did not mark the dawn of a new era but in fact was a recapitulation of the past. During the Paris Peace Conference of 1919, Britain acquiesced in a Wilsonian peace structure that devastated Germany economically and humiliated its people while leaving the Reich's war-making potential intact. At the same time the Treaty of Versailles provided no definitive solution to the problem of French security. When the United States subsequently retreated into isolationism, Britain, weakened by the war and by subsequent war debts-reparations arrangements, was left to face the continental aggressors virtually alone. Similarly, the forces of nationalism and isolationism circumscribed American foreign economic policy during and immediately after World War II to such an extent that it reduced rather than enhanced British power, diminishing London's ability to maintain a balance of power on the Continent and defend its vital interests in the eastern Mediterranean. The same forces kept the United States from participating in either a global or a regional collective security system. Hamstrung by the great power veto and other provisions of its charter, the United Nations was doomed to impotency from the outset. Moreover, the United States not only refused through 1946 to join a Western European union but also did its utmost to keep one from being formed.

Fortunately for Great Britain, however, there would be no twenty-year interregnum in the history of American interventionism following World War II. The Great War left the European nation-state system greatly weakened but still intact. World War II created a void. Joseph Stalin and the Soviet Union stepped forward to take the place of Adolf Hitler and Nazi Germany as anti-heroes in the eternal struggle between good and evil that existed in the minds of most Americans. The isolationist-interventionist cycle in American foreign policy became compressed. The "retreat from responsibility" lasted three years rather than twenty, its strategic phase ending with the Truman Doctrine and its economic phase with the Marshall Plan.

Something remains to be said of the principal actors in the Anglo-American drama. Surely they were prisoners rather than masters of events. All deluded themselves into thinking that they could prevail over domestic institutions, special interests, political factions, and transnational alliances that stood in the way of their worldview and their personal ambition, but they were wrong. John

Maynard Keynes came closest to seeing the total picture, but he was tragically unrealistic about his ability to influence the course of history. He believed that his mastery of the financial imperatives of Britain's position and his vision of a multi-lateral economic system at the international level nurturing planned national economics at various stages of development would enable him to lead the Western world into a new era of peace and prosperity. His faith that his own inspired intuition could triumph over more parochial forces was misplaced. His vision and the edifices that it gave rise to—the International Monetary Fund, the International Bank for Reconstruction and Development, and the Anglo-American Financial Agreement of 1946—were as flawed by American nationalism and isolationism as had been the Versailles peace structure during an earlier era. In refusing to acknowledge this and in serving as the advocate for a corrupted multilateralism, Keynes did his country and his reputation a great disservice.

There was another victim of hubris in this story, a man who tried to have much but wound up with little. Despite his magnificent rhetoric, Franklin Roosevelt had no vision of the future other than his own continuation in office. Internationalism and multilateralism were for him devices to divert the attention of Congress and the masses while he pursued a pragmatic foreign policy, protecting American interests and preserving the peace through the force of his personality. There were two major problems with this approach. First, FDR's lack of diplomatic leadership—he refused to try to sell realpolitik to the American people—created a void into which the forces of nationalism and isolationism rushed. The imperatives of American foreign policy during the 1940s—America's refusal to make a permanent military commitment to European security, its determination to protect and expand its economic empire, and its disillusionment with colonialism and power politics—did not circumscribe the Roosevelt administration's foreign policy, they dictated it. And second, Franklin Roosevelt proved to be mortal. Roosevelt's world without Roosevelt was nothing. He was the flywheel of his own mechanism.

Winston Churchill's role in the Anglo-American dialogue was both tragic and absurd. He was magnificent in leading his once-beleaguered country to victory over the massed forces of Italian and German fascism. He was irrelevant in thinking that Britain specifically and Europeans in general wanted to return to an ancien régime of free enterprise at home and imperialism abroad. A majority of Britons were interested in the empire only insofar as it would help preserve the nation's economic self-sufficiency and physical security. In the domestic arena the United Kingdom's search for a middle way, intensified by the events of the 1940s, led it first to embrace Keynesian financial policies and then comprehensive planning and partial nationalization of the economy in an effort to maintain full employment. The British ship of state left the former naval person bobbing in its wake after July 1945. Ironically, and somewhat pathetically, Churchill had proven willing at the second Quebec Conference to sacrifice Britain's long-range economic health and even perhaps its strategic well-being for short-term American aid that he hoped would avert the need for an austerity program. In this way

Churchill hoped that he could prevent his defeat and that of the Conservative party at the next general election. Fortunately for Churchill's reputation, the Morgenthau Plan fell victim to Russia's Polish policy and to bureaucratic infighting in Washington. It was also fortunate that Clement Attlee and not he was prime minister when Britain finally tied itself to a flawed multilateralism in return for a minimal American aid program. Churchill may not have been strong enough to control events, but he was shrewd enough to appreciate the irony of the fact that the fruits of victory over fascism were socialism at home and dependency on the United States abroad. His solace was that in 1946 he could relive the role he had played so well in the 1930s and issue a call to the English-speaking peoples to once again come to the defense of the Western world against the forces of barbarism and totalitarianism.

James Meade and Harry Hawkins led a group of professional economists who entered government service to facilitate the war effort and wound up with a chance, they believed, to make the world over. They, like Keynes, were convinced that ideas were more important and more powerful than personalities, politics, or events. These social engineers were sure that World War II and the chaos it engendered offered a unique opportunity to install devices at the national and international levels that would eliminate the roots of war. Their schemes fell victim to forces beyond their control. They and their plans became pawns in the game of democratic politics. For Britain, and for the United States, given its long-range security interest, multilateralism as modified by those forces became something of a Frankenstein's monster.

Will Clayton represented that genre that was so typically American—the businessman who believed that what was good for his particular enterprise was good for America—and the world. As an international cotton broker, Clayton was naturally attracted to the tenets of free trade. As he prospered, his stature and his vision grew. Like Keynes during World War I, Clayton in the 1930s turned to public welfare and public service. He became a disciple of multilateralism, mastered its nuances, and was able to move in and take control of America's foreign economic policy when Roosevelt and Harry Hopkins began bringing dollar-a-year people to Washington to run the war. Clayton was not politically naive, and he was willing to compromise. But again like Keynes, he proved unwilling to face reality when the machine he served became fatally flawed. The Reciprocal Trade Agreements Act as modified by Congress did not represent multilateralism, but bilateralism. Free convertibility of currencies in the absence of adequate liquidity doomed financial multilateralism to an early death. Will Clayton was neither an isolationist nor a nationalist, merely their unwitting or unwilling servant.

Ernest Bevin never saw himself as master of history or savior of the world. Rather, he self-consciously played the role of hard-headed representative of first his class and then his nation. His goals were more limited than those of many of his contemporaries, and as a result he was more successful in achieving them. Within the context of a mixed and managed economy he intended to increase wage levels and protect individual rights. Neither pure capitalists nor Gosplanites, to use Meade's phrase, would deter him. In foreign affairs he hoped to contain Soviet expansion and protect Britain's strategic outposts. Multilateralism and internationalism were irrelevant. Britain lived in the present and therefore must concentrate on the short run. Bevin realized that the Anglo-American Financial Agreement of 1946 contained pitfalls and risks, but the British people needed homes, work, and food, and it was in the working class's interest for Labour to remain in power. In the international realm, the United Kingdom needed help in forcing the Russians out of Iran and keeping them out of Turkey. Not an enthusiast for world government himself, Bevin shrewdly confronted the Soviets within the context of the United Nations, thus undercutting Anglophobia in the United States among both internationalists and isolationists. That stratagem had as much or more to do with the advent of a get-tough policy in the United States as Churchill's iron curtain speech. Muddle through is what Britain did in 1945–46, and Ernest Bevin was the chief muddler.

Leo Amery epitomized the new imperialist—enlightened, progressive, and irrelevant. He saw Britain's salvation in corporatism and a kind of welfare imperialism. But Britain, Western Europe, and even America had rejected corporatism because planning was inevitably dominated by the largest financial and manufacturing enterprises. It was private collectivism and the first step, both liberals and conservatives charged, toward fascism. Welfare imperialism ignored nationalism no less than welfare capitalism ignored class consciousness and the vigor of the modern labor movement. Because the empire was disintegrating, empire isolationism would result in the isolation of Great Britain; and given the fact that the United Kingdom was not economically self-sufficient, that meant disaster.

Of all the cast of characters in this tale, Harry Truman was less in control of the events and forces that swirled about him than any other. Truman was a man of values without vision. He prized prosperity and individual liberty for his fellow Americans and for the peoples of the world. When he entered office, he had no idea how to create these conditions other than to continue the policies of his predecessor. And he was not entirely sure what those were, especially in the international sphere. Like Roosevelt, he attempted to appease American conservatives with multilateralism without really understanding the original concept or that it had been fatally flawed. Hoping to help Britain back to economic health, he nearly crippled it. Rather quickly the new president learned that merely living up to the letter of the Yalta accords in the anticipation of reciprocity from the Soviets did nothing to restrain Soviet imperialism in Europe and the Middle East. Truman's mediation policy was designed to placate Anglophobes and opponents of power politics while blunting the Soviet expansionist drive. While trying to build trust in Moscow and work toward a community of interest, Truman silently wielded the bomb and the prospect of a postwar reconstruction loan. All his efforts were to no effect—at least as far as Eastern and Central Europe were concerned. Mediation cast the United States in the role of arbiter between equals, but the United Kingdom and the Soviet Union were far from equal in 1945–46. American foreign policy, moreover, accentuated that inequality. The United States cut off lend-lease to Britain and then saddled it with an insufficient loan that left the United Kingdom financially unprotected after July 1947. Given the fact that the American people opposed a permanent United States military presence in Europe, Truman needed a proxy. Due to ignorance and circumstance—the strength of the conservative coalition in Congress—the Truman administration nearly strangled its erstwhile ally.

Henry Morgenthau was the ultimate bureaucratic imperialist, a man who could never have thrived as a traditional democratic politician. The burgeoning federal bureaucracy created by the New Deal and World War II together with FDR's administrative style provided Morgenthau with his opportunity. From his vantage point in the Treasury, he maneuvered to gain control of the American financial establishment and to dominate any international financial system that emerged from World War II. He succeeded to a remarkable degree in achieving both goals. The financial reforms of the New Deal established Treasury control over Wall Street, and World War II coupled with Bretton Woods put Morgenthau and his advisers in a position to determine the contours of the international financial environment. But Morgenthau was no John Maynard Keynes or Harry Dexter White. He had no vision, no plan. The secret to his success was his nationalism. With it he appealed to Congress, the White House, and the American people. But Treasury ascendancy over Wall Street and perpetuation of an American monopoly of the world's gold/dollar supply did nothing to address Europe's reconstruction needs, nor did they solve any of the other momentous problems arising out of World War II. Truly, Henry Morgenthau's reach exceeded his grasp.

The figure who more than any other embodied American foreign policy in 1945–46 was Robert Taft. The senator from Ohio recognized that the United States, unlike most other members of the international community, was economically self-sufficient. The need for overseas markets was an illusion. America, he insisted, should restrict its foreign economic activity to securing sources of raw materials that had been depleted by World War II and to concluding bilateral trade agreements that benefited American manufacturing and industrial interests. Multilateralism was both a relic of a bygone era and the economic phase of an unworkable internationalism that the Democrats were trying to use to perpetuate themselves in power. Taft wished Britain no harm, but he insisted that its interests did not always coincide with America's. If London's efforts to identify Washington with colonialism were successful, the United States would not only be betraying its heritage but alienating forever most of the nonindustrialized world. Taft recognized that internationalism, and, specifically, the administration's campaign for a collective security organization, was a mask for a policy of realpolitik conducted exclusively by the executive. Aside from being undemocratic, such a foreign policy was dangerous. Balance-of-power, sphere-of-interest politics ran the risk of involving the United States in conflicts that had no bearing on its national interest. Like most Americans, Taft revered the law and believed it could be used to solve international disputes. When the United States embarked on peacekeeping ventures, it should limit itself to arbitration, mediation, and support for the World Court.

Like many American isolationists, however, Robert Taft was not immune to the charms of interventionism. He came around to the view that the Axis constituted a threat to the Western Hemisphere and that America was justified in going to war. He came to view the Soviet Union in the same light and was quick to take up the cudgels against godless communism and Soviet imperialism. He supported limited financial aid to Great Britain not to enable that nation to achieve perpetual equilibrium and thus take its place in an interdependent world economy, but to subsidize an ally for the looming struggle with Russia. Economic self-sufficiency and temporary intervention to thwart the ambitions of evil empires bent on world domination—these were the cornerstones of American foreign policy, not multilateralism and internationalism.

If ever an episode demonstrated the inextricable interrelationship between domestic and foreign policy in American history, it was the story of Anglo-American relations from 1941 to 1946. By March 1946, the Truman administration had clearly decided that the Soviet Union was a menace that warranted intervention into European and Middle Eastern affairs and that Anglo-America ought to make common cause against the Kremlin. And yet Washington was willing to supply its principal ally with a paltry $3.75 billion in aid and attached conditions that brought England to the verge of bankruptcy by late summer 1947. In 1941 the Roosevelt administration had come to similar strategic conclusions but its foreign economic policy matched its strategic initiative. Washington made an initial $7 billion installment payment to Great Britain and then followed that with more than $125 billion in outright lend-lease grants. True, the world was at war in 1941 and it was not in 1946. Nonetheless, many American policymakers considered Stalin and the Soviet Union to be reincarnations of Hitler and Nazi Germany. Only such a parallel would have been able to overcome America's war-weariness and ingrained isolationism and galvanize support for a get-tough policy. America's strategic and economic policies converged in 1941 and diverged in 1946 because those leading the charge against Germany were pragmatic liberals and those comprising the cutting edge of interventionism in 1946 were fiscal conservatives and isolationists. The former, typified by Harry Hopkins, were determined to aid the downtrodden and achieve social justice without regard to ideological considerations. Just as they were anxious to furnish whatever aid was necessary to help the victims of unemployment to their feet in the United States, Hopkins and his fellow liberals were willing to provide unlimited aid to the victims of aggression in Europe. Those in the vanguard of the interventionist movement in 1946, however, were probusiness, fiscal conservatives; they were nationalists determined to gain tangible financial and strategic profit from every dollar spent. Only after Britain experienced virtual bankruptcy and a dangerous void materialized in European politics did the liberal pragmatists seize control of the anticommunist phase of the interventionist movement and come to the continent's rescue.

Notes

Abbreviations

BEW	Bureau of Economic Warfare
CCL/CU	Churchill College Library, Cambridge University
CL/CU	Cooper Library, Clemson University
CRL/UC	Center for Research Libraries, University of Chicago
DOS	U.S. Department of State
FDR	Franklin D. Roosevelt
FEA	Foreign Economic Administration
FL/PU	Firestone Library, Princeton University
FRUS	*Foreign Relations of the United States*
HLRO	House of Lords Record Office, London
HM	Henry Morgenthau, Jr.
HST	Harry S. Truman
LC	Library of Congress
LSE	London School of Economics
ML/PU	Mudd Library, Princeton University
ML/UA	Mullins Library, University of Arkansas
ML/UI	Main Library, University of Iowa
NA	National Archives, Washington, D.C.
PRO	Public Record Office, Kew, London
PSF	President's Secretary's File
RL/LSE	Robertson Library, London School of Economics
RTAA	Reciprocal Trade Agreements Act
SL/YU	Sterling Library, Yale University

Chapter 1

1. Kimball, *The Most Unsordid Act*, 24–25, 225, 234–36; Reynolds, *Anglo-American Alliance*, 164. See also Martel, *Lend-Lease*, and Dobson, *U.S. Wartime Aid to Britain*.

2. Despite the mother country's vigorous protests and considerable delay, American Viscose was put on the block in March 1941. Generally regarded as worth £32 million, it was sold in the New York market in a new issue, sponsored by Morgan Stanley and Dillon Read, for a net of $54.4 million or £13.6 million. The commissions paid on this transaction were high and gave rise to grumblings in Great Britain

about a "banker's ramp." Courtalds demanded compensation from the British government to the tune of £44.1 million, including $50 million for goodwill. It was offered £16.7 million. Arbitration produced an award of £27.15 million plus interest. Thus, it cost British taxpayers £13.6 million to satisfy Morgenthau. Kindleberger, *Financial History*, 425.

3. Burns, *Roosevelt*, 60–61. For details of Hopkins's life and career see McJimsey, *Harry Hopkins*.

4. Ibid., 60.

5. Reynolds, *Anglo-American Alliance*, 274.

6. Schlesinger, *Coming of the New Deal*, 188–89; Green, "Conflict over Trade Ideologies," 7–9.

7. Quoted in Schlesinger, *Coming of the New Deal*, 188–89.

8. Quoted in McCloskey, "Magnanimous Albion," 303.

9. Schlesinger, *Coming of the New Deal*.

10. Dilks, *Diaries of Sir Alexander Cadogan*, 553.

11. Acheson, *Present at the Creation*, 89.

12. See also Bohlen, *Witness to History*, 129–30.

13. Winant memo, undated, DOS, *FRUS, 1945*, 6:22–24; *Anglo-American Financial Agreement*, Senate, 193. See also Minutes of the Executive Committee on "Commercial Policy," July 20 and October 23, 1940, RG353, Intra- and Interdepartmental Committee Files, NA.

14. "Some Economic Problems Raised by the Joint Declaration of August 14, 1941," Notter Files, RG59, DOS Records, NA.

15. U.S. Draft Memo of Understanding of Financial Matters, October 30, 1945, 611.4131/5-746, RG59, DOS Records, NA; *Anglo-American Financial Agreement*, Senate, 177–78.

16. Joan Hoff Wilson, *American Business and Foreign Policy*, 2–5; Levin, "Woodrow Wilson," 93–117.

17. For a thoroughgoing defense of the multilateralists and a refutation of the Williams-Kolko thesis, see Eckes, "Open Door Expansionism Reconsidered."

18. Hawkins to Grady, October 18, 1940, RG353, Intra- and Interdepartmental Committee Files, NA.

19. Hawkins to Grady, October 18, 1940, and "The Place of the Trade Agreements Act in Our Present and Future Commercial Policy," undated, RG353, Intra- and Interdepartmental Committee Files, NA.

20. See, for example, Hawkins to Acheson, Welles, and Hull, August 4, 1941, Acheson Files, RG59, DOS Records, NA.

21. Hawkins to Grady, October 18, 1940, and "The Place of the Trade Agreements Act in Our Present and Future Commercial Policy," undated, RG353, Intra- and Interdepartmental Committee Files, NA. See also "Intradepartmental Problems Raised by the Joint Declaration of August 14, 1941," undated, Notter Files, RG59, DOS Records, NA.

22. Green, "Conflict over Trade Ideologies," 12–13. See also "Some Economic Problems Raised by the Joint Declaration of August 14, 1941," Notter Files, RG59, DOS Records, NA.

23. "Questions and Answers concerning the British Loan," undated, box 27, Acheson Papers, HST Library; "The Anglo-American Economic Agreement," January

17, 1946, Fo 371/52950, Foreign Office Records, PRO; Edelsberg to Blaisdell, undated, box 6, Blaisdell Papers, HST Library.

24. *Anglo-American Financial Agreement*, Senate, 56–57. See also Clayton to Vinson, June 25, 1945, 841.51/6-2845, RG59, DOS Records, NA, and "Statement of Foreign Loan Policy by NAC," February 21, 1946, box 424, Official File, HST Papers, HST Library.

25. See Memo of Atlantic Conference—*Point Four*, 1942, box 13, Notter Files, RG59, DOS Records, NA.

26. Memo by Winant with Hawkins and Penrose, undated, DOS, *FRUS, 1945*, 6:22–24.

27. See Welles, *Time for Decision*, 240, and *Seven Decisions*, 100; Berle Diaries, February 1 and 2, 1942, box 213, FDR Library.

28. Memo of conversation between Welles and Cadogan, September 9, 1941, box 14, Hickerson Files, RG59, DOS Records, NA.

29. Bohlen, *Witness to History*, 283.

30. See Murphy, *Brandeis/Frankfurter Connection*.

31. Wilcox, "No Private Collectivism: A Challenge," *New York Times*, March 19, 1944.

32. Schlesinger, *Coming of the New Deal*, 28–29; Interview with Stanley Dixon of KSQ, Des Moines, Iowa, August 5, 1943, box 23, Wallace Papers, ML/UI.

33. Quoted in Schlesinger, *Coming of the New Deal*, 191–92.

34. See, for example, Wallace Diary, November 15, 1943, box 9, ML/UI.

35. Green, "Conflict over Trade Ideologies," 2–3.

36. Interview with Stanley Dixon of KSQ, Des Moines, Iowa, August 8, 1943, notebook 23, box 8, Wallace Papers, ML/UI.

37. Ibid.

38. Wallace Diary, October 19, 1945, notebook 36, box 12, ML/UI.

39. Wallace Diary, October 15, 1943, notebook 24, box 9, ML/UI.

40. Quoted in Blum, *Price of Vision*, 554.

41. See Divine, *Second Chance*.

42. Dulles to Henry Doughton, April 15, 1943, Dulles Papers, FL/PU.

43. See LaFeber, *New Empire*, and Joan Hoff Wilson, *American Business and Foreign Policy*, 2–5.

44. Johnston to Taft, September 9, 1946, box 633, R. Taft Papers, LC.

45. Businessmen of America, Inc.—Economic Program, December 30, 1944 (box 33), and Wallace Diary, December 21, 1944 (box 11), ML/UI.

46. Acheson, *Present at the Creation*, 47.

47. Harrod, *Keynes*, 3, 73, 97–98.

48. See Hession, *Keynes*, 77, 93–114, 129–55, 241–42.

49. Ibid., 191–94, 331–33; "John Maynard Keynes," *The Economist*, April 27, 1946.

50. Hession, *Keynes*, 241.

51. Waligorski, "Keynesian Politics," 1–19.

52. Quoted in Winch, *Economics and Policy*, 139.

53. Harrod, *Keynes*, 4–5.

54. Schlesinger, *Coming of the New Deal*, 404.

55. Quoted in ibid., 406.

56. Keynes to Hopkins, June 17, 1941, box 305, Hopkins Papers, FDR Library.

57. Memo of conversation between Acheson and Keynes, June 20, 1941, box 3, Acheson Files, RG59, DOS Records, NA.

58. Keynes to Hopkins, June 27, 1941, box 305, Hopkins Papers, FDR Library.

59. Memo of conversation between Acheson and Keynes, July 7, 1941, 841.24/6351/2, RG59, DOS Records, NA.

60. Quoted in Van Dormael, *Bretton Woods*, 22.

61. Reynolds, *Anglo-American Alliance*, 275.

62. Quoted in Van Dormael, *Bretton Woods*, 22.

63. Ibid.

64. Ibid.

65. Memo of conversation between Acheson and Keynes, July 28, 1941, 841.24/820, RG59, DOS Records, NA.

66. Quoted in Van Dormael, *Bretton Woods*, 22.

67. Negotiations between the U.S. and G.B. for the Mutual Aid Agreement, December 8, 1944, Notter Files, RG59, DOS Records, NA; Acheson, *Present at the Creation*, 56–57.

68. Memo of conversation between Acheson and Keynes, July 28, 1941, 841.24/8200, RG59, DOS Records, NA.

Chapter 2

1. Schoenfeld, *War Ministry*, 9.

2. Quoted in ibid., 22.

3. Taylor, *Beaverbrook*, x–xi, 135–37.

4. Ibid., xii–xv; Macmillan, *Blast of War*; Nicolson, *Diaries and Letters*, 189–90.

5. Taylor, *Beaverbrook*, 274.

6. Introduction, list 110, series D, Beaverbrook Papers, HLRO.

7. Quoted in Bullock, *Bevin*, 177–78.

8. M. Gilbert, *Churchill*, 1029, n. 1.

9. Dobson, *U.S. Wartime Aid to Britain*, 9.

10. Ibid., 80–81.

11. Schoenfeld, *War Ministry*, 9.

12. Carpenter, "Corporatism in Britain."

13. Barnes and Nicolson, *Amery Diaries*, 11–21.

14. Macmillan, *Blast of War*, 57.

15. Memo by Secretary of State for India, September 2, 1943, W.P. (43) 588, CAB 66, Cabinet Memoranda, PRO; "Amery's Views on Imperial Preference," March 1, 1944, D/150, Beaverbrook Papers, HLRO.

16. Amery memo on "An Expansionist Economy," September 2, 1943, W.P. (43) 588, CAB 66, Cabinet Memoranda, PRO.

17. Ibid.

18. Amery memo on the "Sterling Problem," undated, W.P. (44) 368, CAB 66, Cabinet Memoranda, PRO.

19. Amery memo on "An Expansionist Economy," September 2, 1943, W.P. (43) 588, CAB 66, Cabinet Memoranda, PRO.

20. Amery memo on the "Sterling Problem," undated, W.P. (44) 368, CAB 66, Cabinet Memoranda, PRO.

21. Ibid.

22. T. Johnston to Law, January 20, 1944, PREM 4/44/13, Law Papers, Prime Minister's Records, PRO.

23. Quoted in Dalton Diaries, 131/44, vol. 1, 30, RL/LSE.

24. See, for example, remarks of Col. Walter Elliott in Bliss to Secretary of State, January 4, 1945, 611.4131/11-445, RG59, DOS Records, NA.

25. R. Gardner, *Sterling-Dollar Diplomacy*, 26–27; Reynolds, *Anglo-American Alliance*, 77–78.

26. R. Gardner, *Sterling-Dollar Diplomacy*, 28–29.

27. Macmillan, *Middle Way*, 15.

28. Ibid., 12, 31, 35–36, 95–96, 178, 186. See also Nicolson, *Diaries and Letters*, 252.

29. Macmillan, *Middle Way*, 274.

30. Ibid., 266–67, 279, 281, 287.

31. "The Tory Reform Committee," Gallman to Secretary of State, March 27, 1944, 841.00/1708, RG59, DOS Records, NA.

32. Johnstone to Churchill, February 26, 1942, PREM 4/17/31, Prime Minister's Records, PRO.

33. *New York Times*, May 27, 1942.

34. *New York Times*, March 22, 1942; R. Gardner, *Sterling-Dollar Diplomacy*, 34–35; Burridge, *British Labor*, 23–24.

35. Burridge, *British Labor*, 14–15.

36. Bullock, *Bevin*, 1; Kraus, *Men around Churchill*, 121–23.

37. Dalton Diaries, November 29, 1943, vol. 1, 19/149, RL/LSE.

38. Anderson, *Cold War*, 82–83.

39. Bullock, *Bevin*, 338–39.

40. R. Gardner, *Sterling-Dollar Diplomacy*, 24–26; Bullock, *Bevin*, 199–202.

41. *New York Times*, September 27, 1942; Bullock, *Bevin*, 190–91.

42. Reynolds, *Anglo-American Alliance*; M. Gilbert, *Churchill*, 359–60 (quotation).

43. See Reynolds, *Anglo-American Alliance*, 272.

44. Goodheart to HM, September 14, 1944, book 771, HM Diaries, FDR Library.

45. Quoted in M. Gilbert, *Churchill*, 181.

46. Colville, *Fringes of Power*, 736.

47. Quoted in M. Gilbert, *Churchill*, 442–43.

48. Ibid., 49–50.

49. Cherwell to Churchill, April 22, 1942, PREM 4/17/3, Prime Minister's Records, PRO.

50. Keynes to Henderson, April 5, 1942, T247/67, Keynes Papers, Treasury Records, PRO.

51. Comments from Keynes, January 29, 1942, T247/69, Keynes Papers, Treasury Records, PRO.

52. Keynes to Henderson, May 9, 1942, T247/67, Keynes Papers, Treasury Records, PRO.

53. Keynes to Henderson, April 5, 1942, T247/67, Keynes Papers, Treasury Records, PRO.

54. Comments on the "Treasury Note on External Monetary and Economic Policy," undated, T247/67, Keynes Papers, Treasury Records, PRO.

55. Keynes to Henderson, April 5 and 9, 1942, T247/67, Keynes Papers, Treasury Records, PRO.

56. Comments on the "Treasury Note on External Monetary and Economic Policy," undated, T247/67, Keynes Papers, Treasury Records, PRO.

57. Keynes to Cohen, October 9, 1941, T247/69, Keynes Papers, Treasury Records, PRO.

58. Burns, *Roosevelt*, 125–31. For a cogent account of this meeting, see Theodore A. Wilson, *First Summit*.

59. Dilks, *Diaries of Sir Alexander Cadogan*, 1.

60. Ibid., 565–66.

61. Ibid., 604.

62. "History of Negotiations with Respect to Point Four of the Atlantic Charter," January 10, 1945, Hickerson Files, RG59, DOS Records, NA.

63. Memo of conversation between Welles and Cadogan, August 9, 1941, box 14, Hickerson Files, RG59, DOS Records, NA.

64. "History of Negotiations with Respect to Point Four of the Atlantic Charter," January 16, 1945, Hickerson Files, RG59, DOS Records, NA.

65. Ibid.

66. Ibid.

67. Memo on Atlantic Charter, undated, Notter Files, RG59, DOS Records, NA.

68. Ibid.

69. "History of Negotiations with Respect to Point Four of the Atlantic Charter," January 16, 1945, Hickerson Papers, RG59, DOS Records, NA.

70. Ibid.

71. Hawkins to Acheson, July 10, 1942, Notter Files, RG59, DOS Records, NA.

72. "History of Negotiations with Respect to Point Four of the Atlantic Charter," January 10, 1945, Hickerson Files, RG59, DOS Records, NA.

73. Kraus, *Men around Churchill*, 102–5; *New York Times*, September 22, 1943.

74. Wood to Eden in Keynes to Harrod, April 19, 1942, T247/67, Keynes Papers, Treasury Records, PRO.

75. Acheson, *Present at the Creation*, 58.

76. Keynes to Harrod, April 19, 1942, and Keynes to Hopkins, July 11, 1941, T247/67, Keynes Papers, Treasury Records, PRO.

77. Comments from Keynes, January 29, 1942, T247/69, Keynes Papers, Treasury Records, PRO.

78. Harrod, *Keynes*, 515.

79. M. Gilbert, *Churchill*.

80. Quoted in Mee, *Meeting at Potsdam*, 28–29.

81. Quoted in Thorne, *Allies of a Kind*, 121.

82. Quoted in letter found with HM Papers, FDR Library.

83. Quoted in Reynolds, *Anglo-American Alliance*, p. 84.

84. Wallace Diary, May 22, 1943, notebook 21, box 7, ML/UI.

85. Ryan, *Vision of Anglo-America*, 2.

86. Reynolds, *Anglo-American Alliance*, 41.

87. Acheson, *Present at the Creation*, 60.

88. Halifax to Eden, January 5, 1942, reel 12, Halifax Papers, CCL/CU.

89. Quoted in Thorne, *Allies of a Kind*, 104.

90. Churchill to Halifax, January 1, 1942, PREM 4/17/3, Prime Minister's Records, PRO.

91. Ibid.

92. Halifax to Eden, December 29, 1941, PREM 4/17/3, Prime Minister's Records, PRO.

93. Eden to Halifax, January 17, 1942, reel 2, Halifax Papers, CCL/CU.

94. Memo of conversation between Acheson and FDR, January 29, 1942, box 3, Acheson Files, RG59, DOS Records, NA.

95. Ibid.

96. Acheson to FDR, January 29, 1942, box 23, Acheson Files, RG59, DOS Records, NA.

97. Halifax to War Cabinet, January 30, 1942, PREM 4/17/3, Prime Minister's Records, PRO; Memo of conversation between Halifax, Opie, Acheson, and Feis, January 30, 1942, Acheson Files, RG59, DOS Records, NA.

98. Kimball, *Churchill and Roosevelt*, 1:345.

99. Ibid., 346.

100. Quoted in Lowenheim et al., *Roosevelt and Churchill*, 5.

101. Roosevelt to Churchill, February 11, 1942, series D, Beaverbrook Papers, HLRO.

102. Dominion Office to Dominion Governments, February 13, 1942, PREM 4/17/3, Prime Minister's Records, PRO.

Chapter 3

1. Quoted in Van Dormael, *Bretton Woods*, 31.

2. Ibid., 7–8; Keynes to Henderson, September 5, 1942, T247/67, Keynes Papers, Treasury Records, PRO.

3. Keynes to Henderson, September 5, 1942, T247/67, Keynes Papers, Treasury Records, PRO.

4. Keynes to Harrod, April 19, 1942, T247/67, Keynes Papers, Treasury Records, PRO.

5. Keynes to Ashton-Gwatkin, April 25, 1941, T247/69, Keynes Papers, Treasury Records, PRO.

6. Van Dormael, *Bretton Woods*, 31–54.

7. Comments of Keynes on British financial policy, January 29, 1942, T247/67, Keynes Papers, Treasury Records, PRO.

8. Quoted in ibid.

9. Quoted in ibid.

10. Van Dormael, *Bretton Woods*, 34–35.

11. Ibid.

12. Keynes to Caine, April 29, 1942, T247/67, Keynes Papers, Treasury Records, PRO.

13. Van Dormael, *Bretton Woods*, 36–37; Keynes to Caine, April 29, 1942, T247/67, Keynes Papers, Treasury Records, PRO.

14. R. Gardner, *Sterling-Dollar Diplomacy*, 77.

15. Clarke, *Anglo-American Economic Collaboration*, 72.

16. Booth, " 'Keynesian Revolution,' " 103, n. 3.

17. Quoted in Harrod, *Keynes*, 528.

18. Clarke, *Anglo-American Economic Collaboration*, 30–31.

19. Memo by the Lord Privy Seal, March 6, 1944, series D, Beaverbrook Papers, HLRO.

20. Bullock, *Bevin*, 204.

21. Van Dormael, *Bretton Woods*, 39.

22. Quoted in ibid., 53.

23. See Heclo, *Government of Strangers*, 37–38, 52–55, 98–99.

24. See Burns, *Roosevelt*, 354–55.

25. For an extensive explanation of the decision-making process see Allison, *Essence of Decision*. Also helpful are "American Political and Bureaucratic Decision-Making," in Pfeffer, *No More Vietnams?* 44–115, and Barnet, *Roots of War*.

26. Louis, *Imperialism at Bay*, 87.

27. See R. Gardner, *Sterling-Dollar Diplomacy*, 5–6.

28. Winant to Hopkins, August 22, 1941, box 305, Hopkins Papers, FDR Library.

29. Quoted in Thorne, *Allies of a Kind*, 115.

30. See Schlesinger, *Coming of the New Deal*, 33–34. Schlesinger's contention that "Above all, his [Morgenthau's] highest ambition was plainly not for himself . . . it was to serve Franklin Roosevelt" is clearly wrong. See also Burns, *Roosevelt*, 8.

31. Ickes Diaries, August 1, 1943, 8038, LC.

32. See Blum, *Morgenthau Diaries*, 279, and Kimball, *The Most Unsordid Act*, 225.

33. The State-Treasury rivalry was perhaps the most intense in wartime Washington because these two agencies displayed more organizational cohesiveness than other bureaucracies. H. G. Nicholas observed that while State and Treasury officials continually referred to the attitude of the department, others had as their frame of reference their "boss"—Ickes, Nelson, Crowley, and so forth. Nicholas, *Washington Dispatches*, xi.

34. Morgenthau to White, December 14, 1941, book 473, HM Diaries, FDR Library.

35. Reese, *Harry Dexter White*, 19–114.

36. "The Goal of International Dealings," November 13, 1939, box 2, White Papers, ML/PU.

37. Van Dormael, *Bretton Woods*, 41.

38. Harrod, *Keynes*, 537–38.

39. Acheson, *Present at the Creation*, 123.

40. Quoted in Van Dormael, *Bretton Woods*, 43.

41. Ibid., 44–45.

42. Quoted in ibid., 46.

43. Ibid., 51–54; R. Gardner, *Sterling-Dollar Diplomacy*, 73–74.

44. R. Gardner, *Sterling-Dollar Diplomacy*, 73–74.

45. Van Dormael, *Bretton Woods*, 54.

46. Reynolds, *Anglo-American Alliance*, 28.

47. Acheson, *Present at the Creation*, 38–39.

48. Schlesinger, *Coming of the New Deal*, 183.

49. Acheson, *Present at the Creation*, 37.

50. Memo on Atlantic Charter—*Point Four*, undated, and "Some Economic Prob-

lems Raised by the Joint Declaration of August 14, 1941," undated, box 13, Notter Files, RG59, DOS Records, NA.

51. Van Dormael, *Bretton Woods*, 59–62.
52. Berle to Hull, September 28, 1942, box 214, Berle Papers, FDR Library.
53. Conclusions of the War Cabinet, April 18, 1943, W.C. (43) 50, CAB 65, Cabinet Conclusions, PRO.
54. Cherwell to Churchill, January 2, 1943, PREM 4/18/4, Prime Minister's Records, PRO.
55. Ibid.; Amery memo on "An Expansionist Economy," September 2, 1943, W.P. (43) 588, CAB 66, Cabinet Memoranda, PRO.
56. Keynes memo on "International Economic Arrangements," February 11, 1942, PREM 4/17/4, Prime Minister's Records, PRO.
57. Van Dormael, *Bretton Woods*, 71–75.
58. Quoted in Berle Diaries, August 16, 1943, box 215, Berle Papers, FDR Library.
59. Van Dormael, *Bretton Woods*, 71–75.
60. Ibid., 76.
61. Ibid., 77.
62. Quoted in ibid., 77.
63. Ibid.
64. Quoted in ibid., 77.
65. Ibid., 90–91.
66. War Cabinet Conclusions, July 27, 1943, W.M. (43) 106, CAB 65, PRO. Churchill, for one, argued that India ought to have to absorb the debt: "Any attempt on our part to make repayment on this scale must . . . result in putting an unbearable burden on the backs of British work people." England could justifiably file a counterclaim in light of all it had done to defend India from conquest by Japan. As usual, however, the prime minister did not speak for the majority. Amery argued that unilateral repudiation was out of the question. Maintenance of the empire and sterling area depended on faith and goodwill. Moreover, repudiation would prompt the Indians to immediately shut down their war plants and the British armies would be denied a vital source of material. The latter argument was obviously compelling, and Bevin, Dalton, and Attlee once again joined the empire isolationists, this time in ruling out repudiation of the Indian debt.
67. Meade Diaries, 1/1, 4–22, RL/LSE.
68. Ibid., 21–22.
69. Ibid., 112.
70. R. Gardner, *Sterling-Dollar Diplomacy*.
71. Meade Diaries, 1/1, 52–80, RL/LSE.
72. Ibid., 23.
73. Meade Diaries, 1/1, 70, RL/LSE.
74. Quoted in Van Dormael, *Bretton Woods*, 105.
75. Cherwell to Churchill, October 4, 1943, PREM 4/17/4, Prime Minister's Records, PRO.
76. Ibid.
77. Van Dormael, *Bretton Woods*, 106–9.
78. Ibid.

Chapter 4

1. Darilek, *Loyal Opposition*, 26, 29.
2. Bohlen, *Witness to History*, 210.
3. Darilek, *Loyal Opposition*, 53.
4. Quoted in ibid.
5. Ibid., 76.
6. Quoted in ibid., 77.
7. Quoted in ibid., 78.
8. Ibid., 125–26; "Truman Group Asks Pay for Lend-Lease," *New York Times*, November 6, 1943.
9. Folger to FDR, November 12, 1943, box 77, Byrnes Papers, CL/CU.
10. Martel, *Lend-Lease*, 8–9.
11. Hawkins to Acheson, January 27, 1943, box 3, Acheson Files, RG59, DOS Records, NA.
12. Ibid.
13. Bunn to Acheson, January 24, 1943, box 3, Acheson Files, RG59, DOS Records, NA; Bohlen, *Witness to History*, 210.
14. "The Pooling and Deficit Theories of Lend-Lease," undated, box 5, Clayton-Thorp Papers, HST Library.
15. Ibid.
16. Ibid.
17. Ibid.
18. Ibid.
19. Law memo on "Reciprocal Aid to U.S.," October 25, 1943, W.P. (43) 477, CAB 66, Cabinet Memoranda, PRO.
20. Blum, *Morgenthau Diaries*, 122–26.
21. Wood to Eden, March 16, 1942, PREM 4/17/3, Prime Minister's Records, PRO.
22. Blum, *Morgenthau Diaries*, 123.
23. Ibid., 126.
24. Ibid., 127.
25. Keynes note on HM, May 2, 1941, T247/113, Keynes Papers, Treasury Records, PRO.
26. Keynes to Eady and Procter, October 14, 1942, T247/67, Keynes Papers, Treasury Records, PRO.
27. Ibid.
28. Blum, *Morgenthau Diaries*, 131.
29. Wallace Diary, undated, notebook 19, box 6, ML/UI.
30. Cherwell to Churchill, November 11, 1943, PREM 4/17/5, Prime Minister's Records, PRO. See also "The British Dollar Balances," undated, Hickerson Files, RG59, DOS Records, NA.
31. HM and Crowley to FDR, January 4, 1944, book 690, HM Diaries, FDR Library.
32. Ickes Diaries, January 1, 1944, 8503, LC.
33. "May Ask British Cash on Machines," *New York Times*, December 29, 1943; Ickes Diaries, January 1, 1944, 8503, LC.
34. Quoted in Woods, *Roosevelt Foreign Policy Establishment*, 94.

35. Cherwell to Churchill, November 11, 1943, PREM 4/17/5, Prime Minister's Records, PRO.

36. Quoted in Blum, *Morgenthau Diaries*, 133.

37. Burns, *Roosevelt*, 400–401; Blum, *Morgenthau Diaries*, 134; Ickes Diaries, January 1, 1944, 8503, LC.

38. HM and Crowley to FDR, January 4, 1944, book 690, HM Diaries, FDR Library.

39. Quoted in Blum, *Morgenthau Diaries*, 136.

40. Hull to FDR, December 31, 1943 (book 690), and Conference in Secretary Hull's Office, January 7, 1944 (book 692), HM Diaries, FDR Library.

41. Blum, *Morgenthau Diaries*, 136–37.

42. Stettinius to FDR, February 22, 1944, box 49, PSF, FDR Papers, FDR Library.

43. FDR to Churchill, February 25, 1944, book 703, HM Diaries, FDR Library.

44. Anderson to Churchill, February 24, 1944, PREM 4/17/5, Prime Minister's Records, PRO; Padmore to E. A. Hoff, March 17, 1944, D/150, Beaverbrook Papers, HLRO.

45. Meeting in Secretary Hull's Office, March 13, 1944, book 692, HM Diaries, and Berle Diaries, March 13, 1944, box 215, FDR Library.

46. Reynolds, *Anglo-American Alliance*, 261. For a detailed discussion and analysis of the British foreign policy establishment's evolving attitude toward the Soviet Union see Rothwell, *Britain and the Cold War*.

47. Carlton, *Eden*.

48. See Ross, "Foreign Office Attitudes."

49. Eden memo on "Policy towards Russia," January 28, 1942, W.P. (42) 48, CAB 66, Cabinet Memoranda, PRO.

50. Resis, "Soviet Influence," 416–23.

51. Eden memo on "Policy towards Russia," January 28, 1942, W.P. (42) 48, CAB 66, Cabinet Memoranda, PRO; Memo of conversation between Eden and Hull, March 15, 1943, box 19, Notter Files, RG59, DOS Records, NA.

52. Memo by N. B. Ronald, February 1943, T247/72, Keynes Papers, Treasury Records, PRO.

53. Eden memo on "Policy towards Russia," January 28, 1942, W.P. (42) 48, CAB 66, Cabinet Memoranda, PRO.

54. Reynolds, *Anglo-American Alliance*, 264–65.

55. Eden memo on "Policy towards Russia," January 28, 1942, W.P. (42) 48, CAB 66, Cabinet Memoranda, PRO.

56. Amery memo on "Europe and the Post-War Settlement," November 12, 1942, W.P. (42) 524, CAB 66, Cabinet Memoranda, PRO.

57. Reynolds, *Anglo-American Alliance*, 263; Eden memo on "Post-War Settlement," July 1, 1943, W.O. (43) 292, CAB 66, Cabinet Memoranda, PRO; Ickes Diaries, May 23, 1943, LC.

58. Kimball, *Churchill and Roosevelt*, 2:130.

59. Albert Resis argues that during World War II neither Britain, the United States, nor the Soviet Union planned the division of Europe into East-West blocs. Stalin feared the formation of an anti-Soviet bloc in Europe, believing that it would act as a spearhead for an anti-Soviet, global movement even while the Allies worked in close harmony to defeat Hitler. Churchill feared a division that would leave the United Kingdom alone to face the USSR and strip it of its territory. Resis, "Soviet Influence."

60. Reynolds, *Anglo-American Alliance*, 261.

61. Quoted in Sherry, *Preparing for the Next War*, 43–44.

62. Quoted in Smith, *American Diplomacy*, 75.

63. See, for example, Wooley, "Quest for Permanent Peace," 18–27.

64. Knight, "Nonfraternal Association," 8–9.

65. Quoted in ibid., 9.

66. See, for example, War Cabinet Conclusions, April 13, 1943, W.M. (43) 153, CAB 65, PRO, and Gaddis, *Origins of the Cold War*, 8–9.

67. See, for example, Berle Diaries, April 4, 1942, box 213, Berle Papers, FDR Library.

68. Lowenheim et al., *Roosevelt and Churchill*, 196.

69. Burns, *Roosevelt*, 400–401.

70. Ryan, *Vision of Anglo-America*, 76–78.

71. Quoted in Smith, *American Diplomacy*, 65.

72. Green, "Conflict over Trade Ideologies," 110–11; Acheson, *Present at the Creation*, 106.

73. Harriman to FDR, July 5, 1943, box 157, Hopkins Papers, FDR Library.

74. Wallace Diary, September 28, 1943, notebook 23, box 8, ML/UI.

75. Stimson to FDR, August 10, 1943, rolls 5–8, Stimson Diaries, SL/YU. Following a trip to America in spring 1943, Eden reported to the War Cabinet that FDR was dissatisfied with Standley and wanted to replace him with Davies. War Cabinet Conclusions, April 13, 1943, W.M. (43) 153, CAB 65, PRO. For a detailed analysis of the second front issue, see Stoler, *Politics of the Second Front*.

76. Sherry, *Preparing for the Next War*, 159–60.

77. Ibid., 168.

78. Stimson Diaries, November 21, 1943, rolls 5–8, SL/YU.

79. McCloy to Hopkins, November 25, 1943, book 8, Sherwood Collection, Hopkins Papers, FDR Library.

80. Harriman and Abel, *Special Envoy*, 178–79.

81. Louis, *Imperialism at Bay*, 4.

82. Ibid., v.

83. Quoted in ibid., 198.

84. Reynolds, *Anglo-American Alliance*, 223–24.

85. Ibid., 58–59.

86. Fitzsimons, *Foreign Policy*, 19.

87. See Thorne, *Allies of a Kind*, 36–39; Louis, *Imperialism at Bay*, 7–8.

88. Smith, *American Diplomacy*, 92–93.

89. Langer, "Harriman-Beaverbrook Mission."

90. Hopkins to Harriman, February 3, 1944, box 335, Hopkins Papers, FDR Library.

Chapter 5

1. See Memo of conversation between Law and Berle, June 8, 1943, box 215, Berle Papers, FDR Library.

2. Quoted in Harrod, *Keynes*, 569.

3. Ibid.

4. Article VII, Questions for Mr. Law, February 5, 1944, D/150, Beaverbrook Papers, HLRO.

5. M. Gilbert, *Churchill*, 993–94, 682, n. 1; Draft Section on Monetary Policy for Law Report, undated, FO 800/431, Law Papers, Prime Minister's Records, PRO.

6. War Cabinet memo by Lord Privy Seal on "Anglo-American Discussions under Article VII," February 9, 1944, D/150, Beaverbrook Papers, HLRO.

7. Ibid.

8. Dalton Diaries, February 14–17, 1944, vol. 1, 30, RL/LSE.

9. War Cabinet Conclusions—Confidential Annex, February 23, 1944, W.M. (44) 24, CAB 65, PRO.

10. Cherwell to Churchill, March 15, 1944, PREM 4/17/10, Prime Minister's Records, PRO.

11. Van Dormael, *Bretton Woods*, 121–22.

12. Matthews, "Taft," 507–12; Patterson, "Alternatives to Globalism," 672–85.

13. Quoted in Darilek, *Loyal Opposition*, 28.

14. Ibid.

15. Quoted in Patterson, "Alternatives to Globalism," 670.

16. Spanier, *Truman-MacArthur Controversy*, 158–59.

17. *New York Times*, January 30, 1943.

18. Address of Robert A. Taft to War Veterans Club of Ohio, May 6, 1944, box 802, R. Taft Papers, LC.

19. Ibid.

20. See Joan Hoff Wilson, *American Business and Foreign Policy*, 14–19.

21. Quoted in Van Dormael, *Bretton Woods*, 111.

22. O'Connell to HM, March 17, 1944, book 711, HM Diaries, FDR Library.

23. Conversation between White and HM, January 8, 1944, book 719, HM Diaries, FDR Library.

24. Wallace to FDR, January 28, 1942, notebook 13, box 5, Wallace Diary, ML/UI; Acheson, *Present at the Creation*, 70.

25. Woods, *Roosevelt Foreign Policy Establishment*, 64.

26. Quoted in Schlesinger, *Coming of the New Deal*, 431.

27. McHale, "National Planning," 213.

28. Jones to Glass, July 5, 1943, box 176, Jones Papers, LC.

29. Ickes Diaries, July 4, 1943, 1946, LC.

30. Jones to Glass, July 5, 1943, box 176, Jones Papers, LC.

31. Conversation with FDR, May 8, 1943, box 14, Smith Diaries, FDR Library.

32. FDR to Hull, June 3, 1943, box 88, Byrnes Papers, CL/CU.

33. Conversation with FDR, July 15, 1943, box 14, Smith Diaries, FDR Library. See also Berle memo, June 27, 1942, box 214, Berle Papers, FDR Library.

34. Wallace Diary, January 10, 1944, notebook 33, box 11, ML/UI.

35. Ickes Diaries, January 1, 1944, 8499, LC.

36. "Bretton Woods," February 15, 1944, book 819, HM Diaries, FDR Library.

37. Ibid.

38. Ibid.

39. Quoted in Van Dormael, *Bretton Woods*, 118. See also HM to Anderson, April 10, 1944, PREM 4/17/8, Prime Minister's Records, PRO.

40. Anderson to Churchill, April 13, 1944, PREM 4/17/8, Prime Minister's Records, PRO.

41. Winant to HM, April 12, 1944, book 720, HM Diaries, FDR Library.

42. Dalton Diaries, March 23, 1944, vol. 1, 30/80, RL/LSE.

43. Dalton Diaries, April 14, 1944, vol. 1, 30/102, RL/LSE.
44. War Cabinet Conclusions—Confidential Annex, April 14, 1944, W.M. (44) 49, CAB 65, PRO; Foreign Office to Opie, April 15, 1944, book 721, HM Diaries, FDR Library.
45. White, Luxford, Bernstein, Smith meeting, April 17, 1944, book 722, HM Diaries, FDR Library.
46. Van Dormael, *Bretton Woods*, 125–26.
47. HM to FDR, April 21, 1944, book 723, HM Diaries, FDR Library.
48. Quoted in Blum, *Morgenthau Diaries*, 249–50.
49. Nicholas, *Washington Dispatches*, 135.
50. Van Dormael, *Bretton Woods*, 124.
51. White, Luxford, Bernstein, Smith meeting, April 17, 1944, book 722, HM Diaries, FDR Library.
52. Van Dormael, *Bretton Woods*, 136–37.
53. Cassaday to Hull and HM, April 26, 1944, book 724, HM Diaries, FDR Library.
54. Ibid.
55. Cassaday to Hull and HM, May 13, 1944, box 10, White Papers, ML/PU.
56. Van Dormael, *Bretton Woods*, 144–45.
57. Quoted in ibid., 147.
58. Blum, *Morgenthau Diaries*, 251–52.
59. Quoted in Van Dormael, *Bretton Woods*, 153–54.
60. Ibid.
61. "Delegates Search for Warm Clothes," *New York Times*, July 2, 1944; Van Dormael, *Bretton Woods*, 168–69.
62. "Morgenthau Opens Conference," *New York Times*, July 3, 1944.
63. Van Dormael, *Bretton Woods*, 78–79, 173–74.
64. Acheson, *Present at the Creation*, 124–25.
65. Meeting of American Technical Committee in White's office, September 14, 1943, box 7, Acheson Files, RG59, DOS Records, NA.
66. Keynes to Hopkins, July 22, 1944, T247/45, Keynes Papers, Treasury Records, PRO.
67. Van Dormael, *Bretton Woods*, 161; Cherwell to Churchill, June 26, 1944, PREM 4/17/7, Prime Minister's Records, PRO.
68. Delegation meeting, July 12, 1944, book 753, HM Diaries, FDR Library.
69. Blum, *Morgenthau Diaries*, 254–55.
70. HM to FDR, June 29, 1944, book 748, HM Diaries, FDR Library.
71. Delegation meeting, February 7, 1944, book 749, HM Diaries, FDR Library.
72. Ibid.; "The Monetary Conference," *New York Times*, July 1, 1944.
73. Preliminary Report on Public Opinion, July 10–11, book 752, HM Diaries, FDR Library.
74. Van Dormael, *Bretton Woods*, 183–84.
75. "$10 Billion Total Seen for Exports," *New York Times*, July 4, 1944.
76. Van Dormael, *Bretton Woods*, 179–82.
77. Instructions to American Delegation, July 1, 1944, book 749, HM Diaries, FDR Library.
78. Kenwood and Lougheed, *Growth of the International Economy*, 22–36.
79. R. Gardner, *Sterling-Dollar Diplomacy*, 261; Delegation meeting, July 1,

1944, book 749, HM Diaries, FDR Library; Memo on Bretton Woods, June 30, 1944, Acheson Files, RF59, DOS Records, NA.

80. Instructions to American Delegation—Fund, July 1, 1944, book 749, HM Diaries, FDR Library.

81. Green, "Conflict over Trade Ideology," 29.

82. Ibid.

83. Quoted in Van Dormael, *Bretton Woods*, 170.

84. Blum, *Morgenthau Diaries*, 260–65; HM to FDR, July 22, 1944, book 757, HM Diaries, FDR Library.

85. Van Dormael, *Bretton Woods*, 191–97.

86. Quoted in ibid., 197–99.

87. Blum, *Morgenthau Diaries*, 274, 276.

88. U.S. Delegation meeting, July 12, 1944, book 753, HM Diaries, FDR Library.

89. U.S. Delegation meeting, July 2, 1944, book 749, HM Diaries, FDR Library.

90. Keynes to Hopkins, July 22, 1944, T247/45, Keynes Papers, Treasury Records, PRO.

91. "Conference Adds 3 Days to Talks: Snarled on Bank," *New York Times*, July 18, 1944.

92. Quoted in Van Dormael, *Bretton Woods*, 209.

93. Quoted in ibid., 222.

94. "Conference Adds 3 Days to Talks: Snarled on Bank," *New York Times*, July 18, 1944.

95. Quoted in Van Dormael, *Bretton Woods*, 220.

96. See, for example, Cherwell to Churchill, May 7, 1942, PREM 4/17/4, Prime Minister's Records, PRO.

97. "Ode to the Ninth Floor," undated, T247/45, Keynes Papers, Treasury Records, PRO.

98. Keynes to Hopkins, July 22, 1944, T247/45, Keynes Papers, Treasury Records, PRO.

Chapter 6

1. "Needs and Instrumentalities for International Capital Movement after the War," April 18, 1942, box 10, Acheson Files, and "Postwar International Economic Policies in Their Relation to Domestic Policies," August 24, 1942, box 81, Notter Files, RG59, DOS Records, NA.

2. Berle to Dunn, October 14, 1944, box 715, Berle Papers, FDR Library.

3. Batt to Hopkins, July 7, 1944, box 9, Hopkins Papers, FDR Library.

4. Currie to Hopkins, July 20, 1944, box 5, Clayton-Thorp Papers, HST Library.

5. Ibid.

6. Ibid.

7. "Foreign Capital Position of the U.S. and G.B.," September 2, 1943, box 82, Notter Files, RG59, DOS Records, NA.

8. Taft memo on "Phase II Lend-Lease," August 25, 1944, box 10, Taft Papers, LC.

9. Currie to John S. Fischer, July 20, 1944, box 5, Clayton-Thorp Papers, HST Library.

10. "Foreign Capital Position of the U.S. and G.B.," September 29, 1943, box 82, Notter Files, RG59, DOS Records, NA.

11. Berle to Dunn, October 14, 1944, box 215, Berle Diaries, FDR Library.

12. "For World Recovery," *New York Times*, December 3, 1944.

13. Hickerson to Achilles, June 22, 1944, box 2, Hickerson Files, RG59, DOS Records, NA; *The Economist*, April 29, 1944.

14. Collado to Hull, March 27, 1944, box 2, Hickerson Files, RG59, DOS Records, NA; Cox to Hopkins, June 21, 1943, box 137, Hopkins Papers, FDR Library; Stettinius Calendar Notes, March 18, 1944, box 14, Office of European Affairs Records, RG59, DOS Records, NA.

15. Acheson to Keynes, April 27, 1944, T236/439, Eady Papers, Treasury Records, PRO.

16. Woods, *Roosevelt Foreign Policy Establishment*, 107–8; Catton, *War Lords of Washington*, 8.

17. Stettinius to FDR, April 7–29, 1944, box 95, PSF, FDR Papers, FDR Library.

18. Ibid.; Stettinius to Hull, HM, and Crowley, April 19, 1944, book 722, HM Diaries, FDR Library.

19. Law to Churchill, April 18, 1944, PREM 4/17/6, Prime Minister's Records, PRO.

20. Ibid.

21. Ibid.

22. Anderson to Churchill, April 26, 1944, PREM 4/17/6, Prime Minister's Records, PRO.

23. Dalton Diaries, June 21, 1944, vol. 1, 30, RL/LSE.

24. Anderson to Halifax, June 10, 1944, T247/124, Keynes Papers, Treasury Records, PRO.

25. Hopkins to Winant, July 26, 1944, box 10, Hopkins Papers, FDR Library.

26. Conference Report for Rosenman, November 15, 1943, box 28, Rosenman Papers, FDR Library.

27. "Congressional Attitudes toward the Use of Executive Agreements as Instruments of Foreign Policy," July 19, 1943, box 2, Hickerson Files, RG59, DOS Records, NA.

28. Cox to Crowley, March 27, 1944, box 20, Cox Papers, and H. M. White, Bell, et al. meeting, May 5, 1944, book 728, HM Diaries, HM Papers, FDR Library; Darilek, *Loyal Opposition*, 125–26.

29. "Lend-Lease and Exports" (March 25, 1944) and "The Life of Lend-Lease" (September 2, 1944), *The Economist*.

30. Hull to FDR, July 1, 1944, box 91, PSF, FDR Papers, FDR Library.

31. Dalton Diaries, June 30, 1944, vol. 1, 30, RL/LSE.

32. "Congressional Attitudes toward the Use of Executive Agreements as Instruments of Foreign Policy," July 11, 1943, box 2, Hickerson Files, RG59, DOS Records, NA; Hull, Acheson, Hawkins, Vandenberg conference, July 7, 1944, box 10, C. Taft Papers, LC.

33. *New York Times*, February 16, 1944.

34. Ibid.

35. "Landon Assails 'Nazi New Dealers,'" *New York Times*, February 13, 1943.

36. Vandenberg to Dulles, July 2, 1944, box 25, Dulles Papers, FL/PU.

37. Taft-Stinebower conversation, December 12, 1944, box 8, C. Taft Papers, LC.

38. Berle to Hull, June 21 and July 7, 1943, box 58, Hopkins Papers, FDR Library.

39. F. M. Eaton to Hopkins, July 7, 1944, box 9, Hopkins Papers, FDR Library.

40. "Keep Lend-Lease, President Asks," *New York Times*, August 24, 1944.

41. "Lend-Lease and Civilian Production—U.S. & U.K.," August 21, 1944, box 9, Hopkins Papers, FDR Library.

42. Quoted in Thorne, *Allies of a Kind*, 385–86.

43. Ibid.

44. Eady to Ronald, May 20, 1944, T236/439, Eady Papers, Treasury Records, PRO; Thorne, *Allies of a Kind*, 387.

45. Meade to Law, July 11, 1944, FO 800/431, (found with) Law Papers, Prime Minister's Records, PRO.

46. "Lend-Lease Supplies for Britain in Stage II—Note for President of U.S.A.," September 4, 1944, box 5, Clayton-Thorp Papers, HST Library; Anderson and Lyttleton memo on "Supplies in Stage II," July 31, 1944, W.P. (44) 149, CAB 66, Cabinet Memoranda, PRO; Lyttleton to Churchill, August 4, 1944, PREM 4/18/6, Prime Minister's Records, PRO.

47. Meeting between Currie, Coe, Batt, Eaton, Hawkins, Taft, et al., August 23, 1944, box 10, C. Taft Papers, LC.

48. Eaton to Hopkins, July 7, 1944, box 9, Hopkins Papers, FDR Library. See also G. N. McReady, Commander, British Army Staff, Combined Chiefs, to Hopkins, August 10, 1944, and Nelson to Hopkins, September 20, 1944, box 335, Hopkins Papers, FDR Library.

49. "Lend Lease," July 8, 1944, series D, Beaverbrook Papers, HLRO.

50. Gen. John H. York to Hopkins, August 11, 1944, box 161, Hopkins Papers, FDR Library.

51. Reed to Crowley, Currie, Cox, and Acheson, September 5, 1944, and Hopkins to Leahy, September 7, 1944, box 335, Hopkins Papers, FDR Library.

52. Quoted in Thorne, *Allies of a Kind*, 450.

53. Quoted in Louis, *Imperialism at Bay*, 376.

54. Quoted in Thorne, *Allies of a Kind*, 392.

55. Quoted in ibid., 490.

56. Ibid., 479–80.

57. Somervell memo on "Lend-Lease Policy after the Defeat of Germany," September 7, 1944, box 335, Hopkins Papers, FDR Library.

58. Quoted in Thorne, *Allies of a Kind*, 450.

59. "Lend-Lease and Civilian Production—U.S. and U.K.," August 21, 1944, and Batt to Hopkins, June 24, 1944, box 9, Hopkins Papers, FDR Library.

60. Brand to Hopkins, August 14, 1944, box 10, Hopkins Papers, FDR Library.

61. Halifax to Foreign Office, July 25 and August 7, 1944, Halifax to Foreign Office, August 7, 1944, Meade to Churchill, August 9, 1944, and Halifax to Foreign Office, August 14, 1944, PREM 4/18/6, Prime Minister's Records, PRO.

62. Note of a meeting between Anderson and HM, August 11, 1944, T247/51, Keynes Papers, Treasury Records, PRO.

63. Ibid.; Memo of a meeting in Chancellor of the Exchequer's Office, August 11, 1944, White Papers, ML/PU; White to HM, April 14, 1944, box 721, HM Diaries, FDR Library; Meade to Private Office, August 11, 1944, PREM 4/17/5, Prime Minister's Records, PRO. See also Meeting between HM, White, and Brand, August 24, 1944, box 764, HM Diaries, FDR Library.

64. Hopkins memo of conference with FDR, August 18, 1944, box 10, Hopkins Papers; Treasury meeting regarding Foreign Financial Policy Board, August 19, 1944, box 764, HM Diaries, FDR Library.

65. Conversation between HM and FDR, August 19, 1944, box 764, HM Diaries, FDR Library.

66. Cherwell to Churchill, September 7, 1944, PREM 4/18/6, Prime Minister's Records, PRO.

67. Hopkins to FDR, September 8, 1944, box 332, Hopkins Papers, FDR Library.

68. Conversation between Taft and Matthews, September 20, 1944, box 7, C. Taft Papers, LC.

69. Hull to FDR, September 4, 1944, box 2, Hickerson Files, RG59, DOS Records, NA. See also Collado and Fetter memo on "The British Gold and Dollar Position in Relation to Lend-lease Operations," September 13, 1944, box 5, Clayton-Thorp Papers, HST Library; and Blum, *Morgenthau Diaries*, 368.

70. HM to FDR, September 12, 1944, box 722, HM Diaries, FDR Library.

71. Hathaway, *Ambiguous Partnership*, 58–59.

72. Cherwell to Churchill, September 17, 1944, PREM 4/18/6, Prime Minister's Records, PRO.

73. Cherwell to Churchill, September 12, 1944, PREM 4/18/6, Prime Minister's Records, PRO.

74. Memo of conversation, Quebec, September 13, 1944, box 6, Presidential Diaries, HM Papers, FDR Library.

75. Blum, *Morgenthau Diaries*, 368; Conversation between Taft and Matthews, September 20, 1944, box 7, C. Taft Papers, LC.

76. Forrestal Diaries, October 20, 1944, Quebec, ML/PU.

77. Blum, *Morgenthau Diaries*, 313.

78. Stimson Diaries, September 6, 1944, roll 9, SL/YU.

79. Ibid., 369.

80. Quoted in Hathaway, *Ambiguous Partnership*, 63.

81. Prime Minister to Deputy Prime Minister, Chancellor of the Exchequer, and War Cabinet, September 14, 1944, PREM 4/18/6, Prime Minister's Records, PRO.

82. Memo of conversation, Quebec, September 13, 1944, book 6, Presidential Diaries, HM Papers, FDR Library. See also "Note Made by McCloy after Meeting in Hull's Office," September 20, 1944, roll 119, Stimson Dairies, SL/YU.

83. Ibid.

84. Memo of conversation, Quebec, undated, book 6, Presidential Diaries, HM Papers, FDR Library.

85. Ibid.

86. "Purpose of U.K. Reverse Lend-Lease Records," October 13, 1944, box 1, Clayton-Thorp Papers, HST Library; *New York Times*, October 23, 1944; "Proposed Book on German Demilitarization," November 3, 1944, box 791, HM Diaries, FDR Library.

87. "Political Background," September–October 1944, T247/67, Keynes Papers, Treasury Records, PRO.

88. Hickerson to Stettinius, January 2, 1944, box 12, Hickerson Files, RG59, DOS Records, NA.

89. McCloy notes on meeting with Hull, September 20, 1944, roll 9, Stimson Diaries, SL/YU.

90. Forrestal Diaries, December 3, 1944, p. 76, ML/PU.

91. Hull to FDR, September 17, 1944, box 1, Havlik Files, RG59, DOS Records, NA; Hull to FDR, September 17, 1944, box 332, Hopkins Papers, FDR Library; Hull to Winant, September 19, 1944, box 5, Clayton-Thorp Papers, HST Library. See also Meeting between Hull, Stimson, and HM, September 20, 1944, box 773, HM Diaries, FDR Library.

92. Conversation between HM and Forrestal, October 20, 1944, p. 46, Forrestal Diaries, ML/PU.

93. Harry L. Whitney to James L. McCamey, November 22, 1944, box 12, Hickerson Files, RG59, DOS Records, NA. In November FEA had showered State with a cluster of statistics designed to prove that American exporters had not taken advantage of White Paper restrictions to capture markets formally controlled by Great Britain. It was true that total British exports had declined from £470.8 million in 1938 to £232.2 million for 1943 (49 percent), but the decline was much less if one compared prewar and current figures for areas not occupied by the enemy. Taking only those markets still open, British exports had declined only about 30 percent (£332 million to £232 million). Although United States exports were 114 percent of the 1938 level in 1943, 81.5 percent of that total was confined to the Western Hemisphere with 46 percent going to Canada.

94. Statement made by Crowley to Byrnes, July 7, 1947, box 94, Byrnes Papers, CL/CU.

95. FDR to Crowley, September 19, 1944, box 335, Hopkins Papers, FDR Library. See also Hull to Hopkins, September 19, 1944, and Hopkins to FDR, September 23, 1944, box 335, Hopkins Papers, FDR Library.

96. Quoted in Thorne, *Allies of a Kind*, 396.

97. Prime Minister to Chancellor of the Exchequer, September 15, 1944, PREM 4/18/6, Prime Minister's Records, PRO.

98. Keynes to Waley, July 1, 1944, T247/6512, Keynes Papers, Treasury Records, PRO.

99. "Decisions of Policy Affecting the Financial Position in Stages II and III," September 28, 1944, T247/72, Keynes Papers, Treasury Records, PRO.

100. War Cabinet Conclusions and Minute 7, Confidential Annex, September 18, 1944, W.C. (44) 123, CAB 65, PRO.

101. Conversations between Taft and Batt, and Lynch and Taft, September 18, 1944, box 7, C. Taft Papers, LC.

102. Conversations between Taft and Clay, and Taft and Denby, September 2, 1944, box 7, C. Taft Papers, LC.

103. Conference with Hopkins, September 26, 1944, box 775, HM Diaries, FDR Library.

104. Conversation between Hawkins and Taft, September 27, 1944, box 7, C. Taft Papers, LC.

105. Conversation between Taft and Denby, and Taft and Lynch, September 27, 1944, box 7, C. Taft Papers, LC.

106. Hull to FDR, October 2, 1944, box 12, Hickerson Files, RG59, DOS Records, NA.

107. Keynes to Anderson, July 21, 1944, T247/65, Keynes Papers, Treasury Records, PRO; HM-White conversation, September 20, 1944, box 773, HM Diaries, FDR Library.

108. Keynes to Anderson, October 4, 1944, T247/65, Keynes Papers, Treasury Records, PRO.

109. Ibid.

110. Foreign Financial Policy Committee, October 6, 1944, box 780, HM Diaries, FDR Library.

111. Orchard to Stettinius, October 7, 1944, box 5, Clayton-Thorp Papers, HST Library.

112. Hopkins to FDR, October 10, 1944, box 335, Hopkins Papers, FDR Library; Stimson Diaries, October 18, 1944, roll 9, SL/YU.

113. "Proposed Book on German Demilitarization," November 3, 1944, box 791, HM Diaries, FDR Library; Conversation between Taft and Krock, October 21, 1944, box 7, C. Taft Papers, LC.; "British Ask More on Lend-Lease," *New York Times*, November 3, 1944.

114. Keynes to Chancellor of the Exchequer, October 21, 1944, T247/124, Keynes Papers, Treasury Records, PRO.

115. Ibid.

116. See Stoff, *Oil, War, and American Security*.

117. "Prospects for Post-War Export Trade," February 17, 1944, series D, Beaverbrook Papers, HLRO.

118. Cox to Hopkins, November 11, 1944, box 173, Hopkins Papers, FDR Library. See also Meeting of Combined Committee on Mutual Lend-Lease, October 29, 1944, and "British Phase II Discussions; White Paper and Export Policy," October 23, 1944, box 12, Hickerson Files, and Meeting of Combined Committee on Mutual Lend-Lease, October 25, 1944, box 1, Havlik Files, RG59, DOS Records, NA.

119. Whitney to Coe, November 9, 1944, box 2, Havlik Files, RG59, DOS Records, NA.

120. "Use of Lend-Lease Articles and Commercial Policy," undated, box 2, Havlik Files, DOS Records, NA.

121. Kurt Lowenstein to Currie, Cox, et al., November 14, 1944, box 17, Hickerson Files, and Meetings of Combined Subcommittee on Mutual Lend-Lease Aid, November 4 and 13, 1944, box 1, Havlik Files, RG59, DOS Records, NA.

122. Keynes to Brand, October 26, 1944, T247/66, Keynes Papers, Treasury Records, PRO.

123. Burns, *Roosevelt*, 515–18.

124. Ibid., 532.

125. Keynes to Hopkins, November 6, 1944, T247/65, Keynes Papers, Treasury Records, PRO.

126. Broadcast over Blue Network by Henry J. Taylor, November 6, 1944, box 792, HM Diaries, HM Papers, FDR Library.

127. Keynes to HM, November 16, 1944, box 17, Hickerson Files, RG59, DOS Records, NA.

128. *New York Times*, December 2, 1944.

129. G.B. and U.S. (Future Lend-Lease Arrangements), *Parliamentary Debates* (Hansard), Commons, November 30, 1944, 5th series, vol. 406.

Chapter 7

1. "The New Liberalism," *The Economist*, February 12, 1944.
2. Joan Hoff Wilson, *American Business and Foreign Policy*, 161.
3. Quoted in ibid., 160–61.
4. Culbertson to Hull, October 6, 1944, rolls 54–56, Hull Papers, CRL/UC.
5. Culbertson memo concerning the recommendation of the "Corporation," December 11, 1944, and Gilpatrick to Taft and Clayton, January 24, 1945, box 1, Clayton-Thorp Papers, HST Library.
6. Taft to Luce, October 21, 1944, box 7, C. Taft Papers, LC.
7. Taft-Stevenson conversation, October 14, 1944, box 7, C. Taft Papers, LC.
8. Baruch memo on "European Reconstruction," October 28, 1944, Baruch Papers, ML/PU. See also Keynes to Halifax, December 9, 1944, T247/65, Keynes Papers, Treasury Records, PRO, for Forrestal's faith in Baruch.
9. Douglas H. Allen to Clayton, January 21, 1945, box 1, Assistant Secretary for Economic Affairs Office Files, RG59, DOS Records, NA.
10. Townsend to Clayton, July 21, 1945, box 1, Clayton-Thorp Papers, HST Library.
11. *Who's Who in America, 1944–45* (Chicago, 1944), 23:62.
12. Bidwell memo on "Postwar Agreements on Commercial Policy," January 1944, box 210, Hopkins Papers, FDR Library.
13. Ibid.
14. Memo by Winant with Hawkins and Penrose, London, undated, DOS, *FRUS, 1945*, 6:22–24. See also E. F. Penrose memo on "Organization of International Economic Reconstruction," April 29, 1944, box 12, Hickerson Files, RG59, DOS Records, NA.
15. Bidwell memo on "Postwar Agreements on Commercial Policy," January 1944, box 210, Hopkins Papers, FDR Library.
16. Memo of conversation between Cripps and Feis, June 9, 1942, Hickerson Files, box 12, RG59, DOS Records, NA.
17. Marwick, *War and Social Change*, 153–57.
18. Marwick, *Home Front*, 127–28.
19. Hazell to Bevin, November 22, 1940, Bevin Papers, CCL/CU.
20. Harris, *Beveridge*, 409–10, 430–31; Marwick, *War and Social Change*, 164.
21. Jones, *Diary with Letters*, 503; Nicolson, *Diaries and Letters*, 264, 281; Attlee to Churchill, 1943, box 2, folder 2, Attlee Papers, CCL/CU.
22. Meade Diaries, 1/3, 68–69, 105, 120–21, 225–27, RL/LSE.
23. Ibid., 120–21.
24. Ibid., 27.
25. Meade Diaries, 1/4, 10–11, RL/LSE.
26. Booth, " 'Keynesian Revolution,' " 106–15; Meade Diaries, 1/3, 2–124, RL/LSE.
27. Bullock, *Bevin*, 313; Dalton Diaries, February 24, 1944, vol. 1, 30, RL/LSE; Winant memo on "Article VII Conversations," February 4, 1943, box 53, PSF, FDR Papers, FDR Library. See "Private Enterprise Urged by Lyttleton," *New York Times*, November 7, 1944, and Winch, *Economics and Policy*.
28. Dalton Diaries, January 21, 1944, vol. 1, 30, RL/LSE.

29. Beaverbrook to Baruch, August 18, 1944, D/127, Beaverbrook Papers, HLRO.

30. Dalton Diaries, May 19, 1944, vol. 1, 30, RL/LSE.

31. Bell to Glasser, July 14, 1944, box 758, HM Diaries, FDR Library; Winch, *Economics and Policy*, 270–73.

32. Booth, " 'Keynesian Revolution,' " 116; Winch, *Economics and Policy*, 269.

33. Quoted in Brady, "Toward Security," 1.

34. Ibid.

35. Ibid., 22, n. 5; 28, n. 18.

36. Burns, *Roosevelt*, 41, 48–49, 53, 353.

37. Warken, *National Resources Planning Board*, 188–89.

38. White to HM, May 12, 1942, box G, White Papers, ML/PU.

39. Quoted in "American Reactions to the Beveridge Report," 1943, T247/72, Keynes Papers, Treasury Records, PRO.

40. Ibid.

41. Burns, *Roosevelt*, 386–87.

42. Quoted in ibid., 387.

43. Brady, "Toward Security," 138–39; Warken, *National Resources Planning Board*, 200.

44. Quoted in Brady, "Toward Security," 139–40.

45. Ibid.

46. Nicholas, *Washington Dispatches*, 49.

47. Quoted in Brady, "Toward Security," 141–43.

48. Washington Embassy to Foreign Office, February 6, 1945, FO 371/44571, Foreign Office Records, PRO.

49. Brady, "Toward Security," 210–14.

50. Conversation between HM, Nathan, White, et al., October 1, 1944, box 781, HM Diaries, FDR Library.

51. Brady, "Toward Security," 217; Conversation with FDR, January 1, 1945, vol. 14, Smith Diaries, FDR Library.

52. Hopkins memo, November 10, 1944, box 335, Hopkins Papers, FDR Library.

53. Laski to FDR, December 5, 1944, box 53, PSF, FDR Papers, FDR Library.

54. Brady, "Toward Security," 235–38.

55. Ibid.

56. Conversation between HM, Stettinius, and FDR, January 19, 1945, vol. 6, Presidential Diaries, HM Papers, FDR Library.

57. Cunningham to Taft, January 16, 1945, box 859, R. Taft Papers, LC.

58. Cullen to Wallace, January 2, 1944, box 176, Jones Papers, LC.

59. Quoted in Paul Gore-Booth to Foreign Office, undated, FO 371/44571, Foreign Office Records, PRO.

60. "Fight on Limiting Power of Wallace Goes to the House," *New York Times*, February 15, 1945.

61. "Senators Oppose Naming of Wallace," *New York Times*, January 23, 1945.

62. Weekly Political Summary, January 1945 (FO 371/4453), and Paul Gore-Booth to Foreign Office, January 29, 1945 (FO 371/44571), Foreign Office Records, PRO; Treasury Group discussion, February 2, 1945, box 815, HM Diaries, FDR Library; Halifax to Foreign Office, March 11, 1945, FO 371/44356, Foreign Office Records, PRO.

63. Brady, "Toward Security," 278–29; Winch, *Economics and Policy*, 275–76.

64. Winch, *Economics and Policy*, 276.

65. United Nations Organization, February 7, 1945, box 7, Naval Aide File, HST Papers, HST Library.

66. For the British view of FDR's thinking at this point, see Law minute on Article VII negotiations, February 2, 1945, FO 371/45679, Foreign Office Records, PRO.

67. L. Gardner, *Architects of Illusion*, 116; Schlesinger, *Coming of the New Deal*, 486; "Challenges Dewey to Keep Hull's Pacts," *New York Times*, October 20, 1944.

68. Clayton had been named to head the War Surplus Property Agency because he favored disposal of surplus war plants, aircraft, and machinery on a businesslike basis according to socially neutral principles. That is, he, like conservatives in Congress and the business world, wanted war plants sold to the private sector and not operated by the government. In fact, all surplus items should be sold to the highest bidder and not distributed according to a preference system designed to aid disadvantaged groups in the economy as some liberals advocated. Dobney, "Reconversion Policy." Hopkins's statement that Clayton would get into trouble on the domestic scene probably stemmed from his belief that Clayton was too rigidly conservative for many New Dealers.

69. Acheson, *Present at the Creation*, 309; "Export Subsidy Results," *New York Times*, October 22, 1944.

70. Clayton to Hopkins, November 18, 1944, box 329, Sherwood Collection, Hopkins Papers, FDR Library.

71. Executive Order, March 21, 1944, box 712, HM Diaries, FDR Library.

72. Memo to FDR, August 19, 1944, box 764, HM Diaries, FDR Library.

73. Hull to FDR, September 26, 1944, box 781, HM Diaries, FDR Library.

74. Smith to FDR, September 27, 1944, box 781, HM Diaries, FDR Library.

75. Conversation with FDR, January 1, 1945, vol. 14, Smith Diaries, FDR Library.

76. See Stimson Diaries, November 27, 1944, roll 119, SL/YU; and Harriman and Abel, *Special Envoy*, 272.

77. Bohlen, *Witness to History*, 166.

78. Ickes Diary, October 18, 1943, 8271, Ickes Papers, LC; State Department Reorganization, January 15 and November 21, 1944, box 8, C. Taft Papers, LC.

79. Hopkins to FDR, November 28, 1944, box 338, Hopkins Papers, FDR Library.

80. FDR to Clayton, November 29, 1944, box 338, Hopkins Papers, FDR Library.

81. Stettinius Files, December 15, 1944, vol. 1, RG59, DOS Records, NA; Wallace Diary, November 28, 1944, notebook 32, box 11, ML/UI; Opie-Pasvolsky conversation, December 21, 1944, FO 371/44555, Foreign Office Records, PRO.

Chapter 8

1. Washington Embassy to Foreign Office, February 6, 1945, FO 371/44571, Foreign Office Records, PRO.

2. "Export or Die," *The Economist*, January 27, 1945.

3. Law on Article VII, February 7, 1944, W.P. (44) 81, CAB 65, Cabinet Conclusions, PRO.

4. Dalton Diaries, February 11, 1944, vol. 1, 30, RL/LSE.

5. Ibid.; War Cabinet Conclusions, February 11, 1945, W.M. (44) 18, CAB 65, PRO.

6. Dalton Diaries, April 27, 1944, 30, and September 14, 1944, 31, vol. 1, RL/LSE.

7. "A Policy of Expansion," April 17, 1944, D/50, Beaverbrook Papers, HLRO.

8. *Parliamentary Debates* (Hansard), Commons, 5th series, vol. 406, 104–7.

9. Ibid., 113.

10. Ibid., 462.

11. Ibid., 633–34.

12. Ibid.

13. Note by Prime Minister, February 26, 1944, PREM 4/18/1, Prime Minister's Records, PRO.

14. Churchill to Anderson, July 13, 1944, PREM 4/18/4, Prime Minister's Records, PRO.

15. Churchill to Eden, April 3, 1944, PREM 4/17/1, Prime Minister's Records, PRO.

16. Cherwell to Churchill, March 15, 1944, PREM 4/17/10, Prime Minister's Records, PRO.

17. Minute by Minister of State on Article VII, February 2, 1945, FO 371/45679, Foreign Office Records, PRO.

18. Halifax to Foreign Office, January 31, 1945, FO 371/45679, Foreign Office Records, PRO.

19. Memo by Secretary of State's Staff Committee, March 5, 1945, DOS, *FRUS, 1945*, 6:24–25.

20. Winant memo with Hawkins and Penrose to Secretary of State, undated, DOS, *FRUS, 1945*, 6:22–24.

21. *1945 Extension of RTAA*, 11.

22. Hawkins to Grady, October 18, 1940, and "The Place of the Trade Agreements Act in Our Present and Future Commercial Policy," Executive Committee on Commercial Policy, July 20 and October 23, 1940, box 42, Intra- and Interdepartmental Committee Files, RG 353, NA.

23. Clayton to Madeline Thompson, April 30, 1945, box 7, Clayton-Thorp Papers, HST Library; Taft to Landon, April 17, 1945, box 10, C. Taft Papers, LC.

24. Acting Secretary of State to Winant, March 5, 1945, 840.50/3-545, DOS Records, RG 59, NA; *1945 Extension of RTAA*, 1.

25. Patterson, *Mr. Republican*, 35, 127, 129, 218, 252.

26. "The Christian Ideal and Political Action," January–February 1945, box 10, C. Taft Papers, LC.

27. Taft to Landon, April 17, 1945, box 10, C. Taft Papers, LC.

28. Taft to Dewey, April 20, 1945, box 10, C. Taft Papers, LC.

29. Matusow, *Farm Policies*, 81–82.

30. Henningson, "Agricultural Trade and Development Policy," 11.

31. Quoted in ibid., 10.

32. Ibid., 11. See also Beddow, "Economic Nationalism or Internationalism," 66.

33. David W. Little memo on "Congressional Attitudes towards Use of Executive Agreements as Instruments of Foreign Policy," July 19, 1943, box 12, Hickerson Files, RG59, DOS Records, NA.

34. Martin J. Gillen to John A. Ritchie, September 3, 1943, box 706, C. Taft Papers, LC.

35. Ibid. See also Address of Robert A. Taft to War Veterans Club of Ohio, May 6, 1944, box 802, R. Taft Papers, LC.

36. Report on Trade Agreements Renewal, July 2, 1945, box 10, C. Taft Papers, LC.

37. *1945 Extension of RTAA*, 6–7.

38. Ibid., 20–50.

39. Quoted in R. Gardner, *Sterling-Dollar Diplomacy*, 159.

40. Stettinius to Wagner, March 31, 1945, box 2, Clayton-Thorp Papers, HST Library.

41. Address by Stettinius to Chicago Council on "Foreign Relations," April 4, 1945, roll 53, Hull Papers, CRL/UC.

42. *1945 Extension of RTAA*, 10–14.

43. R. Taft notes on Dumbarton Oaks, undated, 1945, box 613, R. Taft Papers, LC.

44. C. Taft to Dewey, May 4, 1945, box 10, C. Taft Papers, LC; R. Taft notes on Dumbarton Oaks, undated, 1945, box 613, R. Taft Papers, LC; R. Gardner, *Sterling-Dollar Diplomacy*, 158.

45. Luncheon meeting with Raymond Buel and James Angell, June 25, 1945, box 10, C. Taft Papers, LC.

46. "Postwar Commercial Policy," February 16, 1944, box 12, Hickerson Files, RG59, DOS Records, NA.

47. Henningson, "Agricultural Trade and Development Policy," 12.

48. *1945 Extension of RTAA*, 487.

49. Memo by Clayton for Hawkins, April 28, 1945, lot 122, box 13143, RG59, DOS Records, NA.

50. Winant to Secretary of State, June 28, 1945, 560 AL/6-2845 Tel., RG59, DOS Records, NA.

51. See, for example, Winant to Hull, March 24, 1945, box 329, Sherwood Collection, Hopkins Papers, FDR Library.

52. Memo by Executive Committee on "Economic Foreign Policy," July 21, 1945, 611/6031 Exec. Co./7-1645, RG59, DOS Records, NA.

53. Van Dormael, *Bretton Woods*, 246–49.

54. Conversation between Ned Brown and HM, December 24, 1944, box 757, HM Diaries, FDR Library.

55. "Mr. Aldrich's Monetary Plan," *New York Times*, September 19, 1944.

56. Bell to HM, April 6, 1945 (box 834), and Conversation between HM, Burgess, White, et al., January 4, 1945 (box 822), HM Diaries, FDR Library; Halifax to Foreign Office, February 11, 1945, FO 371/44535, Foreign Office Records, PRO.

57. Cox to HM, July 26, 1944, box 759, HM Diaries, FDR Library.

58. Treasury discussion, February 5, 1945, box 816, HM Diaries, FDR Library.

59. Louis P. Birk to HST, June 22, 1945, box 356, Official File, HST Papers, HST Library.

60. Luxford to HM, August 18, 1944 (box 763), HM-Luxford conversation, August 6, 1944 (box 750), Luxford-Tobey conversation, August 15, 1944 (box 762), and Banker's Report on Bretton Woods, September 2, 1944 (box 773), HM Diaries, FDR

Library; E. E. Holmes to FDR, August 25, 1944, box 4351, Official File, HST Papers, HST Library.

61. White to HM, March 1, 1945, box 824, HM Diaries, FDR Library.

62. Darilek, *Loyal Opposition*, 125–26.

63. "Dewey Supports World Fund, Bank," *New York Times*, June 8, 1945.

64. "Fight on Limiting Power of Wallace Goes to House," *New York Times*, February 15, 1945.

65. "FDR Presses World Money Plan" (February 13, 1945) and "World Fund Bill Offers Surprises as Given Congress" (February 16, 1945), *New York Times*.

66. Van Dormael, *Bretton Woods*, 251; Bretton Woods, February 16, 1945, box 720, HM Diaries, FDR Library.

67. Bretton Woods, March 22, 1945, box 831, HM Diaries, FDR Library.

68. Quoted in Van Dormael, *Bretton Woods*, 254–55.

69. Ibid.

70. Bretton Woods, March 24, 1945, box 832, HM Diaries, FDR Library.

71. *New York Times*, March 4 and 15, 1945.

72. Baruch memo, July 26, 1944, box 14, Baruch Papers, ML/PU.

73. Bretton Woods, March 24, 1945, box 832, HM Diaries, FDR Library.

74. Luxford to HM, April 5, 1945, box 834, HM Diaries, FDR Library.

75. HM to FDR, August 19, 1944, box 764, HM Diaries, FDR Library.

76. Feltus to HM, April 25, 1945, box 840, HM Diaries, FDR Library; Conversation between Taft and Clayton, May 10, 1945, box 10, C. Taft Papers, LC; Van Dormael, *Bretton Woods*, 256.

77. *Congressional Record*, House, 79th Cong., 1st sess., vol. 91, pt. 4, 5577.

78. "Bretton Woods Urged by Truman," *New York Times*, June 6, 1945.

79. *Congressional Record*, House, 79th Cong., 1st sess., vol. 91, pt. 4, 5542.

80. Ibid., 5657–58.

81. Ibid., 5647.

82. "House Test Backs Bretton Program," *New York Times*, June 7, 1945; *Congressional Record*, House, 79th Cong., 1st sess., vol. 91, pt. 4, 5677–79, 5684.

83. Ibid., 5569.

84. Bretton Woods, April 13, 1945, HM Diaries, box 837, FDR Library.

85. *Congressional Record*, Senate, 79th Cong., 1st sess., vol. 91, pt. 6, 7625–26.

86. Ibid., 7571–72, 7575, 7622.

87. Ibid., 7575, 7622.

88. Ibid.

89. Conversation between Luxford and Tobey, August 15, 1944, box 762, HM Diaries, FDR Library.

90. "Taft Presses Fight on Bretton Woods," *New York Times*, July 18, 1945.

91. *Congressional Record*, Senate, 79th Cong., 1st sess., vol. 91, pt. 6, 7678, 7774, 7769.

92. Ibid., 7769.

93. See, for example, Winant to Hull, March 24, 1943, box 329, Sherwood Collection, Hopkins Papers, FDR Library.

94. Keynes to Anderson, July 21, 1944, T247/65, Keynes Papers, Treasury Records, PRO.

95. Van Dormael, *Bretton Woods*, 2222. See Einzig to Hargreaves Parkinson, February 5, 1944, I/14, Einzig Papers, CCL/CU.

96. Van Dormael, *Bretton Woods*, 224–26, 228–30.

97. Ibid.

98. "The Bretton Woods Conference"—Memo by Chancellor of the Exchequer, January 22, 1945, W.P. (45) 46, CAB 66, Cabinet Memoranda, PRO.

Chapter 9

1. Carlton, *Eden*, 199, 202–3, 209–10, 212–13, 225.

2. See Ryan, *Vision of Anglo-America*, 98.

3. Wallace Diary, May 22, 1943, notebook 21, box 7, ML/UI.

4. Eden memo on "Anglo-Soviet Relations," June 14, 1944, W.P. (44) 323, CAB 66, Cabinet Memoranda, PRO.

5. F. Gilbert, *End of the European Era*, 332–33. For changing Foreign Office attitudes toward Soviet Union and European balance of power, see Rothwell, *Britain and the Cold War*.

6. See W. J. Gallman to Secretary of State, March 27, 1944, 841.00/1708, RG59, DOS Records, NA.

7. See, for example, Watt, *Succeeding John Bull*, 90–104, and Ryan, *Vision of Anglo-America*, 13–20.

8. Quoted in Dalton Diaries, February 1, 1944, vol. 1, 30, RL/LSE.

9. J. F. Carter to Stettinius, July 25, 1944, 841.0017-2544, RG59, DOS Records, NA.

10. Stettinius Files, December 7–23, 1944, vol. 12, RG59, DOS Records, NA.

11. Beaverbrook to Halifax, August 29, 1944, D/182, Beaverbrook Papers, HLRO.

12. Halifax to Foreign Office, January 28, 1945, FO 371/44535, Foreign Office Records, PRO.

13. Thorne, *Allies of a Kind*, 138.

14. John Carter Franklin to Stettinius, July 25, 1944, 841.06/7-2544, RG59, DOS Records, NA.

15. Halifax to Foreign Office, July 7, 1945, FO 371/44535, Foreign Office Records, PRO.

16. Halifax to Foreign Office, January 28, 1945, FO 371/44535, Foreign Office Records, PRO.

17. Ibid.

18. Nicolson, *Diaries and Letters*, 385.

19. Quoted in Thorne, *Allies of a Kind*, 515.

20. Michael Wright to Philip Broadmead, January 7, 1945, FO 371/44555, Foreign Office Records, PRO.

21. Quoted in Thorne, *Allies of a Kind*, 138–39.

22. Summary of a report on "Anti-British Feeling in the United States," 1944, T247/72, Keynes Papers, Treasury Records, PRO.

23. Ibid.

24. Minute by Campbell, December 27, 1944, FO 371/44555, Foreign Office Records, PRO.

25. Mastny, *Russia's Road*, 71–72, 110, 181–82.

26. Jones, *Diary with Letters*, 507–8.

27. Grigg to Montgomery, July 25, 1944, 9/8/18, Grigg Papers, CCL/CU.

28. Claire Booth Luce et al. to Hull, March 15, 1944, box 10, C. Taft Papers, LC.

29. "British Policy towards Nations of Western Europe: The American Position," April 13, 1944, box 10, Hickerson Files, RG59, DOS Records, NA.

30. "Principal Problems in Europe," September 26, 1944, roll 5, Berle Papers, FDR Library.

31. Smith, *American Secretaries of State*, 1–25.

32. See Noble, "Conservatism in the USA," 637–39.

33. Acheson to Stettinius and Hull, January 28, 1944, box 27, Acheson Papers, HST Library.

34. Schnabel, "History of the Joint Chiefs of Staff," 14–15.

35. Kimball, *Churchill and Roosevelt*, 3:709.

36. Ibid., 3:767.

37. Memo on "Joint U.S.–U.K. Relations in Connection with Approach to Third Countries," November 10, 1944, Clayton Papers, HST Library.

38. Harriman and Abel, *Special Envoy*, 227.

39. Ibid.

40. Smith, *American Diplomacy*, 142–43.

41. David Carlton, Anthony Eden's most recent biographer, cites Churchill's enthusiasm for the percentages deal as evidence that it was Churchill, rather than Eden, who was the principal exponent of appeasing the Soviet Union in 1944. Carlton, *Eden*, 231. In a recent article in the *Journal of Contemporary History*, Lothar Kettenacker makes no distinction between the two, labeling them both appeasers and chastising them for refusing to admit that their approach to Stalin differed very little from Chamberlain's dealings with Hitler. More to the point, he argues along with Vojtech Mastny that Britain's conciliatory approaches to prewar Germany and postwar Russia were not temporary aberrations but symptoms of Britain's irreversible decline in power. Kettenacker, "Anglo-Soviet Alliance," 435–36.

42. Quoted in Green, "Conflict over Trade Ideologies," 64–65.

43. Ibid., 64–65. See also Watt, *Succeeding John Bull*, 104.

44. Quoted in Gaddis, *Origins of the Cold War*, 164. Eduard Mark argues, in fact, that from the time it was apparent that the Soviet Union would survive Hitler's onslaught, U.S. policymakers anticipated Soviet predominance east of the Elbe. They labored under no illusions of omnipotence and knew it would be futile to resist anyway. American policy toward Eastern Europe, he argues, consisted neither of a utopian bid to rid the Continent of spheres and power politics (orthodox) nor a Machiavellian bid to dominate (revisionist), but a search for stable spheres that would preserve the interests of the major victors. Mark, "American Policy toward Eastern Europe," 313–14.

45. Gaddis, *Origins of the Cold War*, 199–200.

46. Ryan, *Vision of Anglo-America*, 28–30.

47. *Parliamentary Debates* (Hansard), Commons, 5th series, vol. 508, 1671–73.

48. Roberts to C.F.A. Warner, April 30, 1945, FO 371/47854, Foreign Office Records, PRO.

49. Roberts to C.F.A. Warner, April 25, 1945, FO 371/47882, Foreign Office Records, PRO.

50. War Cabinet Conclusions, April 3, 1945, W.M. (45) 39, CAB 65, PRO.

51. Anderson, *Cold War*, 40–45. For a comprehensive analysis of the Polish issue in Anglo-American relations see Ryan, *Vision of Anglo-America*, 73–119.

52. Bohlen, *Witness to History*, 212.

53. Donovan, *Conflict and Crisis*, xiv–xvii. See also Ferrell, *Off the Record*.

54. Donovan, *Conflict and Crisis*, xiv–xvii.

55. Stettinius Files, March 18–April 7, 1945, vol. 5, RG59, DOS Records, NA; Gaddis, *Origins of the Cold War*, 201–2; Harriman and Abel, *Special Envoy*, 447–49.

56. Donovan, *Conflict and Crisis*, 34–35, 43.

57. Gaddis, *Origins of the Cold War*, 204; Grew to HST, May 1, 1945, box 172, PSF, HST Papers, HST Library.

58. Gaddis, *Origins of the Cold War*, 224–25.

59. Vandenberg to Taft, May 2, 1945, box 613, R. Taft Papers, LC.

60. Green, "Conflict over Trade Ideologies," 153–54.

61. Ibid., 157.

62. See Mee, *Meeting at Potsdam*.

63. For an explication of the open-door concept, see William Appleman Williams's *Tragedy of American Diplomacy* (New York, 1962); for its application to the 1943–45 period, see Gabriel Kolko's *Politics of War* (New York, 1968).

64. See Ambrose, *Eisenhower and Berlin*.

65. Sherry, *Preparing for the Next War*, 182.

66. Ibid., 173.

67. Bert Andrews on MacArthur at Leyte, November 22, 1944, vol. 2, Forrestal Diaries, ML/PU.

68. Halifax to Foreign Office, May 5, 1945, FO 371/44536, Foreign Office Records, PRO.

69. Unknown correspondent to Wallace, May 2, 1945, notebook 34, box 12, Wallace Papers, ML/UI.

70. Davies to Byrnes, May 10, 1945, box 191, Byrnes Papers, CL/CU.

71. Quoted in Hathaway, *Ambiguous Partnership*, 36–37.

72. HST to Eleanor Roosevelt, May 10, 1945, in Ferrell, *Off the Record*, 21–22.

73. Latest Opinion Trends, May 24, 1945, box 175, PSF, HST Papers, HST Library.

74. HST Diary, June 7, 1945, in Ferrell, *Off the Record*, 44.

75. Quoted in Knight, "Nonfraternal Association," 15–18.

76. Churchill to HST, June 4, 1945, box 7, Naval Aide File, HST Papers.

77. Balfour to Halifax, May 21, 1945, FO 371/44536, Foreign Office Records, PRO.

78. Orme Sargent minute, May 31, 1945, FO 371/47882, Foreign Office Records, PRO.

79. Anderson, *Cold War*, 88.

80. Clements, *Byrnes*, 2.

81. Quoted in Hathaway, *Ambiguous Partnership*, 149.

82. Gaddis, *Origins of the Cold War*, 239.

83. HST Diary, July 7, 1945, in Ferrell, *Off the Record*, 48.

84. Gaddis, *Origins of the Cold War*, 238.

85. Ibid., 241; J. E. C. Hill minute, May 16, 1945, FO 371/47853, Foreign Office Records, PRO.

86. Donnelley minute, June 2, 1945, FO 371/44536, Foreign Office Records, PRO.

87. Prime Minister to President, May 12, 1945, box 4, Map Room Files, HST Papers, HST Library.

88. Fitzsimons, *Foreign Policy of the British Labour Government*, 31–32; McCloy Memo for State, War, Navy Committee, July 19, 1945, box 4, Naval Aide File, HST Papers, HST Library.

89. Quoted in Dilks, *Diaries of Sir Alexander Cadogan*, 765.

90. Quoted in Gaddis, *Origins of the Cold War*, 243.

Chapter 10

1. Qoted in Hathaway, *Ambiguous Partnership*, 179.

2. Ibid, 180.

3. Quoted in Pelling, "The 1945 General Election," 400.

4. "British Policy Ferment involving Postwar Objectives," October 17, 1942, box 10, Hickerson Files, RG59, DOS Records, NA.

5. Coe to Secretary of State, February 13, 1945, 841.00/2-1345, RG59, DOS Records, NA.

6. "Second Draft Declaration of Policy for the 1945 Annual Conference," March 1945, 2/9, Bevin Papers, CCL/CU.

7. "British Policy Ferment Involving Postwar Objectives," October 17, 1942, box 10, Hickerson Files, RG59, DOS Records, NA.

8. Bullock, *Bevin*, 233–34; Bracken to Beaverbrook, August 28, 1944, D/165, Beaverbrook Papers, HLRO.

9. "British Political Ferment involving Postwar Objectives," October 17, 1942, box 10, Hickerson Files, RG59, DOS Records, NA.

10. Churchill to Attlee, May 22, 1945, 2/2, Attlee Papers, CCL/CU; Pelling, "The 1945 General Election."

11. Quoted in Nicolson, *Diaries and Letters*, 470. See also Winant to Secretary of State, June 13, 1945 (841.00/6-1345), July 2, 1945 (841.00/7-245), and July 7, 1945 (841.00/7-745), RG59, DOS Records, NA.

12. Bartlett, *Post-War Britain*, 16.

13. Ibid., 17.

14. "The Real Issue," *The Economist*, June 23, 1945.

15. Foot, *Bevan*, 25.

16. Dalton Diaries, July 25, 1945, vol. 1, 33, RL/LSE; Watt, *Personalities and Policies*, 57–78.

17. Dalton Diaries, July 12, 1945, vol. 1, 33, RL/LSE.

18. Dilks, *Diaries of Sir Alexander Cadogan*, 776.

19. Dalton Diaries, February 25, 1946, vol. 1, 34, RL/LSE.

20. Foot, *Bevan*, 33–34.

21. Watt, *Personalities and Policies*, 61–62.

22. Dalton Diaries, March 27, 1945, vol. 1, 32, RL/LSE.

23. *Parliamentary Debates* (Hansard), Commons, 5th series, vol. 413, 904–5.

24. Quoted in Fitzsimons, *Foreign Policy of the British Labour Government*, 26–27.

25. Quoted in Knight, "Nonfraternal Association," 30.

26. Bullock, *Bevin*, 98–99.

27. Bevin to William Whitelaw, March 21, 1946, and Lyall Wilkes to Bevin, March 22, 1946, 6/2, Bevin Papers, CCL/CU.

28. Fitzsimons, *Foreign Policy of the British Labour Government*, 27; Burridge, *British Labour*, 158.

29. As Ritchie Ovendale points out, the three foreign policy alternatives considered by the Attlee government were not mutually exclusive. While clinging to the Commonwealth and empire, and encouraging Western Europe to coalesce into a third force, the foreign secretary chose to give the Anglo-American alliance first priority. Ovendale, *Foreign Policy of the British Labour Governments*, 7.

30. See, for example, Halifax to Foreign Office, August 11, 1945, FO 371/4437, Foreign Office Records, PRO.

31. Quoted in Weekly Political Summary, July 1945, FO 371/44537, Foreign Office Records, PRO.

32. Forrestal Diaries, July 29, 1945, vol. 2, ML/PU.

33. Halifax to Foreign Office, July 28, 1945, FO 371/4437, Foreign Office Records, PRO.

34. Gaddis, *Origins of the Cold War*, 257–58.

35. Quoted in Green, "Conflict over Trade Ideologies," 64–65.

36. Quoted in Sherry, *Preparing for the Next War*, 199.

37. JCS to Secretaries of War and Navy, September 19, 1945, SWNCC no. 282, State-War-Navy Coordinating Committee Case Files, CRL/UC; Sherry, *Preparing for the Next War*, 198–99, 218.

38. B. E. F. Gage minute, August 20, 1945, FO 371/44574, Foreign Office Records, PRO.

39. Quoted in Anderson, *Cold War*, 89–90.

40. Ferrell, *Off the Record*, 49.

41. Clements, *Byrnes*, 3–7.

42. See Walter Brown Chronicle of London Foreign Ministers' Conference, August 11–September 20, 1945, box 629, Byrnes Papers, CL/CU.

43. Anderson, *Cold War*, 89–90.

44. Brown Chronicle, September 20, 1945, box 629, Byrnes Papers, CL/CU; Memo of conversation by C. E. Bohlen, September 16, 1945, 740.0019, RG59, DOS Records, NA; Gaddis, *Origins of the Cold War*, 265–66.

45. Brown Chronicle, September 20, 1945, box 629, Byrnes Papers, CL/CU.

46. Blum, *Price of Vision*, 490.

47. Gaddis, *Origins of the Cold War*, 276; Knight, "Nonfraternal Association," 66.

48. *Parliamentary Debates* (Hansard), Commons, 5th series, vol. 14/4, 38; Halifax to Bevin, December 21, 1945, FO 371/44574, Foreign Office Records, PRO.

49. Dalton Diaries, October 5, 1945, vol. 1, 33, RL/LSE.

50. Quoted in Knight, "Nonfraternal Alliance," 66.

51. Halifax to Bevin, December 21, 1945, Foreign Office Records, FO 371/44574, PRO.

52. Quoted in Knight, "Nonfraternal Association," 67.

53. DeConde, *American Foreign Policy*, 216.

54. Quoted in Bohlen, *Witness to History*, 255.

55. Gaddis, *Origins of the Cold War*, 280.

56. James P. Warburg to Dean Acheson, October 31, 1945, box 27, Acheson Papers, HST Library.

57. Dulles to Halleck, November 19, 1945, Dulles Papers, FL/PU.

58. Mundt and Bolton to HST, October 25, 1945, box 186, PSF, HST Papers, HST Library.

59. "The Chairman's Letter—Republican National Committee," October 15, 1945, box 175, PSF, HST Papers, HST Library.

60. "Stop World War III," January 1946, box 613, R. Taft Papers, LC.

61. Donnelley minute on Balfour to Gage, September 12, 1945, FO 371/445741, Foreign Office Records, PRO.

62. Balfour to Paul Mason, January 11, 1946, FO 371/51627, Foreign Office Records, PRO.

63. Halifax to Foreign Office, September 2, 1945, FO 371/44538, Foreign Office Records, PRO.

64. Mason minute, January 25, 1946, FO 371/51627, Foreign Office Records, PRO.

65. Brogan minute on "Political Situation in U.S.," January 1, 1946, FO 371/51606, Foreign Office Records, PRO.

66. Donnelley minute on Weekly Political Summary, March 27, 1946, FO 371/51607, Foreign Office Records, PRO.

67. Michael Butler to Orme Sargent, January 10, 1946, FO 371/56763, Foreign Office Records, PRO.

68. Balfour to Mason, January 11, 1946, FO 371/51627, Foreign Office Records, PRO.

69. Weekly Political Summary, November 3, 1945, FO 371/44539, Foreign Office Records, PRO.

70. Gaddis, *Origins of the Cold War*, 293; Knight, "Nonfraternal Association," 87–88.

71. Donnelley minute on Weekly Political Summary, January 8, 1946, FO 371/51606, Foreign Office Records, PRO.

72. Donnelley and Gage minutes on Weekly Political Summary, January 24, 1946, FO 371/51606, Foreign Office Records, PRO.

73. Ibid.

74. Gaddis, *Origins of the Cold War*, 299.

75. Matthews to Acheson and Byrnes, February 11, 1946, box 10, Hickerson Files, RG59, DOS Records, NA.

76. Quoted in Bohlen, *Witness to History*, 175.

77. Knight, "Nonfraternal Alliance," 85–86.

78. Gaddis, *Origins of the Cold War*, 303–4.

79. Halifax to Foreign Office, February 17, 1946, FO 371/51606, Foreign Office Records, PRO.

80. Donnelley minute, January 4, 1946, FO 371/44574, Foreign Office Records, PRO.

81. Roberts to Christopher Warren, January 9, 1946, FO 371/56763, Foreign Office Records, PRO.

82. Roberts to Foreign Office, March 2, 1946, FO 371/568140, Foreign Office Records, PRO. See also Donnelley minute, February 22, 1946, FO 371/51606, Foreign Office Records, PRO.

83. Anderson, *Cold War*, 100–101.

84. Ferrell, *Off the Record*, 80.

85. Gaddis, *Origins of the Cold War*, 287–89.

86. Anderson, *Cold War*, 107.

87. Donnelley minute, January 17, 1946, FO 371/51606, Foreign Office Records, PRO.

88. Knight, "Nonfraternal Association," 86.

89. Quoted in ibid.

90. Gaddis, *Origins of the Cold War*, 305.

91. Quoted in Knight, "Nonfraternal Association," 87.

92. Brandt to HST, January 14, 1946, box 186, PSF, HST Papers, HST Library.

93. *The Economist*, March 1946.

94. Weekly Political Summary, January 18, 1946, FO 371/51606, Foreign Office Records, PRO.

95. Gaddis, *Origins of the Cold War*, 311–12.

96. Donovan, *Conflict and Crisis*, 195. See also Hess, "Iranian Crisis," and Kuniholm, *Cold War in the Near East*, 304–37.

97. The latest and most comprehensive discussion of the Fulton speech—its origins and its implications—is in Harbut, *Iron Curtain*, 152–208.

98. Weekly Political Summary, August 6, 1945, FO 371/44539, Foreign Office Records, PRO.

99. "Sinews of Peace"—BIS Advance Release, March 5, 1946, box 115, PSF, HST Papers, HST Library.

100. Arkin to HST, May 5, 1946, box 771, Official File, HST Papers, HST Library.

101. Halifax to Bevin, March 9, 1946, FO 371/51624, Foreign Office Records, PRO.

102. Ibid.

103. Quoted in Blum, *Price of Vision*, 556.

104. Schnabel, "History of the Joint Chiefs of Staff," 105–6.

105. Donnelley minute, March 5, 1946, FO 371/51606, Foreign Office Records, PRO. Henry B. Ryan argues that while the Truman administration unquestionably knew what was in the Fulton address, His Majesty's Government, or at least Whitehall, did not. Ryan, "Churchill's 'Iron Curtain' Speech," 895–96.

Chapter 11

1. According to Ritchie Ovendale, by December 1946 Britain needed 400,000 more troops than anticipated; the British military establishment totaled almost 1,500,000. Defense expenditure consumed 18.8 percent of the national income, compared to 10.6 percent in the United States. Ovendale, *Foreign Policy of the Labour Governments*, 7.

2. Eady to Sir A. Barlow, March 16, 1945, T247/71, Keynes Papers, Treasury Records, PRO; Coe to HM, April 10, 1945, box 835, HM Diaries, FDR Library.

3. Hathaway, *Ambiguous Partnership*, 21.

4. See "Survey of British Political Parties," May 14, 1945, 841.00/5-1445, RG59, DOS Records, NA.

5. See War Cabinet Conclusions, May 4, 1944, W.C. (45) 58, CAB 65, PRO.

6. Eady to Barlow, March 16, 1945, T247/71, Keynes Papers, PRO.

7. See, for example, Halifax to Anderson, January 13, 1945, T247/51, Keynes

Papers, PRO, and "The Financial Problems of Postwar Britain," undated, box 216, Berle Papers, FDR Library.

8. See, for example, Conversation with President, October 30, 1944, box 14, Smith Diaries, FDR Library.

9. R. Gardner, *Sterling-Dollar Diplomacy*, 138–40. See also Memo of a meeting in Lord Keynes's office, March 7, 1945, box 835, HM Diaries, FDR Library; Acheson to Dunn, August 4, 1944, box 13, Acheson Files, RG59, DOS Records, NA; and Hull to FDR, September 17, 1944, box 332, Hopkins Papers, FDR Library.

10. FDR to Churchill, February 10, 1945, PREM 4/18/4, Prime Minister's Records, PRO.

11. War Cabinet Conclusions, March 23, 1945, W.C. (45) 35, CAB 65, PRO; Dalton Diaries, April 12, 1945, vol. 1, 32, RL/LSE; Beaverbrook to Churchill, January 29, 1945, D/150, Beaverbrook Papers, HLRO; Bullock, *Bevin*, 350–51; Churchill to FDR, February 13, 1945, in DOS, *FRUS, 1945*, 6:21.

12. Note of Conversation in Lord Keynes's Room, March 7, 1945, FO 371/45850, Foreign Office Records, PRO; Brand to Eady, February 1, 1945, T236/449, Eady Papers, Treasury Records, PRO.

13. Rosenman to FDR, March 8, 1945, box 28, Rosenman Papers, FDR Library.

14. Wm. H. Taylor Memo of a Meeting in Office of Lord Keynes, March 7, 1945, box 835, HM Diaries, FDR Library. See also Note of Conversation in Lord Keynes's Room, March 7, 1945, FO 371/45850, Foreign Office Records, PRO.

15. Eady to Keynes, March 27, 1945, T247/49, Keynes Papers, PRO.

16. A. L. Overton to Keynes, May 26, 1945, Eady Papers, Treasury Records (T236/436), Eady to Keynes, March 27, 1945 (T247/49), and Waley to Eady, June 7, 1944 (T247/65), Keynes Papers, Treasury Records, PRO; Eady to Keynes, March 6, 1945, T236/436, Eady Papers, Treasury Records, PRO.

17. Eady to Keynes, March 27, 1945, T247/49, Keynes Papers, Treasury Records, PRO.

18. Ibid. See also Treasury meeting on "Finance of Stage III," March 28, 1945, T236/449, Treasury Records, PRO; Donnelley minute on Article VII, January 22, 1945, FO 371/45679, Foreign Office Records, PRO.

19. Keynes memo on "Overseas Financial Policy in Stage III," April 17, 1945, D/150, Beaverbrook Papers, HLRO.

20. R. W. Ashton-Gwatney to Eady, March 5, 1945, T236/436, Eady Papers, Treasury Records, PRO; Keynes memo on "Overseas Financial Policy in Stage III," April 17, 1945, D/150, Beaverbrook Papers, HLRO; Beaverbrook to Keynes, April 17, 1945, T247/50, Keynes Papers, Treasury Records, PRO.

21. Bracken to Beaverbrook, May 2, 1945, D/128, Beaverbrook Papers, HLRO.

22. See, for example, Conference with President, April 26, 1945, box 1, Smith Diaries, FDR Library.

23. British Division Weekly Summary, April 19, 1945, box 6, Blaisdell Papers, HST Library.

24. See, for example, "A New Era in World Trade," April 14, 1945, box 1, Clayton-Thorp Papers, HST Library, and Truman, *Memoirs*, 48, 153.

25. J.R.S. to Padmore regarding Churchill-FDR conversation at Potsdam, July 20, 1945, PREM 4/18/6, Prime Minister's Records, PRO.

26. Donovan, *Conflict and Crisis*, xi; Rosenman to Baruch, April 5, 1945, box 29, Rosenman Papers, FDR Library.

27. Baruch memo, July 26, 1944, box 15, Baruch Papers, ML/PU.

28. Baruch to Hopkins, December 2, 1944, box 335, Hopkins Papers, FDR Library.

29. Baruch to FDR (January 22, 1945) and Baruch to Truman (April 20, 1945), box 15, Baruch Papers, ML/PU.

30. British Division Weekly Summary, April 19, 1945, box 6, Blaisdell Papers, HST Library; Hathaway, *Ambiguous Partnership*, 143–44.

31. Memo on "British Empire Lend-Lease Aid," January 20, 1945, box 60, Byrnes Papers, CL/CU.

32. DOS to President, June 14, 1945, box 1, Havlik Files, RG59, DOS Records, NA.

33. Halifax to Foreign Office, March 30, 1945, FO 371/45850, Foreign Office Records, PRO; White to HM, January 30, 1945, box 814, HM Diaries, FDR Library; "Lend-Lease 'Fact' Answer 'Fiction' " (February 8, 1945), "End of Lend-Lease in Peace Pledged" (February 6, 1945), "Lend-Lease" (March 15, 1945), and "Senators Extend Lend-Lease Act; Reject Taft Curb" (April 11, 1945), *New York Times*.

34. Crowley to Baruch, February 13, 1945, box 68, Baruch Papers, ML/PU.

35. "Russia's Postwar Foreign Policy: By Regions," February 5, 1945, vol. 2, Forrestal Diaries, ML/PU; Mee, *Meeting at Potsdam*, 6; Hathaway, *Ambiguous Partnership*, 146; Henry D. Larcade (R-La.) to HST, April 27, 1945, box 1009, Official File, HST Papers, HST Library.

36. J.S.M., Washington to Foreign Office, April 19, 1945, FO 371/45850, Foreign Office Records, PRO.

37. RAF Delegation, Washington to Air Ministry, Whitehall, May 4, 1945, FO 371/45850, Foreign Office Records, PRO.

38. Conference with the President, April 26, 1945, box 1, Diary, Smith Diaries, FDR Library.

39. Blum, *Morgenthau Diaries*, 447–48.

40. Brand to Eady, February 1, 1945, T236/449, Eady Papers, Treasury Records, PRO; J.S.M. to Brand, May 4, 1945, and Foreign Office to Brand, May 5, 1945, FO371/45850, Foreign Office Records, PRO; Ben Smith to Leo Crowley, May 7, 1945, box 1, Havlik Files, RG59, DOS Records, NA.

41. Brand to Keynes, May 17, 1945, T247/124, Keynes Papers, Treasury Records, PRO.

42. Blum, *Morgenthau Diaries*, 447–48.

43. Group discussion, May 23, 1945, box 848, HM Diaries, FDR Library.

44. Cherwell to Churchill, May 25, 1945, PREM 4/18/6, Prime Minister's Records, PRO.

45. Churchill to FDR, May 28, 1945, box 4, Naval Aide File, HST Papers, HST Library.

46. Hathaway, *Ambiguous Partnership*, 145–46. The half-loaf position taken by the State Department appeared clearly in a dispute that arose in early June concerning not the amount of aid promised Britain by the United States in Phase II but whether or not there had been a commitment to provide "old" or "new" supplies. The British took the position that Roosevelt and Churchill had been talking about new aid or requisitions to be submitted by London during the period between V-E Day and V-J Day. Even though certain FEA staffers had made statements in early May to the British Supply Council that indicated they had accepted the requisition interpretation, by fall

the Americans were arguing that the Quebec agreement referred to supplies previously ordered but not delivered as well as new requests. Because lend-lease on a delivery basis involved supplies previously requisitioned during Phase I, the amount of new money needed even to meet the figures Roosevelt and Churchill had settled on at Quebec would be much less. DOS to President, June 14, 1945, box 1, Havlik Files, DOS Records, RG50, NA.

47. Brand to Keynes, June 23, 1945, T247/50, Treasury Records, PRO.

48. Conversation between Crowley and Smith, June 1, 1945, box 1, Daily Record, Smith Diaries, FDR Library; Conversation between Cramer (FEA) and Fetter (DOS), June 4, 1945, box 1, Havlik Files, RG59, DOS Records, NA; A. V. Griffin to Clearance Committee, May 25, 1945, Clayton Files, RG59, DOS Records, NA.

49. Brand to Keynes, June 25, 1945, T236/449, Eady Papers, Treasury Records, PRO.

50. Treasury group discussion, June 5, 1945, box 852, HM Diaries, FDR Library.

51. Stimson to Byrnes, July 11, 1945 (box 5), and Vinson to Byrnes, July 12, 1945 (box 1), Naval Aide File, HST Papers, HST Library; Conversation between Crowley and Smith, June 28, 1945, box 1, Daily Record, Smith Diaries, FDR Library.

52. Grew to HST, June 28, 1945 (box 175), Subject File, and HST to Churchill, July 17, 1945 (box 4), Naval Aide File, HST Papers, HST Library.

53. J.R.S. to Padmore regarding Churchill-HST conversation on Potsdam, July 20, 1945, PREM 4/18/6, Prime Minister's Records, PRO.

54. Ismay to Peck, July 20, 1945, PREM 4/17/15, Prime Minister's Records, PRO.

55. British Chiefs of Staff to Prime Minister, July 20, 1945, Ismay to Peck, July 20 and 23, 1945, Hallis to Jacob, July 22, 1945, Sinclair to Churchill, July 27, 1945, and Attlee to HST, July 31, 1945, PREM 4/17/15, Prime Minister's Records, PRO. See also Churchill to HST, July 24, 1945, box 2, Naval Aide File, HST Papers, HST Library; and Grew to Winant, August 1, 1945, 800.24/8-145 tel., RG59, DOS Records, NA.

56. Ibid.

57. Clayton to Crowley and Acheson, August 12, 1945, box 98, Cox Papers, FDR Library.

58. Thayer to Cox, August 14, 1945, box 98, Cox Papers, FDR Library.

59. See Crowley to Baruch, December 26, 1944, box 173, Hopkins Papers, FDR Library.

60. Byrnes to HST, August 8, 1945, box 177, PSF, HST Papers, HST Library.

61. Byrnes to Winant, August 18, 1945, 800.24/8-1845, RG59, DOS Records, NA; Immediate Release, August 21, 1945, box 98, Cox Papers, FDR Library.

62. Foot, *Bevan*, 52.

63. Acheson, *Present at the Creation*, 172–73.

64. Memo of telephone conversation between Brown and Hawkins, August 19, 1945, 800.24/8-1945, RG59, DOS Records, NA.

65. Byrnes to certain American diplomatic missions, August 20, 1945, 800.24/8-2045, RG59, DOS Records, NA.

66. John Forshay to HST, undated, box 1038, Official File, HST Papers, HST Library.

67. See, for example, United Packinghouse Workers of America, August 27, 1945, box 1038, Official File, HST Papers, HST Library.

68. Cropper to HST, August 24, 1945, box 1038, Official File, HST Papers, HST Library.

69. Wise to HST, August 31, 1945, box 1038, Official File, HST Papers, HST Library.

70. Crowley to HST, August 21, 1945, box 1057, Official File, HST Papers, HST Library.

71. Balfour to Foreign Office, August 22, 1945, T236/2684, Eady Papers, Treasury Records, PRO.

72. Meeting on termination of lend-lease, August 21, 1945 (T236/1684), Treasury memo to Keynes, August 13, 1945, and Note of a meeting in Foreign Secretary's office, August 20, 1945 (T236/1684), and Bridges and Eady to Dalton, August 20, 1945 (T236/439), Eady Papers, Treasury Records, PRO; *Parliamentary Debates* (Hansard), Commons, 5th series, vol. 413, 955–58.

73. Memo for President, April 20, 1945, Presidential Diaries, vol. 7, HM Papers, FDR Library.

74. Vinson to HST, August 8, 1945, reel 14, Vinson Papers, HST Library; Green, "Conflict over Trade Ideologies," 36–38.

75. Byrnes to Crowley, undated (drafted September 3, 1945), 811.516 Export-Import Bank/9-345, RG59, DOS Records, NA.

76. Grew to certain diplomatic and consular offices, June 15, 1945, 811.51/6-1545, RG59, DOS Records, NA.

77. Byrnes to Crowley, undated (1945), 811.516 Export-Import Bank/9-345, RG59, DOS Records, NA.

78. Halifax to Foreign Office, August 7, 1945, FO 371/4437, Foreign Office Records, PRO.

79. *Congressional Record*, House, 79th Cong., 2d sess., vol. 91, pt. 4, 5681. In fall 1945 the NAC endorsed a $100 million credit to Belgium, $316 million to France, $100 million to the Netherlands, $100 million to the Netherlands East Indies, and $6 billion to Russia. The money was earmarked for short-term relief and reconstruction, and for payment for lend-lease goods still in the pipeline. The credit to Russia, of course, was never extended. Crowley to NAC, September 2, 1945, in DOS, *FRUS, 1946*, 1:1103–4.

80. Brand to Keynes, July 23, 1945 (T236/450), and Brand to Keynes, June 25, 1945 (T236/449), Eady Papers, Treasury Records, PRO.

81. Brand to Eady, July 2, 1945, Brand to Keynes, June 12, 1945, and Eady to Keynes, June 14, 1945, T236/449, Eady Papers, Treasury Records, PRO; Halifax to Foreign Office, July 13, 1945, FO 371/4437, Foreign Office Records, PRO.

82. Keynes to Eady, Bridges, and Padmore, June 21, 1945, T236/449, Eady Papers, Treasury Records, PRO.

83. Ibid.

84. Note of a Treasury meeting, July 30, 1945, T236/450, Eady Papers, Treasury Records, PRO. See also Keynes to Eady, Bridges, and Padmore, June 13 and 21, 1945, T236/449, Eady Papers, Treasury Records, PRO.

85. Donovan, *Conflict and Crisis*, 109. See also Vinson to HST, July 19, 1945, box 4, Naval Aide File, HST Papers, HST Library, and Wallace Diary, October 19, 1945, notebook 36, box 12, ML/UI.

86. Edward F. Pritchard to Vinson, August 17, 1945, reel 14, Vinson Papers, HST

Library. See also Rep. George B. Schwabe (D-Okla.) to HST, October 4, 1945, box 1010, Official File, HST Papers, HST Library, and Donovan, *Conflict and Crisis*, 113–14.

87. Clayton to Vinson, June 25, 1945, 841.51/6-2545, RG59, DOS Records, NA.

88. Edelsberg to Blaisdell, August 13, 1945, box 6, Blaisdell Papers, HST Library.

89. Clayton to Vinson, June 25, 1945, 841.51/6-2545, RG59, DOS Records, NA.

90. Ibid.

91. Memo of conversation by John M. Leddy, July 9, 1945, 841.50/7-945, RG59, DOS Records, NA.

Chapter 12

1. Memo of conversation, August 3, 1945, 611.41315, RG59, DOS Records, NA.

2. Harrod, *Keynes*, 593–94; Memo of conversation, August 3, 1945, 611.4131/5-146, RG59, DOS Records, NA; Memo of conversation between Keynes, Clayton, et al., August 3, 1945, and Taylor to White, August 8, 1945, reel 21, Vinson Papers, HST Library.

3. Clayton and Collado to Byrnes, Acheson, Thorp, and Phelps, August 17, 1945, 611.4131/8-1745, RG59, DOS Records, NA.

4. Keynes to Bridges and Padmore, August 16, 1945, T236/439, Eady Papers, Treasury Records, PRO.

5. Eady to Hopkins, February 10, 1945, T236/439, Eady Papers, Treasury Records, PRO.

6. Eady to Bridges, undated, T236/439, Eady Papers, Treasury Records, PRO.

7. Clarke, *Anglo-American Economic Collaboration*, 55–56.

8. Cherwell to Churchill, July 4, 1945, PREM 4/17/15, Prime Minister's Records, PRO; Dalton Diaries, August 3, 1945, vol. 1, 33, RL/LSE.

9. Meade Diaries, 1/4, 102–3, RL/LSE.

10. Keynes memo on "Our Overseas Financial Prospects," August 13, 1945, T137/50, Keynes Papers, Treasury Records, PRO. See also Balfour to Dalton, August 13, 1945, T236/439, Eady Papers, Treasury Records, PRO; Harrod, *Keynes*, 596–97; Cabinet Meeting, August 16, 1945, CAB (45) 23, CAB 128, vol. 1, Cabinet Conclusions, PRO.

11. Knight, "Nonfraternal Association," 57–58.

12. Note of a conversation between Bevin and a deputation of U.S. congressmen, August 22, 1945, T236/439, Eady Papers, Treasury Records, PRO.

13. Bullock, *Bevin*, 386.

14. Acheson to certain American missions, September 10, 1945, 611.4131/9-1045, RG59, DOS Records, NA; Meade Diaries, 1/4, 140–41, RL/LSE.

15. Pritchard to Vinson, August 22, 1945, reel 21, Vinson Papers, HST Library.

16. Ibid.; Coe to Vinson, August 25, 1945, reel 21, Vinson Papers, HST Library.

17. Byrnes to HST, undated, reel 21, Vinson Papers, HST Library.

18. Vinson to HST, August 30, 1945, reel 21, Vinson Papers, HST Library.

19. Clayton to Members of the U.S. Top Group, September 13, 1945, reel 21, Vinson Papers, HST Library.

20. Lord Keynes at Press Conference, September 12, 1945, box 633, R. Taft Papers, LC.

21. Proposals for financial arrangements in sterling area and between U.S. and U.K., Cabinet, September 12, 1945, T247/50, Keynes Papers, Treasury Records, PRO; R. L. Horne to Hall B. Larry, September 11, 1945, NAC Staff Document 4-1945, National Advisory Council Files, U.S. Department of Treasury Records, RG63, NA. See also Acheson to Byrnes, September 14, 1945, 740.00019 Council/9-1445, RG59, DOS Records, NA.

22. Minutes of meeting of U.S. Top Committee, October 6, 1945, 611.4131/5-146, RG59, DOS Records, NA.

23. Hickerson to Clayton, September 14, 1945, 611.4131/9-1445, RG59, DOS Records, NA.

24. Foreign Office to Keynes, September 26, 1945, T236/439, Eady Papers, Treasury Records, PRO.

25. Meeting with Top British Group, September 19, 1945, 611.4131/9-1845, RG59, DOS Records, NA.

26. Minutes of a meeting of Financial Committee, September 20, 1945, reel 21, Vinson Papers, HST Library.

27. "President Urges Writing Off Debt from Lend-Lease," *New York Times*, August 31, 1945.

28. Weekly Political Summary, 9/1-7, FO 371/44538, Foreign Office Records, PRO.

29. Hickerson to Clayton, September 14, 1945, and Hickerson to Achilles, September 19, 1945, 611.4131/9-1945, RG59, DOS Records, NA; McCloy to Clayton, September 19, 1945, box 6, Havlik Files, RG59, DOS Records, NA.

30. McCloy to Acheson, September 23, 1945, Clayton Files, RG59, DOS Records, NA.

31. Keynes to Treasury, October 5, 1945, FO 371/45707, Foreign Office Records, PRO.

32. Collado to Clayton, September 20, 1945 (611.4131/9-2045), and Clayton to HST, September 24, 1945 (841.51/9-2445), RG59, DOS Records, NA.

33. Keynes and Halifax to Bevin and Dalton, September 26, 1945, T236/439, Eady Papers, Treasury Records, PRO.

34. Keynes to Dalton, September 26, 1945, T247/47, Keynes Papers, Treasury Records, PRO.

35. Keynes to Eady, September 4, 1945 (T247/50), and Keynes to Dalton, September 26, 1945 (T247/47), Keynes Papers, Treasury Records, PRO.

36. Hall-Patch to Butler, September 25, 1945, FO 371/45702, Foreign Office Records, PRO.

37. Dalton Diaries, August 1945, vol. 1, 34, RL/LSE.

38. See, for example, Halifax to Foreign Office, September 17, 1945, FO 371/4438, Foreign Office Records, PRO.

39. "The Terms of Assistance," September 26, 1945, T236/439, Eady Papers, Treasury Records, PRO.

40. Bevin and Dalton to Halifax and Keynes, September 26, 1945, T236/439, Eady Papers, Treasury Records, PRO; Winant to Byrnes, October 3, 1945, 841.51/11-345, RG59, DOS Records, NA.

41. Hall-Patch to Butler, October 17, 1945, FO 371/45706, Foreign Office Records, PRO.

42. Donnelley minute on Weekly Political Summary, October 14, 1945, FO 371/

44538, Foreign Office Records, PRO.

43. Dalton Diaries, October 5, 1945, vol. 1, 33, RL/LSE.

44. Keynes to Bevin and Dalton, September 27, 1945, FO 371/45701, Foreign Office Records, PRO.

45. J.S.M. to Cabinet Offices, September 27, 1945 (FO 371/45701), and Hall-Patch to Butler, September 27, 1945 (FO 371/45702), Foreign Office Records, PRO.

46. Keynes to Dalton, October 1, 1945, and Keynes to Dalton, October 1, 1945, T247/47, Keynes Papers, Treasury Records, PRO; Hall-Patch to Butler, September 27, 1945, FO 371/45702, Foreign Office Records, PRO.

47. Keynes to Dalton, October 1, 1945, T247/47, Keynes Papers, Treasury Records, PRO.

48. Keynes to Eady, October 1, 1945, T236/439, Eady Papers, Treasury Records, PRO.

49. Keynes to Dalton, October 1, 1945, T247/47, Keynes Papers, Treasury Records, PRO.

50. "Financial Negotiations and Commercial Policy," Cabinet Meeting, October 5, 1945, FO 371/45702, Foreign Office Records, PRO.

51. Eady to Dalton, October 4, 1945, and Eady to Trend, October 4, 1945, T236/439, Eady Papers, Treasury Records, PRO; Dalton to Keynes, October 2, 1945, and Note of telephone conversation between Keynes and Eady, October 1, 1945, T247/47, Keynes Papers, Treasury Records, PRO.

52. Minute by R. Ashton-Gwatkin, October 3, 1945, FO 371/45701, Foreign Office Records, PRO.

53. Cripps to Leisching, October 27, 1945, FO 371/45705, Foreign Office Records, PRO.

54. Dalton to Keynes, October 8, 1945, FO 371/45702, Foreign Office Records, PRO; Winant to Byrnes, September 19, 1945, 611.4131/9-1945, RG59, DOS Records, NA.

55. Leisching to Cabinet Offices, October 28, 1945, FO 371/45706, Foreign Office Records, PRO.

56. Waley to Hickerson, September 17, 1945, 611.4131/9-1745, RG59, DOS Records, NA.

57. Eady to Dalton, October 4, 1945, T236/439, Eady Papers, Treasury Records, PRO; "Financial Negotiations and Commercial Policy," Meeting of Ministers, October 5, 1945 (FO 371/45702), Keynes to Dalton, October 12, 1945 (FO 371/45703), J. E. Cochran minute, October 9, 1945 (FO 371/45703), J.S.M. Washington to Cabinet Offices, October 2, 1945 (FO 371/45703), and Keynes to Foreign Office, October 7, 1945 (FO 371/45702), Foreign Office Records, PRO. See also Winant to Byrnes, September 24, 1945 (611.4131/9-2445), and Winant to Byrnes, October 3, 1945 (841.51/11-345), RG59, DOS Records, NA; and Status of British Financial Negotiations, undated, reel 21, Vinson Papers, HST Library.

58. Notes on Taylor-Winant conversation, November 6, 1945, reel 21, Vinson Papers, HST Library.

59. Halifax to Foreign Office, October 2, 1945 (FO 371/44539), and Halifax to Cripps, October 16, 1945 (FO 371/45703), Foreign Office Records, PRO.

60. Hall-Patch to Butler, October 25, 1945, FO 371/45704, Foreign Office Records, PRO.

61. Keynes to Dalton, October 23, 1945 (FO 371/45705), and Hall-Patch to Butler, October 19, 1945 (FO 371/4507), and October 25, 1945 (FO 371/45704), Foreign Office Records, PRO.

62. Keynes to Dalton, October 18, 1945, FO 371/45704, Foreign Office Records, PRO.

63. Ibid.

64. Meeting of ministers on "Financial and Commercial Policy," GEN89, November 5, 1945 (FO 371/45708), and Minute by R. Ashton-Gwatkin, October 31, 1945 (FO 371/45706), Foreign Office Records, PRO.

65. Dalton Diaries, November 6, 1945, vol. 1, 33, RL/LSE.

66. Chancellor to Keynes and Halifax, November 6, 1945, FO 371/45707, Foreign Office Records, PRO; Keynes to Vinson, November 6, 1945, T247/47, Keynes Papers, Treasury Records, PRO.

67. Memo for President on "Status of British Financial Negotiations," November 10, 1945, box 172, PSF, HST Papers, HST Library; Keynes and Brand to Dalton, November 11, 1945 (FO 371/45709), and Hall-Patch to Coulson, November 9, 1945 (FO 371/45709), Foreign Office Records, PRO.

68. Hall-Patch to Coulson, November 15, 1945, FO 371/45711, Foreign Office Records, PRO.

69. *Parliamentary Debates* (Hansard), Commons, 5th series, vol. 413, 486. See also Sir Waldron Smithers to HST, September 2, 1945, box 236, Official File, HST Papers, HST Library.

70. Ibid., 512.

71. Note on conversation between U.S. congressmen and Bevin, August 22, 1945, T236/439, Eady Papers, Treasury Records, PRO.

72. "Dalton Is Praised on British Budget" (October 25, 1945) and "Attlee Flies to U.S. for Talks to Shape Atomic Age Society" (November 10, 1945), *New York Times*.

73. Quoted in Blum, *Price of Vision*, 512.

74. Foot, *Bevan*, 21.

75. "The Administration Speaks Out," *The Economist*, November 17, 1945; Lamont to Baruch, November 15, 1945, and Baruch to Lamont, November 19, 1945, box 70, Baruch Papers, ML/PU.

76. Memo for Will Clayton, November 19, 1945, box 68, Baruch Papers, ML/PU.

77. Hall-Patch to Coulson, November 9, 1945, FO 371/45709, Foreign Office Records, PRO.

78. Hall-Patch to Butler, October 6, 1945, FO 371/45703, Foreign Office Records, PRO.

79. Saltonstall et al. to HST, December 10, 1945, box 184, PSF, HST Papers, HST Library.

80. Silver to Baruch, November 6, 1945, box 68, Baruch Papers, ML/PU; Cellar to Clayton, November 1, 1945, box 1, Clayton Files, RG59, DOS Records, NA.

81. Attlee to Halifax, November 27, 1945, FO 371/45711, Foreign Office Records, PRO.

82. Keynes to Eady and Bridges, November 20, 1945 (FO 371/45710), Dalton memo on "Washington Financial Talk," November 22, 1945, GEN.89/13 (FO 371/45710), and Attlee to Halifax, November 24, 1945 (FO 371/45710), Foreign Office Records, PRO.

83. The cabinet had accepted rather reluctantly a suggestion from its delegation that in order to protect Britain from the possible consequences of having to pay 2 percent interest on a very large loan over a fifty-year period, the United Kingdom was entitled, without argument, to cancel the interest in any year in which its export income did not reach a fixed figure (£866 million). In addition, under this, the so-called London Waiver, Britain was entitled to approach the American government for postponement of its annual installment payment during any period in which three conditions existed. Britain would automatically be entitled to defer if (1) there was a breakdown in multilateral clearing in which Britain was able to sell less than 75 percent of its exports to countries with freely convertible currencies (that is, creditor countries like the United States and Canada), (2) an international trade depression occurred as certified by the IMF, and (3) the IMF declared a scarcity of dollars. Clayton and Vinson subsequently rejected the London waiver on the grounds that the scarcity-of-dollars provision would be a red flag to Congress. They proposed an alternative, the Washington Waiver, in which Britain's ability to pay would be based on its gold and dollar reserves. This was, the Americans explained, to reassure Congress that Britain could not take advantage of the interest waiver by citing export income when it was in a strong reserve position. But the Attlee government, angered by America's rejection of the London Waiver, would have nothing to do with the Washington Waiver. If Britain accepted the principle, Dalton told his colleagues, "We should . . . expose ourselves to the risk of an American audit of our affairs, which we will not have." (Dalton memo on "Washington Financial Talks," November 22, 1945, FO 371/45710, Foreign Office Records, PRO.) In consequence, Attlee told the Washington delegation on the twenty-fourth to forget both the Washington and London waivers and to substitute a provision stipulating that either nation was entitled to approach the other with regard to a modification of the agreement if its working threatened to burden international commerce. (Attlee to Halifax, November 24, 1945, FO 371/45710, Foreign Office Records, PRO; "The Waiver, Deferment, and Pari Passu Principle," November 21, 1945, T247/47, Keynes Papers, Treasury Records, PRO; J.S.M. Washington to Cabinet Offices, November 7, 1945, FO 371/45708, Foreign Office Records, PRO.)

84. Keynes to Dalton, November 25, 1945 (FO 371/45710), Brand to Dalton, November 27, 1945 (FO 371/4571), and Eady to Keynes, November 27, 1945 (FO 371/45711), Foreign Office Records, PRO.

85. Meade Diaries, 1/4, 153–54, 156, 168–72, RL/LSE; Clarke, *Anglo-American Economic Collaboration*, 63.

86. Clayton to Vinson, November 27, 1945, reel 21, Vinson Papers, HST Library; Blum, *Price of Vision*, 526–27; Minutes of meeting of U.S. Financial Committee, November 28, 1945, Havlik Files, RG59, DOS Records, NA.

87. U.S. Draft Memo of Understanding on Financial Matters, November 30, 1945, 611.4131/5-146, RG59, DOS Records, NA; Keynes to Dalton, December 6, 1945, FO 371/45713, Foreign Office Records, PRO.

88. Dalton Diaries, December 7, 1945, vol. 1, 33, RL/LSE.

89. Einzig to Anonymous, August 16, 1944, 1/14, Einzig Papers, CCL/CU.

Chapter 13

1. Dalton Diaries, July 12, 1945, vol. 1, 33, RL/LSE.

2. "The Dollar Loan," *The Economist*, December 8, 1945; Keynes from Eady,

December 7, 1945, FO 371/45714, Foreign Office Records, PRO.

3. Quoted in "London Grows Bitter over American Loan," *New York Times*, December 6, 1945.

4. "Second Thoughts," *The Economist*, December 15, 1945.

5. Quoted in Clarke, *Anglo-American Economic Collaboration*, 71.

6. "British Get 55-Year, 2% Loan," *New York Times*, December 7, 1945.

7. "Attlee Beats Off Vote of Censure," *New York Times*, December 7, 1945; Eden to Halifax, January 17, 1946, A4.410.15, Halifax Papers, CCL/CU; "Keynes Optimistic on Pact Approval," *New York Times*, December 9, 1945.

8. *Parliamentary Debates* (Hansard), Commons, 1945–46, 5th series, vol. 417, 421–43.

9. Ibid.

10. Memo of Keynes-Taylor conversation, January 24, 1946, box 11, White Papers, ML/PU.

11. *Parliamentary Debates* (Hansard), Commons, 1945–46, 5th series, vol. 417, 455.

12. Ibid., 465.

13. Ibid., 669–70.

14. Ibid., 720.

15. Dalton Diaries, December 14, 1945, vol. 1, 33, RL/LSE.

16. *Parliamentary Debates* (Hansard), Commons, 5th series, vol. 417, 735, 746.

17. "Beaverbrook Hits Loan, Bretton Plan" (December 15, 1945), "Loan Plan Decried in HLRO" (December 18, 1945), and "Lords Bitter at U.S." (December 19, 1945), *New York Times*; Keynes to Vinson, December 20, 1945, T247/128, Keynes Papers, Treasury Records, PRO.

18. Hedlund, "Congress and the British Loan," 60–61.

19. Halifax to Foreign Office, January 10, 1946, FO 371/52949, Foreign Office Records, PRO. See also Acheson, *Present at the Creation*, 144–45.

20. Quoted in Patterson, *Congressional Conservatism*, 13.

21. Quoted in ibid., 15.

22. For a discussion of the South and internationalism, see George B. Tindall, *The Emergence of the New South, 1913–1945* (Baton Rouge, 1967), 687–88; Alfred O. Hero, Jr., *The Southerner and World Affairs* (Baton Rouge, 1965), 78–92, 100–104; Wayne Cole, "America First and the South 1940–1941," *Journal of American History* 22, no. 1 (February 1956): 36; and Charles O. Lerche, Jr., "Southern Internationalism—Myth and Reality," in Patrick Gerster and Nicholas Cords, eds., *Myth and Southern History* (Chicago, 1974), 258.

23. Bailey to Wallace, October 13, 1945, notebook 36, box 12, Wallace Papers, ML/UI.

24. Ibid.

25. See also Kenneth McKellar to HST, November 6, 1945, Official File, HST Papers, HST Library.

26. Taft address to War Veterans' Club of Ohio, May 6, 1944, box 802, R. Taft Papers, LC.

27. William J. Reardon to Taft, February 12, 1945, box 613, R. Taft Papers, LC.

28. Taft on Dumbarton Oaks Proposals, undated, 1945 (box 613), Taft Address to War Veterans' Club of Ohio, May 6, 1944 (box 802), and E. E. Lincoln to Taft, August 26, 1944, and H. E. Smith to Taft, May 5, 1944 (box 710), R. Taft Papers,

LC. See also "Taft Doubts Congress Will Approve World Financial Stabilization Plan," *New York Times*, July 12, 1944.

29. Hedlund, "Congress and the British Loan," 50–51; Vardaman to Truman, February 13, 1946, box 802, Official File, HST Papers, HST Library.

30. Dulles to Vandenberg, December 17, 1945, box 27, Dulles Papers, FL/PU.

31. Vandenberg to Dulles, December 19, 1945, box 27, Dulles Papers, FL/PU; Paul Gore-Booth memo on conversation with Dulles, February 6, 1946, FO 371/52591, Foreign Office Records, PRO. See also Rep. Parnell Thomas to HST, January 30, 1946, box 802, Official File, HST Papers, HST Library.

32. Quoted in Hedlund, "Congress and the British Loan," 54.

33. Acheson, *Present at the Creation*, 141–42.

34. Ibid., 73; Conversation between Coe and O'Connell, December 18, 1945, box 2, O'Connell Papers, HST Library.

35. Conference with President, December 19, 1945, box 1, Diary, Smith Diaries, FDR Library.

36. Dalton Diaries, February 25, 1946, vol. 1, 34, RL/LSE.

37. Baruch to Snyder, January 14, 1946 (box 16), Baruch to Wallace, February 15, 1946 (box 72), Baruch to Byrnes, December 11 and 24, 1945 (box 16), and "Why We Are Entering into This Transaction," February 16, 1945 (box 12), Baruch Papers, ML/PU.

38. Acheson to Keynes, January 2, 1946, T247/128, Keynes Papers, Treasury Records, PRO.

39. Keynes to Treasury, October 8, 1945 (FO 371/45704), Halifax to Foreign Office, January 18, 1946 (FO 371/52949), Halifax to Prime Minister, December 21, 1945 (FO 371/52949), and Conversation between B. E. F. Gage and John Allison, February 8, 1946 (FO 371/54052), Foreign Office Records, PRO.

40. Hedlund, "Congress and the British Loan," 75–86; Conversations between White and O'Connell, January 9 and 18, 1946, box 2, O'Connell Papers, HST Library; J.S.M. to Cabinet Offices, January 30, 1946, FO 371/52950, Foreign Office Records, PRO.

41. Luxford to Vinson, October 12, 1945, reel 21, Vinson Papers, HST Library.

42. Acheson to Menafee and Bunn, January 3, 1946, box 27, Acheson Papers, HST Library.

43. Acheson remarks to the Platform Guild Conference, January 3, 1946, box 27, Acheson Papers, HST Library.

44. Quoted in *New York Times*, January 31, 1946.

45. Conversation between Lynch and McConnell, February 13, 1946, box 2, O'Connell Papers, HST Library.

46. Keynes to Bridges, February 8, 1946, T247/47, Keynes Papers, Treasury Records, PRO.

47. T. M. Whiteback to John Coulson, February 6, 1946, FO 371/52950, Foreign Office Records, PRO. See also Keynes to Brand, February 8, 1946, FO 371/52950, Foreign Office Records, PRO; and Keynes to Bridges, February 8, 1946, T247/47, Keynes Papers, Treasury Records, PRO.

48. Satterwhite to Secretary of State, February 25, 1946, 841.796/2–2546, RG59, DOS Records, NA; Hedlund, "Congress and the British Loan," 46–47.

49. February opinion poll on British loan, February 8, 1946, box 12, Hickerson Files, RG59, DOS Records, NA.

50. Donnelley minute on Weekly Political Summary, February 6, 1946, FO 371/51606, Foreign Office Records, PRO.

51. Gage minute on Weekly Political Summary, February 23, 1946, FO 371/51606, Foreign Office Records, PRO.

52. "Truman Proposes Quick Loan Action," *New York Times*, December 8, 1945; Weekly Political Summary, February 15, 1946, FO 371/51606, Foreign Office Records, PRO.

53. Hedlund, "Congress and the British Loan," 86.

54. Patterson, *Congressional Conservatism*, 148.

55. *Anglo-American Financial Agreement*, Senate, 2.

56. Kennan to Secretary of State, January 29, 1946, 611.4131/1-2946, RG59, DOS; British Embassy, Moscow, to Foreign Office, January 18, 1946, FO 371/52949, Foreign Office Records, PRO.

57. Harriman to Secretary of State, April 4, 1945, vol. 2, Forrestal Diaries, ML/PU.

58. Ibid.; Byrnes Press Conference, October 17, 1945, box 554, Byrnes Papers, CL/CU; Acheson to American Embassy, Warsaw, September 21, 1945, reel 21, Vinson Papers, HST Library.

59. Quoted in Blum, *Price of Vision*, 558.

60. R. Gardner, *Sterling-Dollar Diplomacy*, 242; Coppock to Wilcox, February 21, 1946, box 3, Clayton-Thorp Papers, HST Library; "Barkley Sees Pay, Prices up 10%–20%," *New York Times*, March 5, 1946.

61. *Anglo-American Financial Agreement*, Senate, 415.

62. Ibid., 79–89.

63. Ibid., 234–35.

64. Ibid.

65. Ibid., 250–53, 463–64; Bridges to Halifax, March 12, 1946, FO 371/52952, Foreign Office Records, PRO.

66. Breck to Keynes, January 5, 1946, T247/128, Keynes Papers, Treasury Records, PRO.

67. See Office of War Mobilization and Reconversion to HST, March 4, 1946, box 48, Official File, HST Papers, HST Library; *Anglo-American Financial Agreement*, Senate, 341, 389, 365, 373–75; American Economic Association to Editor, *New York Times*, October 7, 1945; J.S.M. Washington to Cabinet Offices, March 8, 1946, FO 371/52950, Foreign Office Records, PRO; "The Loan to Britain," *New York Times*, December 7, 1945; Allan Sproul to Keynes, December 27, 1945, T247/47, Keynes Papers, Treasury Records, PRO; Statement of Winthrop Aldrich, March 13, 1946, box 3, Berle Papers, FDR Library.

68. Conversation between Ferguson and O'Connell, March 14, 1946, and Conversation between Burgess and O'Connell, March 19, 1946, box 2, O'Connell Papers, and Vardaman to HST, February 13, 1946, box 802, Official File, HST Papers, HST Library. See also R. C. Dickerson to Fulbright, February 19, 1946, file 22, Fulbright Papers, ML/UA.

69. Dalton Diaries, March 29, 1946, vol. 1, 34, RL/LSE.

70. B. R. Hennes to *The Houston-Chronicle*, April 6, 1946, Jones Papers, LC; Conversation between Ferguson and O'Connell, February 27, 28, and March 6, 1946, O'Connell-Wallace conversation, March 19, 1946, and O'Connell telephone calendar, March 19, 1946, box 2, O'Connell Papers, HST Library; Frank Lee to Keynes,

April 4, 1946, T247/47, Keynes Papers, Treasury Records, PRO.

71. *Anglo-American Financial Agreement*, Senate, 443, 481.

72. Ibid., 391–92.

73. Quoted in Knight, "Nonfraternal Association," 110.

74. Quoted in Hedlund, "Congress and the British Loan," 192.

75. Ibid., 96.

76. "The Loan Hearings," *The Economist*, March 23, 1946. See also *Anglo-American Financial Agreement*, Senate, 391–92; Keynes to Dalton, March 7, 1946, FO 371/52951, Foreign Office Records, PRO.; "Mr. Churchill and the Loan," March 14, 1946, FO 371/52953, Foreign Office Records, PRO.

77. "Random Reflections from a Visit to USA," April 4, 1946, T247/47, Keynes Papers, Treasury Records, PRO; Dalton Diaries, March 29, 1946, vol. 1, 34, RL/LSE.

78. Hedlund, "Congress and the British Loan," 100–101; *Congressional Record*, Senate, 79th Cong., 2d sess., vol. 92 (April 17, 1946).

79. Hedlund, "Congress and the British Loan," 108–9. See also Ashton Williams to Byrnes, April 18, 1946, box 510, Byrnes Papers, CL/CU; and Brand to Eady, April 22, 1946, FO 371/52955, Foreign Office Records, PRO.

80. Weekly Political Summary, April 1946, FO 371/51607, Foreign Office Records, PRO; Conversation between O'Connell and Wilcox, April 18, 1946, box 3, O'Connell Papers, HST Library.

81. Quoted in Hedlund, "Congress and the British Loan," 112–15.

82. Quoted in ibid., 115.

83. Halifax to Byrnes, October 19, 1945 (811.24500/11-1945), Byrnes to Bevin, December 10, 1945 (811.34553B/12-1045), Furber memo of conversation, March 19, 1946 (811.3459013), Dennison to Hickerson, April 22, 1946 (811.34590/4-2246), Gallman to Byrnes and Dunn, April 25, 1946 (811.24500/4-2546), Acheson to Harriman, April 27, 1946 (811.24500/4-2546), George A. Lincoln to Byrnes, May 1, 1946 (811.24500/5-146), Lincoln to Gen. John E. Hull, May 2, 1946 (811.245900/5-246), Matthews memo of conversation, May 2, 1946 (811.245900/5-246), and Harriman to Byrnes, May 9, 1946 (841.014/5-946), RG59, DOS Records, NA.

84. Quoted in Hedlund, "Congress and the British Loan," 119.

85. Ibid., 120; Conversation between Byrnes and Bevin, May 2, 1946, box 638, Byrnes Papers, CL/CU.

86. Hedlund, "Congress and the British Loan," 123.

87. B. W. Anderson to Clayton, January 12, 1946, box 1, Clayton-Thorp Papers, HST Library; Green, "Conflict over Trade Ideologies," 33.

88. *New York Times*, April 18, 1946; Hedlund, "Congress and the British Loan," 98.

89. Conversation between Dierkes and O'Connell, March 18, 1946, box 2, O'Connell Papers, HST Library.

90. Quoted in Hedlund, "Congress and the British Loan," 141.

91. Conversation between Wolcott and Brand, June 6, 1946, FO 371/52957, Foreign Office Records, PRO.

92. Hedlund, "Congress and the British Loan," 127–28.

93. "British Credit," May 16, 1946, box 133, Cox Papers, FDR Library.

94. Quoted in Hedlund, "Congress and the British Loan," 132–33.

95. Conversation between Ferguson and O'Connell, May 15, 1946, box 3, O'Connell Papers, HST Library.

96. Halifax to Foreign Office, undated, FO 371/51628, Foreign Office Records, PRO.

97. Cabinet Conclusions, October 4, 1945, C.M. (45) 38, CAB 128, vol. 1, PRO; J. G. Donnelley and Paul Mason minutes on Weekly Political Summary, October 11, 1945 (FO 371/44538), and May 17, 1946 (FO 371/51607), Foreign Office Records, PRO.

98. Hathaway, *Ambiguous Partnership*, 277; State-War-Navy Coordinating Committee Memo on Palestine, June 21, 1946, box 184, PSF, HST Papers, HST Library.

99. Attlee to HST, May 10, 1946 (box 6, Naval Aide File), and Attlee to HST, June 10, 1946, and HST to Attlee, June 5, 1946 (box 170, PSF), HST Papers, HST Library.

100. Sabbath to HST, June 12, 1946, box 772, Official File, HST Papers, HST Library.

101. Ibid.

102. Wagner et al. to HST, June 20, 1946, box 184, PSF, HST Papers, HST Library.

103. Dalton Diaries, January 8, 1946, vol. 1, 34, RL/LSE.

104. *Anglo-American Financial Agreement*, House, 62.

105. Ibid., 451.

106. Ibid., 370.

107. *Anglo-American Financial Agreement*, House, 357. See also Conversation between O'Conner and O'Connell, May 14, 1946, and Conversation between O'Connell and Spence, June 5, 1946, box 3, O'Connell Papers, HST Library; and Jones to Spence, June 3, 1946, *Anglo-American Financial Agreement*, House, 621–23.

108. Notes on the loan, May 23, 1946, FO 371/52956, Foreign Office Records, PRO.

109. Judson to Foreign Office, May 22, 1946, FO 371/52956, Foreign Office Records, PRO.

110. Hedlund, "Congress and the British Loan," 145.

111. Conversation between O'Connell and Bernstein, June 13, 1946, and Conversation between Niles and O'Connell, July 2, 1946, box 3, O'Connell Papers, HST Library; Inverchapel to Foreign Office, June 26, 1946, FO 371/51608, Foreign Office Records, PRO.

112. Frank McNaughton to Don Birmingham, July 5, 1946, box 1, McNaughton Papers, HST Library.

113. "Dr. Stephen Wise Speaks for the British Loan," undated, box 802, Official File, HST Papers, HST Library.

114. Conversation between Hallahan and O'Connell, July 3, 1946, and Conversation between O'Connell and Dierkies, July 8, 1946, box 3, O'Connell Papers, HST Library; Inverchapel to Foreign Office, July 3, 1946 (FO 371/51608), and Inverchapel to Parliamentary Undersecretary, July 4, 1946 (FO 371/52957), Foreign Office Records, PRO.

115. McNaughton to Birmingham, July 12, 1946, box 1, McNaughton Papers, HST Library.

116. Hedlund, "Congress and the British Loan," 172.

117. Quoted in Knight, "Nonfraternal Association," 118.

118. Ibid., 119–20; Statement by the President, July 15, 1946, box 802, Official File, HST Papers, HST Library.

Bibliography

This bibliography is organized as follows:

A. Manuscript Sources
B. Published Official Documents
C. Journals and Newspapers
D. Books
E. Articles
F. Dissertations and Other Unpublished Manuscripts

A. Manuscript Sources

Official Documents

Great Britain
  London
    Public Record Office
      Cabinet Conclusions, CAB 65
      Cabinet Conclusions, CAB 128
      Cabinet Memoranda, CAB 66
      Foreign Office Records, FO 371
      Prime Minister's Records
        Prime Minister's Office Files
        Richard Law Papers, PREM 4
      Treasury Records
        Sir Wilfrid Eady Papers, T236
        John Maynard Keynes Papers, T247

    House of Lords Record Office
      Lord Beaverbrook Papers

United States
  Hyde Park, New York
    Franklin D. Roosevelt Library
      Adolf Berle Diaries
      Adolf Berle Papers
      Oscar Cox Papers
      Harry Hopkins Papers
      Henry Morgenthau, Jr. Diaries
      Henry Morgenthau, Jr., Papers

Franklin D. Roosevelt Papers
  Map Room Files
  Official File
  President's Personal File
  President's Secretary's File
Samuel Rosenman Papers
Harold Smith Diaries

Independence, Missouri
  Harry S. Truman Library
    Dean Acheson Papers
    Assistant Secretary for Economic Affairs (Clayton-
      Thorp) Papers
    Thomas C. Blaisdell, Jr., Papers
    Will Clayton Papers
    Frank McNaughton Papers
    Joseph O'Connell Papers
    Harry S. Truman Papers
      Map Room File
      Naval Aide File
      Official File
      President's Secretary's File
        Subject File
    Fred Vinson Papers

Washington, D.C.
  Library of Congress
    Harold Ickes Diaries
    Jesse H. Jones Papers
    William D. Leahy Papers
    Charles P. Taft Papers
    Robert A. Taft Papers

  National Archives
    Intra- and Interdepartmental Committee Files,
      Record Group 353
    U.S. Department of State Records, Record Group 59:
      Dean Acheson Files
      Assistant Secretary for Economic Affairs
        Files
      Will Clayton Files
      Decimal Files
        Hubert Havlik Files
      John D. Hickerson Files
      Harley A. Notter Files
      Office of European Affairs Records
      Edward R. Stettinius Files
    U.S. Department of Treasury Records, Record Group 63
      National Advisory Council Files

Private Collections

Great Britain
  Cambridge
    Churchill College Library, Cambridge University
      Clement Attlee Papers
      Ernest Bevin Papers
      Paul Einzig Papers
      Sir Percy Grigg Papers
      Lord Halifax Papers
      Sir Archibald Sinclair Papers

  London
    Robertson Library, London School of Economics
      Hugh Dalton Diaries
      James Meade Diaries

United States
  Chicago, Illinois
    Center for Research Libraries, University of Chicago
      Cordell Hull Papers
      State-War-Navy Coordinating Committee Case Files

  Clemson, South Carolina
    Cooper Library, Clemson University
      James F. Byrnes Papers

  Fayetteville, Arkansas
    Mullins Library, University of Arkansas
      J. William Fulbright Papers

  Iowa City, Iowa
    Main Library, University of Iowa
      Henry A. Wallace Diary
      Henry A. Wallace Papers

  New Haven, Connecticut
    Sterling Library, Yale University
      Henry L. Stimson Diaries

  Princeton, New Jersey
    Firestone Library, Princeton University
      John Foster Dulles Papers

    Mudd Library, Princeton University
      Bernard Baruch Papers
      James V. Forrestal Diaries
      Harry Dexter White Papers

B. Published Official Documents

Anglo-American Financial Agreement: Hearings before the Committee on Banking and Currency, U.S. House of Representatives, 79th Cong., 2d sess. (Washington, D.C., 1946).

Anglo-American Financial Agreement: Hearings before the Committee on Banking and Currency, U.S. Senate, 79th Cong., 2d sess. (Washington, D.C., 1946).

Congressional Record

1945 Extension of Reciprocal Trade Agreements Act: Ways and Means Committee, U.S. House of Representatives, 79th Cong., 1st sess. (Washington, D.C., 1946).

Parliamentary Debates (Hansard)

U.S. Department of State, *Foreign Relations of the United States, 1945*, vols. 1 and 6 (Washington, D.C., 1946); *1946*, vol. 1 (Washington, D.C., 1947).

C. Journals and Newspapers

Economic History Review
The Economist
New York Times

D. Books

Acheson, Dean. *Present at the Creation: My Years in the State Department*. New York, 1970.

Allison, Graham T. *Essence of Decision*. Boston, 1971.

Ambrose, Stephen E. *Eisenhower and Berlin, 1945: The Decision to Halt at the Elbe*. New York, 1967.

Anderson, Terry H. *The United States, Great Britain and the Cold War, 1944–1947*. Columbia, Mo., 1981.

Barnes, John, and Nicholson, David, eds., *The Leo Amery Diaries*. London, 1980.

Barnet, Richard J. *Roots of War*. New York, 1972.

Bartlett, C. J. *A History of Post-War Britain*. London, 1977.

Blum, John Morton. *From the Morgenthau Diaries*. Vol. 3, *Years of War, 1941–1945*. Boston, 1967.

———. *The Price of Vision: The Diary of Henry A. Wallace, 1942–1946*. Boston, 1973.

Bohlen, Charles E. *Witness to History, 1929–1969*. New York, 1973.

Bullock, Alan. *The Life and Times of Ernest Bevin*. Vol. 2, *Minister of Labour, 1940–1945*. London, 1967.

Burns, James McGregor. *Roosevelt: The Soldier of Freedom*. New York, 1970.

Burridge, T. D. *British Labour and Hitler's War*. London, 1976.

Carlton, David. *Anthony Eden: A Biography*. London, 1981.

Catton, Bruce. *The War Lords of Washington*. New York, 1948.

Clarke, Sir Richard. *Anglo-American Economic Collaboration in War and Peace, 1942–1949*. Oxford, 1982.

Clements, Kendrick A., ed. *James F. Byrnes and the Origins of the Cold War*. Durham, N.C., 1982.

Colville, John. *The Fringes of Power: 10 Downing Street Diaries, 1939–1955*. New York and London, 1955.

Dallek, Robert. *Franklin D. Roosevelt and American Foreign Policy*. New York, 1979.

Darilek, Richard E. *A Loyal Opposition in Time of War: The Republican Party and the Politics of Foreign Policy from Pearl Harbor to Yalta*. Westport, Conn., 1976.

DeConde, Alexander. *A History of American Foreign Policy*, vol. 2. New York, 1978.

Dilks, David, ed. *The Diaries of Sir Alexander Cadogan, 1938–1945*. New York, 1972.

Robert A. Divine, *Second Chance: The Triumph of Internationalism in America during World War II*. New York, 1967.

Dobson, Alan P. *U.S. Wartime Aid to Britain, 1940–1946*. London, 1986.

Donovan, Robert. *Conflict and Crisis: The Presidency of Harry S. Truman, 1945–1948*. New York, 1977.

Ferrell, Robert H., ed. *Off the Record: The Private Papers of Harry S. Truman*. New York, 1980.

Fitzsimons, Matthew A. *The Foreign Policy of the British Labour Government, 1945–1951*. Notre Dame, Ind., 1953.

Foot, Michael, *Aneurin Bevan: A Biography*. London, 1962.

Gaddis, John L. *The United States and the Origins of the Cold War, 1941–1947*. New York, 1972.

Gardner, Lloyd C. *Architects of Illusion: Men and Ideas in American Foreign Policy, 1941–1949*. Chicago, 1970.

Gardner, Richard N. *Sterling-Dollar Diplomacy: Anglo-American Cooperation in the Reconstruction of Multilateral Trade*. Oxford, 1956.

Gilbert, Felix. *The End of the European Era: 1890 to the Present*. New York, 1970.

Gilbert, Martin. *Winston Churchill*. Vol. 5, *The Prophet of Truth*. Boston, 1977.

Harbut, Fraser J. *The Iron Curtain: Churchill, America, and the Origins of the Cold War*. New York, 1986.

Harriman, Averell, and Abel, Elie. *Special Envoy to Churchill and Stalin, 1941–1946*. New York, 1975.

Harris, José. *William Beveridge: A Biography*. Oxford, 1972.

Harrod, Roy F. *The Life of John Maynard Keynes*. New York, 1951.

Hathaway, Robert M. *Ambiguous Partnership: Britain and America, 1944–1947*. New York, 1981.

Heclo, Hugh. *A Government of Strangers: Executive Politics in Washington*. Washington, D.C., 1977.

Hession, Charles H. *John Maynard Keynes*. New York and London, 1985.

Jones, Thomas. *A Diary with Letters, 1931–1950*. New York, 1950.

Kenwood, A. G., and Lougheed, A. L. *The Growth of the International Economy, 1820–1960*. Albany, 1972.

Kimball, Warren F. *The Most Unsordid Act: Lend-Lease, 1939–1941* (Baltimore, 1969).

———. *Churchill and Roosevelt: The Complete Correspondence*. 3 vols. Vol. 1, *Alliance Emerging, October 1933–November 1942*. Vol. 2, *Alliance Forged, November 1942–February 1944*. Vol. 3, *Alliance Declining, February 1944–April 1945*. Princeton, 1984.

Kindleberger, Charles P. *A Financial History of Western Europe*. London, 1984.

Kraus, René. *The Men around Churchill*. Philadelphia, 1941.

Kuniholm, Bruce R. *The Origins of the Cold War in the Near East: Great Power Conflict and Diplomacy in Iran, Turkey, and Greece*. Princeton, 1980.

LaFeber, Walter. *The New Empire: An Interpretation of American Expansion, 1860–1898*. Ithaca, 1963.

Louis, William Roger. *Imperialism at Bay: The United States and the Decolonization of the British Empire, 1941–1945*. New York, 1977.

Lowenheim, Francis L.; Langley, Harold D.; and Jonas, Manfred; eds. *Roosevelt and Churchill: Their Secret Wartime Correspondence*. New York, 1975.

McJimsey, George. *Harry Hopkins*. Cambridge, Mass., 1988.

Macmillan, Harold. *The Middle Way: A Study of the Problem of Economic and Social Progress in a Free and Democratic Society*. London, 1938.

―――. *The Blast of War, 1939–1945*. New York, 1968.

Martel, Leon. *Lend-Lease, Loans and the Coming of the Cold War: A Study in the Implementation of Foreign Policy*. Boulder, 1979.

Marwick, Arthur. *The Home Front, the British and the Second World War*. London, 1944.

―――. *War and Social Change in the Twentieth Century*. New York, 1974.

Mastny, Vojtech. *Russia's Road to the Cold War: Diplomacy, Warfare, and the Politics of Communism, 1941–1945*. New York, 1979.

Matusow, Allen J. *Farm Policies and Politics in the Truman Years*. Cambridge, 1967.

Mee, Charles L., Jr. *Meeting at Potsdam*. New York, 1975.

Murphy, Bruce A. *The Brandeis/Frankfurter Connection: The Secret Political Activities of Two Supreme Court Justices*. New York, 1982.

Nicholas, H. G., ed. *Washington Dispatches, 1941–1945*. Chicago, 1981.

Nicolson, Nigel, ed. *Harold Nicolson: The War Years, 1939–1945*. Vol. 2, *Diaries and Letters*. New York, 1967.

Ovendale, Ritchie, ed. *The Foreign Policy of the British Labour Governments, 1945–1951*. Leicester, England, 1984.

Patterson, James T. *Congressional Conservatism and the New Deal: The Growth of the Conservative Coalition in Congress, 1933–1939*. Lexington, Ky., 1969.

―――. *Mr. Republican: A Biography of Robert A. Taft*. Boston, 1972.

Peffer, Richard M. *No More Vietnams?* New York, 1968.

Reese, David. *Harry Dexter White: A Study in Paradox*. New York, 1975.

Reynolds, David. *The Creation of the Anglo-American Alliance 1937–1941: A Study on Competitive Cooperation*. Chapel Hill, 1981.

Rothwell, Victor. *Britain and the Cold War, 1941–1947*. London, 1982.

Ryan, Henry Butterfield. *The Vision of Anglo-America: The US-UK Alliance and the Emerging Cold War, 1943–1946*. Cambridge, England, 1987.

Schlesinger, Arthur, Jr. *The Age of Roosevelt*. Vol. 2, *The Coming of the New Deal*. Boston, 1958.

Schoenfeld, Maxwell. *The War Ministry of Winston Churchill*. Ames, Iowa, 1972.

Sherry, Michael S. *Preparing for the Next War: American Plans for Postwar Defense, 1941–1945*. New Haven, Conn., 1976.

Smith, Gaddis. *American Diplomacy during the Second World War, 1941–1945*. New York, 1965.

―――. *The American Secretaries of State and Their Diplomacy: Dean Acheson*. New York, 1972.

Spanier, John. *The Truman-MacArthur Controversy and the Korean War*. Cambridge, 1959.

Stoff, Michael B. *Oil, War, and American Security: The Search for a National Policy on Foreign Oil, 1941–1949*. New Haven, Conn., 1980.

Stoler, Mark A. *The Politics of the Second Front: Diplomacy in Coalition Warfare, 1941–1943*. Westport, Conn., 1977.

Taylor, A. J. P. *Beaverbrook*. New York, 1972.

Thorne, Christopher. *Allies of a Kind: The United States, Britain and the War Against Japan, 1941–1945*. London, 1978.

Truman, Harry S. *Memoirs*. Vol. 1, *Year of Decisions*. Garden City, N.Y., 1955.

Van Dormael, Armand. *Bretton Woods: Birth of a Monetary System*. New York, 1978.

Warken, Philip W. *A History of the National Resources Planning Board, 1933–1943*. New York and London, 1979.

Watt, D. C. *Personalities and Policies: Studies in the Formulation of British Foreign Policy in the Twentieth Century*. Notre Dame, Ind., 1965.

_____. *Succeeding John Bull: America in Britain's Place, 1900–1975*. Cambridge, Mass., 1984.

Welles, Sumner. *The Time for Decision*. New York, 1944.

_____. *Seven Decisions that Shaped History*. New York, 1950.

Wilson, Joan Hoff. *American Business and Foreign Policy, 1920–1933*. Boston, 1973.

Wilson, Theodore A. *The First Summit: Roosevelt and Churchill at Placentia Bay, 1941*. Boston, 1969.

Winch, Donald. *Economics and Policy: A Historical Study*. London, 1969.

Woods, Randall B. *The Roosevelt Foreign Policy Establishment and the 'Good Neighbor': The United States and Argentina, 1941–1945*. Lawrence, Kans., 1979.

E. Articles

Booth, Alan. "The 'Keynesian Revolution' in Economic Policy-Making." *Economic History Review* 36, no. 1 (February 1983): 103–23.

Carpenter, L. P. "Corporatism in Britain, 1930–45." *Journal of Contemporary History* 11, no. 1 (January 1976): 3–25.

Dobney, Frederick J. "The Evolution of a Reconversion Policy: World War II and Surplus War Property Disposal." *The Historian* 36, no. 3 (May 1974): 498–519.

Eckes, Alfred, Jr. "Open Door Expansionism Reconsidered: The World War II Experience." *Journal of American History* 59, no. 4 (March 1973): 910–45.

Hess, Gary R. "The Iranian Crisis of 1945–46 and the Cold War." *Political Science Quarterly* 89, no. 1 (March 1974): 117–46.

Jones, Byrd L. "Lauchlin Currie, Pump Priming, and New Deal Fiscal Policy, 1934–1936." *History of Political Economy* 10, no. 4 (Winter 1978): 509–24.

Kettenacker, Lothar. "The Anglo-Soviet Alliance and the Problem of Germany, 1941–1945." *Journal of Contemporary History* 17, no. 3 (July 1982): 435–58.

Langer, John Daniel. "The Harriman-Beaverbrook Mission and the Debate over Unconditional Aid for the Soviet Union, 1941." *Journal of Contemporary History* 14, no. 3 (July 1979): 463–82.

Levin, N. Gordon, Jr. "Woodrow Wilson and World Politics." In N. Gordon Levin, Jr., ed., *Woodrow Wilson and the Paris Peace Conference*. Lexington, Ky., 1972.

McCloskey, Donald N. "Magnanimous Albion: Free Trade and British National Income, 1811–1881." *Explorations in Economic History* 17, no. 3 (July 1980).

McHale, James M. "National Planning and Reciprocal Trade: The New Deal Origins of Government Guarantees for Private Exporters." *Prologue* 6, no. 3 (Fall 1974): 189–99.

Mark, Eduard. "American Policy toward Eastern Europe and the Origins of the Cold War, 1941–1946: An Alternative Interpretation." *Journal of American History* 68, no. 2 (September 1981): 313–36.

Matthews, Geoffrey. "Robert A. Taft, the Constitution and American Foreign Policy, 1939–53." *Journal of Contemporary History* 17, no. 3 (July 1982): 507–22.

Noble, David. "Conservatism in the USA." *Journal of Contemporary History* 13, no. 4 (October 1978): 635–52.

Patterson, James T. "Alternatives to Globalism: Robert A. Taft and American Foreign Policy, 1939–1945." *The Historian* 36, no. 4 (August 1974): 670–88.

Pelling, Henry. "The 1945 General Election Reconsidered." *The Historical Journal* 23, no. 2 (1980): 399–414.

Resis, Albert. "Spheres of Influence in Soviet Wartime Diplomacy." *Journal of Modern History* 53, no. 3 (September 1981): 417–39.

Ross, Graham. "Foreign Office Attitudes to the Soviet Union 1941–45." *Journal of Contemporary History* 16, no. 3 (July 1981): 521–39.

Ryan, Henry B. "A New Look at Churchill's 'Iron Curtain' Speech." *The Historical Journal* 22, no. 4 (1979): 895–920.

Wooley, Wesley T., Jr. "The Quest for Permanent Peace—American Supranationalism, 1945–1947." *The Historian* 35, no. 1 (November 1972): 18–31.

F. Dissertations and Other Unpublished Manuscripts

Beddow, James B. "Economic Nationalism or Internationalism: Upper Midwestern Response to New Deal Tariff Policy, 1934–1940." Ph.D. dissertation, Oklahoma State University, 1969.

Brady, Patrick G. "Toward Security: Postwar Economic and Social Planning in the Executive Office, 1939–1946." Ph.D. dissertation, Rutgers University, 1976.

Green, Philip E. "Conflict over Trade Ideologies during the Early Cold War: A Study of American Foreign Economic Policy." Ph.D. dissertation, Duke University, 1978.

Hedlund, Richard P. "Congress and the British Loan, 1945–1946: A Congressional Study." Ph.D. dissertation, University of Kentucky, 1976.

Henningson, Berton E. "Shaping an Agricultural Trade and Development Policy for the United States: The Office of Foreign Agricultural Relations during World War II." Ph.D. dissertation, University of Arkansas, 1981.

Knight, Wayne Stone. "The Nonfraternal Association: Anglo-American Relations and the Breakdown of the Grand Alliance, 1945–1947." Ph.D. dissertation, The American University, 1979.

Schnabel, James F. "The History of the Joint Chiefs of Staff and National Policy, Vol. 1: 1945–1947." Ms. in the Division of Modern Military Records, National Archives, February 1979.

Waligorski, Conrad P. "Keynesian Politics: Political and Social Assumptions of John Maynard Keynes." Paper delivered at the 1979 Meeting of the Western Social Sciences Association.

Index